CONTENTS

OF THE

THIRD VOLUME.

University Buildings.

I. SCHOOLS, LIBRARY, SENATE-HOUSE.

II. PRINTING-HOUSE, MUSEUMS AND LECTURE-ROOMS FOR NATURAL SCIENCE, OBSERVATORY, FITZWILLIAM MUSEUM, SELWYN DIVINITY SCHOOL.

PART III.

ESSAYS ON THE COMPONENT PARTS OF A COLLEGE.

THE
ARCHITECTURAL HISTORY
OF THE
UNIVERSITY OF CAMBRIDGE

THE

ARCHITECTURAL HISTORY

OF THE

UNIVERSITY OF CAMBRIDGE,

AND OF THE

COLLEGES OF CAMBRIDGE AND ETON.

BY THE LATE

ROBERT WILLIS, M.A., F.R.S.

JACKSONIAN PROFESSOR IN THE UNIVERSITY OF CAMBRIDGE,
AND SOMETIME FELLOW OF GONVILLE AND CAIUS COLLEGE.

EDITED WITH LARGE ADDITIONS,

AND BROUGHT UP TO THE PRESENT TIME,

BY

JOHN WILLIS CLARK, M.A.

LATE FELLOW OF TRINITY COLLEGE, CAMBRIDGE.

VOL. III.

The right of the University of Cambridge to print and sell all manner of books was granted by Henry VIII in 1534. The University has printed and published continuously since 1584.

CAMBRIDGE UNIVERSITY PRESS

CAMBRIDGE

NEW YORK NEW ROCHELLE MELBOURNE SYDNEY

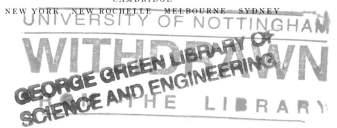

Published by the Press Syndicate of the University of Cambridge
The Pitt Building, Trumpington Street, Cambridge CB2 1RP
32 East 57th Street, New York, NY 10022, USA
10 Stamford Road, Oakleigh, Melbourne 3166, Australia

First published 1886
Reprinted with a new Introduction 1988

Printed in Great Britain at the University Press, Cambridge

British Library cataloguing in publication data
Willis, Robert, 1800–1875
The architectural history of the University of
Cambridge and of the colleges of Cambridge and Eton.
1. University of Cambridge – Buildings – History
2. Eton College – Buildings – History
I. Title II. Willis, Clark John
727'.3'0942659 LF110

Library of Congress cataloguing in publication data
Willis, Robert, 1800–1875
The architectural history of the University of Cambridge and of the colleges of Cambridge and Eton by Robert Willis: edited with large additions and brought up to the present time by John Willis Clark.
p. cm.
Reprint. Originally published: Cambridge: University Press, 1886. With new introd.
ISBN 0 521 35323 8 (set). ISBN 0 521 35851 5 (pbk set)
1. University of Cambridge – Buildings – History. 2. Eton College – Buildings – History. I. Clark, John Willis, 1833–1910. II. Title.
LF110.W7 1988
727'.3'0942659–dc 19 87-37555

ISBN 0 521 35320 3 hard covers (vol. 1)
ISBN 0 521 35848 5 paperback (vol. 1)
ISBN 0 521 35321 1 hard covers (vol. 2)
ISBN 0 521 35849 3 paperback (vol. 2)
ISBN 0 521 35322 X hard covers (vol. 3)
ISBN 0 521 35850 7 paperback (vol. 3)
ISBN 0 521 35323 8 hard covers (the set)
ISBN 0 521 35851 5 paperback (the set)

LIST OF ILLUSTRATIONS

IN THE

THIRD VOLUME.

Printing-House.

Museums and Lecture-Rooms for Natural Science.

Observatory.

Fitzwilliam Museum.

Selwyn Divinity School.

The Collegiate Plan.

The Gateway.

The Chambers and Studies.

THE MASTER'S LODGE.

THE HALL, THE KITCHEN, ETC.

THE LIBRARY.

The Chapel.

The Style of Collegiate Buildings.

The Tennis-Court, etc.

ERRATA IN THE THIRD VOLUME.

P. 15,	*line*	11,	*for*	next	*read*	the third
301	,,	29	,,	Thomas	,,	James

UNIVERSITY BUILDINGS.

I.

Schools, Library, Senate-House.

CHAPTER I.

[HISTORY OF THE SITE[1].

THE present site of these buildings is bounded on the north by Senate-House Passage; on the west by part of the street anciently called Milne Street, but now Trinity Hall Lane; on the south by King's College; and on the east by part of High Street or Trumpington Street, sometimes called Senate-House Hill (fig. 1).

Until the Senate-House was built (1719—30), the thoroughfare called Senate-House Passage did not exist; but communication between Milne Street and High Street was effected by a narrow street called School Street. This street has been fully described in the History of King's College[2], and the direction of it is shewn on Loggan's ground-plan (fig. 2). It will therefore be only necessary to state here that the portion in front of the Schools was called "North Schools Street;" and the portion which led from the Schools to High Street "East Schools Street," "Glomery Lane," or "S. Mary Lane." School Street derived its name from the number of Schools which stood in it. Besides the Schools proper belonging to the University the names of the following have been preserved.

[1] [Professor Willis had only collected materials for this chapter.]

[2] [Vol. i. 318.]

At the north-west corner of North School Street and Gonvile Hall Lane was a theological School, called the School of S. Margaret. It is first mentioned in 1369, when it was given to Michael House. Near it stood a building containing three Schools, given to the same College in 1377[1]. In 1440 we find on the south side of East Schools Street a building called "Gramerscole," with another called "Art Scole" next to it on the east[2]. The former—called also the "School of Glomery" and "Le Glomery Halle," must have been the original home of the "Master of Glomery," and the University "School of Glomery," the position of which has hitherto been a mystery[3]. No record of the foundation of this School has been preserved, but it was evidently of great antiquity, for in 1328—29 we find two Schools described as standing opposite to it at the corner of North School Street and East School Street[4], and the name "Le Glomery Lane," which was derived from it, already applied to East School Street.

It will be seen from Loggan's ground-plan (fig. 2), that the site which we are considering was divided by School Street into three portions, which, for convenience of description, may be designated western, eastern, and south-eastern. We will first relate the history of the western portion, containing the original site of the Schools, and the site of the Old Court of King's College; deferring that of the eastern and south-eastern portions until we come to the building of the Senate-House.

The site of the Schools, as will be seen from the plan (fig. 1) is an irregular piece of ground measuring about 135 feet from north to south, by about 100 feet from east to west. It was bounded on the south, west, and north by the site of King's College, part of which also extended into the angle between the buildings which stood on the southern and western sides of the

[1] [These Schools afterwards became the property of King's College, as has been already related. Vol. i. 320. Vol. ii. 416.]

[2] [History of King's College, Vol. i. 320.]

[3] [Observations on the Statutes of the University of Cambridge. By George Peacock, D.D., 8vo. 1841, p. xxxvi.]

[4] [MSS. Baker, ii. 165. MSS. Harl. Mus. Brit. 7029. Baker quotes the following record from the muniments of Clare Hall: "duas scolas simul jacentes...in venella vocat' le Glomery Lane, super Corneram ex opposito Scolæ Glomeriæ, in longitudine a domo Thome de Codenham versus venellam 31 pedum, in latitudine vero 21 pedum. 2 Edw. III. (1328—29)."]

Schools Quadrangle, and, as the plan shews, was composed of four pieces. The first, taking them in order of date of acquisition, was given to the University by Nigel de Thornton, a physician, shortly before 1278[1] (1); the second was purchased in 1421 from Trinity Hall (2); the third, part of the garden of Crouched Hostel, between 1421 and 1440 (3); the fourth in 1459, from Corpus Christi College (4). We will next describe these pieces more minutely, for which purpose it will be convenient to begin with the last.

This ground (4) was leased to the University, 25 March 1459, by John Botwright, Master of Corpus Christi College, and the Fellows of the same, for 99 years at an annual rent of two shillings. The following passage, translated from the lease, not only describes the piece minutely, but is also our principal authority for the history of Thornton's ground. The piece demised is stated to be:

"A certain piece of ground lately vacant, formerly a garden, leased by the aforesaid College to William Bedell, although a short time since Schools of Civil Law were built on some portion of the aforesaid ground. It contains in length thirty standard feet (*pedes de standardo*), and in breadth twenty-nine and a half feet (*pedes pauli*), as may be seen by the stone fence which protects the ground on all sides, and extends as far as the chair of the old Civil Law School. It is situated in Cambridge, in the Parish of S. Mary by the Market, and is bounded on the south by a vacant plot which was lately bought for the use of the University from William Hulle Prior of S. John's, Jerusalem, (Clerkenwell); and on the north by a vacant plot under the walls of the new Schools (*infra novas Scolas*), which plot was lately acquired by the aforesaid University through the gift of Nigel de Thornton, doctor in medicine. The east head abuts on the highway commonly called Scolelanes; and the west head upon the aforesaid vacant plot which was lately, as aforesaid, given to the University by the aforesaid Nigel de Thornton."

This document—which is preserved in a volume called the

[1] [The history of this donation is extremely obscure. It appears from the Great Inquisition taken 7 Edward I. (1278—79) that Roger de Redelingfield (called also Roger de Thornton) held certain messuages of the gift of his uncle Nigel, a physician, which messuages were afterwards proved to belong to the University, and that Roger de Redelingfield was connected with them only as chaplain of a chantry which his uncle had founded for the repose of his soul.] Various documents relating to a litigation about, and a subsequent settlement of, this property are preserved by Hare (paper copy in 3 vols.), i. pp. 35, 36, 42, 47, 143. They are abstracted in the Borough Rate Report, p. 55.

White Book (*Liber albus*) of Corpus Christi College[1], because it was bound in white leather—is accompanied by a most interesting plan or sketch of the Schools as they then existed, of which a facsimile, on a reduced scale, is here given (fig. 3). On each of the pieces of ground composing the site a brief description is written, with measurements, which occasionally supplement those given in the document or obtainable from

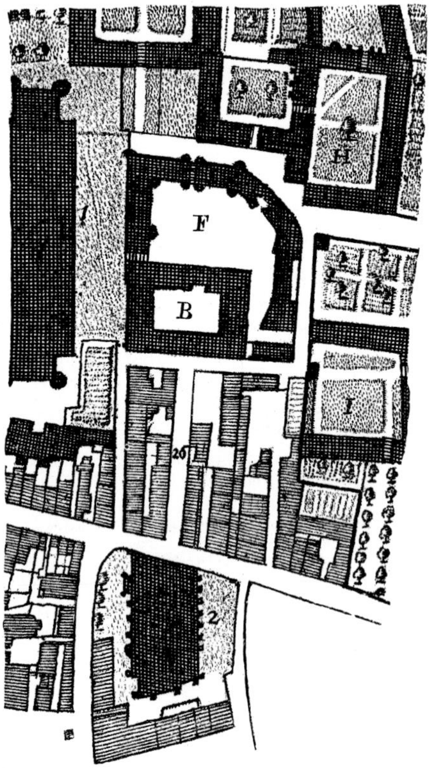

Fig. 2. Ground-plan of the site of the Schools, Senate-House, etc., enlarged from Loggan's Map of Cambridge, 1688.

1 [The full title is: "Memoranda Collegii Corporis Christi et beate Marie Cant' edita per Magistrum Iohannem Botwright sancte theorie professorem et capellanum domini Regis Henrici VI^{ti}, Rectorem de Swaffham Market, Magistrum siue Custodem Collegii predicti, electum in festo Sancti Marci Evangeliste Anno Domini 1442."]

Fig. 3. Sketch of the site and buildings of the Schools Quadrangle, drawn about 1459; reduced about one-half from a photograph of the original in the "White Book" of Corpus Christi College.

other sources. The streets bounding the site are lettered North Schools Street (*vicus scolarum borealis*), and East Schools Street (*vicus scolarum orientalis*) respectively; while on the piece leased by Corpus Christi College, which adjoins the wall bounding the whole site on the east, we read: "Ground of Corpus Christi College, containing in length 30 feet, and in breadth 29 feet, as is evident from the ancient stone wall surrounding it." Within this piece of ground is a rude representation of a Doctor of Law, seated in a chair, beneath which is written: "Chair of Civil Law, with the stone wall belonging to Corpus Christi College." On the west side of this ground a second plot, of about the same size, is designated: "This ground is the remainder of the school of Civil Law, placed upon the ground of Nigel de Thornton; which ancient school was removed in 1459, under the direction of Dr John Gay and Dr Thomas Heywood." On the open space beyond are the words: "Ground of Nigel de Thornton, containing in its greater length through the Canon-Law Schools 90 feet (*pedes pauli*); which ground is a vacant plot, or garden, belonging to the Schools Court." Again, on the north side of the site there is a rude representation of a building called Theology Schools (*Scole theologie*), across which is written "Ground of Nigel de Thornton, containing from the College plot to the Doctor of Theology's chair 60 feet[1]." This latter measurement represents exactly the distance from the College ground to the wall of the Theology School; but the distance from School Street to the outside of the west wall of the Canon Law School (now called Arts School), is actually 100 feet, and from the same street to the outside of the east wall of the same school, 68 feet. It must be remembered, however, that we do not know what was the exact length of the feet designated *pedes*

[1] [The descriptions translated in the text are written as follows on the sketch: "Fundus collegii corporis christi continens in longitudine xxx pedes, et in latitudine xxix, vt patet vndique per pinnaturas lapideas antiquas. Cathedra iuris ciuilis et ibi pinnatura lapidea collegii corporis christi. Iste fundus est residuum Scole Juris ciuilis positus et situatus supra fundum magistri Nigelli de Thornton que quidem scola antiqua removebatur Anno domini 1459 pro tunc magistris operis nouiter inchoati magistro Johanne Gay et magistro Thoma Heywood sacre theorie professoribus. Terra magistri Nigelli de Thorton (*sic*) continens in longitudine maiori per scolas canonum iiij^{xx} et x pedes pauli, qui est vacuus fundus seu ortus curie scolarum. Terra Nigelli de Thornton continens a fundo collegii iij^{xx} pedes usque cathedram doctoralem theologie."]

pauli. From these pieces of information it may be concluded generally that the ground given by Thornton (1) supplied the site for the greater portion of the Schools Court, and probably for the Theology School also, though it is doubtful whether that School was built on his ground, or on some other the history of which is now lost. The fact that the words quoted above are written across the building would lead us to the former conclusion; but, on the other hand, the language used in the lease seems intended to define that Thornton's ground extended no farther than the south wall of the School, a view which is confirmed by the measurements given on the sketch. A conveyance, preserved in the Registry of the University[1], dated 19 May, 1396, seems to refer to this ground before it passed into the hands of Corpus Christi College. Margaret Suhard, Prioress of the Benedictine house of S. Leonard at Stratford le Bowe, conveys to Thomas Kelsal and others a curtilage in School Street, bounded by the Hostel of the Holy Cross on the south, School Street on the east, a garden of Trinity Hall on the west, and a curtilage belonging to Trinity Hall on the north. The sketch (fig. 3) shews a vacant strip of ground on the east side of the Schools' quadrangle, which may be intended to represent the last-mentioned garden, to which, however, we have not been able to find any allusion in other documents.

The piece acquired from Trinity Hall (2) lay to the west of Thornton's ground. It was leased to the University 8 January, 1421, at an annual rent of two silver pennies, and is described in the lease in a passage which may be thus translated:

> "a parcel of ground lying between a garden of the aforesaid Hall on the east, and ground belonging to the aforesaid University on the west; abutting towards the north upon the new chapel in School Street, and towards the south upon a certain garden of the Hostel of the Holy Cross. On this parcel of ground there is now standing a certain stone wall of a building belonging to the University which has of late been newly built."

The "garden of the aforesaid Hall" is that which was purchased by the Commissioners of King Henry the Sixth for the site of the Old Court of King's College, and conveyed by them

[1] [It has been copied by Hare, paper copy in 3 vols., i. 253; and abstracted in the Borough Rate Report, p. 56.]

to the King 22 January, 1440—41[1]; and by "the ground belonging to the University" that given by Nigel de Thornton is evidently meant. The language used in the lease must be taken to signify that the piece demised lay eastward of the former, and westward of the latter. The "stone wall newly built," which was standing on this ground, must have belonged to the building of which a sketch is given on the plan referred to above, marked Canon Law School (*Scole canonum*), with the New Library (*Libraria noua*), above it.

The "garden of the Hostel of the Holy Cross," usually called Crouched Hostel (4), had been bought by the University from William Hulle, Prior of the Hospital of S. John of Jerusalem, 11 March, 1431—32; and when the greater part of it was sold in 1440 to King Henry the Sixth[2], it was expressly stipulated that a piece measuring 68 feet from east to west, by 10 feet from north to south, should be reserved, because it was required "for the erection of new schools (*pro novis scholis super dictam parcellam edificandis*)."

The history of the site of the Old Court of King's College has been already related[3]. The buildings erected upon it were used by King's College until the completion of the new buildings in 1828. Those buildings were not commenced until 1824; but the intentions of the College had become known in 1822, when notice to quit was served upon the tenants of the houses in Trumpington Street[4]. Accordingly, at the beginning of 1823, the Vice-Chancellor, Henry Godfrey, D.D., President of Queens' College, wrote to the Provost of King's College intimating the willingness of the University to treat for the purchase of the site and buildings of the Old Court, which would evidently be of little use to the College when their new buildings were once occupied. The Provost replied (24 February) enclosing the following Minute, which had been entered in the Congregation Book of King's College:

[1] [Vol. i. p. 318.]

[2] [Vol. i. p. 319. King's College Muniments A. 71. This piece is lettered (fig. 3): "Fundus nuper domini Willelmi Hulle prioris sancti Johannis Jerusalem in Anglia perquisitus ad vsum vniuersitatis per magistrum Willelmum Bassett pro tunc cancellarium...continens in longitudine sexaginta viij pedes et in latitudine x pedes." Immediately beyond this piece is shewn the entry to King's College, lettered: "Porta introitus ad nouum collegium domini Regis."]

[3] [Vol. i. p. 317.]

[4] [Ibid. p. 564.]

"It is the present intention of King's College to dispose of the Old Court, as soon as they have completed their projected buildings, and they would have greater satisfaction in treating with the University, than with any individual, being aware how important an addition it would be to the public library."

Notwithstanding this prompt and favourable reply, no further steps appear to have been taken by the University until the following Michaelmas Term, when Syndics were appointed (24 November) to treat with King's College for the purchase of the Old Court. At the beginning of 1825 it was agreed that the property should be valued. The valuer appointed by the University having reported that the site and buildings were worth £6300, or £6500, the Syndics offered £7500, which was declined (22 April, 1825). No further steps of importance were taken until March, 1826, when it was valued for the College at £14,525. The Syndics offered £12,000, which the College refused, but agreed to take £13,125. A Grace however to accept this offer was rejected 2 November, 1826[1]; and a subsequent proposal "that the Vice-Chancellor be empowered to buy for a sum not exceeding £12,000" was equally unsuccessful (20 March, 1827). Two years afterwards, however, King's College took the initiative, and offered to sell for £12,000; the Syndics recommended that the offer be accepted (26 March, 1829); their report was confirmed by the Senate (3 April)[2]; and the property was conveyed to the University at the end of the same year (25 November).]

CHAPTER II.

History of the Schools Quadrangle.

[The buildings disposed round the quadrangular area of which the acquisition has just been recorded, were finished before the end of the fifteenth century; and no important change, either in appearance or arrangement, was effected until the beginning of the eighteenth century. Loggan's print there-

[1] [The numbers, in the Black-Hood House, were: *placet*, 27, *non-placet*, 36.]

[2] [The numbers, in the White-Hood House, were: *placet*, 26, *non-placet*, 12.]

fore (fig. 4), dated 1688, may be considered as recording their original appearance; and it will be constantly referred to in the following attempt to trace their architectural history, the early portion of which, it must be premised, is extremely obscure. At the present day these buildings are usually spoken of as the University Library; but this destination has been the result of gradual absorption, and originally they contained all the rooms required for the public life of the University.]

The north side of the quadrangle was erected first[1]. The foundation is said to have been laid by Sir Robert Thorpe, Master of Pembroke Hall 1347—64, and afterwards Lord Chancellor of England. The date of the foundation has not been recorded; but "our great schools in School Street" are mentioned in a lease dated 15 February, 1347[2]. Sir Robert died suddenly, 29 June 1372, leaving his goods to the disposal of his executors, one of whom, Richard de Treton, afterwards Master of Corpus Christi College 1376—77, caused 40 marks to be given to the University. With this sum, and some other help, the walls were carried up until they came almost to the level of the first floor, when the work was stopped for some years for want of funds. We do not know how it came to be resumed, but in 1398 (20 June) Eudo de la Zouch, Chancellor of the University, agreed with the executors of Sir William Thorpe that a service should be held for the repose of the souls of Sir William Thorpe (brother of Sir Robert), and of his wife Lady Grace Thorpe, 6 May and 19 November in each year, "because they (the executors) had

[1] The following account of the building of the north side of the Schools Quadrangle has been partly derived from the chapter on the Building of the Public Schools (*Scholarum Publicarum Extructio*) in the "Academiae Historia Cantabrigiensis" appended to Archbishop Parker's Treatise "De Antiquitate Britannicae Ecclesiae," Fol. 1572; and partly from a more diffuse history drawn up by himself in English apparently to furnish materials for the former work. The original is among the MSS. at Corpus Christi College. It has been copied by Baker, MSS. xix. 93. MSS. Harl. Mus. Brit. 7046.

[2] [This document is one of those relating to Thornton's property. It has been copied by Hare, paper copy in 3 vols., i. 143, and abstracted in the Borough Rate Report, p. 56. The Chancellor, John de Crachal, and the University grant to William de Alderford, Presbyter, Master of Arts, certain lands, "Ac eciam decem solidos et duos denarios [annui] redditus singulis annis percipiendos de magnis scholis nostris in vico scholarium (*sic*) Cantabrigie."]

Fig. 4. The Schools Quadrangle, from Loggan's print, taken about 1688. A, Divinity School; B, Regent House; C, Library; D, Lesser Library; E, School of Medicine and Law; F, Bachelors School; G, Consistory; H, Court of the Proctors and Taxors; I, Sophisters School.

caused to be built Divinity Schools, together with a Chapel for the souls of the aforesaid William and Grace his wife[1]."

"For which Convention, the Executors of William Thorpe went forward with the Divinity Scholes, paved the Floors, made the Stalls there with the Doctor's Chair, the Plancher above that, and paved it, and made the Partition between the Regent and non-Regent House, and so finished the same perfectly, saving the Battlement on the East side; making also from the ground the Porche, with the foundation, and the volte as it standeth at this day, where the University Hutch is.

In which Porch the Doctors of Divinity were wont to open their Questions to the Answerer, as the Disputers in Philosophy used to declare their Questions in the Little scholes, now the Consistory of the Vice Chancellor. The executors of which William Thorpe caused also the windows to be glazed[2]."

The work is said to have been completed in the year 1400[3].

The western side of the quadrangle was next built, but there are no documents to shew when or how it was begun and carried to its completion. It is mentioned as in existence in 1438 in a petition addressed by the University to King Henry the Sixth, in which the petitioners set forth that from time immemorial they have been seised "of divers tenements and ground on which stand certain buildings for students in Theology and in Civil and Canon Law; and moreover a common library, with a Chapel of exceeding great beauty[4]." Again, in 1440, the garden sold by Trinity Hall to King Henry the Sixth is described as bounded on the east by the "new schools of

[1] [Senior Proctor's Book, fol. 49, No. 184. Commiss. Doc^{ts}. i. 411. The decree proceeds as follows: "Insuper vnanimi concensu...concedimus...quod quilibet incepturus, siue recturus et lecturus in sacra theologia in scolis edificandis per predictos executores iurabit tactis sacrosanctis in die inceptionis sue quod quolibet die quo contingat ipsum legere in scolis annotatis quod finito psalmo *Ad te leuaui* non recedet a predicto loco quousque dixerit psalmum *De profundis* pro animabus predictorum Willelmi et domine Gracie consortis sue." A curious relic of this custom is mentioned in the "Diary of Abraham de la Pryme," ed. Surtees Society 1869, under the year 1694. After describing the ceremony of his degree he adds: "Upon that as he [the Vice Chancellor] has done with them [the incepting Bachelors] one by one they rise up, and, going to a long table hard by, kneel down there and say some short prayer or other as they please."]

[2] [Archbishop Parker's English History of the Schools. The west window still contains the Royal Arms in the centre, flanked by those of Thorpe.]

[3] "Ut jam cernimus, tota [schola] per cohæredes predictos ad finem perducta est anno 1400" are the words of Archbishop Parker, but he gives no authority. The same statement is made by Dr Caius (Hist. Cant. Acad. ii. 81).

[4] [Hare (paper copy, in 3 volumes), ii. 128. b.]

theology and canon law[1];" and in 1458 a Grace of the Senate, to be quoted below, speaks of the Canon Law School as begun but not yet finished. The sketch of the Schools (fig. 3), to which reference has been already made, shews on the west side of the quadrangle a building in two floors, of which the lower is lettered Canon Law Schools (*Scole canonum*), and the upper, New Library (*Libraria noua*): and the University Accounts for 1454 and the following years contain numerous entries for the leaden roof of the New Chapel and Library[2]; for general repairs of the same buildings; for the chaining and binding of books; and especially for their custody and preservation during a fire in King's College in 1457[3].

[The appearance of the Schools in the middle of the 15th century, will be readily understood from the sketch (fig. 3). On the north side of the area stood the Theology School; and on the west the Canon Law School with the new Library above it. The ground bought from William Hulle, not yet built upon, extended along the whole south border of the site. Next to this ground stood the old Civil Law School, entered from North School Street by a door in the east boundary-wall of the quadrangle, lettered, "small gate of entrance to the old Law Schools (*parua porta qua itur ad antiquas scolas iuris*);" and a few feet beyond it, in the same wall, was a second and larger gate, lettered, "great gate of entrance to the court of the New Schools (*magna porta ad intrandam curiam nouarum scolarum*)."]

The history of the building of the south side is very satisfactorily recorded. In 1457 (5 July) a Syndicate was appointed with full powers for making all necessary arrangements for building "a New School of Philosophy and Civil Law or a Library[4];" and in the following year (9 April, 1458) the Chan-

[1] [Vol. i. p. 318.]

[2] [Univ. Accounts 1454. fol. 2[a]. "It'...pro plumbo noue capelle et librarie...vj marc." "It'...pro pauiamento noue capelle xl[s]."]

[3] [Ibid. 1457. fol. 10[a]. "Item doctori thome Stoyle pro diuersis expensis factis per ipsum circa saluacionem communis librarie tempore quo ignis estuabat in regali collegio v[s]. vj[d]."]

[4] [The Grace (Grace Book A. fol. 6. a.) concedes to the Syndics "plenam et plenariam potestatem disponendi prouidendi excogitandi pro edifficacione Noue Scole philosophie et iurisciuilis vel librarie;" words which are evidently intended to include the selection of plans, and the provision of funds.]

cellor, Laurence Booth, Lord Bishop of Durham, Mr Robert Woodlarke, Mr Nicholas Gay, Mr Thomas Haywoode, and the two Proctors, were appointed to supervise the building-work, to make all purchases, and to conclude all bargains thereunto appertaining[1]. Provision for collecting the necessary funds was made at a later date in the same year (30 June) by a second Grace[2], the preamble of which sets forth that "whereas the Schools of Philosophy and Civil Law are in a state of irremediable decay and ruin, and must shortly fall to the ground unless some remedy be speedily provided, the said Schools are to be built on ground belonging to the University, next to the School of Canon Law which has already been built and set up there;" and that the funds to be collected are to be applied to that purpose, "and also to the completion of the latter School."

The work was commenced immediately, and proceeded regularly, for in each succeeding year the Accounts contain entries for money paid to the officers who would now be termed the Building Syndicate. Progress however was extremely slow, probably through want of funds, for in 1466 the Chancellor, William Wilflete, Master of Clare Hall, goes to London to solicit subscriptions[3]. It may be presumed that he was successful, for in the same year (25 June) a contract was drawn between the Syndicate on the one part, and William Harward and William Bacon of Halsted in Essex, carpenters, on the other part, for making the floor, the roof, all the doors and windows, and the roof of the "vice," or staircase. They were to receive £23. 6. 8. besides £10 paid in hand on the day of signing the contract; and the work was to be completed by 1 August, 1467. This contract is one of the most instructive in its descriptions that I have met with; and as the floor and roof in question are still in existence, it admits of accurate interpretation. It will therefore be given at length in a subsequent chapter, when we compare the existing structures with their recorded history. In the same year stone was bought for the win-

[1] [Grace Book A. fol. 11. b.]

[2] [Ibid. fol. 11. a.]

[3] [Univ. Accounts 1466. fol. 38. b. "Item deliberatum est magistro Wolflet Cancellario pro exspensis suis quas habuit London procurando bona pro edificacione noue scole xvij^{s}. ix^{d}."]

dows, and a contract was entered into for glazing them[1]. The document however has not been preserved. The Accounts shew that the work went on regularly during the years 1467, 1468, and 1469, in which year, notwithstanding the provision that the roof was to be finished in 1467, we find timber being brought in, and a crane set up for raising it. In the following year, however, the crane is taken down again[2]; and it is therefore probable that the completion of the whole building took place in 1470 or 1471; but it is difficult to determine this with absolute accuracy, as entries referring to the conclusion of the south range of the Schools are mixed up with others referring to the commencement of the east range.

The south building was entered through a "vice," or turret-staircase, at the north-east corner (fig. 4), which rose to a sufficient height above the roof to be called the Schools Tower (*Turris scolarum*)[3]. It contained the Schools bell, and is therefore sometimes called the Schools Belfry (*campanile scolarum*)[4]. It was so placed that it formed part of the east range, which was commenced in 1470, when the first payment is made "for building two new schools next the schools gate." The narrative which has been already quoted records the work as follows:

> "Further, the little Schole, now the Place of Judgment for the Vice Chancellor, and the other Schole where the Doctors sitt, were built at the charges of the University; and the Library over that [was] built by Thomas Rotheram, then Chancellor both of the Realm and University, Bishop of Lincoln, and afterwards Archbishop of York, besides the Schole Gate, with the jawmes as it standeth, by him especially, and certain other; As Humfrie Duke of Glocester sometime gave 20 marks; And the Earle of Oxford (whose Chaplain the said Rotheram was) gave 10*li*; whose Arms are inward, on the wall of the Little Library."

The Accounts contain few entries which throw any light upon the progress of the work. It may be suggested that, as

[1] [Ibid. 1466. fol. 38. b. "Item pro lapidibus pro fenestris noue scole x^{s}. v^{d}. Item pro vino tempore quo fecimus pactum...pro vitrifacione noue scole vi^{d}." Ibid. fol. 39. a. "Item pro vitreacione noue scole pro Indenturis xij^{d}."]

[2] [Ibid. 1469. fol. 60. a. "In primis solut' carpentariis pro vectura et ammocione meremii et cuiusdam machine vocat' le craane stantis in exteriori curia noui collegii pro operibus vniuersitatis xij^{d}." Ibid. 1470. fol. 64. a. "Item pro deposicione le crane erecte in orto collegij Regis pro noua fabrica vniuersitatis iiij^{d}."]

[3] [Ibid. 1470. p. 64. a. "Pro fenestris in turri scolarum xxj^{d}."]

[4] [Ibid. 1512—13. p. 299. "Item pro meremio ... pro campanili supra scolas iij^{s}. Item pro reparacione campane scolarum ij^{s}."]

it was principally paid for by subscription, the Accounts of receipts and payments would not be entered in the Books of the University. The last entries referring to it are to be found in the Accounts for 1473, when it was probably nearly finished; and in 1475 (13 May) the University caused the name of Thomas Rotherham to be entered among its principal benefactors, because he had "completed the schools, together with a new library over them, which latter he had furnished with everything needful, and enriched with numerous volumes of great value[1]."

The design of the east façade, which was destroyed in 1754, as will be related in the next chapter, has fortunately been preserved by Loggan. The east building occupied the space between the staircase above mentioned, and the Theology School. Including the staircase, it was about 69 feet long, but the ground-plan (fig. 5) shews that the total width could not have exceeded fifteen feet; or eleven feet between the walls[2]. The gate of entrance was in the centre of the distance between the staircase and the Theology School (fig. 4); and therefore, as was so common in medieval buildings, it was neither in the centre of the façade nor in the centre of the east side of the inner quadrangle. The space above the arch was ornamented by three shields. The central shield bore the Royal Arms, supported by lions; that on the right the Arms of Archbishop Rotherham, three stags trippant; that on the left cannot be determined with certainty.

[A description of the west side of the gate, or of part of it, has been preserved by Sandford in his account of King Richard the Third:

"Over the gate of the Library at *Cambridge*, on the inside in a Compartment of Stone, is carved *a Rose*, supported on the right side with *a Bull*, and on the left side by *a Boar*. The latter of which, *viz.* the *white Boar*, was his [King Richard the Third's] Cognisance, which gave occasion to the Rhime which cost the maker his life:

The Cat, *the* Rat, *and* Lovel *the* Dog
Rule all England *under the* Hog[3]."

[1] [Commiss. Doc^{ts}. i. 414.]

[2] [On the plan attached to Archbishop Parker's History it is noted that the width of the central gateway was seven feet two inches, and the depth eleven feet.]

[3] [Genealogical History of the Kings of England, Fol. 1677, p. 405. The distich, written by William Colyngbourne, is given rather differently in Holinshed, p. 746, "The Cat, the Rat, and Lovel our Dog, Ruleth all England under a Hog." The favourites alluded to are Sir William Catesby, Sir Richard Ratcliffe, and Francis Lord Lovel, Lord Chamberlain of the King's household.]

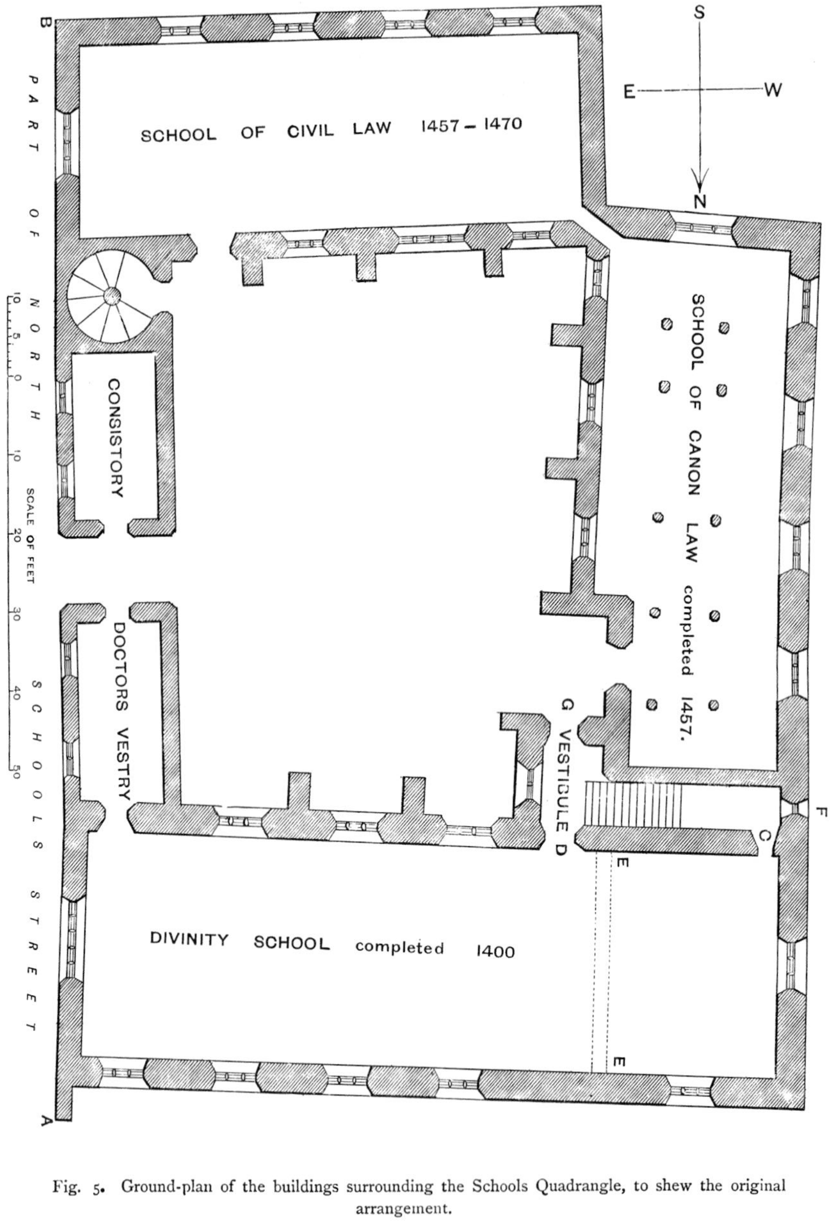

Fig. 5. Ground-plan of the buildings surrounding the Schools Quadrangle, to shew the original arrangement.

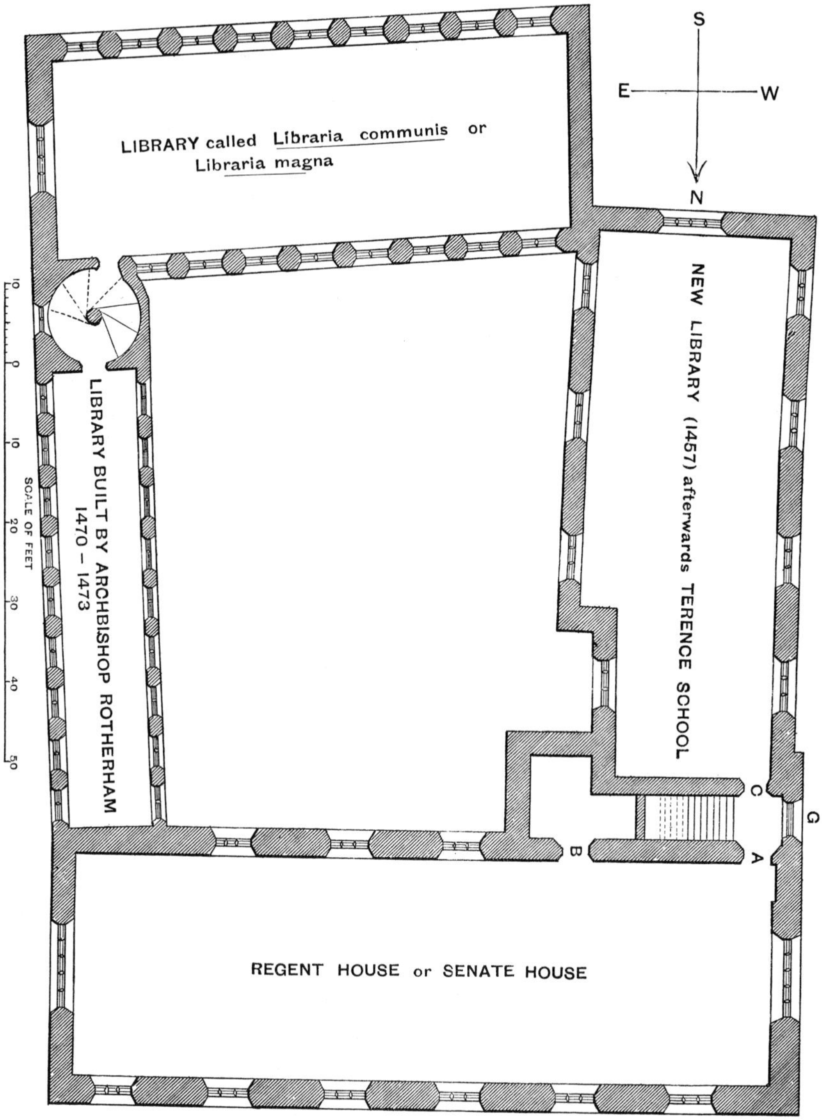

Fig. 6. Plan of the first floor of the Schools Quadrangle, to shew the original arrangement.

A rose was a cognisance of King Edward the Fourth; and a black bull was sometimes used by him as a supporter, just as a boar was used by King Richard the Third, both as Duke of Gloucester and as King. It may therefore be suggested that these devices were intended to commemorate the reign of the former, in which the structure had been built, and some special benefaction of the latter; and it is not improbable that Archbishop Parker, or the scribe whom he employed, may have written Humphry, when he should have written Richard, in the record of those who had contributed to the building of the Library and the Gateway.

In the elevation of the east front of the Schools which illustrates Archbishop Parker's Essay (fig. 7), the gate is ornamented with three coats of arms, as shewn by Loggan, and, further, with a rose, a portcullis, and two flowers which seem to be intended for a daisy and a fleur-de-lis. This drawing however is proved to be inaccurate, not only from Sandford's statement that the rose was on the other side of the gate, but from comparison of the Royal Arms, which fortunately have been preserved, with the representation there given of them. When the façade was pulled down in 1754, the arch, the carved spandrels, and the side-niches, were purchased by Sir John Cotton, and in 1758 set up as the entrance to the courtyard of his house at Madingley, near Cambridge[1]. Of the shields, that bearing the Royal Arms was alone preserved. It is now inserted in a wall which was built above the arch, and which is terminated by a pediment. The niches also now terminate in pinnacles of similar character. A daisy and a portcullis, carved in relief, are inserted in the wall beneath the shield. This

[1] [Cole (MSS. xxxiii. 388. MSS. Add. Mus. Brit. 5834) gives the following account of the disposal of the materials of this gateway: "The Society of Corpus Christi College gave to me, by the means of my late worthy friend Dr Barnardiston the Master [1764—78] several Loads of good Free Stone which the late Master and present Bishop of Lincoln [Dr John Green, Master 1750—64] had purchased on the pulling down the Front of the present Scholes and Library.... The Bishop bought them on an Idea of new building his College...and lying in their way, and mouldring by the Weather, especially the Clunch among the other Stones, he kindly...gave them to me. They were part of the curious Gate-Way, built by Bishop Rotheram, the cheif part of which Sir John Cotton purchased, and again erected at Madingley, where it makes a handsome Entrance to the Court Yard."]

shield, while differing considerably from the representation of it given by Archbishop Parker, closely resembles that of Loggan. On these grounds, therefore, we may accept his drawing as the more accurate of the two, and conclude that the daisy, portcullis, and other devices, did not decorate the east front, but were added to some other part of the building at a later period, probably during the reign of King Henry the Seventh.]

The quadrangle, as thus completed, subsisted with but few changes, until the reign of King George the First; but, before we narrate the alterations then introduced, we will briefly describe the use made of the different parts of it and mention the few historical facts which concern our present purpose. The appropriation of many of the schools has been changed from time to time, as the subjects of study, and modes of teaching, in the University, have varied; and for want of attention to these changes, some confusion and apparent contradiction has arisen between the accounts of different historians[1].

The north side has always had the Theology School, to which Archbishop Parker adds the Hebrew School, on the ground-floor. Above there was at first a chapel, used as well for the chantry service of the Founder and other benefactors as for the deliberations and ceremonials of the Senate. The ancient Graces of the Senate are invariably dated from the "New Chapel of the University" (*nova capella Universitatis*)[2], and though the Reformation put an end to its employment as a chapel, the ancient name "New Chapel" was retained until the eighteenth century. The room was divided into the Regent

[1] [The authorities for these points are: (1) the plan above described (fig. 3), and the documents in the Registry of the University; (2) Archbishop Parker's History, dated 1572, to which is appended an elevation of the four sides of the quadrangle with their designations referred to by letters; (3) the account of the building of the Schools in Dr Caius' History, dated 1574; (4) Fuller's History; (5) the description at the foot of Loggan's print (fig. 4), dated 1688.]

[2] [The usual form was: "Acta sunt hec Cantabrigie in plena congregacione nostra in noua capella universitatis."] The following entries illustrate the celebration of Divine Service in the Chapel: Univ. Accounts 1475—76. "Item pro 2^bus candelis ad altare in capella xij^d." Ibid. 1491—92. "Item pro missis ... in capella Vniuersitatis ij^s. ij^d." Ibid. 1500—1501. "Item pro duobus cereis ... pro exequiis et missis in capella Vniuersitatis vj^d." Ibid. 1522—23. "Item pro tinctura panni cooperientis altare in scolis xvj^d." Ibid. 1556—57. "Pro duobus pannis holosericis pro summo altari in scolis iiij^li." A "small chapel" (*parua capella*) is mentioned in 1512—13.]

House and non-Regent House, which Fuller characterises as "having something of chapel character and consecration in them[1];" and the two are frequently spoken of together as "The Regent House."

The ground-floor of the west side was built, as we have seen, for Canon Law; but this subject having been prohibited by the Royal Injunctions of 1535[2], Dialectics, otherwise termed Logic, took possession of the school. The upper floor of the same building, built originally for a Library, was used for the "Humanities" or Terence School in the early part of the sixteenth

Fig. 7. Gate of entrance to the Schools, from Archbishop Parker's History.

century; and when the Terence lecture was changed for one of Rhetoric in 1549 by the Visitors of King Edward the Sixth, that subject was taught in the same school[3]. In Archbishop

[1] [Fuller, ed. Prickett and Wright, p. 160.]

[2] [Cooper's Annals, i. 375.]

[3] [Dr Caius says of the west side of the quadrangle (Hist. Cant. Acad. p. 80): "In his superioribus [scholis] nostro tempore [defined by him (Ibid. p. 53) to extend from 12 Sept. 1529 to 29 Sept. 1545] professio erat humaniorum literarum, inferioribus dialecticæ;" and Archbishop Parker, speaking of the Grace of 1458, says: "provisum fuit tam de illis scholis perficiendis quam Terentiana quondam schola, in qua jam juris civilis lectiones et disputationes fiunt; necnon ut inferiores dialecticæ

Parker's time Civil Law, Greek, and Rhetoric, were taught there; but these, when Fuller wrote, had given way to Physic and Law, while on the ground-floor were "the philosophy, commonly called the bachelors' schools;" an arrangement which, as Loggan shews, still subsisted in 1688.

The south side was intended originally to contain "a school for Philosophy and Civil Law, or a Library;" and the upper floor was used for the latter purpose until the establishment of the Regius Professorships of Theology, Civil Law, Physic, Hebrew, and Greek, in 1540, the school beneath being shared by Civil Law and Philosophy. After 1540, however, Civil Law was removed to the west side of the quadrangle, as already mentioned, and in 1547 a Grace of the Senate directed that the lectures of the Regius Professor of Divinity (*Theologia regis*) should be given in "the old library;" which, according to Dr Caius, was shared by the Regius Professors of Greek and Physic[1]. The room as thus appropriated is spoken of in the University Accounts as "the new School[2];" "upper Theology School (*Theologica schola superior*);" "new Theology School;" "new divynitie scholes;" and "hier divinytie scholes." We have seen that Archbishop Parker transfers Greek to the first floor of the west side; but Fuller restores it to the south side, placing beneath it "the logic or sophister schools, where (in term time) daily disputations, and the bachelors' commencement is kept;" schools which had hitherto been appropriated to Philosophy. Civil Law, however, has since returned to the school in which it was originally placed. It should also be mentioned that in 1559—60

scholæ perficerentur." The plan appended to his essay designates this school: "Civilis, Græca, Rhetorica." The Injunctions of King Edward the Sixth (Lamb, Documents, p. 141) direct: "Terentii lectio in rhetoricam vertatur, et hujus professor declamationum in scholis moderator erit quemadmodum dialectices professor sophismatum." The old names survived the abolition of the lectures, for the following entries occur in the University Accounts, 1554—55; "Item pro reparatione plumbi terentiane schole xxiij^{s}. vj^{d}." Ibid. 1558—59; "Item pro iij^{bus}. fenestris ligneis in scholis Theologie et humanitatis xiiij^{d}."]

[1] ["In hac scholarum parte professio est hodie inferiùs philosophiæ, vt prius; superiùs professio Theologiæ, linguæ Græcæ, et medicinæ fundationis regiæ, cum tamen nostro tempore superior eius pars bibliotheca communis erat, nec in ea vlla scientiarum professio fuit." Caius, *ut supra*, p. 81.]

[2] [The University Accounts for 1547—48 shew that it was fitted up as a school by Stephen Wallis, for whom see Vol. ii. p. 562.]

a school on this side of the quadrangle is spoken of as the Mathematical School[1].

The east side contained originally two small schools. According to Dr Caius one of them (that on the left hand) was used for what he calls "a questionists' school;" the other as a waiting-room for those who attended the disputations in Theology. In 1571—72 the former was fitted up to serve the double purpose of a Registry, and the Vice-Chancellor's Court, or Consistory:

"Item to Matthew Stokys bedell, to glase and to make thowse on the sowthe syde of the Scoole gatys a consistorie for the Vicechauncelors and an office for the Regester to kepe the bokes and recordys of thuniversitie in ....ix^{li}. ix^{s}."

Fuller describes the latter as "a vestry where the doctors robe themselves, and have a convenient inspection into the divinity schools:" a destination probably identical with that mentioned by Dr Caius[2]. In 1688 the room on the south side of the gate is designated by Loggan "Consistory," and that on the right side "Court of the Proctors and Taxors."

[It has been already stated that no important structural alteration took place in the schools until after 1715. Some minor works however require a brief notice. In 1583—84 a general repair was carried out; the walls were underpinned, and the spouts shewn by Loggan were made[3]. In 1639—40 the battlements were repaired, at a total cost of nearly £103; and in 1646—7 a carpenter is paid for "timber used for supporters." This entry evidently marks the period when doubts began to be entertained of the security of the floors; and accordingly they were supported in each school by a double row of columns. In 1659—60 we find a charge "for cutting needlesse stone out of the windowes to gaine light" in the Divinity School, which

[1] [University Accounts, 1559—60, fol. 78. b.: "pro pecunia soluta collegio corporis Christi pro schola mathematica ij^{s}."]

[2] [Dr Caius (*ut supra*) uses the following words: "Quartam et orientalem partem ...cuius summa pars bibliotheca est, ima quondam quæstionistarum scholæ, procerumque statio ad disputationes Theologicas audiendas confluentium, iam autem tribunal est Procancellarii cum subselliis aptis et fabricatis pro eius assessoribus."]

[3] [Univ. Accounts, 1583—84, fol. 145: "Item to Mr Stokys bedell for makyng spowtes abowt the schooles, for mending the leades, for stone, and vnderpynnyng the whalles of the schooles as apereth by three bylles xix^{li}. xij^{s}. vij^{d}."]

probably indicates the removal of a transom similar to that shewn by Loggan in the Arts School. In 1662 (4 July) the Senate decreed that a room, described in the Grace as situated between the schools of Theology and Philosophy, should be fitted up as a Registry, for the greater security of the documents belonging to the University[1].

Between 1676 and 1678 a general repair, much more extensive than the previous one, was carried out, at a cost of more than £800. The entries in the Accounts refer chiefly to labour and materials, without specific reference to the work done. It appears to have included a thorough repair of the roofs, both in lead and timber, and of the exterior and interior stone work; with a renewal of the fittings of some of the rooms, especially of the Regent House[2]. The woodwork was executed by Cornelius Austin; and it was probably at this time that in the Schools of Arts and Law the fluted columns which still exist were built round the old "supporters" set up thirty years before. Further, Austin is paid "for 32 foot of oake for 8 capitalls," which are proved to have been in the Divinity School by a receipt from the same workman for the value of the old stone foundations of the columns in that School[3].

The following extracts from the Accounts for these two years are worth quotation:

"For a new dore-case to the Divinity Schooles......... 08 . 10 . 00
For a new ouall to give light to the starecase............ 02 . 10 . 00

[1] ["Cum ad Academiæ honorem ac columitatem conducat plurimùm, ut rescripta Regum, Senatus hujus consulta, cæteraque Reipublicæ nostræ munimenta in loco aliquo tuto ac solenni custodiantur, quæ hactenus inter Oppidanorum ædes, incendijs, rapinis, multisque casibus obnoxia delitescunt, Placet vobis vt in posterum intra publicas scholas asserventur: et vt vacivo loco, qui inter scholas Theologicas et Philosophicas interjacet, cura domini Procancellarij (qui pro tempore fuerit) Archivum publicum Academiæ impensis clathris et forulis instruatur, quo munimenta prædicta possint accuratius et ad vsum hujus Senatûs accommodatius asservari." Univ. Accounts 1661—62: "To John Adams the Carpenter his bill for timber, dealebord, and worke for floaring and wainscoating the roome at the West end of the Divinity Schooles for the Registrar's office according to the Grace of the Regent house 036 . 08 . 00. Item to Hutton a bricklayer for a partition wall and plaistering worke...022 . 03 . 03."]

[2] [The extent of the repair is shewn by the following entry at the conclusion of the Account for 1678: "To Robert Grumbold, for overseeing the severall Workmen, Carpenters, Joyners, Painters, Plummers, Glaziers, Smiths, etc., and measuring their Works ... 002 . 10 . 00."]

[3] [Univ. Accounts 1677—78. *Recepta*. "Item recepto a Corn: Austin pro rejectis lapideis fundamentis antiquarum columnarum in Scholâ Theologicâ 000 . 12 . 00."]

For making of a Arch in the going up of the stare-case and working the old stone; for the seates in the starecase out of the old ston	02 . 10 . 00
To John Kendall the Plummer for lead and work over the Regent House and little Library	09 . 03 . 00
To [the same] for lead [etc.] over the Regent House and Great Library	01 . 15 . 00
To [the same] for lead [etc.] over the great Library, and over the Physick schooles	23 . 08 . 00
To Robert Grumbold for paueing and other work done in the Divinity Schooles	47 . 11 . 00
To [the same] for Paveing and Materialls for the Regent and Non Regent House	47 . 10 . 00
To Cornelius Austin for Wainscoting and making seats, and other work about the Divinity Schooles, after deduction for old Wainscot board and old Timber	100 . 02 . 00
To him for the Screene in the Regent house with all the carving belonging to it	030 . 00 . 00
To him for Wanscot, and Seates, and Elbowes in the non-regent house	015 . 00 . 00
For 48 yeards of windscoot (*sic*) in the Non-Regent house with the carving work at 6 shillings per yard	014 . 08 . 00
To Wiseman for painting the Kings and the University Armes over the Skreene in the Regent house	001 . 15 . 00"

In 1772—73 a Syndicate "appointed for the Repairs of the Divinity Schools" directed "that the Columns in the said Schools shall be cover'd plain and not fluted, with a plain Base, Pedestal, and Capital of the Doric Order[1]."]

We will in the next place trace the history of the Library; confining ourselves for the most part to the rooms and book-cases, without reference to the books, an investigation which would lead us beyond the limits of the present work[2].

It has been already shewn that the room on the first floor of the west side of the quadrangle was built for a Library, and was certainly used as such; and though subsequently it was used also as a school, it need not be assumed on that account that its original intention was wholly abandoned. The new Library, on the first floor of the south side, was fitted up as soon as it was completed, for in 1473 the Proctors made a

[1] [Minutes of the Syndicate, 29 July, 1773.]

[2] [The history of the contents of the Library has been admirably narrated in "The University Library. Papers contributed to the Cambridge University Gazette, 1869," by Henry Bradshaw, University Librarian. 8vo. Cambridge, 1881.]

catalogue of the books in it[1]. The document unquestionably refers to the south Library, for it enumerates the contents of eight stalls on the north side, and of one stall and eight desks on the south side. This collection was altogether independent of Rotherham's Library on the first floor of the east side, which was fitted up soon after it was completed. The south Library was called the common library (*libraria communis*), or the great library (*libraria magna*); while the east library was called the Chancellor's library (*libraria domini cancellarij*)[2]. Afterwards, as Dr Caius records, the former was designated "the public library," or "the old library." It contained the more ordinary books and was open to everybody. The latter was designated "the private library" or "the new library." The more valuable books were kept in it, and only a few privileged persons were admitted to it[3]. When Archbishop Parker's plan was drawn, this was the only room designated "University Library (*Bibliotheca Academiæ*)." A Grace recommending the conversion of the old Library into a school for the Regius Professor of Divinity, because "in its present state it is no use to anybody," had been passed in 1547[4]; and we may conclude that "pilferers (*suffurantes*)," as Dr Caius calls them, had by that time so far reduced the number of volumes in both collections, notwithstanding the precautions taken to preserve one at least from depredation, that a single small room was sufficiently large to contain the scanty remnants of the old collection, of which he enumerates about 180 volumes[5].

1 ["Registrum M^{ri} Radulphi Songer et Ricardi Cokeram Procuratorum Cant' compilatum Anno domini millesimo cccc^{mo}. lxx^{o}. tercio." It has been printed from the original in the Registry of the University by Henry Bradshaw, University Librarian, Cam. Antiq. Soc. Antiquarian Communications, ii. 239.]

2 [These names appear in the University Accounts for 1477 and 1478.]

3 [Hist. Cant. Acad. p. 89. "Cum duæ bibliothecæ erant, altera priuata seu noua, altera publica seu vetus dicebatur. In illa optimi quique, in hac omnis generis ex peiori numero ponebantur. Illa paucis, ista omnibus patebat."]

4 [Grace-book Δ, fol. 19. b. "Item conceditur vt dominus vicecancellarius et procuratores vestram habeant authoritatem formandi ex vetusta bibliotheca novam scholam theologicam quoniam vt nunc est nulli est vsui et formosior schola ex ea formari potest quam vlla est reliquarum."]

5 [The same tale of pillage is told by Fuller (p. 160): "This library formerly was furnished with plenty of choice books, partly at the cost of Archbishop Rotheram [etc.]. But these books by the covetousness of some great ones, and carelessness of the library loosers (for library keepers I cannot call them) are for the most part embezzled to the great loss of the University, and learning in general." There is a curious entry

This state of things lasted until 1574, when Archbishop Parker gave some books to the library "to be placed at the north end of the said library, in certain lockers appointed for the same[1];" and Dr Andrew Perne, Master of Peterhouse, who was elected Vice-Chancellor in that year

"being also of a public spirit towards the good estate of this University, backed and countenanced by the Archbishop, set himself to furnish the library, to make it of use and reputation. For which purpose he was come up this year [1574] to London, the better to solicit eminent men to be benefactors to it; having in the mean time his harbour and board at Lambeth with the Archbishop. And he found success in these his commendable pains; for he got books from the Lord Keeper, the Bishop of Winchester, and divers other honourable persons, as well as from the Archbishop. When Perne returned to Cambridge, he was employed in making convenient places and receptacles for the books of each benefactor, that their books might have standings distinct by themselves; that so each giver might be the better remembered to posterity;"

and in a private letter to the Archbishop, dated November, 1574, he dwells upon

"the singular beauty that the comely order of your Grace's books doth bring to the University library, to the great delectation of the eye of every man that shall enter into the said library;"

and adds, at the end of the letter,

"I do send to your Grace also a paper containing the form of the length and bigness of those three places, wherein my Lord Keeper mindeth to grave the names of all his books. The which I send unto your Grace, for that there might be the like drawn of all my Lord of Winchester's books, the which shall be at your Grace's pleasure[2]."

The mention of the north end of the Library, in the first of the above extracts, shews that Rotherham's Library was still

in the Accounts for 1572—73, which may account for the disappearance of many volumes: "Item for dressing the librarye and removing the old bookes ij^s^." A Catalogue of these books made in 1573 (Grace-book Δ, p. 350 (*b*), enumerates 177 volumes; and a note at the end records: "Moste parte of all theis bookes be of velam and parchment, but very sore cut and mangled for the lymned letters and pictures."]

1 [These words occur in the deed by which the Archbishop gave University Street to the University, as recorded in Chapter III.]

2 [Life and Acts of Matthew Parker. By John Strype. Ed. 1821, ii. 407, 408. The Lord Keeper, Sir Nicholas Bacon, gave 73 volumes; Archbishop Parker 100; Robert Horne, D.D., Bishop of Winchester, 50; and James Pilkington, D.D., Bishop of Durham, 20.]

the only one in use. Twelve years afterwards, however, 16 December, 1586, a Grace passed the Senate, empowering the Vice-Chancellor and Proctors to restore the old Library to its original use, on the ground that many persons of distinction were prepared to give a large quantity of books to the University, provided such restitution were made; and to make arrangements elsewhere for the lectures given, and exercises performed therein[1]. It may be presumed that this direction was obeyed, for the Divinity Lecture was transferred to another School, and an entry in the University Accounts for 1586—87

"Item for the charges of the librarye vt patet per librum .... cxxv^{li}. xiij^{s}. iiij^{d}.[2]"

shews that a very considerable amount of work must have been done in the way of fitting up the room for the reception of books; but it was evidently still used for other purposes than those of a Library, for Fuller records that in his time the Greek Schools were on the first floor of the south side of the quadrangle, and he does not mention the Library. In 1645, however, the University petitioned Parliament to put them in possession of Archbishop Bancroft's Library, which he, by Will dated 28 October, 1610, had bequeathed to the Public Library of the University of Cambridge, should certain other conditions not be fulfilled. The request was granted, 15 February, 1646—47, and the books arrived in 1649[3]. It was necessary that immediate steps should be taken to provide room for so large an addition to the Library, and the following Grace was passed, 3 September, 1649[4]:

[1] [Grace-book Δ, fol. 153. "Cum multi honoratissimi viri parati sunt donare magnam copiam librorum modo antiqua bibliotheca restituatur in pristinum vsum, placet vobis vt dominus vice-cancellarius et domini procuratores possint vestra auctoritate de consensu maioris partis prefectorum collegiorum hoc negocium peragere et constituere ordinem pro illis lectionibus et exercitijs que nunc in illa schola consueverunt peragi."]

[2] [The vouchers for this year are unfortunately missing, and therefore we cannot obtain any detailed information respecting the work. In 1611—12 the materials of some old bookcases were sold, and fetched £3, and we find the following entry (p. 221): "Item for timber...and other furniture for the newe bookes vt patet per billam xix^{li}. xi^{s}. ix^{d}.," but it is impossible to determine where these cases were set up.]

[3] [Univ. Accounts, 1648—49. "Item to M^{r}. Thomas Bucke for Moneys layd out by him for removeing and sorting the Lambeth Bookes 05 . 07 . 08."]

[4] [Grace-book H, p. 56.]

"Whereas the books given to this vniversity by Archbishop Bancroft, and lately removed from Lambeth hither, are more than can conveniently be placed in your publick Library; May it therefore please you that the Greek Schooles may be added to your said Librarie, and fitted for the disposeall of the said books; And that the Professor of the Greek tongue may hereafter reade his lectures in the Law Schools, at such times as no hindrance, or disturbance, may thereby be occasioned to what is there to be done by the Law-Professor."

The room was immediately fitted up with new shelves, and Evelyn, who visited the University 31 August, 1654, though he calls the Schools "despicable" and the Public Library "mean," admits that the latter had been "somewhat improv'd by the wainscotting and books lately added by Bishop Bancroft's library and MSS[1]," and Fuller, writing in the following year, exultingly records:

"At this day the library (or libraries shall I say?) of three successive archbishops, Painfull Parker, Pious Grindall, Politic Bancroft, (on the miscarriage of Chelsea College, to which first they were bequeathed) are bestowed upon Cambridge, and are beautifully shelved, (at the costs, as I am informed, of Sir John Woollaston, Alderman of London, so that our library will now move the beam, though it cannot weigh it down, to even the scale with Oxford[2]."

These extracts enable us to date with accuracy the Classes in the south Library, which, although altered to increase shelf-room, are excellent specimens of the woodwork of that period.

[The East Library, now called the Lesser Library (*Bibliotheca minor*), and possibly the "Inner Library[3]," was fitted up by Austin in 1673—74. He charges in his bill:

"Inprimis for 16 Classes and 2 Halfe Classes with the new Window Boardes, and the old waynscott fitting in betweene them at 5^{li}. 10^{s} per classe .... 93 . 10 . 0."

This entry is proved to refer to the eastern Library by Loggan's print (fig. 4), which shews that there were eight

[1] [Evelyn's Diary, ed. Bray, ii. 96.]

[2] [Fuller's History, p. 160. Fuller has, however, sacrificed truth to his favourite alliteration. The books were really Bancroft's and Abbot's. Parker's had gone to his own college, and the destination of Grindall's is unknown. The statement respecting Sir John Woollaston's benefaction is confirmed to some extent by the absence from the University Accounts of any charge for providing accommodation for the Lambeth Library.]

[3] [Univ. Accounts 1656—57. "For a new lock and key for the inner library 000 . 10 . 08."]

spaces between the windows, and two half spaces at the ends of the room.

Before narrating the next important change which took place in the Library, it will be interesting to quote a description written in 1710, by Zacharias Conrad von Uffenbach:

"1 Aug. In the morning we went into the *collegium publicum*, commonly called *the school*, in which are the *auditoria publica* and the library. It is an old, mean building. We saw below too a small room in which the academic council meets: there is nothing however remarkable in it, except the representation of the senate, copied from an ancient picture, as the inscription upon it states, amongst other matters. Above is the library in two mean rooms of moderate size. In the first, on the left hand side, are the printed books, but very ill arranged, in utter confusion. The catalogue is only alphabetical, and lately compiled on the basis of the Bodleian catalogue. It is also local, indicating where the books are to be sought. In the second room, which is half empty, there were some more printed books, and then the MSS., of which however we could see nothing well, because the librarian Dr *Laughton* (or as they pronounce it *Laffton*) was absent[1]."]

No further need for increased accommodation occurred until 1715, when King George the First presented to the University the Library of John Moore, D.D., Lord Bishop of Ely, which he had purchased after the Bishop's death, 31 July, 1714, for 6,000 guineas[2]. The gift was announced to the Vice-Chancellor, Thomas Sherlock, D.D., Master of Catharine Hall, in the following letter from Charles, second Viscount Townshend, then Secretary of State, which was read to the Senate, 22 September, 1715:

[1] [Visit to Cambridge by Z. C. von Uffenbach July and August, 1710. Translated by Rev. J. E. B. Mayor, M.A., S. John's College, p. 140.]

[2] [An excellent account of the state of politics in Cambridge at this period, and of the circumstances which led to the gift of this Library, will be found in Monk's Life of Bentley, i. 375—378. It was on this occasion that the epigram was written:

"King George observing with judicious eyes
The state of both his Universities,
To Oxford sent a troop of horse; and why?
That learned body wanted loyalty.
To Cambridge books he sent, as well discerning,
How much that loyal body wanted learning."

Sir William Browne, founder of the prizes for odes and epigrams, replied:

"The King to Oxford sent a troop of horse
For Tories own no argument but force;
With equal skill to Cambridge books he sent
For Whigs admit no force but argument."]

"Whitehall 20th September, 1715.

"Reverend Sir,

I have received his Majesty's commands to acquaint you that for the incouragment of Learning, and as a mark of His Royall Favour, he gives to the University of Cambridge the Library of the late Bishop of Ely. It is with great satisfaction I send you this Notice, which I desire you will communicate to the Heads of Houses and Senate.

I am, with the greatest truth and respect,

Sir, Your most obedient humble servant,

Townshend.

Dr Sherlock. Vicechancellor of Cambridge.'

It was obvious that a collection of printed books and manuscripts which exceeded 30,000 volumes[1] could not be accommodated in either of the two rooms then occupied by books; and that one of those used as Schools must be fitted up to contain them. Accordingly a Syndicate was appointed (9 November) consisting of the Vice-Chancellor for the time being; Dr Bentley, Master of Trinity College; Mr Grigg, Master of Clare Hall; Mr Crosse, Fellow of Catharine Hall; Mr Langwith and Mr Bull, Fellows of Queens' College; and Mr Shelton, Fellow of Magdalene College; with instructions to provide for the removal of the books from London[2], and their safe-keeping until cases (*Thecae sive quas vocant classes*) could be provided for them, in whichever School should be considered to be best suited for the purpose. As it was not customary, at the period of which we are speaking, for Syndicates to report from time to time to the Senate, and so to obtain their sanction before proceeding further, we do not know what course their deliberations took; but it is evident that they soon made up their minds to fit up again as a Library the room on the first floor of the west side of the quadrangle, then used as the Law School, for, 26 May, 1716, the following agreement[3] was signed by the Vice-Chancellor, Dr Daniel Waterland, Master of Magdalene College, and three of the Syndics:

1 [Hartshorne, Book Rarities of the University of Cambridge, p. 23, where several particulars respecting the gift of the Library are recorded, states, on the authority of Baker, that the number of printed volumes was 28,965; of MSS. 1790.]

2 [Hartshorne says (*ut supra*, p. 22) apparently on the authority of Baker, that the books arrived 19, 20, etc. November, 1715. The University Accounts shew that they did arrive in the year 1715—16; but no hint is given of the place in which they were bestowed.]

3 [This agreement is preserved in the Registry of the University.]

"1. That Mr Grumbold be allowed 120 pounds for ye Mason and Bricklayers' worke in Altering the Windows in the Law Schools.

2. That Coleman and Austin be Undertakers for ye Building of ye Classes in ye Law Schools, and that ye Classes be built to ye same Height with those of the Old Library and left open at the Top.

3. That the Wainscott of the Law Schools be taken down and the Stones of ye pavement taken up, and laid aside.

4. That [Joseph] Coleman[1] be employed for buying of Wood for the Classes."

At the beginning of the following year, 6 March, 1717, Mr Tillotson, Fellow of Clare Hall, was added to the Syndicate in place of Mr Shelton, who had died in the interval; and a new clause was added to the former instructions, authorising the construction of bookcases, and the fitting up of the Library.

Meanwhile another and most important piece of business had been taken in hand. It will be remembered that the piece of ground between the south and west ranges of the quadrangle belonged to King's College. It was therefore impossible to pass from the old Library to the School which was being fitted up to contain "the King's books," as the royal donation was termed, without descending into the court and ascending the stairs at the north-west angle (figs. 5, 6). The importance of acquiring this piece of ground was speedily recognised; and 2 July, 1716, a special Syndicate was appointed to treat with King's College. The ground was then occupied by the Porter's Lodge belonging to the Old Court; a building which, as Loggan shews in his view of the west end of King's College Chapel (fig. 8), did not rise higher than the sills of the windows on the first floor of the Library. No difficulty appears to have been made by King's College, and 28 January, 1716—17, *Articles of Agreement* were drawn up between the College

[1] [The following certificate (preserved in the Registry of the University) is valuable, as shewing Coleman's share in the work. It is countersigned by Dr Bentley. "I do hereby Certify that Mr Colman, lately deceased, was employ'd by me when Vice-Chancellor (with consent of Syndics) as Undertaker in the work at the Schools, was very serviceable to me in that Affair by his Advice and Direction, drawing the Plan of the Classes, providing Materials, and taking several journeys to Cambridge on purpose to supervise, direct, and forward the Work. For which Services I judge Ten Guineys to be no more than a suitable reward.

DAN. WATERLAND
THO. CROSSE
HEN. BULL.

Magd. Coll. April 2. 1718."]

and the University, by which the latter obtained a lease of the space over the Porter's Lodge on certain conditions. The lease was not executed until 1 January, 1718—19, but, in virtue of the *Articles* the University at once set about building the room which was afterwards called the Dome Room, and which it will be convenient to refer to by that name.

Fig. 8. Part of the south front of the Old Court of King's College, shewing the entrance from the Chapel Yard, the Porter's Lodge, and the south-west corner of the University Library: reduced from Loggan's view of the west front of King's College Chapel.

[The projected alterations began in 1715. A study of the items in the estimates and bills of the different workmen employed enables us to make out with tolerable accuracy the extent of the work done. A new floor was laid down in the

Law School, which then, as will be understood from a comparison of the plan of the first floor of the quadrangle in its old state (fig. 5) with the plan of the same as it is at present (fig. 9), was fifteen feet shorter than the existing west room of the Library; plain roundheaded windows, two to each bay, replaced those of three lights shewn by Loggan (fig. 4); and sixteen classes, which still remain, were set up by John Austin. At the same time the Porter's Lodge belonging to King's College was rebuilt, probably with stronger walls; and considerable alterations were carried out to the east gable of the College buildings, and to the gables of the south and west ranges of the Schools quadrangle, in both of which there were windows[1].

The fitting up of the Dome Room was decided by the following order:

"July 16th 1717. At a meeting of Mr Grigg Vicechancellor; Dr Bentley Master of Trinity; Mr Crosse Senior Proctor; Mr Tillotson; Mr Bull; Syndics appointed by the University for this purpose; it was agreed, by us whose names are subscrib'd, That the Area purchas'd of King's College be fitted up for the Manuscripts, and the room be clos'd, and two equal doors be made, one opening into the old Library, and the other, from the Law-schools, into the Manuscript-Room.

Wm. Grigg Vicechancellor,
Rich. Bentley
Robt. Tillotson
Hen. Bull."

The construction of the existing woodwork is recorded in the Accounts for 1719—20, where the following curious items appear in the bill of Woodward the Carver:

"For two Pillaster Cappatals very large after the Composed Order att 2lb per Cappatal 04 00 0
For Six Angel ones or Double Pillaster ones after the same Order att 4lb per Cappatal 24 00 0
For fore Corner ones after the same Order .... 08 00 0."

The fitting up of the Dome Room was evidently the last work undertaken. The Library had been ready for the books

[1] [The following items may be selected from the University Accounts for 1716—17: "A Bill for work done in Mr. Duns and Mr Adams Chambers at King's College; making good the wainscot where the windows was;" "Pulling down the Porter's Lodge;" "For cutting down and raising the Walls for the Floor in the Law School;" and in those for 1717—18 we find Robert Grumbold employed "pulling down the Great windo and setting vp againe." This was evidently the window in the south wall of the Library, which had previously been in one or other of the gables.]

in the previous year, 1719, for the Accounts for 1718—19 contain a charge "for carrying up the King's Books to the new Library." They had been brought from Ely House to Cambridge in 1715, and in the interval had probably been stored in one of the Schools on the ground-floor. The additional space, however, which had been gained by these changes was found to be wholly insufficient; and though the Dome Room was fitted up with shelves, and a double row of bookcases placed in the middle of the west room extending from floor to ceiling, and from one end of the room to the other, in addition to eight classes on either side, a great quantity of books were still left lying in a confused heap on the ground[1]. It was therefore evident that the Regent-House must be fitted up as a Library; and at the beginning of 1719 (6 March, 1718—19) it was agreed to appoint a Syndicate to acquire a site and generally to take steps for building a new Senate-House, by a Grace which began by stating that "His Majesty's generous present of books rendered it necessary to increase the space in the Library by the addition of the New Chapel." The history of the building of the Senate-House will, however, require a separate chapter; after which we will return to the Library, and carry its history down to the present time.]

CHAPTER III.

[History of the Senate-House[2] Quadrangle; Further History of the Library.

The room on the first floor of the north side of the Schools Quadrangle, though large enough for the ordinary meetings of

[1] [These details are contained in a tract called "Bibliothecæ Cantabrigiensis ordinandæ Methodus," published in 1723, by Conyers Middleton, D.D. who had been appointed Principal Librarian (Proto-Bibliothecarius) 15 December, 1721. See also a letter from Baker to Bishop Kennet (Hartshorne, *ut supra*, p. 22): "The law schools, now almost filled up, will not receive much more than half of the books."]

[2] [Professor Willis had collected materials for this chapter, and had written out some portions of it, but the whole was left in a very unfinished state. The subject has therefore been investigated afresh, in the hope of presenting the history in a form which he would have approved, had he finished it himself. The passages written by him have been incorporated, so far as it was possible to do so.]

the Senate, had been found insufficient for those occasions on which a larger assemblage had to be accommodated. It became therefore customary to use the churches of the Franciscans and the Augustinians for Public Commencements; and after their destruction, the parish church of S. Mary by the Market, as it was then called. This latter building could not have been particularly convenient for such a purpose; and, besides, the employment of a church for ceremonies which after the Reformation were regarded as wholly secular gradually came to be considered a scandal. Moreover, although the room on the first floor of the south side of the quadrangle had been again fitted up as a Library, as related in the last chapter, it was easy to foresee that the space thus gained for books would soon be filled; and in consequence various schemes for the erection of a new Library, as well as of a new Senate-House, beyond the precincts of the Schools Quadrangle, came to be set on foot.

These projects began to take a definite shape at the beginning of the seventeenth century, in consequence of the work which had been accomplished at Oxford by the noble liberality of Sir Thomas Bodley, who between the years 1598 and 1612 had repaired the old public library, which had been allowed to become ruinous. and had built a new eastern wing, at his own expense. The following passage occurs in a letter written from London, 20 August, 1614:

"There is an intention of erecting a new publique library in Cambridge in imitation of that of Oxford. The heads of the howses are the *primi motores*, who are allready about to buy the soile, and to prouide the materials. They promise themselues whatsoever furtherance my Lord Treasurer[1] may giue them, either by his authority or countenance; having lately made choise of him to be their Chancelor. Vpon Tuesday last the body of the University went to Audley end to present him with his patent; 20 Doctors in their formalityes and vpon their footscloths, and fourscore other of a second and inferiour rank. They were very honourably interteyned, and richly feasted[2]."

[1] [Thomas Howard, Earl of Suffolk.]

[2] [Thomas Lorkin to Sir Thomas Puckering, then at Tours. MSS. Harl. 7002, fol. 348. Thomas Lorkin, of Emmanuel College, proceeded B.A., 1600; M.A., 1604; travelled on the Continent with Mr Thomas Puckering, who proceeded B.A. at Peterhouse, 1614. While abroad he wrote letters on the affairs of France to Prince Henry (Life of Henry, Prince of Wales; by Thomas Birch, 8vo. Lond. 1760, p. 250). In after years he continued to correspond with his old pupil.]

At about the same period, Fulke Greville, Lord Brooke, made a proposal to the University. The conditions of his benefaction, called, "Articles touching Sir F. Grevile's intent etc. in the Uniuersitie[1]," unfortunately are neither signed nor dated; but as the first of them stipulates that a sum of £200, which Sir Fulke Greville had deposited in the hands of trustees for the acquisition of a site, is to be repaid to him "upon the first of November 1615, if the grownd whereon this Librarie should stand be not fully prepared for that purpose before the daye and yeare abouesaid," the scheme is probably the one referred to in Mr Lorkin's letter. He further promises to spend on the building £100 yearly for ten years; and, "if the said Librarie be finished within that tyme," to continue the said sum for the maintenance and the repair of the same for ever. The annual outlay of £100 was intended to stimulate the liberality of others, for the third article stipulates that "during the space of the said tenn years, there shalbe disbursed at least £300 more in the building of the forenamed Librarie, vntil it be finished; otherwise this £100 to cease." We do not know why this building-scheme did not prosper. It is evident that the speedy construction of a new library was contemplated at the same period by others, for the will of Dr Stephen Perse, Fellow of Gonville and Caius College, dated 27 September, 1615, contains a bequest of £100 "towards the building of the University Library, to be paid by my Executors within five years after my decease, so that the said Library be within that time in building."

Fourteen years afterwards the scheme was revived, on an extended scale, by George Villiers, Duke of Buckingham, Chancellor 1626—28. He visited the University in March, 1626—27; and then announced his intention of spending £7000 on building a "Commencement House and Library[2]."

[1] [Caius Coll. MSS. 73 (51). On the back of the document, in the same hand as the "Articles," are the words: "220 (altered to 230) ped: longit: 24 ped: latit:". For Sir Fulke Greville, see Vol. ii. p. 171.]

[2] [Joseph Mede, Fellow of Christ's College, writes to Sir Martin Stuteville, 24 March, 1626—27 (Heywood, Cambridge Transactions during the Puritan Period, ii. 357): "We talk here of a magnificent library, which our great Chancellor will build, and bestow no lesse toward it than 7000 lib. presently. All the houses betweene Caius Colledg and S^t. Marys must be pulled downe to make roome. I wish he might never do worse deed; but I doubt, I doubt, etc." The building is here

He seems seriously to have contemplated the immediate prosecution of this design; for he corresponded about it with some of the leading members of the University, and when, 29 January 1627—28, they handed to him a detailed certificate, enumerating the houses which it would be necessary to buy up, and that an initial outlay of at least £1100 would be required for this purpose, he replied "that as soon as some present businesses were dispatcht, he would speedily see this effected[1]." The Duke's intentions were arrested by his assassination, 23 August, 1628. The scheme, however, was not lost sight of. It was warmly taken up and developed by John Cosin, B.D., then Fellow of Caius College; and had been accepted, as he says, by the University, when it was arrested by the Civil War. After the Restoration it was once more revived, as we learn from the following letter addressed to Dean Sancroft by Dr Antony Sparrow, President of Queens' College from 1662 to 1667, when he became Bishop of Exeter. It is not dated, but, from internal evidence, was probably written during his year of office as Vice-Chancellor, 1664—65:

"Mr Deane,

I entreat you when you see my Lord of Duresme, to remember my duty to his Lordship, and to let him know that we have, I hope, made sure of the ground on the side of the Regent Walke, next Caius College, for to build a Theatre, and now we resolve to proceed in that design with as much speed as we can, and the great incouragement to that attempt is his Lordship's noble offer to the University, for which we give him our humble and hearty thanks.

As soon as I can have a convenient opportunity to meet the Heads, I intend to propose a subscription here in our severall Colleges, and then crave the help of our noble friends, to finish what we cannot do of ourselves. Mr Buck hath assured me that his Grace of York, and my Lords of London and Exeter, and others, will promote it, and a friend assures us the like of our Chancellor. The Orator promises to go into the North, and to use his oratory upon some gentlemen there, and Dr Bucknam will help us in our country. By these and divers other friends, which we hope to finde, we conceive the work now fecible, if

described as a Library only; the words in the text are taken from Bishop Cosin's account of it quoted below (p. 38).]

[1] [Ibid. ii. 359. The certificate was signed by: Dr Mawe, Master of Trinity College; Dr Paske, Master of Clare Hall; Dr Wren, Master of Peterhouse; Dr Beale, Master of Pembroke College; Dr Butts, Master of Corpus Christi College; and Dr Eden, Master of Trinity Hall.]

ever; and therefore are resolved to make tryall, if we can rescue God's house from Commencement prophanation. *Faxit Deus!*

When I consider your present pious undertakings for St Paul's and your owne College, I can scarcely thinke it modest to desire your assistance in this, but that I know you delight to do good, and will not be weary of well doing. God reward you for all is and shall be the praier of, Sir, your faithfull friend and servant,

Ant. Sparrow[1].

To Dr Sancroft, Dean of S. Paul's."

Dr Cosin's "noble offer" is contained in the following letter. It is dated 2 February, 1668—69, but the proposal must evidently have been made privately some years previously.

"Whereas the most illustrious Duke of Buckingham the late renowned and most noble Chancellor of the University of Cambridge did (out of his ardent desire to promote piety and learning therein) intend to build a Commencement House and Library there, but was prevented by his untimely death (ever to be lamented by this whole nation) to perfect that his so pious intendment;

And whereas a new and more perfect modell of the said building was by me made and presented to the late sacred Majesty of King Charles the First of ever blessed memory, who was pleased to approve thereof, and to command the then Vice-Chancellor and Heads of the said University, to use their utmost endeavour to procure benefactors, for the finishing of that work, wherein though a fair and considerable progress was then made by subscriptions of many Students, Heads, and Fellows of Colleges in the University, and by other gentlemen abroad, who had formerly related to it; so that the summe then subscribed amounted to no less than eight thousand pounds (which was but the sixth part of what was intended to be gathered for the erecting and perfecting of so noble and pious a work) yet (in regard of the late rebellious and unhappy times) it could not then effectually proceed, but is now worthily undertaken by the present Vice-Chancellor and Heads there;

I do therefore hereby give assurance to the said Vice-Chancellor and Heads, that I will give the summe of one hundred pounds, to be paid unto them or their treasurer and steward appointed for that purpose to be employed about the said work, so soon as I am ascertained that they have purchased all the houses now standing on both sides of the Regent-walke, between King's Colledge and Caius Colledge, where the said Commencement House and Library are to be erected, with a large square area between them surrounded or sided with walkes and arched columnes, the roofe thereof being covered with lead, and fronted with battlements of good hewen stone, according to the patterne and dimensions sett forth in the foresaid modell, and by me reposed in the University Library that now is.

[1] [Correspondence of John Cosin, D.D. Ed. Surtees Society, ii. 383.]

And I doe also give assurance that after all the said houses are purchased in and pulled downe, and the ground made clear for the building and erecting of the said Commencement House and Library, that I will contribute foure hundred pounds more, the same to be paid by one hundred pounds per annum during foure years then next ensueing, if the said work shall be carryed on yearly and vigorously, without stop or delay, according to the modell and patterne thereof before mentioned; and if I shall live so long Bishop of Durham.

In witness whereof I have hereunto sett my hand, this second day of February, Anno Domini one thousand six hundred sixty and eight.

Jo. Duresme (*propriâ manu*)[1].

Before proceeding further it will be desirable to investigate the nature of the property which it was thought desirable to acquire, and which occupied the eastern portion of the site described in the first chapter. It must first be mentioned that until after the completion of the present Senate-House the High Street in front of Great S. Mary's Church was not more than about 25 feet wide, as Loggan's ground-plan shews (fig. 2); and that until 1574 the only approach to the Schools had been through East School Street, which the same plan shews to have been a narrow lane, having a mean width of probably not more than about twelve feet. In that year a new street was made leading directly from the Schools to Great S. Mary's Church, at the sole expense of Matthew Parker, D.D., Archbishop of Canterbury,

"that so a more handsome sight might be of the public Schools, obstructed before by the town houses. This way to the Schools he also paved, and built a brick wall on each side against the Schools, and half way of the street, and topped the walls with square stone; and then gave this way and these walls unto the University[2]."

Archbishop Parker called this thoroughfare "University Street;" but the usual perversity of the public changed the name to "Regent Walk." We learn from a deed, dated 6 August 1574[3], by which the Master and Fellows of Corpus Christi College undertook to keep it in repair, that it was 177 feet 3 inches long; 24 feet 2 inches broad at the east end; and

1 [Ibid. from MSS. Baker, xxx. 454. Baker notes at the end: "From an original, the superscription torn away."]

2 [Life and Acts of Matthew Parker. By John Strype. Ed. 1821, ii. 406.]

3 [The original is in the Registry of the University. A very brief summary of it is given by Strype, Appendix, No. xcvii.]

28 feet 1½ inches broad at the west end. The ground had been purchased partly from King's College, partly from Corpus Christi College.

The ground between University Street and Caius College was an irregular parallelogram, measuring 190 feet on the north side, 123 feet on the east side, and 118 feet on the west side (fig. 1). It was occupied by dwelling-houses, of which the most important had been called originally "S. Mary Ostle," but was then known as the "New Inn," or the "New Angel Inn." It extended from High Street to North School Street, from both of which it had entrances[1]. To the south of it there was another inn called the "Green Dragon," and five tenements, occupied chiefly by tradesmen. The ground on which they stood belonged, with the exception of the "Green Dragon," which was freehold, to Corpus Christi College; and the certificate sent to the Duke of Buckingham, quoted above,

"shewed that it being the chiefest part of the town, and the inhabitants being commodiously fitted there, as well for their good advantage in their trades as for their convenience also and pleasure, who saw not how they should be so well fitted elsewhere, besides the loss of their tenures from a college, and the trouble and charge of removing; they would not therefore be induced to part with their severall interest but upon large terms, above the best rates of purchasing."

The space which intervened between the Regent Walk and North School Street was in like manner occupied by dwelling-houses, the acquisition of which by the University will be narrated when we come to speak of the schemes for building which rendered an extension of the site necessary.

No steps were taken to carry out any of these schemes until the end of 1673, when (2 December) a Grace passed the Senate stating that as a proper and fitting site was required for an Academic Theatre, and as the New Inn was offered to the University at a moderate price, a Syndicate consisting of the Vice-Chancellor and seven members of the

[1] [These measurements, of which the northern is evidently not quite accurate, are given in some memoranda compiled by John Smith, M.A., Master of Caius College, 1764—95 (MSS. Cai. Coll. No. 616), where it is stated that the property "extended from Trumpington Street to the Lane leading from Porta Honoris of Caius College to the publick schools, and lay north on Caius College, and a tenement of Dr Middleton's formerly Mr Lane's." The latter house was at the corner of Trumpington Street and Senate-House Passage (Vol. i. pp. 163, 164).]

Senate should be appointed to carry out the business, and that whatever they thought fit to do in the matter should be accepted by the Senate. They were to be appointed in the most formal manner under an instrument sealed with the University Seal[1]. This was the usual form for the appointment of Syndics at this period. We may presume that they were carefully selected in the first instance; but subsequently the most implicit confidence was reposed in them, and it was not considered necessary that they should refer to the Senate the details of the matter confided to them. The Syndics in question succeeded in purchasing the lease of the property (then held by a Mr James Hinton), and apparently at their own cost, for the price paid for it is not set down in the University Accounts. All that we find is a small charge for the legal expenses incident to the transfer[2]; and in the following year (27 March, 1674) a Grace directed that the lease from Corpus Christi College shall be renewed with the utmost precaution, in order to guard against the College sustaining any loss, or any controversy arising with the University at a future time.

The scheme for building was evidently received with approval; for, at the beginning of the following year (27 March, 1674), the Syndicate was reappointed for two years, with the addition of seven new members. The preamble of the Grace announces: "there is now a strong hope that if the University be true to herself she will not be wanting in friends, eager to stretch out to her their helping hands in the matter of the Theatre which we are undertaking;" and the Syndics are empowered to ask for and to collect subscriptions, to hire work-

[1] ["Lect. 12. Nov: 1673. Concess. 2° Dec: 1673. Cum locum Theatro Academiæ (si Deo visum fuerit) extruendo, parem et idoneum inprimis desideremus; et Novum, quod dicitur, Hospitium, conditione non gravi, vobis redimendum proponatur; Placeat vobis ut Dr Jacobus Fletewood [Provost of King's], Dr Robertus Mapletoft [Master of Pembroke], Dr Theophilus Dillingham [Master of Clare], Dr Radulphus Widdrington, Dr Johannes Carr, Mr Thomas Page, et [M[r]] David Morton, unà cum D° Procancellario, huic negotio exequendo præficiantur; et quod illis, hac in re, expedire videatur, vos ratum acceptumque habeatis. Quo vero dicti Delegati authoritate vestra muniantur, Placeat vobis vt literas vestras habeant Syndicatus, Sigillo vestro Communi sigillatas."]

[2] [Univ. Accounts, 1673—74. "To the Atturney for his drawing and ingrossing the covenants between the University and M[r] Hinton in the purchace of the New Inn, 001. 00. 00."]

men, to buy up houses, and generally to promote the work by every means in their power. In the absence of records other than the Graces confirmed by the Senate, we do not know to what circumstances this jubilant language is to be attributed, unless we may assume that the intentions of the Bishop of Ely, Dr Benjamin Laney, had become known. He died 24 January, 1674—75; and soon afterwards (1 April, 1675) we find the following Grace, in English:

"Whereas the late Reverend Lord Bishop of Ely has left to this University a Legacy of five hundred pounds towards the building a Musæum, or Commencement house, upon Condition the Foundation be layd within one yeare after his decease: And whereas there hath been further incouragement from our Superiours to that designe: May it please you that for the more effectuall expedition of this business, the purchese of houses, the receit and disbursments of money, the hireing of workmen and other transactions needfull for the carrying on of this publick work may be intrusted to the persones hereafter named (to whom the like trust by your Grace was formerly committed:) viz: to the Vicechancellour for the time being; Dr Duport, Dr Fletewood, Dr Mapletoft, Dr Breton, Dr Beaumont, Dr Dillingham, Dr Widdrington, Dr Turner, Dr Barrow, Dr Carr, Dr Paman, Mr Crouch Sen., Mr Page, and Mr Morton; to whome may it please you to add Dr Spencer and Mr Bainbrigg; Soe that whatsoever they, or any five of them (of whom the Vicechancellour is alwayes to be one) shall act or doe in this concerne, may be ratified and established by you to all intents and purposes.

Read April 1st 1675 in the fore noone.
Granted in the after noone of the foresaid day."

There is a tradition that Dr Barrow represented to his colleagues that if they made "the proposed building very magnificent and stately, at least exceeding that at Oxford" which had been completed by Sir Christopher Wren in 1669, "money would not be wanted, as the building went up, and occasion called for it; but that sage caution prevailed, and the matter was wholly laid aside[1]." This result unquestionably happened; for with the exception of a survey of the ground, and the preparation of several plans[2], the nature of which has not been

[1] [Vol. ii. p. 532.]

[2] [Univ. Accounts, 1673—74. "Drawing of severall Maps and Schemes in order to the intended Musæum 004. 00. 00." Ibid. 1675—76. "To Robert Grumbold for surveying ground for the Theator 02. 10. 00." It also appears from a Minute of the Syndics, dated 6 April, 1675 (Senate-House Papers), that an attempt was made to acquire the Rose Inn, but that it was found impossible to do so.]

recorded, no progress whatever was made; and no further steps were taken for nearly half a century.

The impossibility of accommodating Bishop Moore's books without adding the Regent House to the University Library, as explained in the last chapter, brought forward the question of building a new Senate-House once more; and a Syndicate was appointed 6 March, 1718—19, in terms evidently copied from the Grace of 1673 quoted above, to buy up the property on the north side of the Regent Walk. This business seems to have presented but little difficulty. In the course of April and May, 1719, the various pieces, whether freehold or leasehold, were acquired; and Corpus Christi College agreed to part with the fee-simple of the ground for £700[1]. It was, however, the opinion of the Syndics, that the authority of an Act of Parliament must be obtained, in order to confirm this agreement, and early in 1720 the following petition was addressed to the House of Lords. Our information respecting this period is so scanty, that the document may be quoted entire, as a contemporaneous record of the intentions of the University. The petition set forth:

"That his most excellent Majesty having been graciously pleas'd to bestow a very large and valuable collection of Books on the said University, Your Petitioners (as in Duty bound) are desirous of providing such convenient Room as may be capable of recieving the same, by enlarging their Publick Library out of their present Schools and Regent-House, and erecting other publick buildings to answer the purposes thereof, But Your Petitioners finding that the houses adjoyning belong to severall Colleges and to the Regius Professor of Physick, who by the Statute of Queen Elizabeth are restrained from alienating tho' willing so to do

Your Petitioners therefore (as well to show their Duty and gratitude to his Majesty as to make his said Royall bounty the more usefull and effectual,) humbly pray That leave may be given to bring in a bill to enable the corporations Aggregate and Sole, who are entitled to the said adjoyning Messuages and ground, to sell and convey to your Peti-

[1] [These particulars are derived from the Minute Book of the Syndics, which has fortunately been preserved in the Registry of the University. Christopher Green, M.D., Regius Professor of Physic, sold his three leasehold houses for £360: William Lunn, D.D., his freehold, the Green Dragon, for £400: and Thomas Phipps, his leasehold house for £225. The remaining house, in the occupation of Thomas Webster, was sold for a rent-charge of £14 per annum. The sum actually paid to Corpus Christi College was subsequently increased to £846. 13*s*. 4*d*. University Accounts, 1719—20.]

cioners so much thereof as may be convenient for enlarging the Scite of the said publick Buildings[1]."

The Act of Parliament received the Royal Assent 11 June, 1720; and in the course of that year and the next the houses were pulled down, the materials sold, and the ground enclosed with a temporary fence.

In 1721 Mr James Burrough, of Caius College, who afterwards achieved distinction as an architect, and whose name has been especially connected with the Senate-House by tradition, was added to the Syndicate[2]. The following Orders shew that he suggested a plan for the proposed building, but that the execution of it was entrusted to Mr James Gibbs. It is evident, however, that Mr Burrough approved of this course, as he signed both the following Orders:

"Feb. 27th 1721—22. Ordered that Mr Gibbs be sent for from London to give his advice about a Plan and such other directions about ye publick Building as are necessary for that Occasion."

"March 8th 1721—22. Ordered and agreed by us whose names are underwritten that Mr James Gibbs do take with him to London Mr Burrough's Plan of the Intended publick Buildings and make what improvements he shall think necessary upon it, and that the said Mr Gibbs be imploy'd and retain'd to supervise and conduct the said work, and be paid for his assistance and directions therein by the Vice-chancellor for the time being."

It will have been remarked that Gibbs was not consulted until February, 1721—22, although the area to be built upon had come into the possession of the University two years previously. Unfortunately the Minutes of the Syndics do not record the steps previously taken to obtain a design; but it is clear that other architects were either consulted or offered their services, for in 1723—24 the following Order was made:

"Jan: 18: 1723. Order'd that, in Consideration of ye Pains taken severally by Mr James and Mr Dicconson, in coming to Cambridge, measuring the Ground, and drawing Plans for a new Commencement House, tho' we proceeded on another Scheme; the summ of twenty Guineas each be paid to the said two Surveyours."

A general view of the design proposed by Gibbs, and the

[1] [Grace Book I, 23 March, 1719—20. The Resolution of the Syndics to ask for an Act of Parliament is dated 25 August, 1719.]

[2] [Grace Book I, 22 March, 1720—21.]

ground-plan which is here reproduced (fig. 11), are to be found among his published works[1]. No scale is given; but on the assumption that the Senate-House was built of the intended width, which is justified by comparing the east end with the design, it is not difficult to construct one, and to lay down the whole in outline on the plan of the site (fig. 1). The west side (A) of the proposed building was to have been built at a short distance from the front of the Schools, and would have contained the Royal

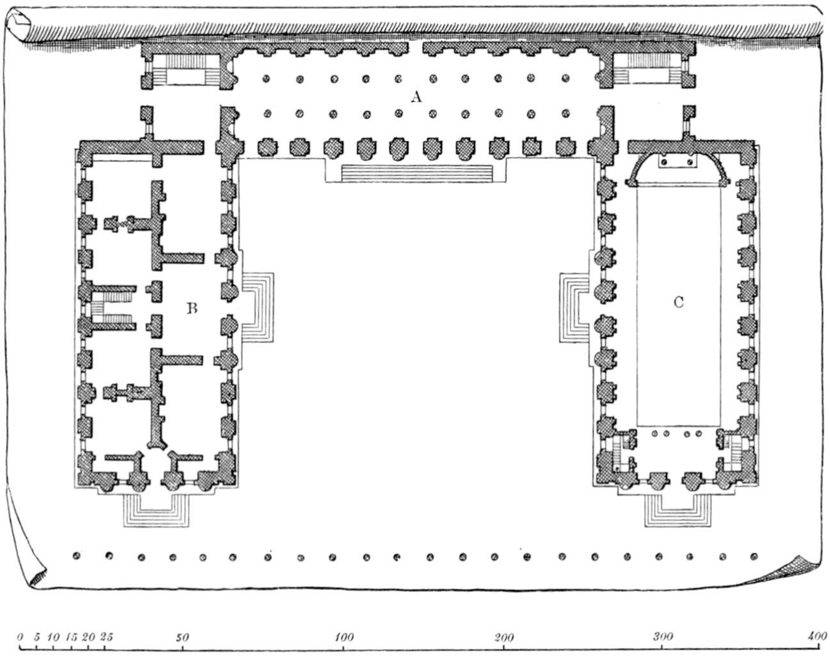

Fig. 11. Ground-plan of the design proposed by Gibbs for "the Publick Building at Cambridge." A. The Royal Library: B. The Consistory and Register Office: C. The Senate-House.

Library on the first floor, with an open cloister beneath. This room, approached by a staircase at either end, would have been 112 feet long, by 27 feet wide. The court, of the same width as the length of the Library, would have had the existing Senate-House, 100 feet long by 50 feet wide, on the north, and

[1] [A Book of Architecture. By James Gibbs. London, 1728. Plate xxxvi.]

on the south a building exactly similar to it in size, and in external appearance, containing the Consistory, Registrary's Office, and other convenient apartments, on the ground-floor. The Printing-House would have occupied the floor above them[1]. The position of the whole edifice was evidently selected with the intention of obstructing as little as possible the view of King's College Chapel from the street; a point which we shall find was strongly insisted upon. It is important to remark before proceeding further, that no opposition to the scheme appears to have been raised for several years, though the Syndics and their architect were alone responsible for it. The Senate was never asked to sanction either the design, or the situation selected for the Senate-House.

The foundation was laid 22 June, 1722, by the Vice-Chancellor, Thomas Crosse, D.D., Master of Catharine Hall, "with four stones: the first in honour of the King; the second of the Prince; the third of the Chancellor of the University; the fourth of the Benefactors[2]." On the same day the Syndics "ordered that a thousand prints of the Model of the publick Building, if there be occasion for so many, be printed by Mr Gibbs' directions[3]," probably with a view of collecting subscriptions; and they also entered into negotiations for a supply of Ketton and Portland stone, and building materials generally, with Christopher Cass, Mason, of London. The contract with him was sanctioned by Grace of the Senate in the following October[4]. On this occasion an opportunity was afforded to the Senate of condemning the scheme, had any objection to it existed; but the Grace passed, so far as we know, without opposition.

The work appears to have proceeded without interruption during 1723, and by the beginning of 1724 the building must have been far advanced, for it was then agreed (9 January) to employ Mr Thomas Phillips and Mr Benjamin Timbrell, car-

[1] [Carter's Cambridge, p. 10.]

[2] [Carter (ibid. p. 11) is our only authority for the date of this ceremony, and for the account of the stones laid.]

[3] [Univ. Accounts, 1721—22. "Paid Mr Gibbs for ye Plate of ye Plan of ye Building and 1000 Prints of it 17. 14. 00."]

[4] [Grace Book, 10 October, 1722.]

penters, for the roof[1]; and in the following month (8 February) to employ Mr James Essex "to make and finish the sashes." At the end of the year estimates were requested from Mr Essex and Mr Cass respectively for the "charge of wainscotting," and the "flooring either by freestone or Marble[2]." The latter material was selected, 11 January, 1724—25; and in the following July the commencement of the internal panelwork was sanctioned:

"July 20. 1725. Order'd that Mr Essex be employ'd for the Wainscot, and that Articles be drawn between the University and him according to the Proposals given in by Mr Essex and alter'd by Mr Gibbs."

The roof must have been completed, and ready for the ceiling, by October, 1725, when we find the following Orders:

"Oct. 5. 1725. Order'd that Mr Isaac Mansfield be employed for the plain Plasterers work, and Mr Artari and Mr Bagutti for the Ornaments of the Cieling in the new Building according to their Proposals."

Up to this time the progress of the Senate-House had been rapid, but, notwithstanding, we shall find that it was not completed for nearly five years. This delay was no doubt partly caused by want of funds, for in 1725 the Vice-Chancellor, William Savage, D.D., Master of Emmanuel College, spent a month in London "procuring Benefactions[3];" but still more by the opposition to the whole scheme which gradually arose in the University. A rival design was suggested, viz. to rebuild the east side of the Schools Quadrangle on a larger scale and a more commodious plan, making it project a little in advance of the old front, but still leaving the Senate-House as a detached building. This was termed the "Detaching Scheme," the original being called the "Attaching Scheme;" and under these names two parties ranged themselves and set up a fierce controversy. The scantiness of records, as already mentioned, makes it extremely difficult to trace the exact progress of events; but, so far as we can ascertain, the opposition declared itself in the following manner.

Notwithstanding the labour of supervising the building of the Senate-House, the Syndics had not been unmindful of the

[1] [The contract with them was sanctioned by the Senate 20 January, 1723—24.]

[2] [Minute of the Syndics, 12 December, 1724.]

[3] [Univ. Accounts, 1724—25.]

rest of the proposed building. In 1723 they began the acquisition of the block of houses between the Regent Walk and North School Street, by treating with Christopher Green, M.D., Regius Professor of Physic, for the house attached to his Professorship. An exchange having been agreed upon, 8 February, 1723—24, confirmed by Grace of the Senate 24 October following, further purchases were projected, and the following Order was made:

"Oct. 22. 1724. Agreed that Dr Gooch be desir'd to apply to the Master and Fellows of Corpus Christi College to set a Price on their Interest in the Houses on the South-Side of the Regent-Walk; in order to the University's purchasing such Interest.

And that He the said Dr Gooch do farther apply to the Provost and Fellows of King's College for so much of the ground belonging to them as will enable Us to bring the West End of St Mary's Church into the Centre-Line of the Regent-Walk."

At that time the parallelogram between East School Street and the Regent Walk was occupied by three properties exclusive of Dr Green's house, the precise situation of which cannot now be discovered. At the west end, nearest to the Schools, was a house which had formerly belonged to Corpus Christi College, the date of the acquisition of which by the University has not been recorded[1]; and east of it were four houses belonging to the same College. These houses occupied the whole space between the two streets as far as High Street, with the exception of a narrow strip at the south-east corner, 77 feet long by 13 feet broad, on which stood some dwelling-houses and four almshouses belonging to King's College. The property at the west end of this block of houses, opposite to the Schools, together with the soil of School Street, must have belonged to the University; for though the above-mentioned houses were not purchased for more than thirty years, it was yet possible to commence building operations immediately on the west side of the proposed quadrangle. The Order, however, is chiefly valuable because it indicates an intention to deviate from Mr Gibbs's accepted plan, according to which, as the ground-plan shews (fig. 1), the centre of the west front of Great S. Mary's Church was not intended to be opposite to the centre of the east front of the Library. We shall see presently that this new scheme emanated from Sir Thomas Gooch, Bart., D.D.,

[1] [It was probably one of the houses acquired by Archbishop Parker.]

Master of Caius College; and it probably caused the architect considerable trouble, for in a letter to the Vice-Chancellor respecting the amount of his charges, written 10 September, 1730, he speaks of the expense he had been put to "in making exterordinary drawings for plates for the use of the University, and other drawings that were made upon account of unhappy differences[1]."

The Order of 22 October, 1724, was succeeded by another, distinctly announcing an intention of commencing operations without delay:

"July y[e] 20th. 1725. Agreed that the New-Regent-House be finish'd with all Speed.

That a Trench, 160 feet long, from y[e] End of King's Coll. gate, to within 40 feet from Caius Coll, be dug, for a new Front to be join'd to the present new wing of the Building.

That the Front-Entrance answer S[t] Mary's, as near as possibly can be contrived."

The carrying-out of these intentions was abandoned, for reasons which we have now no means of discovering, but at the end of 1725 (5 October) an Order was made that the work should be commenced in the following February, "at the furthest;" and though it was again deferred, it was ordered, for the third time, 9 March, 1725—26, and the trenches were actually dug, under the superintendence, as it would appear, of Mr Burrough of Caius College[2]. Shortly before this took place a Grace of the Senate had directed the Syndics to devote their energies to the completion of the remaining sides of the New Building with all convenient speed, and, with that end in view, had invested them with the same authority as they had had before for the North Side[3]. Here again we have a proof that at this time—when the Senate-House was virtually completed, and when therefore an accurate judgment could be formed of the probable appearance of the rest of the building—public opinion in the University was still favourable to the

[1] [This letter is preserved in the Registry of the University.]

[2] [Univ. Accounts, 1726. "Paid for carrying Rubbish from the new foundations 5. 10. 0." The terms of the Minute were: "Agreed that the Order made July the 20th. 1725, be confirm'd, and that the digging of the Trenches be forthwith set about, and that M[r] Burroughs be empower'd to agree with the men that are to dig the Trenches."]

[3] [Grace Book I, 7 February, 1725—26.]

scheme. We do not know to what cause to attribute the change which presently took place. Possibly the trenches, when actually dug, may have made those who inspected them realize more fully the real nature of a scheme of which they had formed a different opinion on paper. Whatever the reason may have been, in the course of the following year the Master of Caius College took alarm. He had been Vice-Chancellor when the scheme of building a separate Senate-House was first projected, and had been continued in office for three years, 1717—19, on account of his vigorous support of it; and one of the Fellows of his College, Mr Burrough, had actively promoted the accepted design, if even he had not been the author of it. It is therefore remarkable that the opposition should have emanated from that College at all; and, still more, that it should not have made itself manifest at an earlier date. Possibly the Master had been absent from Cambridge; for at the commencement of the following letter he speaks of a resolution of the Syndics as recent, which we have seen had been arrived at nearly two years before. In May 1727 he addressed the Vice-Chancellor, Joseph Craven, D.D., Master of Sidney College, in the following terms[1]:

"Reverend Sir,

I am inform'd that at a late Meeting of the Syndics a Resolution was taken for digging Trenches etc to carry on (what is call'd) the attaching Scheme. 'Twill be good News to Me, should I find at my return, that You have Mony enough, or a Prospect of Mony enough, to finish the new Senate-house, to fit up the old one for a Royal Library, and to buy in the Benet-College Lease on the South-side of the Regent-Walk: all which, I think, are of absolute Necessity, and should have ye chief Place in our Thoughts and Care. Were these Things first done, Gentlemen might upon longer Deliberation change their Minds, (as some have already done) about the intended Scheme: at least it might stave of all Suspicion of something else being mean't besides carrying on ye public Building. For my own Part, I am on many Accounts against your last Resolution of proceeding. I think You will do great Injustice to your Royal Benefactor, whose Donation has hitherto been without its Use and Ornament and in this Way is like to be so for many Years to come. I am afraid you will involve yourself and Successors in inextricable Difficulties: and what I am particularly

[1] [Caius Coll. MSS. 635 (3). It is a copy, or draft, of an intended letter, and there is of course no proof that it was ever sent. It is docketed "Letter to Dr Craven, Vice Chancellor," and the subsequent action of the College renders it probable that some intimation of their intentions was given.]

concern'd for, all this will be done to execute a Scheme for which I do in my Conscience believe the whole World will condemn Us; a Scheme that will so effectually shut out all View of that noble fabrick Kings-Chapell, that I wonder how the University or that College can bear it; and a Scheme so injurious to Caius College, that I am fully resolv'd not to bear it. What Ground You have already to build on I my self contracted for: but I am sure I never contracted for the Street in the Front of the Schools, nor could anybody conveigh it to Me.

S[r], I will not enlarge upon a Subject that is well known already; and if it ben't, may come to be so, in a proper Time and Place: and therefore I only desire You on Monday next to acquaint the Syndics that unless Proceedings be stopt, I will immediately pray an Injunction out of Chancery.

I am, with great Respect,
Dear Sir,
Your most obedient humble Servant,

Chichester,
May 31.
1727."

The Master was as good as his word. The Syndics were summoned to appear in Court, 23 October, and there shew cause why the work should not be stopped[1]. The cause having been heard, an injunction[2] was granted, and further progress became impossible. The affidavit put forward by the plaintiffs is worth examination, as setting forth the ground taken by the opponents of the scheme. The Master of Caius College rested his case on the fact that there was a public way on the south side of his college leading from the Gate of Honour to the Public Schools; that the founder, Dr Caius, a very eminent physician, had forbidden the building on that side of any new edifice which might "obstruct the course of the air;" that he himself, while Vice-Chancellor, had purchased for the University certain property on that side for the site of a new Senate-

[1] [Grace of the Senate, 17 October, 1727. "Cum Plures ex Syndicis ad nova vestra Ædificia perficienda Auctoritate Vestrâ constitutis, virtute brevis vulgo vocati *Sub pœnâ* ex almâ Curiâ Cancellariæ emanati, ad comparendum in dictâ Curiâ vicesimo tertio die Octobris instantis teneantur, ut causam reddant quare non fiat breve de operibus vestris inhibendis, ad querelam Magistri et Sociorum Collegij Gonvil et Caij in Universitate Cantabrigiensi, juxta tenorem depositionis vulgo vocatæ *Affidavit*, modo lectæ: Placeat Vobis ut Syndici dictis operibus jam præfecti, ad Jura Universitatis contra prædictos Querentes Universitatis sumptibus defendenda Vestrâ Auctoritate muniantur."]

[2] [Grace of the Senate, 5 May, 1729.]

House, but that neither he nor any one else could purchase the public street; and lastly:

"that the University have lately appointed Syndics, whereof the Vice-Chancellor is always one, to carry on the said public Buildings, and that tho' (as the Relator is inform'd) many Persons of the best Understanding in Architecture do affirm that the said Buildings may be better carry'd on in another Way, and tho' the Street on which they intend to build is what they have no Right to make such Use of, yet they have order'd Trenches to be dug in order to lay a Foundation in the said public Way and to carry up a Building of 45 feet in Height; [and that not an open Arch, but the Pedestal of an Arch, will be set against the Gate][1] within a very small Distance from the South-Side of the said College, whereby during the Time of building (which may be these twenty Years) their Passage to the Schools will be reduc't by Trenches [and] be but about two feet wide, and that too under the Droppings from the Tiles: but also for all Time to come as well the commodious View and Passage they now enjoy, as likewise the Health of the Members of the said College is like to be greatly injur'd[2]."

The suit was a protracted one, and judgment was not delivered until 25 June, 1730, when the Court "saw no cause to give the plaintiffs any relief," on the ground that a suit respecting a public way did not concern a court of equity[3]. No further attempt, however, was made to revive what Dr Gooch calls the "attach'd scheme;" and the trenches, which were partially filled up on the occasion of the visit of King George the Second in 1728[4], were never re-opened. Before

[1] [The words between square brackets are additions to the original draft.]

[2] [Caius Coll. MSS. 635 (5). The affidavit, like the letter to the Vice-Chancellor, is only a rough draft, with many erasures and some omissions of words.]

[3] [A copy of the Lord Chancellor's decree is in the Registry of the University; the reasons for it are given in the correspondence preserved in Caius College. MSS. 635 (7).]

[4] [The King came to Cambridge 25 April, 1728. The following Minute had been made by the Syndics in anticipation of his visit: "April 5th, 1728. Agree'd that that part of the Trench that is dug cross the Regent Walk, and the Western Trench leading to Kings and Cajus College be filled up with the Bricks provided for laying the Foundation, and the Rubbish in the Senate House Yard; And that the Paving of the Regent Walk be repaired, and Rails set up round the rest of the Trenches upon the occasion of his Majesty's visiting the University." The Syndics did indeed make the following Order, 17 July, 1730: "Agreed that Mr Essex and Mr Ogle be appointed to make agreement with persons to dig what remains to be dug, and to clear those trenches already dug, to be laid before Mr Vice Chancellor for his approbation, and upon the obtaining that to sett the Persons to work immediately, pursuant to the order dated July 20. 1725, and that the Vice Chancellor be impowered

leaving this part of our subject, however, we will quote a letter[1] from the architect, in which his scheme is ably defended:

"Sir,

I here send you my Reasons why the three sides of the Publick Building at Cambridge should be joyned togeether and not detach'd, and are as followes:

1st. The Conveniency of passing dry from one part of the Building to the other is not to be neglected.

2dly. As one united Building will appear more Beautifull in it self, so it will skreen the Inferior Building of Cajus College, which being seen betwixt the detach'd Buildings will have a disagreeable look and a very bad effect, which must be allowed by all impartial Judges.

3dly. It will be a great loss to the University to have the present Schools pulled down which must be done if the detach'd Scheme takes place.

4thly. I conceive the Scheme as projected by Dr Gouch is impracticable, For to bring St Mary's Steeple to answer the middle opening of the intended Library, the South Building must come within 18 feet or ther abouts of Kings College Chapell, which I believe that College will not suffer for many reasons which are obvious.

5thly. The Difference between the expence of an Insular or Detach'd Building, and that of a continued and attach'd Building is very great and therefore deserves your consideration where money comes in so slowly that the Building is already at a stand for want of a Supply. If the Building be joyned the back parts may be plain, and the Expence will be only layd out on the Ornaments of the Principal Fronts which are most in view. But if the Buildings are detach'd the same order must return upon the ends, the Charge of which has been already felt in part, which might have been saved if that part of the Building which fronts Cajus College had been kept plain.

For these Reasons I proposed at first that the three Sides of the Publick Building should be joyn'd—which was then agreed to by the Syndics as I have printed it; and indeed I don't know for what reason it should be otherways, since the joyning it renders it more convenient, more Beautifull, and less chargeable than the other impracticable wild Scheme.

Sir, I am with all respect
Your most obliged humble Servant
Ja: Gibbs.

London, 2^d of May
1728."

A statement on the opposite side had been addressed to Dr Gooch by Mr John James[2], one of the architects who had

to agree for bricks and other materials to be employed in laying the foundation of the new front;" but there is no evidence that the Order was ever acted upon.]

1 [The letter, preserved in the Registry of the University is endorsed "For Mr Burford, Bursar of King's College."]

2 [Vol. i. p. 195.]

been consulted at the commencement of the work. It will be interesting to compare his letter with that written by Mr Gibbs:

"Revd Sir,

I was from home on Saturday last that I could not acknowledge the favour of yours by the last post.

I have considered the Sketch you sent me and remember well the Disposition of every part of it.

I think there is no doubt but the Detachments of the Senate house in the North, and the Consistory etc. on the South, from the front of the Building which is the Library, would be altogether as beautiful as the Conjunction of the West Ends of those Buildings with the Library; but in that Case, perhaps, it may be absolutely necessary to make some Communications with the Library, by Porticos of Columns only, which neither obstruct the View or Air. The Detachment of these Buildings might also be a means of preventing the spreading of Fire from one to the other, if such should happen, tho' in any of the Designs I have seen of Mr Gibbs's for this Work, I never found them detached. This, Sir, is all I can say at present upon this head. I remain with great Respect and Obligation,

Reverend Sir
Y^r most humble and
most obedient servant
Jn James.

Grenwich Hospital
12 August 1729[1]."

We will now return to the Senate-House. The glazing and the plasterwork were finished in the course of 1726[2]; during the three following years the wainscotting proceeded slowly; and in 1730 we find the charges for the Portland stone steps at the east end and on the south side, with those for the dwarf walls and iron railings. This same year saw the long-deferred completion of the structure internally,—the exterior of the west end being still left rough, in expectation of the revival of the "Attachment" scheme—and it was opened by the ceremonies of a Public Commencement, 6 July, 1730[3]. The building work had therefore occupied exactly eight years. The cost had been £16,386, of which £13,000 had been spent on the building, the rest upon the site and other expenses[4].

[1] [Caius Coll. MSS. 635 (9).]

[2] [The Univ. Accounts for the year ending 3 November, 1726, contain payments in full to Mr Essex for sashes and glazing, and to Mr Bagutti for ornaments.]

[3] [Cooper's Annals, iv. 208. Monk's Bentley, ii. 292.]

[4] [This is the amount arrived at in "An Account of the Expences of building the *Senate-House*"; Caius Coll. MSS. 621 (10). Professor Willis notes: "The payments

Before leaving the Senate-House it will be desirable to relate the history of the five memorial statues which have been placed in it at different times, taking them in the order of the date of their arrival.

1. KING GEORGE THE FIRST; by Rysbrack[1].

In 1736 (29 October) a Grace passed the Senate, setting forth that whereas the credit and the duty of the University were alike concerned in commemorating and handing down to posterity the liberality of King George the First, now departed this life, some celebrated sculptor should be employed to make a marble statue of him, to be placed in the Public Library, in perpetual memory of his gift. This intention of the University having been conveyed to Lord Townshend, he asked, through his son, to be allowed to defray the cost of the statue; and on learning that such a proposal would be agreeable, he addressed the following letter to the Vice-Chancellor:

Rainham, Dec. 2, 1736.

"Sir

As soon as I heard of the University's having resolved to pay a publick Mark of its respect to the late King, by erecting, in the Library, a Statue in Honour of that truely great and good Prince; my Veneration for his Memory and my Zeal for the University made me very desirous to have this Resolution, so much to its Honour, carryed into Execution as soon as possible. The indulging me therefore in the Request I took the Liberty to make by my Son, has made me very happy.

I have a Heart full of Gratitude for the Honour the University has done my Family; and tho' in the way of Life, to which Age and Infirmities have reduced me, I can myself be of little Use to it, my Son may however, I hope, be of more. My Prayers, good Wishes, and all the Assistance I can give shall ever attend his Endeavours for its Interest and Service.

I am now, Sir, to return you my most humble Thanks for your obliging

made to Gibbs may serve to shew his share in the work, and I therefore add them: Univ. Accounts 1721—22, 'P^d Mr Gibbs for the Plate of the Plan of the Building and 1000 Prints of it 17.14.00.' Ibid. 1722—23. 'Gave Mr Gibbs Surveyour by order of Syndicks 50.00.00. P^d do the Engravers bill for a Copper Plate 23.11.00. P^d do the Printers Bill for 500 Prints 10.00.00.' Ibid. 1723—24. 'P^d Mr Gibbs 50.00.00.' These sums produce a total of £151. 5*s*. 0*d*. After the completion of the building he wrote to the Vice-Chancellor (10 Sept. 1730) stating that he was usually paid at the rate of 5 per cent. on the total outlay, but that 'out of that respect I have for the University, I only charge the halfe I have from any other person, which is two and a halfe per cent of the whole Charge of this building now compleated, what that amounts to I leave that to your books, I don't know the expence exactly. I have received one hundred pounds upon account and no more ever since the Building was begunne.'" The Accounts do not shew that any further payments were made to him.]

[1] [On the statue are the words "RYSBRACK. Fecit."]

Letter, and must beg you would do me the Justice to believe that I am with the most perfect Esteem and respect,

Sir
Your most obedient Humble
Servant
Townshend."

This letter was read to the Senate at the next Congregation after its receipt[1], and formal thanks were returned to Lord Townshend on the same day, 8 December, 1736. The sculptor selected was Rysbrack; and the statue arrived at Cambridge in November, 1739. Meanwhile, however, Lord Townshend had died (June, 1738); and the cost was defrayed by his son, to whom a long letter of thanks was addressed by the University, 16 November, 1739. The following inscriptions are on the pedestal:

GEORGIO
OPTIMO PRINCIPI
MAGNÆ BRITANNIÆ REGI
OB INSIGNE EJUS IN HANC ACADEMIAM
MERITA
SENATUS CANTABRIGIENSIS
IN PERPETUUM
GRATI ANIMI TESTIMONIUM
STATUAM
MORTUO PONENDAM
DECREVIT.

CAROLUS
VICECOMES TOWNSHEND
SUMMUM TUM ACADEMIÆ TUM REIPUBLICÆ
DECUS
PRO EXIMIA QUA REGEM COLUERAT PIETATE
PROQUE SINGULARI QUA ACADEMIAM FOVERAT
CARITATE STATUAM
A SENATU ACADEMICO DECRETAM
SUMPTIBUS SUIS E MARMORE
FACIENDAM LOCAVIT.

CAROLUS FILIUS
VICECOMES TOWNSHEND
VIRTUTUM ÆQUE AC HONORUM PATERNORUM HERES
STATUAM
QUAM PATER MORTE SUBITA ABREPTUS
IMPERFECTAM RELIQUERAT
PERFICIENDAM
ATQUE IN HOC ORNATISSIMO
ACADEMIÆ LOCO COLLOCANDAM
CURAVIT.

[1] [This appears from a note in the Grace-Book, where the letter is copied. The original has not been preserved.]

It was originally intended, as we have shewn, that the statue should be placed in the Library; but it appears, from the terms of the last inscription, to have been placed in the Senate-House in deference to Lord Townshend's wishes[1]. The change was not sanctioned by Grace of the Senate. The statue was placed in the middle of the north side[2]. In 1884 (7 Feb.) a Grace of the Senate authorized the removal of this statue and of that of King George the Second to the Library, where they have been placed at the west end of Cockerell's Building.

2. ACADEMIC GLORY; by John Baratta.

A few years after the arrival of the statue of King George the First, Peter Burrell, M.B. of S. John's College, presented to the University a statue which he had bought at the sale of Cannons, the seat of the Duke of Chandos. It had been executed at Florence in 1715, by John Baratta[3], and was said to represent *Glory*. At Cannons it had stood near a statue of the Duke of Marlborough, in honour of his victories. It was probably presented to the University in 1745, the year in which Mr Burrell took his degree; and it was immediately placed in the Senate-House, on the south side, opposite to the statue of King George the First[4]. For what next happened we will quote the diary of the Rev. Henry Hubbard[5], of Emmanuel College, for 14 December, 1748, on which day the Duke of Newcastle was elected Chancellor of the University:

"A Grace also passed the Caput and was read in the 2 Houses, importing: 'That whereas the Statue, called *Glory*, had been put up without any Decree of the Senate first had, That the Thanks of the University should be given to Peter Burrell Esq. for the said Statue, and that it should be removed out of the Senate-House and placed where the Syndics for the Library should think proper.'...Rejected in the Non-Regent House: Placets 26, Non Placets 67.

As soon as this Grace was rejected, another was offered: 'That Thanks should be given to Mr Burrell for the Statue by Dr Fogg, Mr Mortlock, and

[1] [The Vice-Chancellor visited Lord Townshend in 1739: Univ. Accounts 1738—39: "Coach-hire to Lord Townshend about the King's Statue o. 5. o. Rysbrack's servants at setting up the Statue o. 7. 6."]

[2] [The Foreigner's Guide, etc., 1748, p. 15.]

[3] [On an ornament behind the statue are these words: IOANNES BARATTA FECIT FLORENTIAE ANNO MDCCXV.]

[4] [MSS. Cole xxxi. Add. MSS. Mus. Brit. 5832.]

[5] [Henry Hubbard, S. Catharine's Hall, A.B. 1728, A.M. 1732; migrated to Emmanuel Coll., where he was elected Fellow; S.T.B. 1739; Registrary of the University from 1758 to 1778. His diary begins 10 October, 1741, and ends 5 November, 1769. A copy of it was made by Cole (MSS. Cole li. Add. MSS. Mus. Brit. 5852). In a note dated 1780, Cole records of Mr Hubbard that he "was the most active and shining Man in the Senate House and University, for the support of good Discipline and the Credit of the Place; and tho' at that Time we idle People used to call him a busy officious meddling Man, yet it was very happy that he was so."]

M[r] Courtail;' and passed the Caput. Upon this, another was offered, by the Persons who promoted that in the morning, and passed the Caput, containing only the latter Part of the former Grace, expressed in the same Words to this Purpose, viz: 'That the Statue, called the Statue of *Glory*, should be removed from the Senate House, and placed where the Syndics for the Library should think proper.'

Dec. 16. The Grace to return Thanks to M[r] Burrell passed both Houses without Opposition. The Grace to remove the Statue, rejected by the Non-Regents. Placets 5, Non-Placets 47.

N.B. It was pleasantly observed, That it looked odd, That a Grace should be proposed with so much Warmth, to remove Glory out of the Senate House, immediately after the Duke of Newcastle was chosen Chancellor."

The reason for this opposition is said to have been either that the statue really represented Queen Anne, or that it was thought to resemble her[1].

On a label of black marble, at the feet of the statue, is the line: CVNCTI ADSINT·MERITAEQ·EXSPECTENT·PRAEMIA·PALMAE; and on the pedestal the following inscription:

GLORIAE · AETERNAE
ALMAE · MATRIS · ACADEMIAE
SACRUM
OB
DOCTRINAE · FELICITER · EXCULTAE
PERPETUAM · LAUDEM
ET
EXCOLENDAE
FELICEM · OPERAM
L · M · P
PETRVS · BVRRELL
IN
PIETATIS · SVAE · ET · FIDEI
PVBLICVM · ARGVMENTVM
A·M·DCC·XL·VIII·

[1] [A very amusing account of the whole affair will be found in Nichols' Illustrations of Literature, i. 64—70, with "A Dialogue in the Senate-House at Cambridge," between a *Stranger* and a *Beadle*. The latter, after explaining that the statue had been originally intended for *Fame*, proceeds:

"In doubt at first what Nymph's, what Heroine's name
What Queen's was best adapted to the Dame;
At length, by vote unanimous, we made her
A sovereign goddess, and as such display'd her:
But fearing lest the Senate should disown,
As *George's* friends, his *Adversary's* stone,
Inscrib'd with bits of verse, and scraps of prose,
(The verse at least is classical) we chose
To make and call her ACADEMIC GLORY,
Still in disguise a Queen, and still a TORY."]

3. Charles Duke of Somerset; by Rysbrack.

In 1750, Frances, Marchioness of Granby, and Charlotte, Lady Guernsey, daughters of Charles Seymour, Duke of Somerset, Chancellor of the University from 1689 to 1748, offered a statue of their late father[1]. The statue, by Rysbrack[2], arrived in 1756, and was placed at the east end of the Senate-House, on the left of the entrance. The inscriptions on the pedestal are:

CAROLO
DVCI SOMERSETENSI
STRENVO IVRIS ACADEMICI DEFENSORI
ACERRIMO LIBERTATIS PVBLICAE VINDICI
STATVAM
LECTISSIMARVM MATRONARVM MVNVS
L. M. PONENDAM DECREVIT
ACADEMIA CANTABRIGIENSIS
QVAM PRAESIDIO SVO MVNIVIT
AVXIT MVNIFICENTIA
PER ANNOS PLVS SEXAGINTA
CANCELLARIVS.

HANC STATVAM
SVAE IM PARENTEM PIETATIS
IN ACADEMIAM STVDII
MONVMENTVM
ORNATISSIMAE FEMINAE
FRANCISCA MARCHIONIS DE GRANBY } CONIVX
CHARLOTTA BARONIS DE GVERNSEY } CONIVX
S. P. FACIENDAM CVRAVERVNT
M·D·C·C·L·V·I·

4. King George the Second; by Wilton.

This statue was given by Thomas Holles Pelham, Duke of Newcastle, Chancellor of the University 1748—68; and shortly before the Duke visited the University, 28 June, 1766[3], had been placed on the south side of the Senate-House, opposite to that of King George the First, the statue of *Glory* being removed to the east end, on the right

[1] [The Grace to return thanks to them for their intended present was passed 29 June, 1750. By the same Grace a Syndicate was appointed to inscribe the Duke's name among the Benefactors of the University, and to select a suitable place for the statue.]

[2] [On the statue are the words: "Mich^{l}. Rysbrack *Sculp^{t}.* 1756."]

[3] [Cooper's Annals, iv. 342. On the statue are the words "I: WILTON sculp^{t}."]

of the entrance. The position of the statue was not sanctioned by Grace of the Senate. The following inscription is on the pedestal:

GEORGIO SECUNDO
Patrono suo, optimè merenti,
Semper venerando;
Quòd volenti Populo,
Justissimè, humanissimè,
In Pace, et in Bello,
Feliciter Imperavit;
Quòd Academiam Cantabrigiensem
Fovit, auxit, ornavit;
HANC STATUAM
Æternum, faxit Deus, Monumentum
Grati Animi in Regem,
Pietatis in Patriam,
Amoris in Academiam,
Suis Sumptibus poni curavit
THOMAS HOLLES
DUX DE NEWCASTLE
AC ACADEMIÆ CANCELLARIUS
A.D.MDCCLXVI.

5. WILLIAM PITT; by Nollekens.

Mr Pitt died 23 January, 1806, and on 21 March following a Grace was offered to the Senate proposing that a Syndicate should be appointed to consider some mark of respect to his memory. This having been rejected in the Caput by the vote of Dr Martin Davy, Master of Caius College, a meeting of members of the Senate was held at Trinity College Lodge on the following Monday (24 March), at which it was resolved to erect a statue by subscription. The strength of feeling in favour of the project among resident members of the University is shewn by the fact that £537. 15*s.* 0*d.* was subscribed in the room; £787. 5*s.* 0*d.* on 25 March; and £373. 5*s.* 0*d.* on 26 March; making a total of £1697. 5*s.* 0*d.* from residents only. Before the subscription was closed it had amounted to £7564. 10*s.* 0*d.*; but of this total a portion was not paid, and a portion was returned to the subscribers. In less than a month after the meeting had been held (18 April), the Secretary, the Rev. John Brown, M.A. of Trinity College, wrote to the University stating that the committee had now "very ample funds;" and "being desirous that the statue should be placed in the most public and honourable situation, do hereby request the University to accept it when completed, and to place it in the Senate House." A Grace to accept the gift, and to agree to the wish of the subscribers, was passed a few days later (23 April); and at the beginning of the following year it was decided that the statue, when it arrived, should be placed opposite to that of the Duke of Somerset, the statue of *Glory*, which then occupied that position, being removed, with the concurrence of Baron Gwydir, son of the donor, to the Law School[1]. The Committee applied to five artists for models of the statue, viz.: Flaxman, Westmacott, Nollekens, Bacon, and Garrard. Canova was also suggested, but, as he could not come to England to execute the work, he was not formally applied to. The artists were instructed that the statue should "correspond in height of figure and pedestal with that of the Duke of Somerset;" and that it was "to be free in every part from emblematical or allegorical devices, and to be in the habit of a Master of Arts, after the manner of the statue of Newton." The design of Nollekens was accepted, and it was agreed (23 March, 1808) that he should receive £3000, provided the statue was finished within three years. It did not, however, arrive until 1812, owing to the difficulty of procuring a proper block of marble. The inscription is the single word: PITT; on the back of the plinth are the words: "Nollekens Ft. 1812"[2].

The Senate-House having been completed, the room in which the Senate had formerly met was added to the Library, as will be related presently. This work accomplished, the project of erecting a south wing which should correspond with the Senate-House, was revived. In 1738 (3 May) a Grace passed the Senate to the following effect: (1) that the south side of the New Building was greatly needed for the Vice-Chancellor's Court, Registrary's office, and other academic purposes, and more especially for the Press, to save the University a heavy annual outlay in hiring buildings belonging to other persons; (2) that certain houses on the south side of the Regent Walk belonging to King's College and Corpus Christi College could be purchased, in virtue of a Grace of the Senate formerly passed for that purpose; (3) that the following persons be appointed Syndics in the usual form for carrying out these

[1] [Grace, 16 January, 1807. "Placeat vobis, ut Statua in hoc Senaculo Gloriæ dicata, et ab eximio Viro Petro Burrell, Armigero, Academiæ olim donata, Honoratissimo Domino Domino Baroni Gwyder, ejusdem Filio unico, huic rei suffragante, in Scholas juridicas transmoveatur; nisi in alium aptiorem locum eam Vobis posthac transmoveri placuerit."]

[2] [Cooper's Annals, iv. 485. Le Keux, ed. Cooper, iii. 57. Minute Book of the Committee, now preserved in the Cambridge Free Library. No. 1743. B.]

objects: the Vice-Chancellor (Dr Richardson, Master of Emmanuel); the Vice-Chancellor for the time being; Dr Gooch, Dr Newcome, Dr Hubbard, Mr Wrigley, Mr Burrough, Mr Burford, Mr Evans, Mr Rutterforth, Mr Yonge, and Mr Cornwallis. The appearance of the name of Dr Gooch among these Syndics shews that the scheme must have been approved of by those members of the "Detachment" party who had been most prominent in their opposition to the former one. It will be observed, however, that the instructions to the Syndics limit them strictly to the purchase of a suitable site for the new building, and that nothing is said about procuring a design or soliciting subscriptions. Soon after their appointment they purchased from Corpus Christi College the lease of the four houses on the Regent Walk[1], but there is no evidence that they negotiated with King's College, or attempted to purchase the ground on which the houses stood, and no further action seems to have been taken by them for fifteen years.

In 1753 (15 December) the Syndicate was increased by the addition of five new members, and they were instructed, besides their former duties, to buy "other houses also, with the ground adjoining, from King's College." This direction evidently refers to the houses on the south side of East School Street, the purchase of which was effected some years afterwards.

Meanwhile the design for a new building seems to have been abandoned, and the attention of the University to have been turned to the desirability of building a new façade to the Library, which, without reviving the obnoxious "Attachment" scheme, should provide a capacious room for the Royal Library on the first floor, with some offices below, and should continue the classical character of the style adopted for the Senate-House. A ground-plan and elevation were designed by Mr Burrough in 1752, and afterwards published by James Essex[2], which fulfil the necessary requirements with great taste and ability. It was of course necessary to pull down the building connecting the Divinity

[1] [The price paid was £350. Univ. Accounts, 1737—38.]

[2] [The print, engraved by Fourdrinier, but without date, is called: "A Design for the Publick Library at Cambridge, made by the late Sr James Burrough, in the Year 1752. Jac^{s}. Essex delin^{t}. 1752." We may infer from Cole (quoted below, p. 65) that it was printed in 1775.]

School and the Law School; but, with this exception, the old buildings were not interfered with, and the new façade was set in front of them. On this account his ground-plan, here reproduced on a reduced scale (fig. 12), is peculiarly valuable; for it supplies the only information now attainable respecting the original arrangement of the west ends of the Divinity School and the Law School. His building would have stood about 12 feet in advance of the Divinity School, and 18 feet in advance of the Law School. In the centre of the façade, approached by a flight of five steps, there was a portico of six engaged composite columns, supporting a pediment. Behind this portico was a corridor, with a central passage into the quadrangle. On the right and left of this passage were two rooms, lighted on the west side only. In the south wing there was a staircase, as at present; and in the north wing a small vestibule, giving access to the Divinity School. On the first floor there was a Library, 70 feet long by 27 feet broad, with a door at either end, and subdivided, by bookcases set at right angles to the walls, into seven compartments on each side, each lighted by a window. The style of the façade, both in the central columns, and the pilasters to the right and left of it, was exactly copied from the adjoining Senate-House.

This design, it will be observed, made no provision for the public offices which were to have been contained in the new building; but it was evidently admired at the time, and was in fact adopted, with trifling modifications, two years afterwards; though the style was altered, and the execution entrusted to a different architect. For this we will again quote Mr Hubbard's diary;

"11 June 1754. A Grace passed, the Preamble of which set forth, 'That the Duke of Newcastle, our Chancellor, had given 500*l.* towards erecting a Front to the Library, and several other great and noble Persons, our Patrons, had contributed to the same'; and the Grace was: 'That the Syndics appointed formerly for contracting with Kings and Corpus Christi Colleges, should take care of the Execution of this Building, according to the Plan recommended by our Chancellor'[1].

[1] ["Cum Illustrissimus Cancellarius vester, pro perpetuâ quâ est in Vos benevolentiâ, eam Bibliothecae partem quæ spectat versus templum Beatae Mariae Virginis de novo aedificari exoptans, in eum usum libras quingentas erogari jussit, cumque alii magni nominis viri, Academiae Patroni et Fautores, pecunias in eundem usum collaturi sunt; Placeat Vobis, ut Syndici, quibus cura committitur domos terrasque a Collegijs Regali et Corporis Christi redimendi caeteraque negotia novum aedificium

Non Regents: Placets 51.

Non-Placets 10. viz. Mess[rs]. Burrough, Smith, Goodrich, Bringloe and Sturgeon of Caius, Nicholson and Smith of Peter-House, Masters C.C.C. Loggon Joh. and Hubbard Emman.

Regents. Placets 33.

Non Placets 6. viz. Mess[rs]. White, Hickes, Norris, Carlos, Atthill."

Upon this passage Cole makes the following observations dated 5 March, 1780:

"The Occasion of this Opposition was this. Sir James Burrough had built the Senate House on a most elegant Plan, and prepared a Front to the Library (which was a Continuation of the same Building,)

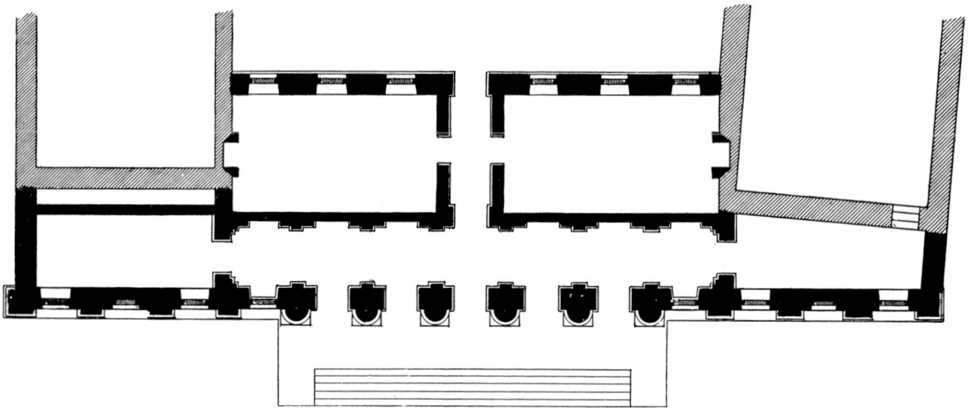

Fig. 12. Ground-plan of the design proposed by Burrough for the east front of the Library.

on the same Plan, as no Doubt was proper: but the Duke, probably advised by other Persons, brought down a new Plan, in another Style of Building, which he was desirous to have executed, tho' inferior to M[r]. Burrough's, and by another Architect: possibly they might think the new one might be executed cheaper, as the former was on a rich Corinthian Plan and Design. Whatever were the Motives, the Friends of M[r]. Burrough, (and he had no Enemies, tho' the Expectants voted for the lucrative Side) thought this not only a great Slight thrown unnecessarily on a very worthy Member and old Servant of the University, who had deserved better, but that the Building a new Front to the Library, on a different Design from that of the adjoining Senate-House, was absurd

spectantia exequendi, huic operi praeficiantur, curentque ut dicta pars Bibliothecae extruatur secundum delineationem quam Cancellarius vobis commendaverit?"]

and ill judged. The World may judge of this Matter, as Mr. Essex has printed within these 4 or 5 years a View of Sir James Burrough's Design; and that of the Duke of Newcastle was published before[1]. It occasioned a great deal of Animosity and ill Temper in the University;

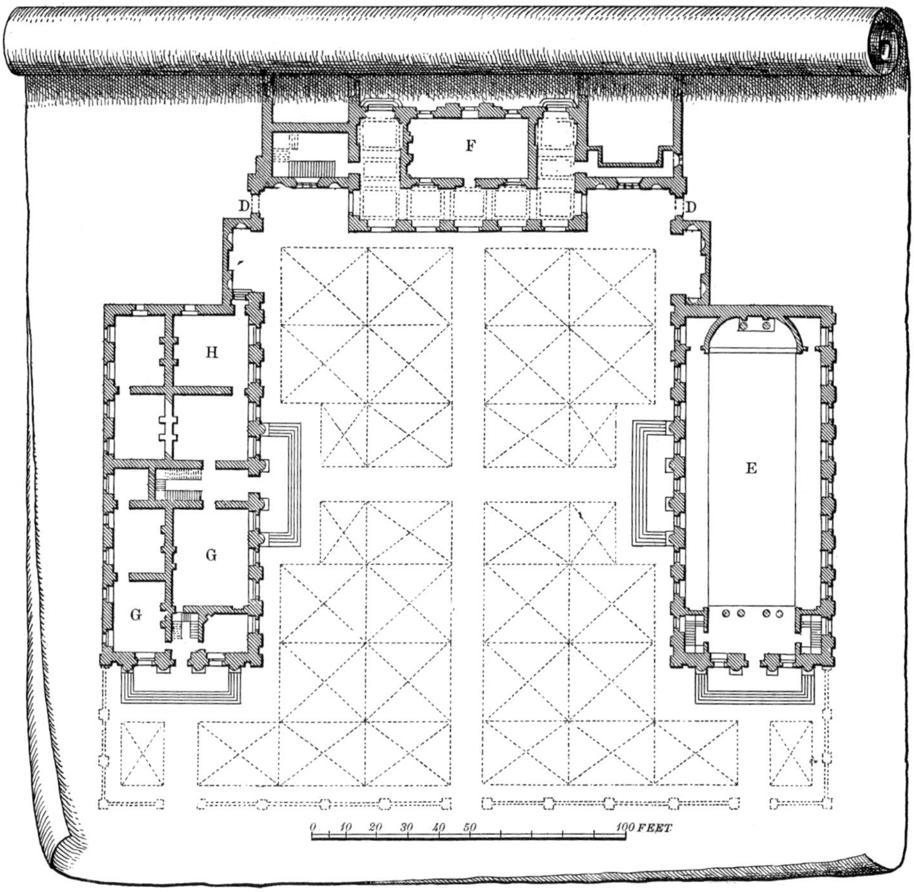

Fig. 13. Ground-plan of the design proposed by Wright, and called by him "The Regent walk, and General plan of the new Building at Cambridge." D. Passages to King's and Caius Colleges; E. Senate-House; F. New Consistory; G. New Registrary's Office; H. Librarian's Room, etc.

[1] [Wright's design, engraved by Fourdrinier, bears no date on the plate, but in the Univ. Accounts for 1753—54 we find "Mr Fourdrinier, Engraver, £19 . 15 . 0," which can refer to no other expense than that of this view of the building, which would be circulated to obtain subscriptions.]

and the Duke, in order to cajole and bring into Temper Mr Burrough, soon after procured him a Knighthood. But the Absurdity of the measure must strike everyone."

The architect selected by the Chancellor was Mr Stephen Wright; and his plan, so far as the Library was concerned, was carried out exactly. He did not, however, confine himself to the Library, as Burrough had done, but gave a ground-plan of a new building (fig. 13) corresponding in dimensions, and it may be presumed, in style also, to the Senate-House. An architectural connexion between the Library and these two structures was provided by the ingenious device of an arcade, surmounted with a coping and a row of stone balls, extending from each end of the new façade to the adjoining structures. The arcade between the Library and Senate-House was actually built[1].

The work began in July 1754, and in the following weeks the Accounts contain charges for "taking down the old building—cutting out doorways into the old Library—working up a doorway at the Senate House—working up part of a window in the Library—lathing and plaistering a pertition in the Law School—digging up the old foundations," and the like. In September the Chancellor came to Cambridge, and inspected the trenches dug for the foundations[2]. The ceremony of laying the first stone took place in April of the following year. Here again we will quote Mr Hubbard:

"April 30. A Levee in Clare Hall Combination [the Master of Clare Hall, Peter Stephen Goddard, D.D. being Vice Chancellor], and at about Half an Hour past 12, the Duke came to the Congregation, where all Masters of Arts were with their Hoods flourished: the Beadles in tufted Gowns, Coifs, and Caps, except Mr Porteus the Junior Beadle, who had on a Master of Arts Gown. From the Senate House a Procession to the laying the first Stone of the New Building, in this Order: First, the Junior Beadle, then the Syndics for the New Building, two and two, Juniors first: then the other two Beadles, the Chancellor, Vice Chancellor, Heads, Doctors, B. D. Masters of Arts, &c. in Order of Seniority, Seniors first. When they came to the Place appointed for the Stone (which was the North Corner of the Front) the Duke performed the Ceremony, speaking a few Words in Latin at the same

[1] [This statement is made on the authority of Dr John Smith, whose account of the completion of the west end of the Senate-House is printed below, p. 70. The arcade appears in a "Prospect of the Senate-House" etc. engraved for The Complete English Traveller, fol. Lond. 1771.]

[2] [Hubbard's Diary, 16 September, 1754.]

Time: the Vice Chancellor read the Inscription upon the Plate, and after that was inserted in the Stone, and Money, according to Custom, put in, all returned to the Senate House, where the Orator [John Skynner, M.A., Fellow of S. John's College,] (from a small Rostrum) made a long Speech; and the Chancellor adjourned the Congregation to Thursday 11 o'clock."

The following is the inscription[1] on the stone:

CONSTANTIAE AETERNITATIQVE SACRVM.
LATVS HOC ORIENTALE BIBLIOTHECAE PVBLICAE
EGREGIA GEORGI I^{MI}
BRITANNIARVM REGIS
LIBERALITATE LOCVPLETATAE
VETVSTATE OBSOLETVM INSTAVRAVIT
GEORGI II^{DI} PRINCIPIS OPTIMI
MVNIFICENTIA
ACCEDENTE
NOBILISSIMORVM VIRORVM
THOMAE HOLLES DVCIS DE NEWCASTLE
ACADEMIAE CANCELLARII
PHILIPPI COMITIS DE HARDWICKE ANGLIAE CANCELLARII
ACADEMIAE SVMMI SENESCHALLI
AC PLVRIMORVM PRAESVLVM, OPTIMATVM,
ALIORVMQUE ACADEMIAE FAVTORVM
PROPENSA IN REI LITERARIAE INCREMENTVM
SPLENDOREMQVE BENIGNITATE

LAPIDEM HVNC IMMOBILEM
OPERIS EXORDIVM
IPSIVS AVSPICIIS SVSCEPTI
AVTHORITATE, PATROCINIO, PROCVRATIONE,
FELICITER, DEO PROPITIO, PERFICIENDI,
CIRCVMSTANTE FREQVENTISSIMA ACADEMICORVM CORONA,
PRID. KALEND. MAI. MDCCLV.
SVA MANV SOLENNITER POSVIT
ACADEMIAE CANCELLARIVS.

The work proceeded without interruption, and the building was practically finished by the summer of 1758, though the Accounts were not closed until 1759. The ceremony of opening the new Library is thus described by Mr Hubbard:

"July 3 [1758]. A grand Levee at Clare Hall. Soon after 11 the Chancellor came to the Congregation, where the Public Orator made a long

[1] [It is printed in the following work: "Carmina ad nobilissimum Thomam Holles Ducem de Newcastle Inscripta, cum Academiam Cantabrigiensem Bibliothecæ Restituendæ Causa inviseret Prid. Kalend. Maias, MDCCLV. Cantabrigiæ Typis Academicis excudebat J. Bentham. MDCCLV." 4to. The Orator's speech was printed in the same year.]

and very elegant Speech, which was received with universal Applause: then a Procession to the New Library: Syndics first, preceded by the Junior Beadle; next the Chancellor, preceded by the other 2 Beadles; then the Vice Chancellor, Noblemen, Doctors, etc. At the upper End of the Room, the Orator made another Speech, addressed to the Chancellor; which was answered by him. Then went back to the Congregation, and passed Degrees."

The expense had amounted to £10,506. 9*s.* 8¾*d.*; and the receipts to £9692. 9*s.*, in which total are included the value of the old materials, and legacies of £500 from Sir Nathaniel Lloyd, Master of Trinity Hall 1710—35, and of £30 from Robert Tillotson, M.A., Fellow of Clare Hall. King George the Second gave £3000; the Chancellor £1000; the Earl of Hardwicke, High Steward, £500; and the Members, the Hon. Edward Finch, and the Hon. Thomas Townshend, £250 each[1].

The arrangement of the new building with reference to the old will be readily understood from the ground-plan of the quadrangle in its present state (fig. 10), on which the former structures are indicated by dotted lines. The ground-floor was intended for the Vice-Chancellor's Court, or Consistory, but in 1795 was fitted up as a Lecture Room for the Professors of Divinity[2]. It was entered by a door in the centre of the façade (*Y* fig. 10), which was removed to the south end (ibid. *Z*) when the room was assigned to the Library in 1880. The following extract from a letter written 18 March, 1754, by the Vice-Chancellor to William George, D.D., Provost of King's College, shews the difficulties which arose in consequence of the ground belonging to the University being so limited in extent, and the special importance of acquiring the piece next to the Library on the south (fig. 1):

"The front of the new building is design'd to be carried on with all possible expedition, and the other day, upon measuring the ground over again, it appear'd that the plan which we are upon cannot be carried into execution without encroaching upon the north west corner of the area before your Lodge. About 25 feet from West to East, and

[1] [A complete list of the subscriptions is given in Cooper's Annals, iv. 293. Cole, writing in 1780, remarks: "Probably most of the Clerical Subscribers, and possibly many of the Layity, put in here as into a Lottery of the Duke of Newcastle's Formation. Translations, Places, and Preferments were what was fished for, and many succeeded to their Heart's Desire." MSS. li. 440. Add. MSS. Mus. Brit. 5852.]

[2] [Cambridge Guide, 1799, p. 25.]

12 from North to South will be wanting, not properly to build upon, but to make good the passage into your College, the end of the building being of necessity to cover the present gate. Your thoughts upon this subject I expect with impatience; and as I am sure my Lord Duke of Newcastle will allways have it in his thoughts to compleat the whole building, I wish a price were set upon the houses formerly mention'd to you. I am persuaded that the Bursars would enter into a negotiation with me if they have your permission[1]."

While the façade of the Library was in progress the Syndics succeeded (in the course of 1757) in purchasing all the property between the Regent Walk and East School Street[2]; but the ground was not cleared until 1769[3], when the houses were pulled down, and the materials sold.

It was next determined to finish the west end of the Senate-House, which, as mentioned above, had been left in rough brick-work, and to improve the west end of Great S. Mary's Church, which, after the removal of the intervening houses, would directly face the new east front of the Library.

The former work was undertaken at this particular time in consequence of a legacy from Sir James Burrough, who had died

[1] [Documents in the Registry of the University, Library, vol. 31. 2. 40.]

[2] [These particulars and the descriptions of the property given above are derived from the conveyances in the Registry of the University, and from the Univ. Accounts for 1756—57. Corpus Christi College received £440; and King's College £333.10.0. A Grace to seal the conveyances passed the Senate 21 January, 1757.]

[3] [Grace, 24 April, 1769. "Cum Ædes quædam ab Australi latere Ambulacri Regentium, completo jam Senaculi Ædificio et occidentali parte Ecclesiæ beatæ Mariæ, Offensioni sint Omnibus, et Academiæ Dedecori; Placeat Vobis, ut, quam primum fieri poterit, diruantur." Cam. Chron. 12 May, 1769. "The houses in the Regent Walk lately purchased by the University, are now pulling down, and the ground we hear is to be entirely cleared and levelled by the 10th of June, which will greatly add to the beauty of the Senate-House, Royal Library, etc." Cole defines the position of these houses (MSS. xlii. 139. Add. MSS. Mus. Brit. 5843): "May 2, 1769. As the old Range of Houses on the South Side of the Regent Walk are now immediately going to be pulled down by the University, in Order to have the Space clear of them before the approaching Celebrity of the Chancellor's Installation, with a View, as is supposed, that a Subscription may be opened towards erecting a Building correspondent to the elegant Theatre or Senate House, I went into the first of them, exactly fronting the west window of the South Isle of Great St. Mary's Church, now this year newly rebuilt, as was the West Window of the North Isle also, at the University Expence; or rather fronting the South Side of the Church yard, or South Porch of St. Mary Major's Church: in Order to see whether there was any Furniture or Wainscote worth removing to Milton, where I am now going to repair, and in a manner, rebuild an old House belonging to King's College, which I have taken a long lease of."]

in 1754, and bequeathed £150 to the University for that purpose. In 1766 (16 June) a Grace passed the Senate, drawing attention to the unfinished state of the building, and to the above-mentioned legacy, and appointing a Syndicate to obtain plans and estimates; which, contrary to the usual practice at this time, were to be submitted to the Senate for their approval. The following account[1] of the progress of the work was drawn up, probably soon after its completion, by Mr John Smith, who had succeeded Sir James Burrough as Master of Caius College, and was appointed Vice-Chancellor in November, 1766.

"On Friday the 28th November, the Syndics appointed June 16, 1766, met, and Mr. Essex laid before them a design marked N° 1, for caseing the West End of the Theatre, and an estimate of the Expence of the work in Portland stone, amounting to 1077*l.* The Syndics were of opinion that the West End, according to that Design, would not correspond enough with the other parts of the building, and that it ought to be enriched with Pilasters, and Entablature, and Dressing; and that the Windows should be dressed, and the Entablature carved, in the same manner as they are on the fronts and east end; and Mr. Essex was directed to draw a Design according to that Idea."

"The Design marked N°. 2 with the Estimate exceeding the former 310*l.* drawn by Mr. Essex were laid before the Syndics December 3, and approved of by them[2]. On Tuesday the 27th of January, 1767, the Masons began to erect Scaffolds to take down the Balls and Copeing of the Stone Arches which connected the publick Library with the Theatre at its West End. The Masons raised and finished the wall which is above the Arches and Balls and carryed them from the Library to the street by Caius Gate before the middle of May; at that time the trench was dug 14 feet deep and the foundation laid; and the work was brought to the level of the ground June the 15th. The work was stopped from the 15th of June to the 3d. of August; when 100 Ton of Portland stone or more, which had been long waited for, was brought up and landed; and on the next day, the 21st of August, at 10 o'clock in the morning, the first Stone which is in height one foot, one inch, was laid by me at the South West Angle of the Pediment of the West End; and on the upper Face of the said Stone, which is 2 *ft*, 5¾ *in*, by 1 *ft*, 6 *in*, are cut the following words: POSVIT IOANNES SMITH PROCAN. MDCCLXVII.

1 [Caius Coll. MSS. No. 616.]

2 [The execution of the work was sanctioned by the Senate 15 December, 1766; but there is nothing in the words of the Grace to shew that the actual design was submitted to the Senate: "Cum formula occidentale latus Senaculi quadrato lapide obducendi, et sumptus ad id absolvendum erogandi, à vestris Syndicis in eam rem constitutis examinati et approbati fuerint; Placeat Vobis, ut latus illud secundum istam formulam ab iisdem Syndicis perficiatur; Et ut quicquid ab iis vel a majori parte eorum (quorum unus sit Dnus. Procancellarius) in hoc opere exequendo conclusum fuerit, id a vobis ratum firmumque habeatur."]

This Stone was covered with a thin sheet of Lead in order to guard the Inscription on the 27th of August. Immediately the Stone in the Second Course, which stands on this, was set. On the 14th September the Base of the angular pilaster at the south-west was first set, and then the Base of the angular pilaster at the North-west. September the 25th. 1767 the first stone of the Shaft of the south-west corner Pilaster was set; and on the 19th of December the work, both of Stone and Brick, was carryed up to the Top of the Pediments over the first Tier of windows and brought to a Level, and cover'd over with Sedge for the Winter.

In the beginning of March, 1768, the Masons, who had been busy during the winter in preparing (cutting out) the Stone for the Pilasters, and carving the Capitals and Mouldings, began to raise the Scaffold and to set the Stone, and the latter end, viz. the 28th, of June, 1768, the West End was finished, the work measured up, and the scaffold struck.

The stone basement for the Iron Pallisades was begun immediately after finishing the West End, and finished in the middle of July, on which the iron pallisades were set [in] August, and the iron gate hung."

The iron fence here mentioned extended "from the north west angle of the Theatre to King's wall[1];" i.e. to the angle of the north wall of King's College Old Court facing Gonville Hall Lane. It was made to correspond with the fence which had been already set up at the east end, and along the north side, of the building. The total cost of the works above described, including the fence, had been nearly £1754.

Meanwhile the west end of Great S. Mary's Church had been undertaken. In 1767 (6 July) a Grace directed the Vice-Chancellor to treat with Trinity College and with the Parish for certain hovels (*ædiculæ*) which encumbered the west end of the north and south aisles, with a view to their destruction; and, 27 October in the same year, the houses having been pulled down, the Syndics who had charge of the Senate-House were empowered to repair the walls of the Church against which the houses had abutted. This they did in the course of 1768.

"The Scaffolding was begun to be raised at the West End of the North Isle of St Mary's Church Monday July the 24th; and the West Window and Battlements of the Isle were finished in the month of August, and those belonging to the South Isle were finished the first week in November 1768[2]."

The iron railings westward of the Church were put up in 1769[3].

[1] [Caius Coll. MSS. No. 604.]
[2] [Dr Smith's Notes, *ut supra*.]
[3] [Minute of the Syndics, 24 April, 1769.]

The appearance of Senate-House Yard, as it was called, after these alterations had been carried out, has been preserved in an engraving by P. S. Lamborn, which, though undated, was evidently published between 1768 and 1770[1]. The whole space is represented as open, and we learn from the University Accounts for 1762, in which year it was levelled, and otherwise improved, that it was gravelled. This space is traversed by the Regent Walk, which, as heretofore, led direct from the central arch of the façade of the Library to the west door of Great S. Mary's Church (fig. 1). The iron railings in front of the Senate-House are several feet in advance of the steps, and they terminate abruptly at the Regent Walk. West of the Senate-House we see the railing in front of the Gate of Honour of Caius College, and the arcade mentioned above (p. 66), surmounted with a row of stone balls, rebuilt in prolongation of the façade of the Library towards the north. It must be remembered that Senate-House Yard was at this period still bounded on the south by the houses on the south side of School Street, the acquisition of which by the University has been already recorded in the History of King's College[2]. A brief reference to the transaction is however necessary in this place.

We have seen that the purchase of houses from King's College was made an instruction to the Syndics appointed in 1753; and that in 1754, when the façade of the Library was being set out, the Vice-Chancellor wrote to the Provost, mentioning his wish to acquire certain houses belonging to the College. These stood at the corner of High Street and School Street, with a frontage of 144 feet to the former, and 102 feet to the latter, abutting westward on a wing of the Provost's Lodge. No definite steps however were taken respecting their acquisition until 1769, when a Syndicate was appointed (1 February) to conclude terms of purchase with the College; and the conveyance was sealed 4 December in the same year. The price paid was £1920. No immediate use was made of them ; and no revival of the

1 [The plate is dedicated to the Duke of Grafton, First Lord Commissioner of the Treasury, and Chancellor of the University of Cambridge. As the Duke's Administration lasted from 1768 to 1770, and he was Chancellor 1768—1811, the print must have been engraved between 1768 and 1770, probably in 1769, before the Installation, to attract subscriptions.]

2 [History of King's College, Vol. i. p. 545—548.]

building scheme was attempted until 1783, when a Grace was passed (28 June), stating: (1) that the south wing of the new building had long been wanted by all persons; (2) that, having regard to the increased wealth of the University, there was a hope that the scheme, though extensive and difficult, might now be undertaken under good auspices, and carried to a successful issue at no distant date; and suggesting the appointment of Syndics to buy any buildings which might be desirable; to obtain designs and estimates; and at the earliest opportunity to submit such as they approved of to the Senate for their sanction.

These Syndics (the number of whom was increased more than once) entered into an agreement with King's College in 1786 by which the College ceded to the University a considerable portion of the Provost's Lodge on condition, among other things, of receiving back about half the site of the houses sold seventeen years before. The University further agreed to pull down the old houses, and to erect a brick wall (*AB*, fig. 1) between their property and that of the College.

The houses were pulled down between 1787 and 1789, and the wall built. This having been completed, and the whole area thrown open, various schemes for fencing it were proposed. In 1789 the iron palisades which had been erected on the completion of the Senate-House were taken down, and re-erected in their present position[1]; and in 1791 the Senate authorized the fencing in of the remainder of the area. In the course of 1792 the fence was completed as far as the abovementioned wall (fig. 1) under the direction of Mr John Soane, Architect[2]; and the area within it was turfed and paved[3].

1 [Minutes of the Syndicate, 14 May, 1789. "Agreed that the Palisades on the East side of the area of the Senate house be taken down, and that Palisades be erected from the corner of the Senate house steps to the corner of the steps of the intended building according to a plan drawn by the Syndics for the direction of the Surveyor employed by the Commissioners of the Paving Act."]

2 [Grace, 11 March, 1791. Minute of the Syndicate, 31 March, 1792.]

3 [Minute of the Syndicate, 6 July, 1792. "Agreed that from the Front Gate next to the east end of the Senate-House a flat stone Pavement of a due Width not less than that of the said Gate be laid down to the End of the Cloister and parallel to the Senate-House; and that a similar Pavement be carried from the other Front Gate to the other End of the Cloister. Agreed likewise that a similar Pavement be laid within the Palisades from Gate to Gate, and that the Space within these Pavements be laid out in a Grass-Plot, and that proper Cess-Pools be made."]

Meanwhile the new building had not been neglected. In 1785 Mr Brettingham, Architect, gave plans and estimates, but they were evidently not approved, as they were not submitted to the Senate[1]. In 1791 Mr John Soane, Architect, was consulted, and the following definite instructions were given to him:

"April 13th. 1791. At a meeting of the Syndics...it was agreed that Mr Soane be desired to distribute the Interior space of the said intended Building into the following Rooms, viz: A musæum, a picture-gallery, a large Lecture Room, which may serve also for a Music Room, a smaller Lecture Room, and a Registrary's office, and to lay his plan before the said Syndics as soon as he can conveniently."

His plans, which still exist[2], shew a building exactly resembling the Senate-House externally, and divided, as well as the space would admit, into the required apartments. The Senate, however, rejected them by a majority of two votes, 13 December, 1791; but the ground of the opposition has not been recorded. No rival design appears to have been suggested; nor, so far as we know, did the Syndics make any subsequent attempt to obtain one which might be more satisfactory to the Senate. It is curious that no one seems to have thought of using the ground-plans suggested by Gibbs or Wright, either of which would have provided the required apartments. In 1797 an attempt was made to obtain more ground from King's College, but the proposal was declined[3]; and after that date the scheme for a new building appears to have been definitely abandoned.

We will now return to the Library, and narrate the changes introduced after the completion of the Senate-House.

In August, 1730, it was decided that the Regent House should be dismantled, and fitted up as a Library; the old wainscot being used for the repair of the Sophisters School on the ground-floor of the west side of the quadrangle, now the Arts School. These changes were directed by the following Grace, in English:

"5 August 1730. Whereas the Schools appointed for Batchelors and Sophisters are rendered unfit for performance of their Exercises,

[1] [Univ. Accounts, 1784—85.]

[2] [They are preserved in the Registry of the University.]

[3] [Vol. i. p. 547.]

May it please You that those Schools be fitted up for that purpose, and the materials for Floor Wainscot and Seats belonging to the Old Senate House be employ'd to this use, and that Room be order'd for enlargement of the Library, and rendred commodious for Reception of the Books given by his late Majesty, till you have a Building more suitable to the Munificence of Our Royal Benefactor."

The Accounts shew that the work, so far as the School was concerned, was completed in the course of 1731; but that the fitting up of the Regent House occupied nearly four years. It was entrusted to James Essex, and the payments to him "towards Flooring and Classing the Old Senate House for the reception of the King's Books" begin in 1731; but the books were not moved in until 1734, as shewn by the following entries in the University Accounts:

"To 4 Scholars for assisting in Setting up the King's books and in making the Catalogue 61 3 0

To Labourers in the Library for Removing and Cleaning books...... 13 9 3"

While this work was proceeding, an alteration to the west room of the Library was undertaken under the direction of the same architect. At that time this room was shorter, and at the north end, narrower, than it is at present (fig. 7), and the only means of passing from it to the Regent House was by crossing the landing of the staircase. It was accordingly determined to remove the staircase, and to make the Library, and consequently the room under the north end of it also, of a uniform width throughout. This scheme was sanctioned by the Senate 26 June, 1732[1], and was probably carried out without delay, the door at the south-west corner of the Regent House (*A*, fig. 9) being blocked, and the present entrance from the west room, with the panelwork, being constructed in place of it. In May of the next year a door was made out of the East Library into the Regent House[2], so as to complete the communication

[1] ["26 June 1732. Cum Senaculum vetus jam sit classibus instruendum, ut Regii muneris receptui magis sit accommodum: Placeat Vobis ut Gradus amoveantur, et ut Bibliotheca qua angustior est amplificetur."]

[2] ["23 May 1733. Cum instet tempus Bibliothecæ Regiæ disponendæ, Placeat Vobis, ut aditus pateat ex Bibliothecæ vestræ parte Orientali ad Senaculum vetus."]

between the four rooms which then, as now, were devoted to the purposes of a Library[1].

A description of the Library written in 1748, after these alterations had been carried out, but before the new east room had been built, is worth quotation:

"The old Library, consisting of eighteen Classes, is situate at the South End of the Court, over the Law-school. That Part of the Library given to the University by King *George*, consisting of 30,000 Volumes, takes up the Galleries on the West and North Side of the Court, over the Philosophy and Divinity-Schools, containing twentysix large beautiful Classes. The Manuscripts are in the Gallery on the East Side of the Square; where are also some *Indian* Pagods, a Mummy, and other Curiosities[2]."

The printed books having been at last accommodated, attention was turned to the Manuscripts, and the "Square Room" as it was called, between the south and west libraries, the construction of which in 1716 has been already narrated, was altered for their reception. In 1750 and 1751 Mr Essex was employed to construct a new roof with a glazed cupola surmounted by a pine-apple; and suitable furniture was provided[3]. In 1752 (6 July) the Senate was informed that the cases were ready for the Manuscripts, and leave was obtained to set them in order in the course of the ensuing summer[4]. It is curious to remark that at the same time doubts about the stability of the floor began to be entertained; and that a few days after the above Grace had been sanctioned a fresh agreement was made with King's College to the following effect:

"July 15. 1752. The Provost and Fellows of King's College consented to the erecting arches under the square room in the Publick

1 [Unfortunately no details of these interesting works are to be found in the Accounts or bills of workmen. Mr Essex was always paid in gross, "for work done;" and the bills contain little else than charges for labour and materials. In 1733 the bricklayer heads his account: "Work done at the Schools, viz. cutting down windows, carrying away Rubbish, Turning an Arch for a Doorway and pointing the Ceiling." The doorway is probably that which leads from the west room to the north room of the Library.]

2 [The Foreigner's Companion etc. By Mr Salmon. London, 1748, p. 17.]

3 [Univ. Accounts 1749—50; 1750—51.]

4 ["6 July 1752. Cum Plutei in Bibliotheca Academica Codicibus manuscriptis recipiendis destinati jam confecti sint: Placeat Vobis ut dicti Codices in ordinem hac æstate redigantur, eorumque Catalogi a Bibliothecariis vestris describantur, utque necessarij sumptus suppeditentur juxta mentem Curatorum Bibliothecæ vestræ."]

Library at the expence of the University. And in consideration that it will be attended with some inconvenience to the said College, the University is to be at the expence of building them a staircase there[1]."

This work appears to have been carried out in the course of the same year; and two years later the cases were fitted with doors of brass wire-work. The MSS. were probably moved in when the old east library was destroyed to make way for the new façade, for in 1763 we find the following description of the room:

"In the South West Angle is a handsome square Room enlightned with a Cupola, lately fitted up with Doors of Brass Wire-work for the Reception of Manuscripts and other valuable Books: and here likewise are preserved a Mummy, a *Chinese* Pagod, and many other Curiosities[2]."

From the dates given in the above narrative it will be seen that the arrangement of Bishop Moore's Library was a more than usually remarkable instance of the delay which seems inseparable from all University work. The books had arrived in 1715, but nineteen years elapsed before the printed books were really available for study; and thirty-seven before the manuscripts were placed in the room which had been specially constructed for them in 1716.

We have seen that the new east room was completed in 1758, but no attempt was made to fit it up with suitable book-cases for nearly twenty years. The words of a Grace which passed the Senate 23 March, 1787, indicate that the old cases, which must have been singularly unsuitable, had been made use of up to that time. A Syndicate was then appointed to procure more convenient book-cases; to rearrange the Library; and to print a Catalogue of it, if they thought proper. As usual, they did not hurry themselves; for the agreement with Charles Humfrey, Carpenter, of Cambridge, is dated 1 November, 1787, and the cases were not completed until 1790[3]. The cases constructed by him are the eight large cases which

1 [Registry of the University, Library vol. 31. 2. 39.]

2 [Cantabrigia Depicta, Cambridge, 1763, p. 23. The Univ. Accounts for 1759—60 shew that the upper portion of the room was not fitted up until 1760: "Mr Essex, for upper Doors and Shelves in the Manuscript Library; and for the long Desk with sliding Doors and Shelves £62. 3. 4."]

3 [Univ. Accounts 1788—89; 1789—90. The total cost was £827. 3. 4.]

project from the east and west walls; and the four half-cases which stand against the north and south walls.

Before we conclude this chapter it should be mentioned that the connexion of the Geological Museum with the Library dates from the time of Dr John Woodward's original bequest. He died 25 April, 1728, and his collections came to Cambridge in the course of the same year[1]. There is no evidence to shew where they were originally deposited; but in 1735[2] the room at the north end of the Arts School, now the 'Novel Room,' was fitted up for their reception. This arrangement was not directed by Grace of the Senate; and it is only from the description of Cambridge already quoted that we know which room is referred to in the Accounts.

"On the West Side [of the Schools' Quadrangle] opposite to the Gate, are the Philosophy-Schools, where Disputations are held in Term-time....At the North End of the Philosophy-School, is the Room where Dr *Woodward's* Fossils, a vast Quantity of Ores, Minerals, and Shells, with other Curiosities well worth the viewing, are reposited[3]."

The room at the west end of the Divinity School was fitted up as a Registry in 1662, as has been already recorded (p. 23). This arrangement subsisted until 1831, when a Syndicate was appointed "to inspect the room where the records of the University are kept, and to see whether a more suitable place cannot be found for them." They reported that the room was damp and dark, that the records were rapidly perishing, and that it would be well to remove them to a room in the Old Court of King's College. This suggestion having been approved by the Senate, the room on the first floor of the south side, formerly the Combination Room, was fitted up for them, and an entrance to it was made from the west end of the Law School. In 1836, when the Old Court was pulled down, as will be narrated in a subsequent chapter, the Registry was transferred to a room at the south end of the ground-floor in the Pitt Press; and in 1848 to the large room on the first floor over the gate of entrance, originally built for a Syndicate Room[4].]

1 [Univ. Accounts, 1727—28.]

2 [Ibid. 1734—35.]

3 [The Foreigner's Companion, etc. p. 17.]

4 [These particulars are derived from notes made by Joseph Romilly, M.A., Registrary, preserved in the Registry.]

CHAPTER IV.

DESCRIPTION AND COMPARISON OF THE BUILDINGS OF THE SCHOOLS QUADRANGLE.

[BEFORE narrating the extension of the Library carried out in the present century, we will compare the buildings surrounding the Schools Quadrangle with the recorded facts of their history.

Professor Willis, after stating that the quadrangle was built between 1370 and 1475, makes the following notes on it in its present state: "As each side in succession was undertaken as a complete work, it afforded a series of interesting specimens to illustrate the gradual changes of the Perpendicular period. The soft stone, however, of which the tracery of the windows was made, has led to their destruction in the parts that remain; for nothing is now left in the windows except the monials.... The form of the window-heads in the Divinity School is of an earlier character than that of the other windows.... The details and forms of the west and south building are alike, as might be expected from the fact that these two buildings were carried on in immediate succession to each other.... A good series of doorways remains in this quadrangle; but the remainder of the details have been so altered and patched as to be of little value for study."

Notwithstanding these expressions it will still be worth our while to examine the buildings in detail; for the removal of the plaster from the north, west, and south sides of the quadrangle in the course of the repairs to the internal walls directed by Grace of the Senate 6 June, 1867, and the alterations in the Arts School which are now proceeding (January, 1884), have exposed numerous details and cleared up several difficulties. Besides the evidence supplied by the buildings themselves, this investigation will be greatly assisted by the elevation illustrating Archbishop Parker's essay, across which are written the length and breadth of most of the rooms as they existed in his time, as well as by Loggan's general view (fig. 4) and the view of the west side included in his picture of the Old Court of King's College (fig. 14).

The limits of the original west front are very satisfactorily determined by the buttress and quoins still standing at the north-east angle (fig. 10, *A*); and by the quoins at the south-east angle (ibid. *B*). If these points be connected we shall obtain the

Fig. 14. Exterior of the west side of the Schools Quadrangle; reduced from Loggan's view of the Old Court of King's College.

general outline of the west front next to North School Street, of which the elevation is shewn by Loggan (fig. 4).

If the plan drawn in 1752 by Mr Burrough (fig. 12) be accurate, the north building was rectangular; and its eastern gable made an angle with the rest of the façade (fig. 5). It was

91 feet long by 28 feet wide between the walls on the ground-floor. The wall which crosses the room from north to south (fig. 10, *EE*), cutting off a space 22 feet long from the west end, appears to be original[1]; for Parker gives the length of the Divinity School (which occupied the ground-floor until 1856) as 67 feet, a dimension which corresponds exactly with the distance between that wall and the east wall. On the other hand it must be remarked that the portion of wall against which the north end of this cross-wall abuts is of exactly the length required to contain one window and two spaces, of the same dimensions as those still existing in other parts of the same wall. It is difficult to examine this wall accurately, for Cockerell's building advances to within a short distance of it, but, so far as it can be examined, there does not appear to be any trace of a sixth window. Botwright's plan (fig. 3) shews seven windows on this side, but the existing windows have every appearance of being original, and it is quite possible that his sketch may have been drawn from memory, for no windows at all are shewn on the first floor. Loggan shews that there was originally a window of five lights in the eastern gable, and a window of three lights in the western gable (figs. 4, 14).

A third window (*W*, fig. 10) has been blocked by the insertion of a door-case brought from some other position; and, before the east side of the quadrangle was built (1470—75) there may have been a fourth window, in the space between the easternmost window and the east gable. When the classical façade was erected (1755—58), an irregular space was added to the Divinity School, the shape of which was ingeniously concealed by two additional pillars and a dais approached by steps.

The room on the first floor, now the catalogue-room of the Library, was originally lighted by six windows on the north side, of which one only, the easternmost, is now open; and probably by four on the south side, for there are traces on the surface of the wall (*CD*, fig. 9) against which the eastern building abuts which indicate the presence of a window behind the book-cases. This window has been indicated in outline

[1] [As the age of this wall is uncertain, it has been indicated by dotted lines on the ground-plan of the buildings in their original state (fig. 5).]

on the plan. Each gable contained a window of five lights (figs. 4, 14).

Professor Willis remarks in the passage quoted above that the form of the heads of the windows in the Divinity School is of earlier character than that of the other windows. Two of these original windows still remain in the west gable, and their peculiar form is shewn in the elevation of the west side in its present state (fig. 18).

The roof of the catalogue-room is open, and divided into six compartments by tie-beams encased in plaster-work. This plaster-work is carried up to the roof, which is divided into panels of the same style, enriched with a variety of ornaments. No record of the construction of this beautiful work has been preserved, but as the arms of Jegon appear upon it at the west end, we may conclude that it was put up either by John Jegon, D.D., Master of Corpus Christi College 1590—1602, or by his brother Thomas Jegon, D.D., who held the same office, 1602—18. Dr John Jegon was Vice-Chancellor for three years in succession, 1596—97, 1597—98, 1598—99, and again 1600—1601, when he was made Dean of Norwich. It is not improbable that he presented this roof to the University to commemorate a tenure of office which was at that time without precedent. Dr Thomas Jegon held the office of Vice-Chancellor for one year only, 1608—1609.

Archbishop Parker makes the length of the Regent House the same as that of the Divinity School, namely, 67 feet, a measurement which it is exceedingly difficult to interpret. As all his other measurements are perfectly correct, so far as we are able to judge, it would be rash to assume that this measurement is altogether erroneous. The total length of the room in its old state must have been nearly 91 feet. We know nothing about its arrangements, except that in 1676 a screen was set up in it, to divide the Regent and the Non-Regent Houses. It may be suggested that Parker's measurement was taken when part of the east end was still divided off for a Chapel, and only a portion of the room was available for the meetings of the Senate. It must, however, be admitted that the coincidence of length between the upper and lower rooms is suspicious.

This room was originally entered through a large and picturesque doorway (fig. 15) at the west end of the south wall (*A*, fig. 9). This doorway, the existence of which had previously been unsuspected, was discovered during some alterations to the west room in the summer of 1883. A smaller door (ibid. *B*) about twenty feet to the east of it, was discovered at the same time. The larger door was approached by a flight of stairs contained in the building in the north-west angle of the quadrangle, the external appearance of which has been preserved by Loggan (fig. 4). The stairs were removed in 1732, when the west room was altered for the reception of Bishop Moore's books, and the ancient arrangements were completely forgotten until the removal of the plaster from the walls in the interior of the quadrangle in 1867 revealed a portion of the doorway on the ground-floor through which the Divinity School had been originally entered (*D*, fig. 10, fig. 5). In January 1884, in the course of some alterations to the Arts School, the foundations of the wall containing the original door of entrance to that school (fig. 4) were discovered; and leave was then obtained to make an excavation in the quadrangle, with the view of discovering the exact dimensions of the building shewn by Loggan. The foundations then laid bare have been laid down on the plan of the ground-floor in its present state (fig. 10); and the results deduced from them on the attempted restoration of the original ground-plan (fig. 5).

The foundations in the court (*GH*, fig. 10) are clearly those of the east wall and buttress, and of part of the south wall, of the projecting building shewn by Loggan. The rest of the foundation of the south wall is covered by the modern east wall and buttress of the Arts School (*XD*). The foundation discovered within that school, *IKL*, may be assigned with certainty to that portion of the original east wall of the School which contained the doorway (fig. 4). This foundation was traced as far as the partition between the Arts School and the Novel Room. On taking up part of the floor of this latter room, a wall, undoubtedly ancient, was found to extend across it from east to west (ibid. *MN*). It was two feet thick, and about eighteen inches high, having evidently been left to support the modern floor. This wall did not reach quite so far as the modern east wall; nor could the connexion of it with the previously discovered foundations be accurately determined. The ground between its east end and the partition between the Novel Room and the Arts School, was filled with a confused mass of rubble-work, the precise extent of which could not be ascertained. At the same

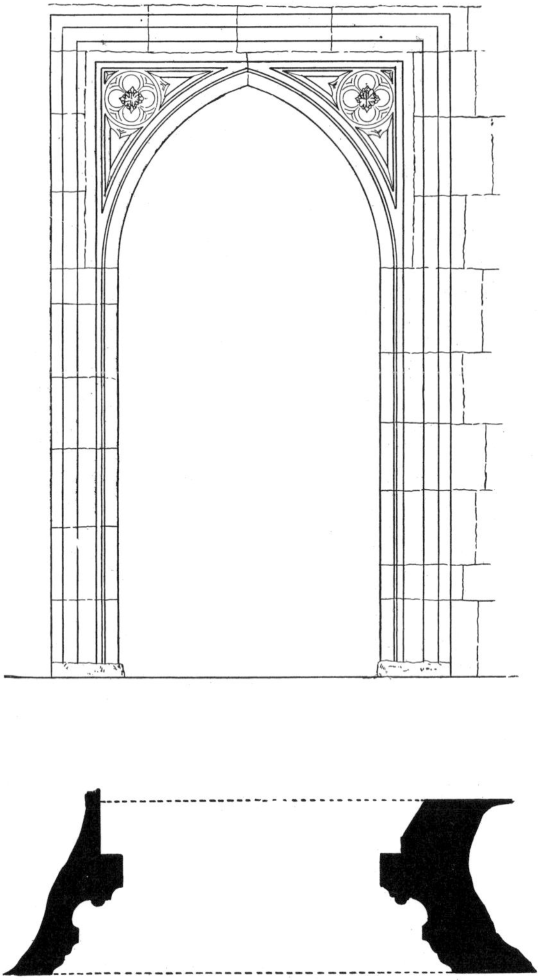

Fig. 15. Elevation of the door of entrance to the Regent House (*A* fig. 6).

time a small door (ibid. *C*) was discovered at the south-west corner of the Divinity School.

There can be no doubt that the wall *MN* represents the wall which formed the south side of the staircase which led up to the old Senate-House, or Regent House; for the distance from that wall to the south gable-wall of the Arts School is just 68 feet, the length which Archbishop Parker assigns to the

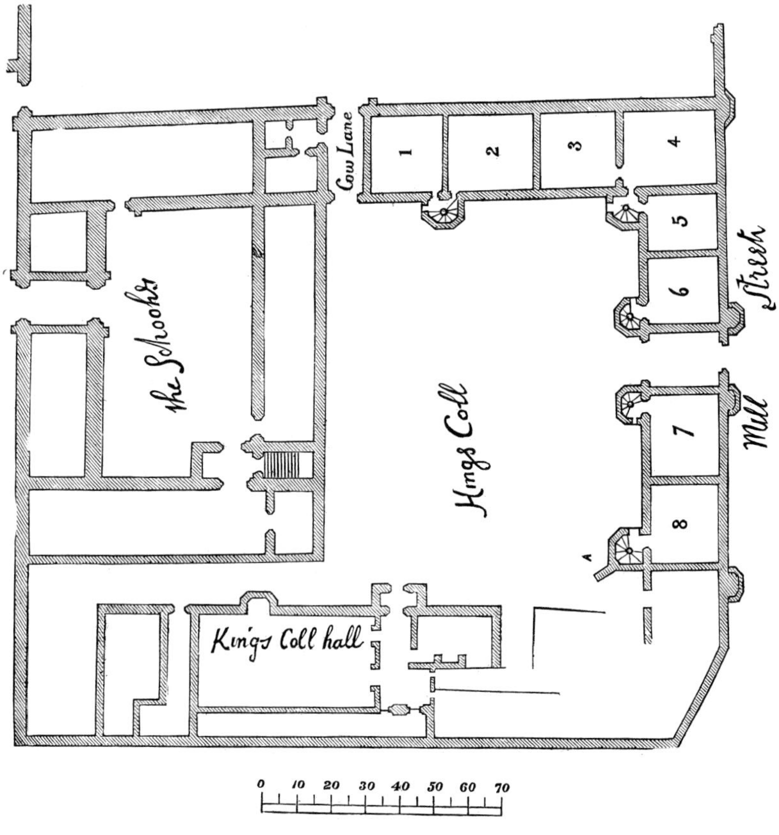

Fig. 16. Ground-plan of the Schools Quadrangle, and of the Old Court of King's College; reduced from a plan of Clare Hall made about 1635.

School. Again, a staircase in this position is shewn on the plan of the Schools Quadrangle which forms part of the plan of Clare Hall taken about 1635 (fig. 16); and the general accuracy of that plan is confirmed by the consideration that the entrance to the most important room in the University would not have been placed so completely in one of the corners that part of the west wall had to be cut away to receive the door when open, had it not been necessary to diminish the steepness of the ascent to it as far as possible. The small door at the south-west corner of the Divinity School evidently gave access to the space under the stairs, and the small door above (*B*, fig. 9)

Fig. 17. Section to shew the arrangement of the staircase leading to the Regent House. A. door of entrance to the Regent House; B. smaller door, leading to a closet over the stairs; C. door leading to space under the stairs; D. door of entrance to the Divinity School; E. window of vestibule; F. window lighting space under the stairs; G. window lighting the staircase.

to a closet over the vestibule (fig. 5). The probable direction of the stairs, and their relation to these doors, has been shewn on an elevation of part of the south wall of the north building (fig. 17).

If we now turn to Loggan's view of the west side (fig. 14), we shall see that he shews three windows, one above the other, between the windows which lighted the north building and the west building, then lighted by four windows on each of its two floors, and that the wall containing those windows was in the same plane as the wall of the gable. The largest of these three windows (*G*, fig. 17) would of course light the landing of the staircase, and the narrow slit beneath it (ibid. *F*), the space under the stairs. The upper slit probably lighted an approach to the roof, the precise position of which cannot now be ascertained.

Fig. 18. Elevation of the north end of the exterior of the west side of the Schools Quadrangle; from a photograph.

The present condition of the west wall is shewn in the elevation (fig. 18). The two buttresses *P*, *Q*, were erected by Mr G. G. Scott in 1864. The round-headed window, which is nearest to the southernmost buttress (*Q*) and lights the Music Room, is probably part of the work done in 1662, when the present Newspaper Room was fitted up as a Registry, and the wall *TV* (fig. 10) was built. When Loggan's print was taken this room was lighted only by a narrow slit. The window of the Novel Room (*R*, fig. 18) is probably part of the alterations of 1732. The two windows over this belong to the same period, when the original wall was pulled down, and the wall of the west building was prolonged as far as the gable of the north building, partially blocking the old doorway (figs. 9, 17, *A*). These windows evidently indicate the extent of the piece then added to the west room; and it will be observed that some quoins still exist in the wall just beyond them (fig. 18) which appear to mark the south-west angle of the building containing the staircase. The position of these quoins has been marked on the ground-plan (*S*, fig. 10), and it will be seen that they do not correspond with the termination of the wall *MN*, although they do correspond tolerably well with the foundations discovered in the quadrangle. It may be suggested that we have before us two states of the north building. The recorded dates have shewn us that it was erected first, and it is evident that the building containing the staircase must have been part of the original structure, for otherwise there would have been no means of approaching the upper floor. This view is confirmed by the peculiar arrangement of the Arts School, for the wall containing the door of entrance would never have been set behind the rest of the wall had it not been necessary to avoid interference with the door through which the staircase-building was entered. This building, in its original state, was probably of the same width on both its east and west sides, but, when the Arts School came to be set against it, the width of the stairs was diminished, and the School was made of the length assigned to it by Archbishop Parker. It should be observed that the plan dated 1635 (fig. 16) assigns to the staircase-building a uniform width from east to west. The entrance to the small vestibule at the foot of the stairs was in the south wall (fig. 4; *G*, fig. 5). When the vestibule was destroyed in 1732, and the original entrance to the Divinity School blocked by the prolongation of the east wall of the Arts School, a new entrance was obtained by converting the westernmost window on the south side into a door (*W*, fig. 10), the old door-case being probably made use of, for the hood-mold shews that it had been originally intended for external use. Loggan shews that the vestibule was lighted by a small window of two lights in the east wall (fig. 4).

The west building was erected soon after the completion of the north building, but, as explained above (p. 11), we know nothing about the precise date of its commencement, though we find it mentioned as in existence in 1438. Its progress was slow, like that of other University buildings, and it was still unfinished in 1457. Its original features have been almost wholly obliterated by successive alterations and repairs.

The appearance of the east front in 1688 has been preserved by Loggan (fig. 4). The School on the ground-floor was entered through a door which still exists, though removed to about three feet in advance of its original position. This was done in 1732, when the wall containing it (*XD*, fig. 10) was built. It is of different construction to the rest of the east wall of the School, being composed of various materials instead of rubble laid in regular courses, and the buttress (*H*) is evidently a modern imitation of the older buttresses beyond. The School was lighted by three windows, each of three lights, subdivided by a transom. These windows still exist—but the transom, and the tracery which Loggan shews in two of them,—have been removed ; and the window nearest to the Law School has been turned into a door, in order to provide access to the gallery at the south end which was probably built in the course of the last century. The west side was lighted by four windows, as already mentioned; and the alterations now in progress (March, 1884) have shewn that originally there was a large window of three lights in the south gable (fig. 5). This must have been blocked when the Porter's Lodge of King's College was set against it, and the freshness of the fragments of the tracery built into the brickwork with which the window was filled, shews that it must have been destroyed soon after its original construction. The sill and jambs are entire, and the pieces of tracery are sufficiently complete to be replaced in their original position. The design of this window (fig. 19) was probably the same as that of the other windows in the School, with the exception of the transom, which was evidently wanting.

The floor above is now supported by six fluted columns of wood (fig. 10). It has been found that these columns encase plain hexagonal shafts of older construction, resting on small stone bases which are also hexagonal. These are probably the "supporters" put up in 1647. There were originally at least ten of these shafts, for two have been discovered within the partition dividing off the Novel Room (*a, b,* fig. 10); and the bases of two more at the south end (ibid. *c, d*).

The School above (fig. 6) was no doubt of the same size as the School below, as Archbishop Parker has stated, and as we see must have been the case from the plan of the ground-floor (fig. 5), part of which has been indicated by dotted lines upon that of the first floor (fig. 9). It must have been entered through a door at the north-west corner (fig. 6, *C*), approached by the

Fig. 19. Window at the south end of the Arts School, restored from the fragments of tracery discovered in March, 1884.

stairs which led to the Regent House. It was lighted by four windows in the east and west walls respectively, and probably by a window in the south gable also (p. 33). When this School was fitted up as a Library the windows were altered, a new floor was laid down, and the present flat ceiling was probably made. The walls are certainly higher than they were originally, as will be seen by comparing Loggan's view of the west front (fig. 14) with the elevation of the west front in its present state (fig. 18). The quoins at the top of the north-west corner of the building there shewn must have stood clear of the wall next to them on the south; and, moreover, the deep wooden cornice above the windows in the west room is clearly, by the style, a work of the eighteenth century. On the other hand, we know that the staircase at the north end was not taken away until 1732; and the terms of the Grace directing the removal, "that the stairs be taken away, and the narrower part of the Library be made broader," shew that the area of the room was not altered when it was first fitted up as a Library. Moreover the joint in the floor (*ab*, fig. 9), exactly above the partition dividing the Arts School from the Novel Room below, indicates the extent of the piece added in 1732; and the narrower width of the piers (E, F, G, H) between the windows at that end, while the windows themselves are of the same width throughout, shews that the builder found a difficulty in accommodating his work to that which had been executed sixteen years before. The evidence of the joint, however, does not prove that the room may not have been a few feet longer before the alteration; it only shews that the floor was taken up and relaid between that point and the wall of the room which is now the Catalogue Room. It is probable that Grumbold's work in 1716, described as "altering the windows in the Law School," included the removal of the eight three-light windows, and the replacing of them by sixteen round-headed windows[1], two of which were in the wall over the door of the Arts School, afterwards taken down and rebuilt; and that in the course of the work carried out in 1732 these windows were replaced in the new wall, and two more on each side were added to them, completing the full number of twenty by which the room is now lighted.

The Law School, built between 1457 and 1471 (p. 12) was originally 67 feet long, as Archbishop Parker states. The material employed was red brick, instead of the rubble used for the north and west sides. It is entered through a door at the

[1] [In the Univ. Accounts for 1716—17 the painter charges "for 16 caisments and 16 freames painted 3 times in oyle in the new libery." As there is a single casement only to each window, this entry proves that Grumbold made sixteen windows in the course of the first alteration. These have been numbered 1—16 on the plan (fig. 9).]

south-east corner of the quadrangle, which is evidently in the original position, for the west wall of the east building coincided very nearly with the corresponding wall of the present building (fig. 10). It was lighted by three windows in the north wall, the second of which, counting from the door, was of four lights; and by four windows, each of three lights, in the south wall. There was also a window of four lights in the east gable (fig. 4); but recent researches have shewn that there was no window in the west gable. The westernmost window in the north wall was blocked, like the window in the Arts School close to it, in the last century, in order to provide a door to the gallery at the west end. The six fluted columns which support the roof, and the panelwork, are evidently, by their style, a part of the same work.

It has now been discovered (March, 1884) that a narrow passage, about five feet long, seven feet high, and three feet wide, led from this school into the Arts School at the north-west corner (figs. 5, 10). The floor of this passage was four feet six inches above the level of the floor of the Arts School, and probably at the same height above that of the Law School. It may be suggested therefore that it provided a communication from a gallery in the one school to a gallery in the other, and that it was blocked when it was thought better to provide a separate entrance to each of the two galleries from the quadrangle.

The Library on the first floor was 67 feet long, like the School below. It was lighted by eight windows in the north wall, and by nine windows in the south wall, each of two lights (fig. 6). There was also a window of four lights in the east gable (fig. 4), and probably a window in the west gable also. It was entered by a door, fortunately left intact when the east building was erected, in the north-east corner (*I*, fig. 9), approached by the "vice," or turret-stair, which abutted against it at that point.

The contract for the ceiling of the lower school, and for the floor, ceiling, and roof of the upper school or library (p. 13), dated 25 June, 1466, is as follows:

"This endenture made the .xxv. day of Juyn the sixt yeere of the Regne of Kyng Edward the fourth, betwix Maister William Wylflete nowe beyng Chauncellor of thvniuersite of Cambrigge Maister Nicholas Gay Maister William Smyth Maister Edmond Connesburgh Doctours of the same vniuersite, Maister William Wyche and Maister William Langton nowe being proctours of the said vniuersite sufficiently and lawfully deputed and ordeyned by the hool congregacion of Regentes and non Regentes of the forsaid vnyuersite for to purvey rewle surveye and gwyde the werke of the new scoles in the same vniuersite of that oon partie And William Harward of Halsted in the Counte of Essex Carpenter, and William Bakon of the same Towne and Counte Carpenter of that othir partie, Witnesseth :

That the same William Harward and William Bakon haue made feythfull promysse and couenaunt with the forsaid Doctours and proctours in the name of alle thvnyuersite aforsaid, For alle the tymbre, cariage, and werkmanship for the Floores and Rofe of the said new scoles, forto be parfitly made of tymbre and werkmanship benethe specified, tofore the Feest of Seynt Petir that is called *Ad uincula sancti Petri* that shalbe in the yeer of oure Lorde M[l].CCCC.lxvij. in maner and fourme that foloweth :

That is to sey : the nethir floore shal haue .vj. Dormauntes in breed of xvj ynches square ; the gistes shalbe .viij. ynches in breede and .v. ynches thyk with braces and pendauntes and with Angels and enbowed for the dormauntes ; And alle the gistes of the same floore shal haue an hool casement enbowed ; And betwix gist and gist shalbe .viij. ynches ; And the bords that it shalbe plaunched with shalbe ynche thyk ; And the bordes shalbe lynyd and leyd on hye on the gistes.

And a Roofe for the said Scole shal haue .vj. right bemes with ioppijs purloynes, braces, pendauntes with angels, and alle shalbe enbowed as longith vnto the Werke. And the same Roofe shal haue a dowble Roofe ; that is to sey first bemes right, like to the dormauntes of the floore, with crosse dormauntes, and the ioppijs so that alle the gistes of the flore shal rest vpon the crosse dormauntes and on the said ioppijs ; whiche gistes shalbe .viij. ynches in brede and .iiij. ynches thyk and borded in lyke wyse as the lougher flore shalbe.

And from euery beme a leyrn stood with .ij. braces into the beme and .ij. into the crownetree which shal lye vpon the said studdes, and bere the sparres with a purloyn on bothe sydes in the myddist of the said sparres with punchions fro the bemes to bere the same. And the said sparres shalbe .viij. ynches in brede at the fote and .vj. ynches at the toppe, and .vj. ynches thyk at the fote, and .v. in the toppe, and shal ryse fro the said beme in the myddist .iij. fote and an half. Also the said Roofe shal haue sufficient leedlathis of herty ooke sufficiently dried ; And alle this tymbir shalbe white oke, not doted, nor storvyn, nor sappy, to hurt the beawty or thynbowyng of the werke.

Also thei shal make alle the dores and wyndowes, and the Roofe of the vice of the staire. And the same dores and wyndowes shalbe like of strength and makyng of the dores and wyndowes of the other new scoles there.

And the said carpenters shal semblaby fynde alle the bord and tymbre for the said dores and wyndowes and for the Roof of the vice aforsaid.

And for alle the tymbir and borde aboue rehersed, cariage of the same, and werkmanship of Carpentrie in maner and fourme aboueseid, to be done and perfourmed, the forsaid Doctours and proctours shal paie or do to be paid vnto the said William Harward and William Bakon whan it shalbe seen vnto the said Doctours and proctours expedient and behoueful for the perfourmyng of the couenauntes aforsaid .xxiij^{li}. vj^{s}. viij^{d}. of lawfull money of Englond, ouer x^{li}. to the same Carpenters paid in hand the day of the makyng of these presentes.

And to alle these couenauntes abouewriten on eythir partie as is abouesaid wel and truly to be holden, perfourmed, and kept The same parties byndeth theym yche of hem to other alternatly fast by these presentes[1]."

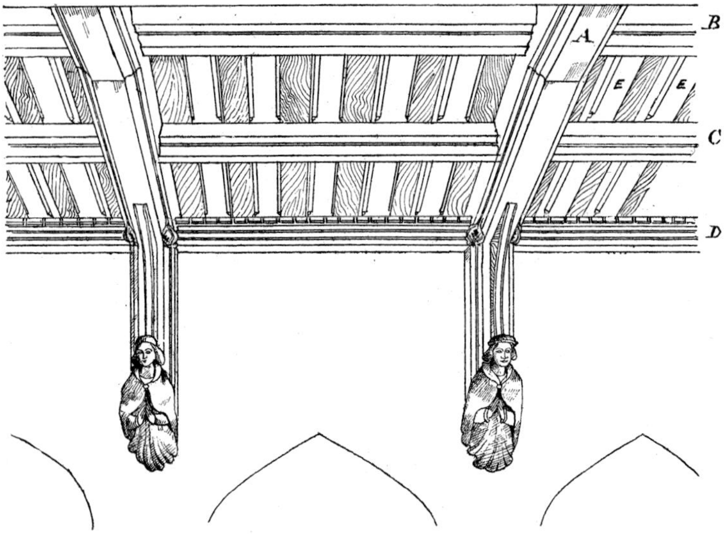

Fig. 20. Roof of the south room of the Library in its present state. A. main beam; B. "crosse dormaunte;" C. purlin; D. "joppye," or cornice; E. joists.

The above contract provides in the first place for the floor of the Library, and the roof of the Law School below. The latter—spoken of as *nethir floore*, and *lougher floore*—is to have six main beams (*dormauntes*), each 16 inches square. The joists (*gistes*) between these main beams are to be 8 inches broad, 5 inches thick, and 8 inches apart, with their edges hollowed out into the molding called a "casement." The boards of the floor, which are to lie across the joists, are to be one inch thick, and made to fit accurately (*lynyd*). Each main beam is to have a brace and pendant, with an angel, as is ordered to be provided

[1] [Registry of the University, *Charters, etc.* No. 112.]

for the roof above. This part of the work was destroyed when a plain flat ceiling was put on to the School, probably in the last century.

The roof of the Library was partly concealed by a modern ceiling until about 1864, when it was removed, and the original construction exposed to view (fig. 20). This roof, with the timbers above it, was fortunately examined and measured by Professor Willis in January, 1860, and from his drawings and measurements the accompanying section (fig. 21) has been prepared. The addition of the upper storey renders the study of the construction impossible at the present time.

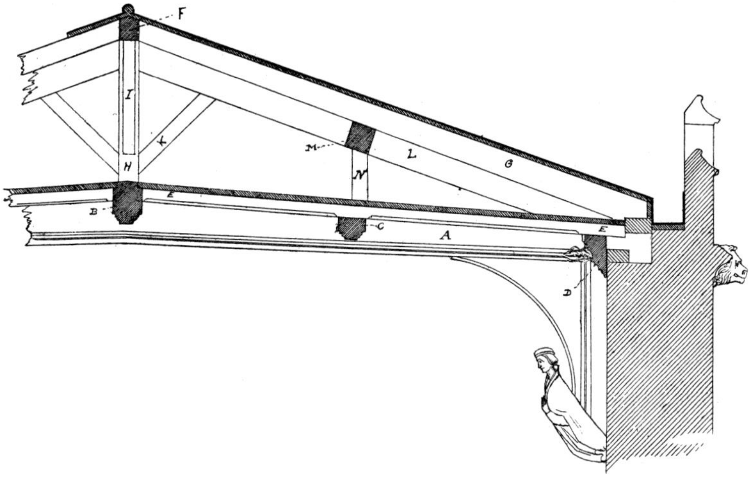

Fig. 21. Section of the roof of the south room of the Library, from drawings made by Professor Willis. A. main beam; B. "crosse dormaunte;" C. purlin; D. "joppye," or cornice; E. joists; F. ridge-piece, or "crowntree;" G. spars; H. king-post, or "leyrn stood;" I, K. braces; L. upper beam; M. purlin; N. punchion.

The roof is to have six main beams (*right bemes*) (*A*) "like to the dormauntes of the floore," a direction which doubtless means that they are to resemble them in size and disposition. There are now nine of these beams, and there were evidently once ten, which shews either that the School was lengthened after the contract was drawn, or, more probably, that it was thought desirable to increase the number so as to have one between each pair of windows besides one at each end of the room[1]. It is further provided that there shall be a "crosse dormaunte" (*B*), purlins (*purloyns*) (*C*), and "joppyes" or cornices (*D*), so arranged that the joists (*E*) may rest upon the cross dormant at one end, and the "joppy" at the other. These joists are to be 8 inches broad by 4 inches thick, and the boards which rest upon them are to be laid in the same manner as those of the floor below.

The pitch of the roof is defined by the direction that the spars (*G*) are to rise in the middle three and a half feet. From each of the lower beams a king-post (*leyrn stood*, *H*) is to rise to the ridge-piece (*crownetree*, *F*), which is to "lye vpon the said studdes," that is, to be supported by them. Each king-post is to have two braces, one pair of which (*I*) is to extend to the ridge-piece, and the other (*K*) to the beam (*L*), by which Professor Willis understands an upper beam, visible, as he notes, when he made the section, and not the lower beam before-mentioned. The ridge-piece is to carry the spars, in the middle of which—by which the middle point between the ridge-piece and the wall plate is to be understood—there is to be a purlin (*M*), mortised into the upper beam[2], and supported from the lower beam by a "punchion" (*N*). It is specified that the spars are to be eight inches broad, and six inches thick at the foot, and to taper upwards so as to be six inches broad and five inches thick at the top.

The east building has been already described (p. 15), and the two floors have been laid down in accordance with the measurements given by Archbishop Parker, and with Loggan's view (fig. 4). The plans (figs. 5, 6) sufficiently explain themselves, and need no further description.

When the new building was erected on the east side of the quadrangle (1755—58), the old walls were made use of as far as possible, as shewn by the different hatchings employed on the plans (figs. 9, 10). A partition-wall was built across the east end of the Law School, cutting off about eight feet from this School, and from the Library above, in order to provide

[1] [Of the ten which evidently once existed, that against the east wall would be removed when the staircase was built in 1755.]

[2] [Professor Willis notes: "Thus the king-post or 'lierne stud' has four braces in the usual way, for the purlins are mortised into the upper beam."]

room for a staircase. This wall blocked part of the easternmost window on the south side, which, however, is still visible on the exterior; and the west wall to the central building blocked half the easternmost window on the north side (fig. 9).]

CHAPTER V.

HISTORY OF THE EXTENSION OF THE LIBRARY IN THE PRESENT CENTURY.

IT has been already shewn that the buildings surrounding the Schools Quadrangle contained originally all the rooms required for the public life of the University; viz. Senate-House, Registry, Library, Lecture-Rooms for the Professors in the different faculties; and it should be further mentioned that the same buildings served to a certain extent as a Picture Gallery and a Museum. Such an arrangement, however, was incompatible with the growth of the University, and we have seen that a separate Library had been contemplated so early as the end of the sixteenth century, and that a new Senate-House was actually constructed in the eighteenth. Again, the establishment of Professorships in the Natural Sciences compelled the University to provide lecture-rooms, which, for want of space in the original schools, were situated in various parts of the town. Most of these rooms were ill-adapted to the purposes for which they were used; and their distance from each other caused great inconvenience both to Professors and students. Museums, moreover, were wholly wanting.

As interest in the Natural Sciences increased, the evils of such a state of things became intolerable; and early in the present century the attention of the University was directed to the necessity of making some attempt to remedy them. In May, 1818, the Syndics of the Woodwardian Museum of Geology stated "that it was desirable that a larger room should be built, with a contiguous room for the accommodation of the Lecturer;" in 1821 a special Syndicate considered the building of a Museum for that collection; and in 1824 another Syndicate reported that "the want of rooms for public lectures and examinations is becoming every year more urgent[1];" and in 1828 a *Statement*, of which the late Dr Whewell is now known to have been the author, gave detailed information on the subject, and suggested a scheme for providing at least temporary accommodation for the Professors of Botany, Mineralogy, Geology, and Anatomy. This document, as a valuable contemporary record, shall be given at length:

"*The following Statement is respectfully offered to the Members of the Senate.*

Great difficulties arise every term, and serious detriment to the University is occasioned, from the want of sufficient Lecture-Rooms, and Rooms for Scientific Collections.

In consequence of this want, it is often scarcely or not at all possible for the Professors to give their Lectures so that they may be convenient and serviceable to the Students: and the benefit of accessible and instructive Museums—still more of Collections improving with the increase of science and scientific zeal—is altogether lost.

The Woodwardian Collection of GEOLOGY was accepted on condition of the University placing it in a room admitting of its being habitually exhibited; and is so highly valued by the University, that the Professor is held to the due care of it in a bond of £5000. To this has been added a very extensive series of Specimens, exhibiting the structure of almost every part of England. This Collection is contained in a room originally unworthy of it, and unfit for the purpose, and at present incapable of receiving additions; while the state of the science makes it more than ever necessary that such a collection should be every year enlarged. Indeed the Professor has been compelled, by absolute want of space in the Woodwardian Museum, to retain in his own apartments a considerable portion of the specimens belonging to the University.

There is no lecture-room at the disposal of the Woodwardian Professor; and he is hence compelled to make irregular and incommodious arrangements, that he may be enabled to use the nearest lecture-room when it is not occupied by the Norrisian Professor of Divinity.

The BOTANICAL Collection is of considerable extent, and is rapidly increasing. A room is appropriated to it, which, however, is inadequate to its proper exhibition, and, what is still worse, to its preservation: being exposed to damp: so that the Professor has perpetually the mortification of finding his labours wasted by the destruction of his specimens. The adjacent lecture-room belongs in part to the Botanical Professor.

[1] [Report, dated 10 March, 1825, of a Syndicate appointed 17 May, 1824, "to consider what practicable improvements in the town of Cambridge would be beneficial and ornamental to the University."]

The MINERALOGICAL Collection was purchased by the University of the executors of the late Dr [E. D.] Clarke, for £1500. For the reception of this the University possesses no room whatever; nor for lectures on this science. When it became necessary to remove the Collection from the Botanical Museum, where it had been kept, the present Professor found himself under the necessity of receiving it into a room adjacent to his own, where it cannot be exhibited, nor even properly preserved.

The ANATOMICAL Collection consists principally of the Museum of the late Sir B. Harwood, purchased by the University for £360; together with a set of beautiful Wax Models bought from Florence, for £200. Of this collection, the former portion is placed in a room adjacent to the lecture-room; which is incapable of properly holding, much less of displaying it: and where many of the dry preparations are already destroyed, and all the others are greatly injured, by the very great dampness of the place. The models, from defect of space, are concealed in a dark closet belonging to the ancient chemical room; and like the rest, are undergoing serious injury for want of better accommodation.

The Professor of CHEMISTRY has no room appropriated to him in which it is possible for him to lecture; and is obliged to lecture in the room belonging to the Jacksonian and Botanical Professors, at times inconvenient to himself and his class.

The Professor of PHYSIC has no room in which to give his lectures, and is obliged to make use of the very inconvenient and confined lecture-room of the Professor of Anatomy.

The Professor of MODERN HISTORY delivers his lectures in a room under the Anatomical lecture-room, which was originally intended for the lectures on Chemistry. This room is, in many respects, inconvenient, and has generally been found inadequate to the proper reception of the students desirous of attending the lectures.

The Professor of GREEK has no lecture-room, and delivers his lectures every year in a room in Trinity College, which, though inconveniently small, happens to be capable of being used for this purpose.

The PLUMIAN Professor is destitute of any room whatever for the delivery of his lectures on NATURAL PHILOSOPHY: and it seems to be difficult for him to make even a temporary arrangement; so that without some provision of this kind he will be compelled, on this account alone, to discontinue his lectures. Indeed the nature of his lectures requires, that he should have a room besides his lecture-room for the reception of his apparatus: or, at least a room in which the apparatus can remain undisturbed, as was the case with the late Professor Vince.

The LUCASIAN Professor of MATHEMATICS is directed by the foundation of his office to deliver lectures, and it is understood to be the intention of the present Professor to do so. He has no lecture-room.

It is manifest, that with regard to the various sciences of Natural History, Museums easily accessible and well-arranged are of paramount importance. And the continual progress of such sciences cannot be understood, except the Museums be capable of admitting the objects whhic illustrate this progress. It is beyond a doubt, also, that if the

University were possessed of space for the reception and exhibition of such collections, the regard of its members towards it, their zeal for science, and numberless opportunities perpetually occurring, would augment and complete its stores.

This is what is in fact going on in other places. Not to mention considerable collections of various kinds and extensive lecture-rooms established by institutions less resembling our own, the sister University is daily growing in this scientific wealth. The Ashmolean Museum has assumed the character of a distinguished collection of Natural History. Oxford has been supplied with casts of the most remarkable specimens of Osteology in the Paris collection, by the kindness of Cuvier and the liberality of the French Government; a donation which could not have been accepted here, for want of the room necessary for its reception; and the Anatomical School in that University has made extensive purchases in Comparative Anatomy, at the recent sale of Brookes's Museum.

Without some provision for lecture-rooms and for Collections, in addition to what Cambridge now possesses, she will have the mortification to see herself left behind in the cultivation of such studies as are above-mentioned; at a time when her Professors are as zealous as they have ever been, and are not charged with incapacity; when her Students are daily growing in activity and intelligence; and when her scientific possessions are such as to offer no mean foundation for future times to raise into complete collections.

Under these circumstances, a year or half a year of procrastination is by no means unimportant with regard to time and opportunities lost. In Natural History especially, space devoted to Museums and lecture-rooms would certainly produce, in no long period, an advantageous effect.

It seems desirable that the Collections of Botany, Mineralogy, Geology and Anatomy, should have their Lecture-Rooms and Museums adjacent to each other; and in this manner, perhaps one or two lecture-rooms with four separate Museums might be made to answer for all the four sciences. The site lately occupied by the warehouses of the old Press, and contiguous to the present Anatomical Museum, contains a space of about 50 yards by 45 yards, and is immediately at the disposal of the University. It is at present a source of annual expense, and entirely useless; the buildings being unoccupied and ruinous. If this space were employed for the Museums and Lecture-Rooms just mentioned, the room now occupied by the Botanical Professor might be left at the disposal of the Professor of Chemistry, to whom it is better adapted: and in this manner he might share the lecture-room of the Jacksonian Professor, each having a separate room besides; an arrangement which would be convenient so far as those Professors are concerned.

Without comparing the site just mentioned with any other situation, it seems thus to have advantages which make well worth the while of the University to apply it immediately to the purposes which have been pointed out, where the need is so urgent and so important.

It appears from what has been said, that if, after the erection of such a Museum as is now proposed, the University should find itself in the possession of other space applicable to such purposes, there could be no difficulty in discovering worthy and desirable uses to which it might be turned.

Dec. 9, 1828."

These suggestions, though clear and practical, do not appear to have found favour with the University, probably because the acquisition of the Old Court of King's College, as related above (p. 9), seemed to provide the space so long needed in the immediate neighbourhood of the Schools which had been associated by immemorial tradition with all the studies of the University; and no time was lost in attempting to take advantage of it. The Senate agreed to purchase it 3 April, 1829; and 6 May following a Syndicate was appointed to consider how it could be "converted to Academic use." This Syndicate, afterwards known as "The First Syndicate," consisted of the following persons: Mr Ainslie, Master of Pembroke College, Vice-Chancellor; Dr John Kaye, Bishop of Lincoln, Master of Christ's College; Dr Haviland, Regius Professor of Medicine; Mr Whewell, Professor of Mineralogy; Mr Hustler, Registrary, Jesus College; Mr Carrighan, S. John's College; Mr Peacock, Trinity College; Mr Shelford, Corpus Christi College; Mr Lodge, Magdalene College; Mr King, Queens' College. Dr Procter, Master of Catharine Hall, was added to the Syndicate 29 October following.

The appointment of this Syndicate in 1829 marks the commencement of a controversy which agitated the University during the next eight years; for the first stone of the north wing of the new library, called Cockerell's Building, was not laid till near the end of 1837. The intervening period was spent in attempts to obtain a design which should fulfil the conditions demanded of the Architects consulted, and at the same time satisfy the Senate. The rejected designs have not been preserved in the University; but, as several persons wrote pamphlets to support a scheme which they advocated, or to criticize one which they condemned, it is not difficult to understand the main points at issue[1]. We do not propose to describe minutely designs which,

[1] [The pamphlets are: Observations on the Plans for the New Library, etc. By a member of the First Syndicate [Rev. G. Peacock, M.A. Trin. Coll.]. 8vo.

for good reasons, were set aside, but, after a careful study of the above authorities, and the reports and other documents issued by the several Syndicates, to narrate, as briefly as is consistent with clearness, the different steps of the controversy.

It is probable that some at least of the members of the First Syndicate had made up their minds on the course to be adopted before they were appointed[1]; for, although they were allowed a whole year within which to prepare a Report to the Senate, they issued the following document 2 July, 1829. It was signed by all the Syndics except Bishop Kaye and Mr King:

"Pembroke Lodge, July 2, 1829.

The Syndics appointed to consider of the arrangements concerning the 'Old Court lately purchased of King's College,' beg leave to report to the Senate:

That they consider it necessary that provision should be made, not merely for a large increase of the accommodation of the Public Library, but likewise for four additional Lecture-Rooms, for Museums of Geology, Mineralogy, Botany, and if practicable, of Zoology, for a new office for the Registrary, for an additional School for the Professor of Physic, and for other purposes connected with the dispatch of the ordinary business of the University:

That they consider the extent of ground, now the property of the University, including the site of the present Library, as amply sufficient for all these objects:

That they consider it expedient to make application to four Architects, for complete plans, elevations and estimates, to be forwarded to the Vice-Chancellor, on or before the 1st of November next: and that the Syndicate should be authorized to give the necessary instructions;

Cambridge, 1831 (1 January). Reply to Observations, etc. By a member of both Syndicates [Rev. W. Whewell, M.A. Trin. Coll.]. 8vo. Cambridge, 1831. An Answer to Observations on the Plans for the New Library; being a defence of the design presented by Messrs Rickman and Hutchinson. 8vo. Birmingham, 1831. A few remarks on the "New Library" question. [By a member of neither Syndicate [Rev. H. Coddington, M.A. Trin. Coll.]. 8vo. Cambridge, 1831. Remarks on the Replies to the Observations on the Plans for the New Library, etc. By a member of the First Syndicate [Rev. G. Peacock, M.A. Trin. Coll.] 8vo. Cambridge, 1831. Letter to the Members of the Senate of the University of Cambridge. By William Wilkins, Esq. 8vo. Cambridge, 1831 (9 February). An Appeal to the Senate, on the subject of the Plans for the University Library. By William Wilkins, A.M., R.A. 8vo. Cambridge, 1831 (15 April). Observations upon the Report made by a Syndicate appointed to confer with the Architects who were desired to furnish the University with Designs for a New Library. By George Peacock, M.A. Cambridge, 8vo. 1835.]

[1] [Mr Coddington's pamphlet, p. 4.]

to offer the sum of 100 Guineas to each of the three Architects whose plans shall not be adopted; and to make a further report to the Senate before the end of next Term."

The adoption of this Report was unopposed, and it was confirmed by the Senate four days afterwards (6 July). Applications were immediately addressed to Mr Cockerell, Mr Rickman, Mr Burton, and Mr Wilkins, who severally accepted the terms of the competition. The following instructions, with ground-plans of the existing buildings, were forwarded to them[1].

"Instructions for Architects respecting the Building of Museums, Lecture-Rooms, Schools, etc. and additions to the Public Library.

[1] It is required to provide for four Schools of Divinity, Law, Physic, and Arts; for an Office for the Registrary; for Museums of Geology, Mineralogy, Zoology, and Botany, for three or four Lecture Rooms, for Workshops and Unpacking Rooms connected with the several Museums, for a Model Room for the Jacksonian Professor, and also for the Apparatus of the Plumian Professor, for a very large increase of accommodation for Books for the Public Library, including a Room for the Librarian and Syndics, a Reading Room, &c.

[2] It is proposed to place the four Schools *en suite* on the side next to King's Chapel. They are to be so constructed as to communicate with each other, when required, by large *double* folding doors, and thus to form a series of Examination or Lecture Rooms: the Professors' Pulpits must be moveable, or so constructed as not to interfere with these latter objects: the Law Schools to be placed at the East end, the Divinity at the West, and to be somewhat longer than the other two: Galleries must be placed at the East end of the Law Schools, and at the West end of the Divinity Schools, for the accommodation of the Heads, Professors, Doctors, etc.

[3] At the Eastern end of the Law Schools, it is proposed, if practicable, to place the Registrary's Office and Record Room, the first about 20 feet by 15 feet, communicating with the Law Schools and Record Room; the Record Office about 30 feet by 20 feet, and to be Fire-Proof, and to admit of being perfectly ventilated and warmed.

[4] On the North and Western sides are to be placed *en suite* the series of Museums of Geology, Mineralogy, Zoology and Botany: and in that order the first being on the site of the present Divinity Schools, about 70 feet in length: the second about 30 feet, and the last 20 feet: the rest of the space to be allotted for the Zoological

[1] [Mr Peacock's first pamphlet, p. 2. The Instructions are printed from one of the original copies preserved in the Registry of the University; and the paragraphs have been numbered for facility of reference. In the original the different sites mentioned are indicated by letters, which evidently refer to the plan which accompanied the Instructions. This, unfortunately, has not been preserved.]

Museum: they must all admit of communication when required, by sliding Double Doors: no provision to be made by the Architect for the fittings of these rooms: with each Museum there must be connected a Workshop, or Unpacking Room, the two longest for the Geological and Zoological Museums.

[5] All these Schools and Museums must be well lighted, and admit, as much as possible, of perfect ventilation: the airing of them, by heated air, to be provided for according to the most approved plans, which may likewise serve for the Library above. On the space between this range of Museums and Senate House passage, it is proposed to place two Theatres, for Lecture Rooms, one capable of containing from 400 to 500 people, the other from 250 to 300: also a smaller Lecture Room, capable of containing about 100 people: they must admit of communication with the Museums, and also with a Model Room for the Jacksonian Professor (about 40 feet by 30 feet), and the small Lecture Room with the Room for the apparatus of the Plumian Professor: the entrances to the Theatres and Workshops to be from the Senate House passage: the Lecture Room which is to be used by the Plumian Professor must be so placed, as to admit the *introduction* of the Sun's light for two or three hours in the middle of the day: the Lecture Rooms also to be provided with desks: any of these Rooms may be placed on the First Floor, if such plan be more convenient and do not interfere with the arrangements of the Library.

[6] The Library to occupy the whole of the first floor, above the Registrary's Office, Schools, and Museum, so as to form a complete square; the front of the present Library (that is the first floor), to be extended towards King's Chapel and Caius College, over the Schools and Museum: a projecting Room towards Senate House Lane on the first floor opposite the West end of the Senate House, for the use of the Librarian and Syndics: the Cross Library to be retained, either supported entirely on arcades, or with a passage through the centre: this may be extended also towards Senate House Passage, if practicable and consistent with the other objects described above, so as to form a Reading Room: the Books to be placed on projecting cases as in the Library of Trinity College, which must be so constructed as to admit hereafter of the addition of galleries.

[7] In case it is found that there is not on the South side sufficient space for the four Schools and the Registrary's Office and Record Room, a portion of the West side may be taken, and in that case the Divinity School would be on the West side opposite Clare Hall: to supply the space thus taken from the Museums, the Geological Museum may be placed on the East side, reaching from the Senate House passage to the South side of the North Library, being about 80 feet long.

---

[8] The SYNDICS in proposing the above arrangements beg to be understood as merely suggesting such plans as appear to them to be most convenient,—but leave it to the Architects to make what alterations or modifications they may think right.

[9] The several fronts to be of Ketton or Bath Stone, or any other which the Architects may prefer.

[10] No particular style of Architecture is prescribed.

The Plans and Estimates to be sent to the VICE-CHANCELLOR on or before the 1st of *November* next: the Plans to be drawn to a scale of 8 feet to an inch: there must be four elevations in outline of the several fronts, and two perspective views, namely South-East and South-West: to be *drawn*, and tinted in Indian ink.

CAMBRIDGE,
July 1829."

These instructions, we are told, were the joint production of the entire Syndicate, with the exception of Bishop Kaye, who does not appear to have taken any part in the deliberations[1].

"They were considered to be such as embodied, most completely, the great objects which the University had in view, and the opinions entertained by the different Members of the Syndicate of the best mode of effecting them; they suggested a precise arrangement of the succession and position of the several rooms, chiefly for the purpose of making their views more intelligible to the Architects, than could have been done by any more general statement of the wants of the University; but it was mentioned in the instructions themselves, and more expressly afterwards in private communications to the Architects, that they were perfectly at liberty to make such an arrangement and combination of the parts of the building as in their judgment would most completely satisfy the various purposes for which it was intended, and would be best adapted to all the circumstances of the site.

The Architects were referred to different Members of the Syndicate for further information connected with the instructions, and for the purpose of supplying any omissions in them: and it was through such channels that an enquiry was made whether any of the present buildings could be retained with advantage.

No sum was mentioned as the limit of the expense for which funds could be provided by the University, either now or hereafter: but it was signified to the Architects, that no part of the present Library or Schools could be removed, before provision had been made in the new buildings for the reception of the books and for carrying on the ordinary business of the University; it was therefore perfectly understood that the two parts of the buildings must be completed at different and probably distant periods of time; and it was merely considered necessary to have a complete plan in the first instance, with a view to its ultimate completion as one great and uniform design[2]."

The Architects were ready with their plans at the time appointed, 1 November, 1829. Messrs Rickman and Hutchinson,

[1] [Mr Peacock's first pamphlet, p. 5.]

[2] [Ibid. p. 5.]

Mr Wilkins, and Mr Burton were content with a single design each; Mr Cockerell sent two. The second of these, which extended the principal building to the extremity of the ground belonging to the University on every side[1], and is further interesting as reviving a project originally suggested by Mr Gibbs, and nearly realised by another architect in 1791, as previously narrated, is thus described by Mr Whewell:

"Besides his Plan constructed in agreement with the suggestions of the Syndicate, which he called No. 1, Mr Cockerell sent down another, No. 2, in which the most striking feature was a *double* of the Senate-House (with the exception of its centre portion being an open colonnade) placed opposite to it, at the other extremity of the present front of the Library. This Design excited considerable admiration, as a fine specimen of architectural invention: but I do not think that any one looked upon it as offering any probability of execution; or examined the arrangements of it as a project to be entertained[2]."

The Syndicate did not make the plans public until they had studied them themselves, and made their own decision, which they communicated to the Senate in a singularly brief Report:

"Sidney Lodge, *Nov.* 25, 1829. That they unanimously agree to recommend Mr Cockerell's Design (No. 1) for the New Library and other Public Buildings, as being, in their opinion, upon the whole, best adapted to answer the purposes which the University have in contemplation."

To this document the Vice-Chancellor—Dr Chafy, Master of Sidney Sussex College—appended the following notice:

"The Vice-Chancellor begs to inform the Members of the Senate, that he has directed all the Plans and Designs which have been submitted to the consideration of the Syndics, to be placed in the Public Library, for their general Inspection."

It will have been observed that the two Syndics, Mr King and Dr Procter, did not sign the Report. It was however explained afterwards that they had not abstained from signing because they dissented from it, but because they were absent from the last meeting; and that "the word 'unanimously' was added at the request of a most distinguished Member of the Syndicate, who had expressed some doubts respecting the preference given to Mr Cockerell's plan, but whose opinion

[1] [Mr Peacock's first pamphlet, p. 18.] [2] [Reply to Observations, etc. p. 8.]

had been determined in its favour by some observations made at the time[1]."

The plans suggested by Mr Cockerell and his competitors have not been described in detail in any of the pamphlets, and we are therefore unable to give any account of them. We may presume, however, that they conformed generally to the instructions, and proposed a new quadrangle of about the same breadth as the old, but extending up to Trinity Hall Lane; and that the space between the north range and Senate-House Passage was to be occupied by Lecture Rooms. It is evident that no part of the existing buildings was to be retained[2]. Mr Cockerell's selected plan, however, did not give satisfaction; and the Syndicate was severely blamed for having selected a design which might be the best of those submitted to them, but which is stated to have had many evident defects. Their apologists said that the plan had not been selected with a view to its execution, but because Mr Cockerell had, "more completely than any other architect, satisfied the conditions of the very difficult problem proposed[3]," and was therefore the proper person to prepare all future plans, and to superintend the execution of any one which might finally be adopted. It was objected to this reasoning that the language of their Reports (dated 2 July and 25 November) bound the Senate to a plan, and not to an architect; and that if the second Report were confirmed, the University would be committed to a design which even those who had recommended it could not defend[4]. On reviewing the controversy at the present day it is almost inexplicable that no one seems to have remembered that the obvious way out of the difficulty was to propose a Grace to confirm the Report, to reject it, and to begin again. The excitement, however, which prevailed was so extraordinary that a proposal to confirm the Report dated 25 November, 1829, and another to apply to Mr Cockerell for an amended design, were both withdrawn (26 February, 1830); and an alternative measure was carried without opposition: viz. to appoint a Syndicate to investigate and report upon the state of the University finances. The Grace, as first drawn up, had the following preamble, which

[1] [Mr Peacock's first pamphlet, p. 16.]
[2] [Ibid. p. 6.]
[3] [Ibid. p. 16.]
[4] [Mr Coddington's pamphlet, p. 7.]

deserves quotation as illustrating the feeling then prevalent in the University:

"23 Feb. 1830. Whereas many Members of the Senate are of opinion that the cost of carrying into effect any one of the Plans proposed for a new Library, Lecture-Rooms, and Museums, is much beyond the resources of the University; and that the present Library may be enlarged, and the requisite Lecture-Rooms and Museums obtained at a moderate expence: the following Grace will be offered to the Senate on Friday next."

The Grace as confirmed by the Senate, proposed (1) to appoint the Vice-Chancellor (William Chafy, D.D., Master of Sidney Sussex College); Dr Kaye; Dr Ainslie; Dr Turton, Regius Professor of Divinity; Mr Higman, Trinity College; Mr Hustler, Jesus College; Mr Gwatkin, S. John's College; and Mr King, Queens' College, to report on the funds of the University Chest; and (2) "to defer the question of destroying the Library, and building a new one, until their Report be published." The precise result at which this Syndicate arrived is not known, though we find an announcement that their Report would be made public at a Congregation to be held 12 May, 1830[1]. Whatever may have been the tenour of this Report, an idea was evidently prevalent that the University could not safely accept Mr Cockerell's plans; for a fortnight later (26 May), a Grace was introduced to pay 100 guineas to each of the four competing architects, on the ground that the University was not in possession of funds sufficient to build the proposed buildings in accordance with any of the suggested designs. This Grace, however, was successfully opposed[2], because it was considered that the Report of the Syndicate inviting the competition, which the Senate had adopted 6 July, 1829, implied that one of the four was to be employed, and that they had devoted their time and talents to the service of the University on the faith of it[3].

[1] [Grace Paper, dated "Sidney Lodge, 8 May, 1830." Mr Romilly notes: "This Report, *if ever printed*, is not to be found." Mr Peacock had certainly seen it, for he says in his first pamphlet (p. 56): "A report of a Syndicate made in the month of April last [April, 1830], made the disposable capital of the University about £13,000, after all claims upon it were satisfied, and after leaving a balance of £5,000 ...in the hands of the Vice-Chancellor."]

[2] [It was opposed in the Black Hood House by Richard Sheepshanks, M.A., Trinity College, and lost by 18 votes to 16.]

[3] [Mr Coddington's pamphlet, p. 8.]

Meanwhile Mr Cockerell had sent down a new plan, which is said to have borne a general resemblance to his rejected design (No. 2)[1]. It was chiefly valuable, however, as shewing that he, at least, would be willing to modify his plans to meet the wishes of the University; and, this having become generally known, Mr Thorp of Trinity College was enabled to get carried without opposition, 31 May, 1830, what Mr Peacock calls "a conciliatory grace." He named a Syndicate with the following instructions: (1) to consider the extension of the Library and the construction of Museums and Lecture Rooms, respect being had to the Graces already passed on the subject; (2) to inquire into the means whereby funds could be acquired; (3) to report on these questions either together or separately before the end of the following term. This Syndicate, commonly known as the Second Syndicate, consisted of the following persons: The Vice-Chancellor; Dr French, Master of Jesus College; Dr Ainslie, Master of Pembroke College; Dr Turton; Professor Whewell; Mr Martin Thackeray, King's College; Mr Graham, Christ's College; Mr King, Queens' College; Mr Charles Blick and Mr William Jones, S. John's College; Mr Sheepshanks, Trinity College; Mr William Hildyard, Trinity Hall; Mr Joseph Studholme, Jesus College; Mr Lodge, Magdalene College; Mr Joseph Cape, Clare Hall; Mr Shelford, Corpus Christi College; Mr Dawes, Downing College; Mr Griffith; and Mr Gibson. To these were added subsequently (11 June, 1830) Mr Willis, Caius College; Mr Charles Smith, Peterhouse; and (17 November), Dr Chafy, and Dr Clark, Professor of Anatomy[2].

Soon after the appointment of this Syndicate, the Vice-Chancellor addressed the following circular to each of the four architects:

"Sidney Lodge, June 23, 1830.

Sir,

The Designs for the Enlargement and Improvement of the Public Library and adjoining Buildings at Cambridge, which have been sent to the Vice-Chancellor by the four Architects who were applied to for that Purpose, have not met with the general approbation of the

[1] [Mr Whewell's pamphlet, p. 9.]

[2] [It is worth notice that in the Grace of 11 June this Syndicate is described as "for consulting respecting the enlarging the Library and the disposal of King's Old Court;" and in that of 17 November as "the New Library Syndicate."]

Senate. I have been requested therefore by the Syndics to enquire whether those Architects are disposed to alter their Designs, agreeably to such Instructions as may hereafter be given to them.

It may be proper now to state, that, altho' the Syndics wish to have a general Plan of Improvement, which shall embrace the Public Library, Schools, etc., it is not proposed to extend the Improvement, at the *present Time*, beyond the Old Court of King's College. The Completion of the Design, will, in all Probability, be postponed to a distant Period.

You will also be pleased to understand that the Syndics do not undertake to guarantee any further Remuneration to those Architects whose Plans may not be adopted by the Senate, than that which has already been offered.

Your early Answer to this Letter of Inquiry will oblige

Sir,

Your very obt Servant,

W. CHAFY, V.C."

The architects all replied in the affirmative, and, accordingly, instructions which had been carefully prepared at successive meetings of the Syndicate, were sent to them in the course of July[1]. These instructions do not differ from those issued by the first Syndicate so materially as to make it necessary to print them in full. The Schools, as before, § 2, are to be placed on the south side, and the Museums on the north side, of the proposed quadrangle. The Library is to occupy the first floor, above the Museums; and the Lecture-Rooms are to be placed between the Museums and Senate-House Passage, as before. The arrangement of the Museums, however, differs slightly from that formerly suggested, § 4, and the Museum of Zoology is omitted altogether:

II. "In the line of the present North Library, on the ground floor, are to be placed the Museums of Geology, Mineralogy, and Botany: the first being at the Western extremity of this line, 70 feet long; the next, to the East of this, 30 feet long, the rest of the North side being appropriated to the Botanical Museum and other uses; a Lecture Room for the Plumian Professor being provided at its Eastern extremity."

At the end of the document the order in which the works are to be undertaken, their cost, and their style, are precisely indicated:

IX. "It is intended to execute at present only a part of the plan, and to leave the whole of the existing Library untouched; connecting

[1] [Mr Whewell's pamphlet, p. 13.]

it temporarily with the additions to it which shall be first built. It is proposed to begin with the Museums forming the North side, between the present Registry and the Western boundary of the ground; adding on the West side a room to be occupied by the Botanical Professor till the rest of the plan can be executed; the storey above these rooms forming the addition to be at present made to the Library. It is proposed also to build the Lecture Rooms adjoining Senate-House Passage, providing as soon as possible one Lecture Room and an accompanying Model Room for the Jacksonian Professor.

X. The sum to be at present expended not to exceed £25,000; and estimates of the expense of the part described in the last paragraph to be sent along with the Plans.

XI. The fronts to be of stone.

XII. The style of Architecture to be Grecian.

XIII. The Plans and Estimates of the whole Building to be sent to the Vice-Chancellor, on or before the 10th of October next; the Plans to be drawn to a scale of 8 feet to an inch."

Three of the architects, Mr Cockerell, Mr Wilkins, and Messrs Rickman and Hutchinson, sent amended designs to the Vice-Chancellor, who shortly afterwards (28 October, 1830) informed the Senate that "the new Designs for the Enlargement of the Public Library are deposited in the Library for their Inspection."

The difficulty of recommending a particular design was felt to be very great, more especially as no preponderance of opinion in favour of any one of the three could be ascertained. Moreover, while Mr Wilkins and Messrs Rickman and Hutchinson had conformed to the instructions, Mr Cockerell had "completely rejected both their principle and their details[1]." His design, however, found a powerful advocate in Mr Peacock, whose two pamphlets, the second of which is said to have had the advantage of Mr Cockerell's own supervision[2], were written to commend it to the Senate. Mr Whewell, on the other hand, criticized it severely, and supported that by Messrs Rickman and Hutchinson, appending a "Defence" of their design to his own "Reply" to Mr Peacock's "observations." The third design, that by Mr Wilkins, met with but little attention; and though Mr Peacock admits that it was "superior to that of Mr Rickman," and that it had not "experienced from the Members of the University the attention which it merits[3]," neither he nor others attempted to bring it prominently forward.

[1] [Mr Whewell's pamphlet, p. 16.] [2] [Mr Wilkins's Appeal, p. 1.]
[3] [Mr Peacock's first pamphlet, p. 51.]

It would be beside our purpose to do more than indicate the merits of these rival designs[1]. All three architects proposed to sweep away the old buildings entirely. In Mr Rickman's design the façade of the main building was coextensive with that of the present Library; and the north and south sides stood, in part, upon the ground occupied by the Divinity School and the Law School respectively. His internal quadrangle measured 110 feet from east to west, by 63 feet from north to south. Round this, on the ground-floor, the required apartments were arranged, in the following order, beginning at the south-east corner: Record Room, Registry, School of Law, School of Physic, School of Divinity. On the west side, opposite to Clare Hall, was the School of Arts. On the north side were the Museums of Geology, Mineralogy, Botany; and lastly, the Plumian Professor's Lecture Room. The space between the north side of the main building and Senate-House Passage contained two large lecture-rooms, and a model-room for the Jacksonian Professor. The Library occupied the whole of the first floor, above the Schools and Museums. The design of Mr Wilkins closely resembled that of Mr Rickman, both having been arranged in strict conformity with the instructions.

Mr Cockerell, on the contrary, carried his buildings to the extreme limit of the ground on all sides; and arranged the required Schools and Museums, including the Museum of Zoology, round the quadrangle in much the same order as Mr Rickman had done. There was, however, an important difference between the two designs. Mr Cockerell placed his façade—a double Corinthian portico—in advance of his main building; so that all four sides of his quadrangle were available for Schools and Museums on the ground-floor, and for a Library on the first floor. Moreover, he provided a basement story, containing workrooms, storerooms, a residence for an attendant, etc. His internal quadrangle measured 95 feet from east to west, by 100 feet from north to south; but this extensive area was curtailed by a great lecture theatre which rose on the north side of it, from the basement to the level of the first floor.

[1] [The designs of Cockerell and Rickman were circulated by Mr Peacock with his first pamphlet; that by Mr Wilkins was published by himself shortly after the appearance of his Appeal to the Senate in April, 1831.]

The Syndicate did not make their selection until the end of the Michaelmas Term, when they reported to the Senate, 10 December, 1830:

> "That taking all circumstances into consideration, they have agreed to recommend Messrs Rickman's and Hutchinson's Design for the New Library and other Public Buildings to the Senate for their adoption; subject to such modifications as a Syndicate, to be appointed for superintending the execution of the Plan, may deem it expedient to suggest to the Senate for their approbation."

This Report was signed by the Vice-Chancellor and twelve members of the Syndicate. The next step was to empower the same Syndicate (15 December) to consider how the necessary funds were to be obtained. They reported early in the following term (15 February, 1831), "that it appeared to them expedient to raise £30,000, in order to defray the expense of erecting that part of the intended buildings which it is proposed to execute at present." It was suggested that half this sum might be contributed by the University Chest; and that half might be raised by a loan, to be repaid in thirty years, the annual interest being defrayed partly out of surplus revenue, partly by charging £500 per annum to the Library Fund. This scheme, though generally condemned in the different pamphlets, passed the Senate without opposition. The original Report, however, which advised the adoption of Rickman's design, was never presented to the Senate for confirmation, and the whole scheme was once more laid aside, for reasons which it is now impossible to discover.

Nearly four years elapsed before any definite step was taken, for it was not until 14 March, 1834, that a Syndicate consisting of the Vice-Chancellor (Mr King, President of Queens' College); Mr Frere, Master of Downing College; Professor Whewell; Mr Hughes, St John's College; and Mr Calthrop, Corpus Christi College, was appointed to confer with the architects who, as the Grace reminded the Senate, "have, in accordance with your own decision, prepared designs for a new Library." The Vice-Chancellor informed the architects that "the University has been compelled to abandon the intention of building a new Library," and offered each of them 100 guineas. In a subsequent letter to Mr Cockerell he expressly states that this change of intention had been caused by deficiency of funds. After a long correspondence the architects, with the exception of Mr Cockerell, accepted the sums offered to them, and the Syndicate having informed the Senate of what had passed (31 May, 1834), a Grace to pay £105 to Mr Burton, Mr Rickman and Mr Wilkins, was introduced and agreed to without opposition.

The position in which the University was now placed, after six years of discussion, was no doubt felt to be discreditable; and it is not surprising that early in the following year (14 March, 1835) a Grace to raise the necessary funds by subscription should have been agreed to. The preamble stated that whereas the Old Court of King's College had been bought for £12,000 with the intention of building a Library and other edifices to be dedicated to literature and science; and whereas it was notorious that the University was too poor to undertake such a work out of its own resources; that a Syndicate should be appointed to solicit subscriptions, provided (among other things) that the existing Library should not only not be destroyed, but not even be in the slightest degree interfered with, until the new buildings were ready for the reception of books. The Syndicate was a very large one, consisting of the Heads, Bursars, and Tutors of all the Colleges; all the Professors; the Deputy High Steward; the Public Orator; the Librarian, and the Registrary; the Vice-Provost of King's College; the Vice-Master of Trinity College; the President of St John's College; and ten Masters of Arts. Their efforts were thoroughly successful, and before the beginning of the following Michaelmas Term more than £20,000 had been promised.

The improved circumstances in which the University was now placed were at once taken advantage of, and a Syndicate, which may be termed the Third Syndicate, was appointed (18 November, 1835) to report "on the best method of carrying out the wishes of the University, both as regards the building of a new Library, and those other matters which were intended when the Old Court of King's College was purchased." This Syndicate, in which every College except Emmanuel College was represented, consisted of the Vice-Chancellor; the Hon. G. Neville, Master of Magdalene College; Dr French, Master of Jesus College; Professor Sedgwick; Professor Miller; Mr Tatham, and Mr Snowball, S. John's College; Mr Lodge,

Magdalene College; Mr Peacock, Mr Whewell, Trinity College; Mr Craufurd, King's College; Mr Worsley, Downing College; Mr Willis, Caius College; Mr Ash, Christ's College; Mr Calthrop, Corpus Christi College; Mr Lodington, Clare Hall; Mr Fennell, Queens' College; Mr Hildyard, Trinity Hall; Mr Corrie, Catharine Hall; Mr Heaviside, Sidney College; Mr Hodgson, Peterhouse; Mr Arlett, Pembroke College.

This Syndicate set to work with the utmost alacrity; for within one week of their appointment they published the three following Reports:

"Report (A).

Emmanuel Lodge, November 25, 1835.

The Syndicate appointed 'to consider and report to the Senate, upon the best measures to be adopted for carrying into effect the wishes of the University, with regard to the Additions to the Library, &c.' beg leave to Report as follows:

That the sum of £20,895 has been subscribed for building a new Library, and for accomplishing the other important objects contemplated in the purchase of the Old Court of King's College.

That it appears to the Syndicate, to be the duty of the University, to second by all the resources at its command, the great and generous efforts which have been made by public bodies, by individual members, and by friends, in furtherance of objects of the utmost importance to its welfare.

That they therefore recommend the appointment of a special Syndicate for making enquiries with regard to any funds at present in the possession of the University which may be available for the above mentioned purposes, and also with a view to any other pecuniary resources which may be hereafter employed in the prosecution of this undertaking.

They further beg leave to state,

That the amount of the present Subscriptions, and the prospect of future Contributions will in their opinion fully warrant the University in taking immediate steps for the commencement of this work on a scale commensurate with the just expectations of the Contributors and Members of the University at large[1]."

"Report (B).

Emmanuel College, Nov. 25, 1835.

The Syndicate [etc.] beg leave to recommend,

That the ground for the erection of the Buildings proposed be cleared, and the old materials disposed of without delay; and further recommend, that Mr Elliot Smith be directed to take immediate steps

[1] [A note was appended to this Report: "A statement of particulars with regard to the Sum actually paid in and now invested will be laid on the Registrary's Table."]

for the sale and removal of those materials, and for the temporary enclosure of the ground.

The Syndicate however, considering it probable that the University or some public body connected with the University, may be disposed to re-erect or restore on some other site, the Old Gateway of King's College, (as a venerable and beautiful Specimen of Architecture), recommend that it should for the present be left undisturbed.

They also recommend, That, until proper accommodation shall have been provided for the Registrary and the Records, that part of the Old Court of King's College in which the Registrary's Office is now placed, be left standing."

"Report (C).

Emmanuel Lodge, Nov. 25, 1835.

The Syndicate [etc.] beg leave to recommend,

That the four Architects formerly applied to for Designs for a New Library, Museums, and Lecture Rooms, be informed that the project of erecting such buildings has been resumed, and that they be invited again to send in Designs, modified or amended, in reference to the following Instructions:

The entire Building for which Designs are required, is intended to contain Schools of Divinity, Arts, Law, and Physic, to be placed if possible *en suite*, and to serve as Lecture Rooms for those Professors who have no Apparatus to exhibit: a Registrary's Office and Record Room, each of moderate dimensions, with easy access from the Senate House: Museums of Geology, Mineralogy, Botany, &c., the first of considerable size; with such accommodation connected with them as the circumstances of the site will conveniently allow: two or three Lecture Rooms for the Scientific Professors, connected as much as possible with their Museums, the one appropriated to the Plumian Professor, to be so placed as to admit of the introduction of the Sun's light for Optical experiments: a Room for the apparatus of the Plumian Professor: a Room for the Vice-Chancellor for holding Syndicates or other uses: and also apartments for the residence of a Porter or Keeper in the basement story or elsewhere.

The whole of the second floor to be appropriated to the Library, which will be required to accommodate not less than 30,000 Volumes; also a Reading Room, a private Room for the Librarian, and separate rooms for Manuscripts and Books of great price and rarity.

The part of this Building which is required to be executed immediately, is to be confined to the Old Court of King's College, and not to interfere materially with the use of the existing buildings: immediate accommodation must be afforded for the Geological and Mineralogical Collections, with one or more Lecture Rooms connected with them: the largest Lecture Room will not be required to hold more than 200 persons: the part of the New Library to be built must be sufficient to hold all the Books in the present Library, with the probable additions for some years: and proper access must be made to it, both from the present Buildings and elsewhere.

All the Fronts to be of Stone.

The sum to be expended, in the first instance, is not to exceed £25,000.

The Designs to be sent in to the Vicechancellor on or before the 18th day of February, 1836: and the selection of one of the four Architects to be made on the 18th of March, on the principle adopted in the selection of the Design for the Fitzwilliam Museum, viz.:

That each Member of the Senate deliver to the Vicechancellor a Vote in favour of that particular Design, which he prefers.

That two hours, viz. from 12 to 2, be allowed for receiving such votes.

That the Vicechancellor, Proctors, and Scrutators, examine the votes received; and if there shall be an actual majority of the whole number of votes in favour of some one Design, then such Design shall be deemed to be *selected* to the exclusion of the rest, for the purpose of being subsequently referred to the consideration of a Syndicate: but if there shall not be an actual majority in favour of any one Design, then the Design, in favour of which the smallest number of votes has been given, shall be deemed to be finally excluded.

That the same process be (if necessary) repeated successively, with the remaining Designs, until all shall have been excluded, except one, which shall be deemed to be *selected* for the purpose of being referred for further consideration to a Syndicate, who shall report whether such design be in accordance with the Instructions: and that for the purpose of preventing delay, such Syndicate be appointed at some Congregation on or before the 24th of March.

The Architect whose Design shall be chosen shall be considered as the Architect for the Additions of the Library, &c. but it will be competent for the University to make any alterations which they may think expedient in the character and details of that Design.

It is understood that the Architects may make any use of their Designs sent in on a former occasion, which they may think proper."

The first two Reports were signed by the Vice-Chancellor and fourteen Syndics, the latter by twelve Syndics only. All three however passed the Senate without opposition at the next Congregation (2 December). Three of the architects, Messrs Cockerell, Rickman, and Wilkins, sent in fresh designs, which were exhibited to the Senate 14 April, 1836; and, 11 May, that of Mr Cockerell was selected by a large majority[1]. On the same day a Syndicate was appointed to inquire whether his design was in conformity with the instructions. They reported in the affirmative 18 May; and further, that the portion which was to be executed immediately might be built for a sum not exceeding £25,000, but that Mr Cockerell "declined to pledge himself to this precise sum, as the amount of the expenditure

[1] [The votes were: Cockerell 60; Rickman 9; Wilkins 0.]

may be materially affected by the nature of the stone and other materials employed." A Grace to confirm this report was prepared, but the ambiguity of Mr Cockerell's language caused it to be vetoed on the caput (25 May) by Dr Webb, Master of Clare Hall, and further progress was once more delayed. The destruction of the Old Court of King's College, which had been already commenced, was suspended (11 June) and the former Syndicate was reappointed to confer again with Mr Cockerell. They reported (24 November) that the portion marked for immediate execution, which, as we learn from a subsequent document "comprehended the whole of the Western side, and also parts of the North and South sides of the new Quadrangle[1]" might be built for £25,000. The adoption of this Report was opposed, but was carried (30 November) by twenty-two votes against five; and a building Syndicate was appointed (7 December) "to confer with Mr Cockerell (1) as to retaining any part of the present walls of the old Building purchased of King's College; and (2) as to any alterations which may be thought expedient in the character and details of his Design."

No ground-plan or elevation of Mr Cockerell's design has been preserved in the University, so far as we have been able to discover; and our knowledge of it is mainly derived from an engraving by Mackenzie in Le Keux's Memorials of Cambridge. This shews that the east side of the quadrangle was set several feet in advance of the east ends of the north and south sides; and that it was entered through a noble portico, supported by a range of columns, and surmounted by a row of statues[2]. The style, as there shewn, is Ionic; but the actual building is Corinthian. The south wing was no doubt intended to resemble the north wing exactly, and the west side, opposite to Clare Hall, was to abut against the north side in such a manner

[1] [Report, dated 8 March, 1837, of a Syndicate appointed 7 December, 1836, to confer with Mr Cockerell.]

[2] [A large engraving of the building in progress, from the West, drawn by Mr Cockerell himself, but unfortunately without date, exhibits the building in section, so as to shew the construction; and a very rough ground-plan, not drawn to scale, is sketched on a piece of paling in the foreground. A detailed ground-plan is given in the Companion to the British Almanac for 1840, p. 238, but the authority from which it is derived is not stated. This plan is reproduced in Observations on some recent University Buildings, by Francis Bashforth, M.A. 8vo. Camb. 1853.]

as to widen the street considerably. A western portico had been originally intended, but this was suppressed before the work began. The probable extent of the whole building has been indicated by dotted lines on the ground-plan of the site (fig. 1).

The Syndicate appointed 7 December, 1836, occupied several months in the preparation of their Report, which was not published until 8 March, 1837. They informed the Senate in the first place that "no part of the Walls of the Old Building can be retained so as to form part of the Walls of the New Library;" and secondly, proposed a number of alterations which Mr Cockerell had embodied in a new set of plans. These alterations need not be specified, as neither the old nor the new designs are before us. Lastly, it was suggested that the work should begin by the building of the north side of the quadrangle. This part of the Report, as referring to an existing building, shall be quoted entire:

"The rise which has taken place in the prices of building materials since Mr Cockerell furnished his original design induces him to advise now, that, instead of the portion just mentioned [the West side, and parts of the North and South sides of the quadrangle], the entire North side, the architecture of which is of a less expensive character, should be the part selected for erection in the first instance: and he states, from an accurate Estimate founded on the basis of present prices, that this part may be built, and prepared for the reception of its fittings for the sum originally proposed to be expended.

Mr Cockerell states that, independently of the question of expense, a considerable advantage would be obtained by this course of proceeding from the circumstance of the North side being a complete Building in itself.

The Syndics beg leave to add that by this plan accommodation will be afforded for the Geological and Mineralogical Collections with one Lecture-Room attached to them; and also, according to Mr Cockerill's computation, for 180,000 volumes. Although the light in the proposed Building and also in the present Library will be partially obstructed from their proximity to each other in one quarter, no material inconvenience will, in the judgment of the Syndicate, result to either.

Convenient access may be obtained to the proposed Building from the present Library.

Mr Cockerell advises, in case his present proposal should be approved of, that the Walls of the Old Court be taken down to the level of the string-course, which is about 15 feet from the ground; and that the materials thus obtained be used in the foundation of the New Building; the remaining part of the Walls being employed in the formation of temporary workshops."

This Report was confirmed by the Senate 16 March, 1837; and the work began shortly afterwards. Mr Cockerell was authorised, 12 June, to raise the foundations to the surface of the ground; and 1 July, a contract with Messrs J. and C. Rigby, Builders, of London, for £23,945, was recommended by the Syndicate to the Senate. This contract was not sealed until 18 October following; but in the meantime the work had proceeded, and the ceremony of laying the first stone took place 29 September. The following brief notice of the ceremony is worth quotation:

"The first stone of [the new University Library] was laid by the Vice-Chancellor [Gilbert Ainslie, D.D. Master of Pembroke College], but, owing to the resident members of the University being now very few, and the anxiety of proceeding immediately with the work preventing any delay, the proceedings were strictly private. The Vice-Chancellor was accompanied only by the Master of Jesus College, the Vice-Master of Trinity College [Rev. John Brown], the Registrary [Rev. Joseph Romilly, Trin. Coll.], the Senior Proctor [Rev. Francis Martin, Trin. Coll.], Professor Peacock, Mr Whewell, and two or three other Members of the Senate. The Architect was also present.

The stone was laid at the north-west pier of the third window on the north side of the building. The stone having been lowered, and the Vice-Chancellor having given it the accustomed stroke with the mallet, he took off his cap, and pronounced the following prayer: 'I pray that this building may redound to the glory of God by the propagation of true religion and the encouragement and increase of sound learning.' The proceedings terminated with three times three shouts.

The following is the inscription on the stone:

'SEPT. 29. A.D. MDCCCXXXVII. VICTORIÆ . I.
JOH . JEFFRIES . MARCHION . CAMDEN . CANC.
GILBERTO . AINSLIE . ITERVM . PROCANC.
CAR . ROB . COCKERELL . ARCHIT.'

The stone is from Whitby, and is peculiarly cheap as well as good[1]."

The work proceeded without interruption, and by the be-

[1] [Partly from the Cambridge Chronicle, 30 Sept. 1837: partly from notes added by Mr Romilly. It should be mentioned that in the course of the work the arcade described above (p. 77) was sold, 17 August, 1838. The auctioneer's hand-bill describes it as: "The Stone Wall at the North End of the East Front [of the Public Library], being 45 ft. 6 in. long, 16 ft. 6 in. high, and the thickness 2 ft. 9 in. including the brickwork at the back. It contains Four beautiful well-proportioned Arches, and the Coping is surmounted by Nine Balls. It will be sold in one Lot; excepting the Balls, which will be lotted in Pairs."]

ginning of 1840 Mr Cockerell certified that the contractors had "satisfactorily completed the substantial works of the New Library." The fittings were undertaken next, and were completed in about two years, as the last payment to the contractors was made in November, 1842. Rather more than five years had therefore been occupied in the work. It is difficult to estimate the total cost exactly, as no detailed accounts were published; but it could not have been less than £35,000. The subscriptions, with interest, had amounted to £23,410. 3*s*. 11*d*. and the difference between this sum and the amount expended was defrayed out of the Library Fund[1].

No proposal has since been made to complete Mr Cockerell's design; and even the ground-plan, as mentioned above, has not been preserved. The gradual increase of books has however, rendered extension of space in the Library necessary, which has been provided partly by additional bookcases, partly by gradually adding to it rooms originally intended for other purposes, partly by new buildings.

In 1856 (27 October) the Library Syndicate proposed to add the Divinity School—which at that time was used as a storeroom—to the Library, and to provide an approach to it from the room above by an iron spiral staircase; and at the same time to make arrangements for connecting with it the Newspaper Room, the Music Room, and the Novel Room. This work was carried out in the course of 1857[2].

The additional space thus provided was not great; and, 7 March, 1860, the Annual Report of the Syndicate contained the following passage:

"The Syndics beg to call attention to the fact that all the available space in the Library is fast being filled, and that therefore an early consideration of the best mode of obtaining additional accommodation for the rapidly increasing collection is absolutely necessary. They would suggest that a distinct Syndicate should be appointed to consider this important subject."

In consequence of this recommendation a Syndicate was appointed (25 October), and reported:

[1] [Report of Syndicate, 5 December, 1839. The sum required was raised by the issue of bonds of £300. The fittings of the Geological Museum were paid for out of the Woodwardian Fund, Grace 3 June, 1840.]

[2] [Fourth Annual Report of the Syndicate, 17 February, 1858.]

"That in their opinion it is desirable that the University should take steps for providing other Lecture Rooms instead of those under the Library, and that the present Schools and Lecture Room under the old Library Buildings should be given up for the purposes of the Library."

This recommendation raised questions so difficult of solution that the Report was never presented to the Senate for confirmation; and the subject of Library extension was not reopened until 1862, when the Rev. George Williams, B.D., Senior Fellow of King's College, put forward a scheme[1] for extending the south wing of the Library westward, up to the limit of the ground opposite Clare Hall, with a continuation northward to join the old gateway; and for adding, if the University thought fit, an additional story to the old south building. This scheme, which was supported by the advice of a practical surveyor, met with general approval; and a fresh Syndicate was appointed (15 May) to consider the whole question of Library extension. This Syndicate reported (10 December) that they had consulted George Gilbert Scott, Esq., Architect, from whom they had received drawings and estimates, not only for the buildings suggested above, but also for the west range of the Old Court. The whole was estimated to cost "about £15,800, in addition to a certain outlay not estimated for improving the present South front, and adding buttresses to it." The scheme however will be best understood by the following passages from a letter written by Mr Scott to the Syndicate 22 November, 1862:

"I submit to you herewith three plans and a perspective sketch of the proposed extension of the University Library. The plans shew, as you are aware, the addition of buildings occupying the site of the Old Court of King's College, and in the main reproducing that Court, subject to such variations as the altered purpose suggests, among which may be specially mentioned the increase of width to the building on its Southern side. I have preserved the present width of the Western side both to avoid unduly diminishing the Court, and to preserve the design of the exquisite Gateway.

Besides this, however, I have supposed that an additional story will be added to the Southern wing of the present Library.

I am of opinion that the cost of either the Southern or Western wing or side of the Court would be (including fittings) about £11,500 to £12,000, reckoning that the Southern wing comprises the building

[1] [University Library Extension. A Letter to the Vice-Chancellor of the University of Cambridge. By George Williams, B.D. Senior Fellow of King's College. 8vo. Cambridge, 1862. (28 March).]

from A to B on the plans, with a temporary wall to close it at B, in case the western side is not carried on in the first instance.

The cost of the upper story of the present Southern range of Library I reckon at about £3,800, or perhaps a little more; in addition to which there would be required a certain outlay in improving that front and adding buttresses to it. I suppose the New Buildings to be faced throughout with stone.

It seems to me that these additions will give very excellent space for books and other purposes, and probably at a cheaper rate than it could readily be obtained in any other way. It would also be attended with the advantage of restoring in some degree the ancient Court and its beautiful Gateway—one of the architectural gems of Cambridge. This Court might at a future time be covered with glass if found desirable.

I would mention that the Library on the first or middle floor would be of such a height as to admit of galleries."

The stability of the old walls having been questioned, Mr Scott sent the following description of them in a second letter addressed to the Vice-Chancellor, 4 March, 1863:

"They are of brick both within and without to a depth of a foot or fourteen inches, the centre being filled in with a mixture of brick, clunch, or compact chalk, and a very hard thin-bedded stone cemented with very excellent mortar. In fact, [my Practical Assistant] says, that *we could not make a better wall;* indeed, it took a very long time to cut into it, it was so firmly cemented together.

In facing with stone (which I suppose would be considered necessary for the sake of appearance) I should not see any objection to cutting carefully into the brickwork and inserting the ashlar; binding it firmly at intervals and setting it in Roman cement. The wall will bear it perfectly well."

Notwithstanding this very decided expression of opinion, the adoption of the Report was opposed, but carried by a very large majority (12 March)[1]. A new Syndicate was appointed to supervise the building-work (20 March); and the Provost and Fellows of King's College having conveyed to the University the ground required for the erection of buttresses (24 June, 1863), the plans were matured, and the contract was ready for signature at the beginning of 1864. The first stone was laid by the Rev. George Williams, 21 May, 1864.

The scheme for completing the quadrangle by the erection of a west range—the ground-floor of which would have been used as a Divinity School—was abandoned, and the work undertaken consisted of the south range only (fig. 1), together

[1] [The numbers were 61 to 5.]

with the proposed third floor above the old Common Library on the south side of the Schools Quadrangle. The new rooms were all ready for occupation at the beginning of 1867[1]; and the bookcases, which were not ordered until the following year (18 March, 1868), were finished in the course of that summer. The rooms on the ground-floor, intended for the Librarian, and for a receiving and unpacking office, were assigned "for the present[2]" to general University purposes, and have continued to be thus used up to the present time.

Lastly, in 1880, the New Divinity School having been completed, the old Divinity Lecture-Room was added to the Library; and a new office for the registration of books borrowed and returned was made out of the south entrance to the quadrangle.

CHRONOLOGICAL SUMMARY.

1347. 15 February. The "Great Schools" in School Street mentioned.

1398. 20 June. Decree of Eudo de la Zouch, Chancellor, for an annual service for the souls of Sir William and Lady Grace Thorpe, because Sir William's executors had built Divinity Schools and a Chapel.

1400. Divinity School and Chapel completed (Parker).

1421. 8 January. A piece of garden-ground leased from Trinity Hall.

1424. Books left to the Library by Richard Holme, Warden of King's Hall.

1431—32. 11 March. The Hostel of the Holy Cross bought from William Hulle.

1438. The west side of the Schools quadrangle mentioned.

1439. Before this year a catalogue of the books in the Library had been made.

1440. The Hostel of the Holy Cross sold to King Henry VI. Reservation of a piece for the erection of new schools. The "New Schools of Theology and Canon Law" mentioned.

1454. New Chapel and Library mentioned in the University Accounts.

1457. 5 July. Syndicate appointed to build a new School of Philosophy and Canon Law, or a Library.

1458. The Canon Law School mentioned in a Grace of the Senate as begun but not yet finished.

[1] [The contract with Messrs Jackson and Shaw for £14,500 was accepted 11 February, 1864; and the last payment to them was sanctioned 28 February, 1867. In that term the upper room in the new building was used for examinations (Grace, 28 March, 1867).]

[2] [Report of the Council of the Senate, 27 May, 1867; confirmed by Grace, 6 June, 1867.]

1458.	9 April. Syndicate appointed to supervise the building of the new School.
	30 June. Grace to provide the funds required for the new School, and for the completion of the Canon Law School.
1459.	25 March. Ground in School Street leased from John Botwright, Master of Corpus Christi College.
1466.	25 June. Contract for the roof, floor, windows, and roof of staircase in the Civil Law School. Stone bought for the windows, and contract made for glazing them.
1470.	The south side of the quadrangle completed, and the east side begun.
1473.	The books in the Library catalogued by the Proctors.
1475.	13 May. Thomas Rotherham enrolled among University Benefactors.
1547.	Grace to convert the old Library into a School for the Regius Professor of Divinity.
1574.	Archbishop Parker, Bishop Horne, Bishop Pilkington, and Sir Nicholas Bacon, give books.
	6 August. Deed between Archbishop Parker and Corpus Christi College respecting the repair of University Street or Regent Walk.
1583—84.	General repair to Schools; spouts made.
1586.	16 December. Grace to restore the old Library to its original use.
1596—1601.	Ornamental ceiling to New Chapel, Dr Jegon, Vice-Chancellor.
1615.	27 September. Dr Stephen Perse bequeaths £100 to the building of the Library. Scheme of Sir Fulke Greville for a new Library.
1626—27.	March. Visit of the Duke of Buckingham. He promises £7000 for a Commencement House and Library.
1639—40.	Battlements repaired at a cost of £103.
1645.	Petition of the University for Archbishop Bancroft's books.
1646—47.	Timber bought for "supporters."
1649.	Arrival of Archbishop Bancroft's books.
	3 September. Grace to fit up the Greek Schools as a Library. Sir John Woollaston gives bookcases.
1659—60.	"Needless stone" cut out of windows in Divinity School.
1662.	4 July. Room at west end of Divinity School fitted up as a Registry.
1668.	2 February. Dr Cosin's offer towards the building of a Theatre.
1673.	2 December. Purchase of the Lease of the New Inn.
1673—74.	Austin fits up the East room of the Library with new bookcases.
1675.	1 April. Grace appointing a Syndicate to supervise the building of a Commencement House.
1676—78.	General repair. Columns in certain schools made by Cornelius Austin. New screen and fittings for Regent House.
1715.	20 September. King George the First gives Bishop Moore's books to the Library; and, (9 November) Syndicate appointed to provide for the safe keeping of them.
1716.	26 May. Law School to be fitted up as a Library by Coleman and Austin.
1716—17.	28 January. Agreement between the University and King's College for the space above the Porter's Lodge.
	Construction of the Dome Room in progress.
1717.	6 March. Syndicate empowered to have bookcases made.
1718—19.	6 March. Syndicate appointed to buy property on the north side of the Regent Walk. Grace for the building of a new Senate-House.

1719.	Bishop Moore's books placed in the Library.
1720.	Fittings of the Dome Room being made by Woodward.
	11 June. Royal Assent to Act of Parliament to enable owners of property to sell to the University.
1721—22.	27 February. Conclusion of Syndics to consult Mr Gibbs.
1722.	22 June. First stone of Senate-House laid by the Vice-Chancellor.
	10 October. Contract for building-stone with Christopher Cass.
1723—24.	20 January. Contract for the wooden roof.
	8 February. " with Essex for the sashes.
	8 February. Acquisition of Dr Green's house, between the Regent Walk and East School Street.
1724.	22 October. Order to buy houses belonging to Corpus Christi College between the Regent Walk and East School Street.
1724—25.	11 January. Marble to be used for floor of Senate-House.
1725.	20 July. Order to dig the foundations of the front of the New Building (Attachment Scheme).
	20 July. Essex to put up the wainscot according to Gibbs' design.
	5 October. The Plaster ceiling to be executed.
	" Second order to begin the New Building in February.
1725—26.	7 February. Grace of the Senate to proceed with the west and south sides of the New Building.
	9 March. Third order to dig trenches for the New Building.
1726.	Completion of plaster work in Senate-House.
1727.	31 May. Dr Gooch, Master of Caius College, writes to the Vice-Chancellor condemning the Attachment Scheme.
	23 October. Syndics summoned to appear before Court of Chancery.
1728.	5 April. Trenches filled up in anticipation of visit of King George II.
1730.	Steps of Senate-House completed: iron railings put up.
	25 June. Judgment of Court of Chancery non-suiting the Plaintiffs.
	6 July. Senate-House opened by a Public Commencement.
	August. Grace to fit up the old Senate-House as a Library.
1732.	26 June. Staircase to be removed, and Library to be widened.
1733.	23 May. Door to be made out of East Library into the old Senate-House.
1734.	Books moved into the old Senate-House.
1735.	Room fitted up for Dr Woodward's fossils.
1736.	2 December. Letter of Lord Townshend, offering to present a statue of King George I.
1738.	Houses on the S. side of the Regent Walk purchased from Corpus Christi College.
1739.	November. Arrival of the Statue of King George I.
1745.	A Statue of *Glory* presented by Peter Burrell, M.B.
1748.	14 December. Thanks returned to Mr Burrell for the Statue of *Glory*.
1750.	New roof and cupola constructed for the Square Room.
	Statue of the Duke of Somerset offered by his daughters.
1752.	Design for the new façade to the Library made by Mr Burrough.
	6 July. MSS. to be removed into the cases which are ready for them.
	15 July. Agreement with King's College to build arches under the Dome Room.

1753. 15 December. Syndics directed to buy property from King's College, on the S. side of East School Street.

1754. 11 June. The same Syndics to preside over the erection of the new façade of the Library according to the plan of the Duke of Newcastle.

1755. 30 April. First stone laid of the new façade.

1756. Arrival of the Statue of the Duke of Somerset.

1757. The houses between the Regent Walk and East School Street bought.

1758. 3 July. East room of Library opened by Chancellor.

1766. Arrival of the Statue of King George the Second, given by the Duke of Newcastle.

16 June. West end of Senate-House to be finished.

1767. January. Arcade between Senate-House and Library pulled down.

6 July. West end of N. and S. aisles of Great S. Mary's Church to be cleared of the houses abutting against them, and the walls to be repaired.

21 August. First stone of west front of Senate-House laid by the Vice-Chancellor.

1768. Repair to west end of Great S. Mary's Church carried out.

28 June. West front of Senate-House finished.

1769. May. Ground between the Regent Walk and East School Street cleared.

4 December. Houses belonging to King's College at the corners of High Street and School Street bought.

1773. Columns in Divinity School cased with classical woodwork.

1783. 28 June. Appointment of Syndics to undertake the south building.

1786. 26 December. Agreement with King's College.

1787. 1 November. Contract with Charles Humfrey for bookcases in the East Room of the Library.

1791. 13 December. Mr Soane's plans for the south building rejected by the Senate.

1812. Arrival of the Statue of Mr Pitt, purchased by subscription.

1827. 25 November. The Old Court of King's College bought for £12,000.

1829. 6 May. Appointment of "The First Syndicate."

2 July. Report, advising application to four architects.

July. Instructions for architects.

25 November. Conveyance of the Old Court of King's College to the University for £12,000.

25 November. Report of Syndicate, recommending Mr Cockerell's design.

1830. 26 February. Appointment of a Syndicate to ascertain what funds exist for the building of a new Library.

31 May. Appointment of "The Second Syndicate."

Instructions for architects.

23 June. Letter of the Vice-Chancellor to the four architects suggesting amendment of their designs.

10 December. Report of Syndicate, recommending Rickman's design (now presented to the Senate).

1831. 15 February. Report of Syndicate shewing how funds may be raised for the new buildings.

1834. 14 March. Appointment of a Syndicate to confer with the architects.

1835. 14 March. Appointment of a Syndicate to raise the necessary funds by subscription.

18 November. Appointment of "The Third Syndicate."

25 November. Publication of three reports, recommending: (A) that the new building be commenced without delay, £20,895 having been subscribed; (B) that the ground be cleared; (C) that the four architects be again applied to.

1836. 14 April. Designs sent in by Cockerell, Rickman, and Wilkins.

11 May. Cockerell's design selected.

24 November. Report stating that the north and west sides of the proposed quadrangle may be built for £25,000.

7 December. Appointment of a "Building Syndicate."

1837. 8 March. Report of the Building Syndicate recommending: (1) various alterations, and (2) the construction in the first instance of the north side only.

12 June. Mr Cockerell authorised to raise the foundations to the level of the ground.

1 July. Contract with Messrs Rigby for £23,945 recommended to the Senate.

29 September. First Stone laid by the Vice-Chancellor.

18 October. Contract with Messrs Rigby adopted.

1840. Building-work completed.

1842. Fittings completed.

1856. Divinity School added to the Library.

1862. Proposal to extend the south wing of the Library westward; and to add a new story to it.

15 May. Syndicate appointed to consider the whole question.

10 December. Report, recommending a plan by G. G. Scott, architect.

1863. 12 March. Mr Scott's plan adopted.

1864. Contract for a new south wing signed. First stone laid 21 May, by Rev. George Williams.

1867. Completion of new south wing.

1880. Divinity Lecture-Room added to Library.

1884. Arts School added to Library.

UNIVERSITY BUILDINGS.

II.

Printing-House, Museums and Lecture Rooms for Natural Science, Observatory, Fitzwilliam Museum, Selwyn Divinity School.

IT was explained in the last section that all the buildings required for the public life of the University were originally grouped round the Schools Quadrangle; but that gradually, as additional space was required for the Library, it became necessary to erect new buildings on other sites. The history of the most important of these, the Senate House, has been already narrated. It now remains to investigate that of the rest of the University Buildings; but, as they can hardly be said to possess an architectural history at present, our account of them will of necessity be extremely brief. We will begin with the Printing-House, the right of appointing three stationers or printers having been granted to the University by King Henry the Eighth in 1534[1].

CHAPTER I.

HISTORY OF THE PRINTING-HOUSE, COMMONLY CALLED THE PITT PRESS.

THE site of the University Printing-House, commonly called "The Pitt Press," is bounded on the north by Silver Street, on the east by Trumpington Street, on the south by Mill Lane,

[1] [Cooper's Annals, I. 368. Dyer, "Privileges of the University", I. 107.]

and on the west by the Black Lion Yard, and a dwelling-house not the property of the University.

Before narrating the history of the acquisition of this site, and of the erection of the existing buildings, we will notice, very briefly, the different places in which printing is known to have been carried on previously; confining ourselves strictly, as in other cases, to information about buildings, to the exclusion of that which concerns printers, or works produced by them[1].

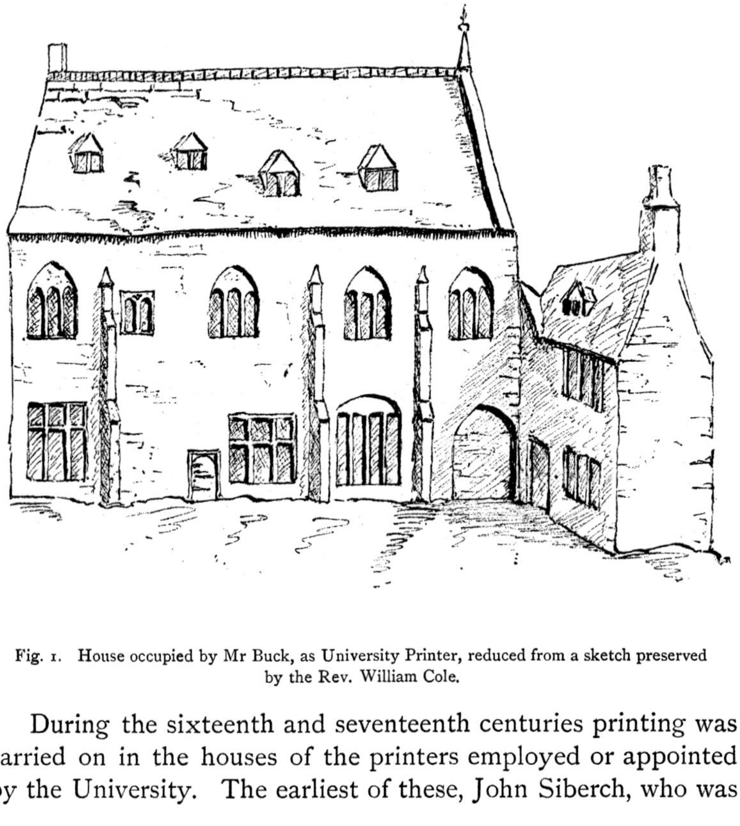

Fig. 1. House occupied by Mr Buck, as University Printer, reduced from a sketch preserved by the Rev. William Cole.

During the sixteenth and seventeenth centuries printing was carried on in the houses of the printers employed or appointed by the University. The earliest of these, John Siberch, who was

[1] [Those interested in the history of the Cambridge Press should consult: "Brief Annals of the Cambridge University Press," in 'Scholæ Academicæ,' by C. Wordsworth, M.A., 8vo. Cambridge, 1877; and 'Biographical Notes on Cambridge Printers from 1821 to the present day,' by R. Bowes, published in the Camb. Antiq. Soc. Communications, 1884—85. I have to thank my friend Mr Bowes for most of the information here given.]

printing in 1521 and 1522, occupied a house opposite to S. Michael's Church, called The Royal Arms (*Arma regia*), now part of Gonville and Caius College[1]. Thomas Thomas (1582—88), and John Legate (1588—1607), resided in the parish of S. Mary the Great, either on the Regent Walk, or in one of the houses abutting on the Church. In the controversy between Leonard Green and his partner Thomas Buck in or about 1622, it is made a cause of complaint against the latter that he had taken "the Angel"—probably the Angel Inn opposite Great S. Mary's Church—and set up a printing-press there[2]; but a few years afterwards he had removed to a house which stood near the north-west corner of the old Botanic Garden, as will be explained below in the History of the New Museums, described as

> "all that capitall messuage or tenement called the Augustine fryers, wherein the said Thomas Buck now dwelleth, together with the printing house, and all other houses, yards, orchards, [etc] thereunto belonging[3]."

Cole has preserved a rough sketch of this house, of which a reduced copy is here given (fig. 1). He describes it as

> "The West Prospect of what remains of the Priory of S^t^. Austin in Cambridge, late the Dwelling House of Mr Buck, and now the House belonging to the Curator of the Botanic Garden. It was taken Jan. 19, 1770, by Mr Tyson, Fellow of Bene't College, from a Chamber Window in that College, and just opposite to it. It is drawn rather too short at the North end[4]."

Again, when attending the sale of the effects "of the late Mr Buck in his house in Free School Lane," 25 November, 1746, he remarks:

> "which said House, tho' just behind the East End of St Benedict's Church and Corpus Christi College, is nothing more than the Refectory of the Austin Friers, and is compleat; only made into 3 Stories[5]."

In 1655 the University obtained from Queens' College a lease of their ground at the corner of Silver Street and Queens'

1 [History of Gonville and Caius College, Vol. I. p. 160.]

2 [Allegations preferred by Leonard Green against Thomas Buck, in the Registry of the University, 'Press Documents,' 33. 1. 11.]

3 [Agreement between Thomas Buck and Roger Daniel, Ibid. 33. 1. 19.]

4 [MSS. Cole, xlii. 260. Add. MSS. Mus. Brit. 5843.]

5 [Ibid. iv. fol. 43. b. Add. MSS. Mus. Brit. 5805.]

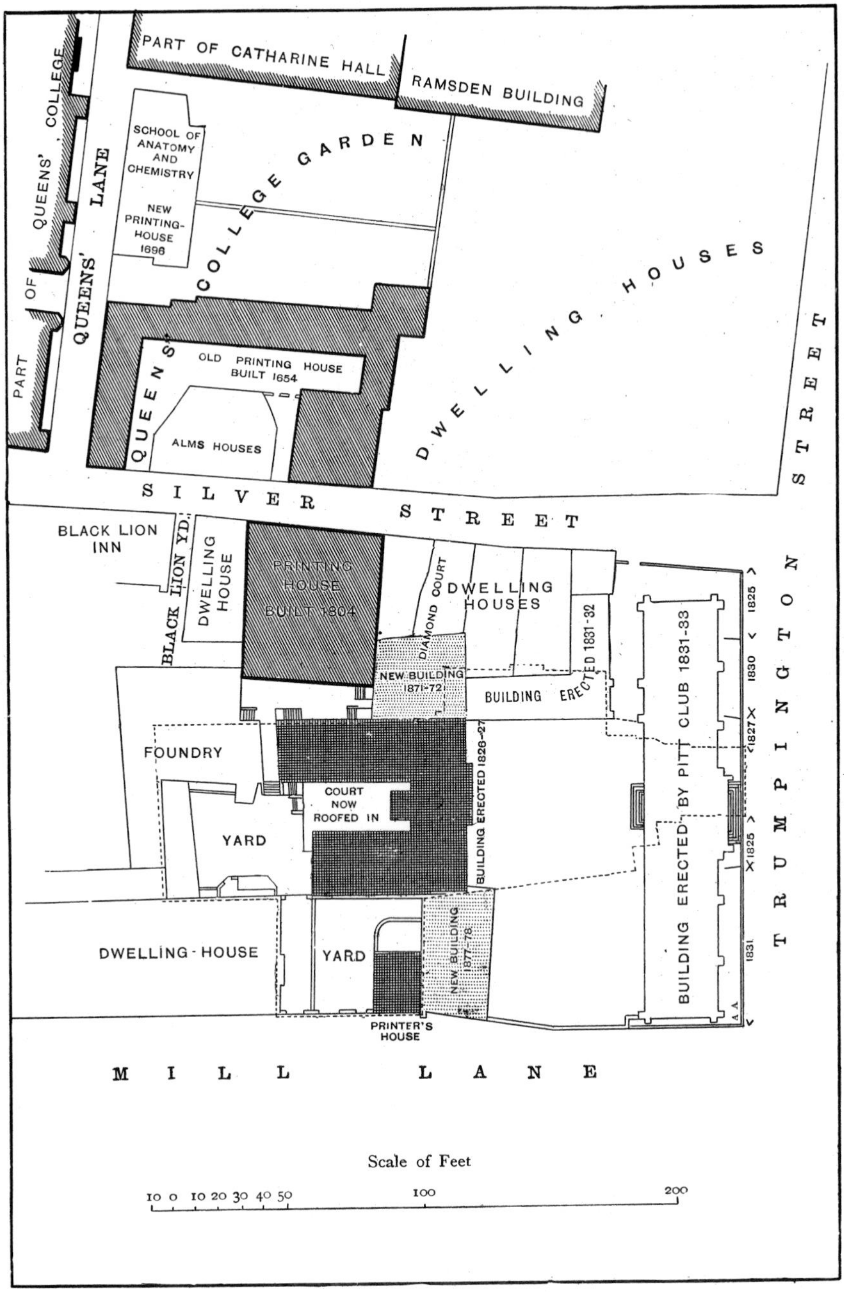

Fig. 2. Ground-plan of the sites of the old and new Press.

Lane[1]. On part of this site John Field, who had been appointed Printer in 1654, "built the large Shop or Printing-house now [1753] in use[2]." In 1696, however, when great efforts were made to renovate and improve the University Press, mainly at the instigation of the Duke of Somerset, elected Chancellor in 1689, who "contributed largely himself, and procured considerable Benefactions from others, towards reestablishing and supporting our Press[3]," a second, or new printing-house, was built, to the north of the former[4]. The two houses were used until 1716, when the more modern building was made over to the Professors of Anatomy and Chemistry, because, in the words of the Grace, it was of no use to the University for any other purpose (*Academiæ alioquin infructuosum*)[5], and the business of printing was carried on in the older house, which stood at the corner of Silver Street and Queens' Lane, with a range of warehouses extending from it eastward behind the almshouses belonging to Queens' College and returned beyond them to the street, so as to form three sides of a small court (fig. 2). Cole, writing in 1780, has recorded the following description of these houses among some notes on Dr Plumptre's MS. History of Queens' College:

"Query, if the Orchard before the College Gates does not mean the Garden lately belonging to Mr Alderman Bentham, as Printer to the University, contiguous to his House in Silver Street, being the S. W. Corner of that Street: the Printing House makes the South Side of the Garden, Mr Hayles's House [at the corner of Trumpington Street and Silver Street] and others the East End, Catharine Hall Lodge and M^rs. Ramsden's New Building take up the whole North Side, and the West Side is occupied by the Anatomy Schole contiguous to S^t. Catharine Hall, and the Printer's House which reaches to the Angle of the Strete: the Printer's House and Offices make a sort of Quadrangle or Square:

1 [History of Queens' College, Vol. II. p. 1. History of St Catharine's College, Ibid. pp. 78—86.]

2 [Carter's Cambridge, p. 469.]

3 [This sentence is taken from the Service for the Commemoration of Benefactors, in the Registry of the University.]

4 [In the Univ. Accounts for 1696—97 Grumbold is paid "for drawing the scheme of the new printing-house;" but, as no further charges for it are set down, the cost was probably defrayed out of the subscription set on foot in 1696 for the purpose of placing the Press on a new footing. See Monk's Bentley, I. 73; and the letter written by the Duke of Somerset to the Vice-Chancellor, 29 June 1696, printed by Wordsworth, *ut supra*, p. 384.]

5 Grace of the Senate, 10 October, 1716.

I think it belongs to Queens' College: I know Mr. Stokes the Bedel lived in it, Temp. Elizabeth[1]."

This building was evidently found to be inconvenient, for a new Printing-house was included in the scheme suggested by Gibbs in 1715 for the Senate House, Library, &c., and probably in that suggested by Wright in 1753, but, as has been already related, the south wing, which would have contained it, was never erected[2]. This failure may have induced the Syndics of the Press to turn their attention to the acquisition of a site for themselves; for, in 1762 they "agreed to purchase, for £170, a house called the White Lion[3]." The position of this house, probably an Inn, is not defined, but, if we are right in supposing that it supplied the site for "a new warehouse for the printing-office," erected in 1786[4], and altered into a Printing-office in 1804[5], it was on the south side of Silver Street, nearly opposite to the old buildings.

It may therefore be stated that the acquisition of the present site began in 1762, and the erection of the present buildings in 1804, for the house built in that year is still standing (fig. 2). After this time the business of the Press was probably carried on almost entirely in the new house, which is described in 1809 as "a commodious brick building, situated in Silver Street, with a stereotype foundry adjoining[6]."

As the business of the Press increased, the limited extent of this building was found to be extremely inconvenient; and in January, 1821, the Syndics recommended to the University the acquisition, for £5060, of a large messuage adjoining it on the south, then belonging to Mr James Nutter[7]. This property, the

1 [MSS. Cole xlviii. 243. Add. MSS. Mus. Brit. 5849.]

2 [History of the Schools, etc., Chapter III.]

3 [Syndicate Book (preserved in the Registry of the University), 1737—87, p. 117. A Grace to carry out this suggestion passed the Senate 21 October, 1762.]

4 [Univ. Accounts, 1785—86.]

5 [Minutes of the Press Syndicate, 20 April, 1804. "Agreed also that Mr Watts with the assistance of Mr Humphreys shall prepare a plan for altering the Warehouse into a Printing office."]

6 [Dyer's 'Privileges of the University of Cambridge,' Vol. II. *History of the University Press*, p. 30. Harraden's Cambridge, p. 185.]

7 [The Grace, sanctioned 24 January, 1821, was in the following terms: "Quum in Typographeo vestro, ex angustiis loci, multa detrimenta atque incommoda subinde exoriri soleant; quumque, in remedium mali istius, Preli Typographici Curatores pactionem inierint cum Domino Nutter, ut facultate a vobis impetratâ, quasdam

area of which is about one-third of the whole site of the Press, had formerly been an inn called "The Cardinal's Hat," or "The Cardinal's Cap." It extended from Trumpington Street on the east to the Black Lion Yard on the west; on the north it adjoined the Printing-office then in use, and on the south a portion of it reached as far as Mill Lane[1]. The space thus acquired—the boundaries of which have been indicated by dotted lines on the plan (fig. 2)—was large enough to contain the additional buildings required, without waiting for the acquisition of the adjoining houses. Moreover, the condition of the older buildings, as evidenced by the following Report, dated 29 June, 1824, rendered immediate action necessary:

"We, the undersigned Syndics of the Press, having been requested to enquire into the general state of its concerns, have in the course of our enquiries directed our attention to the condition of the Buildings, which we find to be so dilapidated and so inadequate to the effectual conducting of the business, that the University will at no distant period be obliged to incur a very considerable expense in rebuilding the premises situated near Catharine Hall, as well as in making essential alterations in those on the opposite side of Silver Street. In making this statement we do not merely express our own opinion, but also that of an eminent London Printer, to whose assistance we have found it necessary to have recourse in the prosecution of our enquiries."

The Syndics therefore lost no time in obtaining plans from Mr James Walter, Architect. They were exhibited to the Senate in October 1825, and were evidently approved of, for early in the following year (26 April, 1826), the Senate authorized the sealing of a contract with Mr Spicer Crowe, Builder. The buildings specified, consisting of the printing-house on the west side of the quadrangle, and a dwelling-house for the printer fronting Mill Lane, were completed in January, 1827[2].

domos illius quinque mille et sexaginta librarum pretio redimerent: Placeat Vobis, ut pactio ista rata ac firma habeatur, atque ut summa prædicta e cista communi, usibus istis destinanda, erogetur." The conveyance was sealed 6 May, 1824.]

[1] [In 1792 the southern boundary is described as the "Common Ditch" and the "King's Ditch." The Inn had been established from very early times. It is mentioned in King's College Mundum Book, 1492—93 (*Feoda et Regarda*): 'et sol' pro vino apud Cardynall Hatte...xij^{d}.' In 1670 it became the property of Cornelius Austin, Joyner, whose work has been so often met with.]

[2] [These particulars are derived from documents preserved in the Registry of the University. Various hatchings have been employed upon the plan (fig. 2) to denote the work of different periods.]

We have next to relate the circumstances which led to the connexion of the name of Mr William Pitt with the University Press. It has been already related in the History of the Senate House, that the University had shewn a disposition to honour his memory by allowing his statue to be placed in the Senate House; and subsequently, in 1813, by accepting £1000 offered by the committee for managing the statue, to found the Pitt Scholarship. These circumstances may have induced the London Pitt Club to turn their attention to Cambridge when considering the purposes to which the surplus funds at their disposal might best be devoted. It is said that the Bishop of Gloucester and Bristol, James Henry Monk, D.D., who had been Professor of Greek from 1808 to 1823, and would therefore have had ample opportunity of learning the condition of the University Press, was the first to suggest the propriety of connecting Mr Pitt's name with an extension of it. The first definite proposal was contained in the following letter addressed to the Vice-Chancellor, John Lamb, M.A., Master of Corpus Christi College, by the Marquis Camden, Chairman of the Committee and Chancellor of the University:

"Arlington Street, May 25th, 1824.

Sir,

I have the Honor to inform you that I am just returned from a Meeting of the Committee appointed to consider of the disposal of the surplus of Money subscribed, many years ago, for the Erection of a Statue to the memory of Mr Pitt[1].

I am, now, authorized by that Committee to state to you, Sir, that which I had the Honor of personally communicating to you at Cambridge: 'the disposition of that Committee to recommend to a general Meeting of Subscribers to the Fund above-mentioned the Disposal of a considerable Sum of Money for the Erection of an handsome Building connected with the University Press at Cambridge;' but, as it will be necessary to state to the general Meeting how far the University is disposed to find and provide a proper Scite for the erecting such Building, near or opposite to Pembroke College, I now trouble you on that subject, and I request you will have the goodness to inform me how far I may be authorized to inform the General Meeting of the Disposition of the University to find and provide a proper Scite as above-mentioned

[1] [Annual Register for 1802, Vol. xliv. p. 184. "A subscription for the purpose of erecting a statue of [Mr Pitt] was set on foot, and was almost immediately filled to a considerable amount. But at his instance, who could not receive such honours during his life-time, and on maturer consideration, the sum so raised was vested in the public funds in the names of trustees to accumulate till his demise, and then to be appropriated to the fulfilment of the original intention."]

for the erecting of an handsome Building, which the Committee is desirous should be erected on such a scale as to be a distinguished Ornament to the University, and tend to perpetuate the Name and Memory of Mr Pitt.

I have the Honor to remain, Sir,

Your most obedient humble Servant

CAMDEN.

P.S. The general meeting is appointed for the 11th of June."

The next letter shews that the answer of the Vice-Chancellor had been favourable to the project; and that the subscribers, on their part, had offered no objection to it:

"Arlington Street, June 21st 1824.

Sir,

I have the Honor of enclosing to you the Copy of a Resolution entered into by the general Meeting of Subscribers for the Erection of a Statue of Mr Pitt.

This Resolution was unanimously adopted by those who composed that general Meeting, and they felt they could not devote the surplus of the Fund at their Disposal to any object so satisfactorily as to that which is adopted by them, and to which they are led to hope the University of Cambridge is equally inclined.

They feel that it will be a most flattering addition to the Character and reputation of Mr Pitt that his Name should be connected with that Press from which emanate works of enlightened Literature and profound Science, and they trust they shall be enabled to add to the magnificent Improvements now proceeding at Cambridge by the Erection of a Building which will adorn and decorate the University.

They also trust that University will feel an high Degree of Satisfaction in enrolling the Name of Pitt among its Benefactors, more especially as that eminent Person mainly attributed his success in public Life to his Education within its Precincts.

I have the honor to remain, Sir

Your most obedient humble servant

CAMDEN.

At a Meeting of the Subscribers for erecting a Statue of the late Right Hon. William Pitt, called by Public Advertisement, and held at the Thatched House Tavern, on Friday, the 18th of June, 1824:

Marquis Camden in the Chair:

It was proposed by the Lord President of the Council, seconded by the Lord Archbishop of Canterbury, and unanimously resolved:

'That the surplus of the Fund, after defraying the Expense of the Statue in Hanover-Square, as resolved at the former Meeting on the 11th instant, be applied to the Erection of a handsome and appropriate

Building at Cambridge, connected with the University Press; such building to bear the name of Mr Pitt.

That the Committee be desired to take the necessary steps for carrying into execution this Resolution.'"

The question was referred to a Syndicate which had been appointed in the previous May "to consider what practicable improvements in the Town of Cambridge would be beneficial and ornamental to the University." They suggested (28 June) that the above Resolution should be at once communicated to the Senate, and that the Vice-Chancellor; William Webb, D.D., Master of Clare Hall; John Croft, M.A., Christ's College; and William Whewell, M.A., Trinity College, should be appointed a Syndicate "with power to purchase houses or leases of houses for the purpose of making exchanges with the Proprietors of the houses between Silver Street and Mill Lane fronting towards Trumpington Street, the sum to be so expended not to exceed £5000." This Grace passed the Senate without opposition, 1 July, 1824; and 8 December following a second Grace authorized the Syndics to expend a further sum of £3000 on the same objects.

Four years elapsed before the Committee began to consider seriously the nature of the proposed building. In the course of 1828, however, seven architects were communicated with, and asked to send in designs in conformity with plans and specifications submitted to them[1]. We do not know who these architects were, or how many complied with this request, but early in 1829 the Committee made choice of the design submitted to them by Mr Blore, and the Marquis Camden introduced him to the Vice-Chancellor in the following letter:

"Arlington Street, April 5th 1829.

Sir,

I have been encouraged by the Bishop of Lincoln [John Kaye, D.D., Master of Christ's College] to address you on the Subject of the Press at Cambridge, and I venture to give this Letter to Mr Blore the Architect to be delivered to you by him.

The Committee who have had the Management of the Money devoted to the object of the Press, and who are desirous it should be

[1] [Letter from the Secretary of the Committee to Mr Blore, dated 4 December, 1828. This letter, and the others which passed between the Committee, the University, and Mr Blore, with the Minutes of the Committee, have been kindly lent to me by my friend, the Rev. E. W. Blore, M.A., Fellow of Trinity College. The three letters from the Marquis Camden to the Vice-Chancellor are preserved in the Registry of the University.]

connected with the Name of Mr Pitt, have decided upon a Plan designed by Mr Blore. That Person is going to Cambridge, upon other Business entrusted to him there, and during the Period he is there I have thought it desirable he should confer with the Authorities at Cambridge on the Subject of Accommodation which may be to be found in the proposed Building for the Business connected with the Press itself, as that subject has frequently been mentioned to the Committee.

It is necessary to premise, that the Committee is desirous that an handsome Room should be included in the Design, together with a staircase leading to it, but that the Committee would be most desirous any Accommodation could be given to the Press in the Building to be erected which did not interfere with those Parts which they think should be ornamented.

Mr Parker, now employed by the University, met Mr Blore here, and appeared to think great and sufficient accommodation can be given to the Press consistent with what the Committee deem proper as to Decoration.

Keeping in view that wish of the Committee I beg in their Name to inform you that every possible anxiety is felt by those who compose it to meet the liberal conduct of the University as connected with this object. The Bishop of Lincoln and the Master of Clare Hall have corresponded with me on this subject and it is at the suggestion of the former I beg to repeat I have ventured to address you and to recommend Mr Blore to your notice.

I have the honour to remain [etc.]

CAMDEN.

The Vice Chancellor of Cambridge."

When these plans were drawn, the frontage towards Trumpington Street, which the Syndics had succeeded in purchasing, consisted only of the properties on each side of Mr Nutter's messuage, acquired in 1825 and 1827 respectively, and of the house at the corner of Silver Street, acquired in 1825. The width of the frontage available for a building was therefore hardly equal to the mean width of the original purchase[1], and Mr Blore's building had been designed for this restricted site. In the course of 1830, however, the purchase of the remaining houses was either effected or rendered certain[2], and the University authorised the Committee (3 July) "to erect at their own expence, under the superintendence of the Syndics of the Press, a New Building to be called the Pitt Press, between Silver Street and Mill Lane." Mr Blore was asked to furnish new

[1] [The dates of the purchase of the different houses composing the frontage are written on the plan (fig. 2).]

[2] [It appears from a study of the Graces of the Senate and of the University Accounts, that the total cost of these purchases was £11,925. 14*s*. 4*d*.]

designs in conformity with what Lord Camden terms "the new state of things," but he appears to have made objections, which were overcome with difficulty, and it was not until the beginning of the following year (3 March, 1831) that the Committee made the following Minute:

"The Committee desire Mr Blore to prepare new Plans suited to the more extended Site now offered; and for this purpose to proceed to Cambridge, and confer with the Authorities and the Printer there, and ascertain the whole Extent of the particular Accommodation that may be required; and when he has completed the Elevation of the Building and Plans of the interior Arrangement, and received the Approbation of the Syndicate of such Elevation and Plans, that he will wait upon the Committee at their next Meeting, for the purpose of laying before them such Plans so approved.

They further inform Mr Blore, that the whole Site between Mill Lane and Silver Street has been obtained by the University, and that the Plan which the Committee now direct him to prepare must comprehend a Design for the Elevation of the whole Front. That part which is to be erected at the Expence of the Committee to be begun as soon as possible: the other, which the University propose to build, will be to be erected at their convenience and also at their expence.

They likewise inform Mr Blore that it will be necessary in the Estimate of the Building to limit the Cost of that part of the Building which is to be erected at the Expence of the Committee to the sum originally mentioned viz. £9000. The probable Expence to the University should also be stated with accuracy to that body.

Mr Blore was called in and the Committee instructed him accordingly, and they also desired that Mr Martin [their Secretary] would write to the Vice Chancellor, informing him that Mr Blore had been instructed to proceed to Cambridge, and to make the fullest communication to the Syndicate upon every part of this Subject."

These directions were immediately carried out, and at the end of April

"The Drawings for the front of the Pitt Press approved by the Press Syndicate at Cambridge were submitted to the Committee, who approved generally of the same, and resolved that the Building should be erected agreably to the above designs; and Mr Blore received instructions to take the necessary measures for carrying the resolution of the Committee into immediate effect[1]."

Our information respecting the share of the work to be borne by the University is unfortunately extremely defective. It would seem that the first proposal of the Pitt Committee made in 1824, included all the buildings required for the com-

[1] [Minute of the Committee, 25 April, 1831.]

pletion of the Press; but that before many months had elapsed it was discovered that they would be unable to expend so large a sum as they had at first supposed, because it had turned out that the statue in Hanover Square would be more costly than was at first supposed[1]. It therefore became necessary for the University to defray the cost of those buildings which could not be included in the range next Trumpington Street. A Grace sanctioning an outlay not exceeding £2000 for this purpose passed the Senate 11 June, 1831, and the building which forms the north side of the quadrangle was at once commenced[2], from a design by Mr Blore, and completed in March, 1832.

The first stone of the façade towards Trumpington Street was laid by the Marquis Camden with the usual solemnities, on Tuesday, 18 October, 1831. It bore the following inscription:

IN · HONOREM ·
GVLIELMI . PITT ·
HVJVS · ACADEMIÆ · OLIM · ALVMNI ·
VIRI · ILLVSTRIORIS · QVAM · VT · VLLO · INDIGEAT · PRÆCONIO ·
ÆQVALES · ET · AMICI · SVPERSTITES ·
CVRATORES · PECVNIARVM · TVM · AB · IPSIS · TVM · AB · ALIIS ·
FAMÆ · EJVS · TVENDÆ ·
ERGO · COLLATARVM ·
HOC · ÆDIFICIVM · EXTRVI · VOLVERVNT ·
LAPIDEM · AVSPICALEM · SOLENNIBVS · CÆREMONIIS · STATVIT ·
VIR · NOBILISSIMVS ·
IOANNES · JEFFRIES · MARCHIO · CAMDEN ·
ASSISTENTIBVS · EI · HONORATISSIMIS · COMITIBVS · CLARENDON ·
ET · HARROWBY ·
HONORABILI · ADMODVM · BARONE · FARNBOROVGH ·
HENRICO · BANKES · ARMIGERO ·
TOTA · INSPECTANTE · ET · PLAVDENTE · ACADEMIA ·
DECIMO · QVINTO · CAL · NOVEMB · ANNO · M · DCCC · XXXI ·
GEORGIO · THACKERAY · S · T · P · COLL · REGAL · PRÆS ·
ITERVM · PROCANCELLARIO ·

[1] [Minute of the Improvement Syndicate, 26 November, 1824. "The Master of Clare Hall stated that a letter had been received from Marquis Camden intimating that since his former communication it appeared that more money would be required for the Statue of Mr Pitt than was at first contemplated, and that in consequence there would be a less surplus applicable to the Pitt Press." The statue, in bronze, by Chantrey, cost £7000. It was set up in 1831.]

[2] [Mr Blore's notice inviting tenders "for erecting additional Press and Ware Rooms," dated 28 June, 1831, appears in the Cambridge Chronicle for 1 July, 1831.]

The building then commenced occupies the whole frontage towards Trumpington Street. It consists of a range of chambers in three floors, with a square central tower of considerable height, under which is a wide passage into the quadrangle beyond. Above this passage is a large and lofty room, intended for the meetings of the Press Syndicate, but now used as the Registry of the University. The style of the building is Late Perpendicular; the material, stone towards the street, and brick towards the interior quadrangle. It was at first intended that the north and south ends also should be of brick, but this was changed for stone while the building was proceeding. Moreover in the first design the four pinnacles of the central tower were not all of the same size, the two towards the street being larger than those towards the court; and the roof was of a higher pitch. These features were all altered in deference to the suggestions of George Peacock, M.A., Fellow of Trinity College. The work occupied about eighteen months, and the total cost was £10,711. 8*s*. 9*d*. On Tuesday, 28 April, 1833, the Marquis Camden solemnly delivered the key to the Vice-Chancellor, William Webb, D.D., Master of Clare Hall. The following account[1] of the ceremony is worth quotation:

"The Pitt Press having been completed, Tuesday last was appointed for the Vice Chancellor to receive the key of the building from the Marquis Camden and a deputation of the Pitt Committee.

"A Congregation was held in the Senate House at eleven o'clock, after which a procession was formed, consisting of nearly all the members at present resident in the University. Having arrived at the building, the Marquis Camden, accompanied by the members of the Committee, proceeded into the grand entrance hall, and having invited the Vice-Chancellor to the door, spoke as follows:

"'Mr Vice-Chancellor and Gentlemen of the University of Cambridge: Whilst I place in your hands the key of this building, to be disposed of for the purposes for which it was erected as the University of Cambridge may now direct, I wish that it had fallen to some other of my friends and colleagues to address you upon this occasion, so interesting to us, and I trust, by the mode in which we are met by the University, equally interesting to them; but I do not pretend to deny that I have personally felt so much interest during the progress of this undertaking that I have the highest satisfaction in thus witnessing its conclusion.

"'The idea of connecting the name of Mr Pitt with the Press of that University to which he owed his education and so much of his fame, was met by all parties with

[1] [Abridged from the Cambridge Chronicle, 1 May, 1833.]

zeal and enthusiasm. The University have displayed an activity and liberality in providing this magnificent site which could only have been prompted by an admiration for the character of Mr Pitt. The Committee, animated by a personal respect and affection towards their contemporary, have endeavoured to cause to be erected on this site, such a building as might prove an addition to the other great improvements already perfected in this place, and which, from its peculiar destination, will unite the name of Mr Pitt with all those works of religion, morality, and science, which will in future emanate from it, and diffuse throughout the world the connexion of his name with erudition and learning. The manner in which the University have met the efforts of that Committee of which I am the unworthy representative on this occasion, deserves their warmest acknowledgments, and, if it were necessary, imprints still more deeply their respect for the place of their education.

"'Sir, you have caused this ceremony to be attended by all the undergraduates as well as by the dignitaries of the University. Let me call the peculiar attention of all to this ceremony, and allow me to impress on the undergraduates that we, Mr Pitt's contemporaries, have been witnesses of his uniting the closest study with the utmost cheerfulness, and, when not employed in solving the most abstruse problems, he has engaged the admiration of his friends and companions, by the liveliest sallies of wit and imagination. Let his example stimulate you to the greatest exertion during your residence in this place, so well calculated to provide for your instruction in every department of literature and science.'

"His lordship then presented the key of the building to the Vice-Chancellor, who said:

"'It is most gratifying to me, my Lord, to be the person upon whom devolves the honour of receiving at your lordship's hands the key which puts the University in possession of a building for which it is indebted to the kindness and liberality of yourself and your illustrious colleagues. Like that erected in our sister University, which bears the name of one of the greatest statesmen of former days, that of Clarendon, this is dedicated to the memory of him whose counsels upheld, and whose guidance preserved, this country amid the torrent of anarchy and infidelity which overwhelmed the neighbouring nations, raising it to a dignity and eminence which rendered it the refuge and sanctuary of religion and virtue. These were the principles which guided his policy; his loyalty to his king was founded upon his reverence for, and his duty to his God; for he felt that this kingdom could flourish only through the union of Church and State. What more appropriate monument then could be erected to the memory of Pitt than this building, the chief purpose and object of which is to send forth to the world the Word of God; and could he, with prophetic eye, when residing in yon neighbouring college, whose proudest boast is to number him among her sons—could he have beheld such a structure, bearing his name, raised for such a purpose, and erected by such friends, even his own eloquence would have scarce sufficed to express the feelings of his heart. My Lord, the edifice with which you have adorned this University, and the illustrious name it bears, will add a fresh stimulus to our exertions in the dissemination of truth, the extension of science, and the advancement of religious knowledge; and I humbly trust that nothing will ever issue from these walls but such works as may conduce to the furtherance of these important objects.

"'My Lords and gentlemen, in the name of the University of Cambridge I beg most cordially to thank you for this building, which forms so noble an addition to those which are already the pride and ornament of this University, and for which we are indebted to the munificence of a long and splendid train of royal and illustrious benefactors.'

"At the conclusion of the Vice-Chancellor's speech, the deputation, and a considerable number of members of the University, passed through the entrance hall to an ante-room at the foot of the principal staircase, where a handsome printing-press had been fixed for the occasion, from which Marquis Camden and the other members of the deputation printed off a copy of the inscription on the foundation-stone.

"The company then went upstairs into the Syndicate Room, where they partook of a cold collation given by the Press Syndicate, and afterwards returned to the Senate House[1]."

Since this time the buildings have been gradually extended in various directions as increased business rendered further space necessary. In 1863 certain cottages in Black Lion Yard were pulled down, and their site utilised for a foundry; in 1871—72 an addition to the machine-room and warehouses was built on ground previously occupied by houses in a small court called Diamond Court, opening from Silver Street; and in 1877—78 a large building in three floors and a basement was erected in the south-west corner of the quadrangle under the superintendence of W. M. Fawcett, M.A., architect, on a site purchased in 1866 from Ebenezer Bird Foster, Esq.[2]

[1] [After the completion of the new buildings, the ground and buildings of the old Press, which, after several renewals of the lease, had been bought by the University from Queens' College in 1819 for £750 (Grace, 26 March, 1819), were resold to Queens' College for £3500 (Grace, 2 December, 1835), and in 1836 were conveyed to Catharine Hall (Vol. II. p. 85).]

[2] [Grace of the Senate, 16 June, 1866.]

CHAPTER II.

History of the Museums and Lecture-Rooms for Natural Science.

[The site of these Museums is bounded on the south by Pembroke Street, and Downing Street, formerly Dowdiver Lane; on the east by the open space now called S. Andrew's Hill, but formerly Hog Hill, or the Hog Market, or the Beast Market, and Corn Exchange Street, formerly Slaughter House Lane, or Fair Yard Lane; on the north by the Corn Exchange, the estate of E. J. Mortlock, Esq., and some dwelling houses; and on the west by Free School Lane, formerly Luthburne Lane, and the estate belonging to the trustees of Stephen Perse, M.D., commonly called the Perse School.

The principal portion of this ground was bought, 16 July 1760, by Richard Walker, D.D., then Vice-Master of Trinity College, from Richard Whish, Vintner, of Cambridge, and conveyed by him to the University 25 August, 1762, in trust for the purposes of a Botanic Garden. His motives for making this donation, and for selecting this particular piece of ground, have been recorded by himself[1]:

"We have generally had Titular Professors of Botany, but nothing worth mentioning left behind them: Dr *Martyn* indeed within our memory, laboured much to bring this Science into repute; read public Lectures for several years; perambulated the Country with his Scholars, shewing them the *Cambridgeshire* Plants where Mr *Ray* had described them to grow, and making many additions to that Catalogue: but this Gentleman's private affairs took him from us, much esteemed for his great knowledge of Plants[2].

[1] [A short Account of the late Donation of a Botanic Garden to the University of Cambridge. 4to. Cambridge 1763. The pamphlet is anonymous, but is referred to by Dr Walker in his Will, dated 14 January, 1764, as "my account of the Garden, printed in the year 1763." For Dr Walker's Will, with other documents referring to the Botanic Garden, see Endowments of the University of Cambridge, pp. 246—261. The originals of all the documents referred to in the text are preserved in the Registry of the University.]

[2] [John Martyn, Professor of Botany 1733—61, began to lecture at Cambridge in 1727, on the declared incompetence of Richard Bradley, who had been elected the first Professor in 1724. He was succeeded by his son Thomas Martyn, elected 2 February, 1762. See Memoirs of John Martyn, and of Thomas Martyn, Professors of Botany in the University of Cambridge. By G. C. Gorham, B.D. 8vo. 1830.]

About fifteen years ago, the learned Physician Dr *Heberden*, was so kind as to oblige the University with a Course of Experiments, upon such plants as he then found amongst us, in order to shew their uses in Medicine[1]. This was entering into the practical and principal part of Botany, to which we had been strangers, since the abovementioned Association. But this Doctor's great Abilities in his profession soon after called him from us, much lamenting the want of a Public Garden, furnished with sufficient variety of Plants for making the like Experiments.

These considerations, particularly Dr *Heberden's* most useful attempt, put the present Vice-Master of Trinity College upon finding out a proper situation for such a Garden; who, with the assistance of his Friend Mr [Philip] *Miller*[2], of *Chelsea*, called in for his great experience and judgement in such an affair, after several treaties that failed, at last pitched upon and purchased the *Mansion House* in *Free School Lane* (formerly part of an old Monastry) with near five Acres of Garden about it, well walled round, quite open to the South, conveniently sheltered by the Town on the other quarters, with an antient water-course through the midst of it[3]."

The conveyance to Dr Walker divides the site into four sections[4]:

[1] "All that House and Ground lying and being on the West side of Fair Yard Lane in Cambridge, at the South end of the said lane, containing in Length 24 feet and in Depth 60 feet within the walls;

And also all that Close called the Tainter Yard, as it is now walled in, formerly demised to Henry Stegg, Gentleman...lying and being between the Orchard late in the tenure of James Thornbrow Junr. on

1 [Dr Heberden's lectures were delivered "about the year 1748." Ibid. p. 117.]

2 [Author of The Gardener's Dictionary, first published in 1731.]

3 [A proposal to lay out a Botanic Garden had been made in 1588 by John Gerard, author of the celebrated "Herbal," to William Cecil, Lord Burleigh, then Chancellor of the University, but it is doubtful whether the suggestion was ever conveyed to the University. His letter is printed by Cooper: Annals, ii. 458. In 1695—96 the scheme was revived, and the Vice-Chancellor (John Eachard, D.D., Master of S. Catharine's Hall) sets down in his Accounts: *Expences uncertaine;* "Spent in London about October 20th about the Physick-Garden £2. 0. 0. Laid out towards the Physick-Garden as appears in the booke £48. 2. 7." Part of this sum was probably spent in obtaining the advice of "Mr Loudon the King's Gardener," who visited Cambridge three times in 1696. The Cambridge Portfolio, p. 81, quoting a note of expenses drawn up by Dr Eachard. The ground, the situation of which has not been recorded, was actually laid out, for in the University Accounts for 1696—97 (with a note that the items refer to the previous year) we find: "To Robert Grumbold for measuring the intended Physick-garden...05. 0. 0." In 1731 an attempt was made to buy the estate of a Mr Brownell of Willingham (Life of Martyn, *ut supra*, p. 114), but without success.]

4 [They have been numbered for convenience of reference.]

the North part, and the Common Highway on the South part, the East side containing 75 yards, the South side 126 yards, and the West side 16 yards, within the walls...."

The lease of this, held from the Corporation of Cambridge, was assigned to Dr Walker by the vendor of the rest of the property, who, in consideration of £1600, further conveys:

[2] "All that freehold Capital Messuage or Tenement heretofore part or reputed part of the Saint Austin Fryery scituate standing and being in the parish of Saint Edward...in a certain street or Lane there called Free School Lane, formerly in the tenure or occupation of Thomas Buck..."

[3] "Also all that Garden Ground containing by Estimation one acre and three roods...situate in the Parish of S. Edward aforesaid with the messuage or Tenement therein standing as the same were heretofore in the occupation of Thomas Brewer late of John Thornborough..."

[4] "And also all that moiety or full half part of and in all those several Messuages or Tenements scituate and being in Free School Lane ...now or late in the Tenure or Occupation of William Bridges, Anthony Knights, William Belsher, John Conde, John Key, and Francis Clarke ...all which said last mentioned premisses were heretofore purchased by the said Thomas Buck of Theophilus Burdet etc."

The property held on lease from the Corporation [1] was leased to the University 28 March, 1783, for 999 years, and the lease, to which a map is fortunately appended, describes the larger portion of it as:

"that piece or parcel of ground heretofore a Close, and called the Tenter Yard, now converted into and used as part of the Botanic Garden..., as the same is now walled in on the East, South, and West parts, containing by Admeasurement in length on the East side, from the South East corner of the said Messuage[1]...next Hog Hill to the Common High-Way, Two Hundred and Thirteen Feet; on the South Side, next the said High Way leading towards Pembroke Hall, Three Hundred and seventy Eight Feet; and on the West Side, Forty One Feet; And the North side thereof Extendeth and runneth along on the outside of the Ditch, where a Wall lately stood from the North End of the said West side through the said piece of Ground to that part of the same Ditch which is opposite to the South West Corner of the Garden belonging to the said Messuage..., And from the outside of the said Ditch at that Place to the said South West Corner of the said Garden, and from thence along by the South side of the said Garden, and South End of the said Messuage or Tenement, to the North End of the East Wall next Fair Yard Lane aforesaid."

This description, though the measurements cannot be exactly fitted to the ground in its present state, enables us

1 [This messuage is the house in Fair Yard Lane [1].]

to identify the close in question with the piece shewn by Loggan (fig. 2) on the south side of the King's Ditch. The house and garden-ground included in the lease were situated at the north-east corner of the close, beyond the King's Ditch (fig. 1). The lease describes them as:

"All that messuage or Tenement, situate and being on the West side of the South End of Fair Yard Lane in the Parish of Saint

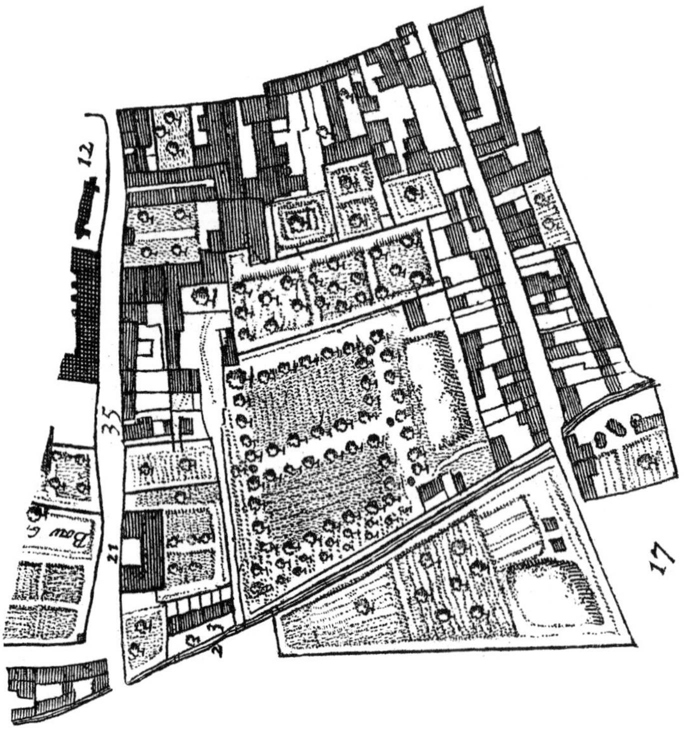

Fig. 2. Site of the New Museums, enlarged from Loggan's map of Cambridge, 1688. The following explanation of the references is given on the margin of the original: 12. St Benett's Church; 17. The Hogg Market; 21. The Free Schoole; 23. The Almes houses; 35. Free School Lane.

Edwards,...containing by Admeasurement in length next the said Lane twenty six feet, and in Depth fifteen Feet, with the Garden Ground lying behind and belonging to the same messuage, the East end of which said Garden Ground next the said Messuage.... containeth... Twenty Six Feet; the West End Thirty Eight Feet Eight Inches; the

North Side Forty Eight Feet Eight Inches from the corner of the North End of the said Messuage; And the South side Fifty Four feet, from the corner of the South End of the same Messuage."

This property was leased by the University, 15 March, 1786, to John Mortlock, Esq., for 999 years, at an annual rent of one shilling[1]. It subsequently passed through several hands,

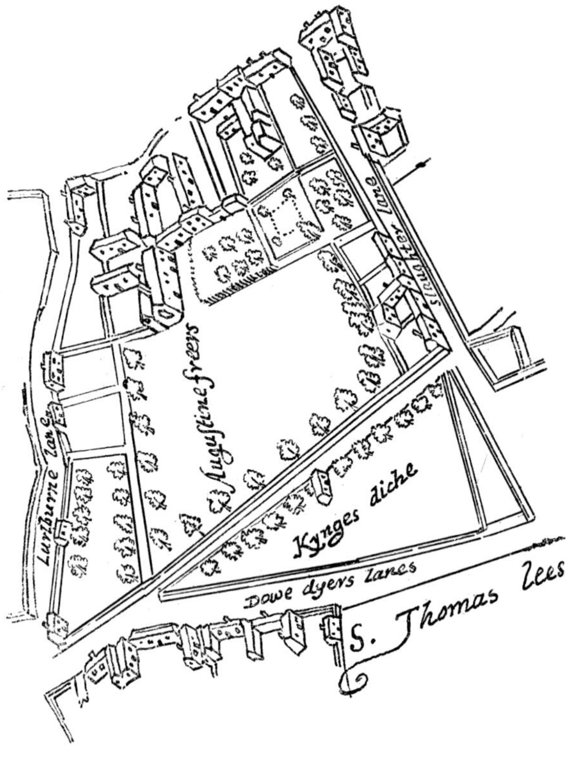

Fig. 3. Site of the New Museums, reduced from Hammond's map of Cambridge, 1592.

and was finally repurchased by the University in 1873 for £505. 12*s.* 3*d.*

The dimensions and the exact position of the "messuage

[1] [It was at first agreed (Grace, 16 December, 1785) that the property then used as the workhouse of S. Edward's Parish should be leased to Mr Mortlock for 40 years; but, by a second Grace, 8 March, 1786, the term was extended to 999 years from Lady Day, 1783.]

reputed part of the Saint Austin Friery" [2], are unfortunately not given in any of the documents relating to it; but a little research will enable us to ascertain them approximately. The messuage is stated to be "in a certain Street or Lane called Free School Lane." It is evident therefore that it had a frontage to the Lane; and Cole, writing in 1746, notes that it was situated "just behind the East End of St Benedict's Church and Corpus Christi College," as has been already related (p. 131); and the sketch which he gives of it, dated 1770, there reproduced, was taken "from a Chamber Window in that College, and just opposite to it." In 1783 the house had become ruinous, and the Governors of the Garden appointed by Dr Walker's Will were authorised by Grace of the Senate (21 February[1]) to sell it to John Mortlock, Esq., for £150. The conveyance to him, dated 24 June, 1784, describes the property as:

"All that the site and ground whereon the capital messuage or Tenement, heretofore part, or reputed part, of the Austin Friery in Free School Lane,...lately stood, together with the Court Yard or Ground lying before it next to Free School Lane aforesaid, as the same Site and Ground are now inclosed and seperated from the Botanic Garden there ...by a Brick wall erected around it by the said John Mortlock;

And also all that messuage or Tenement, Yard and Garden thereto adjoining now let out on lease to William Roberts Esquire and in the tenure or occupation of Robert Gee Gentleman...except and always reserved unto the [University] the Messuage or Tenement now in the occupation of John Salton the Gardner of the said Botanic Garden, and a passage of sixteen feet in width leading from Free School Lane aforesaid to the said Botanic Garden."

The ground leased to Mr Roberts is described in the lease to him, dated 27 June, 1772, as:

"All that piece...of ground...on the north side of the Court Yard of the Botanic Garden estate...(on part whereof certain Tenements were formerly set and builded and which have been lately taken down)... together with full and free liberty of Ingress and Regress to and into the same by and through a certain way or passage leading thereto out of the lane called Free School Lane."

[1] [The Grace appointing the Governors of the Garden to be Syndics to settle the whole question, begins with the following sentence: "Cum ex Fundatoris præscripto Jus vobis sit, Ædes quaslibet Domosque in Usum Horti Botanici assignatas vendendi, aliasque vicissim vel Terras vel Tenementa earum Loco coemendi: Cumque Conditiones certæ quædam proponuntur, quibus Domus illa præcipua et primaria, quæ vetustate fere collapsa corruit, in altera cedat jura, et subruenda funditus tradatur."]

The passage sixteen feet wide reserved in the above conveyance is known to have been situated on the north border of the existing property (fig. 1); and the portion sold was therefore to the north of it. This may be identified, so far as the frontage is concerned, with a piece of garden-ground 44 feet wide, now the property of Mr Mortlock, which intervenes between the north wall of the Cavendish Laboratory and certain dwelling houses, which, though modern, are on the site of ancient ones. The extent of it eastwards cannot now be ascertained.

The "capital messuage," which Cole decides to have been the Refectory of the Augustinians, and which is evidently represented on Hammond's map (fig. 3) by the large building at the north-west corner of the ground there designated "Augustine freers," must have formed a portion of the west side of the conventual quadrangle. When Mr Mortlock's present stables (fig. 1) were built in 1873, considerable remains were discovered of a building which, from its architectural style, clearly belonged to the same convent, and probably formed part of the east side. As no remains or foundations have ever been found, so far as we know, on the south side, it may be safely conjectured that the church was on the north side, the south side being left open. The garden-ground [3], belonging to the same house, extended, according to Hammond, as far as the King's Ditch (fig. 3).

The history of the tenements in Free School Lane [4] is extremely obscure. They formed part of Mr Buck's estate, and when the rest of the property was conveyed to Dr Walker, it was intended that they, or at any rate some considerable portion of them, should continue to belong to Mr Richard Whish. By an error, however, they were included in the conveyance, and, in order to secure their reservation, Dr Walker released them by a separate deed, 25 July, 1760[1]. They subsequently became an Inn called "The Three Cups." In after years we find them divided into two dwelling-houses, with an office behind one of them, which was bought by the University 24 December, 1856, the houses being bought in 1862 and 1871 respectively. The three dwelling-houses to the south of them

[1] [This deed was sent to the Registry of the University with the other title-deeds of the property.]

were bought in 1872, 1874, and 1875[1]. These latter had always been quite distinct from the original property.

In order to complete the history of the site, before proceeding to that of the buildings, it may be here mentioned that the warehouses at the north-east corner, under lease from the Corporation of Cambridge to Messrs Headly, were purchased in 1881; the tenements to the north of the cottages purchased in 1873, as above related, in 1883; and the intervening piece in 1884. None of these require any special description.

The principal buildings which stood on the ground originally bought by Dr Walker were: (1) greenhouses and other buildings required for the Botanic Garden, the cost of which was principally defrayed by subscription; (2) a Lecture-Room for the Professor of Botany. Dr Walker, in his *Regulations for the Botanic Garden*, had directed:

"That the room on the ground floor of the principal Messuage, with an apartment at the end of it, be appropriated for the reading of Lectures on Botany, and for the use of the Reader; that the unfurnished room above-stairs be set apart for the reception of Books on Botany and other Sciences relating thereto; and also of a *Hortus Siccus* or Collection of dried Plants; and the tapestry room above-stairs be for the use of the Governors when they meet there, and that the plaister building below be in part pulled down, and fitted up to make a suitable apartment and bed-chamber for the Curator to reside in[2]."

These directions were carried out so far that Professor Thomas Martyn was able to lecture in what was then called "the great house[3]." After it had been sold, as above related, in 1784, it became the duty of the University to accommodate the Professor of Botany in some other place. The Jacksonian Professor, moreover, appointed for the first time in 1783, had no lecture-room, and, as the founder, Richard Jackson, had directed

[1] [The extent of these houses has been shewn on the plan (fig. 1).]

[2] [Endowments of the University, *ut supra*, p. 250.]

[3] [Cole has preserved the following advertisement, from the Cambridge Chronicle of 26 March, 1763 (MSS. xxxiii. Add. MSS. Mus. Brit. 5834).

"Sid. Coll. Mar. 23. 1763.

"On Monday 18 April, at the great House in Free Schole-Lane, will begin a Course of Lectures in Botany, by T. Martyn M.A. Prof. The first Course 2 Guineas, the 2d. Course 1 Guinea, Ever after Gratis. The Lectures will begin exactly at 2 o'clock. Gentlemen who propose to attend are desired to send in their names.

Note. The Professor intends to read gratis to those who subscribe ten Guineas towards the Support of the Botanic Garden."]

his trustees to augment the salary of the "Head Gardener of the University Physic Garden," and had enumerated Botany among the subjects which his Professor might select for investigation, it appeared natural that he should deliver his lectures in or near the Botanic Garden. A Syndicate was therefore appointed, 26 May, 1784, consisting of the five Governors of the Garden; Thomas Martyn, M.A., Professor of Botany; Isaac Milner, M.A., Jacksonian Professor[1]; William Elliston, D.D., Master of Sidney Sussex College; Robert Tyrwhitt, M.A., Jesus College; James Lambert, M.A., Trinity College; Mark Antony Stephenson, M.A., Clare Hall, "to erect a building wherein the Professor of Botany and the Jacksonian Professor may deliver public lectures, provided that they limit the cost of such building to £1500."

These Syndics did not make up their minds hastily, for it was not until the beginning of December that they selected a site, and drew up the following Minute:

"3 December 1784. Agreed by the Syndics appointed to erect a Botanical and Chemical Lecture Room that the peice of Ground at the South East corner of the Botanical Garden is a proper Spot and be therefore accepted, and the Vice Chancellor is desired to apply to Mr Brettingham for a plan[2]."

Mr Brettingham's plan, which was sent in the course of 1785[3], was evidently not approved of, and no further action appears to have been taken until February, 1786, when the same Syndics adopted a plan suggested by Mr Bradwell, bricklayer, and Mr Kaye, carpenter, both of Cambridge. These workmen undertook to erect the building for £1406, but this sum was found insufficient, and early in the following year the Syndics obtained leave from the Senate to expend a further sum of £200[4].

1 [In 1782 Mr Milner had obtained leave from Queens' College to fit up as a Laboratory a portion of the offices on the west side of the River Cam.]

2 [Minutes of Syndicates 1778—1803, preserved in the Registry of the University. For Mr Brettingham see above, p. 74.]

3 [Univ. Accounts, 1784—85: *Exp. Ordinary and Extraordinary*: "Plans and Estimates, Mr Brettingham Architect, £48. 16. 6."]

4 [The preamble of the Grace, 9 March, 1787, sets forth the reasons as follows: "Cum Syndicis vestris summa ædificiis in horto Botanico extruendis erogata parum sufficere videatur, tum propter lateribus impositum vectigal, tum propter interna quædam opera quæ Professoribus ipsis necessaria esse constat."]

The building then erected (fig. 1) was of the simplest character, consisting merely of a lecture-room 40 feet long, by 28 feet broad, with a private room for the Professor of Botany at the south end, and for the Jacksonian Professor at the north end. The material employed was brick, with stone dressings.

Although the arrangement of this ground as a Botanic Garden does not directly concern our present purpose, it may be briefly described. The usual entrance to the garden was from Free School Lane, through a small Renaissance archway[1] opening into the passage specially reserved when the ground to the north of it was sold in 1784. On the right of this passage, at its east end, stood the curator's house. There was a second entrance from Pembroke Street, through a handsome pair of wrought-iron gates, which still exist. From these gates a broad gravel walk led straight across the garden to the centre of a range of greenhouses built against the north wall. At a distance of about 175 feet from the gates, this walk was carried, by a wooden bridge, over a long narrow pond, which crossed the garden from east to west, and divided it into two unequal divisions. That between the pond and the street contained the herbaceous plants, arranged in a series of parallel beds; that between it and the greenhouses was laid out in other beds, not quite so formal, for less hardy plants. The site of the lecture-room, built 1786, had been originally appropriated to grasses, and to a nursery for shrubs. It should be added that before the above-mentioned gates in Pembroke Street were set up, the entrance to the garden on that side was through a small doorway at the south-west corner, the traces of which may still be seen in the boundary wall[2].

It was mentioned above (p. 133) that a house adjoining the old Press had been assigned to the Professors of Anatomy and Chemistry in 1716[3]. The accommodation thus provided was extremely inconvenient and inadequate, with no possibility of

[1] [This doorway, taken down when the Cavendish Laboratory was built, was re-erected within that building.]

[2] [These details have been described from a plan of the garden called Prospectus Horti Botanici Cantabrigiensis, bound up with a copy of T. Martyn's Catalogus Horti Botanici Cantabrigiensis, 8vo., Cambridge, 1771, now in the Botanical Library; and from the description of the garden, with a plan dated 1838, in The Cambridge Portfolio.]

[3] [The lecture-room for Anatomy in this building is figured by Ackermann, ii. 290.]

extension. The Professor of Chemistry soon abandoned it, and made use of the rooms in the Botanic Garden which had been built for the Jacksonian Professor in 1786. The Professor of Anatomy was obliged to lecture and to display his collections as well as he could in the old building; but the dearth of space elsewhere was so great that he shared his lecture-room with the Professors of Physic and of Modern History. For Mineralogy no provision whatever was made when the Professorship was founded in 1808; and Geology continued until 1840, as related above (pp. 78, 121), to occupy a room which the late Professor Sedgwick described as "small, damp, and ill-lighted, and utterly unfit for a residence or a lecture-room." The graphic *Statement* circulated by Professor Whewell in 1828, which has been already given at length (pp. 98—101), called the attention of the University to the evils resulting from this state of things, and in the next year the *Instructions to Architects* for the building which was intended to replace the old Library and Schools, directed them to provide Museums and Lecture-Rooms for Geology, Mineralogy, Zoology, Botany; and a Model-room for the Jacksonian Professor. This scheme, however, as already related, was not carried out, Geology and Mineralogy alone being accommodated in Cockerell's building, nor had the wants of Anatomy and Chemistry been so much as recognised. In 1831 however the commencement of negotiations for the sale of the ground and buildings of the old Press compelled the University to appoint a Syndicate (23 February, 1831), consisting of the Vice-Chancellor; John Haviland, M.D., Regius Professor of Medicine; William Clark, M.D., Professor of Anatomy; James Cumming, M.A., Professor of Chemistry; John Croft, M.A., Christ's College; Charles Currie, M.A., Pembroke College; and Joseph Studholme, M.A., Jesus College, to consider the whole question. Their Report, dated 18 February, 1832, suggested the following scheme:

"It appears to the Syndicate that sufficient accommodation may be secured to the Professor of Chemistry by a slight addition on the northern extremity of the buildings now standing in the Botanic Garden.

These buildings are placed in a recess of the Garden, 24 feet distant from the boundary wall of Downing-street, and have behind them an irregularly triangular space of about 230 square yards bounded by Downing-street and by St Andrew's Hill.

The Syndics find that this irregular space (which appears to be of little value for the purposes of the Garden), together with that gained by extending the front of the present building 24 feet up to Downing-street, will afford a sufficient area for the erection of buildings to be appropriated to the use of the Professor of Anatomy—viz. a Museum, Lecture Room, Dissecting Room, and private Room: whilst, by a corresponding extent of frontage on the northern extremity, the symmetry of the building will be preserved, and the additional accommodation of an Apparatus Room and a private Room be secured to the Professor of Chemistry.

If the Anatomical Lecture Room, which may be so placed as to be contiguous to that in which the Botanical Collection is now preserved, be raised to the height required for the Museum, a Lecture Room on the ground floor and another above it may be obtained on the same site, and thus sufficient accommodation will be afforded to every Professor concerned."

This Report was confirmed 22 February, and the Syndics were reappointed, with authority to consult an Architect. They obtained a plan from Mr Charles Humfrey, a local builder, by which accommodation was to be provided for Anatomy and Chemistry, and also for Mineralogy, by raising part of the buildings, as suggested above, to a greater height. The former building was estimated to cost £2500, the latter £600. This part of the scheme was rejected by the Senate, while they accepted the former (6 April, 1832).

The buildings were begun in June, 1832, and completed in about twelve months. It was then found that the cost had exceeded the estimate by so large a sum that Mr Humfrey felt it necessary to address a verbose Report to the Syndicate, in which he attempted to justify the changes which he had introduced into the plan, and which were to a great extent the cause of the increased expenditure. The Syndicate published this Report 24 June, 1833; and it appears to have been received with much surprise and disapprobation, for early in the following year a special Syndicate was appointed to investigate the whole question. They recommended (10 March, 1834) that the demands of the contractor, Mr John Fromant, and those of other persons, should be settled[1], but they prefaced their recommendations with the following passage:

[1] [The recommendations were divided into three Graces, which passed the Senate 14 March, 1834. The Grace to pay Mr Fromant was opposed, but carried by 10 votes to 6.]

"The Syndics have examined the New Buildings in the Botanic Garden, and to the best of their judgment they are well and substantially built. The cost of erecting these New Buildings has however very much exceeded that which the Senate expected, and without giving any opinion on the merits of the great alterations made in the original design, the Syndics consider that they only discharge their duty to the University, by stating that they find upon enquiry, that those alterations were mainly effected without any consultation with the Syndics or any Member of the Syndicate appointed more especially to superintend the erection of the Buildings."

The buildings then erected included two rooms for the use of the Professor of Chemistry at the north end of the old building, and the octagonal Museum, with a private room, a lecture-room, and a closet for dissection, all of which are still used by the Professor of Anatomy. The total cost (including fittings) appears to have been nearly £3630.

The buildings of which we have just completed the history, though inconvenient and ill-arranged, sufficed for more than thirty years for the use of the Professors of Anatomy, Physic, Botany, Chemistry, and Applied Mechanics, as the Jacksonian Professor came gradually to be designated. The obligation, however, of providing better accommodation for them, and their rapidly increasing collections, was never wholly lost sight of; and when the Natural Sciences Tripos had been established, the first examination for which was held in 1851, prompt action became imperative. The publication, moreover, of the evidence of the scientific Professors by Her Majesty's Commissioners of 1850, drew public attention to the subject.

The removal of the Botanic Garden to a new site[1], commenced

[1] [The old site had become too small, the soil was worn out, and it was closely surrounded by houses. An amusing account of the damage done by the depredations of the jackdaws who built in the adjoining chimneys and steeples will be found in Loudon's Mag. of Nat. Hist. vi. 397. A private Act of Parliament (1 William IV. cap. 5), which received the Royal Assent 30 March, 1831, enabled the University to obtain the present site, by exchange with the Master and Fellows of Trinity Hall. The removal, however, could not be effected at once, as the ground was held under a lease, which did not expire until Michaelmas, 1844. The Report of the Syndicate recommending the exchange, dated 26 May, 1830, confirmed by the Senate 31 May, 1830, proposed "to enable the Trustees of the present Botanic Garden to dispose of the old Garden on building leases, or for the purpose of converting it into a Market Place, or for such other purposes as may appear advisable." In 1841 this site was suggested for the County Courts.]

in 1846, having been practically completed by the end of 1852, a Syndicate was appointed, 2 February, 1853, with instructions to lay before the University, before the end of the Easter Term, a scheme for legally acquiring the site of the old garden[1], and, in the second place, for building new Museums and Lecture-Rooms. This Syndicate consisted of the Vice-Chancellor; Henry Philpott, D.D., Master of S. Catharine's Hall; Henry Wilkinson Cookson, D.D., Master of Peterhouse; James Cartmell, D.D., Master of Christ's College; William Hallows Miller, M.D., Professor of Mineralogy; Robert Willis, M.A., Jacksonian Professor; George Gabriel Stokes, M.A., Lucasian Professor; John Newton Peill, M.A., Queens' College; Francis France, M.A., S. John's College; Francis Martin, M.A., Trinity College; Godfrey Milnes Sykes, M.A., Downing College; William Marsh, M.A., Trinity Hall; John Fenwick, M.A., Corpus Christi College.

The first question submitted to them was easily dealt with, and they issued a Report (7 March, 1853), shewing how the garden might legally become the property of the University. This Report was confirmed by the Senate, 11 March; and, 29 July following, an order of the Court of Chancery vested the ground in the Chancellor, Masters, and Scholars, on consideration of the payment of £3,448. 4*s*. 4*d*. to the Governors of the Garden.

The second question entrusted to the Syndicate required far longer consideration, and their Report upon it is dated 31 December, 1853. The preparation of it had been entrusted to a Sub-Syndicate consisting of Dr Cookson, Professor Miller, Professor Stokes, and Professor Willis, but it was mainly, if not entirely, the work of Professor Willis[2]. On this account, and also from the care and minuteness with which the wants of the

[1] [The words of the Grace are "qui deliberent quid tandem agendum sit quo situs Horti Botanici veteris usui Academiæ inserviat, et qui de ea re cum fidejussoribus Horti Botanici conferant;" but the action taken by the Syndicate shews that they took the view of their duties stated in the text.]

[2] [This is proved by letters, preserved among his papers, from those whom he consulted while he was engaged upon it. Among these may be mentioned two from George Peacock, M.A., then Dean of Ely, who, among other criticisms, strongly advocated the construction of an entrance from Pease Hill. Writing 26 December, 1853, he says: "I am very much in earnest about the entrance from Pease Hill:...it is the only mode of bringing the lecture-rooms, &c., into the proper vicinage of the great mass of the academical population."]

University at that period are stated and discussed in it, it is quoted without abbreviation :

"The annual Programme published under the authority of the Vice-Chancellor, shews that the majority of the Professors deliver their Lectures in places not originally intended for that purpose, and that the actual number of real Lecture-Rooms is exceedingly small.

For the consideration of the accommodation required, the Professors may be divided into two classes : namely, Literary Professors, including all those whose lectures require neither Museums, Laboratories, nor any other appendage to the Lecture-Room; and Scientific Professors, who lecture upon various branches of Natural and Experimental Science, each of which requires Museums, Laboratories, or Apparatus-Rooms, in connexion with the Lecture-Room. A Literary Professor requires the use of a lecture-room only during the time which is occupied by the delivery of the lecture, and the assembling and dispersion of his audience. A Scientific Professor, on the contrary, must occupy the room in most cases for several hours, for the purpose of arranging the specimens, apparatus, and drawings required for the lecture, of giving private explanations of them, and allowing the inspection of them by the Students after the lecture, and for taking them away afterwards. From the nature of University education, which compels every Student to attend College Lectures in the early part of the morning, it is found that there are not more than three hours, or at most four hours, during which the attendance of Students can be secured at Professorial Lectures. As also each Scientific Professor lectures during four or more days in the week in full Term, it results that nearly every one of them requires the entire and exclusive possession of the Lecture-Room during the term which is selected for his course.

The number of Literary Professors is twelve, two of whom (the Regius Professors of Law and Hebrew) lecture in every Term, two others (the Margaret and Norrisian Professors of Divinity) during two Terms, and the remainder for one Term each. Some of these Professors, from the nature of their subjects, have limited classes; but others, especially the Professors of Divinity, require accommodation for at least 350 Students. The Programme shews that at present five courses in all are delivered by the Literary Professors in the Michaelmas Term, nine in the Lent Term, and four in the Easter Term. The lectures begin at various hours from eleven to two. The places are : the Schools of Arts and of Law, the Lecture-Room under the front of the University Library, the Geological Lecture-Room, and various apartments borrowed from the Colleges or the Pitt Press[1]. Of these places the Lecture-Room under the Library is the only one fitted with rising benches. It will accommodate about ninety persons, and the flat floor may perhaps, when crowded, contain seventy or eighty more; but the room is very low and ill ventilated. It was not originally intended to receive an audience, but was appropriated to Professorial

[1] [The following list of the Lecture-Rooms in the University, and of the Professors by whom they were used, is taken from the evidence forwarded to Her Majesty's

Lectures by a Grace of the Senate in 1794, and fitted up accordingly. The Arts and Law Schools, although capacious, are encumbered with pillars and other obstructions, and have no rising benches.

It is recommended therefore that one large Lecture Theatre, expressly adapted for Literary Lectures, and capable of accommodating about 400 Students, be erected for these Professors. As at least two lectures could be delivered in this Theatre in the same day, and as many of these Professors lecture three times a week only, it is manifest that one such Theatre would relieve the wants of this portion of the Professorial body; the more especially as the removal of the lectures of the Lucasian and Plumian Professors to the new buildings, which will be proposed in a subsequent part of the Report, would leave the Lecture-Room under the Library completely at liberty for Professors.

The teaching of Astronomy, the Mechanical and Physical Sciences and their practical applications, and Chemistry, is divided amongst the Lucasian, Chemical, Plumian, Lowndean, and Jacksonian Professors. The distribution of these subjects amongst these Professors has somewhat varied at different periods, according to the taste or habits of the persons who have held the appointments. But the actual accommodation afforded in the shape of museums, laboratories, and other apartments, as well as of apparatus and assistants, all which are necessary for the successful prosecution and teaching of these various subjects, is miserably deficient; with the exception of the excellent and well-appointed Observatory under the charge of the Plumian Professor. The remaining accommodation consists of a single Lecture-Room in the Botanic Garden, for the use of the Chemical and Jacksonian Professors, conjointly with the Botanical Professor, to which Lecture-Room are attached several rooms and laboratories. The Lucasian, Plumian, and Lowndean Professors have to make shift with Lecture-Rooms not originally erected for the purpose, and unprovided with private rooms, or any other apartments.

It appears from the evidence of the Anatomical Professor[1], that the buildings appropriated to his subject require considerable additions, for the purpose of separating Human Anatomy from Comparative Anatomy, and for the accommodation of the new Professor, required by the

Commissioners by Professor G. G. Stokes, Lucasian Professor of Mathematics, 20 December, 1851. Report, etc., Evidence, p. 98.

Arts School.	Lady Margaret's Professor of Divinity.
Law School.	Regius Professor of Civil Law.
Addenbrooke's Hospital.	Regius Professor of Physic.
Downing College.	Downing Professor of the Laws of England. Downing Professor of Medicine.
A room in the Pitt Press.	Regius Professor of Greek. Lord Almoner's Reader of Arabic. Lowndean Professor of Astronomy, etc.
Trinity College.	Professor of Moral Philosophy.
Observatory.	Plumian Professor of Astronomy, etc.
S. Catharine's Hall.	Professor of Arabic.]

[1] Report of Her Majesty's Commissioners, etc. 1852. Evidence, p. 107.

increased work added by the establishment of the Natural Sciences Tripos. The principal apartments wanted, in addition to those now assigned to Anatomy, are a lecture-room, a dissecting-room, a workshop for preparing specimens, mounting skeletons, &c. a museum, and a private room. These are required for the purpose of separating the Human from the Comparative Anatomy. A private room for the Regius Professor of Physic, and additional dissecting-rooms for Students are also necessary. But as these two subjects are of a similar nature, it is desirable that their buildings, especially the museums, should be in contiguity, although provided with separate entrances. Yet the ground upon which the Anatomical Museum and its appendages stand is hemmed in between the streets and the Jacksonian lecture-buildings, so as to make contiguous additions impossible. It is recommended therefore that the whole of the original buildings, including those assigned to the Chemical, Botanical, and Jacksonian Professors, with the great Lecture-Room, be given up to the Anatomical department, and that the three above-mentioned Professors be accommodated elsewhere. This department would thus be provided with the Lecture-Room required, and the other rooms, if put into thorough repair, with the necessary alterations, and the addition of a Museum, would supply the wants already enumerated.

An entirely new building must consequently be erected for the accommodation of the Lucasian, Chemical, Plumian, Lowndean, and Jacksonian Professors, and to these should be added the Professors of Botany and Mineralogy, for the reasons stated below.

For Botany, the University possesses a valuable Herbarium, and other collections, and a small especial library. A portion of these collections is at present packed in boxes, and useless to the students. The subject itself is always attractive, and the Professor requires the use of a large Lecture-Room. Botany therefore, if ejected as proposed from the old buildings, must also be accommodated in the new one.

The Mineralogical Museum is now arranged in a room under the new wing of the University Library, which is by no means sufficient for the display of the Collection. But the Professor is compelled to carry on his private investigations in the vaults below, which also contain part of the collection in drawers, and various lecture apparatus, and he is unprovided with a laboratory. The connexion between Chemistry and Mineralogy requires that provision should be made for them in the same building, so that the Students of each may make use of the laboratories. The room now occupied by the Mineralogical Collection is wanted by the Geological Professor.

Seven Professors have therefore to be provided with Lecture-Rooms, and the apartments respectively required for their subjects. Of these Professors we may assume that two at least may lecture during two Terms, and the remaining five during one Term, so that we have nine courses distributed over three Terms. Three Lecture-Rooms will be necessary, and will probably be sufficient in the first instance to supply these courses, as the Mineralogical lectures may be delivered in a room adjoining the Museum, and if other Professors wish to lecture during two Terms they may not find it necessary to occupy the room for more than three days in the week, so that two separate courses may go on in the same room during the same Term. But a fourth Lecture-Room at least should be provided for in the plan, to be added if required in future.

The present Jacksonian Lecture-Room is capable of accommodating nearly 150 persons on the benches, every one of whom can see and hear perfectly. Its construction is exceedingly simple and practical, and ample room is given for the Lecturer to display apparatus and diagrams. With some changes in the mode of lighting and other details, and with an additional space that would extend its accommodation to 200 persons, this room would become an excellent model for the proposed new Lecture-Rooms. It offers a most favourable contrast to the Lecture-Theatres which architects usually erect, in which the audience are disposed in circular rows described about the Lecturer as a centre, and hemming him in on all sides so as to leave him no room for apparatus, and also placing the eyes of the audience in every possible position with respect to his drawings and machinery; whereas these almost always require to be presented for explanation in the same direction to all the listeners.

Every one of the seven Professors will require one or more private rooms, the workshops, so to speak, of his own subject, wherein to perform private experiments, to arrange or construct apparatus, to prepare specimens, make drawings for lectures or other purposes, and keep portions of apparatus that are his own property or that may be unfitted for a place in the rooms open to the University; one or more rooms for the use of Students in Chemistry and other branches of experimental science should be added.

A suite of Rooms, for the formation of a collection of Philosophical apparatus, should be provided to receive models, machinery, and apparatus of all kinds that admit of being disposed in order for public inspection. The University at present possesses no apparatus for physical or mechanical science, with the exception of that employed at the Observatory. In the Natural Sciences, collections have been formed and have become the property of the University, either by private gift or by purchase; and the University has from time to time erected Museums for the reception and display of such Collections, without which its members necessarily lose the advantages of studying them.

It is now proposed to apply the same principles to physical and mechanical science, by erecting a suite of proper Rooms, provided with glass cases and other convenient fittings, in which the various Professors may deposit those portions of their apparatus which are suitable for public inspection, instead of keeping the whole locked up in their private rooms, as they are now compelled to do.

If this system be carried out, and aided by grants from the University funds or from private liberality, for the purchase of apparatus, the expense of which has been hitherto entirely thrown upon the Professors, a collection would be made and preserved for the use of Students and future Professors. Under the present system each Professor upon quitting office is obliged to sell his apparatus at a great sacrifice; and thus very curious and instructive collections have been dispersed, and lost to the University, which would have given a very interesting picture of the various phases of scientific research from time to time, besides their actual utility. Such collections are usually attached to lecture-rooms on the continent.

We may now state in detail the apartments required by each Professor, in addition to his Lecture-Room.

The Lucasian Professor requires a private room, as well as a working room, in which to fit up and experiment upon the apparatus of his Lectures. In these rooms, as well as in his Lecture-Room, the aspect and mode of introducing the light must be particularly attended to.

The Chemical Professor requires a laboratory and private room with a Balance-room, and other usual appendages. The modern method of teaching Chemistry is to instruct Students in the actual practice of the laboratory, in addition to the course of Lectures. For this purpose a Students Laboratory must be constructed, separated from the Laboratories and Lecture-Room of the Professor, and fitted up with distinct working places for the Students. A room about forty feet long, and fifteen wide, will accommodate fourteen Students, but the plan should comprise the easy addition of more room if required.

The Plumian and Lowndean Professors of Astronomy require each a private room, and one room for Students, so arranged that it may contain astronomical instruments of the smaller kind, by which the use and management of them may be familiarized.

The Botanical Professor requires a Museum, the area of which should be at least 1300 feet, and well lighted. It should be in immediate connexion with the Lecture-Room. There must be a moderately sized private room, with good light for making lecture-drawings, and for microscopic examinations; and also an unpacking room. It is not necessary that these should be all on the same floor.

The apparatus required by the Jacksonian Professor for lectures on manufacturing machinery, steam-engines, &c. is necessarily bulky. Much of it may be disposed in the Museum of Apparatus, but he requires, in addition, a room of the nature of a workshop, in which apparatus may be fitted together and adjusted for use in the Lecture-Room; and the frames and unsightly portions of lecturing machinery stowed away. This room should be contiguous to the Lecture-Room. He also requires a private room and a small laboratory fitted with a forge, and furnace for melting metals, &c.

The Mineralogical Professor requires a Museum, which may consist of two well lighted rooms. His Lecture-Room, on account of the large number of objects to be exhibited, must be immediately contiguous to, and on the same floor with, the Museum. But, for this subject, raised seats are not necessary for the audience, and the room therefore need not be loftier than proper ventilation requires. A small room to stow away lecture-stands, frames, and similar objects, should be attached, together with a private room in which Mineralogical Observations, such as measurements of angles, determinations of specific gravities, blowpipe examinations, &c. may be carried on by the Professor without interruption from the persons visiting the Museum. The whole establishment of Mineralogy may be contained in the upper floor of the proposed Building, as the objects of the Collection are not bulky, and do not require very lofty rooms, but they must be well lighted, and convenient access should be made to the chemical Laboratories below, one of which may be assigned to the Professor. Most original researches in Mineralogy require a chemical Laboratory.

On the whole it appears that the new Building will be required to contain at least three Lecture-Rooms, besides the large Theatre for the Literary Professors, (if it be determined that it be contained in this same establishment). Also a Museum of Philosophical apparatus, a Botanical Museum, a Mineralogical Museum, and a Student Laboratory for Practical Chemistry, one or more rooms for Students in other subjects, and the private rooms and workshops respectively required by the seven Professors, as already enumerated. As many chemical processes produce corrosive vapours which are injurious to delicate apparatus and to machinery, the Lecture-Room assigned to mechanical and Physical Lectures should not be the same as that given to Chemistry, and the laboratories must be placed as far apart from the museums of apparatus as possible. The entire building must be thoroughly warmed and well supplied with water.

To plan and carry out so complicated an edifice requires the experience of a first-rate Architect; and it is recommended that such an one be selected, and that he be requested to design the new Buildings, and the alterations of the old ones, and to prepare the estimate.

The Syndicate recommend that the style be as plain as possible, and the material brick. That there be no unnecessary expenditure upon architectural decoration; but that the Architect be requested to display his skill rather in the perfect adaptation of the various apartments to their use, and in their convenient juxtaposition, as well for their respective Professors, as for the ready admission of visitors to the Museums, without interference with the parts appropriated to the Professors and their Pupils; and lastly, that each especial portion be arranged after consultation with the Professor to whose department it may belong, each Professor being requested to put in writing a minute account of the number and size of the apartments he may wish for, their proportions, juxtaposition, the nature of their lighting, fittings, and every other particular.

The Syndicate also recommend that this work be entrusted to Mr Salvin, not only on account of his well known ability and high standing in his profession, but because he has recently given to the University, in the alterations and additions of Trinity Hall and Caius College, proofs of his especial skill in the planning of complicated and commodious buildings upon sites limited in space, awkward in form, and connected with previous structures.

The selection of the site for the Building in the Botanic Garden must be made with care, so as to interfere as little as possible with the employment of the remaining ground, and on this point the opinion of the Architect must be taken.

Previous to the commencement of the work the entire ground will require to be thoroughly drained. Its soil is very retentive of water, and accordingly the old Lecture-Room, and all its surrounding groups of buildings, are so damp, as to occasion serious damage to the apparatus and specimens contained in them."

This Report gave general satisfaction, and 8 February, 1854, a Grace passed the Senate, authorising the Syndicate to obtain plans, and an estimate of cost, from Mr Salvin. He was accordingly instructed, 17 February, to base his design on the recommendations contained in the Report, and on further information to be supplied by Professor Willis[1]. This information was obtained by sending a circular to each Professor, requesting him to furnish exact particulars in writing of the rooms required; and great care was taken to provide, as far as possible, the full accommodation asked for. The plans were laid before the Syndicate at the beginning of May, and were generally approved, as being in accordance with the instructions. These plans have not been preserved, but their provisions will be understood from the description by Professor Willis:

"The proposed building is located on the north side of the old Botanic Garden; the extreme width is 230 feet, and the greatest distance from the north wall is 108 feet, including a court-yard behind, 35 feet wide. It occupies in width the whole of the northern boundary, with the exception of a road at the western end of the façade, which road is a continuation of the entrance from Free-School Lane, and furnishes access to the front of the building and to the garden on that side.

The building is disposed into three principal masses, of which the centre is occupied by the large Theatre for the Literary Professors, beneath which is the Museum of Philosophical Apparatus. The right wing of the building contains on the ground-floor a Lecture-Room for the Chemical Professor; annexed are the private rooms, &c. appertaining to this Professorship, and behind this wing is placed the Students' Laboratory. An ample staircase conducts to the upper floor, upon which is located the Mineralogical Lecture-Room, Museum, and other rooms connected with that department. The left wing of the building has on the ground-floor a Lecture-Room for the Jacksonian and Botanical Professors, with rooms for apparatus, &c. belonging to them, and the necessary staircases for access to the upper floor. The Botanical Museum extends along the western front of the building, and the upper floor of this wing is appropriated to the Lecture-Room of the Lucasian, Plumian, and Lowndean Professors, with their private rooms and other apartments for apparatus and students practice.

This summary account will shew that the proposed building includes all the Lecture-Rooms and other rooms which are enumerated in the general description [in] the Report of the Syndicate, and that in accordance with that description the mechanical and physical portion of the

[1] [Minute of the Syndicate, 17 February, 1854.]

edifice is widely separated from that which is devoted to Chemical subjects. It remains to explain in detail the apartments assigned to each Professor in conformity with the written accounts of their wishes.

It must be premised that the great Theatre for the Literary Professors is capable of containing 400 persons, and is approached by the two principal staircases, one on the east side and the other on the west, which lead to two separate doors of entrance in the front of the building. Annexed to the Theatre at the head of the eastern staircase is a small room for the use of the Lecturer, with a separate entrance to the Lecture-Table. The three lesser Lecture-Rooms for the Mechanical, Physical, and Chemical departments are arranged as nearly as possible in conformity with the present Jacksonian Lecture-Room, and will hold about 200 persons each. The Mineralogical Lecture-Room is smaller.

We may now take the separate Professorships as nearly as possible in the order in which they are placed in the Report.

The Lecture-Room of the Lucasian Professor is placed at the south-west corner of the building; the direction of the seats is from north to south. For the purpose of arranging optical experiments, this room, besides the ordinary windows, has one in the west wall and one in the south wall, especially formed for the reception and management of the Heliostat. The one in the west wall corresponds to an opening in the seats through which the sun's rays may be directed upon the Lecture-Table. The remaining windows are provided with shutters that can be conveniently closed when the Lecturer desires to exclude light. A door from the platform leads to a room for the stowage of frames and other Lecture-apparatus of an unwieldy description. Beyond this is a room for the private study and place of delicate apparatus. These apartments have a separate entrance from the principal staircase adjoining, and the private room has a Heliostat window on its southern side. In the roof above is 'a loft for Optical experiments intended for the use of any Professor, or member of the University, who may be engaged in researches that require such a place;' it is seventy-five feet long, and lighted by a lucarne window at its eastern and western extremities.

The Lecture-Room of the Lucasian Professor is also assigned to the Plumian and Lowndean Professors of Astronomy. A door in the north wall of its platform opens to a passage which gives access to three rooms, lighted from the court, and intended for the private rooms of the Plumian and Lowndean Professors respectively, and for their common Apparatus-room. The walls of the north-west corner of the court are carried up higher than the others, so as to provide a room over the Plumian room, surmounted by a flat uncovered area clear of the roof, and intended for Students practice in Astronomical Observation.

The Botanical Museum is contained in a long narrow wing of the building which is erected against the return wall of the ground, immediately opposite to the entrance from Free-School Lane. This Museum, in exact accordance with the written instructions of the Botanical Professor, is arranged 'in two stories, the lower of which is the general Botanical Museum, consisting of two rooms of 42 ft. by 18 ft., above which are placed two rooms of the same dimensions for the Herbarium.

They are all lighted on one side (the west), and provided with a separate door in the west wall, and a staircase which also serves for the Optical Lecture-Room.

The great height of the two stories of Lecture-Rooms in the front of the building allows the small rooms at the back which face the court to be arranged in three stories. Thus the Botanical unpacking room is placed on the ground-floor, and the private room above it, the two being under the Plumian private room. The rooms under the Lowndean private room and Astronomical Apparatus-room may be assigned to any purpose that may arise, for example, for the use of Students. Beneath them are the private room and laboratory of the Jacksonian Professor.

The Botanical Lecture-Room is also assigned to the Jacksonian Professor. The platform has a door on the northern extremity leading to the Botanical apartments, and another at the southern extremity opening to the Jacksonian Apparatus-room, which is immediately under the Lucasian private rooms. This room has a separate entrance from the principal western staircase, and also a door of communication with a room intended for a workshop. The latter is lighted by a skylight, as it forms the lower part of a small court or well, which is employed in giving light to the passages and staircases of the upper floor. The private room and laboratory of the Professorship are placed on the ground-floor of the back rooms as already described, and are immediately opposite to the workshop last mentioned.

For the purpose of providing a ready internal access to all parts of the building, a corridor traverses it, beginning from the western door, and extending in a direct line very nearly to the eastern boundary. Doors placed in this corridor may be closed when required.

The rooms already described are separated from the Chemical establishment by the central mass of building, the ground-floor of which is divided by the corridor into two spaces, each about 53 ft. by 18 ft., and each well lighted by large windows, and applicable to the reception of the proposed collection of Philosophical Apparatus.

The ground-floor of the eastern wing, which is assigned to Chemistry, is arranged very nearly in the same manner as that of the western wing. The Lecture-Room has a room annexed to it on the south front, which is intended for the use of the Chemical Professor. On the north side is a range of Student Laboratories in one story, which may be extended as required about the sides of the court, and which have an independent access. There is also placed next to this court a set of small rooms in two stories corresponding to those on the opposite wing, but less in number and therefore occupying a smaller space. These are assigned to the Balance-room, Private Laboratory, Closet for Chemicals, Students Apparatus-Room, and Mineralogical Laboratory. The latter, for the convenience of the Professor, is placed near the foot of the staircase which ascends to his department.

The upper floor of this wing is appropriated to Mineralogy. The Mineralogical Museum consists of two apartments 38 ft. by 22 ft. each, connected by a short passage, and each lighted on both sides. The Lecture Room is approached through the Museum, and beyond it is the

Professor's private room, 40 ft. long, and 10 ft. wide, lighted by a window at each end. These long and narrow dimensions are required to suit the peculiar nature of his observations. A stowage room for Lecture-frames and Apparatus opens to the Lecture-Room.

[It is further proposed to alter] the old Jacksonian Lecture-buildings, for the purpose of providing the Professor of Comparative Anatomy with a set of apartments completely distinct from those appropriated to Human Anatomy, as recommended in the Report, and in conformity with a communication subsequently received from the Professor of Anatomy.

The only additions to the present building in the proposed Plan are the Museum for Comparative Anatomy, and the Dissecting-room for the Students of Human Anatomy; the latter being erected upon the space at present occupied by the Chemical Laboratory, the form and fittings of which are entirely antiquated, and of a nature to render the apartment useless for any other purpose, and make its demolition imperative.

The remaining work indicated in this Plan consists merely of some changes in the doors and windows of the existing building, and in a new roof to the room at present occupied by the apparatus of the Jacksonian Professor. This roof is in very bad repair, and must be removed. The staircase of the Museum is placed on a portion of the area of the room, and a private room for the Professor is added above it.

The two departments of Human Anatomy and Comparative Anatomy are completely separated, without even a door of communication from one to the other, and they have separate entrances. In the department of Human Anatomy the public entrance, the Museum, and Lecture-Theatre remain as at present; but the present Private-room of the Professor is assigned to the Regius Professor of Physic, the Professor of Human Anatomy is lodged in the present Botanical Museum, and the dimensions of the present Pupils Dissecting-room are slightly enlarged so as to serve for the Professor. A large well-lighted room (32 ft. by 15 ft.) is erected, as already stated, on the site of the present Chemical Laboratory for the dissections of the Students, and the present Dissecting-room of the Professor is removed altogether.

The proposed Museum of Comparative Anatomy is of an oblong form (80 ft. by 40 ft.), and has a gallery running round of 5 feet in depth, and 12 feet from the floors. The walls are 26 feet in height, and it is lighted by a large oblong lantern with windows on every side. These arrangements are in conformity with the directions contained in Professor [Clark's] letter, and the apartments described by him as requisite for carrying on the work of the Professorship of Comparative Anatomy are provided for as follows:

(1) The Lecture-room is the existing Jacksonian Room.

(2) The Professor's Private Room, requiring good light for making drawings and microscopic observations, is placed over the present Jacksonian Apparatus-room, and reached by a staircase that also serves the gallery of the Museum. This room is well lighted by three windows to the east.

(3) The Professor's Working-room for dissecting and injecting and for mounting skeletons is placed in the present Chemical Professor's

larger room (21 ft. × 24 ft.), which is well lighted and admits of being fitted up with a boiler, sink, hot-hearth, sand-bath, and oven, as required.

(4) The private Laboratory of the Chemical Professor is converted into a servant's room for cleaning and tying jars, in which can be fitted a boiler and a forge.

(5) A room for cases and for the reception of objects, some of which may be of a large size, is obtained in the part of the present Jacksonian Apparatus-room which remains after the staircase is taken out, as shewn in the Plan.

(6) Two yards are enclosed for the exclusive use of the department of Comparative Anatomy, one of which is a portion of the present yard, now common to the entire group of buildings. This yard has a door in the Corn-Market, which supplies a private entrance to the establishment. The public entrance to the Lecture-room and Museum is the present one in the Botanic Garden.

ROBERT WILLIS."

When however the question of cost came to be considered, it was found that it would amount to at least £23,166, to meet which the University had not more than about £5000 then available. It was therefore suggested that the Colleges should "assist in the execution of a work which is urgently required, not only for the credit of the University as compared with other similar institutions, but also for the actual education of the students of the colleges in various departments both of literature and science[1]." This proposal was coldly received[2], and, as no other means of raising funds suggested itself, the scheme was of necessity laid aside for a considerable period.

No further steps were taken until 1860, when the question was reopened by the Council of the Senate, who wisely began with the question of finance. At their suggestion the "University Property Syndicate" was instructed to inform the Senate what amount of money could be devoted to the erection of new buildings[3]. They reported, 16 March, 1861, that there was about £13,500[4] in hand, which was obviously insufficient, and proposed:

[1] [This sentence occurs in a Report of the Syndicate dated 20 May, 1854.]

[2] [Trinity College agreed, 30 October, 1854, to contribute £4000, in the course of four years, "provided a sum sufficient for carrying out the scheme can be raised by the contributions of the colleges"; and other Colleges made proportional offers; but it was found impossible to arrive at any joint scheme of contribution.]

[3] [Grace, 22 November, 1860.]

[4] [This sum consisted of the balance in the Chest 3 November, 1860; £500 paid to the Vice-Chancellor by the Syndics of the Press under the authority of the following Grace passed 22 November, 1860: "Placeat vobis ut pecuniæ, a Syndicis Preli

(1) the immediate formation of a special Fund to be called "The Museums and Lecture-Rooms Building Fund," to which the above sum should be paid over, and which should also receive £1000 a year from the University Chest, together with any sums which the Syndics of the Press might choose to pay from time to time to the Vice-Chancellor; (2) an increase in the capitation tax, estimated to produce about £750 a year; (3) loans from surplus funds belonging to the Syndics of the Press, the Library, and the Fitzwilliam Museum. These proposals were discussed in the Arts School 17 April, and were on the whole favourably received, with the exception of the increased tax. Thereupon the Council of the Senate recommended the adoption of proposals (1) and (3) only, which were agreed to unanimously (25 April); and shortly afterwards, having ascertained the views of the Library and Press Syndicates, they obtained leave (2 May) to borrow £5000 from the latter, and £6553. 11*s.* 5*d.* Consols from the former. By these means the funds available for building purposes amounted to nearly £20,000 in money before the design had been prepared by the architect, a sum which had risen to £27,000 before the end of 1861[1].

While these questions were being discussed, the former Syndicate, which does not appear to have met since 1854, was reinforced (7 March, 1861) by the addition of four new members, viz. William Whewell, D.D., Master of Trinity College; Edward Harold Browne, B.D., Norrisian Professor of Divinity; Arthur Westmorland, M.A., Jesus College; and John Lamb, M.A., Caius College. Their first act on reassembling was to nominate a Sub-Syndicate consisting of Dr Cookson, Professor Willis, and Professor Miller, "to obtain fresh information from the respective Professors upon the subject of their requirements in new Lecture Rooms and Museums, and to examine the plans of Mr Salvin[2]." They decided that it would be desirable and necessary to make many changes in the disposition of the buildings. The scientific Professors were requested to revise the statements of their respec-

vestri typographici in Cistam Communem relatæ, in publicis nummis vestro nomine collocentur, non nisi speciali Senatus gratia in usus quosvis erogandæ"; and £7274. 8*s.* 8*d.* Consols, of which £3842. 2*s.* 1*d.* represented the price received for the Old Press, as mentioned above, p. 144.]

[1] [Report of the Syndicate, 16 December, 1861.]

[2] [Minute of the Syndicate, 8 June, 1861.]

tive requirements, and, in accordance with the altered instructions thus obtained, Mr Salvin, assisted at all points and on all occasions by Professor Willis[1], as before, prepared an entirely new set of plans. This second design was estimated to cost £26,475. 11*s.* 0*d.*, exclusive of the architect's commission, and the salary of the clerk of the works; the increase being due, as was stated, to the greater extent of the building, the cost of the deep foundations, and the complete draining of the site, which, for some unexplained reason, had not been included in the former estimate. The new plans were ready at the beginning of December, 1861, and were submitted to the Senate, 16 December, as "admirably arranged, and in every way fulfilling the various and complicated purposes for which they were designed," with a recommendation that tenders should be obtained immediately for their erection[2]. A description of them, as in the former case, was prepared by Professor Willis, and circulated with the Report. This is printed entire. A comparison of it with the description of the former design, and with the ground-plan of the present buildings (fig. 1), will readily shew what changes had been introduced[3].

"The proposed Buildings are arranged about a quadrangular court, 138 ft. from north to south, and 114 ft. from east to west, and occupy about three-fifths of the old Botanic garden. The outer walls of the quadrangle are separated from the irregular eastern and western boundaries of the garden by a space of about forty feet in breadth, and are in closer proximity to the northern boundary, but the south front is 150 feet from Pembroke Street, leaving space sufficient for a future building in that street if required. This front consists of two square masses or towers connected by a lower building, having a carriage archway in the centre. The western tower has the Lecture-Room of the Jacksonian and Botanical Professors on the ground-floor, and that assigned to the Lucasian, Plumian, and Lowndean Professors above.

The Apparatus-Room and private room of the Jacksonian Professor are contained in the lateral one-storied appendage on the west side of the tower; and the apparatus and private rooms of the three last-named professors extend along the upper story of the intermediate building, the lower floor of which is occupied by the Museum of Philosophical Apparatus.

[1] [The share taken by Professor Willis is shewn by the numerous letters which passed between him and Mr Salvin while the plans were being got ready.]

[2] [This account of the design of 1861 is derived from the Report of the Syndicate dated 16 December, 1861.]

[3] [Mr Salvin, writing to Professor Willis 10 December, 1861, points out that the buildings in the first plan contained 844,720 cubic feet, those in the second 982,744 cubic feet.]

The Natural Sciences are disposed in the remaining three sides of the quadrangle, Human Anatomy excepted, which is retained in the buildings especially erected for its reception in 1831. Chemistry also remains in its ancient position. In the new quadrangle Botany is placed on the ground floor of the west side, in contiguity with the Lecture-Room which it shares with the Jacksonian Professor: Mineralogy on the first floor, having its Lecture-Room at the north end. Comparative Anatomy occupies the east side of the quadrangle, with a museum on a single floor, of which it is proposed at present to erect only about one-half. Its Lecture-Room, Dissecting-Rooms, &c., are placed on the ground-floor of the eastern tower, and in the lateral one-storied building which corresponds to the Jacksonian appendage at the other extremity of the façade. Above the Lecture-Room of Comparative Anatomy is the Zoological Museum. The north side of the quadrangle is reserved for Geology, whenever it may be required to remove it from its present position beneath the University Library. Thus the Natural Sciences of Botany, Mineralogy, Geology, Comparative Anatomy, and Zoology, will be placed in a connected series of Museums.

The Theological and Literary Professors, namely those who require neither Museums, Laboratories, or other appendage to the Lecture-Room, except a small private room, are located in a detached building at the entrance gate in Free-School lane. This building contains two Lecture-Rooms, one on the ground-floor, 39 ft. by 32 ft., which will seat 250 persons; and another on the upper floor, 48 feet square, capable of accommodating more than 400 persons. There is also a spacious double staircase to the latter Lecture-Room, and an entrance corridor which leads to the buildings of the principal quadrangle. Beyond this corridor, on the left hand, is a building which projects from the north end of the quadrangle. Its ground-floor contains rooms for a porter or keeper of the buildings, below the private rooms of the Mineralogical Professor.

It must be remarked that any of the Lecture-Rooms in the building may be employed as Examination rooms, by the contrivance of applying desks in front of the rising benches.

The Report of Dec. 31, 1853, recommended that 'the style of the buildings be as plain as possible, and the material brick. That there be no unnecessary expenditure upon architectural decoration; but that the architect be requested to display his skill rather in the perfect adaptation of the various apartments to their use, and in their convenient juxtaposition, &c.' Accordingly, the only portions of the proposed buildings in which architectural symmetry and decoration are employed, are the south front facing Pembroke Street, and the west front in Free-School Lane. These are designed in a simple and suitable Italian style, capable of being carried out in brick[1] with stone dressings. The remainder of the buildings within and without the quadrangle are of plain brick.

The apartments respectively assigned to the Professors have been arranged in conformity with written reports of their requirements,

[1] [When this Report was discussed in the Arts School, Professor Willis said that "red not cream-coloured brick" would be used.]

originally furnished by these gentlemen at the request of the Syndicate, contained in the Report of Dec. 31, 1853, and revised by them during the present year. It remains to explain in detail the manner in which these requirements have been embodied in the present plan.

The Lucasian Professor is placed at the south-west corner of the upper floor of the building. His Lecture-Room has a western and a southern outward wall, in each of which is a window especially formed for the reception and management of a Heliostat. The one in the west wall corresponds to an opening or horizontal trunk through the rising seats, by which the solar ray may be directed upon the Lecture-table. The remaining windows are provided with shutters, that can be conveniently closed when the Lecturer desires to exclude light. Contiguous to the east wall of the Lecture-Room are two rooms, one for private study and delicate apparatus, the other for the stowage of frames and unwieldy Lecture apparatus. Both of these are lighted from the south, and the doors of communication so arranged that the Heliostat ray from the west window of the Lecture-Room may be transmitted into them if required. The rooms have also a separate entrance from the staircase without.

A loft for Optical experiments is arranged in the roof of the western range. It consists of a long narrow gallery, or garret, extending from the north gable to the staircase at the south end of that range. A ray of sunlight, received upon the mirror of a Heliostat placed at a window in the south wall of the Lecture-Room, is transmitted directly through an opening in the north wall, and thence over the staircase into and along the gallery. The total distance from the Heliostat to the north gable of the gallery is 220 feet. Near the north extremity of the gallery its width is increased, by a transept in the roof, for the convenience of arranging apparatus. Access to the gallery is obtained by a flight of steps from its southern extremity, which descends to the landing of the Lecture-Room staircase, and thus at once to the rooms of the Lucasian Professor. In consequence of the difference between the height of the Museums in the western wing [which are] in two stories of 12 ft. each, and of the Lecture-rooms which are 20 ft. high, the floor of this optical gallery is only 6 ft. above that of the Lucasian apartments.

The Lecture-Room of the Lucasian Professor is also assigned to the Plumian and Lowndean Professors of Astronomy, and three rooms, lighted from the south and connected with the Lecture-Room by doors opening into a short passage, are intended for the private rooms of the Plumian and Lowndean Professors, respectively, and for a common Apparatus-Room.

Upon the roof of the Lecture-Room tower a clear flat uncovered area, fifteen feet square, surrounded by a parapet, is constructed, which is reached by means of a staircase next to the Lecture-Room. The transverse division-wall which separates the Lecture-Room tower into two portions is carried up to the level of this platform, so as to serve as a foundation for two stone slabs upon which Astronomical instruments can be placed for students practice in observation.

The Jacksonian Professor is provided with an Apparatus-Room of the same dimensions as that which he at present occupies in the old building, and in addition with a private room that may be used as a workshop and unpacking-room.

The Museum of Philosophical Apparatus is placed on the ground-floor of the central portion of the façade. Two rooms, of a total length of 80 feet, are assigned to it; and it is conveniently accessible from the Jacksonian Lecture-Room, and also, by means of the staircase at the north-west angle, from the apartments of the Professors on the upper floor. This Museum is introduced in accordance with the Report of the Lecture-Room Syndicate, Dec. 31, 1853, and is intended for the reception of models, machinery, and apparatus of all kinds, that admit of being disposed in order for public inspection. It must be furnished with glass cases and other convenient fittings, in which the various Professors of Physical and Mechanical science may deposit those portions of their apparatus which are suitable for public inspection, and which may also serve for the reception of such instruments of Philosophical research as may become the property of the University by gift or purchase.

The Botanical Museum occupies the great part of the ground-floor of the western side of the quadrangle. It consists of two rooms, respectively 62 and 35 feet long and 24 broad, lighted by windows on the west side. Its entrance is at the north end. At the south end is placed the private room, unpacking-room, &c. of the Professor, which is in communication with his Lecture-Room, held in common with the Jacksonian Professor.

The upper floor of this side of the quadrangle is appropriated to the Mineralogical Professor. His Museum is placed in two rooms, each 63 feet long and 24 broad, with windows on both sides. His Lecture-Room is at the north end of the Museum. A staircase, constructed between the north boundary-wall of the ground and the gable of the building, leads up to a passage on the east side of the Lecture-Room and Museum, and thus, by two doors, gives independent access to them. A short wing projects from the west side, and contains the Professor's Laboratory, Apparatus-Room, and private room. The latter, from the peculiar nature of his observations, requires considerable length. It has at the west end a window with a bracket for a Heliostat, the ray from which can be transmitted along a distance of 38 feet within the room, or beyond it, through a door, so as to reach the Lecture-Table.

The lower story of this wing (partly fitted up as a Porter's Lodge) also contains a small Laboratory for Mineralogical students.

The Museum of Comparative Anatomy is placed on the eastern side of the quadrangle. In dimensions it is 100 feet long and 40 feet broad, which, according to [Professor Clark's] statement, will be sufficient to hold the present collection. Its position on the ground, however, admits of a future elongation to the extent of 80 feet. To facilitate this, it is proposed to construct the gable with a large archway, closed by a wall. Thus, whenever the additional structure is completed, this wall can be readily removed, and the whole will be laid in one.

On the south of this Museum is placed the Lecture-Room, 43 feet by 32 feet, in contiguity with which is the Professor's Room, 21 feet by 18 feet; also a room, 26 feet by 15, for dissections, mounting skeletons,

&c.; a servants room, and a spare room for stowing packing-cases, and objects in preparation for the Museum. These rooms are contained in the lateral one-storied wing of the façade, and are all well lighted and are in communication with the back-yard on the east of the Museum.

The room above the Anatomical Lecture-Room is assigned to Zoology.

It is proposed that the Chemical Professor should retain the present Jacksonian Lecture-Room and also occupy the room now appropriated to the Jacksonian Professor, as well as the rooms to the north of it which were erected for Chemistry in 1831, and that these should receive the addition of an upper story to the north of the Lecture-Room, with other necessary alterations, to adapt them to the present state of the science and for the reception of students in Practical Chemistry.

ROBERT WILLIS.

Dec. 14, 1861."

These plans, when first exhibited to the Senate, excited almost universal disapprobation. The Divinity Professors objected that they had not been consulted, and could not accept the proposed lecture-rooms in Free-School Lane, because they thought that such a course would prejudge the question of a Divinity School, which they were most anxious to see erected in some central part of the University. Members of the Senate in general thought the design needlessly mean and ugly, and distrusted the competence of the architect. The Syndicate did their best to conciliate these two classes of objectors. They explained that the two lecture-rooms in Free-School Lane were not intended as a final provision for all the literary Professors, but merely as an attempt to give temporary accommodation to some of them; and further, that none of the new lecture-rooms were to be assigned irrevocably to any class of Professors. This explanation, which was accepted by the four Professors of Divinity, was publicly stated at a discussion in the Arts School (15 March, 1862), at which many of the general objections were brought forward and answered, more or less completely. The general tone of the discussion, however, had been so unfavourable to the whole scheme, that the Council of the Senate referred it back to the Syndicate for further consideration. They thought it best to withdraw that portion of it which related to the erection of the building in Free-School Lane and to the borrowing of money from the Library; and further, requested Professor Willis to confer with Mr Salvin in the hope of rendering his design more acceptable by slight modifications[1]. An amended design having been sent down, the Syndicate issued a fresh Report[2] (27 March), in which they announced the withdrawal of the obnoxious lecture-rooms, the consequent reduction of expenditure, and the attempt to modify the design. In consequence of these changes, and of a unanimous expression of approval from the scientific Professors, the design was adopted, 4 April, 1862, by a majority of sixty-three[3].

This decision, however, did not by any means terminate the difficulties which the scheme was destined to encounter. It will be remembered that Mr Salvin had estimated the cost of the new buildings, exclusive of suggested alterations to the old ones, at £26,475. 11*s.* 0*d.* This estimate, by the withdrawal of the lecture-rooms in Free-School Lane, was reduced to £19,692. 6*s.* 0*d.* When, however, tenders came to be received, it was found that the lowest, that of Messrs George Smith, exceeded this reduced estimate by £7,251. 14*s.* 0*d.* The Syndicate had no alternative but to propose the acceptance of this tender to the Senate. In doing so, they attempted, by a carefully worded Report, 23 May, 1862, to excuse the architect, and to explain to the Senate the nature of certain changes which they proposed to introduce into the design, so as to bring the outlay within the prescribed limits. The passages in which this was attempted are the following:

"The lowest of these Tenders exceeds the estimate of Mr Salvin by more than £7000; a discrepancy partly due to the more accurate knowledge of the extent of deep foundation required, and of the nature of the drainage, acquired since that estimate was prepared, and partly from the introduction of many altered details into the designs during their preparation for the specifications.

As the sum is so much greater than that which the Syndicate were led to expect, they requested Mr Salvin to review the designs for the purpose of ascertaining what parts of the buildings would admit of being separated from the whole and reserved for future erection, as the funds at the disposal of the University might permit; and also of extracting from the specifications all details that could be changed or dispensed with, so as to reduce the expense of construction without

[1] [Minute of the Syndicate, 19 March, 1862.]

[2] [The correspondence with the Professors of Divinity, the letter from the scientific Professors, and the Report, dated 31 December, 1853, were circulated with this Report.]

[3] [The numbers were: Placet 77, Non-placet 14.]

impairing the efficiency of the buildings. It appears from his report that the Museum of Comparative Anatomy is the only part of the buildings that can be conveniently separated from the others for subsequent erection, and that this will remove from the tenders the sum of £2,364. 14*s*. 3*d*. It also appears that by postponing the laying out of the inner quadrangle with its embankments, dwarf walls, stone steps, iron gates, &c. and by simplifying the details of the inside fittings of the rooms and museums in ceilings, cornices, &c. by the substitution of deal doors for wainscot and other like changes, which will not materially affect the appearance, and in no way interfere with the efficiency, of the rooms, or the stability of the structure, a farther sum of £2,469. 17*s*. 1*d*. will be removed; thus making a total reduction of the tenders by £4,834. 11*s*. 4*d*."

The publication of this Report revived all the hostility to the plans which had formerly existed, but which it was believed had been effectually removed. The extent and the intensity of this became manifest when the Report was discussed in the Arts School, 31 May; and though the violence of some of the speeches, shewing that those who uttered them were opposed rather to science in general than to any particular design for Museums, caused a slight reaction in public opinion, and though the person most interested in the speedy erection of a Museum of Comparative Anatomy, Professor Clark, made known his approval of the temporary suppression of it, the adoption of the Report was negatived, 30 May, by a majority of twenty-three[1].

In the course of the following Michaelmas Term a Memorial, to which a large number of signatures was attached, was presented to the Council of the Senate "requesting that immediate steps be taken for proceeding with the erection of New Museums and Lecture Rooms." In consequence of this Memorial, the Council issued a short Report, recommending that:

"as a necessary preliminary to taking any further step in the matter, a Syndicate be appointed to ascertain what liabilities have been already incurred by the University in engaging an architect, and obtaining plans, specifications, and tenders for building; and to consider what course of proceeding it may be desirable to adopt in the matter[2]."

Shortly afterwards (11 December), a Syndicate was proposed to the Senate in accordance with the above Report, and elected without opposition[3]. The persons selected were: Henry Wilkinson Cookson, D.D., Master of Peterhouse; William Henry

[1] [The numbers were: Placet 44, Non-placet 67.]

[2] [Report of the Council of the Senate, 1 December, 1862.]

[3] [The words used in the Grace were "secundum relationem Concilii Senatus de

Bateson, D.D., Master of S. John's College; George Edward Paget, M.D., Caius College; William Hallows Miller, M.D., Professor of Mineralogy; George Downing Liveing, M.A., Professor of Chemistry; John Roberts, M.A., Magdalene College; Isaac Todhunter, M.A., S. John's College; Samuel George Phear, M.A., Emmanuel College; Charles Gray, M.A., and John Willis Clark, M.A., Trinity College; and John Clough Williams Ellis, M.A., Sidney College.

The first act of these Syndics was to ask Mr Salvin for "a statement of his claims upon the University to the present time[1]." He replied that they amounted to £1402. 9*s.* 0*d.* for the two sets of plans; viz. £579. 3*s.* 0*d.* for the first, and £823. 6*s.* 0*d.* for the second, but that the latter sum would be deducted from the usual architect's commission if the second design were carried out; and further, that the surveyor's charges amounted to £426. 0*s.* 0*d.* It appeared therefore that under any circumstances the University would be compelled to pay £1005. 3*s.* 0*d.*; and, if it abandoned Mr Salvin, and began afresh with a new architect, that £1828. 9*s.* 0*d.* would have to be sacrificed.

Early in the following year (24 February, 1863) the Syndicate issued their Report. Having pointed out to the Senate the claims of Mr Salvin, as above stated, they expressed their conviction that it would be impossible, with the limited funds at the command of the University, to erect buildings which should be ornamental throughout, and yet large enough to give even the minimum of accommodation required; that, in their opinion, the scheme for building Museums and Lecture-Rooms ought properly to be divided into two parts, the plain and the ornamental, the former of which, placed on the back part of the ground, might be erected immediately, and supply the most urgent wants of the scientific Professors; while the latter, on the frontage towards Downing Street, might be reserved for additions and extensions. Next, after alluding to the evils of postponement, or of erecting temporary buildings, it was shewn that no real

novis Museis et Lectorum cameris exstruendis datam 1mo Decembris 1862 constituantur [Syndici] ea lege ut ad vos ante finem termini proximi quadragesimalis de dictis rebus ad vos referant."]

1 [Minute of the Syndicate, 12 December, 1862.]

advantage would be gained by beginning afresh with a new architect. Mr Salvin's buildings were skilfully arranged, and well adapted to their complicated purposes. Moreover, he proposed to place them at a distance of 150 feet from the south boundary-wall of the site, thus leaving space sufficient for a building in front of them. This distance might be extended to 170 feet by reducing the length of the proposed western wing, so as to reduce the estimated cost, and increase the space for the ornamental building which the Senate might wish to erect at some future period. The Report ended by definitely recommending: "that the Vice Chancellor be authorised to contract with Messrs George Smith and Co. for the completion of the work at a sum so much lower than the reduced tender mentioned in the former Report, dated 23 May, 1862 (£22,109. 8*s.* 8*d.*), as the above-mentioned reduction of 20 feet in the length of the western wing of the building may appear to require."

This Report, which was signed by all the Syndics except Mr Todhunter, was regarded in the University as an ingenious device for extricating the Senate from the difficulty in which it had placed itself by the adverse vote of 30 May, 1862. The most determined, however, of those who had voted in the majority on that occasion were extremely indignant. They chose to consider that "the sole duty of the Syndicate was to retire Mr Salvin[1]," and when they found that the scheme which they so bitterly detested was again brought forward, they endeavoured, by raising a cry of unconstitutional conduct against the Council, by aspersing Mr Salvin's character, and by throwing doubts on the necessity for such buildings at all, to persuade the Senate to reject the scheme a second time. A Grace to confirm the Report was, however, carried by a majority of 21 votes, 20 March, 1863[2].

The further history of Mr Salvin's buildings, as they may be

[1] [These words are quoted from a fly-sheet by C. B. Clarke, M.A., Queens' College, dated 3 March, 1863. Fly-sheets on the same side were written by W. M. Campion, B.D., of the same College, and by A. Long, M.A., King's College, who gave the first "non-placet" in the Senate-House on both occasions. These fly-sheets were answered by Professor C. C. Babington, Dr Drosier, Professors Challis, Stokes, and Adams, who published a joint statement, and by J. W. Clark, who addressed himself chiefly to the question of Mr Salvin's charges, shewing that he had acted in strict accordance with the rules of his profession.]

[2] [The numbers were: Placet, 83; Non-placet, 62.]

called in order to distinguish them from others subsequently erected, need not detain us long. At the beginning of June a Syndicate was appointed to superintend the building-operations[1], and, 9 June 1863, at three o'clock in the afternoon, the ground was handed over to the architect and contractor, in whose presence the foundation-stone was laid by Professor Liveing, but without any formal ceremony[2].

Soon after the work had been begun a difficulty arose about the ownership of the eastern boundary-wall of the Old Botanic Garden. As there appeared to be no hope of arriving at any satisfactory arrangement with the occupiers of the adjoining tenements, it became necessary to modify Mr Salvin's design. After some consideration it was decided to omit one of the four proposed rooms in the eastern annex, and to use the ground thus obtained for a roadway to the back of the buildings, which Mr Salvin had neglected to provide. The accommodation lost by this change was supplied in a small detached building.

It will be remembered that a previous Syndicate had been compelled to advise the temporary omission of the Museum of Comparative Anatomy. The inconvenience of this postponement having become more manifest as the rest of the work proceeded, Professor Clark wrote to the Vice-Chancellor, 27 September, 1863, offering to lend the sum required (£2364. 14*s*. 3*d*.) at a nominal rate of interest. This liberal offer was at once accepted by the Syndicate, and by them made known to the Senate, 24 October, in the Report which recommended the small alterations above described. This Report was confirmed by the Senate 12 November, and the Museum was commenced soon afterwards[3].

The work proceeded without interruption: the west wing was ready for occupation in November, 1864[4]; the Museum of Zoology, as the large room in the east wing was then called, in February, 1865[5]; and the Museum of Comparative Anatomy in

[1] [This Syndicate (appointed by Grace of the Senate 4 June, 1863) consisted of: the Vice-Chancellor; Dr Cookson, Dr Bateson, Dr Paget, Professor Liveing, and James Lempriere Hammond, M.A., Trinity College.]

[2] [Minute of the Syndicate, 9 June, 1863.]

[3] [The contract was sealed 16 December, 1863.]

[4] [Report of the Syndicate, 1 November, 1864.]

[5] [Minute of the Syndicate, 25 February, 1865.]

June of the same year[1]. In the course of the summer and autumn wall-cases were provided, and the collections were removed from the Old Museum[2]. While this work was proceeding, the old Anatomical Schools were altered so as to adapt them to the requirements of the Professors of Anatomy and Chemistry[3]. This work was substantially completed by the beginning of the Michaelmas Term. The fitting up of the Museums of Mineralogy and Botany was undertaken next, according to plans suggested by Professor Miller and Professor Babington[4], and cases and cabinets were ordered gradually, year by year, according to the state of the Maintenance Fund created by Grace of the Senate 31 May, 1866. The whole building was therefore built and occupied in rather more than two years from the commencement.

The University next turned its attention to the want of instruction in Heat, Electricity, and Magnetism, subjects to which the scheme of examination for Honours in the Mathematical Tripos approved by the Senate 2 June, 1868, had given new prominence. A Syndicate appointed 25 November, 1868, to consider how these subjects might best be taught, reported (27 February, 1869) in favour of founding a special Professorship; and of supplying the Professor with the means of making his teaching practical, in other words, of giving him a Demonstrator, a Lecture-Room, a Laboratory, and several class-rooms, with a sufficient stock of apparatus. Requirements such as these could not be satisfied in any of the rooms then unoccupied in the new buildings, but "additional buildings specially designed for this branch of science" were required. Such buildings, it was added, would probably cost not less than £5000; and apparatus and fittings about £1300 more. In conclusion they suggested the appointment of a special Syndicate to investigate the means of raising this sum. A new Syndicate was accordingly appointed, 13 May, 1869, which suggested (29 March, 1870), among other

[1] [Minute of the Syndicate, 1 June, 1865.]

[2] [Report of the Syndicate, 2 June, 1865; confirmed by Grace, 8 June, 1865. Minute of the Syndicate, 6 October, 1865.]

[3] [Report of the Syndicate, 18 March, 1865, confirmed by Grace, 1 April, 1865.]

[4] [Ibid. 19 October, 1865, confirmed by Grace, 2 November, 1865. The first cabinet was placed in the Museum of Mineralogy at the beginning of 1866. Minute of the Syndicate, 3 May, 1866.]

schemes for raising money, an increase in the Capitation Tax. This recommendation, respecting which the Syndics themselves were not unanimous, was disapproved of by the Senate, and the Report containing it, though reissued in an amended form (31 May), was never presented for confirmation, and the University separated for the Long Vacation without arriving at any conclusion. At the beginning of the Michaelmas Term the Vice-Chancellor received the following letter from the Duke of Devonshire, Chancellor of the University:

"HOLKER HALL, GRANGE, LANCASHIRE,
10 *October*, 1870.

"My dear Mr Vice-Chancellor,

I have the honor to address you for the purpose of making an offer to the University, which, if you see no objection, I shall be much obliged to you to submit in such manner as you may think fit for the consideration of the Council and the University.

I find in the Report dated 29 February, 1869, of the Physical Science Syndicate, recommending the establishment of a Professor and Demonstrator of Experimental Physics, that the buildings and apparatus required for this department of Science are estimated to cost £6300.

I am desirous to assist the University in carrying this recommendation into effect, and shall accordingly be prepared to provide the funds required for the building and apparatus, so soon as the University shall have in other respects completed its arrangements for teaching Experimental Physics, and shall have approved the plan of the building.

I remain, [etc.]

DEVONSHIRE."

This letter was published to the University 13 October, 1870, and soon afterwards (28 October) the Heads of Colleges agreed that the sums required to be raised for the expenses incurred under the Cambridge Improvement Acts should be levied by assessment, instead of being paid out of the University Chest as heretofore. By this arrangement the annual expenditure of the University was so far reduced that the Council of the Senate was enabled to propose (28 November) the immediate foundation of a Professorship of Experimental Physics. This recommendation having been approved (9 February, 1871), a Syndicate was appointed (2 March), to consider the question of an appropriate site for a building, to take professional advice, and to obtain plans and estimates.

This Syndicate consisted of the Vice-Chancellor; Henry Wilkinson Cookson, D.D., Master of Peterhouse; William

Henry Bateson, D.D., Master of S. John's College; Professors Adams, Humphry, Liveing, Maxwell[1], Miller; John Willis Clark, M.A., and Coutts Trotter, M.A., of Trinity College. They reported (18 November) that they could find no position more suitable than the ground adjoining Free School Lane, at the entrance of the old Botanic Garden (fig. 1). This site had the advantage of being easy of access, and far enough from the principal thoroughfares to be free from much vibration. At the same time they presented a complete design, not only for a Laboratory, but also for a Porter's Lodge adjoining it, prepared by W. M. Fawcett, M.A., Architect, with the concurrence, so far as the scientific buildings were concerned, of Professor Liveing and Mr Trotter, who, since the appointment of the Syndicate, "had visited the principal buildings for Physical Science recently erected at home or abroad, for the purpose of ascertaining the best arrangements." They further announced that:

"The plans have been submitted to the Chancellor and approved by him; and although Mr Fawcett's estimate for the building is greater than the amount contemplated when his Grace's munificent offer was made, the Syndicate have the pleasure to state that he has intimated his wish to present the building complete to the University."

The lowest tender, that of Mr John Loveday of Kibworth, Leicester, amounted to £8450. This having been accepted by the Senate (12 March, 1872), a contract with him was sealed 11 April, and the work was commenced shortly afterwards. The building, which, to commemorate the munificence of the Chancellor, it was agreed to call "The Cavendish Laboratory," was practically completed by the Michaelmas Term, 1873, during which the Lecture-Room and Laboratory for students were first used; but it was not ready for experimental work until Easter, 1874[2]. It

[1] [James Clerk Maxwell, M.A., Trinity College, had been elected the first Professor of Experimental Physics 8 March, 1871, and added to the Syndicate 16 March.]

[2] [Reports of Professor Maxwell, dated 1 May, 1874, and 14 April, 1875, appended to the Eighth and Ninth Annual Reports of the Museums and Lecture-Rooms Syndicate, dated 20 May, 1874, and 20 April, 1875. It should be mentioned that while the building was proceeding a claim of £600 for injury to ancient lights was put forward by Corpus Christi College (22 November, 1872). After some correspondence, a special Syndicate was appointed to consider the question. They were advised that the injury could not be substantiated. This opinion, with the reasons for it, having been communicated to the College by the Vice-Chancellor, the Master was instructed "entirely to forego" the claim for compensation. Report of the Syndicate, dated 21 May, 1873. Camb. Univ. Reporter, p. 73.]

was formally inaugurated 16 June, in the same year, when the letter of thanks written by the Public Orator, R. C. Jebb, M.A., Trinity College, was read by him to the Chancellor in the Senate-House. His Grace replied, and then handed the key of the building to the Vice-Chancellor.

The building is arranged in three floors, with the main frontage towards Free School Lane, and a wing returned eastwards as far as the ground will allow. The Porter's Lodge is on the south side of the entrance, so arranged as to command both the entrance and the court beyond. The Lecture-Room is placed immediately over the entrance and Porter's Lodge, advantage being taken of the rising seats to obtain height for the chamber-floor of the Lodge. The lecture-table is immediately over a division-wall, so as to be perfectly firm for experiments. The laboratories, class-rooms, and private rooms are chiefly in the eastern wing. The style is a plain Gothic, worked in stone in the western building, and in white brick with stone dressings in the other.

A students Laboratory was added to the Department of Chemistry in June, 1872[1].

The next addition to the New Museums was the building in three floors which extends from the Museum and Lecture-Room of Zoology and Comparative Anatomy to Corn Exchange Street. The necessity of providing new work-rooms and class-rooms for Comparative Anatomy and Physiology was first brought forward in 1872 by Mr J. W. Clark and Mr Michael Foster, who, as Trinity Prælector in Physiology, had used since 1870 the two rooms in the central building, intended originally for a Museum of Philosophical apparatus[2]. The Museums and Lecture-Rooms Syndicate reported, 25 October, 1872, in favour of the scheme laid before them, which included a design by Mr Fawcett, and their Report was confirmed by the Senate[3], but, with the exception of the purchase of part of the site, as above-mentioned, in the following year, no steps were taken at that time. At the beginning of 1876, the want of additional rooms having become more urgent than ever, in consequence of the

[1] [Grace, 6 June, 1872.]

[2] [Minute of the Syndicate, 17 June, 1870.]

[3] [Grace, 21 November, 1872. It was non-placeted, but carried by a majority of 50 votes.]

appointment of several officers in the interval, the increase of students, and the establishment of a class in Animal Morphology in October, 1875, under the superintendence of Francis Maitland Balfour, M.A., Trinity College, to accommodate which the Professor of Zoology had given up his own private room, the subject was revived, and, a scheme for temporary accommodation having been dismissed as impracticable, it was decided that it would be better to sacrifice the old eastern wing, which Mr Fawcett had previously been instructed to preserve, and to ask him for an entirely new set of designs. These, after the approval of those for whose use they were intended had been obtained, were introduced to the Senate in a Report of the Museums Syndicate, dated 6 March, 1876, which, after discussion and amendment, was confirmed by the Senate without a division (30 March). By a subsequent Grace (4 May) leave to obtain tenders was granted, and that of Messrs Bell, amounting to £8500, having been accepted (15 June), the buildings were commenced without delay.

In the interval between 4 May and 15 June, the Syndicate, acting on the advice of the architect, had determined to use concrete instead of wood for the floors; and subsequently, 22 February, 1877, they obtained leave to construct a roof of the same material, as being less costly and more durable. During the same period a difficulty arose respecting ancient lights with the owner of a house in Corn Exchange Street, and the contract was divided into two portions; viz. for the western portion of the building, together with the ground floor of the portion facing Corn Exchange Street; and for the upper floors of the latter portion. The former portion was ready for occupation by the beginning of 1878; but, in consideration of the above-mentioned difficulty, the commencement of the latter was not authorised by the Senate until 31 May, 1877. The contractors proceeded with the work immediately, and the building was nearly finished, when, 18 February, 1878, a slab of concrete which formed the northernmost compartment of the roof next Corn Exchange Street gave way, and fell to the ground, carrying with it the floors beneath it. It is unnecessary to detail in this place the steps which the Syndicate thought proper to take in consequence of this deplorable accident; it will be sufficient to state that they decided (30 August), after long and careful consideration, and consultation with experts, that the concrete floors throughout the whole of the new buildings should be removed, and replaced by wood[1]. The progress of the building was greatly retarded by this alteration, and the rooms were not finally ready for occupation until the end of January, 1879.

The first floor of this building was appropriated to the Department of Physiology; the rest of the rooms were assigned temporarily to the Professor of Anatomy, the Professor of Zoology and Comparative Anatomy, the Jacksonian Professor (James Dewar)[2], and the Superintendent, partly as work-rooms, partly as private rooms and class-rooms[3].

It was necessary to make this new wing abut against the Museum of Zoology, since called "The Bird Room," in such a manner as to block the windows on the east side. To compensate for this loss of lights a skylight was added; and increased accommodation was obtained by the construction of a gallery.

We must next briefly narrate the establishment of the department of Mechanism. Professor Willis, as Jacksonian Professor, had given lectures on Mechanism, but, on his death in 1875, it was decided that his successor should be a Chemist, and a separate Professorship of Mechanism was established by Grace of the Senate, 25 May, 1875, to which James Stuart, M.A., Trinity College, was elected, 17 November in the same year. For a time he occupied the three rooms originally erected for the Jacksonian Professor, using one as a museum, the other as a workshop, and sharing the lecture room with the Professor of Botany, but at the beginning of 1877 he drew the attention of the Museums Syndicate to the want of a workshop for his engineering pupils, and also of a room in which they might be taught mechanical drawing[4]. In the following year (8 March, 1878) he announced the successful formation of a practical class, and

[1] [A complete narrative of the whole transaction, with all the documents given at length, will be found in a special Report of the Syndicate, dated 23 October, 1878. Camb. Univ. Reporter, No. 258. The course taken was approved by the Senate 14 November, 1878.]

[2] [Elected to the Jacksonian Chair 13 April, 1875.]

[3] [Thirteenth Annual Report of the Museums Syndicate, 27 May, 1879. Camb. Univ. Reporter, p. 665.]

[4] [Eleventh Annual Report, 9 May, 1877. Ibid. p. 424.]

repeated his demand for a new workshop[1], a demand which he shortly afterwards supplemented by an offer that, if the University would build it, he would furnish it with the necessary tools and fittings at his own expense. This liberal proposal having been reported to the Senate, and accepted by them, a workshop, about fifty feet long by twenty feet broad, was erected in the course of the Long Vacation of 1878, in the garden at the back of the Botanical Museum (fig. 1), and opened at the beginning of the following Michaelmas Term[2]. The instruction supplied by Professor Stuart proved so attractive, that in December, 1880, he found it necessary to ask not only for an extension of the workshop, but also for the erection of a room in which mechanical drawing might be taught, to the necessity for which he had before alluded. These requests were granted by the Senate, 16 December, 1880, and carried out at the beginning of the following year. The drawing-office was placed at right angles to the former building, in the garden to the south of the Cavendish Laboratory. A further extension of the workshop was carried out in 1882, by the erection of a building in two floors at its south-west corner[3], to which a Foundry was added in 1884. At the same time the adjoining dwelling-house was utilised as a temporary museum and store-room[4].

We have next to notice the changes introduced into the central block of buildings. In the summer of 1880 the two large rooms called "Museums of Philosophical Apparatus" were thrown into one[5]; the through-passage being placed at the east end. The large room thus formed has since served the double purpose of a Library[6] and an Examination Hall.

It was mentioned above that when the eastern wing was constructed a room was provided in it for Mr Balfour's class in Animal Morphology. This class, in consequence of the en-

[1] [Twelfth Annual Report, 14 May, 1878. Camb. Univ. Reporter, p. 516.]

[2] [Report of the Syndicate, 10 May, 1878, confirmed 6 June. Thirteenth Annual Report, 27 May, 1879. Ibid. p. 665.]

[3] [Report of the Syndicate, 2 December, 1881; confirmed 23 February, 1882.]

[4] [Report, 19 February; confirmed 20 March, 1884.]

[5] [This change had been sanctioned by the Senate 6 June, 1878, but for various reasons the work was not undertaken at that time.]

[6] [By an arrangement with the Cambridge Philosophical Society, confirmed by the Senate 2 June, 1881, their Library was moved into this room in the course of the Long Vacation of that year, and made accessible to the University.]

thusiasm excited by his admirable teaching, soon became so large that the accommodation was found to be wholly inadequate. Mr Foster also had soon a similar complaint to make respecting his own department. A joint representation was therefore made to the Syndicate, in consequence of which the question of additional accommodation was carefully considered. After discussing various ways for providing it, the Syndicate recommended the addition of a third floor to the central building, which would give space for a class-room and two private rooms[1]. This difficult work was carried out with complete success in the Long Vacation of 1882, but Mr Balfour unfortunately did not live to see the work completed. His teaching, however, was carried on so successfully by his friend and pupil Adam Sedgwick, M.A., Trinity College, that in 1884 it was found necessary to add a third floor to the adjoining west wing of the Museums[2] in order to provide an additional laboratory, class room, and private room. This work was carried out with complete success in such a novel manner that the method of operation must be described in detail.

When the existing rooms were examined by a builder, peculiar difficulties presented themselves, for it was found that the ceiling of the Mineralogical Museum was nailed to the beams of the roof, and it appeared that this ceiling must be sacrificed, and the roof taken to pieces. Had this course been adopted, the cases containing the collection of minerals must have been temporarily removed, thereby entailing a large amount of labour, and the closing of the Museum for several weeks. Under these circumstances the Museums and Lecture-Rooms Syndicate applied to Professor Stuart and Mr Lyon (Superintendent of the Mechanical Department) for their opinion. They replied that the roof could be lifted up bodily to the required height, the ceiling being left behind untouched; and further, that the cost would be at least £1000 less than the builder consulted had stated. Under these circumstances they were requested to carry out the work under their personal supervision[3].

[1] [Report of the Syndicate, 28 April; confirmed 11 May, 1882.]

[2] [Report, 24 May; confirmed 10 June, 1884.]

[3] [Report of the Syndicate, 24 May, 1884; confirmed by the Senate 12 June.]

The following was the method adopted in carrying out the operation of lifting the roof. On each side of the principal timbers of the roof, holes were made in the walls under the wall-plates, and new timbers were slid in and placed with their ends on the two walls. It was then ascertained how much weight these new timbers would have to carry in supporting the ceiling, and what their deflection would be when their load came upon them. After being screwed down with a "jack" to give them the required deflection, every rafter which carried the ceiling of the Mineralogical Museum was attached to them by means of hoop-iron slings; and, when the operation was complete, the nails fastening these rafters to the principal timbers of the roof were very carefully cut so as to leave the ceiling hanging entirely by the new timbers. So nicely was the deflection calculated, that no timber moved upwards or downwards more than the eighth of an inch when the load came upon it. Next, an iron beam on either side of the principal was slid under the wall-plate, and these also, six and twenty in number, were made to rest on the two walls, which have a clear span of twenty-five feet. The lifting of the roof then began. It was accomplished by means of twelve screw-jacks, one of which was placed under the end of each of the principal timbers on the same wall. Any straining of the roof was prevented by working all the jacks simultaneously, the men giving each jack half a turn at the word of command of the Superintendent. All the principal ends being thus lifted one foot, packing was put across the two iron beams on either side of each principal, and the principal was lowered on to it; the jacks were then all taken to the other side of the building and a similar process was carried out there. Brick pillars were built temporarily on the iron beams to carry the principals while the roof was being lifted the necessary twelve and a half feet so as to leave the walls of the new storey perfectly free from strain while they were being built. Finally, when the walls were complete, the roof, which had been lifted a few inches too high, was lowered on to them and made secure. Not a single slate or nail in the roof was broken or strained, and the whole work of lifting the roof and building the exterior walls was completed in seventeen working days, the weight lifted being fifty tons, and the total length of roof one hundred and ten feet[1]. At the same time a second floor was added to the western annex, in order to supply class-rooms and private rooms for the teaching of Physiological Botany[2].]

CHAPTER III.

History of the Observatory.

[Thomas Plume, D.D., Christ's College, Archdeacon of Rochester, directed by his will, dated 2 September, 1704, that a sum of about £1800 should be placed in the hands of certain Trustees, for the following purposes: to erect an Observatory, to stock it with Instruments, to maintain a Professor of Astronomy and Experimental Philosophy, and to buy or build a House for the Professor in or near the said Observatory[3]. The sum was obviously inadequate for these various purposes, and it was therefore agreed to lay it out in the purchase of an estate at Balsham in Cambridgeshire, the annual income of which should be devoted to the objects indicated by the testator[4]. Meanwhile, 5 February, 1705—6, Roger Cotes, M.A., Fellow of Trinity College, having been elected first Professor, the Master and Seniors agreed: "that he and his Successors after him in the said Professorship of what College or Place soever they shall be, have the Rooms and Leads of the King's Gate for a dwelling and Observatory, so long as the Trustees or Electors for the said Professorship shall think fit." This Conclusion was presented to Dr Plume's Trustees in the form of an Instrument under the College seal, 9 February, 1705—6, and the Observatory over the

[1] [This description of the work has been most kindly communicated by my friend James Lyon, M.A., Clare College.]

[2] [Reports, 19 February and 22 April; confirmed 15 May, 1884.]

[3] [In Dr Plume's Will the Observatory is placed first; in the letters patent of Queen Anne, the Professor's salary is placed first, and the Observatory House and Instruments second.]

[4] [Letters Patent of Queen Anne, 11 June, 1707, printed in Endowments of the University of Cambridge, p. 54.]

Great Gate (fig. 1) was probably begun soon afterwards. The cost was defrayed partly by subscription, partly by Trinity College, but, as it formed part of the buildings of that College, its history has been already related, and need not be repeated here[1]. It was handed over to the College by Dr Plume's Trustees in 1792, no use having been made of it for at least fifty years, and it was taken down in 1797.

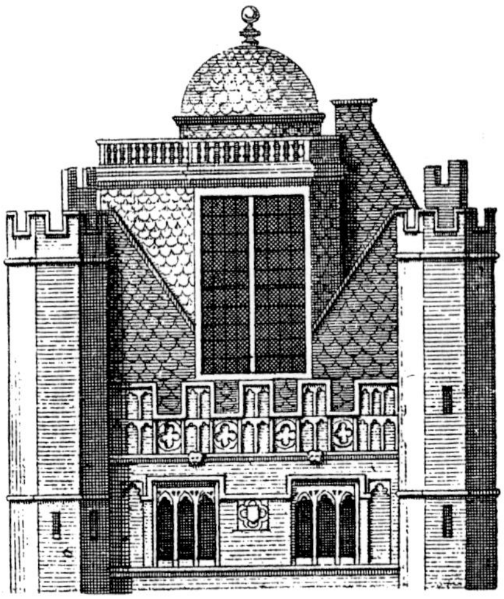

Fig. 1. Upper story of the east front of the Great Gate of Trinity College, with the Observatory: from a view taken in 1740.

Two years before this act on the part of Dr Plume's Trustees, a Grace had passed the Senate, 25 May, 1790, the preamble of which set forth, that "students of Astronomy greatly desired a building, in which they might properly pursue astronomical observations;" and the Grace proceeded to nominate a Syndicate to consider and report upon the matter. The Syndics appear to have obtained a plan, but beyond a single entry to this effect in the University Accounts[2], we know nothing about their proceedings.

[1] [History of Trinity College, Vol. ii. pp. 499, 500.]

[2] [Univ. Accounts, 1796—97 (*Exp. ordinary and extraordinary*). "Mr Gibson, for Plans for an Observatory, 24. 6. 0."]

No further steps were taken until 1817, when a Grace passed the Senate (3 December) to the effect that the erection of an Observatory in the University was greatly to be desired, and nominating Syndics to report within three months on a suitable site, on the funds available for such an undertaking, and on all other matters relating thereunto. The Syndics appointed were: the Vice-Chancellor; Isaac Milner, D.D., President of Queens' College; John Kaye, D.D., Master of Christ's College; Samuel Vince, M.A., Plumian Professor; William Farish, M.A., Jacksonian Professor; William Lax, M.A., Lowndean Professor; Thomas Catton, M.A., S. John's College; Bewick Bridge, M.A., Peterhouse; Robert Woodhouse, M.A., Gonville and Caius College; George Peacock, M.A., Trinity College; Thomas Turton, M.A., Catharine Hall; John Frederick William Herschel, M.A., S. John's College; and William Hustler, M.A., Jesus College.

At a meeting held 29 January, 1818, the Syndics made the following Minute:

"1. That the establishment of an Observatory will be beneficial to the University and to the Nation:

2. That the expenses of building and furnishing an Observatory will probably not exceed £10,000.

3. That the Funds of the University, considering the probable demands upon them for other purposes, are inadequate to defray the whole of such expenses:

4. That towards defraying them a Grace be proposed to the Senate for the donation of £5,000 from the University Chest; and that a Subscription be opened for raising the remainder of the sum:

5. That an application be made to Government to appoint an Observer and an Assistant, with adequate Salaries:

6. That the above sum of £5,000 be advanced from the Chest, and the work commenced, as soon as £5,000 shall have been raised by Subscription, and a favourable answer received from Government.

7. That the precincts of the University afford several sites proper for the purpose."

The Syndicate was reappointed 8 April, 1818, and the next two years were probably spent in negotiations, for they did not issue their first Report until 24 April, 1820. As this document does not differ, in any important particular having reference to the building, from the Minute quoted above, it need not be transcribed. It was confirmed by the Senate 5 May following, and the £5000 asked for was granted out of the University Chest. On the same day two Syndicates were appointed, the one to collect subscriptions, the other, which may be called the Building Syndicate, to select a proper site, to make arrangements for its purchase, to obtain plans and estimates for the Observatory, to purchase Instruments to the value of £3000, as soon as £10,000 had been collected[1], and to report to the Senate within seven months from the date of their appointment.

The latter Syndicate, which alone concerns our present purpose, consisted of eight members of the first Syndicate, viz. Dr Kaye; Professor Farish; Professor Woodhouse, elected Lucasian Professor, 1820; Mr Catton, Mr Bridge, Mr Turton, Mr Hustler, Mr Herschel, with one new member, James Cumming, M.A., Professor of Chemistry.

The subscriptions came in so rapidly that the Syndicate was enabled to inform the Senate, 2 December, 1820, that more than £5000 had been collected, and that they had therefore ordered certain instruments to the value of about £2,300. With reference to the site and building the Report contained the following clauses:

"The Syndics, after an attentive examination of every situation in the neighbourhood of Cambridge, have unanimously agreed, that the most eligible site for an Observatory is a field belonging to St John's College near the gravel-pits on the Madingley Road; which unites the advantages of a view all round the horizon, not now obstructed, nor likely to be obstructed hereafter in any direction, particularly in the essential one of the meridian; of sufficient elevation; of a clear air, never subject to be disturbed by the smoke of the Town; of a dry soil; and of such a distance from the University as, all circumstances considered, they judge the most desirable.

The Syndics have made application to St John's College, to know if possession of part of this field can be obtained; and have received for answer, that the College is willing and ready to enter into a negotiation for that purpose. And they are endeavouring to ascertain the precise spot which may have the advantage of a very distant meridian-mark, on the tower if possible, or on some part, of Grantchester Church.

With respect to plans of the building; though the Syndics have used due diligence, they have not been able, as yet, to obtain such information concerning the construction of the principal Observatories in this kingdom or abroad, and such suggestions from the most eminent

[1] [This proviso must mean that £3000 was to be spent on instruments, as soon as the whole fund, including the £5000 voted by the Senate, amounted to £10,000.]

practical Astronomers, as would enable them to point out to Architects, with sufficient detail, all those precautions in the fabric of an Observatory, and those dimensions, and that arrangement of the different rooms in it, which would be best adapted to secure stability of the instruments, precision of the observations, and facility in making them."

Lastly, they recommended that the site suggested be approved, and that the time for making their final Report should be extended to the end of the Easter Term. These Graces passed the Senate 12 December, 1820.

When this Report appeared, 1 June, 1821, it announced that S. John's College had agreed to sell six acres and a half of ground, in the field above specified, at the price of £100 per acre, but that as the sale could only be effected by an Act of Parliament, considerable delay would of necessity elapse before the transfer could be effected. It was, however, hoped that, with the consent of the College, preparatory operations might begin in the autumn. "With this view," they added, "the spot which has the tower of Grantchester Church in the meridian to the South, has been ascertained with sufficient accuracy; and this spot will determine the Western end of the Observatory." The following passage, having reference to the plan of the proposed building, is worth quotation, as shewing how much care was taken to procure the best possible design:

"The Syndics having examined plans or descriptions of the principal Observatories of Europe, and having been by the kindness of Mr Rennie favoured with a copy of the plan lately made by him for the intended Observatory at the *Cape of Good Hope*, expect to be able shortly to propose such a description of the buildings, their dimensions, and arrangement, as may enable Architects to furnish them with plans and estimates of the Observatory and dwellings of the Observers; which, as soon as they are procured, will be laid before the Senate for their consideration."

In October 1821 a public advertisement made known that

"The Syndics for building an Observatory in the University of Cambridge are desirous of procuring Plans, Specifications, and Estimates for an Observatory, the Ground Plan of which is already agreed upon[1]; and for two Houses for the Observer and Assistant Observers.

[1] [A detailed ground plan had evidently been prepared by the Syndicate, for Mr Mead begins his description of his design by saying: "The plan of the ground floor

A Premium of one Hundred Pounds will be given for the best Design, and of Fifty Pounds for the second best. Plans to be sent in before the first of January 1822.

Further particulars may be obtained by application to the Rev. the Vice Chancellor.

Cambridge, Oct. 16. 1821."

Thirteen architects sent in designs. The Syndicate, on their own responsibility, adjudged the first prize to that by John Clement Mead, the second to that by William Wilkins[1]. This selection was approved by the Senate, 13 March, 1822. Mr Mead estimated the cost at £8795. 13*s.* —; but the contractors, Messrs Munday and Bushell, undertook to complete the entire structure, with stone facings throughout, for £8,497. 6*s.* 8*d.* before the end of October, 1823. The contract was signed 21 June, and work began on Tuesday, 25 June, 1822[2]. On the day following the Syndicate made the terms of the contract known to the Senate, and prudently stated:

"That it appears, from the information which the Syndics at present possess, that the expenses of completing the Observatory in a manner creditable to the University will exceed the amount of the Subscriptions which have been received; in consequence of which, they think it right to state that, at some future period, an appeal must be made to the liberality of the Senate for further assistance from the Common Chest[3]."

The buildings were completed at the time agreed upon, or shortly afterwards; and the Syndicate then addressed themselves to the task of "collecting and examining the several bills yet undischarged." The cost had reached an amount so large, and so extraordinarily in excess of the contracted price, that it will be interesting to transcribe the totals from the Report dated 17 May 1824, in which the Syndicate admitted, and tried to excuse, their responsibility for this excess:

has been laid out agreeably to the instructions and dimensions specified, and it is presumed little further explanation will be necessary than is contained in the drawings."]

1 [Minute of the Syndicate, 4 March, 1822.]

2 [Letter of the architect to the Vice-Chancellor, 21 June, 1822.]

3 [Report of the Syndicate, 26 June, 1822. This Report was practically confirmed by a Grace of the Senate, 29 June, which continued the Syndicate with their existing powers.]

				£	s.	d.
Purchase of ground				1,008	4	7
Inclosure and laying out of ground				1,472	13	5
Observatory, Observer's and Assistant's House:						
Contract with Messrs Munday	8,497	6	8			
Alterations	1,075	2	8			
Additions: Dome and shutters	2,766	16	1			
Ironwork, chiefly to the houses ...	782	16	3			
				13,122	1	8
Stable, Offices, Garden Wall, etc.				1,518	1	8
Gates				652	14	0
Insurance, etc.				155	15	9
Premiums to architects				150	0	0
Clerk of Works				183	15	0
Architect				978	3	0
				£19,241	9	1

To meet this outlay there was only £11,806. 11*s.* 9*d.* in hand, of which £5000 had been voted by the University, and paid over to the Syndics; £5,705. 18*s.* 7*d.* represented the surplus of the subscriptions after the purchase of instruments as related above; and £1100. 13*s.* 2*d.* consisted of dividends and profits on sale of stock. There was therefore a deficit of £7,434. 17*s.* 4*d.*

The Syndicate admitted that if they had foreseen such an expenditure as that which had actually taken place, when they made their intimation dated 26 June, 1822, they would certainly have applied to the Senate, in the first instance, for a more distinct authority; that the cost of the Dome very far exceeded what they had been led to expect; that the cost of laying out the grounds might have been more effectually controlled, if some of the works had been executed under separate and specific contracts; and they concluded by asking for £5000, to be appropriated to the discharge of the bills which they had examined and approved; though they admitted that a considerable sum would still be required for the final settlement of the accounts connected with the building, exclusive of a further outlay for instruments. We cannot be surprised that the Senate declined, 26 May, 1824, both to grant this sum[1], and to prolong the existence of the Syndicate[2]. After a long negotiation the out-

[1] [The numbers were: Non Placet, 30; Placet, 18.]

[2] [The numbers were: Non Placet, 33; Placet, 12.]

standing bills were reduced by a small amount, and before the end of the year the whole matter was finally settled[1]. From a careful comparison of the different reports and lists of bills it appears that the building, exclusive of the site and the planting of it, could not have cost less than £16,340. 12*s.* 11*d.*, or nearly twice the amount specified in the contract. It is therefore satisfactory to find the Plumian Professor, George Biddell Airy, M.A., Trinity College, stating to the Senate, 26 February, 1828,

Fig. 2. North-west view of the Observatory.

that "all the Astronomers who have seen it, English and Foreign, agree in declaring it to be better adapted to its purpose than any similar building in Europe."

The general appearance of the building will be understood from the woodcut (fig. 2). The principal front, to the west, is

[1] [The Vice-Chancellor was authorised by Grace of the Senate to pay £4000. 4 June, 1824, and £3115. 0. 2, 8 December, 1824.]

about 160 feet long. It is entered through a tetrastyle portico in the Doric style, copied, according to the architect's own statement, "from the Temple of Minerva at Athens." The building is in two floors, and though the general style is Grecian, the symbol of Osiris is introduced as an ornament along the cornice. The south wing contains the apartments of the Professor, the north wing those of his assistant.

An adjoining building was erected in 1835, at the expense of the Duke of Northumberland, then High Steward, and afterwards Chancellor, of the University, to contain a telescope presented by himself.]

CHAPTER IV.

HISTORY OF THE FITZWILLIAM MUSEUM[1].

[RICHARD FITZWILLIAM, Viscount FITZWILLIAM, by will dated 18 August, 1815, bequeathed to the University his pictures, engravings, books, &c., together with £100,000 in the New South Sea Annuities. The will contained the following clauses respecting the building in which these treasures were to be deposited:

"I do hereby...direct that they [the University] shall with all convenient Speed after my Decease, by and out of the Dividends and Annual Proceeds of my said New South Sea Annuities, cause to be erected and built a good substantial and convenient Museum, Repository, or other Building, within the Precincts of the said University, for the reception and preservation of the said Pictures, Books, and other Articles, or to purchase one or more Erections or Buildings for that purpose.

And in the mean time and until such a Museum...shall be erected, built, or purchased as aforesaid, to procure a proper Building for their temporary Reception."

Viscount Fitzwilliam died 5 February, 1816; the bequest was announced to the University by the Earl of Pembroke, the sole executor, 22 February following; and the collection was removed to Cambridge a few months afterwards; but the first

[1] [It will be understood that the documents quoted in this chapter are preserved in the Registry of the University, unless it is otherwise stated.]

stone of the permanent building was not laid until 1837. The reasons for this delay must be briefly investigated.

The first step taken by the University was the appointment of a Syndicate, 17 April, 1816,

"To provide a place for the temporary reception of the Paintings, etc., bequeathed to the University by the late Lord Viscount Fitzwilliam, and to consult and report to the Senate upon a plan for carrying into effect that part of the Will which relates to the erection of a Museum."

The Syndicate consisted of the Vice-Chancellor; Martin Davy, M.D., Master of Gonville and Caius College; George Thackeray, B.D., Provost of King's College; Edward Daniel Clarke, LL.D., Jesus College; Sir Isaac Pennington, M.D., S. John's College; John Hailstone, M.A., Woodwardian Professor; Thomas Jackson, B.D., Norrisian Professor of Divinity; Adam Sedgwick, M.A., Trinity College; William French, M.A., Pembroke College.

They addressed themselves first to the question of temporary accommodation, and after careful examination of buildings suggested to them, decided, in May, to select the Grammar School founded in 1615, by the will of Stephen Perse, M.D., the situation of which has been already alluded to (p. 145). This School, which at that time attracted but few scholars[1], contained a room 66 feet long by 22 feet broad, and 16 feet high, with a fine open roof. The Trustees of the School made no difficulty in allowing the Syndics to take possession of this large room in the first instance, and subsequently of the wing abutting against it to the north, and to make what alterations they thought proper to fit the premises for the reception of pictures and books, the Syndics undertaking to provide a new School-Room and Master's House[2]. The necessary alterations, which included suitable cases for the books and prints, were carried out by William Wilkins, Architect, and the collection was ready for exhibition at the beginning of

[1] ["The school-house now exists almost without scholars; the insufficiency of the salaries prevents a constant attendance of the masters, and therefore but few boys attend—and those receive their lessons very frequently at the Master's lodgings." Harraden's Cantabrigia Depicta, 4to. Cambridge, 1809. The Master of the School informed a Sub-Syndicate deputed to examine the premises that he did not "make much use of this room except during the hot weather." Report, 27 April, 1816.]

[2] [Minutes of the Syndicate, 7 May, 1816.]

the Michaelmas Term, 1816. The larger room served the two-fold purpose of a Library and a Picture-Gallery. The original windows were blocked, and new windows contrived in the sloping roof. Bookcases of wainscot, with wire doors, were ranged along the side-walls; the pictures occupied the space above them. The smaller room contained the cabinet pictures[1]. The collection remained in the Perse School until 1842, when it was placed in the East Room of the University Library, with the concurrence of the Library Syndicate, until the permanent building was ready for it in 1848.

Meanwhile the Syndicate had not been unmindful of the duty of providing a site for a permanent building, but five years elapsed before they were successful. At the first meeting after their appointment, 25 April, 1816, they agreed that it would be desirable to place the proposed Museum in the vicinity of the Senate-House and Library; and as King's College was understood to be about to extend their buildings, it was further suggested that the objects of the College and of the Syndicate might perhaps be combined. At the next meeting (4 May) it was decided to ask for the ground extending from the east end of King's College Chapel to Old King's Lane; in other words, for the entire frontage of the College to Trumpington Street. This resolution was duly forwarded to the College by the Vice-Chancellor; but the Provost returned the very obvious reply, that the Fellows "seemed decidedly adverse to the alienation of that part of the College property[2]." The Syndics next asked Catharine Hall to sell the Bull Inn; but the proposal was declined. Not discouraged by this failure they reported to the Senate (23 January, 1818) that: "upon mature consideration, the ground fronting Trumpington Street, between King's Lane and Catharine Hall, appears to them the most eligible scite for a Museum which their funds would enable them to purchase." The rest of the year was spent in maturing a very elaborate scheme for an exchange of property between the University, King's College, Catharine Hall, and Clare Hall, by which the

[1] [These details have been partly derived from the Cambridge Guide for 1820 and 1830; partly from a contemporary engraving in the Free Library, Cambridge.]

[2] [Letter of the Provost of King's College to the Vice-Chancellor, 27 November, 1816.]

University would have obtained a site sufficiently large for the Museum: King's College, Mr Cory's House, which was greatly needed for the new buildings[1]; Catharine Hall, several houses and piece of ground adjoining to the College; and Clare Hall would have been enabled to effect a long-desired exchange with King's College[2]. This scheme, which is detailed in an undated Report confirmed by the Senate 11 December, 1818, was overthrown at the last moment by the refusal of Catharine Hall. The sites next suggested were the ground opposite to Clare Hall Piece, which, it was thought, "might be obtained for the Museum, a new Botanical Garden, and the proposed Observatory[3]"; the south side of the old Botanic Garden; the "Paschal Yard," belonging to Corpus Christi College, now part of Pembroke College[4]; the north side of the grounds of Downing College[5]; the vacant space on the south side of Senate-House Yard, on which it had formerly been proposed to erect a building equal and opposite to the Senate-House[6]; the area bounded on the west by Trumpington Street, on the south by Bene't Street, on the east by Pease Hill, and on the north by S. Mary's Passage, or a portion of it[7]; and, lastly, the area between Great S. Mary's Church and S. Michael's Church.

[1] [History of King's College, Vol. i. p. 348.] [2] [Ibid. p. 347.]

[3] [Minutes of the Syndicate, 13 October, 1819.]

[4] [History of Pembroke College, Vol. i. p. 125.]

[5] [A Minute of the Syndicate shews that these three sites were discussed 14 December, 1819.]

[6] [History of the Schools, etc. Chapter III.]

[7] [Minutes of the Syndicate, 22 February, 1820. A Report in favour of the portion of this site north of S. Edward's Church was presented to the Senate 17 April, 1820. Among other schemes it was gravely suggested to remove Gonville and Caius College and to build the Museum on its site "of the exact dimensions and proportions of the Parthenon at Athens (the Sculpture omitted)." The author of this curious design is said to have been William John Bankes, M.A., Trinity College, M.P. for the University 1824—26. A lithographed elevation of the whole west side of Trumpington Street, with the proposed alteration carried out, was published by Messrs Colnaghi, 1 July, 1824; and a scheme for raising the necessary funds, about £80,000, was suggested in a fly-sheet dated Commencement Tuesday, 1824. The removal of Caius College had been already suggested by the Syndicate appointed 17 May, 1824, "to consider practicable Improvements in the Town of Cambridge"; and the Minutes of the Syndicate shew that the idea was favourably received by the College. The site suggested was the "New Gardens" belonging to Peterhouse; but the then lessee, Mr Christopher Pemberton, declined to surrender his lease, and no further progress was made.]

These sites were all, for different reasons, dismissed, and 4 January, 1821, "a suggestion having been made that a site suitable for the Museum might possibly be procured on ground in Trumpington Street, the property of Peterhouse, and to the south of that College," the Vice-Chancellor was requested to ascertain, through the Master, whether the Society would be disposed to treat, and on what terms[1]. The negotiations proceeded smoothly, and before the end of the Easter Term, 1821, the Syndicate were able to announce to the Senate (30 May, 1821) that they had obtained, for £8,500, a site bounded on the east by Trumpington Street, and on the other sides by the grove and gardens of Peterhouse[2]. This site had a frontage of 400 feet towards Trumpington Street, with a depth of about 100 feet[3]. In the course of the following year, the Master and Fellows of Peterhouse—who had throughout treated the application of the Syndicate in the most liberal manner—agreed to exchange a portion of the frontage for an increased depth; and further, to remove certain houses which stood between the College and the proposed Museum[4], as soon as the latter should be built, and to lay out the ground as a garden. This alteration was approved by the Senate, and the property was conveyed to the University, 3 April, 1823. Unfortunately the ground was held under eight different leases, for periods which varied from 14 years to 24 years, and the prices demanded by the lessees were such that the Syndicate could not recommend the University to accede to them[5].

No further action was taken for eleven years, and in all probability a still longer period would have elapsed before the plans for a permanent building were even discussed, had not the Perse Trustees intimated to the University, 3 March, 1834, their wish to resume possession of the School. Shortly afterwards (14 March) a Syndicate, which may be designated for convenience the First Syndicate, was appointed "to consult what steps should be taken to provide accommodation for the

1 [Minutes of the Syndicate, 4 January, 1821.]

2 [See the Plan attached to the History of Peterhouse, Vol. i. p. 1.]

3 [The Report of the Syndicate in favour of this site, dated 28 May, 1821, was confirmed by the Senate, 1 June, 1821.]

4 [Some of these houses are figured, History of Peterhouse, Vol. i. p. 5.]

5 [Minutes of the Syndicate, 23 May, 1823.]

Fitzwilliam Collections[1]." The persons selected were: the Vice-Chancellor; George Thackeray, D.D., Provost of King's College; John Kaye, D.D., Master of Christ's College; James William Geldart, LL.D., Regius Professor of Civil Law; John Haviland, M.D., Regius Professor of Physic; Adam Sedgwick, M.A., Woodwardian Professor of Geology; William Hallows Miller, M.A., Professor of Mineralogy; Henry Philpott, M.A., Catharine Hall; William Potter, M.A., Peterhouse.

It does not appear from the Minutes of this Syndicate, or from any of their published reports, that they addressed themselves at all to the question of finding a place for the temporary accommodation of the collection. On the contrary, they reported, 27 May, that the site purchased in 1823 was so nearly out of lease that "they decidedly recommend to the Senate to proceed with as little delay as possible, to build, for the accommodation of the Fitzwilliam Collection, a Museum, or portion thereof"; and they proceeded to point out that the central portion of the site, containing a frontage of 160 feet, would be out of lease at Michaelmas, 1835; further portions at Michaelmas, 1836 and 1837; and the whole site at Michaelmas, 1840. This Report having been published to the University, and favourably received, the Syndicate agreed (23 June, 1834) to propose the following Grace to the Senate:

"To continue the Fitzwilliam Syndicate to the expiration of the ensuing Term, and to empower them to receive Plans and Estimates of a new Museum from such Architects as may be disposed to supply them gratuitously; to be submitted to the Senate for their judgment and selection."

This Grace having been duly passed (28 June), the Syndicate proceeded (21 July) to insert advertisements in the principal newspapers, inviting architects to send in plans and estimates. No precise instructions, as in the case of the Library, were drawn up, the style, the arrangement, and the extent, of the proposed building being left to the judgment of the competitors. The only information supplied to them was contained in the following document:

[1] [The words of the Latin Grace are: "Syndici constituantur qui inquirant quo commode transferantur Libri et Tabellæ Pictæ Fitzwilliamenses."]

"It is intended to provide for the reception of the present Collection, the Bequest of the late Mr MESMAN[1], consisting of about 200 Pictures, and possible future additions.

The portion of the MUSEUM to be first erected is intended to occupy the centre of the site; which will be out of Lease at Michaelmas, 1835. The Sum to be expended upon the erection of this portion of the Museum is not to exceed £40,000.

The portion of the Ground Plan, designated as a part of S. Peter's College Grove, being subject to no Lease, will be available for any purpose connected with the proposed Building.

The Plans and Estimates must be sent to the VICE-CHANCELLOR on or before the 12th of November next."

A supplemental instruction was subsequently issued (12 August):

"The Syndicate do not recommend that provision be made for the residence of a Curator in the central portion of the Museum intended to be first erected, but they are of opinion that provision should be made for ultimately effecting such purpose, either in the wings or in the rear of the proposed building.

The Syndicate have also agreed that the time for sending in the plans and estimates be extended from 12 November next to 10 April, 1835."

The competition had evidently excited extraordinary interest, for thirty-six designs were sent in, representing the work of twenty-seven architects. Their names, arranged in alphabetical order, are: Mr Bardwell, Mr Barnes, Mr Basevi, Mr Bellamy, Mr Brookes, Mr Cheffins, Mr Fowler, Mr Fripp, Mr Hakewill, Mr Inman, Mr Mylne, Mr Pennethorne, Mr Poynter, Mr Rickman, Mr Salvin, Mr Tatham, Mr Taylor, Mr Thomas, Mr Vulliamy, Mr Walter, Mr Wilkins Of these, Mr Inman, Mr Rickman, and Mr Taylor, sent in three designs each, and Mr Vulliamy, four; six others were designated by symbols or mottoes only. Of the latter, the motto *Palmam qui meruit ferat* was known to represent the design of Mr Lappidge. These designs were ready for exhibition at the Pitt Press 15 April, 1835; and, as the final selection was not made until 29 October following, the Senate had ample time for forming a correct judgment on their merits,

[1] [Daniel Mesman, Esq. bequeathed his collection of pictures to his brother, the Rev. Charles Mesman, for his life, with a remainder to the University. He, however, surrendered his life-interest, and the collection was removed to Cambridge in the course of 1834. It was deposited in the large room at the Pitt Press, now the Registry of the University.]

notwithstanding their great number, and probably varied character, but unfortunately no record has been preserved of the style or extent of those which were unsuccessful. With regard to the mode of selection, to regulate which the First Syndicate was reappointed (8 May)[1], it was agreed that there should be two scrutinies: at the first, each member of the Senate should vote for four designs, and at the second, for one. This scheme produced the following result: at the first scrutiny Mr Basevi had 140 votes; Mr Poynter, 105; Mr Lappidge, 102; Mr Bardwell, 65: at the second Mr Basevi had 131 votes; Mr Bardwell, 31; Mr Poynter, 9; and Mr Lappidge, 4.

Mr Basevi's design having been selected, a Syndicate was appointed, 18 November, to ascertain whether it was in conformity with the instructions. On the following day they issued a singularly brief report:

"That, having conferred with Mr Basevi, and having referred to all the Instructions given to Architects respecting Plans for the Fitzwilliam Museum, they are of opinion that Mr Basevi's Design is in conformity with those Instructions."

The next step was to appoint a Syndicate (2 December, 1835)—which we will term the Second Syndicate—to confer with Mr Basevi on any changes which he might think it expedient to make in his design; to decide on the material to be employed; to consider, as far as the nature of the case admitted, what additions it would be possible to make at a future time to the Museum; and lastly, to fence off the site of the proposed building. The Syndics were: the Vice-Chancellor; George Neville, M.A., Master of Magdalene College; George Thackeray, D.D., Provost of King's College; William French, D.D., Master of Jesus College; John Kaye, D.D., Master of Christ's College; William Frere, M.A., Master of Downing College; John Haviland, M.D., Regius Professor of Physic; Adam Sedgwick, M.A., Woodwardian Professor of Geology; Ralph Tatham, M.A., and Charles Merivale, M.A., S. John's College; John Lodge, M.A., Magdalene College; George Peacock, M.A., and William Whewell, M.A., Trinity College; Robert Willis, M.A., Gonville and Caius College; Thomas Worsley, M.A., Downing College; Francis

[1] [They proposed their scheme to the Senate 4 June, and it was confirmed 11 June, 1835.]

William Lodington, M.A., Clare College; Samuel Fennell, M.A., Queens' College; Henry Philpott, M.A., Catharine Hall; Robert Birkett, M.A., Emmanuel College; Henry Calthrop, M.A., Corpus Christi College; William Potter, M.A., and William Hopkins, M.A., Peterhouse; and James William Lucas Heaviside, M.A., Sidney Sussex College.

They first considered the shape and the extent of the site which had been purchased from Peterhouse, and in consequence of a statement made to them by Mr Basevi, that an additional depth of ground would be required to give full effect to his design, they induced the College: (1) to grant to the University an additional space along the west side of the site about twelve feet wide at its central point; (2) to make the new western boundary parallel to Trumpington Street throughout its whole extent, at the distance of 162 feet from it; (3) to make the northern boundary at right angles to Trumpington Street, the University returning to the College a triangular piece of ground at the north-east corner, having a base of about 30 feet frontage to Trumpington Street. In consideration of the additional space thus obtained, it was agreed that the College should receive £1000, and that the clause by which the College had covenanted to lay out the ground between their buildings and the Museum as a garden, should be relaxed so far as to allow of the erection of strictly collegiate buildings upon it, provided that a space 15 feet wide was left between them and the north boundary of the Museum ground[1]. The Senate accepted these new arrangements 2 November, 1836.

It is much to be regretted that the drawings which Mr Basevi submitted to competition in the first instance should not have been preserved, and still more, that he should not have published any description of them. Such a document would probably have given a history of the origin and development of the design, which is said to have been suggested, at least so far as the arrangement of the portico is concerned, by the remains of a Roman building discovered at Brescia in 1820[2]; and, further,

[1] [These details are taken from a Report of the Syndicate, dated 28 October, 1836.]

[2] [A ground-plan of the façade of this building, the columns of which are arranged in the same manner as those of the Fitzwilliam Museum, will be found in the Annali dell' Instituto di Corrispondenza Archeologica, xi. 182, 8vo. Roma, 1839.]

would have explained his reasons for introducing certain features which were subsequently modified, either by himself or by his successors. In the absence of such information the following passages, which occur in a report of the Second Syndicate, dated 13 February, 1837, are of great value:

"(1) The following are the alterations in the design, which are now submitted to the Senate for its approbation:

The length of the façade to be increased six feet, and the height of the building about one foot.

Part of the Attic over each wing of the portico to be suppressed.

The width of the Picture Gallery to be diminished, and that of the Sculpture Gallery and Hall [to be] increased about six feet; the height of the Sculpture Gallery and Hall being also increased four feet, and that of the Library one foot.

(2) In respect to the Materials to be employed, it was originally the intention of Mr Basevi, that the Façade should be of Bath stone, and the other three sides of white brick with stone dressings and a plain cornice; and that the roof should be partly covered with lead and partly with slate: it was also his intention that the pavement in the Sculpture Gallery and Hall should be of stone with dots of marble; that the columns in it should be of Bath Stone; and that all the floors should be of deal.

According to the plan now furnished by him it is proposed that the whole exterior of the edifice shall be of Portland stone, and that the enriched cornice of the façade shall be carried entirely round the building; also that the roof shall be wholly covered with lead: And with regard to the interior it is proposed that the pavement of the Sculpture Gallery and Hall shall be altogether of marble; that the columns shall be of scagliola; and that all the floors shall be of wainscot.

(3) The increase of the site effected by the late exchange with the Master and Fellows of Peterhouse will allow of the erection of the two wings represented in Mr Basevi's original design, whenever such additions may be required.

The estimate now furnished by Mr Basevi exceeds that which accompanied his original plan [£40,000] by the sum of £16.800. The whole of this excess however is not owing to the proposed alterations in the Design and Materials; part being due to the expense of such of the external sculpture, as was not included in the former calculation, and part to the rise in the prices of building materials since the original estimate was made."

Mr Basevi subsequently explained that he intended to raise "the square part over the portico" four feet and a half. It was of course necessary to inform the Senate of this further alteration, the above Report having been published before the receipt of

Mr Basevi's letter[1]. It was therefore announced in the following Grace, which passed without opposition, 3 March, 1837:

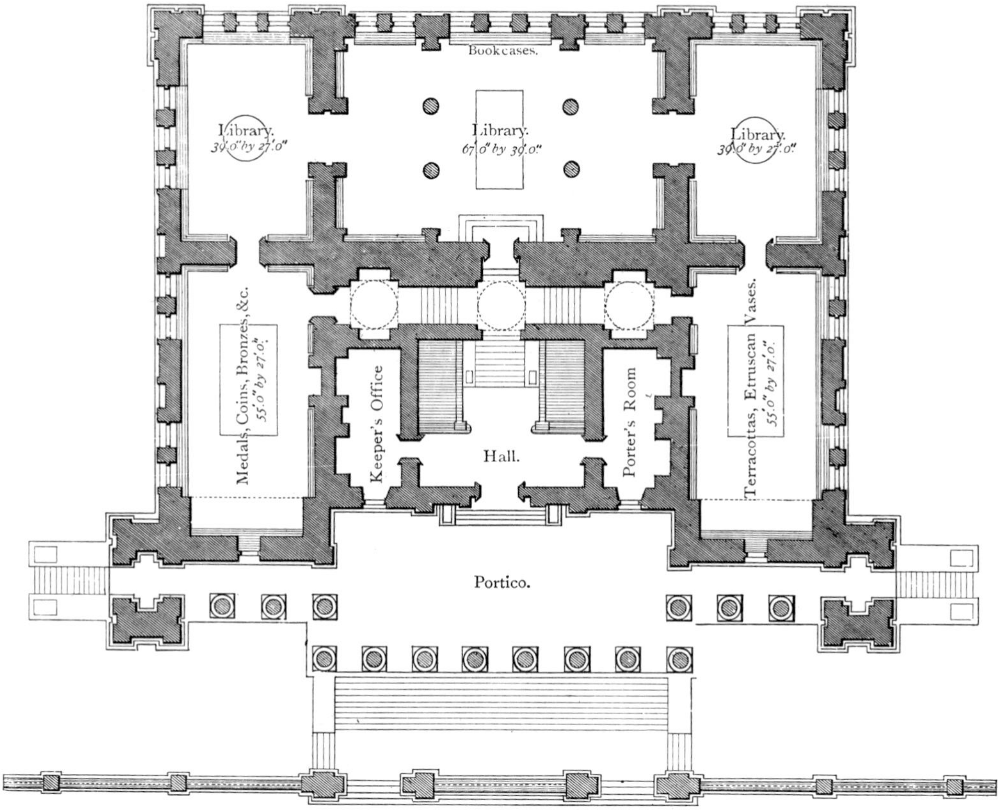

Fig. 1. Ground plan of the Fitzwilliam Museum, as designed by George Basevi: from a lithograph drawn and published by himself in 1837.

[1] [The words between inverted commas occur in a letter addressed by Mr Basevi to the Vice-Chancellor, 21 February, 1837. The Vice-Chancellor's reply has not been preserved, but Mr Basevi wrote again, 24 February; "I am truly concerned to hear that I have caused unnecessary trouble both to yourself and the Senate by not having earlier alluded to the increased height the Elevation would exhibit of the centre part of the Fitzwilliam building. I trust I shall meet with indulgence when I explain, that at the time of the competition, I had not fully determined, to my own satisfaction,

"To adopt the Report of the 13th instant of the Fitzwilliam Syndicate, with the understanding that the height of the whole Building is to be increased about one foot, as stated in the Report, but that the height of the centre part comprehending the Sculpture Gallery and Hall is to be increased four feet and a half: and with the further understanding that the cost of the Sculpture of the Pediment is not included in the estimate."

Mr Basevi's final arrangements will be understood from the ground-plan (fig. 1) and the general view of the exterior (fig. 2), both drawn by himself, and published at the beginning of 1837[1]. The central doorway admitted to a vestibule of moderate size, on each side of which was a room for the attendants. Two staircases ascended to the first floor, and a third staircase, opposite to the door, descended to a second vestibule or passage, which contained the entrances to the Library on the west side, and to the rooms on the north and south sides, intended for Vases and Coins respectively. It will be observed that the door which admitted to this vestibule was as wide as that through which the building was entered, and that the floor of the vestibule was only ten steps below the level of the Hall. This arrangement was probably intended to ensure sufficient light. The floor of the Library and the other rooms was reached by staircases from the second vestibule. It was also intended that these rooms should all communicate with each other. The entrance-hall was lighted by three domes, in addition to the side-windows.

The main features of the design having been settled, a Third Syndicate was appointed, 10 March, 1837, consisting of ten members of the Second Syndicate, viz. Dr French, Mr Worsley, Professor Haviland, Professor Peacock, Professor Willis, Mr

the height this centre portion ought to be for its due effect in every point of view, and had merely assumed in my geometrical elevation the altitude I proposed to work out in the Perspective. Thus from never having precisely determined a height I had not considered the additional 4½ feet an actual alteration of the design, but rather viewed it in the light of an alteration of the drawing, and probably should not have recollected or even alluded to the point, but for the discrepancy visible between the original and improved elevations."]

[1] [Mr Basevi to Rev. G. Peacock, 4 February, 1837. "I trouble you, as you permitted me, with the prints of the Museum, and shall be obliged by your distributing them as you suggested. I have at length completed my Estimate, and [am] using Portland stone for the whole of the exterior—Wainscot floors for the galleries and Libraries—Marble for the Hall—and all the other improvements. The amount is £56,800, which I hope the University will be able to afford. The use of Portland stone makes a difference of about £5000 in round numbers."]

Fig. 2. The Fitzwilliam Museum, as designed by George

lithograph drawn and published by himself in 1837.

Tatham, Mr Lodge, Mr Whewell, Mr Hopkins, Mr Philpott; and one new member, John Graham, D.D., Master of Christ's College. Their duties were to confer with Mr Basevi as to any alterations which might be thought advisable in the details of his design; to advertise for tenders; and further, to superintend the progress of the work. Accordingly, they at once (14 March) advertised for tenders for excavating the earth to a proper depth for the concrete foundations, and for supplying materials to make the concrete; and authorised Mr Basevi to engage a staff of labourers. This work was probably commenced at once, for in May following they obtained authority from the Senate to carry up the brick foundations to the level of the ground. At the same time they announced the completion of the new design for the Entrance Hall, and recommended its adoption[1]. Tenders for "building the carcase[2]" of the Museum were received early in September, and that of Messrs Hicks of London, for £33,262, was accepted. Soon afterwards, however, the contractors discovered a serious error in their calculations, and withdrew their offer. The Syndicate then proposed the acceptance of the tender of Mr George Baker, of London, for £35,838. This recommendation was confirmed by the Senate, 25 October, 1837. Meanwhile the architect had not been unmindful of the decorative portion of the building, and a contract had been entered into with William Grinsell Nicholl, sculptor, for the capitals of the Corinthian columns and pilasters, the frieze under the cornice of the side porticoes, the lunette over the entrance-door, four sculptured panels in the façade, and the vases, chimæras, and other decorative objects of the façade[3]. The same artist was subsequently authorised to execute the sculpture of the pediment —representing the nine Muses—from a design supplied by Mr Eastlake[4]; and the four lions at the foot of the staircases leading to the north and south entrances of the colonnade[5].

[1] [This Report, dated 24 May, was confirmed 31 May, 1837.]

[2] [This is the term used in the Report of the Syndicate, dated 11 October, 1837, in which they recommended the adoption of Messrs Hicks' tender.]

[3] [This was sanctioned by the Senate 19 April, 1837. The total cost was £3,180.]

[4] [Grace, 15 November, confirming a Report of the Syndicate dated 1 November, 1837. Mr Basevi's own design for the sculpture (fig. 2) seems to have been intended to commemorate Viscount Fitzwilliam.]

[5] [Minute of the Syndicate, 7 June, 1839.]

The first stone was laid by the Vice-Chancellor, Gilbert Ainslie, D.D., Master of Pembroke College, on Thursday, 2 November, 1837. The following account of the ceremony[1] is worth quotation:

"At twelve o'clock the members of the University assembled in the Senate-House, and at about half-past twelve they walked in procession round the Senate-House Yard, and thence down the centre of Trumpington Street to the site of the Museum.

A considerable portion of the site had been inclosed, and fitted up with stages, one of which was appropriated to ladies, another to Members of the Senate, a third to undergraduates, and a fourth to gentlemen not members of the University.

The stone which had been prepared for the occasion was from the Isle of Portland, and weighed nearly five tons. After it had been elevated to the height of about four feet, the Vice Chancellor read the following inscription, which had been written by Dr Graham, Master of Christ's College[2], and engraved on a copper tablet:

HAS · ÆDES
RICARDVS · VICECOMES · FITZWILLIAM
ADMIRABILI · MVNIFICENTIA · ET · IN · ALMAM · MATREM · PIETATE
PECVNIIS · TESTAMENTO · LEGATIS
EXTRVI · JVSSIT
IN · QVAS · LIBRI · PICTÆ · TABVLÆ
ALIAQVE · ELEGANTIORVM · ARTIVM · MONVMENTA
IPSIVS · DONA
RECIPERENTVR
LAPIDEM · AVSPICALEM · STATVIT
GILBERTVS · AINSLIE · S · T · P ·
COLLEGII · PEMBROCHIANI · CVSTOS
ACADEMIÆ · ITERVM · PROCANCELLARIVS
QVARTO · NON · NOVEMB · ANNO · DOMINI · MDCCCXXXVII ·
REGINÆ · VICTORIÆ · I
JOANNE · JEFFREYS · MARCHIONE · CAMDEN · ACADEMIÆ · CANCELLARIO
GEORGIO · BASEVI · ARCHITECTO

This tablet having been deposited in a case made of lead and let into an under stone, and the first stone having been lowered to its proper place, the Vice-Chancellor performed the ceremonies incidental to the occasion, after which he spoke as follows:

[1] [Abridged from the Cambridge Chronicle, 4 November, 1837.]

[2] [This statement rests on the authority of Joseph Romilly, M.A., Registrary.]

'Gentlemen of the University,

At a time when our University is so actively exerting itself to keep pace with the spirit of improvement which pervades the whole country, we cannot but hail with satisfaction and delight the auspicious commencement of this noble work. Learning indeed and science have long flourished amid our venerable Halls; the merit and praise of being the first to encourage the more elegant and polite arts must for ever be coupled with the name of Viscount Fitzwilliam. To his liberality we owe not only the magnificent structure which is about to be erected in this place, but many choice and excellent productions of the Sculptor's and Painter's skill. From the cultivation of the more refined arts we may naturally expect to derive the ordinary benefits which they at all times confer upon civilised communities. But it is not necessary to limit our expectations within such narrow limits, since there is just reason to look forward to other advantages allied to those which result from our severer philosophical studies. For things, when rightly viewed, whether they be the works of nature or of human genius, afford ample cause to admire and adore that Great Being, who is alike the author of all material objects and of the intellect which is exercised upon them. Such reflections we should be always anxious to cherish; and thus, having the honour of the Supreme Being as the aim of all our efforts, we may the more freely indulge in the hope that His benevolence and favour will guide them to a happy termination.'

The Public Orator then stepped forward, and delivered a long Latin Speech appropriate to the occasion."

The work proceeded without interruption, and the principal part of it must have been completed by the beginning of 1841, when the Syndicate agreed (25 March) to obtain authority from the Senate to take down the house occupied by the clerk of the works, and for Mr Basevi to contract "for inclosing the front of the Museum with a Portland Stone Balustrade and Iron Gates according to design; and for completing the Portico Steps and Landing." In the following June the completion of this part of the building was undertaken; and similar authority was obtained "to authorise Mr Basevi to make contracts with Messrs Baker, Mr Nicholl, and Messrs Hutchinson, for executing the ornamental Plaister Ceiling of the Portico and side Colonnades, and Frieze around the ceiling, with the various works incident hereto[1]." These works probably occupied the whole of the year 1842, for the decoration and fitting of the interior was not considered until May, 1843. Mr Basevi then wrote the following

[1] [The balustrade, etc., cost £3650; the ceiling £1878. A Grace to authorise the former expenditure passed the Senate 1 April; the latter 22 June, 1841. In 1842 a Grace to authorise the enclosure of the north and west sides of the ground, "the former with a Portland Stone architectural wall, and the latter with an Iron palisade" designed by Mr Basevi, was offered and rejected.]

letter to the Syndicate, which, though of no great interest for our present purpose, is quoted entire, as almost the only document remaining to inform us of the architect's original intentions:

"Gentlemen,

I beg to inform you that I estimate the expense of finishing the interior of the Fitzwilliam Museum according to the accompanying drawings and particulars at the sum of Thirty thousand three hundred and fifty pounds.

This estimate includes wainscot Bookcases for the present collection of books and prints—also the warming of the building.

It likewise includes £120 for carving an enrichment in the upper member of the architrave round the ceiling of the Portico which the time did not allow to be completed with the ceiling.

I have the honor to be, [etc.]

George Basevi Junr.

17 Savile Row
May 22, 1843."

The following "Description of the Materials proposed to be used in the several Apartments of the Fitzwilliam Museum" accompanied the above letter:

"*Entrance Hall and Corridor leading to the lower suite of rooms.*

The floors to be of marble, laid in compartments.

The steps to be of veined marble.

The balustrade of the staircase and gallery to be of scagliola.

The walls from the ground-floor to the level of the gallery-landing, and the dado, base, and surbase round the Gallery, and the Corinthian columns and pilasters and the pedestals on which they stand, to be in scagliola in imitation of various marbles.

The walls of the Hall and Corridor to be of Keene's or Martin's cement highly polished: casts from the Phigalian Marbles[1] to be set in a frieze level with the capitals of the columns.

The side vaultings of the ceilings to be of plaster highly enriched. The centre vault prepared for fresco or oil painting.

The doors into the picture galleries to be of mahogany.

The door from the portico into the hall to be of oak and bronze.

Large Picture Gallery.

The floors to be of the best wainscot.

The walls to be of stucco.

The doors and archway dressings to be of scagliola to design.

[1] [Casts of these marbles, together with those of the Panathenaic Procession from the frieze of the Parthenon, had been purchased, on Mr Basevi's recommendation, from the Trustees of the British Museum, in 1837. Minutes of the Syndicate, 19 December, 1836; and 16 January, 1837.]

Casts from the Elgin frieze to be fixed round the room in a frieze under the cove of the ceiling.

The ceiling of the lantern to be of plaster highly enriched, with Caryatides supporting the longitudinal and transverse beams.

Dome Rooms.

The floors to be of the best wainscot.

The walls of stucco.

The pilasters supporting the domes to be of scagliola.

The arched ceilings and domes to be of plaster highly enriched; farther explained by the accompanying drawing.

The style of the side rooms to be similar.

Lower suite of Rooms.

The style to be Grecian Doric according to the original approved design.

The floors to be of best wainscot.

The columns and pilasters of scagliola in imitation of granite.

The walls of Keene's or Martin's cement polished.

The ceilings to be of plaster in the trabeated style, with cornices appropriately enriched.

The doors to be of mahogany and the dressings round them to be of scagliola in imitation of granite.

The windows to be glazed with plate glass in wainscot frames.

George Basevi, Junr.
22 May 1843."

The Syndicate made this estimate known to the Senate, 24 May, 1843, announcing at the same time that the funds would fall short of the whole amount of the estimate by about £12,000, and suggesting that the money required should be raised by the issue of bonds. Mr Basevi's designs were exhibited in the University Library, and were evidently admired, for the Report was confirmed by the Senate, 31 May; but no progress was made during that year. At the beginning of 1844 Mr Basevi was authorised to proceed with "the preliminary works in the interior of the Museum," and, 22 May following, to settle the terms of a contract with Messrs Baker for the completion of the whole at a cost not exceeding £28,350. These preparations for the decoration of the interior were, unfortunately, the last works in connexion with the Museum which he was permitted to superintend; for, on Tuesday, 14 October, 1845, he was killed by falling through an opening in the floor of the west tower of Ely Cathedral.

In consequence of this sad event, the following Report, signed by all the Syndics, was issued, 9 December, 1845:

"The FITZWILLIAM SYNDICATE conceive that the great loss which the University has suffered by the lamented death of Mr BASEVI, the architect of the New Fitzwilliam Museum, makes it proper for them to offer to the Senate a Report describing the state in which the designs for the building are left; and to bring under the notice of the Senate the state of the engagements made with the Contractors for the execution of the work:

The Syndicate find by an examination of the drawings left by Mr Basevi (which have been sent for their inspection by his brother Mr N. Basevi) that the designs for the greater part of the work remaining to be executed, are in a forward state; but they conceive that these designs not having been perfected, require, for the completion of the work, the assistance of an architect of the same order as Mr Basevi in professional eminence and skill.

The Syndicate think it highly desirable that the building should be completed with a close adherence to Mr Basevi's intentions, so far as they appear in a settled form in his designs.

The Syndicate have also ascertained by inquiry of Mr N. Basevi and of Mr Baker, the state of the pending engagements with Mr Baker; and the results of this inquiry will be laid upon the Registrary's table.

The Syndicate, considering the high professional character of Mr Cockerell and the confidence already reposed in him by the University, beg leave to recommend that Mr Cockerell be appointed Mr Basevi's successor as architect of the New Fitzwilliam Museum, with instructions to adhere as closely as may be to Mr Basevi's designs in carrying on the work to its completion."

This Report having been confirmed by the Senate 15 December, the Syndicate reported further, 5 March, 1846:

"That in conformity with the Grace of December 15, 1845, they have obtained from Mr COCKERELL designs for the completion of the Hall and Staircases of the Fitzwilliam Museum, for which parts of the building Mr BASEVI had not left designs in a settled form.

That the Syndicate beg to express their entire concurrence with Mr COCKERELL'S views as to the mode of finishing this part of the Museum; and to recommend that he be requested to prepare working drawings and estimates corresponding with his designs, with a view to a Contract being made for the execution of the work."

This Report was confirmed a few days afterwards, 11 March; and in consequence of its acceptance the Syndicate made the following Minutes at subsequent meetings:

"14 May, 1846. Agreed that Mr Cockerell be requested to make a detailed estimate, and to procure from Messrs Baker a tender, for the architectural completion of the South Library, according to the designs this day submitted by him to the Syndicate.

And also that he be requested in like manner to procure a tender from Messrs. Baker for the Book Cases designed by him for this room, with a view to the designs and the tender being submitted to the Senate.

Agreed also, that Mr Cockerell be requested to procure a tender from Messrs. Baker for the architectural completion of the Hall and Staircase, according to his Report and the designs submitted to this meeting.

22 May, 1846. Agreed to request the Vice-Chancellor to propose a Grace to the Senate to authorise Mr Cockerell to make a Contract on behalf of the University with Messrs. Baker for the Book Cases to be placed in the South Room on the ground-floor of the Fitzwilliam Museum; and further, to authorise Mr Cockerell to give orders for preparing the stone to be used for the stairs and columns of the Hall of the Museum in accordance with [his] recommendation."

The Grace respecting the book-cases passed the Senate without opposition (11 June)[1]; and, 3 July following, the Syndicate requested the Vice-Chancellor to propose the following Graces, having reference to the Hall and Staircases:

"1. To authorise Mr COCKERELL to expend a sum not exceeding £1,000 for altering the lantern in the Fitzwilliam Museum according to the Plan approved of by Grace of the Senate on the 11th March last.

2. To authorise Mr COCKERELL to contract for red Granite Columns for the Hall of the Fitzwilliam Museum in lieu of Scagliola, and for fixing the same, at a cost not exceeding £1,000, in conformity with the recommendation of Mr Cockerell approved of by the Syndicate on the 14th May last."

The first of the above Graces did not pass without opposition[2], the following brief paper, written by John James Smith, M.A., Gonville and Caius College, being circulated against it:

"That *alteration* of the plan left by the late Architect, was expressly guarded against by the Senate.

That the arrangement, which it is now proposed to *alter*, was made by the Architect *deliberately*, deliberately recommended by the Syndicate, and approved by the Senate.

That the cost of such alteration is an *addition* of expenditure scarcely warrantable.

July 5th, 1846."

[1] [Their cost was £1666. 15. 0.]

[2] [The numbers were: in the Black Hood House; Placet 7, Non Placet 6: in the White Hood House; Placet 13, Non Placet 7. The late period of the year (6 July) at which the Congregation was held may account for the smallness of the numbers.]

The Syndicate had exhibited Mr Cockerell's designs, with a letter explanatory of them[1]; but unfortunately neither the designs nor the letter have been preserved in the University. It is known, however, that the only structural alterations of importance which he carried out were the substitution of a central lantern for the three domes designed by Mr Basevi; and a change in the arrangements of the staircases which led from the entrance-hall to the picture-galleries and basement. He decided to ascend to the former by a single central staircase instead of by two lateral staircases; and to descend to the latter by two lateral staircases instead of a single central staircase.

These works were carried out in the course of 1846 and 1847. At the end of the latter year, the £12,000 which the Vice-Chancellor had been authorised to raise by bond having been all spent, the Syndicate came to the conclusion that it would be very undesirable to lay any further burden on the income of the Museum by procuring an additional loan, and that it would be better to suspend the further progress of the works "until the available funds of the Fitzwilliam Trust are adequate to the completion of the Museum." The Report containing these recommendations, dated 9 December, 1847, having been confirmed by the Senate, 14 December, the Library and Galleries were got ready for the reception of the collections, and they were moved in in the course of 1848. When the accounts were made up, it was found that the building had already cost £91,550. 9*s.* 10*d.*

No proposal to clothe the bare brickwork of the Entrance-Hall with suitable decoration was made until 1870, when, a sufficient sum having accumulated, the Syndicate of Management, in their Annual Report, dated 22 March, stated their opinion that it ought to be completed without delay; and further, 22 October following, requested the Vice-Chancellor to draw the attention of the Council of the Senate to the paragraph in question. In consequence of this representation a Syndicate was appointed (24 November) to consider what steps should be taken in the matter. This Syndicate consisted of the Vice-Chancellor; Robert Phelps, D.D., Master of Sidney Sussex College; William Henry

[1] [This is known from a note appended to the Report dated 11 March, 1846.]

Bateson, D.D., Master of S. John's College; William Hepworth Thompson, D.D., Master of Trinity College; William Selwyn, D.D., Lady Margaret's Professor of Divinity; Robert Willis, M.A., Jacksonian Professor; George Downing Liveing, M.A., Professor of Chemistry; Edward Henry Perowne, B.D., Corpus Christi College; Thomas George Bonney, B.D., S. John's College; Andrew Long, M.A., King's College; William Bennet Pike, M.A., Downing College; John Willis Clark, M.A., Trinity College; and Edmund Henry Morgan, M.A., Jesus College.

In their first Report, dated 27 May, 1871, they stated that "having formed an opinion that it would be expedient to revert in its main features to the design of Mr Basevi, the original architect of the building, they consulted Mr Edward M. Barry, R.A., Architect, upon the subject; and having found that he concurred with them in this view of the question, they requested him to prepare plans shewing what changes of structure would in his judgment become necessary for the purpose of giving effect to this decision." Mr Barry furnished them with the following Report, which will be readily understood by reference to Mr Basevi's ground plan (fig. 1).

"21 Abingdon Street, 4 May, 1871.

Mr Basevi's original design for the staircase in the Fitzwilliam Museum provided for two flights of ascending steps to the first floor, one on each side of a central descending flight to the ground floor. It is now proposed to carry out in principle this arrangement. Before doing so, it may be well to consider some points of detail which may have an important influence on architectural effect and convenience. The central portion of the staircase is only 33 feet square, which is a small space when considered in relation to the design proposed. The latter may in fact be described as a proposal to place a large staircase in a small space. Another point to be considered is the short distance between the doorway and the first step of the descending flight, and it may be feared that the architectural effect may not be satisfactory under these circumstances. To ascend a considerable flight of steps under the portico, in order to descend immediately another flight of steps to the ground-floor, is a proposal open to grave objections. * * *

The design which accompanies this report is an attempt to deal with the question in accordance with the principle of Mr Basevi's plan, and to obviate, as far as possible, the foregoing objections. It carries out Mr Basevi's idea of a double flight of steps to the upper floor, while modifying the design of the descending flight.

There are at present 4 steps, of an aggregate height of 2 feet, in front of the principal door. These steps may be removed without injury to the architectural effect, and it is therefore proposed to dispense with them, and to lower the floor of the entrance-hall 2 feet. Looking to the smallness of the several dimensions, the staircase may be advantageously enlarged by taking into it the two side-rooms under the upper corridors [marked Porter's Room and Keeper's Office], thus giving the whole staircase a width of 64 feet, instead of 33 feet as at present. The side-rooms are now of little use, and are lost to the general effect of the interior. A double descending flight of steps to the ground floor may be constructed in the space thus gained, sufficient headway being obtained by lowering the floor of the Hall as before described. By this arrangement there would be a double flight of steps, 10 feet wide, to the ground floor, and a double flight of steps, 9 feet wide, to the upper floor. The dimensions of the staircase would also be considerably enlarged.

It would be desirable to form new doorways into the sculpture-room on the ground-floor, one doorway to be at the foot of each flight of stairs. The present central doorway might be stopped up, and treated as an ornamental recess, with a borrowed light to assist in giving light to the ground-floor corridor. By these arrangements a larger amount of light and cheerfulness would be obtained in the staircase generally[1].

EDWARD M. BARRY."

This Report was confirmed by the Senate, 7 June, 1871, and the changes recommended, which were estimated to cost £2000, were commenced immediately. In November the Syndicate published a further Report from Mr Barry:

"The structural alterations of the staircase are now completed, and the necessary temporary accommodation provided to give public access to the collections. The time has therefore arrived when the permanent completion of the staircase may be advantageously considered.

The walls of the upper portion of the staircase are still unfinished, although the necessary preparations for niches and other architectural features have been made at the time of their erection. It is proposed to adhere to the existing design in respect of these features, and to complete the internal plastering in accordance with them. In connection with this work would be the provision of permanent doors to the galleries, the doors being of wainscot, with suitable dressings of a dark-coloured marble.

It would be desirable to admit more light into the staircase, and with this view it is proposed to remove the present central skylight, and to substitute for it one of larger size. This may be done with very little architectural disturbance of the design of the ceiling, by suppressing the uppermost cove immediately under the existing skylight, and by making the new skylight the whole size of the circular shaft or lantern. There would be a considerable increase of light by this arrangement. It is also proposed to enlarge the windows in the

[1] [A few unimportant sentences have been omitted from this Report for the sake of brevity.]

semicircular spaces over the cornice in the side-walls. These spaces are not wholly occupied by the windows, but are divided into three parts. Two of these parts are solid, and the central and larger part forms the window. It is proposed to widen the windows so that they may fill the whole semi-circular space. This change would further increase the light in the staircase without injury to its architectural effect.

It is proposed to complete the ceiling in accordance with the present design, with the two exceptions above described.

The lower portion of the staircase is already partly completed. It is proposed to add a balustrade with pedestals, and other architectural features as shown in the accompanying model. The balustrade would be of alabaster, and the handrail and other portions of the work of Sienna marble. The small columns to the openings on the ground-floor would be of green marble. The walls of staircases and corridors on the basement floor would be plastered, and finished in accordance with the style of the building. The floors where left rough are proposed to be finished with marble margins and mosaic panels of ornamental design. The windows might be filled with grisaille glass, and some moderate amount of coloured decoration applied to the ceilings and walls. Leaving for future consideration the advisability of further outlay under this head, and the provision of glass and mosaics of a high artistic character, I estimate the cost of the finishings described in this report at about £11,000, and consider that a period of 12 months will suffice for their completion.

EDWARD M. BARRY.

3 November, 1871."

The Senate authorised the adoption of these proposals (30 November), though not without some expression of adverse opinion[1], and the work was executed in the course of 1872. As usual, there was a considerable difference in price between the estimated and the actual cost, which had risen to £12,180; and, in addition to this total, new bronze external doors were ordered at a cost of £700, and rooms for the attendants constructed in the basement. Mr Barry next suggested the following additional works, which shall be described in his own words:

"My designs for the completion of the staircase, as described in my former reports, and as contracted for at the cost above given, were based, as I have previously stated, on the retention of the present architectural forms of the niches, wall-panelling, and doors, but before proceeding with the final completion of the three doorways to the

[1] [Discussion of the Report in the Arts School, 22 November, 1871. Camb. Univ. Reporter, p. 83.]

Picture Galleries on the upper landing of the staircase, I wish to draw the attention of the Syndicate to Mr Basevi's design for the same. It shows a more elaborate treatment of these doorways than I have yet proposed, with carved figures or Caryatides supporting a handsome entablature. On mature consideration, I think the architectural effect of the staircase would be much improved by the adoption of this design for the principal central doorway facing the great entrance, and should strongly recommend it, if the additional cost be not considered an insuperable objection. The figures would be of white marble, on marble pedestals, and the entablature of alabaster. The door frames would also be of marble. For the two doorways to the side-galleries, I should suggest a simple treatment, without figures, but with the architectural details of marble and alabaster. On the ground-floor of the staircase, I should be glad to make a slight modification of my first proposal, and to employ double instead of single columns to support the upper landings. This addition would, in my opinion, greatly increase the architectural effect of this portion of the building. I would further suggest that the present unsightly window-frames, on each side of the entrance-doorway, under the portico, should be removed, and their place supplied by plate-glass, with an ornamental grating towards the portico. I would at the same time slightly enlarge the windows, so as to increase the light in the interior of the staircase. I estimate the cost of these additions to the doorways, columns, and windows at £2200.

I have also given my attention to the questions which were left for future consideration, viz. filling the windows with grisaille glass, laying down in the Hall, and on the landings, ornamental mosaic pavements, and the treatment of the ceilings, niches, and walls with a moderate amount of painting and gilding. I should recommend that the six semicircular windows should be filled with grisaille glass, which would intercept but little light. The pavement might be of Roman mosaic in small tesseræ, principally of a light colour, with stone and marble margins. Some of the more prominent members of the ceiling, and the capitals of the columns, might be relieved with gilding, and the niches and walls painted in sober and appropriate colours. I estimate the cost of these works at £3980.

EDWARD M. BARRY.

6 December, 1872."

The decoration of the Entrance-Hall, which was completed by the end of 1875, differs in some details from that suggested by Mr Barry in his Reports. The openings in the wall between the ascending and descending staircases are lined with green Genoa marble; the plinth and rail of the ascending staircases are of Siena marble, the balustrades of red Devonshire marble, instead of alabaster; and the same materials are employed for the dwarf balustrades between the red granite columns in the side-galleries.

The Phigalean frieze, which Mr Basevi had placed along the side-walls, in continuation of the capitals of his columns, was removed; and the niches, instead of being left, as he had indicated, as simple round-headed openings, devoid of ornament, like those shewn in his design for the façade (fig. 2), are now enriched with fluted columns, painted in imitation of Siena marble, and bearing a small entablature and carved pediment. The door into the great picture-gallery is ornamented with Caryatids of white marble, bearing a rich alabaster cornice, above which are the arms and supporters of Viscount Fitzwilliam. The doors into the side-galleries are treated in a plainer manner, with suits of moldings worked in green and red marble, and an alabaster cornice above of less elaborate design.

The cost of Mr Barry's work amounted to at least £23,392[1]; and we have already seen that the work previously executed had cost £91,550. 9*s.* 10*d.* The total cost of the Museum has therefore amounted to £114,942. 9*s.* 10*d.*

Lastly, it may be mentioned that in 1839[2] it was decided by the Syndicate "that the inscription upon the Frieze of the Portico be MUSEUM VICE-COMITIS FITZWILLIAM"; but that up to the present time the Founder has not been distinctly commemorated in any way.

The memorial statue of H.R.H. Prince Albert, in his robes as Chancellor of the University, by John Henry Foley, R.A., was placed in the Entrance-Hall in 1877. The history of this statue must be briefly recorded.

Soon after the death of the Prince a meeting of the members of the Senate was held in Queens' College Hall, 13 February, 1862, the President, George Phillips, D.D., being Vice-Chancellor, to consider the propriety of erecting by subscription a University Memorial to the late Chancellor. This was at once agreed to, but there was a difference of opinion as to the form which the memorial should take; some being in favour of a Museum for Natural Science, others of a bronze statue to be placed in the Senate House Yard. Ultimately, however, these dissentients gave way in favour of a marble statue, of at least the size of life, an opinion which was endorsed by non-resident members of the University at a meeting held in London, at Devonshire House, 28 Feb-

[1] [Report of the Building-Syndicate, 6 December, 1872.]

[2] [Minute of the Syndicate, 25 October, 1839.]

ruary, 1862. The selection of a sculptor was entrusted to the Duke of Devonshire, Chancellor, who named Mr Foley. The statue, the execution of which had been retarded by various causes, was offered to the University by the Duke of Devonshire, Chancellor, as chairman of the Executive Committee of the subscribers, 17 May, and accepted by the Senate 25 May, 1870. It was the wish of the sculptor that it should be placed in the centre of the west wall of the central Picture Gallery, so as to face the door of entrance, and he advocated this position for his work in the following words:

"To render this site more effective, and to allow of the pictures being arranged at each side within defined spaces, I propose the formation of an arch, unpierced, but otherwise similar to those at either end of the room, making within its boundary a shallow recess which would form an effective background to the Statue. I cannot feel that this change would be injurious to the effect of the room; it would but render it more uniform throughout[1]."

If this site were disapproved of, Mr Foley suggested the south side of the south-western gallery, or the north side of the north-western gallery. The next step was to appoint a Syndicate (2 June, 1870) to consider the best site for the statue. They reported (28 October) that they could not recommend any of the three positions indicated by Mr Foley, on the ground (1) that such prominence ought not to be given to any person except the Founder of the Museum, Viscount Fitzwilliam; and (2) that the floor was not sufficiently strong to sustain the weight of the statue without important structural alterations. At their request, Mr Foley had visited Cambridge, and, having made a fresh examination of the Fitzwilliam Museum, and of the Senate House, had stated that, in deference to the views of the Syndicate, he was willing to give up the three sites which he preferred, but would suggest either the niche at the east end of the south gallery of the Fitzwilliam Museum, or a site in the Senate House. After careful consideration the Syndicate recommended to place the statue on the north side of the Senate House, opposite to the south door, which they proposed to open, and to remove the statues of King George the First and King George the Second to the west end, on the right and left of the Chancellor's chair[2].

[1] [Letter of Mr Foley, 8 July, 1864.]

[2] [It has been already stated above (p. 57) that in 1884 these statues were placed at the west end of Cockerell's Building in the University Library (Grace 7 February, 1884, confirming a Report of the Senate-House Syndicate, dated 19 November, 1883). The south door of the Senate-House had been opened in 1882, and the statues placed temporarily in the Law School, previous to their re-erection in another position in the Senate-House, as suggested in a previous Report of the same Syndicate (16 March, 1882, confirmed by Grace 25 May).]

This Report having been rejected (8 December, 1870) a fresh Syndicate was appointed (30 March, 1871). They considered that, having regard to the feeling of the Senate, as manifested by the vote of the previous December, it would be useless to suggest any other position in the Senate House; and, after examination of various sites, felt obliged to report "that the Fitzwilliam Museum is the only other building in the University at all adapted for receiving" the statue. They suggested, however, that "if at some time a new building should be erected on the Pembroke Street front of the Museums and Lecture Rooms, it is possible that a more appropriate site might be found there, to which the statue might without difficulty be removed." Finally, after discussing and rejecting the position at the east end of the south picture gallery which Mr Foley had formerly advocated, they recommended that the statue should be placed on the floor of the Entrance-Hall. This Report, dated 2 December, 1871, was confirmed by the Senate (15 February, 1872), and the hall was prepared under Mr Barry's direction for the reception of the statue. It arrived in Cambridge 31 July, 1876, and was placed in the Museum in the course of 1877. The formal ceremony of unveiling it was performed by His Royal Highness the Prince of Wales, 22 January, 1878[1]. Mr Foley received £1200 for the statue, and £420 for the pedestal, which bears the following inscription:

ALBERTO
VICTORIAE REGINAE CONIVGI
REGIAE DIGNITATIS CONSORTI
CANCELLARIO SVO
ACADEMICI CANTABRIGIENSES

On the plinth of the statue are the words: J. H. FOLEY, R.A. Sc. London, 1866.

We have next to narrate the erection of a Museum of Classical and General Archæology, the classical division of which, though on a separate site, forms part of the Fitzwilliam Museum.

The clause in Viscount Fitzwilliam's Will which declares that his bequest is made to the University, "for promoting the increase of learning and the other great objects of that noble foundation," justified the formation of a gallery of ancient art in connexion with the Museum. Moreover, a small collection of casts from ancient statues had been presented in 1850 by John

[1] [Cambridge University Reporter, 4 February, 1878.]

Kirkpatrick, M.A., Trinity College[1], and augmented at a later period by various gifts and purchases. These began soon after the appointment of Sidney Colvin, M.A., Trinity College, to the office of Director of the Museum, 1 April, 1876, who, as Slade Professor of Fine Art, selected for his lectures subjects requiring illustration by casts, as, for instance, *On the recent discoveries at Olympia*, in the Lent Term, 1878. Soon afterwards the Syndicate began "to consider whether any steps can be taken for the formation of a gallery of ancient art in connection with the Fitzwilliam Museum, and what should be the future relations of the Fitzwilliam Museum to the purposes of art-teaching in the University." The want of "an adequate collection of casts from ancient Greek and Roman sculptures, selected and arranged for the purposes of systematic study," became more apparent in the following year, when (8 May, 1879) it was agreed that Art and Archæology should form a special section of the Classical Tripos. In consequence of this extension of the course of classical study, lectures *On the History of Greek Sculpture* were delivered by Mr Charles Waldstein in the Easter Term, 1880, and continued in subsequent years, on the recommendation of the Board of Classical Studies[2]. These lectures, and Mr Waldstein's personal influence, stimulated the University to provide the materials for teaching Classical Archæology with as little delay as possible.

The first question which engaged the attention of the Syndicate was the position of the proposed gallery, which they were anxious to place, if possible, in connection with the Museum. The *Instructions to Architects* published in 1834 (p. 204) had contemplated future additions to the collections, and had spoken of the "wings of the proposed building." These wings had evidently been included in Mr Basevi's original design (p. 207), but, unfortunately, we do not know how he intended to arrange them. The plan of the first floor, which he circulated together with the plan of the ground-floor reproduced above (fig. 1), shews a wing projecting on either side from the north and south ends of the western picture gallery. These wings would have been

[1] [A Grace to affix the University Seal to a letter of thanks to him, written by the Public Orator, passed the Senate 2 November, 1850.]

[2] [Report of the Board, 4 June, confirmed by Grace 10 June, 1880.]

about 50 feet long by 30 feet broad; but, as they are not drawn upon the ground-plan, we do not know how he proposed to support them; and a glance at that plan shews that such an addition would of necessity have deprived the western galleries, there called Libraries, of their north and south lights. The Syndicate, however, were anxious to revert to the principle of lateral extension, and, after informal consultation with an architect, the following scheme was laid before them, which, though subsequently abandoned, deserves to be placed on record:

"The sub-Syndicate are of opinion that it would be undesirable to alter the design and appearance of the Museum by additions to or extensions of the existing block. But they think that separate galleries of the kind required might be constructed in communication with the Museum, as it is, and without injury to its design and appearance, either (*a*) in rear of the existing block, or (*b*) on the ground at either side. The alternative (*a*) would have the advantage that the new buildings would be little seen, and could therefore be erected with greater plainness and at less cost, but is only possible on the supposition that a piece of ground measuring not less than 180 feet by 70 feet can first be acquired from Peterhouse. Alternative (*b*), on the other hand, requires no more than the acquisition from that College of a strip of ground not exceeding 12 feet in width along the northern, and 6 feet in width along the western, boundary of the ground upon which the Museum stands.

The sub-Syndicate therefore are of opinion that alternative (*b*) is the more practicable of the two. According to preliminary designs and estimates which they have caused to be prepared, it appears that two galleries or halls, each 100 feet long by 40 feet wide and 25 feet high, and lighted by skylights, can be erected at a distance of 35 feet from the present Museum, on the ground north and south of the same, and communicating by corridors with the present sculpture-gallery of the Museum, at an approximate cost of £10,000. The cost of furnishing the galleries with the required casts of ancient sculpture would be from £2000 to £3000 more."

This scheme, and a subsequent scheme for building on the ground to the south-west of the Museum, were never submitted to the Senate. The Syndicate reluctantly laid them aside, partly on architectural grounds, partly because they were unable to obtain the necessary extension of the site. They next turned their attention to the possibility of finding a suitable site at no great distance from the Museum; and, after consideration of various positions, decided in favour of a piece of ground belonging to Peterhouse, nearly one-third of an acre in extent, on the west side of the churchyard of S. Mary the Less. This site, the position of which will be readily understood by reference to the plan of Peterhouse, .is approached from Trumpington Street by Little S. Mary's Lane, which bounds it on the north; on the east it is bounded by a branch of that lane leading to Peterhouse; on the south by some of the buildings of Peterhouse; and on the west by the lane leading to Coe Fen. When the Syndicate first tried to acquire it, in 1882, it was occupied by malthouses, which were in good repair, and stated to be capable of conversion, "at a comparatively trifling cost, into excellent sculpture-galleries." The Syndicate therefore recommended the purchase, out of the Fitzwilliam Fund, of the remainders of the two leases under which the property was held, at the price of £1000[1].

Meanwhile it had been represented to the Council of the Senate:

"That a large number of objects illustrative of the history of this country in British, Roman, Saxon, and Mediæval times are at present often discovered in and near Cambridge; that opportunities of securing a collection of these objects for the use of students are likely to become less frequent; and that the valuable collection of the Cambridge Antiquarian Society[2], together with many objects which have been already acquired by private individuals, would not improbably be presented to a University Museum[3]."

In consequence of this representation a Syndicate was appointed (11 December, 1879) "to consider first whether any rooms can be provided temporarily for the immediate reception of objects of the character referred to, and, secondly, what permanent provision can be made for the preparation, arrangement, and display of such collections." This Syndicate, called the "Archæological Collections Syndicate," examined several buildings and sites, all of which they felt obliged to abandon, the former being unsuitable as a temporary receptacle, and the latter for a permanent structure[4]. Under these circumstances it oc-

[1] [Report of the Fitzwilliam Museum Syndicate, 11 March, 1882. Camb. Univ. Reporter, p. 380.]

[2] [This reference was justified by a letter written to the Vice-Chancellor by the Secretary of the Society, 26 May, 1875, and printed in the Appendix to the Report of the "Additional Buildings Syndicate," 3 June, 1875. Ibid. p. 486.]

[3] [Report of the Council, 8 December, 1879. Ibid. p. 161.]

[4] [Reports of the Archæological Collections Syndicate, 1 June, 1880; 26 February, 1881. Ibid. 1 March, 1881.]

curred to them that galleries suitable for General as well as for Classical Archæology might possibly be arranged under the same roof, and with this view they entered into communication with the Fitzwilliam Museum Syndicate, while engaged in negotiating the purchase above described. The scheme for effecting that purchase, and a subsequent scheme for converting the existing malthouses to the purposes of a Museum, which had been prepared under the direction of Professor Colvin, having met with their unanimous approval, the Fitzwilliam Museum Syndicate were able to inform the Senate that their scheme could be made to serve a double purpose. This consideration probably disposed the Senate to regard it with favour, for the slight opposition which manifested itself at first soon disappeared, and the Report recommending it was confirmed by the Senate without a division, 23 March, 1882[1].

The leases in question having been acquired, Peterhouse agreed to cancel them, and to grant a new one to the University for 99 years, at an annual rent of £150. This offer was submitted to the Senate, 22 May, 1882, together with a suggestion that the cost of erecting the proposed Museum, the plans for which had been approved by those for whose use it was intended, should be divided between the Fitzwilliam Museum and the University. The total cost being estimated not to exceed £7000, it was proposed that the former should pay £5000, and the latter £2000. This scheme, after considerable delay, and much discussion, was accepted by the Senate, 7 December, 1882[2], and the building was commenced without delay. When, however, the working drawings came to be prepared by the architect, Mr Basil Champneys, it appeared that the buildings, when completed, would cost nearly £8800, exclusive of the fittings of the four rooms which it was proposed to assign to General Archæology. As however it was proposed to pay this additional sum out of the Fitzwilliam Museum Reserve Fund, the Senate made no objection, and the Report explaining and recommending it, dated 3 March, 1883, was confirmed, 15 March, without opposition. The building was

[1] [Camb. Univ. Reporter, pp. 380, 447.]

[2] [The Report of the Syndicate, rewritten, and much enlarged, was republished 28 October, 1882. Ibid. p. 142.]

practically finished by the end of 1883, but much time was necessarily required for the proper placing of the casts[1], and it was not formally opened until 6 May, 1884.

The building, the ground-plan of which was of necessity dictated by that of the malthouses already existing on the site, consists for the most part of parallel galleries, with a large lecture-theatre, library, and private rooms in the centre. The galleries, which are admirably suited for their purpose, are lighted from the roof. Four rooms, on the south and east sides, are assigned to General Archæology; the rest of the building to Classical Archæology. The total cost was £9739. 18*s.* 7*d.*]

CHAPTER V.

History of the Selwyn Divinity School.

[Due provision had been made for the teaching of Divinity at Cambridge from the earliest times. It has been already shewn that the Divinity School, on the ground floor of the north side of the Schools Quadrangle, is the oldest existing building erected for any University purpose; and in 1794 further accommodation was granted to the Divinity Professors by assigning to them the lecture-rooms under the east room of the Library[2]. When the new Schools and Library were planned in 1829, the architects were instructed to include a new Divinity School in their design, and these instructions were repeated when the scheme was revived in 1835[3]. It came to pass, however, that not only was the erection of the portion of Mr Cockerell's design which con-

[1] [A list of those which it was thought most important to acquire will be found in the Appendix to a Report of the Fitzwilliam Syndicate, 3 March, 1883; Camb. Univ. Reporter, p. 448.]

[2] [The Grace, passed 29 January, 1794, ran as follows: "Cum alia domus præter eas ab Academia jam constructas desideretur, in quâ Professores Lectiones suas publice legant; Placeat Vobis, ut Camera sub Bibliotheca publicâ in parte Orientali sita in hunc finem paretur; et ut summa octoginta librarum ad hoc opus absolvendum e cista communi erogetur; et ut Loculamenta in eâ posita vendantur"; but it was understood that the Norrisian Professor of Divinity should lecture in it, and it was always called "The Divinity Lecture Room."]

[3] [History of the Schools etc., pp. 103, 116.]

tained it deferred, but the old School was rendered useless for its original purpose by the proximity of the north wing of the new Library. The Divinity Professors were therefore confined to the eastern Lecture-Room, and to such temporary accommodation as could be granted to them from time to time. The first definite proposal for the erection of an independent Divinity School is to be found in the following minute of the Board of Theological Studies, dated 7 December, 1858:

"That it would tend to the promotion of Theological study if a Divinity School of sufficient size could be provided; that the room under the portico, called in the ancient plan *Schola Parva*[1], is much too small for the purpose; and this, as well as the Arts School, which is also used at present for Theological Lectures, is often required for other University purposes, which prevents the Professors of Divinity from meeting the students in Theology so frequently as is desirable."

This suggestion was embodied by the Board in their Report, dated 30 December in the same year, but no further steps were taken at that time. Two years afterwards (16 November 1860), William Selwyn, B.D., S. John's College, who had been elected Lady Margaret's Professor of Divinity in 1855, wrote to the Vice-Chancellor offering £1000 for the purpose, and at a meeting of the Board, held shortly afterwards, suggested that additional contributions might be raised by way of a Memorial to his predecessor, John James Blunt, B.D. This scheme was not approved, and no definite action was taken until 1864, when it was agreed (8 December) that an annual gift of £700, contributed by Professor Selwyn, should be regularly invested in the names of certain Trustees, and should ultimately be applied to the erection of a Divinity School[2]. The first stone of the "Scott Building" of the University Library had been laid in May of this same year, as has been already related[3], and

[1] [The plan here referred to is that by Archbishop Parker, described above, History of the Schools, etc., p. 18.]

[2] [Professor Selwyn had applied £700 a year to increase the income of the Norrisian Professorship as long as he and Professor Browne held their respective offices; and proposed further, that in case the Norrisian Professorship should first become vacant, the said sum should be appropriated to the encouragement of Theological learning, in such manner as the Senate, with the consent of the Lady Margaret's Professor, should determine. These arrangements were accepted by the Senate 14 May, 1856. The Norrisian Professorship became vacant in 1864, by the elevation of Professor Browne to the See of Ely.]

[3] [History of the Schools, etc. p. 122.]

advantage was taken of this circumstance by its chief promoter, George Williams, B.D., Senior Fellow of King's College, to make the following suggestion:

"My definite proposal is this: That as soon as that part of the New Library which is now in progress shall be completed, the building shall be carried on without interruption as far as the old Gateway, and that the ground floor of the West side, between the S. W. angle and the Gateway, shall be assigned for a Divinity School. This would give a room 69 feet long by 21 feet wide, interior measurement, which might be divided into a Lecture-Room and Class-Rooms at the option of the Professors[1]."

Attention having been drawn to this suggestion by the Board of Theological Studies in their next Report (29 March, 1865), a Syndicate was appointed (11 May) to consider the matter. They reported (18 May) that the University had no funds available for the proposed extension, and that some of the existing Lecture-Rooms, especially those in the New Museums, would suffice for temporary accommodation. In consequence of this action, the idea of extending the Library as far as the Gateway, and of using the ground floor for a Divinity School, was abandoned. The half-finished angels on the corbels of the room at the south-west angle remain as a witness of what had been intended.

In 1874, the accumulated funds having exceeded £8000[2], a Syndicate was appointed (3 December)

"To enquire as to the best site for a Divinity School; also to enquire what other additional buildings are needed for University purposes; what is the approximate amount of the accommodation required; the best way in which the buildings may be combined; the best sites for the several buildings; and the probable approximate expense."

The members of this Syndicate were the Vice-Chancellor; William Henry Bateson, D.D., Master of S. John's College; Joseph Barber Lightfoot, D.D., Trinity College; George Murray Humphry, M.D., Downing College; George Downing Liveing, M.A.; Edmund Henry Morgan, M.A., Jesus College; Norman Macleod Ferrers, M.A , Caius College; Edward William Blore, M.A., and Coutts Trotter, M.A., Trinity College; George Forrest

[1] [This paragraph is quoted from a short pamphlet, by Mr Williams, dated 6 December, 1864.]

[2] [The exact amount was £8907. 8*s*. 6*d*. 3 per cent. consolidated Bank Annuities. Camb. Univ. Reporter, 14 April, 1874, p. 313.]

Browne, M.A., S. Catharine's College; and James William Cartmell, M.A., Christ's College. Professor Selwyn, whose name had been inadvertently omitted, was added to the Syndicate 10 December.

Professor Selwyn was strongly in favour of building the Divinity School on the most central site possible. He wrote to the Vice-Chancellor (17 December):

"The best site would be the open space on the south side of the Senate-House Square, between the lines (produced) of King's College Chapel and the Public Library.

The building will not be so large or so lofty as the Senate-House; and, while it completes the square of University buildings, will not mar the general view in King's Parade, or that of King's College Chapel, which will be seen high above it, as the Capitol of Rome is seen high above the Temples in the Forum.

Second best site (*sed longo intervallo*) St John's ground, on the North side of All Saints Churchyard.

No other sites appear to me suitable or available."

Subsequently, however, he came to the conclusion that "if the ground between the north and south wings of the Library, opposite to Clare College, could be secured to a Divinity School for ever, without the possibility of invasion[1]," he should prefer that site to the one opposite to S. John's College. The Syndicate, having carefully considered these sites, and also the space left unoccupied in the Old Botanic Garden, reported that it was not expedient in their opinion to occupy with new buildings any portion of Senate House Square; that the whole of the site of the Old Court of King's College should be reserved for the future wants of the Library; and that Natural Science would soon require all the ground in the neighbourhood of the New Museums. They therefore recommended the purchase of the site opposite to S. John's College, as having been agreeable to Professor Selwyn, and suitable for a Divinity School. As Professor Selwyn's benefaction could not be used for any other purpose than for the building of a School, the duty of providing a site devolved upon the University. The price fixed by S. John's College was £3,750[2].

[1] [Letter from Professor Selwyn to the Vice-Chancellor, 25 February, 1875, quoted by the latter in his speech in the Arts School, when the Report of the Syndicate was discussed, 14 May, 1875. Camb. Univ. Reporter, p. 404.]

[2] [Report of the Syndicate, 5 May, confirmed 27 May, 1875: Camb. Univ. Reporter, pp. 382, 436. Professor Selwyn died 24 April, 1875.]

The piece of ground thus acquired (fig. 1) had once been occupied by the Pentionary of S. John's College[1]; when purchased by the University it was partly occupied by the College stables and bakehouse, partly by dwelling-houses.

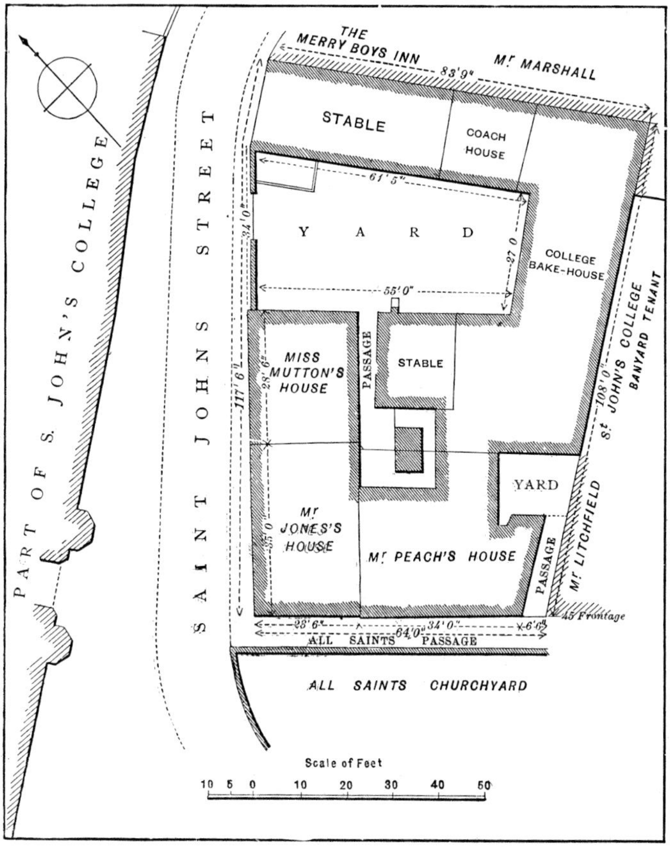

Fig. 1. Plan of the site of the Selwyn Divinity School.

The Syndicate further announced that there would be space on the proposed site for Lecture-Rooms for some of the literary Professors as well as for the Divinity School, a conjunction to which the Professors of Divinity offered no objection. The Syndi-

[1] [History of S. John's College, Vol. ii. p. 248.]

cate returned to this subject in their second Report (5 June) in which they discussed very fully, as they were required to do by the terms of their appointment, the whole question of additional buildings. It would be beside our present purpose to do more than allude to this Report, interesting and valuable as it is; the only passage which concerns our present purpose is that in which they tabulated the reports received from Professors of Languages, and reiterated their conviction that they could be accommodated on a portion of the site of the new Divinity School[1].

The question of a site having been settled, a fresh Syndicate was appointed (28 October) "to consider the subject of erecting a suitable building thereon, to take professional advice, and to obtain plans and estimates for the approval of the Senate." This Syndicate consisted of: the Vice-Chancellor; William Henry Bateson, D.D., Master of S. John's College; William Hepworth Thompson, D.D., Master of Trinity College; Brooke Foss Westcott, D.D., Regius Professor of Divinity; Charles Anthony Swainson, D.D., Norrisian Professor of Divinity; Joseph Barber Lightfoot, D.D., Lady Margaret's Professor of Divinity; John James Stewart Perowne, D.D., Hulsean Professor of Divinity; George Downing Liveing, M.A., Professor of Chemistry; Sidney Colvin, M.A., Slade Professor of Fine Art; John Clough Williams Ellis, M.A., Sidney Sussex College; and Edmund Henry Morgan, M.A., Jesus College.

This Syndicate set to work in a thoroughly systematic manner[2]. They decided to invite three approved architects,

[1] ["I. Reports have been received from Professors of Languages of which the substance is as follows:

(*a*) The Professor of Greek would be glad if a Lecture-Room could be reserved for himself and the Professor of Latin.

(*b*) The Professor of Latin thinks that if the present relation of University and College lectures continues, a Lecture-Room to accommodate a class of about 40 men would be sufficient.

(*c*) Sir Thomas Adams' Professor of Arabic uses his rooms in Queens' College, and the Divinity Lecture-Room; the Professor of Sanskrit his own house and the Divinity Lecture Room. They are satisfied with this accommodation. The Lord Almoner's Reader in Arabic uses the Librarian's Room, but he thinks that if the Oriental Triposes attract a fair number of Candidates, increased accommodation will be necessary." Report, 3 June, 1875. Camb. Univ. Reporter, p. 447.]

[2] [The following particulars are derived from the Report of the Syndicate, dated 18 October, 1876. Camb. Univ. Reporter, p. 51.]

Mr Blomfield, Mr G. G. Scott, and Mr Champneys, to send in competitive designs, and drew up the following *Instructions* for their guidance:

"A Syndicate appointed by the Senate of the University of Cambridge to obtain designs and estimates for a new Divinity School with a view to their being laid before the Senate for approval, has decided to invite three Architects to submit to them designs for the building. They propose to pay fifty guineas to each for his plans and drawings, but in case of any one of the three being employed to carry out the work, this sum will be deducted from the commission to which he will become entitled.

The drawings must include a plan of each floor, an elevation of the two principal fronts, and two sections. The competing Architects are at liberty to supply any additional plans, sections, or elevations which they may think desirable. One or at most two perspective drawings may be added, but must not be in colours.

The scale employed must be throughout that of one-eighth of an inch to a foot.

A plan of the site is annexed; but it is to be observed that the building must be set back not less than six feet from the present boundary line of the property towards St John's Street.

The main accommodation required is:

One large Lecture-Room capable of seating 200, with desks to write upon.

A smaller Lecture-Room to seat 70, also with desks to write upon.

A Library, which might also be used for a class room, with an area of not less than 800 sq. ft. clear of the book shelves.

Four small rooms as private rooms for the Professors.

A Lavatory, &c.

Two rooms for the Porter.

Provision must be made for warming and ventilating the rooms.

The attention of the competing architects is especially directed to the provision of adequate light in the Lecture-rooms.

The Syndicate considers that the building will not cover the whole site, but should occupy the prominent position on the front next All Saints Churchyard and St John's College. It is in contemplation to build hereafter other Lecture-Rooms on that part of the site which shall not be occupied by the Divinity School, but it is intended that the Divinity School shall be the principal feature of any buildings erected on the site. Each architect is requested to indicate in his drawings the relation which he proposes that the supplemental buildings should have to the Divinity School.

The style is to be an English Style of the 16th century; the material red brick and stone.

The cost of the building (the fittings of the Library not included) is not to exceed £8,500.

Each competing Architect should accompany his designs with a statement of their probable cost.

The designs must be sent in to the Vice-Chancellor not later than March 25, 1876.

The Syndicate reserve to themselves the power of taking a Surveyor's opinion upon the arrangements provided by the several designs, and upon the cost of executing them.

The Syndicate has only power to recommend a design: the ultimate choice of an Architect will rest with the Senate.

The Syndicate does not undertake to recommend any of the designs.

If any one of the designs is selected for execution, the drawings thereof shall become the property of the University. Unsuccessful designs will be returned to their authors."

The designs having been sent in, the Syndicate carefully examined them, and having decided that they could not altogether approve any one of them, they had an interview with each of the architects, and explained the objections entertained to his design. The three consented to send in sketches shewing how their plans could be modified, and, these altered designs having been in their turn carefully examined, that of Mr Basil Champneys was selected. As, however, his design still failed to satisfy the Syndicate, they induced him to make further changes in it, after which they recommended it unanimously to the Senate for adoption. In this case the design, as ultimately adopted, was accompanied by a Report, prepared by the architect, a document the absence of which has been often lamented when we have been investigating the history of other buildings. It is therefore given entire.

"The style of the accompanying designs is English Gothic of the early part of the sixteenth century.

The materials are brick and stone, and their distribution is arranged mainly according to practical utility.

The building designed consists of a central block and two wings. The central building, with the Southern or right-hand wing, contains the Divinity Schools and the Porter's Lodge, and the left-hand or Northern wing the Literary Schools. The central block, which contains the largest rooms, is necessarily of greatly superior height to the wings; and the South elevation shews a gable of considerable height rising above the lower buildings of the South wing. A similar arrangement exists in Hampton Court Palace, a building also in the style of the sixteenth century, where the gable of the Banqueting Hall rises above the lower buildings of the quadrangle, and has a very effective appearance. This precedent has been kept in view in the present design.

In order to mark the disengaged angle of the building and to balance the somewhat similar feature in the Master's Court of Trinity

College, an octagonal Corner Turret has been introduced, which would form an oriel window to the Library.

An entrance in the centre gives access to the entire building, and is commanded by the Porter's Lodge.

The Divinity Schools consist of two Lecture-Rooms, a Library, four Professors' Rooms, two Porters' Rooms, and accommodation for stowage and offices. Of the Lecture-Rooms, the smaller is on the ground floor, and is 33 ft. 6 in. × 25 ft. 0 in. and 17 ft. high; the larger is on the first floor, and is 54 ft. 6 in. × 33 ft. 6 in., and in height 17 ft. to the wall-plate and 32 ft. to the ridge of the roof. The Library is 41 ft. 6 in. × 20 ft. 3 in., besides recesses which would give room for book-shelves, and is in height 14 ft. to the wall-plate and 24 ft. to the ridge. The Professors' Rooms have an area of about 300 superficial feet each, and are one of them 10 ft. and the remaining three 11 ft. in height.

As the ground-floor Lecture-Room is 17 ft. in height, and a much less height is sufficient for the Professor's Room, Porter's Room, and passage, which occupy the remainder of the central block, it seemed advisable to utilise the superfluous height by forming a Mezzanine Floor. By this means two good rooms, communicating with each other, are obtained for the Porter, as well as about 584 feet area of stowage room, which is sure to prove serviceable, especially in connection with the Library. The lower room of the Porter's lodgings does not depend for light on that obtained from the cloisters, but light and direct connection with the open air are obtained from above by means of a well-hole.

The staircase of the Divinity Schools is 6 ft. wide, and is placed at the south-eastern corner of the building, having a wide landing on the level of the Library and another on the level of the larger Lecture-Room. It also gives access to the stowage room on the mezzanine floor.

The Literary Schools consist of four Lecture-Rooms, two on the ground and two on the first floor. No. 1 is 31 ft. 6 in. × 23 ft. 6 in. and 17 ft. high; No. 2 is 20 ft. × 19 ft. 6 in. and 13 ft. high; No. 3 is 31 ft. 6 in. × 23 ft. 6 in. and 17 ft. to the collar; and No. 4 is 28 ft. × 19 ft. 6 in., 12 ft. to the wall-plate, and 22 ft. to the ridge; No. 4 is especially adapted to serve as a Museum if required. There is also a large cupboard for stowage on a mezzanine, and the necessary offices.

In all the Lecture-Rooms the window-space has been made as ample as possible. The windows are placed not less than 5 ft. from the floor-line, and in all case there is provision for through ventilation.

A staircase, 5 ft. wide, gives access to the mezzanine and upper rooms, and from the top of the landing a door leads into the large Divinity Lecture-Room. The space under this staircase is used for the Furnace Room, which communicates with an underground chamber, 4 ft. wide, running across the central block of the building, in which hot-water pipes would be packed for the warming of the large Divinity Lecture-Room. A thoroughly efficient system of warming involves the question of ventilation, and the latter must comprise the full and sufficient supply of fresh air as well as the withdrawal of vitiated air. I purpose to employ the low-pressure hot-water system for warming the passages and largest rooms. In the larger Lecture-Room I should warm the air partly by a large open-fire ventilating grate, partly by a very full and efficient supply of fresh warmed air rising from a chamber on the basement and discharged into the rooms at about one foot above the level of the floor through trellis gratings fitted with adjustable valves. In the Lecture-Rooms the grates will be placed near the doorways, both to economise space and to prevent draughts from entering through the doors when opened. In all but the large Lecture-Room mentioned above, I should use open-fire ventilating grates, calculated accurately for the cubical contents of the several rooms. The withdrawal of the vitiated air from the several rooms will be accomplished very simply by the provision of brick flues rising from the upper part of each room and discharging at the highest practicable level. In arranging these flues, care will be taken to utilize the waste heat of the smoke flues, while their success will be guaranteed by the large admission of fresh warmed air to the lower portion of each room.

ESTIMATED COST.

	£
I estimate the cost of the portion of the building comprising the Divinity Schools, at.................	8,375
That of the left-hand wing, comprising the Literary Schools (as extra to the Divinity Schools, the party-wall common to both being included in the above estimate) at	2,998
The warming chamber, which is common to both portions of the building, I estimate at	150
Total......................	£11,523

BASIL CHAMPNEYS, *Architect.*

39, Great Marlborough Street, W.,
Sept. 30, 1876."

This description will be readily understood from the ground-plan (fig. 2). The large Divinity Lecture Room on the first floor occupies the whole space above the small Divinity Lecture Room, the Professor's Room No. I, the Porter's Room, and the south range of the corridor. The Library is over the three rooms for the Professors in the south wing. The two Literary Lecture Rooms on the first floor are directly over those on the ground-floor.

The Report recommending the design of Mr Champneys was confirmed by the Senate 2 November, 1876, and the preparation of the working drawings was commenced at once. The architect soon found that in order to make the north-eastern angle of the Literary Schools rectangular, it would be necessary

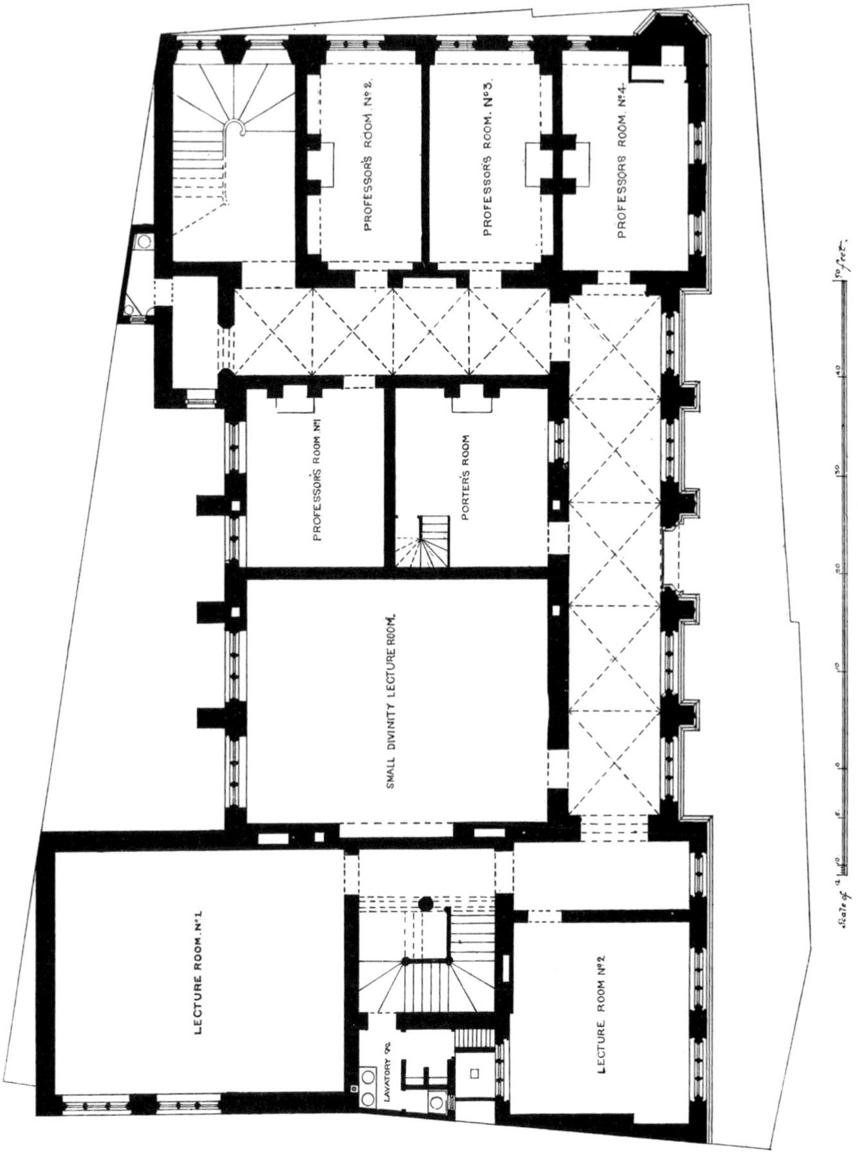

Fig. 2. Ground-plan of the Selwyn Divinity School; reduced from that drawn by Mr Champneys.

to obtain a small addition to the site[1]. This change entailed a slight increase in the size of some of the rooms; and the architect further suggested an increase in the ornamentation of the south front. In consequence, the lowest tender, that of Mr Loveday, of Kibworth, Leicestershire, amounted to £11,977, or £454 in excess of Mr Champney's estimate[2]. The Senate, however, made no objection to the increased outlay, and it was agreed that the contract should be sealed 22 March, 1877[3]. The building was commenced shortly afterwards, and was ready for use in the Michaelmas Term, 1879. There was no opening ceremony, but a short service was held in the School 24 October, on the occasion of the first public use of it for the terminal meeting of Graduates in Divinity. It was formally conveyed to the University, 30 October, 1879, on which day the Vice-Chancellor read to the Senate a Latin letter from the Trustees, announcing the completion of the building, and commending, in well-selected phrases, the piety and liberality of Professor Selwyn[4].

As usually happens in extensive works of this kind, the sum specified in the contract was considerably exceeded, and Messrs Loveday's account ultimately amounted to £15,074. 12*s*. 7*d*.; viz. £11,060. 4*s*. 3*d*. for the Divinity School, and £4,014. 8*s*. 4*d*. for the Literary Lecture Rooms[5]. To this must be added the remuneration of the Architect, and other smaller charges, so that the cost of the whole work could not have fallen far short of £17,000.]

[1] [The seal of the University was affixed to the conveyance of this piece of ground, 25 March, 1878.]

[2] [Report of the Syndicate, 10 March, 1877, confirmed by Grace 15 March: Camb. Univ. Reporter, pp. 299, 319.]

[3] [Ibid. p. 340.]

[4] [The letter, written by the Bishop of Durham and Dr Okes, is printed in the Camb. Univ. Reporter, 4 November, 1879, p. 84.]

[5] [Report of the Syndicate, 4 February, 1880. Ibid. p. 282.]

CHRONOLOGICAL SUMMARY.

PRINTING-HOUSE.

1655. Queens' College lease to the University their ground at the corner of Silver Street and Queens' Lane, on which a Printing-house is afterwards built.
1696. Second Printing-house built, to the north of the former.
1716. The old Printing-house made over to the Professors of Anatomy and Chemistry.
1762. Purchase of "The White Lion."
1786. Warehouse built for the Printing-house.
1804. Warehouse altered into a Printing-house.
1821. The Syndics of the Press recommend the purchase of Mr Nutter's estate called "The Cardinal's Hat."
1824. 25 May. The Marquis Camden offers to the University for a new Printing-house the surplus of a fund subscribed for a statue to Mr Pitt.
18 June. Formal Resolution of the subscribers to the same effect.
1 July. Grace to purchase houses fronting Trumpington Street.
1826. Contract sealed for building new Printing-office and Printer's house.
1829. Mr Blore's design for the proposed Pitt building selected.
1830. Site increased by the purchase of additional houses.
1831. 3 March. Mr Blore asked to prepare a new design.
11 June. Grace to sanction an outlay of £2000 on building the north sid of the quadrangle; Mr Blore to be the architect.
18 October. First stone laid of the façade to Trumpington Street.
1833. 28 April. The building formally made over to the University.
1863. New foundry built in Black Lion Yard.
1871—72. Machine-room and warehouses increased.
1877—78. New building erected at the S.W. corner of the quadrangle.

MUSEUMS AND LECTURE-ROOMS FOR NATURAL SCIENCE.

1588. Foundation of a Botanic Garden suggested by John Gerard.
1696. Plans obtained for a "Physic Garden."
1731. Attempt to buy an estate for the same.
1760—62. Ground purchased and conveyed to the University by Dr Richard Walker in trust for a Botanic Garden.
1760. Dr Walker releases to the vendor of the estate certain messuages in Free School Lane.
1783. Leasehold portion of Dr Walker's estate leased to the University by the Corporation of Cambridge for 999 years.
First election of a Jacksonian Professor.

1784. The "capital messuage" on the Botanic Garden estate sold to John Mortlock and pulled down.

1786. A messuage, part of the same estate, leased by the University to John Mortlock for 999 years.

1786—87. Jacksonian lecture-room built.

1831. New site obtained for the Botanic Garden.

1832—33. Anatomical lecture-room and Museum built.

1846. Removal of the Botanic Garden to the new site commenced.

1853. 2 February. Syndicate appointed to acquire the old Botanic Garden for the University, and to suggest a scheme for building new Museums and Lecture-Rooms.

29 July. The old Botanic Garden conveyed to the University.

31 December. Report on what Museums and Lecture-Rooms it would be desirable to build.

1854. 8 February. Mr Salvin authorised to send in plans and estimate.

May. Mr Salvin's plans laid before the Syndicate.

1856. House in Free School Lane purchased.

1860. 22 November. University Property Syndicate instructed to inform the Senate what funds could be appropriated to new buildings.

1861. 25 April. A "Museums Building Fund" created.

8 June. The Syndicate appointed 2 February, 1853, resume the consideration of plans, and obtain a new design.

16 December. Mr Salvin's new plans submitted to the Senate.

1862. March. House in Free School Lane purchased.

15 March. Mr Salvin's plans discussed in the Arts School, and unfavourably received.

27 March. Design re-issued with modifications.

4 April. Design accepted by the Senate.

23 May. Report of the Syndicate announcing the lowest tender to be greatly in excess of the estimate.

30 May. The scheme rejected.

11 December. Syndicate appointed to ascertain the position of the University with reference to the architect and the plans.

1863. 24 February. Report of the Syndicate reviving Mr Salvin's scheme with modifications.

20 March. Report confirmed.

4 June. Appointment of a Building Syndicate.

9 June. Ground handed over to the contractor.

12 November. Confirmation of the Report of the Syndicate announcing Professor Clark's offer to lend the money required to build the Museum of Comparative Anatomy.

1864. November. West wing of the Museums completed.

1865. February. Museum of Zoology completed.

June. Museum of Comparative Anatomy completed.

1866. 31 May. A Museums "Maintenance Fund" created.

1868. 25 November. Syndicate appointed to report on the best method of teaching Experimental Physics.

1869. 27 February. They recommend the foundation of a special Professorship, with proper appliances.

1869. 13 May. Special Syndicate appointed to investigate the means of raising the necessary funds.

1870. June. The Trinity Prælector in Physiology allowed to use the rooms called Museums of Philosophical Apparatus.

10 October. The Duke of Devonshire, Chancellor, offers to defray the cost of the building and apparatus required for Experimental Physics.

1871. 9 February. Professorship of Experimental Physics founded.

2 March. Syndicate to select site and design for a suitable building.

8 March. First Professor of Experimental Physics elected.

June. House in Free School Lane purchased.

1872—75. Houses in Free School Lane purchased.

1872. 12 March. Tender to build the Cavendish Laboratory accepted.

June. Laboratory for students in Chemistry built.

25 October. The Museums Syndicate advise the erection of new rooms for Comparative Anatomy and Physiology.

1873. House in Corn Exchange Street purchased.

1874. Easter. Cavendish Laboratory completed.

1875. 25 May. Professorship of Mechanism established.

1876. June. New buildings for Comparative Anatomy and Physiology commenced.

1878. Workshop built for Professor of Mechanism.

1880. Museums of Philosophical Apparatus thrown together.

1880—81. Drawing-office and additional workshop built for Professor of Mechanism.

1881. Warehouses in Corn Exchange Street purchased from Mr Headly.

1882. Further extension of the Mechanical workshops. Floor added to the central building for Morphology.

1883. House in Corn Exchange Street purchased.

1884. House in Corn Exchange Street purchased.

Foundry built for the Professor of Mechanism. Floor added to the west wing for Morphology. Class-room, etc. for Physiological Botany built.

OBSERVATORY.

1704. Will of Dr Plume bequeathing £1800 to the University.

1706. The roof of the Great Gate of Trinity College assigned for an Observatory.

1790. Syndicate appointed to consider the building of a new Observatory.

1792. The Observatory on Trinity Gate made over to the College by Dr Plume's Trustees.

1797. The Observatory pulled down.

1817. Syndicate appointed to report on a suitable site for a new Observatory, and on other matters appertaining thereto.

1820. 5 May. Grace to allow £5000 towards the expense of building; appointment of a Syndicate to collect subscriptions, and of a Syndicate to purchase a site.

1821. S. John's College agree to sell a site to the University.

1822. 13 March. Mr Mead's design for an Observatory accepted.

25 June. Building operations begin.

1823. Observatory completed.

1835. Building erected to contain the Duke of Northumberland's telescope.

FITZWILLIAM MUSEUM.

1815.	Will of Viscount Fitzwilliam bequeathing his collections and £100,000 to the University.
1816.	5 February. Death of Viscount Fitzwilliam.
	17 April. Syndicate appointed to provide temporary accommodation for the collections.
	7 May. The Perse School selected as a temporary receptacle.
	October. Collections ready for exhibition.
1823.	Site for a permanent Museum purchased from Peterhouse.
1834.	Designs for the Museum to be obtained.
1835.	Mr Basevi's design selected.
1836.	Additional ground obtained from Peterhouse.
1837.	2 November. The first stone laid by the Vice-Chancellor.
1841.	The building practically completed.
1844.	Contract for the internal fittings.
1845.	14 October. Death of Mr Basevi.
	15 December. Appointment of Mr Cockerell as his successor.
1846.	Mr Cockerell gives designs for completing the Hall and staircases; designs bookcases for the Library; alters lantern in Entrance-Hall.
1847.	9 December. Works suspended for want of funds.
1848.	The collections moved in to the building.
1870.	Completion of Entrance-Hall suggested.
1871.	Mr Edward M. Barry consulted.
	7 June. His Report confirmed by the Senate, and the work begun.
1875.	Completion of the decoration of the Entrance-Hall.
1877.	Statue of H.R.H. Prince Albert placed in the Entrance-Hall.
1878.	The formation of a Museum of Casts first considered by the Syndicate of Management.
1879.	11 December. The "Archæological Collections Syndicate" appointed.
1882.	23 March. A leasehold site acquired from Peterhouse.
	7 December. A Museum for Classical Archæology to be erected out of the Fitzwilliam Fund; for General Archæology by the University.
1884.	6 May. Formal opening of the Museum.

SELWYN DIVINITY SCHOOL.

1858.	The Board of Theological Studies suggest the building of a Divinity School.
1864.	Professor Selwyn's annual benefaction to be devoted to that purpose.
1874.	Syndicate appointed to select a site for the School.
1875.	Purchase of ground from S. John's College.
	October. Syndicate appointed to obtain a design.
1876.	The design by Mr Champneys selected.
1877.	March. Contract sealed, and building commenced.
1879.	School completed and formally conveyed to the University.

PART III.

ESSAYS

ON THE

Component Parts of a College.

1. THE COLLEGIATE PLAN.

2. THE GATEWAY.

3. THE CHAMBERS AND STUDIES.

4. THE MASTER'S LODGE.

5. THE HALL, THE KITCHEN, ETC.

6. THE COMBINATION ROOM.

7. THE LIBRARY.

8. THE TREASURY, OR MUNIMENT ROOM.

9. THE CHAPEL.

10. THE STYLE OF COLLEGIATE BUILDINGS.

11. THE TENNIS COURT, THE BOWLING-GREEN, THE GARDENS, ETC.

I.

THE COLLEGIATE PLAN.

CHAPTER I.

THE FIRST COLLEGIATE BUILDINGS WITHOUT DEFINITE PLAN. THE QUADRANGULAR ARRANGEMENT ADOPTED GRADUALLY. SURVEY OF THE PLANS OF THE COLLEGES OF OXFORD AND CAMBRIDGE. WORKS AND INFLUENCE OF WALTER DE MERTON AND WILLIAM OF WYKEHAM.

THE general plan and disposition of a college, as at present constituted, has so remarkable an analogy with that of a monastery, that we might naturally assume that the former had been copied from the latter upon the first invention of a college. The general inclosure within walls, the disposition into courts surrounded with buildings, the cloister, the refectory with its attendant kitchen and offices, the chapel, the master's lodge recalling the house of the Prior or Abbot, all have their analogies more or less in the monastic buildings, or at least in the canonical establishments. The dormitory, however, in which the whole of the monastic members with a few exceptions slept, was never employed in colleges, where the Scholars, Fellows, and other inhabitants have always been lodged in chambers.

It is the purpose of the following essay to shew that the systematic arrangement, which we now regard as essentially belonging to colleges, was developed very gradually; and it will appear, as we proceed, that it is impossible to maintain any theory of direct derivation of a college from a monastery.

The buildings required in the earliest colleges were very simple, consisting of little else than chambers to lodge the inhabitants, a refectory or hall, and a kitchen with its offices to prepare their food. Their devotions were performed in the parish church[1], their books were kept in a chest in the strong room, and the master, in the majority of them, occupied an ordinary chamber, so that the chapel, the library, the master's lodge, and the stately gateways, which supply so many distinctive features in the later colleges, were wholly wanting in the earlier ones; and it is very interesting to watch them taking their place in succession in the quadrangles. The attempt to erect a quadrangle on a settled plan, containing the chambers and official buildings disposed in order round about the area, in which form all these early colleges now present themselves, was not made till long after their establishment. For, in fact, until the collegiate system had fairly stood the test of a long trial, it was hardly possible to determine what arrangement of buildings would be best adapted for its practical working, while the continual growth and improvement of the system in each successive foundation demanded enlargements and changes. At both Universities the inhabitants of the earliest colleges were in most cases lodged at first in houses already in existence, purchased by the founder together with the ground on which they stood. For instance, the University of Oxford invested the bequest which William of Durham made to them in 1249 in houses, in one of which they settled four Masters of Arts in 1280; but Selverne Hall, the earliest building on the present site of University College, was not purchased until 1332; nor a second Hall, adjacent to the former, until 1343. Into this latter dwelling the Society removed soon afterwards; but it was not until the beginning of the reign of Henry VI. that "they began to pull down their buildings, which stood without any method, and to reduce them into a quadrangular pile[2]." The quadrangle then built, which was much smaller than the present one (begun 1634), was pulled down to make way for it, and its aspect has been preserved to us only in the imperfect designs

[1] [College Chapels will be treated in a separate essay.]

[2] Wood, ed. Gutch, p. 56. Ingram's Memorials of Oxford, Vol. I., University College, p. 9.

of Neele and Agas[1]. According to these authorities the college had a regular closed quadrangle. The hall was on the east side, and the chapel on the south side, but so placed that it could not have had an east window. In the same way the foundress of Balliol College purchased a building called S. Mary's Hall in 1284, "which stood where the southwest corner of the College quadrangle now stands," and removed her scholars thither, having added to it "several convenient places, as Refectory, Kitchen, out-houses, and walks[2]." At the latter end of the fourteenth century irregular additions were made to the buildings for the reception of the increasing number of students, but the regular quadrangle shewn by Loggan was not commenced until the reign of King Henry VI., when the ancient structures were completely swept away, and the foundation of the chapel was not laid until 1521.

It is remarkable that Merton College (fig. 1), which, as mentioned in the Historical Introduction, gave birth to the whole system, should have preserved its primitive buildings better than any of those which succeeded it during the next century. It is evident that the founder did not contemplate the formation of the closed monastic quadrangle which, when once introduced, became the characteristic plan of a college until the Reformation. Yet his buildings are disposed in an unconnected manner about a quadrangular court after the fashion of the outer *curia* of a monastery. The eastern gable and the vestry of his collegiate church occupy the western side, which is completed by the wall of the churchyard. The hall, of which the doorway appears to belong to Merton's original plan, stands detached on the south. The Warden's lodgings, and some other buildings with decorated windows in the style of the church, are on the east and north sides. The latter side has chambers and a gateway next to the street, but built long subsequently, although the entrance must always have been there[3]. No building could ever

[1] Ingram's Memorials, *ut supra*, p. 8. Skelton's Oxonia Antiqua, ed. 1843. Plate 18.

[2] [Wood, *ut supra*, p. 86.]

[3] The building at the north-east corner was a large chamber like a Hall or Refectory, and had windows in the style of the collegiate church. It was pulled down in 1812. It is engraved by Skelton and by Loggan. [The gateway was built 1416, and the chambers between it and the Warden's lodgings were rebuilt 1589. Wood, *ut supra*, p. 17.]

have been intended to join or hide the eastern gable of the quire. In fact, the system of this first college seems to have been to keep the buildings separate : the collegiate quire with its vestry on the right hand of the courtyard ; the refectory opposite to the entrance, with its kitchen and offices beyond ; the Master's *hospitium* on the left ; and the scholars' *hospitium* as a separate dwelling also. On the south side of the church there is now a real quadrangle, called *Mob Quadrangle*, of great

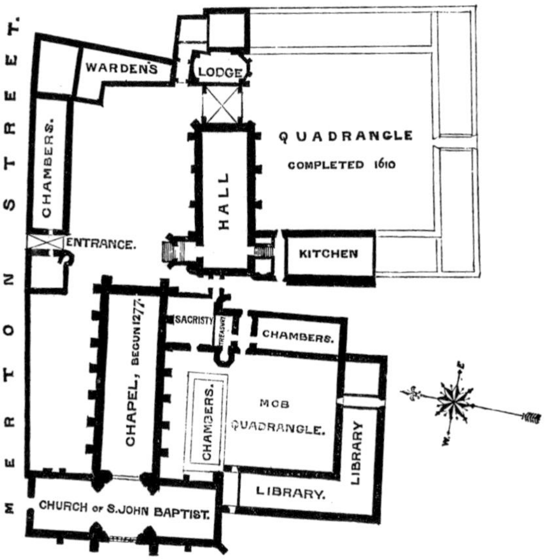

Fig. 1. Ground-plan of Merton College, Oxford.

apparent antiquity, which nevertheless is the result of a gradual accumulation of buildings. The northern side is formed by a range of chambers of the sixteenth century standing within ten feet of the quire buttresses, but, previous to the building of this range, the northern side was formed by the church itself. The eastern side contains the vestry and the treasury, both of Merton's time ; and it is completed by a range of chambers of uncertain date. The west side was at first formed by the wall of the south transept (now covered by the north range), and by part of the library, begun about 1376, long after Merton's time. This library returns and closes the quadrangle on the south.

All Merton's work is in the best style and workmanship of his period, and his church, so far as it goes, is a monumental structure. He commenced his buildings by erecting the quire of the collegiate church, the high altar of which was dedicated in 1277, the year of his death, but the building of the church continued and appears in the bursar's rolls of 1288. In 1278 a new kitchen is mentioned, and in 1304 the steps of the hall, together with a wooden bell turret (*campanarium*). New chambers were built in 1306, and the foundations of the vestry were dug in 1311[1].

The collegiate foundations which succeeded that of Merton were on a smaller scale, and had to struggle with difficulties, as, want of funds, and the premature death of their founders. The latter generally endeavoured to obtain for their scholars a site containing a Hostel or Hall already adapted for students, or which would admit of alterations and additions so as to bring it into a suitable state for their lodging. In succeeding years the funds of these colleges, and the gifts of their benefactors, were first directed to the purchase of surrounding property so as to form a compact site, an operation which frequently occupied a considerable space of time. The twelve scholars of Stapledon Hall, afterwards Exeter College, were settled in S. Stephen's Hall on the present site in 1315, which was gradually enlarged, and additional buildings erected upon it from time to time as required; but this college is remarkable for the extreme confusion and want of arrangement which its buildings retained even to the year 1605, when the formation of the present quadrangle may be said to have been begun. The founder of Oriel College in 1324 first settled his ten students in Tackley's Inn, and three years afterwards removed them to the great messuage called Oriole, or Oriel Hall, on the present site;

[1] [In a copy, made for the use of Professor Willis, of one of the Merton College Account Rolls, extending from 25 July, 1310, to 25 July, 1311, the following entry occurs for the week ending 27 March, 1311: "Item in stipendio duorum operariorum per sex dies ad fodiendum fundamenta vestiarii ij^{s}." The remaining dates are supported by extracts from the Account Rolls printed in the Archæological Journal, II. 142, and in Wood, *ut supra*, p. 17. Compare also *Merton College before the Reformation*, an essay by the present Warden, in The Nineteenth Century for September, 1882.]

"but afterward when certain messuages were purchased that laid on the north side of the said Hall, the Society began to frame their edifices into a quadrangular pile about the latter end of K. Edward III, partly with their own, and partly with the money of certain Benefactors. Which buildings being erected at several times, some of stone, and others of timber and plaister, continued for the most part till an. 1620[1];"

when the buildings of the present quadrangle were begun. In a similar manner the founder of Queen's College in 1340 placed his Provost and twelve scholars in a messuage called Temple Hall; and during the rest of his life enlarged the site by purchasing other tenements and plots of ground. The permanent buildings were not begun until the year of his death, 1349. The views which have been preserved of this college[2] shew that the buildings were arranged about a quadrangular court on the detached system employed by Merton. A gatehouse and chambers stood on the east side of the court, and the chapel on the south side. The eastern gable of the chapel, in which there was a window of five lights with rich flowing tracery, was remote from the street, and completely free from the corner of the gatehouse. The hall was on the west side of the court, but at some distance from the chapel. The intervening space was subsequently occupied by the Provost's lodgings. The library, also detached, stood westward of the chapel. [Little certain information can be obtained about the first arrangements of Durham College (afterwards Trinity College); but it is probable that the greater part of the quadrangle belongs to the fourteenth century, and that the buildings were planned in a quadrangular form from the beginning. In introducing this arrangement the Benedictine founders may have copied the monastic quadrangle to which they were accustomed. The chapel (fig. 2), on the south side, is said to have been completed before 1330; the library, and the rest of the eastern range, before 1381; and the hall and kitchen, on the west side, were probably earlier, to judge from the analogy of other colleges[3].]

We will next examine the arrangements of the earliest colleges at Cambridge. Bishop Hugh de Balsham, founder of Peterhouse, began by settling his scholars in two hostels next to

1 [Wood, *ut supra*, p. 130.]

2 [Views of the old College are given by Loggan and Skelton.]

3 [Wood's account of Trinity College, and Ingram's Memorials of Oxford.]

the Church of S. Peter beyond Trumpington Gates (afterwards called S. Mary the Less), which he granted to them, together with the church. Just before his death in 1286, he bequeathed to them, then fifteen in number, three hundred marks for erecting new buildings, but this sum appears to have been only sufficient to enable them to enlarge their site and to build a refectory, for even in 1395 we find them alleging poverty, and the incompleteness of the necessary buildings; and their quadrangle was not commenced until 1424. The buildings were then

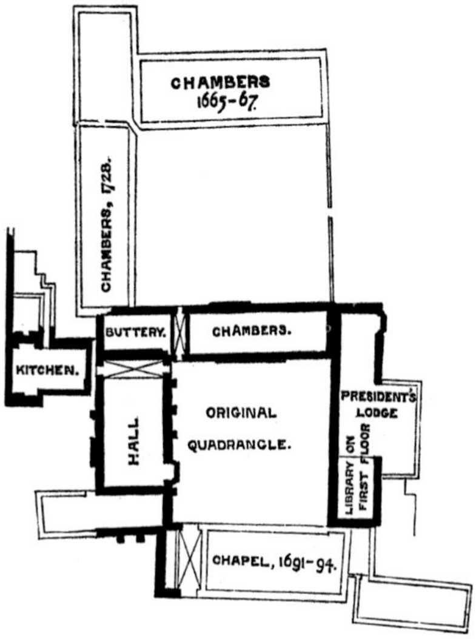

Fig. 2. Ground-plan of Trinity College, Oxford.

carried on continuously until about 1466. The north, west, and south sides were undertaken in succession, the east side being still occupied by the primitive hostels. The chapel and cloisters were not begun until 1628.

The ground which Hervey de Stanton purchased in 1324 for his college of Michael House contained a mansion sufficiently extensive for his scholars to reside in; and it probably served them until William de Gootham's chambers were built between fifty and sixty years afterwards[1]. In the same manner the

[1] [History of Trinity College, Vol. II. p. 398.]

scholars of Richard de Badew were located in the tenements already existing on the site of the present Clare Hall. They were replaced by more suitable structures by the Lady Clare after 1338; but the college was not arranged on a quadrangular plan, so far as we know, until after the fire of 1521. Hammond's view of it, dated 1592 (fig. 3), shews a regular quadrangle, having the entrance on the east side. The chapel was on the north

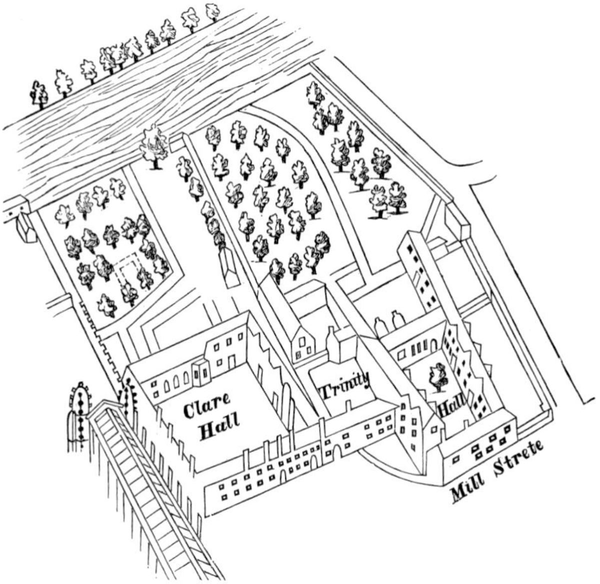

Fig. 3. Clare Hall, reduced from Hammond's map of Cambridge, dated 1592.

side; the hall on the west side; and ranges of chambers on the south and north sides. The Master and the thirty-two scholars of the royal foundation of King's Hall had no special provision made for them, but were placed in the mansion and grounds of Robert de Croyland in 1337. In subsequent years the house was enlarged, and the hall was lengthened; in 1375 the rebuilding of the entire college on a new site was undertaken; but it was not reduced to a regular quadrangular form until about 1420[1].

We come in the next place to the group of four colleges founded at Cambridge in the middle of the reign of King Edward III., namely: Pembroke College, 1346; Gonville Hall, 1348; Trinity Hall, 1350; and Corpus Christi College, 1352. Among these the first closed quadrangles are to be found.

The area of the diminutive court of Pembroke College, the smallest in the University, was completely purchased before 1351, but the buildings were not erected immediately. In the mean time the scholars were probably accommodated in one of the messuages standing on the site. It has been shewn above in the History of the College, that the south side of the quadrangle was begun in the lifetime of the Foundress; and that a papal Bull authorising the construction of a chapel was obtained in 1355. The dates of the different buildings surrounding the quadrangle are uncertain; but it is unquestionably a closed quadrangle, and the first at Cambridge in the plan of which a chapel was included[2].

When Gonville Hall was moved to its present position in 1353, the scholars were placed in the houses of John Goldcorn and Sir John de Cambridge, on the north border of the site. The chapel, occupying part of the south side, was built in 1393, and the chambers which complete that side and form part of the west side, in 1441; but the east side, completing the quadrangle, was not built until 1490, one hundred and forty years after it had been begun[3]. It should be remarked that here also the chapel was a part of the original plan, and that it was placed with its east end free, and with lateral windows, shewing that no chambers were intended to abut against it.

At Trinity Hall the scholars were probably lodged in the first instance in the old building called the Monks' Hostel[4], or in some other building on the site. The founder probably built the hall, and the range next the street. The rest of the west range and the north range were added in 1374; but the chapel was not built until near the end of the following century. It was probably

[1] [History of Trinity College, Vol. II. chapter II.]

[2] [History of Pembroke College, Vol. I.]

[3] [History of Gonville and Caius College, Vol. I. pp. 166—169.]

[4] [History of Trinity Hall, Vol. I. pp. 210, 216.]

intended to stand with the east gable free for a window. The quadrangle of this college is larger than that of any of its predecessors, being about 115 feet long, and in breadth the same as Gonville Court, namely 80 feet. It has the peculiarity of an entrance court interposed between the quadrangle and the street, like the *curia* of a monastery. This feature occurs also at Jesus College, and formed part of the plan of King's College and Eton College. It is also employed at Winchester College.

The quadrangle of Corpus Christi College, built, as shewn in the History of the College, between 1352 and 1377, possesses a simplicity of arrangement which may fairly entitle it to be the first originally planned closed quadrangle, for it consists of a hall-range on the south, containing the hall, kitchen, and Master's lodge; and of chambers on the other three sides. The buildings are low, and of the same height all round. A chapel did not form any part of it.

We must next examine carefully the work of William of Wykeham, who laid the foundation of New College at Oxford in 1379. Hitherto we have seen the collegiate buildings rising slowly and piecemeal, and never completed during the lifetime of their Founder. Now for the first time in the history of collegiate architecture a Founder, having organised a college on a large and comprehensive system, resulting from the experimental essays of his predecessors, purchases a site, and in six years finishes his buildings at Oxford, as well as his preparatory college at Winchester. The two were built between 1379 and 1393, at the beginning of the reign of King Richard the Second, a few years after the foundation of the four Cambridge colleges just described. Wykeham's buildings served as a model for all the large foundations which were subsequently undertaken, and it is from this period that the real history of collegiate architecture begins. Wykeham possessed great practical knowledge of architecture, for, as is well known, he began active life as Clerk of the Works in certain manors to King Edward the Third, and is said to have entered Holy Orders at the King's command, in order to qualify himself for the ecclesiastical preferments with which his master desired to reward his talents and services[1].

[1] Lowth's Life of William of Wykeham, 8vo. Oxford, 1777, p. 17. Wood, *ut supra*, p. 174.

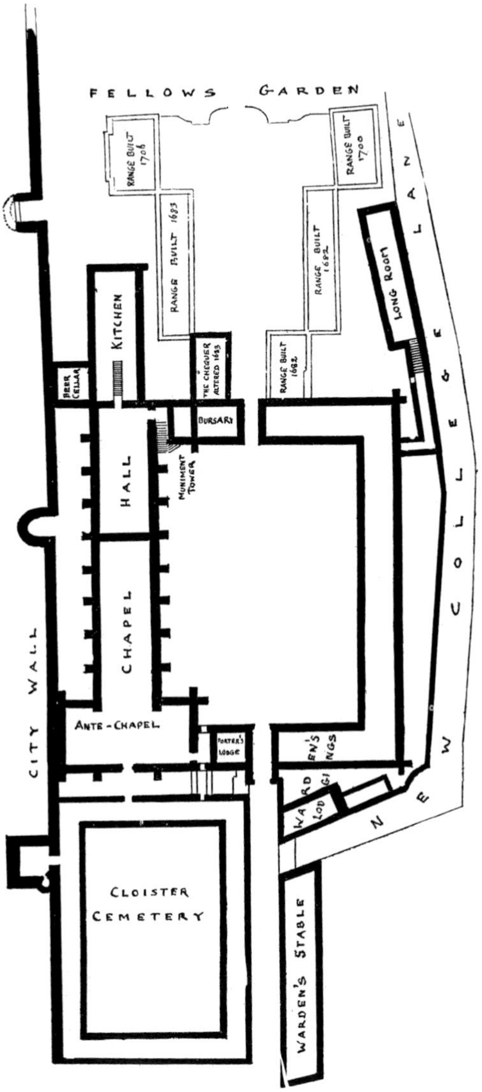

Fig. 4. Ground plan of New College, Oxford.

His professional skill enabled him to design the structures required for the college which he had devised. The number of students which he proposed to accommodate was so much in excess of that contemplated in any previous college, that a more complex organisation was needed, together with buildings of corresponding extent, and their magnitude enabled him to produce architectural effects notwithstanding the noble simplicity of style which he employed. In New College, for the first time, the Chapel, the Hall, the Library, the Treasury, the Warden's Lodgings, sufficient ranges of chambers, the cloister, and the various domestic offices, are provided for, and erected without change of plan. One large quadrangle includes the six first and principal elements of collegiate architecture.

This quadrangle (fig. 4), which measures about 150 feet from east to west, by 125 feet from north to south, is entered on the west side through a tower-gateway, now for the first time introduced. The west and south sides are wholly devoted to chambers; the east side principally to rooms of common use. The upper floor contains the library, the lower the Bursar's rooms. But the most original feature of the arrangement is that the chapel and the hall form a continuous range of building on the north side, the altar of the former being placed against the partition wall which has the high-table of the latter on its other side. The chapel therefore has no east window, but in lieu thereof a lofty pile of tabernacle work and imagery covers the whole surface of the east wall. The antechapel occupies two bays of the seven into which the length of the whole chapel is divided, but it has the novel peculiarity of projecting considerably north and south in the manner of transepts, so that the whole plan looks like a cross church lacking the nave. Hence many have imagined that this plan was imitated from the chapel of Merton College, not remembering that the transepts of the latter were erected forty years after Wykeham's, and that the remains of three western arches, now filled with masonry, shew that a nave with aisles formed part of the original design, this building being heretofore, as now, both a collegiate chapel and a parochial church. No nave, however, was intended at New College, and the statutes furnish a clue to the motives for the large antechapel, by enjoining that disputations in civil law, canon law, and theology are to take place therein[1]. The transverse position of the ante-chapel is an ingenious device to obtain space for it without intruding on the portion of the site intended for the cloister-cemetery, which lies next to the outer western side of the quadrangle, while the lane by which the college is approached runs outside its south wall. A lofty campanile is built against the outer side of the north walk of the cloister, in which is its door of entrance, but it is wholly detached from the chapel. The Warden's apartments are over, and on each side of, the gateway, and his backyard and offices are on the south side of the lane of approach. The butteries and kitchen are in a projecting wing which runs eastward in continuation of the hall into a courtyard external to the east side of the quadrangle.

[The effect of these innovations will be noticed as we proceed. For the present we will continue our enumeration of the collegiate foundations, beginning, as before, with those of Oxford, where three complete quadrangular colleges were built during the reign of King Henry VI., besides the alterations already noticed, by which the buildings of Balliol College and University College were reduced to a quadrangular arrangement.] It will be found that Wykeham's contrivances were copied in most of the succeeding colleges at Oxford, but that they obtained no imitators at Cambridge. Whatever influence the Oxford statutes may have had upon those of Cambridge, it is plain that the architecture of the one had no effect upon that of the other either in respect to plan or design.

The small college of Lincoln (founded 1427) was built in the form of a three-sided quadrangle. The hall and buttery, with the kitchen at the north-east external angle, were begun in 1436; the library and oratory on the north side, and the street front and gateway-tower on the west side, were finished before 1438. The south side was added in 1475.

In 1436 S. Bernard's College (now S. John's) was founded for the Cistercians by Archbishop Chichele, and the buildings

[1] Statutes of New College, p. 57. Oxford Commiss. Docts. Vol. i. "Aliam vero disputationem in navi capellæ collegii nostri prædicti, videlicet, extra chorum ejusdem capellæ, unam videlicet una septimana per civilistas...et aliam alia septimana per canonistas...volumus fieri et haberi...Unam etiam disputationem theologicam faciant inter se collegii nostri Socii theologiæ intendentes, in navi capellæ collegii supradicta."

were immediately erected in the form of a complete quadrangle (fig. 5), with the entrance-tower on the west side. The hall and chapel, on the north side, are in one line of building, imitating New College, with this exception, that the hall is to the west of the chapel and that the latter has no antechapel. The east side is occupied by a library and chambers; and the south side by chambers. This quadrangle, with few and obvious modern

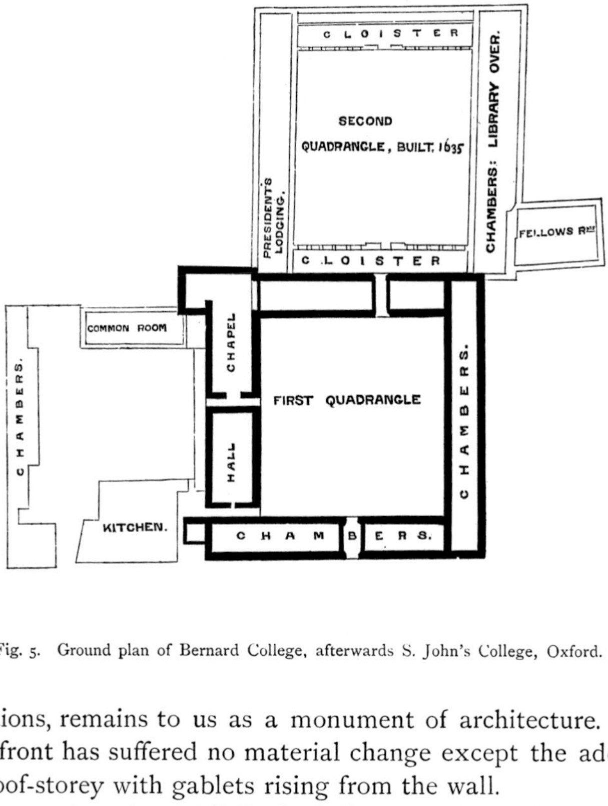

Fig. 5. Ground plan of Bernard College, afterwards S. John's College, Oxford.

alterations, remains to us as a monument of architecture. The street front has suffered no material change except the addition of a roof-storey with gablets rising from the wall.

The quadrangle of All Souls College was begun in 1437, and built in the same style by the same founder in five years, with the exception of a cloister on the north side of the chapel, which was finished in 1491. In this college (fig. 6) the entrance gateway is on the south side. The hall and chapel are in contact on the north side; but, in closer imitation of New College, the chapel is to the west of the hall, and has a transeptal antechapel. Originally the hall stood transverse to the chapel, the quadrangle being too small to allow of their being placed in line. This venerable little quadrangle was allowed to remain nearly intact when the great north quadrangle was built at the beginning of the last century.

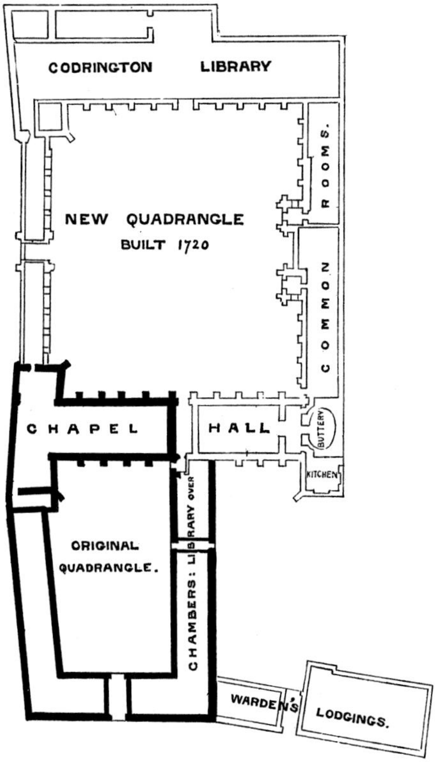

Fig. 6. Ground plan of All Souls College, Oxford.

The first stone of Magdalen College (fig. 7) was laid 5 May 1473, and the buildings were carried on steadily until 1479. The chapel and hall are arranged on Wykeham's system, the chapel having a transeptal antechapel, and its east end being in contact with the table end of the hall, the two together forming a high continuous range on the south side of the quadrangle. A lofty campanile, also evidently suggested by Wykeham's, stands detached from the chapel on the south, but this was not begun until 1492, six years after the founder's death. The monastic cloister, with chambers above it, which is carried round the great quadrangle, is a new feature in that position in collegiate architecture. The south walk of this cloister, abutting against the hall and the chapel, was added in 1490, and probably was not originally intended.

The reign of King Henry the Eighth produced the entire colleges of Brasenose and Corpus Christi, and the quadrangle of Christ Church, so far as Wolsey was permitted to carry it on. The quadrangle of the first was begun in 1509, and "for the most part erected in the time of the two Founders[1]." The gate of entrance, with the Principal's lodgings, was on the east side; the north and west sides consisted wholly of chambers, with the exception of the library at the west end of the former side; the south side had the hall in the centre, westward of which was the buttery, with the chapel above it. The kitchen adjoined the external wall of the hall. The second, begun in 1516, was also erected before the founder died. The entrance is on the north side. This side, and the west side, consisted wholly of chambers; the library occupied the entire first floor of the south side; the hall was at the north end of the east side. The chapel stood external to the quadrangle, at the south-east corner, and on the south side of the chapel there was a small cloister[2]. Both these quadrangles remain to us with only the inevitable changes produced by the requirements of succeeding ages. [The first stone of the buildings of Christ Church, or Cardinal College, as it was called by the founder, was laid 17 July, 1525. The work was carried forward with the utmost despatch, but, being interrupted by the fall of Wolsey in 1529, the college remained unfinished for more than a century. So far as the intended arrangements can be made out, it would have consisted in the main of one great closed quadrangle, measuring 264 feet from north to south, by 281 feet from east to west. The portions erected by Wolsey are the hall on the south side, with its offices and kitchen, external to the quad-

[1] [Wood, *ut supra*, p. 367.]

[2] This cloister was removed in 1706.

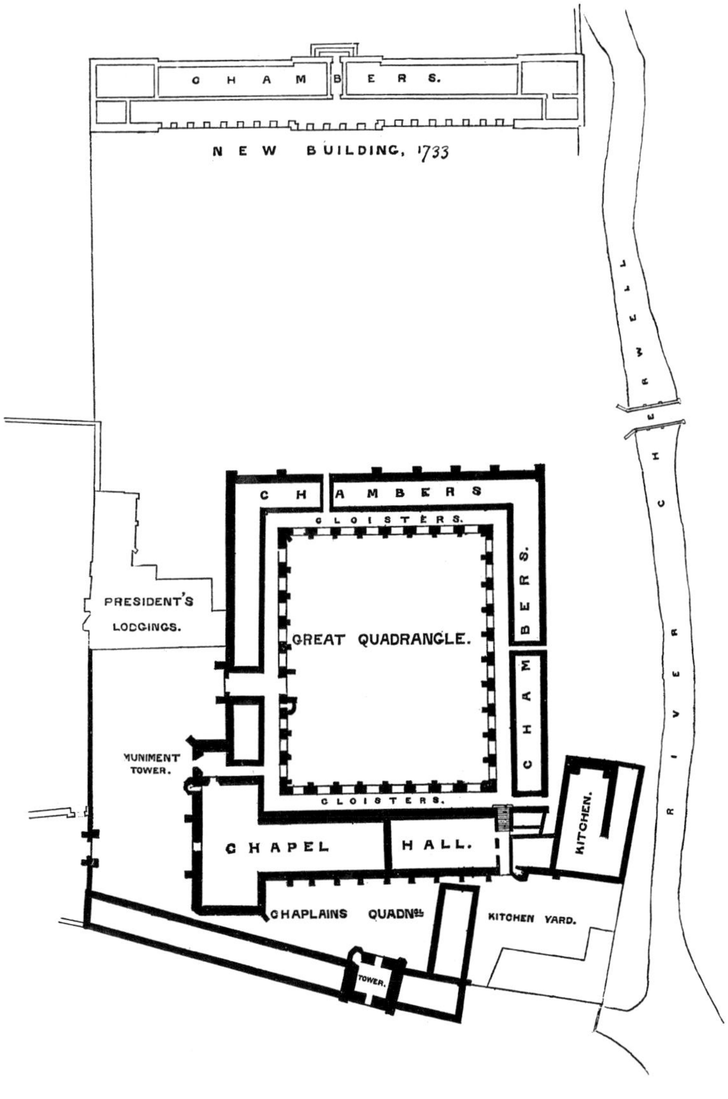

Fig. 7. Ground plan of Magdalen College, Oxford.

rangle; the rest of the south side, the east side, and part of the west side, in the centre of which was the gate of entrance. These would have consisted, as now, of ranges of chambers in two floors. The north side would have been occupied by a large church or chapel. Communication between the different parts of the quadrangle was to be effected by an internal cloister. A library was provided by altering a building which had originally been the refectory of the Priory of S. Frideswide. This formed the north side of a small court to the south-east of the large quadrangle. The south and east sides were formed by other buildings of the priory altered into chambers; and the west side by Wolsey's kitchen.]

Returning to Cambridge, we find that the quadrangle of the Benedictine Hostel founded in 1428, called afterwards Buckingham College, and refounded as Magdalene College in 1542, was planned as a closed quadrangle, though the buildings were never completed. The west side contained the entrance and certain chambers; the Master's lodge and the chapel were on the north side; and the hall and kitchen on the west side[1].

The first stone of King's College in its original position (commonly styled "The Old Court") was laid in 1441. The area which King Henry VI. was able to purchase was of such a peculiar shape that a regular quadrangle could not be attempted; and the further progress of the college was so soon arrested by the founder's schemes of enlargement that the intended arrangement cannot be recovered. The buildings were the work of a firstrate architect, and might well have been restored and preserved, as a monument of collegiate architecture. Unfortunately they were sacrificed to a controversy between the partizans of rival styles of architecture when the plans for rebuilding the University Library were under consideration, and the gateway alone remains. The first stone of the chapel for the enlarged foundation was laid in 1446. The design for the whole college, as contained in the Will of King Henry VI., has been fully described already, and in this place it is only necessary to mention that a closed quadrangle was intended, of which the chapel would have formed the north side; the

[1] [History of Magdalene College, Vol. ii. Chap. II. pp. 339—364.]

west side would have been occupied by the library, the hall, and the Provost's lodge; the south and east sides by chambers. Westward of the chapel there would have been a cloister, like Wykeham's, with a lofty detached campanile[1].

In 1448 Queens' College was founded, and, like the Oxford Colleges of Brasenose and Corpus Christi, the principal quadrangle was completely designed and finished in a few years[2]. It is entered on the east side, which, together with the south side, is occupied by chambers. The hall, kitchen, and butteries are on the west side, and the chapel and library on the north side. The material employed is red brick. It was the work of an excellent architect, and, although its aspect has been much deteriorated, partly by the mutilations of the last century when medieval architecture was despised, partly by the grotesque additions of our own time, it still retains its characteristic features sufficiently to preserve the original idea. It may be regarded not only as a most valuable architectural example, but as a type of the collegiate arrangements of the period.

The little college of Catharine Hall, projected by its founder in the reign of King Henry VI. but stopped by the civil wars, was built and opened in 1473 for two Fellows and some Fellow-Commoners (*commensales*). The chapel was licensed in 1478. Its buildings, such as they were, have all disappeared, but it has been shewn in the History of the College that they were arranged about a quadrangular area[3]. The hall, library, and Master's lodge were on the north side, and the chapel on the south side, projecting eastward beyond the eastern range of chambers. The present college was commenced in 1673.

The transformation of the nunnery of S. Rhadegund into Jesus College was commenced about 1495. The charter was granted in 1497, and the founder died in 1500, leaving his college nearly finished. This college is a very curious and instructive architectural monument, but, as the distribution of the buildings differs entirely from that of every other college in the University, and is merely an adaptation of the structural arrange-

[1] [History of King's College, Vol. i. Chap. IV. p. 350.]

[2] [History of Queens' College, Vol. ii. Chap. II. p. 7.]

[3] [History of S. Catharine's College, Vol. ii. pp. 86—90.]

ments of the nunnery, it need not be further discussed in this essay[1].

The two colleges founded by the Lady Margaret, Christ's College and S. John's College, were probably designed by the same architect. They both have closed quadrangles, which were completed in a few years after their foundation. The quadrangle of the former was begun in 1505 and completed in 1511. It is entered on the west side, which also contains the library and some chambers. The chapel is on the north side; the Master's lodge and the hall with its offices on the east side; and a range of chambers on the south side. S. John's College was begun in 1511, and was formally opened in 1516. The east range, through which it is entered, contained the library and some chambers; the chapel (part of the older Hospital altered to collegiate use), together with the Master's lodge, were on the north side; the hall and its offices on the west side; and a range of chambers on the south side. As an architectural study, as well for beauty as for contrivance, this quadrangle was one of the most notable in the University.

CHAPTER II.

PRINCIPLES OF COLLEGIATE ARRANGEMENT. THIS ARRANGEMENT DERIVED FROM THAT OF A MANOR HOUSE. DESCRIPTION OF THE PLAN OF HADDON HALL.

WE have now reached a point in our enumeration of the foundations of colleges and the disposition of their buildings, at which it will be well to endeavour to determine what were the general principles which governed the arrangement of them.

The historical survey attempted in the previous chapter shews that the collegiate quadrangle was not adopted in either University until after the middle of the fourteenth century. At Cambridge the first closed quadrangle, containing all the buildings required for the collegiate life, was that of Pembroke College, begun immediately after the foundation in 1346. At

[1] [The plan has been fully described in the History of Jesus College, Vol. ii. p. 119.]

Oxford the same arrangement was first employed by William of Wykeham at New College in 1379, and, after it had been once introduced, not only was it adopted in all the colleges founded subsequently, but the earlier colleges reformed, or re-erected, their buildings, so as to bring them into the same form.

The principal or official buildings are always ranged about a single quadrangle, one side of which stands in a street, and the entrance to the quadrangle is through an archway[1] in this side. Exceptions to this rule are found at Peterhouse and Corpus Christi College, Cambridge, which were originally entered from the churchyards of S. Mary the Less and S. Benedict respectively. At Cambridge the entrance is generally not placed in the exact centre of the side of the quadrangle, the only example of such a symmetrical position having been at S. John's College. At Oxford, on the contrary, the later colleges have their entrances in the middle of one side, the only unsymmetrical examples being Balliol College, Merton College, Oriel College, Queen's College, and New College.

At Merton College and Jesus College, Oxford (founded 1571), the hall was placed on the side of the quadrangle opposite to the entrance. This arrangement was followed at Cambridge, where the favourite type of a quadrangle has the hall parallel to, and remote from, the street of entrance and therefore on the opposite side to the gateway. The buttery shews its window in the quadrangle, prolonging the hall; and the kitchen, extending in the same direction beyond the buttery, is usually in the corner of the quadrangle, so as to shew no windows inwards. The Master's lodge is in contact with the opposite extremity of the hall. All these arrangements exist, or once existed, at the colleges of Pembroke, Corpus Christi, Queens', Christ's, S. John's, Trinity, and Emmanuel; and, in addition to the abovenamed colleges, the hall was opposite to the gate of entrance at Peterhouse, Clare Hall, Magdalene College, and Sidney College, and was intended to be in that position at King's College. The exceptions are: Michael House; King's Hall; Gonville Hall, where the hall was not built until 1441 and the chapel had from the first preoccupied the side opposite to the entrance; King's College in its first position, where the

[1] College gateways will be treated in a separate essay.

University Schools were already fixed opposite to the gateway; S. Catharine's Hall[1]; and Jesus College, where the refectory of the nuns of S. Rhadegund was adapted for the collegiate hall. In the modern buildings of S. Catharine's Hall, Clare Hall, Downing College, Corpus Christi College, King's College, and Caius College, the ancient rule has been departed from.

At Oxford, on the contrary, with the exception of the two colleges cited above, and of Lincoln College, no hall is placed on the side opposite to the entrance. Wykeham's peculiar arrangement, by which the hall is built in continuation of the chapel, so as to form one side of the quadrangle, was adopted at S. Bernard's, or S. John's, College, but with this difference, that the chapel is there placed to the east of the hall so as to obtain an east window for the former; at All Souls College, with the change of setting the hall transverse to the chapel; and at Magdalen College in exactly the same form as the original[2]. This plan found no favour at Cambridge[3]. At both Universities there seems to have been an objection to placing the hall near the street of entrance, for the only halls which have their gables in a street are that of Gonville Hall at Cambridge, and at Oxford those of Oriel College in its old position and Corpus Christi College[4].

The chapel[5], when it enters into the quadrangle, is usually, at Cambridge, on the north side. It occupies this position at Clare Hall, Pembroke Hall, and the Colleges of Magdalene, King's, Queens', Christ's, S. John's, and Trinity. The north side was probably selected because it was convenient to reserve the warmer south side for chambers; and it is obvious that the chapel could only be placed on that side of a quadrangle which lies nearest to the east and west direction. It is always set, if

1 [History of S. Catharine's Hall, Vol. i. p. 97.]

2 The same arrangement was adopted subsequently at Wadham College (1611), and at Oriel College when the Hall was rebuilt in 1729.

3 The late buildings of S. Catharine's Hall and of Clare Hall have their hall and chapel in contact, but are too remote in age from Wykeham's buildings to have felt their influence.

4 [Professor Willis notes that Cistercian Refectories stand north and south; Benedictine and others east and west.]

5 The use of Parish Churches as Chapels, and their appropriation, is discussed in the Essay on College Chapels.

possible, so as to leave the east gable free for a great window, which will of course shew itself in the street, or at one corner of the college, according to circumstances. At Cambridge the only chapels which have blank east ends are those of Pembroke Hall, Trinity Hall, and Clare Hall. The east gable of the second of these probably stood free at the beginning; and the arrangement of that of Clare Hall is rather uncertain[1]. At Oxford Wykeham set the example of a blank east wall to his chapel[2], and this blank termination was followed at University College during the reign of King Henry VI.; at All Souls College, 1437; and at Magdalen College, 1473. The little oratories at Oriel College and Lincoln College had also no east windows.

The transeptal antechapel, introduced by Wykeham, was employed in Oxford at All Souls College, Magdalen College, and Wadham College, and the transepts added by Waynflete to the chapel of Eton College were probably suggested by Wykeham's work[3]. Transepts were also added to the old chapel of Queen's College in 1518. At Cambridge there is no example of a transeptal antechapel.

A detached cloister-cemetery formed part of the original plan of New College, All Souls College, and Corpus Christi College at Oxford; and it was directed in the Will of King Henry VI. for King's College, Cambridge, and for Eton College, in imitation of Wykeham.

A cloister extended round two sides at least of the small quadrangle of King's Hall, Cambridge. The quadrangle of Jesus College also was cloistered, but there the feature was probably borrowed from the nunnery which preceded the college. At Oxford the quadrangle of Magdalen College was cloistered; and a cloister was intended at Christ Church.

Trinity Hall and Jesus College, at Cambridge, and Magdalen College, at Oxford, have small entrance-courts.

In addition to the primary quadrangle a few of the colleges

[1] It sometimes happens that the gable is so set as not to fill the angle of the quadrangle. This was the case at Queen's College, Oxford; at Gonville Hall, and probably at Trinity Hall, and Clare Hall.

[2] His chapel at Winchester College, although in one line with the hall, was joined to it at the west end, so as to leave the east gable free.

[3] There is a transeptal antechapel with piers on the Wykehamite plan at Haddon Hall.

had another. At Oxford, Merton College very early acquired the library quadrangle, commonly called *Mob quadrangle;* and a small court at the west end of the chapel at Queen's College seems to have been separated from the irregular primary one, by the building of the transeptal antechapel in 1518. At Cambridge Queens' College has a second quadrangle westward of the principal one, of which the west side dates from the foundation, and the north side, consisting of a cloister, with the gallery of the President's lodge above it, from about 1525. The south side was originally built in the reign of Queen Elizabeth, the existing building having been added in the last century.

[This college was specially selected by Professor Willis for the illustration of his theory that the design for a college at Cambridge, where the peculiar influence of William of Wykeham had been scarcely felt, was derived from the great mansions of the fifteenth century. In support of this view he used to exhibit the ground-plan of Haddon Hall (fig. 7)[1], which was probably selected for comparison on account of the completeness of the mansion originally, and the very slight amount of alteration which it has undergone.

The plan and general architectural character of Haddon Hall may be referred to the fifteenth century, though large portions of the existing buildings were erected in the reign of Queen Elizabeth. It is castellated, but the fortifications must always have been for ornament rather than for defence. There are two courts, separated by a range of buildings containing the hall and other apartments. The lower court and part of the upper court are said to have been built by Sir Henry Vernon,

[1] [This plan is reduced from that given in The History and Antiquities of Haddon Hall, by S. Rayner, 4to. London, 1836. The description is derived partly from his work, partly from Some Account of Domestic Architecture in England, from Richard II. to Henry VIII., 8vo. Oxford, 1859, p. 220, compared with the brief notices to be found in Lysons' Derbyshire, and in Observations on Ancient Castles, by Edward King, 4to. London, 1782. When Professor Willis lectured before the Architectural Congress at Cambridge in 1860, he exhibited coloured plans of the two buildings, and pointed out that "they were so truly similar that he was almost afraid that his hearers would charge him with cooking them." Ground plans of other quadrangular mansions will be found in Old Halls in Lancashire and Cheshire, by Henry Taylor, Architect, 4to. Manchester, 1884. The author shews (p. 9) that the quadrangular form of plan was not generally adopted, at least in those counties, until the fifteenth century.]

who died in 1515; the south and east sides of the upper court are Elizabethan.

The first, or lower court, is entered at the north-west corner through a good gateway-tower of early Perpendicular work. The porter's lodge is on the right of the entrance. The general level of this court is so much above that of the external ground that there is a flight of nine steps just within the gate, and a second flight of four steps leads to the space in front of the hall. These differences of level shew that it must always have been impossible to enter otherwise than on foot, and no horse or carriage could ever have approached the door of the house. The north and west sides are each occupied by a range of chambers in two floors, originally intended, in all probability, for officers and retainers. The chapel is in the south-west corner, standing at an irregular angle, and partly external to the line of wall. It appears to have been originally a small parish church, built long before the castle, and to have been fitted up as a chapel by Sir Richard Vernon, who died in 1452. In some of the windows there are remains of stained glass coeval with the building, and in one of them is the date 1427. The hall, entered from the court through a porch surmounted by a tower, is early in the Perpendicular style, with good windows of two lights, divided by a transom. The lights are trefoiled, with a quatrefoil in the head. Between the two windows on the west side is a large fireplace. The roof is modern, but the screen and music-gallery remain, though mutilated, and have good panelling of early Perpendicular work. The hall, like the chapel, was built by Sir Richard Vernon, whose arms are above the porch.

The passage under the music-gallery, which serves as a through-passage to the second, or upper, court, contains the usual doors to the kitchen and offices. The first door opens into the buttery; the middle door leads along a narrow passage into the kitchen; by the side of the kitchen are the scullery and larders, and beyond them the bakehouse, with its large fireplace and ovens; this has a separate entrance from the upper court, and has no communication with the kitchen. The third doorway leads into the pantry.

At the upper end of the hall, behind the dais, is a low panelled room, with wainscoting of the time of Henry VIII. It appears

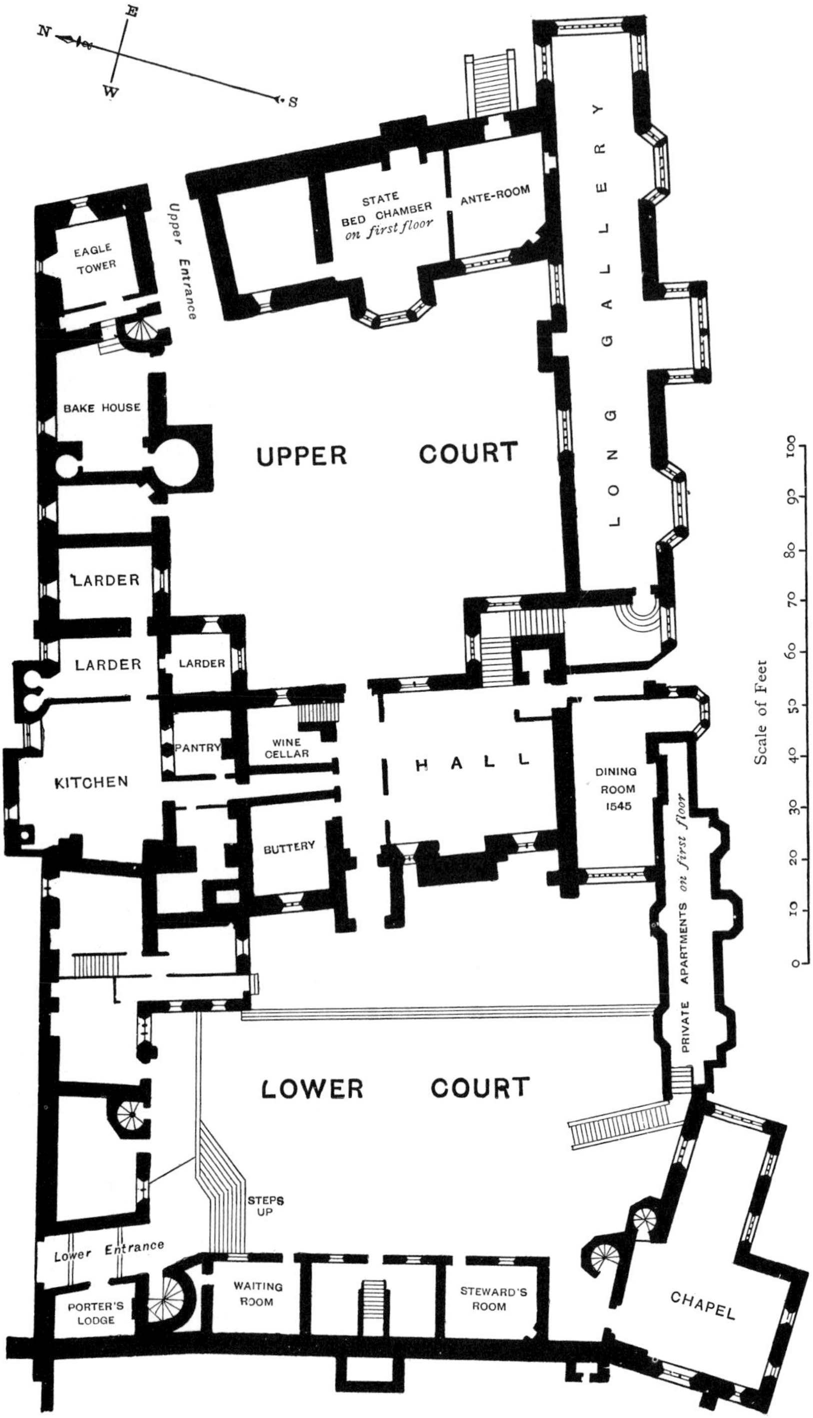

Fig. 8. Ground plan of Haddon Hall, Derbyshire.

to have been built, with the wing which intervenes between it and the chapel, in 1545, that date being carved upon the stone fireplace. At that time it was probably used as the "withdrawing room" to which those who had dined at the high table in the hall retired after dinner. Above it is a more modern drawing-room, of Elizabethan work, connected with which, on the south side of the first court, are three tapestried rooms with oriel windows looking into the garden. These rooms, probably the private apartments of the owner of the mansion, can be approached either by the stone staircase at the south-east corner of the hall, which leads to a vestibule common to them and to the long gallery, or from the first court by a separate flight of steps at the north-east corner of the chapel. This range is said to have been built by Sir John Manners, who died in 1611. One of the leaden water-pipes is dated 1602. The whole south side of the second court is occupied by the long gallery, and the vestibule before-mentioned. The gallery is 109 feet 9 inches long, and only 16 feet 10 inches broad; the height is 15 feet. From the east end of the gallery access is obtained to the rooms on the first floor of the range opposite to the hall, now used as bedrooms for visitors of distinction. This court has a separate entrance at the north-east corner.

If this ground-plan be compared with that of Queens' College their striking similarity will at once be recognised. The orientation of the chapel at Haddon happens to be the reverse of that at Queens' College, but with this exception, and the position of the entrance to the first quadrangle in the angle between two of the sides, instead of towards the centre of one side, the arrangement of the buildings in the two mansions is practically identical. The hall, buttery, and kitchen occupy in both the range between the two courts; the private dining-room beyond the hall is represented at Queens' College by the combination room; the rooms above it by the original Master's chamber; the long gallery in the upper court by the Master's gallery in the second court; the range containing the state bedrooms by that containing the audit room and other chambers; and lastly, the upper entrance into the second court by the passage leading to the bridge.]

CHAPTER III.

MODIFICATIONS INTRODUCED INTO COLLEGIATE ARRANGEMENT BETWEEN THE REFORMATION AND THE PRESENT DAY. WORKS AND INFLUENCE OF DR CAIUS. HIS QUADRANGLE WITH ONE SIDE OPEN FINDS FAVOUR AT CAMBRIDGE, BUT NOT AT OXFORD UNTIL SANCTIONED BY WREN AND HIS FOLLOWERS.

IN tracing the history of collegiate arrangement to our own time we have to consider the erection of new colleges, together with new buildings, rebuildings, and alterations in the older colleges for the sake of procuring additional lodging-room; or for the mere purpose of accommodating them to the mutations of architectural taste. These alterations were begun in the first quarter of the seventeenth century, as noticed by Fuller, who, in recounting the events of the year 1631—32, writes as follows:

"Now began the University to be much beautified in buildings, every college either casting its skin with the snake, or renewing its bill with the eagle, having their courts, or at leastwise their fronts and gatehouses, repaired and adorned[1]."

When a college becomes too small for its inhabitants, increased accommodation may be obtained either by adding more chambers, or by rebuilding the whole. The last expedient generally produces the best result, because the hall and the chapel of the old college necessarily require enlargement to receive additional members, or else become inconveniently crowded, and the old chambers are very often so ill-adapted to modern requirements that they also become condemned. But this sweeping destruction of historical structures associated with the memory of founders and benefactors, to whose generosity the establishments owe their existence, is always to be lamented, and, if possible, to be avoided. It is evident that this feeling prevailed in both Universities, for only six colleges can be said to have been completely rebuilt since the Reformation: namely, at

[1] [Fuller, ed. Prickett and Wright, p. 317.]

Cambridge, Clare Hall (1638) and S. Catharine's Hall (1673); at Oxford, Exeter College (1615), Oriel College (1620), University College (1634), and Queen's College (1693)[1].

The first additional court built after the Reformation was that which Dr Caius erected on the south side of Gonville Hall in 1565 to receive the Fellows and Scholars of his new foundation. In building this court a new principle was introduced. It was formed by two parallel ranges of buildings on the east and west sides, by the chapel and part of the Master's lodge of Gonville Hall on the north side, and by a low wall containing the detached entrance-gateway called the "Gate of Honour" on the south side. The absence of buildings on the south side deserves special attention, because it was the result of a principle distinctly enunciated by Dr Caius in the following clause of his statutes:

"We decree that no building be constructed which shall shut in the entire south side of the college of our foundation, lest for lack of free ventilation the air should become foul, the health of our college, and still more the health of Gonville's college, should become impaired, and disease and death be thereby rendered more frequent in both[2]."

The example of this skilful and eminent physician produced a most extensive practical effect in Cambridge, for, in place of the universal closed quadrangle which had characterised the colleges built before the Reformation, and which it had been their pride to attain to, we now find that the majority of the courts, whether added to old colleges for increased accommodation, or erected for those newly founded, are in the form of quadrangular areas with one side left open, or in other ways provided with the means of ventilation. This will be made more clear by specifying the examples on which the above generalisation is founded.

The new college of Emmanuel, commenced in 1584, con-

[1] [Had Professor Willis lived to complete his work, he would probably have added to this list Balliol College at Oxford, and Pembroke College at Cambridge.]

[2] [Commiss. Docts. ii. 262. "*De non claudendo latere Collegii nostri meridionali.* 30. Præterea statuimus ne quod ædificium construatur quod universum latus Collegii nostræ fundationis meridionale claudat, ne prohibita libera perspiratione aer conclusus vitietur, et valetudinem nostrorum et maxime Collegii Gonevili offendat, ac utrisque morbos acceleret atque mortem." Compare History of Gonville and Caius College, Chapter II. Vol. i. p. 165.]

sisted of two quadrangles, of which the entrance-quadrangle was open to the north in Emmanuel Lane, and the inner quadrangle open to the east. This was followed by the new college of Sidney Sussex (1595), arranged in two quadrangles side by side, both open on the west to the street; and by Nevile's court at Trinity College (1612), formed, like the court of Caius College, by a pair of parallel wings added to the older buildings, and connected along the west side by a wall containing a gate leading to the walks. These examples were all the work of the same architect, Ralph Symons. At Trinity Hall an additional court on the Caius system was formed under Dr Gabriel Harvey, the contemporary of Dr Caius, who built two wings containing the Master's gallery and the library respectively; at Peterhouse, Dr Perne's library (1590), and Dr Richardson's chambers (1632), formed, with the east side of the old quadrangle, a small court closed only by a wall on the side next Trumpington Street; at Pembroke College a second court open to the east was begun in 1610; and at Jesus College the monastic *curia* was converted into a three-sided quadrangle by a range of chambers, begun 1638. Besides these a single wing of chambers was built at Queens' College in the Walnut Tree Court (1616—19), perhaps with a view to the subsequent formation of such a court; and a similar structure at Emmanuel College, the so-called Brick Building (1633—34). Had this been matched by a similar and opposite wing next to the street, the college would have presented the unique disposition of three quadrangles in a series from north to south, open to the north, the east, and the south respectively, yet presenting to the street an unbroken frontage of 400 feet.

These buildings were all erected before the Commonwealth. In fact, the only exceptions to what may be described as the sanitary arrangement during the period between the Reformation and the Commonwealth are at Magdalene College, where the quadrangle was completed by Sir Christopher Wray and other benefactors before the close of the 16th century; at Clare Hall, where a regular closed quadrangle was commenced in 1638; at Trinity College (1597—99); and at S. John's College (1598—1602). These two last-mentioned courts are, however, so spacious that they are not affected by their enclosure with buildings.

In the period which intervened between the Restoration and the beginning of the present century the closed principle was resumed for a short time. The third court of S. John's College became closed by the addition of ranges of chambers on the south and west sides (1669—71)[1]; and Nevile's court at Trinity College by the library (1676—95). Besides these examples, the design for the new quadrangle of S. Catharine's Hall, begun 1673, shews that it was intended to be closed on the east side by a range of buildings in two floors. But Essex, to whose lot it fell to complete the project eighty years after its commencement, had the good taste to give to the college its present agreeable aspect of a three-sided quadrangle with an open iron railing and gates next Trumpington Street.

The innovation introduced by Dr Caius was not approved of at Oxford, for, while it was being generally adopted at Cambridge, eight completely closed quadrangles were built there. These are: Jesus College (1571); Exeter College (1605); Wadham College (1610); Oriel College (1620); University College (1634); and the courts added to Merton College (1610), to Lincoln College (1612), and to S. John's College by Inigo Jones (1631) [under the auspices of William Laud, D.D., then Bishop of London. The following passage from his life[2] shews that this latter extension was prompted by jealousy of the then recent extension of accommodation for students at Cambridge:

"He [the Archbishop] had received his breeding and first Preferments in St *John's* Colledge in *Oxon.* which he resolved to gratifie for the charge of his Education, by adding a second Quadrangle unto that of the first Foundation. * * * Some Benefactor had before enricht the Colledge with a Publick Library, which made one side to his new Building, the other three he added to it of his own. That on the North consisted altogether of several Chambers, for the accommodations of the Fellows and other Students. That on the East of a fair open walk below, supported upon curious Pillars, and bearing up a beautiful Gallery, opening out of the Library, for meditation and discourse: confronted on the other side with the like open walk below, and a suitable Fabrick over that raised up against the Eastern wall of the Ancient Buildings. The whole composure fashioned in an excellent symetry according to the exactest rules of Modern *Architecture;* not only grace-

[1] [It has been shewn in the History of St John's College, Vol. II. p. 274, that Sir C. Wren was consulted respecting the west side of the third court.]

[2] [Cyprianus Anglicus: by P. Heylyn: fol. London, 1668, p. 223.]

ful in itself, and useful to that private house, but a great ornament also to the University. St *Johns* in *Cambridge* shall boast no longer of its precedency before this in a double quadrangle; In which it stands equalled at the least, if not surmounted also by this of *Oxford.* On the twenty-third of *July*, in this present year [1631], he laid the first stone of this new building, not intermitting it (but only during the unseasonableness of the following Winters) till he had brought it to an end, according to his first design and proposition."]

It should, however, be mentioned that the second court of Wadham College, founded 1610, was formed on the Caian principle by the parallel buildings which contain the chapel and the library; but that the second court of Jesus College (1640), although it was left in that state when the civil war broke out[1], appears to have been always intended for the closed form which was given to it by the completion of the library in 1677.

A modification of the principle of which we have been tracing the influence was introduced into Cambridge in 1628, where the addition of the chapel to Peterhouse gave occasion to an original and effective arrangement. This building was placed at the eastern extremity of the great quadrangle, midway between the north and south ranges of chambers. Its eastern gable was thus exhibited in the street, while its western gable formed the centre of the eastern boundary of the quadrangle, which was completed by open cloisters carrying galleries to connect the chapel with the previously erected chambers. These cloisters produced a light and picturesque effect, and provided a thorough ventilation for the two courts. These arrangements were afterwards copied with excellent effect by Sir Christopher Wren, when commissioned by Archbishop Sandcroft to supply a properly orientated chapel for Emmanuel College. As the chapel of Peterhouse had been erected under the auspices of his celebrated uncle, Dr Matthew Wren, when Master of the college, it may well be supposed that its peculiar plan had formed part of the studies of the architectural nephew. It may even have been suggested in the first instance by his father, Dr Christopher Wren, who is recorded to have possessed considerable skill in architecture[2].

[1] [It is shewn in this condition by Loggan.]

[2] [This observation is probably made by Professor Willis on the authority of a passage in Parentalia: or Memoirs of the Family of the Wrens; fol. London, 1750, p. 142.]

The quadrangle with one side open, to which Dr Caius attached so great a value upon sanitary grounds, was adopted by Sir Christopher Wren and his followers, but probably on account of its superior architectural beauty. It was introduced in his time at Brasenose College, Oxford, where a new chapel and Principal's lodgings were built between 1656 and 1663, in such a position as to form, with the south side of the old closed quadrangle, a quadrangle of three sides only. Wren was also employed at Trinity College, Oxford, where a quadrangle open to the east was commenced under his direction in 1665. In a letter which he wrote to the President, Ralph Bathurst, M.D., dated 22 June, 1665, his opinions are rather alluded to than accounted for. It is evident that a prejudice existed in favour of the old closed quadrangle. The paragraphs which concern our present purpose are the following:

> "I am confirmed with Machiavell, or some such unlucky fellow, 'tis noe matter whither I quote trew, that the World is governed by wordes. I perceiue the Name of a Quadrangle will carrie it with those whom you say may possibly be your Benefactors, though it be much the worse situation for the Chambers, and the Beauty of the Colledge, and the Beauty of the particular pile of building; and if I had Skill in enchantment to represent the pile first in one position then in another, that the difference might be evidently seen, I should certainly make them of my opinion; or else I'le appeal to Mounsieur Manzard, or Signior Bernini, both which I shall see at Paris within this fortnight.
>
> But, to be sober, if any body, as you say, will pay for a Quadrangle, there is no dispute to be made; let them haue a quadrangle, though a lame one, somewhat like a three-legged table[1]."

By this language I suppose that we are to understand that Wren wished for a structure extended in one mass, for the sake of an imposing front, but, if that could not be obtained, a quadrangle of three sides of building was to be preferred to a closed one[2]. [It must also be remembered that in his first design for

[1] Memoirs of the Life and Works of Sir Christopher Wren: by James Elmes, 4to. London, 1823, p. 172. [By the kindness of the President and Bursar of Trinity College, Oxford, this transcript has been collated with the original, preserved in their Muniment Room.]

[2] [Wren's design, engraved by Skelton (Oxonia Illustrata, Plate 75), shews an arrangement of buildings very similar to that at New College. Only a portion, however, was executed. The north wing (fig. 2) was finished in 1667, and the foundation of the west side was laid at the same time, but it was not finished until 1682. The south side was not altered to its present appearance until 1728.]

the library of Trinity College, Cambridge, he contemplated a circular building connected with the north and south sides of Nevile's court by dwarf walls[1]. The reasons which induced him to erect the present structure, by which the quadrangle is effectually closed, have unfortunately not been recorded.]

The open quadrangle appears also at Oxford in the garden court of New College (fig. 4), [where a design for a closed quadrangle, one side of which would have been formed by the east side of Wykeham's quadrangle, was deliberately rejected in favour of the existing arrangement, executed by "William Bird, Mason in Oxford, according to a Modell of the same, drawne by himselfe, and delivered in." The position of the new work was regulated by that of an ancient building called "The Chequer"; and Bird's work was limited to altering this, and to building the range opposite to it on the south, together with the two parallel ranges eastward of this last and of "The Chequer" itself. These buildings were begun 31 January, 1681—82, and completed 28 August, 1685[2]. The two ranges at right angles to these were not planned until the beginning of the following century[3]; which shews that the principle which governed the arrangement had been approved, and was still maintained.

The quadrangle which replaced the old and picturesque buildings of Queen's College, of which the first stone was laid 6 February, 1710, is ascribed by tradition to Wren's pupil, Nicholas Hawkesmoore, who was unquestionably the architect of the new quadrangle at All Souls College (fig. 6). The buildings which he executed there are dated 1720—1734, but he had been consulted six years before the earlier of these dates, and his design for the east side of the quadrangle is dated 1717. The Society had evidently intended to pull down the whole of

[1] [History of Trinity College, Vol. ii. p. 533.]

[2] [It is stated in Ackermann's Oxford, i. 157, that the first stone was laid 13 February 1682, and the whole finished in 1684. The dates given in the text are those of the Building-Accounts preserved in the College.]

[3] [The contract for the south building, with "Richard Piddington and George Smith, both of Oxford, Builders," is dated 2 August, 1700; that for the north building, with William Townsend and George Smith, also of Oxford, is dated 1 March, 1706. These particulars of the buildings of New College are due to the kindness of James Edward Sewell, D.D., Warden, and Alfred Robinson, M.A., Bursar.]

the older part of their college, and on this subject Hawkesmoore addressed to them a long letter, dated 17 February, 1714—15, from which the following passage may be quoted. It is not only interesting in itself, but has a direct bearing on the whole question of the way in which collegiate structures should be treated when additions become necessary:

"I must ask leave to say something in favour of ye Old Quadrangle, built by your most reverend Founder, for altho' it may have some faults, yet it is not without its virtues. This building is strong and durable, much more firm than any of your new buildings, because they have not ye Substance nor Workmanship, and I am confident that much conveniency and beauty may be added to it, whereas utterly destroying it wou'd be useing ye founder cruelly and a loss to ye present possessours.

* * * *

Whatever is good in its kind ought to be preserv'd in respect to antiquity, as well as our present advantage, for destruction can be profitable to none but such as live by it.

* * * *

What I am offering at in this Article is for the preservation of Antient durable Publick Buildings, that are strong and usefull, instead of erecting new fantasticall perishable Trash, or altering and wounding ye Old by unskilfull knavish Workmen."

Both these quadrangles are of three sides only, and are closed next to the street by a colonnade, in the centre of which is an ornamental gateway[1].]

At University College, the small second quadrangle, built 1719, consists, like the new buildings at Brasenose, of two ranges at right angles to each other, forming, with the old west side of the college, a quadrangle open to the south; and the quadrangle of Worcester College, begun 1720, is closed on the east side by a wall only. Had the larger quadrangle towards the garden been completed, it would have consisted of two parallel wings connected by a wall, as at Trinity College.

Examples of courts open at the angles are to be found at the Peckwater quadrangle of Christ Church (1705); and at Oriel College, where a court is formed by the Robinson Building (1719), the Carter Building (1730), and the Library (1788), none of which are joined either to each other or to the side of the older quadrangle beyond which they were erected.

[1] [The possible share of Wren in these designs is discussed in a note to Walpole's Anecdotes of Painting, ed. Dallaway, iv. 73.]

It was probably under the influence of Wren that Gibbs designed the quadrangle of King's College Cambridge in 1724 to consist of three separate masses of building completely detached at the corners, so as to ventilate the court, and besides, as he himself states in the text which accompanies his published design, to prevent damage from fire[1]. It is a pity that architects can so seldom be induced to describe their own designs, and to inform posterity of the reasons which induced them to adopt this or that principle of arrangement or outline.

In the present century no uniform rule has been maintained. The quadrangle of Downing College (1803) was planned by Wyatt on the principle of the design published by Gibbs for King's College; an open quadrangle was designed by Wilkins at King's College in 1824; by Brooks at Peterhouse in 1825; and by Rickman at S. John's College in 1827; but on the other hand Wilkins himself resumed the closed principle both at Corpus Christi College and at Trinity College, whilst his open quadrangle at King's College was in progress.

[In the additions to colleges which have been carried out both at Oxford and Cambridge since the above-mentioned works were completed, the detached principle has been maintained, except in "The Master's Courts" at Trinity College, Cambridge (1860—68), both of which are closed.]

[1] [History of King's College, Vol. i. p. 560. Wren had been actually consulted by Hawkesmoore, when he gave a design for a new quadrangle at King's College in 1713 (Ibid. 557), and the advice then given was probably acted upon by Gibbs.]

II.

THE GATEWAY.

THE entrance to the early colleges was usually not marked by any tower, and the eaves or the parapet of the adjoining buildings, as the case might be, were carried over it without any change of level.

Peterhouse was entered from the churchyard of S. Mary the Less through an arch under the gallery leading from the college to the church[1]; and Corpus Christi College from the churchyard of S. Benedict, through a perfectly plain four-centered arch, without even a hoodmold. This entrance still exists, though much disguised since Loggan's print was taken. Pembroke College has an arch of entrance ornamented with a hood-mold, with two coats of arms above it between a pair of oriel windows. The court of Gonville Hall was entered through a plain arch, as we learn from Loggan; but as his print shews only the interior of the quadrangle, we do not know how the entrance was treated on the exterior; but it is evident that it was not marked by any tower. Clare Hall, according to Hammond's plan, dated 1592 (p. 254), was entered through a plain arch-way. Trinity Hall, as Loggan shews, had a kind of gatehouse, of the plainest character, built probably soon after the foundation of the college. The division from the chambers north and south of it was marked by party-walls, which rose above the roofs in a series of steps. It had a large gateway-arch flanked by a postern-arch,

[1] [History of Peterhouse, Vol. i. p. 23.]

which was surmounted by a niche containing a pedestal for a figure[1]. The entrance to the house of Robert de Croyland, after its extension in 1343, appears to have been marked by a gate-house with a chamber over it[2]; and that to Michael House, if we may trust Lyne's print dated 1574, by a distinct tower[3]. These two examples, however, are uncertain. [Magdalene College also was probably entered through a plain archway until the cinque-cento structure shewn by Loggan was put up in 1585[4].]

A remarkable exception to the usual treatment of the entrances to early colleges is afforded by Queen's College, Oxford, which had a lofty gatehouse resembling that of an abbey, occupying more than half of the east side of the quadrangle. This structure was finished, according to Wood, about 1355[5].

The gateway-tower which is now so great an ornament to collegiate buildings was undoubtedly employed for the first time in collegiate architecture between 1379 and 1393, by William of Wykeham, both at New College, Oxford, and in his College at Winchester. At Cambridge the first gateway-tower is that which was commenced at King's Hall in 1426—27, as previously related[6], and has ever since been called King Edward's Tower.

These tower-gateways furnish curious illustrations of the imitative spirit which so strongly influenced medieval architecture. Wykeham's gateway-tower rises plain and square above the parapet-line of the chambers [and is set only a few feet in advance of the walls to the right and left of it, as shewn on the ground-plan of the college (p. 257)]. The exterior face (fig. 1) is at the end of the alley between parallel walls through which the college is approached, and the angles of the tower which rise above these walls have small buttresses. But within the court the angles are unornamented, and the wall of the tower below is flush with that of the chambers, without the slightest projection to distinguish it vertically. In fact the string-course above the ground-floor windows of the chambers runs unbroken over the head of the archway, as if the architect had purposely

1 [History of Trinity Hall, Vol. i. p. 215.]

2 [History of Trinity College, Vol. ii. p. 432.]

3 [Ibid. p. 400.]

4 [History of Magdalene College, Vol. ii. p. 364.]

5 [Wood, ed. Gutch, p. 150. The east front is shewn by Loggan, and the west front by Skelton; Oxonia Antiqua Restaurata, pl. 39, ed. 1843.]

6 [History of Trinity College, Vol. ii. p. 444.]

avoided any detail that would carry the vertical line down to the ground. In the college at Winchester a similar treatment of the external face of the tower is employed, and the string-course breaks upward on the face of the tower-wall in a manner still more distinctly to obliterate the vertical lines of its mass.

The first gateway-tower at Cambridge, on the other hand, has octagonal turrets at the angles, by which the tower is defined from the base upwards.

The pattern of a college gateway having been thus established in the respective Universities, every successive gate-tower in Oxford follows Wykeham's in the absence of angle-turrets and well-defined vertical lines downwards, with the sole exception of Christ Church, which has very elaborate flanking turrets; and every gate-tower in Cambridge has four flanking turrets in imitation of King's Hall, with the exception of that of Jesus College.

In some of the Oxford gate-houses, as in that of Oriel College (1620), and in the second stage of that at S. John's College, the vertical wall is set slightly in advance; at Magdalene College there are slender buttresses on each side from the ground upwards; but at the colleges of Merton; Exeter (north gateway); All Souls; Lincoln; Balliol; Brasenose; Corpus; Wadham; the wall of the tower below the parapet line is wholly undistinguishable from that of the chambers to right and left. In the same manner the staircase-turret which occupies one of the interior angles of the gateway-tower is wholly included in its plan, so as not to project into the court, except at the colleges of Merton, Magdalen, and Brasenose, where it stands at a corner of the tower. [At Corpus Christi College the turret is on the east side of the tower, with which it is connected by one side only; but below the parapet-line of the chambers it is behind the walls of the range above which it rises.

We will now describe Wykeham's gateways in greater detail, and then note the manner in which their arrangements were followed, or departed from, subsequently in other colleges.]

Wykeham's tower-gateway at New College is in three floors, divided by string-courses. The arch of entrance (fig. 1) is a plain four-centered arch, without a hood-mold; the second stage contains simply two square-headed windows also without hoodmolds, each of two lights pointed, divided by a transom; but in the third stage, which rises above the adjoining roofs, he places a central tabernacle-niche, and on each side of it a narrow square-headed window[1], flanked externally by a smaller niche containing a kneeling figure. The string-course rises square

Fig. 1. Entrance-gateway to New College, Oxford, in its present state.

over the central niche, giving additional prominence to it, and breaking the flat surface of the parapet. [On the side next the court the lower stage has two square-headed windows; the upper has a lofty central tabernacle, with a window and small

[1] [These windows are shewn by Loggan, but have since been altered as shewn in the illustration.]

niche on each side of it.] The corresponding gateway at Winchester is in two stages only. The lower of these has at each angle a buttress in two stages, and the arch of entrance is more elaborate than that at New College, having a hood-mold terminating in a corbel. The upper stage has the central tabernacle and the narrow single-light windows described above, but the smaller niches are absent. In neither college were the towers or the buildings crenellated originally. At New College the latter had battlements imposed upon their internal walls in the seventeenth century, but the parapet of the gate is still plain.

The ornamentation of the arch and the wall above it varies, as might be expected, with the importance of the college to which it belongs. In most examples the arch is embellished with a square hood-mold and ornamental spandrels. Even at Wadham College (1610) the running table, or string-course, which marks the division between the ground floor and the first floor of the chambers on each side of the gate, rises square over the Jacobean semicircular arch. The wall above the arch is also treated variously. At Merton College it is not subdivided into stages, but the first floor has a central window of two lights with a square hood-mold, flanked by two handsome tabernacles containing statues, and ornamented above by a piece of sculpture finished with an elaborate cresting. Above this again is a small window of two lights with square hood-mold close under the parapet, which is crenellated [1]. The architect employed by Archbishop Chichele for his colleges of S. Bernard (1436) and All Souls (1437) combined the two tabernacles and central window below, as used at Merton College, with the central tabernacle above, as used at New College. Both these gateways are crenellated. At All Souls College the tower is in four stages, the two highest of which rise above the roof-line of the adjoining chambers. The lowest is occupied by the gate of entrance, the second by a two-light window under a square hood-mold, with a tabernacle on either side, while the third and fourth have each two single-light windows, between which the great central tabernacle rises nearly to the string-course immediately below the parapet. At Bernard College the tower is in three stages,

[1] [This description is derived from the view of the gate given by Loggan. Since his print was taken it has been completely transformed.]

and the central window in the second stage is replaced by an oriel. Both these compositions are in all essential points quite unaltered.

This latter design found great favour, and was copied at Balliol College (1490), as we learn from Loggan, for the tower no longer exists, and at Corpus Christi College (1516); and it was imitated (of course eschewing the tabernacles) at Wadham College (1610), and at Oriel College (1620). At University College, if we may trust the ancient print copied by Skelton[1], the gateway-tower (built at the beginning of the reign of King Henry the Eighth) was in two floors, the second of which contained an oriel between two tabernacles; and, when the college was rebuilt (1635), the same type was employed in a very singular fashion of the pseudo-gothic of that time. On the second stage a tabernacle or niche is set in the middle of the oriel; and in the third stage there are two tall windows, each of two lights divided by a transom, and separated by a second tabernacle. [It also suggested, in all probability, the gateway of Lincoln College (1438), which presents a perfectly plain square tower, flush with the equally plain external wall, and not divided into stages like the others. The arch has no hood-mold; above it is a window of two lights divided by a transom, above which again is a single-light window with a very small tabernacle on either side. None of these windows have hood-molds. The parapet is not crenellated; and the belfry-staircase is within the line of the wall[2].]

In the midst of this series of imitations we meet with two other original designs: at Magdalen College (1475), and at Brasenose College (1509). The tower of the former has a noble oriel in two stages, flanked by very small tabernacles, two on each side one above the other, and a window of three lights above. The parapet is crenellated, and the angle-buttresses, which are themselves unusual, are crowned by the equally unusual addition of pinnacles. At Brasenose College the tower is masked by a peculiar flat projecting screen of Perpendicular panelling and window-lights, surmounted by a small oriel with a niche on either side. Above the oriel is a central tabernacle

[1] Oxonia Antiqua Restaurata, ed. 1843, Plate 18.

[2] [These details are derived from Loggan's print.]

rising into the parapet of the tower, and two small windows each of two lights. The parapet is crenellated.

If we now turn to the Cambridge gateway-towers we find seven specimens of a totally different type, having four flanking turrets, of which one on the interior is sometimes made larger than the others to contain a staircase. The examples are: King's Hall (1427); the Old Court of King's College (1441); Queens' College (1448); Christ's College (1505); S. John's College (1510); Trinity College Great Gate (1518), and the Queen's Gate (1597).

The first of these was rebuilt in its present position in 1600. A ground-plan, however, made before the removal, has fortunately been preserved, and from this we learn not only that the gate had originally four turrets, a fact which had already been made known to us from the Accounts of King's Hall for 1430—31[1], but the original disposition of them is shewn, and we find that three of them were used for closets to the adjoining chambers, and that the fourth was a large stair-turret. The alterations carried out at the time of the removal were so extensive that it would be unwise to base any argument upon the present appearance of the façade[2]. It is now marked out into four divisions by string-courses. The lowest is occupied by the arch; the next has two windows each of two lights, between which is the niche and statue of King Edward the Third; the third has a window of four lights flanked by heraldic insignia; the fourth has two windows, like those in the second; and the whole is crowned by a handsome parapet, panelled and crenellated[3].

The ground-plan of the gate of King's College (fig. 2)

[1] [History of Trinity College, Vol. ii. pp. 444—446.]

[2] [This has been fully described already, Ibid. p. 514.]

[3] [In addition to this description of the gate, which occurs upon a page of notes, Professor Willis has left the following, which, in substance at least, has been incorporated in the History of Trinity College:

"Of the first [gate], King Edward's, it must be remarked that only the arch and front wall between the turrets belongs to the original, the side-turrets are manifestly a reconstruction, and are smaller than the originals, and the hinder-part has been rebuilt without regard to the former disposition. Its present position only requires one ornamental face. But in its former state it was the entrance gateway of the College, and must have had an exterior and an interior façade, one of which, with its flanking turrets, has therefore disappeared."]

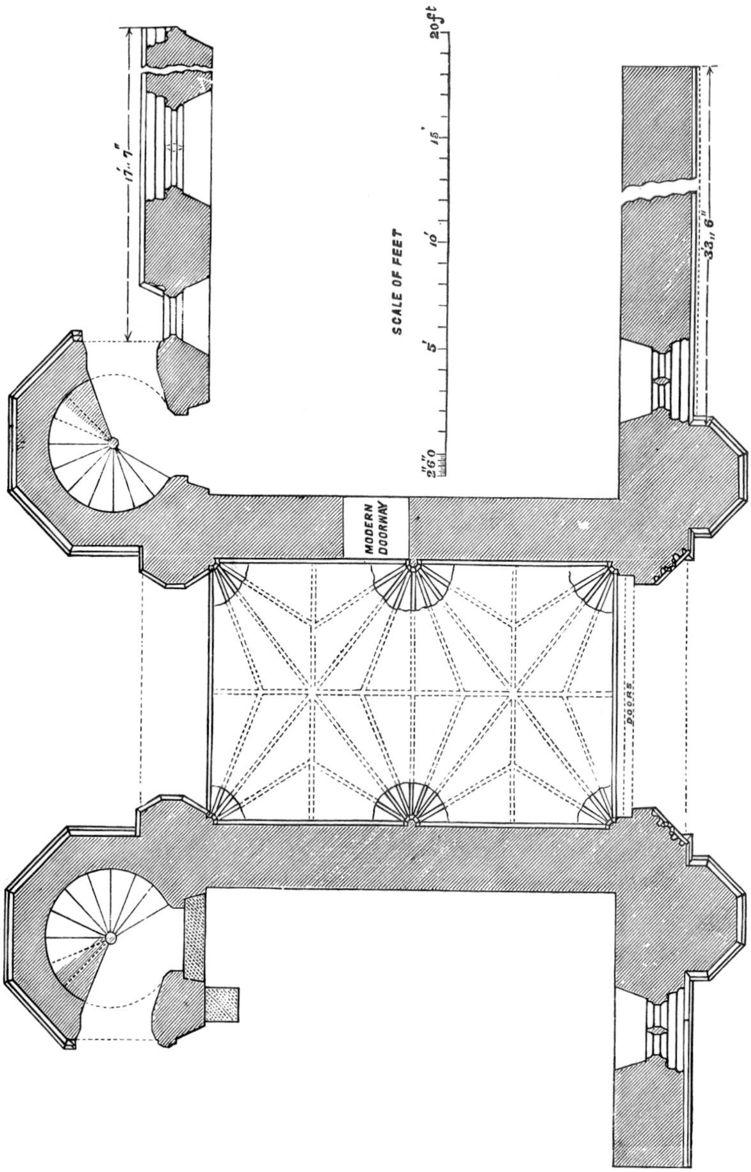

Fig. 2. Ground-plan of the gateway, begun 1441, Old Court of King's College.

shews a different proportion of the turrets. The two next to the street are small, as being merely buttress-turrets[1]; those next to the court are both large enough for each to contain a staircase leading to the chambers above. This gate was never completed, but the fragment which remains shews that it would have been a singularly rich and beautiful specimen of architecture. No portion of the wall is left plain. The arch is surmounted by a band of ornament, above which are two windows, each of two lights divided by a transom, and three tabernacles, one of which is central, and two lateral[2]. A gate-house on a similar plan is directed in the Will of King Henry the Sixth for the entrance to his enlarged college from Trumpington Street[3].

[The two examples already cited, though prescribing the ground-plan of a gate with four turrets, have not exhibited, so far as we can ascertain from the remains which have come down to us, any pattern for the treatment of the façade, such as we have found in Wykeham's gate at New College, Oxford. At Cambridge, this seems to have been left to the taste of individual builders, who followed the general plan laid down by their predecessors, with variations introduced by themselves.] The gate-houses of King's Hall and King's College were both worked in stone; but the next, at Queens' College (1448), is a noble structure of red brick, rising high and tower-like above the two-storied chambers on either side. The external turrets towards Queens' Lane are used, like those of King Edward's Gate, as closets or studies, and are therefore larger, in proportion to those towards the court, each of which contains a staircase, than the corresponding turrets at King's College. The façade is worked in three divisions. The lowest has an arch of entrance with ornamental spandrels; the second a small central tabernacle between two pointed two-light windows; and the third a small central window[4].

[1] [The first stage of these turrets is solid; the second was occupied by closets entered from the adjoining chambers.]

[2] [The interior and exterior façades of this gate are figured in the History of King's College, Vol. i. pp. 328, 329.]

[3] [Ibid. p. 369.]

[4] [It is hoped that the design of this gate, and of those of Christ's College and S. John's College, to be described next, will be understood from Loggan's prints, which have been reproduced in the History of each College.]

The ground-plan of the gate-house at Christ's College differs slightly from that at S. John's College, but, in other respects, as might be expected, the two gate-houses resemble each other very closely. At the former the four turrets are small in proportion to the mass of the gate, and none of them contain staircases. At the latter the external turrets are used as closets, and those towards the court contain staircases. Of these that at the south-west angle is larger than that at the north-west angle, as it was built for a spacious staircase which originally gave access to the library. The curtain-wall is designed in nearly the same manner at both colleges. It is divided into two nearly equal portions by a string-course. The ogee hood-mold over the arch of entrance rises to support a tabernacle which occupies the centre of the upper portion. This portion, in both colleges, is divided internally into two floors. At Christ's College the first floor only has external windows, of which there is one on each side of the tabernacle, of two lights, under a square hood-mold. On the second floor, in lieu of windows, there are sunk panels containing respectively a rose and a portcullis, both crowned. At S. John's College each floor has two windows, each of two lights pointed, with a quatrefoil in the head. In these gate-houses the spandrel-spaces are made higher and larger than elsewhere, in order to display the arms and badges of the Lady Margaret, which we will proceed to describe.

In both examples the rising stem of the hood-mold of the arch has a shield affixed to it bearing the arms of France and England quarterly, crowned, and supported by the antelopes of Beaufort. At Christ's College an eagle collared, the crest of Beaufort, rises out of the crown, and the string-course, which crosses the gate and the flanking turrets at the same level, is carried up square above it, so that it is set in a sort of panel. On each side of it are three ostrich feathers, rising out of a band or coronet, and below them three others, not fastened together. These were badges of John Beaufort, Duke of Somerset, father of the Foundress[1]. The rest of the spandrel-space contains other badges peculiar to the Foundress and her son: the portcullis; the rose *en soleil*, crowned; and the daisy. Daisies are also represented as growing out of the ground on which these badges are set in relief. In the centre of the irregular triangle formed by the arch

[1] [Cooper's Life of the Lady Margaret, p. 126.]

and the rising branches of the hood-mold is a portcullis; and the corbel-heads are carved in a dragon and a greyhound respectively.

At S. John's College the string-course which divides the first and second stages of the gate-house is at a different level from that of the turrets, and is formed of the branch of a vine bearing leaves and fruit. Two portcullises and two roses are set among the foliage. Below this string-course is a band of daisies. Both these bands project outwards in the centre of the façade, and form a bracket for the niche which contains the statue of S. John. Below this bracket the hood-mold of the arch terminates in a handsome finial. The arms of England are placed in the same position as at Christ's College, with the same supporters. Beneath the shield, in the triangular space described above, is a rose *en soleil.* To the right of the central device is a portcullis, to the left a rose, both crowned. The crown of the former has the points composed of bunches of daisies. As at Christ's College the whole ground of the spandrel-space is covered with daisies and other flowers. Over the window to the left of the niche is a rose; over that to the right a portcullis, beneath which are carved eight daisies. Both badges are crowned.]

The Great Gate of Trinity College, built in the first instance for King's Hall (1518—35), has been already fully described and figured[1]. The ground-plan resembles that of S. John's College in the relative size of the external and internal turrets, with this difference, that the turret containing the staircase is not larger than any of the other three. This gate-house, with the gate-house of Trinity Hall, are the only examples in either University which have a small postern-arch by the side of the larger one—an arrangement not uncommon in the gatehouses and towers of abbeys[2]. The Queen's Gate (1597), evidently intended as a copy of King Edward's Gate, need not be further described in this place[3].

The picturesque red-brick gateway-tower of Jesus College (1497), although destitute of angle-turrets, is yet distinguished from the ground upwards by a slight relief; by stone quoins; and by having its string-courses designedly placed at different

[1] [History of Trinity College, Vol. ii. pp. 452, 484, 486.]

[2] The secondary gateway of All Souls College, which has no tower over it, has a postern-arch.

[3] [Vol. ii. p. 516.]

levels from those of the chambers on each side of it[1]. The general disposition of the ornamentation of its arch and of the wall above it furnished the model for the more elaborate gatehouses at Christ's College and at S. John's College. The ogee hood-mold rises upwards, and the stem of its finial terminates under the base of a handsome tabernacle which occupies the centre of the upper stage, with a window on each side of it.

Fig. 3. Exterior view of one of the great doors of Queens' College.

Each of the spandrel-spaces contains a shield, and a larger shield is to be found in the triangular field between the hood-mold and the arch.

[The ponderous wooden doors with which these gateways were originally closed still exist in most of the colleges. That of

[1] [These details will be readily understood from Loggan's print.]

Queens' College, as one of the least altered, is here figured as a specimen (figs. 3, 4). It was evidently the intention of Professor Willis to describe them, and he had made a number of sketches and notes for that purpose. He had not, however, written anything, and his collections are in such a fragmentary state that it has been found impossible to ascertain how he intended to treat the subject. Under these circumstances it has been

Fig. 4. Internal view of one of the great doors of Queens' College.

thought better to omit this portion of his essay altogether, rather than to attempt an investigation the result of which would probably have been very different from his original intentions.

Loggan shews that at some colleges a row of stout posts and rails was set up for a certain distance in front of the principal façade. These were probably originally intended as a protection against the traffic, before foot-pavements were laid down, for we find them only at those colleges which stood in a crowded thoroughfare: viz. Queens', Christ's, S. John's, Magdalene, Trinity, Sidney, Emmanuel. They once existed at Pembroke College also [1]. The rails were about three feet high, and at each end of the row there was a lofty post. The arrangement varies a little in each case, but in all the posts which stood on either side of the great gate were about ten feet high, elaborately carved and ornamented. At Christ's College and S. John's College they bore the rose and portcullis of the foundress. The top was covered with lead, and had one or more iron spikes fixed into it. The whole structure was painted in colours, and the spikes were either painted in a different colour, or even gilt [2].]

[1] [History of Pembroke College, Vol. i. pp. 139, 141.]

[2] [The Bursars' Accounts contain numerous entries referring to these posts and rails, from which the following may be selected: Queens' Coll. Mag. Jour. 1545—46 fo. 134. "Item Dowseo laboranti circa tres postes fixos pro foribus collegii in plateis ...Item Georgio Ray pro duobus spiculis vel aculeis ferreis pro duobus postibus pro foribus sexaginta pondo. Item Richardo Grene pictori pro pingendis tribus postibus in platea positis viridi colore." S. John's Coll. Audit-Book, 1562—63. "Item to the Painter for leyinge the Irons of the greate Postes in oyle and red leade iij^{s}." Ibid. 1614—15. "To a ioyner for cutting a Crowne in wood to set upon the posts of ye gate ij^{s}. vj^{d}." For those at Christ's Coll. see History of the Coll. Vol. ii. p. 226. At Trinity College the lofty posts near the gate had been removed before Loggan's print was taken, but we find the following entries in the Accounts, with further charges for carving the great posts: 1614—15. Sen. Bursar's Accounts, *Extraordinaries*. "Item for guilding the Iron pickes in the greate posts xv^{s}." *Buildings and Out Workes*. "Item to John Smyth for caruing the 8 eschochions on the postes at the greate gates at 3^{s}. and finishing them xxxiiij^{s}."]

III.

THE CHAMBERS AND STUDIES.

THE chambers in all the early colleges, with the exception of King's College, were built in two floors, without garrets, which were added subsequently. This arrangement may be seen with least alteration in the old quadrangle of Corpus Christi College, begun, as explained in the History of the College, in 1352[1]. The detailed narrative of Josselin, there translated, shews that the garrets were added gradually, as required, partly at the expense of the college, partly at that of the occupants. The walls had no parapets, and the roofs terminated in eaves, which discharged the water on to the ground below without the intervention of spouts. This was also the arrangement at Gonville Hall, as appears from Loggan's print; and also from the Matriculation Book of Gonville and Caius College, begun 1560, which mentions only upper and lower rooms (*cubicula superiora et inferiora*). Ranges of chambers in two floors are also to be found at Peterhouse, Pembroke College, Trinity Hall, Queens' College, Jesus College (west range of entrance quadrangle), Christ's College, the first court of S. John's College[2], and the Great Court of Trinity College. In Loggan's prints some of these examples have eaves, some parapets; and all have garrets in the roof. It is probable, however, that neither parapets nor garrets formed part of the original structure.

As further accommodation became necessary, the chambers were built in three floors, the third of which, called a half-storey, extended upwards into the roof for a short distance; and the

[1] [History of Corpus Christi College, Vol. i. pp. 250—254.]

[2] [It is not improbable that there may once have been small garrets or "excelses" (see below, p. 306) in the roof of this court.]

space above it was utilised for a range of diminutive garrets. The half-storey was lighted by dormer windows, the gables of which were in the same plane as the main wall of the building. A good example of this style of building was afforded by the Perse and Legge Buildings at Caius College (figs. 1, 2), built

Fig. 1. The Perse and Legge Buildings, Gonville and Caius College, reduced from Loggan's print, taken about 1688.

1618—19, the arrangements of which will be described in detail below. It was also employed in the ranges which form the north and south sides of the principal court at Sidney Sussex College (1596); on the north side of the second court at

Pembroke College (1610); and in the Walnut Tree Court at Queens' College (1616—19). In some examples the garrets were absent, as in the Founder's Range at Emmanuel College, 1585, as shewn by Loggan; in the second Court of S. John's College (1599); and in Nevile's Court at Trinity College (1612).

Early in the seventeenth century this mode was abandoned, and the ranges of chambers were built in two floors, or, more usually, in three floors, with garrets lighted on both sides by dormer windows in the roof. Examples of ranges built after this fashion are Sir F. Clerke's building at Sidney Sussex College (1628); the Brick Building at Emmanuel College (1632), where the gablets over the windows on the third floor are retained, but rise wholly above the eaves; the Bishop's Hostel at Trinity College (1671), in two floors only; and the buildings which form the principal quadrangle of S. Catharine's Hall, begun 1673. In these four examples the ancient eaves are retained, but in the following they are replaced by parapets: the chambers in Dr Gostlin's Court at S. Catharine's Hall (1634); the quadrangle of Clare Hall, begun 1638; the Fellows' Building at Christ's College, begun 1640; and the third Court of S. John's College, begun 1669. The range on the north side of the entrance-court at Jesus College, begun 1638, differed from these examples in having three floors without garrets[1].

According to primitive arrangements, at Oxford as well as at Cambridge, each chamber, with few exceptions, was occupied by several persons, who dwelt, slept, and pursued their studies therein. [The way in which the chambers were to be assigned, and the number of occupants of each, is commonly defined in a particular statute (*De dispositione camerarum*, or, *De assignatione camerarum*). These rules, often exceedingly minute, supply valuable details respecting the arrangements which obtained in the different colleges to which they refer; and it will be convenient to examine in chronological order the provisions of those which appear most distinctive and important, before explaining the curious contrivances by which so many students were accommodated in so small a space.

It may be stated generally that nearly all the statutes direct

[1] [This Introduction has been compiled from notes made by Professor Willis.]

that in assigning the chambers seniority is to be strictly observed; and that the Master, or in his absence the Vice-Master, is to have supreme authority in making the assignment, and in settling all doubtful or disputed questions.]

The earliest statutes, those for Merton College, Oxford (1270), do not define the number in each chamber; but, by directing that "in every chamber wherein the scholars of the house reside there shall be one of more mature age than the others to take care of them," it is plainly indicated that three at least must have been lodged together. Similarly at Michael House, Cambridge (1324), the number is not defined in the statutes; but the special *Rules for the assignment of chambers*[1], made in 1429, imply that there was usually one person only lodged in each. The statutes of Oriel College, Oxford (1326), are copied from those of Merton; and at Queen's College, in the same University (1340), it is directed that "two persons at least are to be lodged together, unless the rank and position of any scholar entitle him to have a room to himself." At Cambridge, the statutes of Pembroke College (1347) provide that "each of the Fellows, in order of seniority, beginning with the Master, are to select their studies in such manner that in each chamber there may be at least two Fellows[2];" while those of Peterhouse (1344); of Clare Hall (1359); and of King's Hall (1379—80) all direct that two only are to be lodged together. At Oxford, on the contrary, there seems to have been an early tendency to place a larger number in each room, as we have already seen; and at New College (1400) Wykeham places "at least three Fellows or scholars" in each of his upper chambers, and four in each of his lower chambers. Each occupant is to have a separate bed; one of the Fellows is to be older than the others, and it is to be his duty to exercise authority over his chamber-fellows (*camerales*), and from time to time to inform the Warden, the Sub-Warden, and the Deans, of their manners, conversation, and progress in their studies. The corresponding

[1] [These rules have been printed in the Appendix to the History of Trinity College, Vol. ii. p. 677.]

[2] [Old Statutes of Pembroke College, preserved in the College Treasury, A. 12. *Capitulum de forma eligendi Custodem et alios ministros dicti collegii.* "Eligant et predicti socii a custode inchoando, et seriatim descendendo secundum eorum statum in domo, studia sua, ita quod in qualibet camera ad minus sint duo socii."]

statute for King's College, Cambridge (1443), copying as usual the words of Wykeham, diminishes the number of persons in each room, by substituting two and three respectively for the numbers given in his statute. In the next Oxford code, that for the College of All Souls (1445), the eight Senior Fellows are only permitted to have a chamber-fellow (*cameralis*) to lodge with them, but three or two Fellows must be grouped together in the other chambers. At S. Catharine's Hall, Cambridge (1475), the Fellows are lodged two and two together. At Magdalen College, Oxford (1479), Bishop Waynflete increases the number to four in the upper chambers, two of whom are to have "principal beds" (*lecti principales*) and two, "beds on wheels" (*lecti rotales*, Trookyll beddys *vulgariter appellati*). In the lower chambers there are to be two principal beds, and one truckle-bed. The clause respecting the superintendence to be exercised by the elder over the younger occupants, is here enforced with much minuteness. The statutes of Lincoln College, Oxford, on the other hand, drawn up by Bishop Rotherham in the same year, direct that the rooms are to be selected by the Rector and Fellows in order of seniority at the Great Chapter, held on the festival of S. John *ante portam latinam* (6 May); and it would appear that each of the Fellows was to have a room to himself.

The statutes of Christ's College, Cambridge (1506), which have the authority of the Foundress, the Lady Margaret, return to the original Cambridge arrangement of grouping the Fellows two and two in each chamber, and no one, except a Doctor, is allowed to have a chamber to himself. On the other hand the statutes of Jesus College, Cambridge, drawn up by her stepson, Thomas Stanley, D.D., Lord Bishop of Ely (1506—15), assign a single chamber to each Fellow, until the number of Fellows shall exceed the number of chambers. When this has come to pass, two Fellows, beginning with the juniors, are to occupy a single chamber, but they are to have separate beds.

The statutes of Corpus Christi College, Oxford, given in 1517 by Richard Fox, D.D., Lord Bishop of Winchester, return, with a few differences, to the provisions of Bishop Waynflete. Each chamber, whether upper or lower, is to contain two beds, both "high beds" (*cubilia altiora*); or, if that be impossible, one is to be high, the other low, that is, on wheels. A Fellow or

Scholar is to occupy the former, a pensioner (*discipulus*), the latter; and the older men are to supervise and assist their younger chamber-fellows (*concubicularii*). The number is again increased in the statutes of Brasenose College, Oxford (1524), which place three Fellows and Scholars in each of the upper chambers, and four in each of the lower. The Fellows are to sleep alone; the other members of the college either alone, or with a bed-fellow, according as the Principal may direct.

The statute of Corpus Christi College, Oxford, is copied almost literally in the statutes of S. John's College (1555), and also in those given to S. John's College, Cambridge in 1530 by Bishop Fisher. Each room is to have two beds, as above defined; one is to be occupied by a Fellow, the other by two scholars, or at least by one. No one is to have a room to himself unless he be a Doctor or a College Preacher. The second body of statutes given to S. John's College by King Henry VIII. (1535) enacts that each room is to be occupied by two Fellows, or, in the case of College Preachers and the twelve senior Fellows, by one Fellow and two scholars. The junior Fellows are to take in another Fellow or a scholar, if the Master so ordains. In the case of scholars not more than four are to be compelled to occupy the same chamber. In these two codes the number two is prescribed in the case of Fellows; but the scholars are to be more closely packed together. A similar arrangement is made at Trinity College, Cambridge, in the statutes given by King Edward VI. (1547—53); but the number is slightly increased in those given by Queen Elizabeth (1559—60), which minutely define the persons who are to share a chamber. Three is to be the usual number where one is a Fellow; but scholars, pensioners, sizars, and subsizars, are to be placed four together, if possible. These arrangements, so far as the scholars and pensioners are concerned, are copied at Emmanuel College, Cambridge (1585), and at Sidney Sussex College (1598); but in these two Colleges each Fellow is allowed to have a chamber to himself.

In the above enumeration we have omitted the statutes of Magdalene College, Cambridge (1553—54) and of Gonville and Caius College, Cambridge (1572). In both these colleges two persons are to be lodged together; in the former two Fellows who have taken the degree of Bachelor of Arts; in the latter every Fellow is to share his room with an indigent scholar.

The provisions of which we have given a rapid review refer to a system which had arrived at its full development in the course of the sixteenth century. After that period it fell gradually into disuse [1], though it survived in a modified form during the eighteenth century. The statutes of Worcester College, Oxford (1714), place one Fellow, or at most two, in each chamber; and at Cambridge we still find new-comers sharing their rooms with another member of the college. Thus at S. John's College it is mentioned that Ambrose Bonwicke (admitted 24 August, 1710) "had an agreeable chamber-fellow, a very good scholar, a sober and innocent yet chearful companion [2]"; and Dr Samuel Knight, who proceeded to the degree of B.A. at Trinity College, Cambridge, in 1702, speaking of Roger Cotes, who took his degree in the same year, says:

"I could run out many Pages in the just Character of this extraordinary Man, being very intimate with him, and having the Opportunity of knowing him perfectly, by being his Chamber-fellow many Years in *Trinity College* in *Cambridge* [3]."

The choice of a chamber-fellow was of course a matter of great importance. This is illustrated by a letter addressed to Dr Eachard, then Master of S. Catharine's Hall, 19 March 1678—9:

"I intreat you to make choice of a good chamber-fellow for him, by whose converse and company he may receive benefit and furtherance in his work [4]."

The term "chamber-fellow" became gradually shortened into "chum"; and though the practice of lodging two in a room has

[1] In 1652, the *Gesta Book* of Gonville and Caius College contains the following Order: "At a meeting of the Master and Fellows May 17, 1652: Ordered that every fellow, scholar, and student in the College have a chamber de proprio. That no fellow, scholar, or student take any chamber without the leave of the Master. That every fellow, scholar, and student pay rent immediately to the College. That whoever hath the keys of any chamber or study besides his own bring them to the bursar within 7 days, otherwise pay the rent of such chamber or study which he keeps the key of." [It has been suggested that this enlargement of accommodation may indicate nothing more than that great decrease of numbers which began to take place about 1650, as shewn by the number of degrees conferred.]

[2] [Life of Ambrose Bonwicke: ed. J. E. B. Mayor, Camb. 1870, p. 18.]

[3] [Life of Dr John Colet, by Samuel Knight, D.D. 8vo. Camb. 1724, p. 430.]

[4] [The Cambridge Portfolio, i. p. 275. Compare also Life of Bonwicke, *ut supra*, p. 35.]

been long abandoned, the memory of it survived in King's College, Cambridge, until within the last thirty years; every new scholar being, on his arrival, looked after by an older one (his "chum"), who was responsible for his "nib's" strict observance of all college discipline during the first week of his residence.

The internal arrangements of the chambers of colleges have been so completely altered from time to time in accordance with the habits and tastes of their inhabitants that it would be difficult, if not impossible, to discover from their present state what the original dispositions had been, even by the help of the descriptions in the statutes and elsewhere. Fortunately however two building-contracts remain, the one for the erection of the Perse and Legge chambers at Caius College, in 1617—18 and 1618—19 respectively; the other for the erection of the Bishop's Hostel at Trinity College, in 1669[1]; by the comparison of which with the actual buildings their ancient arrangements can be accurately reproduced. [The Bishop's Hostel still exists, but the Perse and Legge Buildings were pulled down in 1868. Their ancient arrangement will however be understood from Loggan's view given above (fig. 1), and from the complete plans and description which Professor Willis prepared before they were destroyed.]

The contract for the Legge Building, dated 18 January, 1618—19, provides, among other things, that it shall be

> "Three stories in heyght with garretts or excelses in the topp of the Rooffe;...the lower storie to be eightene foote wide within the walls and to be parted into foure Chambers, every Chamber to have three convenient Studdies a peece:
>
> the next storie to be ninetene foote wide within the walls, and to be equally devided into foure chambers likewise with two convenient studdies a peece[2]:
>
> and the halfe storie to be equally devided into foure chambers and to have two studies a peece:
>
> and the garretts to be parted into ffoure Roomes, and have two studdies a peece with fyttinges, and convenient Stayres of Oken plancke to leade conveniently to every of the same chambers....
>
> In every of the twelve Chambers one Chimney, with Chimney peeces and borders of white stone cleane and handsomely wrought...:

[1] [For the History of the Perse and Legge buildings see Vol. i. pp. 186, 187; for that of Bishop's Hostel, Vol. ii. pp. 551—560. The two contracts have been printed in full in the Appendix to the History of Caius College, Vol. i. pp. 206—208.]

[2] In the Perse Building each of the chambers in the two stories above the lower storey were to have one study only.

every studdye window to have an iron casement of two foote longe, and every chamber two casements besides the studdies of the same length, for thorow light and ayer; and all the same lights to be well and sufficiently glased with good Burgundie glasse in small quarries well leaded....

All the partitions shalbe made with good and sufficient...Oke tymber and the same and all the studdies to be lathed with hart lathes; and the nine partitions in the seacond and halfe storie...to be lathed on both sydes with hart lath, and to be all plastered over with lyme and hayer workeman lyke; and all the outward dores to be made of Furdeale..., and a sufficient locke and key for every of the outward dores: and also to make a good and sufficient dore for every studdye to be fitted to the dorestead and hanged on sufficient hooks and hinges."

The description of the Perse Building is in exactly the same words, with the necessary variations in the number of chambers, of which there are only three on each floor.

[It will be well to preface the description of the internal arrangements of the two buildings by a brief comparison of them with the contracts, which should be referred to for details. They stood at the north-east corner of the college, the north side of the Perse Building abutting on Trinity Lane, and the east side of the Legge Building on Trinity Street. Both were in three floors, with garrets or *excelses*, as the contract calls them, in the roof. These, having no windows towards the court, are not shewn in Loggan's print (fig. 1). The arrangements of the two ranges were practically the same; but it is with the Legge Building that we are principally concerned, for the reasons given by Professor Willis below. The exact dimensions of the different portions are minutely set down in the contract, and were faithfully carried out, as shewn in the section (fig. 2). The lower storey was eighteen feet wide, and the second storey nineteen feet wide, within the walls, each being nine feet high; the third storey, called a "half-storey," was eight feet six inches high, and evidently of the same width as the storey below it. The precise height and width of the windows in each storey is also given, and those in the half-storey are to have "gable ends with crests and finials of freestone." No windows towards the street are specified for this storey. The garrets, on the contrary, were lighted by twelve small dormers on the street side only. The material was brick, with stone quoins, and stone dressings for the doors and windows.]

In the actual buildings the number of the floors, chambers and staircases in each agrees perfectly with the description in the contract[1], but new partitions have been set up in a manner which is perfectly explicable after the garrets have been examined, for the garret-floor of Legge's Building fortunately retains its original distribution, having been from time immemorial, and apparently from the want of fireplaces, abandoned as a lodging-

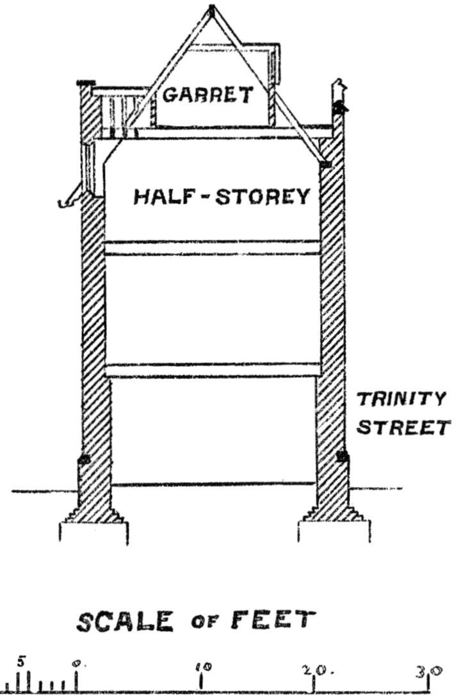

Fig. 2. Transverse section of the Legge Building at Gonville and Caius College, measured and drawn by Professor Willis.

place for students, allowed to fall into a state of dilapidation, and employed solely as a lumber-room for packing-cases and fuel. The contract says that this floor is to be divided into four cham-

[1] [It has been thought better to leave this description exactly as Professor Willis wrote it while the building to which it refers was still standing.]

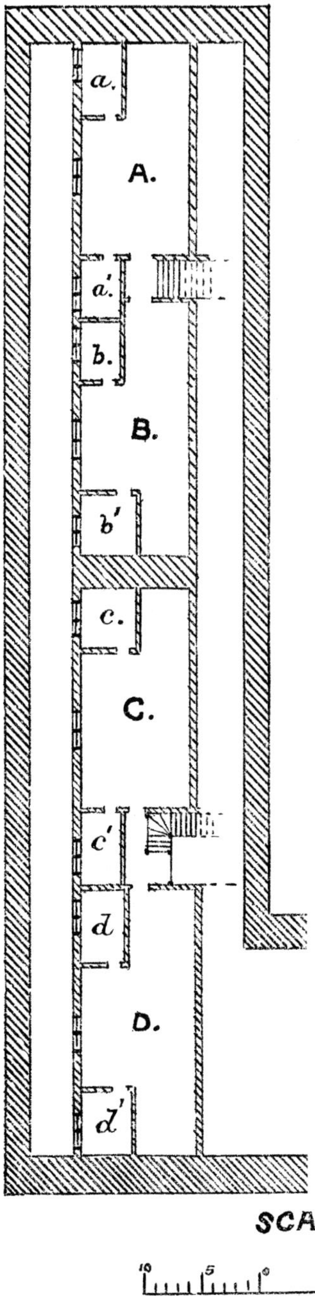

bers, each having two studies. The annexed plan (fig. 3) shews that it is actually divided into four chambers (*A, B, C, D*); and that every chamber has two small closets (*a, a'*; *b, b'*, etc.) parted off by stud-partitions at the corners, which must be the studies mentioned in the contract, for each of them is provided with its own garret-window and door, the chamber itself being lighted by a similar window between the closets. Thus the twelve windows prescribed in the contract are accounted for. The chamber is nine feet wide, and about twenty feet long, but it is only six feet eight inches high, and the roof slopes over it excessively on both sides of the closets. The studies are about four feet wide and from five to six feet long. The two bedsteads were of course placed at the corners of the room opposite to the window-wall, so that the four corners of the chamber were occupied, two by the beds, and two by the studies. We thus obtain the complete arrangement of an Elizabethan college-room, as shewn in the annexed sketch (fig. 4). The windows of the studies being now blocked up, they have hitherto passed, upon superficial observation, for mere

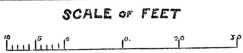

Fig. 3. Plan of the garret-floor of the Legge Building at Gonville and Caius College, measured and drawn by Professor Willis.

closets. The adjoining garret-floor of the Perse Building has been fitted up in later times, the studies swept away, the chambers used as bedrooms for the rooms respectively beneath them, and a chimney formed in the gable for the western garret. The disposition and the number of the windows shews that studies were originally laid out here in the same manner as in the Legge Building.

Fig. 4. Interior of one of the garrets in the Legge Building at Gonville and Caius College, from a sketch by Professor Willis.

These garrets having shewn us that the studies were little cabinets enclosed at the corners of rooms, it becomes easy to trace the arrangement of them in the more complete rooms below which have been altered to suit modern habits. I have planned and carefully examined every one of the twenty-eight rooms in these buildings, and find the traces of the studies in so many of them that I am enabled to restore the whole system.

The contracts have told us that on the ground-floor (fig. 5) each chamber had three studies; and the traces which remain shew, as might naturally be expected, that, since the outer door was in one corner, the three other corners were occupied by the three studies, one in each.

In the Perse Building, which was erected first, the rooms and studies of the ground-floor are regularly and similarly disposed in the manner shewn on the plan. But it is evident that the Legge Building was an afterthought, and that there was not sufficient space between the east end of the Perse Building and Trinity Street to make the two buildings independent. In consequence, the Legge Building abuts against the Perse Building in such a manner that it conceals the single-light windows

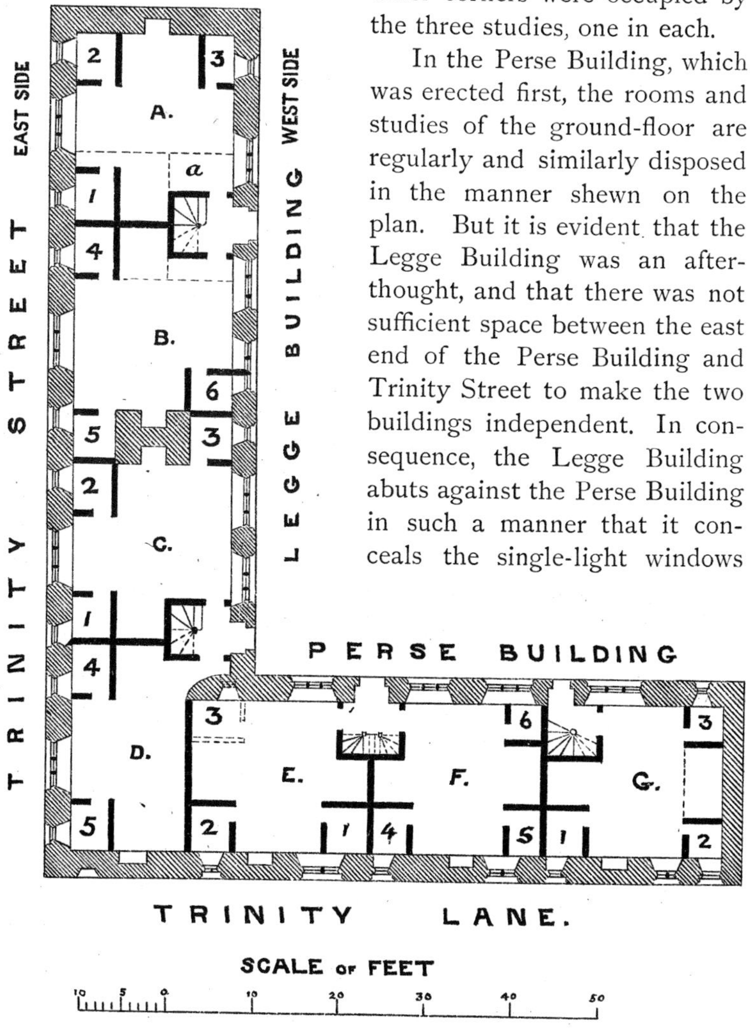

Fig. 5. Plan of the ground-floor of the Perse and Legge Buildings at Gonville and Caius College, measured and drawn by Professor Willis.

which were placed at the south-eastern extremity on each storey to correspond with those at the other end. For example, the study which ought to have occupied the south-east corner of the easternmost room (No. 3, E) loses its light, although the window still remains in the wall. In the two upper floors each chamber, by the contract, had but a single study, which may still be traced in one or other of the northern corners of nearly every room.

In the walls of the Legge Building next the street the windows are disposed so that a three-light window is always flanked by a single-light window, the former for the chamber, the latter for a pair of studies, marked 1, 2; 4, 5, in the alternate chambers; and these (with one exception) are also the positions of the studies in the second and third stories, which have but two studies in each chamber. The southernmost chamber (A) is regularly disposed like those on the ground-floor of the Perse Building, and it has a window of one light next the court for the south-western study (3); but the position of the great chimney-stack in the centre of the building occasions a little irregularity in the plan of the chambers next to it (B, C), and in the rooms above these on the two upper floors the study on the west side of the stack (3) is given to B, and that on the east side (5) to C, their doors opening in the reverse direction to those on the ground-floor. The corner chamber (D) is contracted by the previously existing Perse Building, and I am unable to discover how the three studies were placed, if indeed they were not limited to two in this particular case. On the upper floors above D the two studies are as shewn on the plan (4, 5).

The conversion of the ancient arrangements into the modern is shewn on the plan by dotted lines. Thus in chamber A the studies have all been removed, and the dotted partitions substituted, by which a bed-chamber is substituted for study No. 1, and a vestibule or gyp-room obtained (*a*). A similar arrangement has been made in chamber B, but the width of the study No. 4 has been retained, the west side only having been removed (leaving a trace on the ceiling which shews that it stood four feet six inches from the wall), and the north side continued across to the opposite wall. This, the most usual mode of treating the studies, has been carried out in E, F, and G, and in various other rooms on the upper floors. In such cases the ceiling usually retains traces which shew where the original cross-partition of the study was fixed to it, and thus give the dimensions. The outline of study No. 6 in B is still distinctly marked on the ceiling; it was four feet three inches wide against the window and five feet deep. In the second storey of the Perse Building above E, No. 2, the study has been elongated into a bed-room in the same manner as in B and C; but its original side is retained, shewing the doorway two feet wide, and five feet six inches high, in the position of E, No. 2. This study was four feet six inches wide and five feet six inches long. Traces of a considerable number thus remain, so as to furnish ample authority for the restoration I have given of the whole system. Their widths vary from three feet six inches to nearly five feet, and their depths from four feet six inches to five feet. In the chamber G, study No. 1 has been removed, No. 2 has been elongated into a bed-room as shewn by the dotted line, and No. 3 has been left to serve as a gyp-room.

I have thought it best to begin with these examples, because they give the clearest conception of the ancient chamber and studies of the olden time, and enable us the better to understand the older allusions to them in statutes and other records, of which the earliest that I am aware of is in the statutes of Queen's College, Oxford (1340), which direct that all scholars shall be provided with chambers and studies (*studia*)[1]. Wykeham's statutes (1400) ordain that the studies as well as the chambers (*cameræ et loca studiorum in iisdem cameris*) are to be assigned by the Warden, and that in those lower chambers, which are each provided with four windows and four studies, there are always to be four Scholars or four Fellows[2]. In the

[1] [Commiss. Doc[ts]. (Oxford); Statutes of Queen's College, p. 19. "Scholares etiam omnes habeant cameras et studia, juxta assignationem Præpositi....Copuletque duos ad minus in eadem camera, nisi forte aliud exigat alicujus scholarium dictæ aulæ status vel conditionis preeminentia." The same provisions are made respecting the chambers and studies (*studia*) in an Injunction of the Visitor to All Souls College, Oxford, 1445. Ibid. Statutes of All Souls College, p. 71.]

[2] [Ibid. Statutes of New College, p. 88. "In inferioribus autem cameris dicti collegii, quatuor fenestras et quatuor studiorum loca habentibus, sint semper quatuor scholares vel socii collocati."]

south range of the principal quadrangle of New College (fig. 6), which has suffered the least alteration, each chamber-window towards the court has two lights, and is placed between two small single-light windows, as in the Legge Building at Cambridge, and there are two similar single-light windows opposite to them in the back wall. Thus three studies, marked 1, 2, 3, on the plan, are provided for, one of them being nestled under the landing of the staircase. [The fourth occupant must have used the common bedroom as his study. This view is confirmed by the examination of a chamber at Christ's College, Cambridge, where we have the guidance of an inventory called "An Account of the Chambers, Studies, Inhabitants, and Incomes in the Ould Court, taken Jan. 30, 1655." One of the rooms on the ground

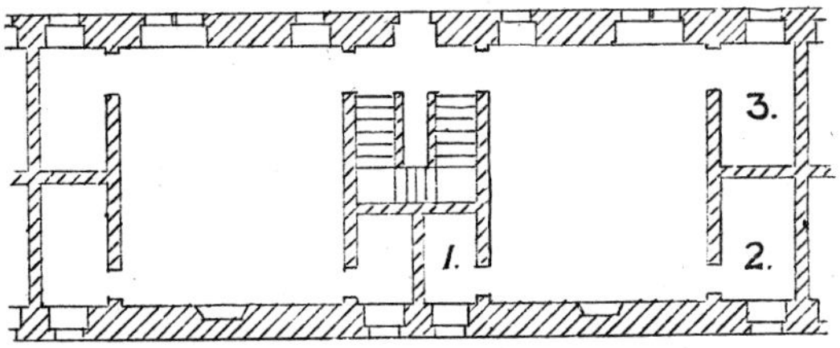

Fig. 6. Ground-plan of part of the south range of the principal quadrangle at New College, Oxford, from Williams' Oxonia Depicta.

floor, there called "Low Chambers," has three studies, and four occupants, whose names are given. The room is on the south side of the court, next to a staircase, with windows towards the court and towards the garden. The three studies are designated as follows: "(1) by the chimney; (2) under the staires; (3) to the court." This is precisely the arrangement at New College.]

In the earlier colleges at Cambridge the stairs run in a single long flight between two parallel partitions to an upper landing, on which, to the right and left, are the outer doors of the upper chambers. The space beneath the landing appears to have been appropriated to one or two studies for the ground-chambers, and the studies of the upper floor are often constructed over the entrance-landing of the staircase. [An instance of this latter arrangement may be cited from S. John's College, where the inventory of the college property in the different chambers, called the "Prizing Book," has fortunately been preserved. The chamber over the butteries, prized 5 April, 1630, contains "The outward chamber"; "The inner chamber"; "The studye"; and "The upper chamber." This contained six studies:

"The studye next ye hall wth 2 shelues, lock and key and a table	o . 12 . o
The studie next vnto it with 3 shelues, a deske, and a table	o . 13 . o
The third study from ye halle with 3 shelues and a table	o . 15 . o
The fourth study from ye halle with a table 4 shelues and a seate	o . 15 . 6
The study next ye new Court with 4 shelues and a table	o . 13 . o
The studye at ye stayers head with lock and key and shelues and seate and table	o . 15 . o"

The ground-plan of S. John's College shews that this room must have had windows on the east and west sides, looking respectively into the old and new courts. Those of the east side would light the four studies, which must have occupied nearly the whole of that side; on the west side there was only one study, leaving the other windows free to light the rest of the room. The last study is described in the next valuation, dated 25 July, 1631, as "The study without the chamber on the staires."] The narrow single-light windows in the outer walls of Peterhouse, Pembroke College, and other early colleges at Cambridge, as well as in some of those at Oxford, indicate this arrangement externally. This form of study, from its natural connection with the structure of the building, is probably the most ancient. But in the greater part of the chambers built after 1590 a staircase is employed which does not extend to the back wall, but has two flights or more to each storey, or else winding stairs are constructed, so as to leave space for studies behind them. This is shewn on the ground-plan of the Perse and Legge Buildings (fig. 5); and will be better understood from the accompanying sketch (fig. 7) representing one of the staircases at the west end of the range on the north side of the second court of Pembroke College (1610). The spectator is supposed to be standing on the first floor, with a chamber-door to his right and left.

[At King's College, Cambridge, where the statutes, as mentioned above, are copied from Wykeham's with certain alterations, it is provided that the chambers and studies (*loca studiorum*) are to be assigned by the Provost and Vice-Provost; the upper chambers are to be occupied by two Fellows at the least; and

Fig. 7. Staircase in the north range of the Second Court of Pembroke College.

the lower chambers, when provided with three studies, by three Scholars or Fellows; but they are to have separate beds, and one is to be older than the others. The buildings of the Old Court, to which these injunctions refer, have been already described; but a portion of what was there said must be repeated[1]. They were in three floors; on each floor the windows, on both sides of the chambers, were of two lights and one light alternately. On the ground-floor and the upper floor the studies were probably arranged on the system which Professor Willis has explained at Caius College; but on the middle-floor, where the chambers were fifteen feet six inches high, a peculiar arrangement was adopted. The single-light window was divided by two transoms into three parts, the central part being filled in with stone-work. The lower portion of these long windows, of which there was one to each room, lighted a narrow slip about five feet wide, separated off from the rest of the room by a transverse partition. This slip—which was termed a gallery[2]—was again divided by a partition into two portions, of which that next to the court served as a vestibule, and the other, lighted by a window in the outer wall, was of course a study. The height of the chambers, however, admitted of the construction of a floor above the vestibule and study, concealed by the stone panel of the window. This floor could either be used as a separate room, or divided into two studies, each of which would be lighted by the upper portion of the long window. It might have been approached in two ways; either by a small staircase or ladder in the interior of the room, as we find was actually the case in one of the chambers at S. John's College, or by the stone external staircase which gave access to the different floors.

The contrivances by which the provisions of the statutes were obeyed, and the seventy[3] members of the college accommodated in twenty-eight chambers, have been recorded in a most curious and interesting "Inventarye of the Stuff in the Colledge Chambers," made in 1598[4], in which the names of the

[1] [This description has been derived partly from the recollections of Professor Willis as stated above (Vol. I. p. 330), partly from Loggan's view of the interior of the court and Burford's view of the exterior (Ibid. figs. 5, 7).]

[2] [The Inventory of these rooms referred to below, made 1598, contains numerous entries such as: "The gallery without furniture"; "Item the gallarye at xxxiij^{s}. iiij^{d}."; "a double casement in the gallarye"; "a gallary with a little table"; "In the gallarye a waynscott cubborde"; "a bedsteade in the gallarye."]

[3] [There were 13 Senior Fellows, 34 Fellows, 6 Junior Fellows, and 17 Scholars.]

[4] [Printed in the Cambridge Antiquarian Society's Communications, Vol. III., by Henry Bradshaw, M.A., Fellow of King's College, and University Librarian.]

occupants are fortunately set down, as well as a list of the furniture.

There were eight chambers on the upper floor, eight on the middle floor, and nine on the ground-floor. Besides these there was a room over the treasury, a room over the pantry, and a room over the old buttery[1]. The Senior Fellows were placed for the most part in the rooms on the middle floor, as being the best; but they usually shared them with a Fellow. Thus we find in the first middle chamber a Senior Fellow and a Fellow; in the second, two seniors (the Vice-Provost and one of the Bursars); in the third the Dean of Arts and another senior; in the fourth two Fellows; in the fifth a senior alone; in the sixth a senior (the Dean of Divinity) and a Fellow; in the seventh a senior and a Fellow; in the eighth a senior (one of the Bursars) and a Fellow. On the storey above, the first upper chamber was occupied by a senior (one of the Bursars) and a junior Fellow; the second by two Fellows; the third by a senior and a Fellow; the fourth by a senior alone; the fifth by a senior and a Fellow; the sixth, seventh, and eighth by two Fellows each. On the ground-floor the first room was occupied by two Fellows; the second and third by a Fellow and three Scholars; the fourth, fifth, and seventh by a Fellow, a junior Fellow, and two Scholars; the sixth by a Fellow and two Scholars; the eighth by two junior Fellows and two Scholars; the ninth by two Fellows and one Scholar. Of the remaining chambers, a senior and a Fellow lived in that over the pantry; and those over the treasury and buttery respectively contained two Fellows each. We have thus accounted for sixty-nine persons; the Fellow whose name does not appear as the occupant of a room was absent at Eton.]

In many instances the windows are so managed that the contiguous studies of two neighbouring chambers are lighted by one window of two or three lights, the partition between them being attached to the mullion, so as practically to produce the effect of two small windows inwards, while outwards a handsome window, uniform with those of the chambers, is substituted for the pair of narrow study-lights, which, according to the older fashion, were interposed between the larger chamber-windows.

[1] [The situation of these rooms has been explained in the History of the College, Vol. I. pp. 325—332.]

The old system had the merit of distinctly indicating the arrangements within; the later system destroys the variety of effect, by substituting a long uniform range of similar windows.

The studies were not always within, or even contiguous to, the rooms of the students who used them; for example, in 1583 a room belonging to the Master of Caius College over the library was fitted up with ten studies at the expense of certain Pensioners, on condition that whoever enjoyed the use of one, should pay a third part of the cost on quitting it, and that finally the rent of them should belong to the Master[1]. In 1652 it was ordered that "whoever have the Keyes of any chamber or study besides his own bring them in to the Bursar within seven days, otherwise pay the rent of such chamber or study[2]." There are also many indications of separate studies hired by students, as for instance at Trinity College in 1554[3]:

"Payd unto Sir Grafton for a Studye wch Syr Knarysborow hayth in the low chamber under Mr Godsalve."

[A few more instances of the arrangement, of which Professor Willis described a typical instance at Gonville and Caius College, remain to be noticed.

The garret-floor of the north range of the first court at Pembroke College, between the chapel and the kitchen, was once fitted with studies on the same system as in the Legge Building. These, as explained in the History of the College (Vol. I. p. 136), had become ruinous, and the windows had been blocked. On ascending the first staircase eastward of the chapel, marked I on the plan of the college (fig. 2), which led to the first floor, a small supplementary flight led up to what had once been the garret-floor. The arrangement of this flight clearly shewed that the fitting-up of the roof-space as chambers had been an afterthought. On ascending the stairs a small passage was reached, which contained two doors. The easternmost of these gave access to a room fifteen feet long, and twenty-two feet six inches wide, arranged exactly as in the Legge Building. Against the north wall there were two studies, each measuring 5 feet 6 inches by 6 feet, and lighted by a small window. Be-

1 Annals of Caius College for the year 1583, p. 143. The paragraph is noted in the margin "Library Studdies"; but in the text they are called "Musea."

2 [This Order has been already quoted at length, p. 303, *note*.]

3 Junior Bursar's Accounts, 25 August, 1554.

tween them a larger window lighted the rest of the room, and there were windows in the south wall also, as Loggan shews. The door at the west end of the passage gave access to a larger room, about 35 feet long, the arrangement of which was less clearly defined, as the ancient partitions were confused by the intrusion of others of more recent date. There had, however, unquestionably been two studies against the north wall, as in the former room, and possibly two others against the south wall, so that four occupants might easily have been accommodated. Studies are alluded to in the statutes of Magdalene College (1554—55); at S. Catharine's Hall in 1577 (Vol. II. p. 88) where Mr Momson's two rooms, spoken of collectively as his chamber[1], had a bed-chamber and two studies, and a single study respectively; at the same college in 1611 (Ibid. p. 111) when John Atkinson, who afterwards built the Legge Building, constructed a range of chambers each of which contained a study and a bed-chamber; and at Emmanuel College in 1632—33 (Ibid. p. 697) where the contract for the Brick Building mentions "all the particions and studyes." Professor Willis also discovered traces of studies, arranged exactly like those described by him above, at Christ's College, and at Sidney Sussex College.]

The contract for building the Bishop's Hostel at Trinity College in 1669, that is to say, fifty years after the Legge Building, and subsequent to the Restoration, is accompanied by an original plan of the ground-floor signed by the contractor Robert Minchin (fig. 8), and the description in the contract[2] stipulates that

"uppon the ground floore there shalbe five outward chambers, and each of those chambers to have made and belonging thereunto two bedchambers and two Studdyes, each of which bedchambers to conteine in length seaven foot, and in breadth five foot and a halfe, and each of the said Studdyes to be six foot long and five foot wide."

This plan, arranged for two chamber-fellows only, exhibits a great advance in symmetry and comfort over the last. Each sitting-room, square in outline, is lighted by two windows, and has three rooms opening into it. Each of these is about

[1] [A similar expression is used by Dr R. Cosin in his bequest to Trinity College in 1594. Vol. II. p. 478.]

[2] [The contract is given at length in the History of Trinity College, Vol. II. pp. 555—559.]

five feet wide by seven feet long, lighted by a separate window. There is also a recess of about the same size on one side of each sitting-room. Manifestly two of these subordinate rooms are the studies, and the remaining one, with the recess, represents the two bed-chambers mentioned in the contract.

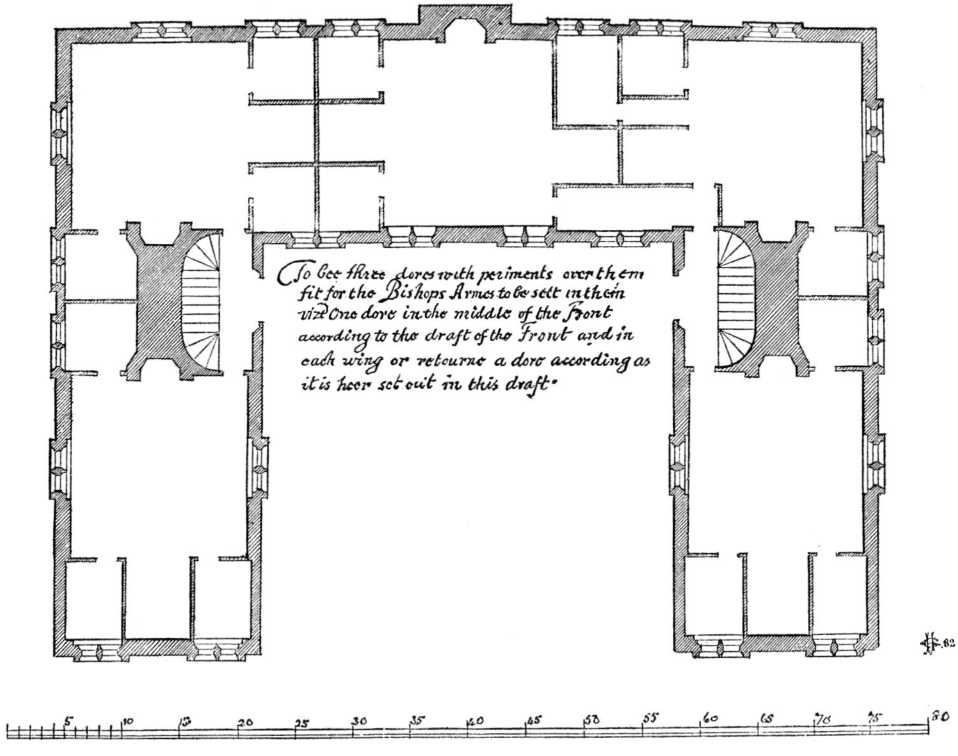
To bee three dores with periments over them
fit for the Bishops Armes to be sett in them
vizt One dore in the middle of the Front
according to the draft of the Front and in
each wing or retourne a dore according as
it is heer set out in this draft.
5 10 15 20 25 30 35 40 45 50 55 60 65 70 75 80

Fig. 8. Ground-plan of Bishop's Hostel, Trinity College, reduced from that appended to the original contract, dated 15 January, 1669.

By this means privacy was obtained in the bed-room as well as in the study, for when one chum retired to the smaller bed-room, the sitting-room became a separate bed-room for the other. In the central room the difficulties of the plan seem to have driven the architect into the older arrangement, in which two bed-recesses are open to the room, possibly closed by curtains.

[A similar arrangement was carried out at New College, Oxford, in 1681. The contract for the building then commenced on the south side of the garden-court, provides that it "shall conteine three Roomes on a floure, with two Studies and two Bedplaces to each roome of sufficient capacity." The plan appended to the contract, part of which is here given (fig. 9), shews how this was done. In room A (which is at the end of the building, with three windows in the eastern wall) two studies and two bed-rooms, marked 1, 2, 3, 4, on the plan, were easily provided, each lighted by a separate window; in the room next to it, marked B, the same number appears, but the middle one (2) had no window. This arrangement still exists, except that the partitions between the studies have been removed. In A, for

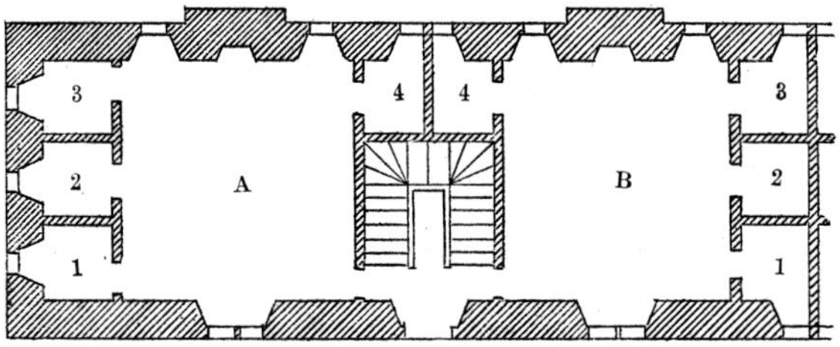

Fig. 9. Ground-plan of part of the south range of the Garden-court of New College, Oxford; reduced from the plan appended to the contract, dated 23 January, 1681.

instance, the rooms marked 1, 2, 3 have become a single bed-room, while the other (4) remains as a store-closet.]

In the early colleges the windows of the chambers were unglazed, and closed with wooden shutters; their floors were either of clay, or tiled; and their walls and ceilings were unplastered. This is distinctly stated by Josselin, who, writing during the reign of Queen Elizabeth, prefaces his minute account of Corpus Christi College, to which reference has been already[1] made, by the general statement that though the Master's Lodge and the Fellows' chambers were at that time glazed and panelled, no work of the kind had been executed in any part of the college before the beginning of the reign of King Henry

[1] [History of Corpus Christi College, Vol. I. pp. 251—254.]

the Eighth. He then proceeds through the college, room by room, and gives the dates of the plastering, panelling, glazing, and flooring, in each. These dates range between 1508 and 1562, two only falling within the previous century. The expense was borne partly by the college, partly by the occupants. [Some curious entries to the same effect are to be found in the *Magnum Journale* of Queens' College for 1539—40. Among other repairs a wooden floor is laid down in the room occupied by a Mr Ashton; and the first entry is a charge for removing the clay with which it had been floored previously[1]. Similar evidence is supplied for Trinity Hall by Dr Warren, but, as he wrote in the first half of the last century, his information is not so valuable for our present purpose. He notes, however, that several rooms had been panelled in the reign of Queen Elizabeth, it may be presumed for the first time. In other colleges the style of much of the existing panelwork shews that it must have been put up at about the same period.]

At Gonville and Caius College the wainscoting of the chambers was not undertaken systematically until the end of the 17th century, when the following Order was made:

> "Oct. 24. 1696. It was agreed that if any fellow desired to have his chamber wainscotted and it was done at the college charge the common chest should receive yearly after the rate of £5 p.c. for their money so laid out[2]."

The Bursar's Books for 1697, 1703, 1729, contain entries for wainscoting the chambers of persons enumerated. In 1754, when the north side of Gonville Court was rebuilt, it was ordered "that the rooms be ceiled and floored and the windows finished with shutters"; and in the next year that all the rooms therein should be wainscoted. The wainscot then put up remains to this day throughout the college; in many rooms the fine dark-coloured oak panels, extending to the ceiling, are in their

[1] [Mag. Journ. 1539—40, fo. 61. "Item...exportantibus aream argillosam a cubiculo dni Ashtoni xiiij^{d}. Item Dowseo contabulanti cubiculum dni Ashtoni 7 diebus, et ingressum cubiculi, et læviganti asseres pro area totius cubiculi, ex iussu presidis iij^{s}. vj^{d}."]

[2] After a sufficient time this wainscot-rent was remitted. In 1787 it is noted that "the two end rooms on the west side of Caius Court ceased to pay 3*l.* per annum wainscot to the College, for they had been wainscotted so long that the College was reimbursed." MSS. Gonv. and Caius Coll. Library, No. 616, p. 110.

original condition, unpainted, but in others they have been painted in light grey.

[When panelwork was not to be obtained, it was usual to hang the walls with some kind of stuff, as green say, dornicks, or perpetuana. For important official rooms tapestry was used, or canvas artificially painted. A wooden molding, called a crest, was fixed to the wall at about eighteen inches from the ceiling, and the hangings were nailed to it[1]. The following extracts from an account for work done to a set of rooms in Trinity Hall, dated 7 January, 1607, may be quoted in this place:

	£	s.	d.
"To the Joyner for waynscoting my Chaumber	6	16	0
For the Iron worke for the two newe portalls	0	5	4
For a lock and key to the settle	0	1	2
For paynting over all the windowes and borders of anticke woorke	0	2	
For remooving the matts and clay and evening the floure in ye bed chaumber	0	2	6
For paynting the cloth in the upper chamber	0	10	0"

The annexed illustration (fig. 10), from a room in the old court of Pembroke College, will give some idea of this early wainscoting, and of the appearance of one of the "portalls" with its prominent hinges.]

The studies which we have been describing were not necessarily a part of the structure, but rather of the nature of fixtures which could be set up in a corner of the room against a window, and be removed at pleasure. The study (6) in the chamber marked B in the Legge Building at Caius College (fig. 5) is an excellent example of this arrangement. [In the statutes of Magdalene College (1554—55), studies, there called *musæa*, are classed with other articles nailed to the walls, and are not allowed to be removed without the Master's permission[2];] and the Bursars' Books of the different

1 [The "Prizing Book" of S. John's College gives several instances of this in 1627, as: "Thirty-six foote of Inch bourd for ye Ledge and Creste to ye chamber; For 63 yards of dornix 4^li; For tape, Tenter-hookes, rings, and Nayles; For fittinge and sewinge Curtains and hangings"; and again: "The bed chamber. Ledges for the painted cloth; Canvas and paintinge at ij^s. per yard."]

2 [Commiss. Docts. (Cambridge) III. 358. *De Cubiculorum Distributione.* "Musæa denique singula exstructa aut extruenda, vitrum ac casulæ fenestris imposita ac alia

Colleges contain instances, which might be indefinitely multiplied, to shew that studies were actually put up and taken down according to the fancy of the tenant of the chamber for the time being. The following are good examples of this custom:

"Item to the Carpenter for setting vpp a studdie in Mr Sparrowes Chamber ij^s^.

Item to a Carpenter for ij dayes worke in taking downe a studdie in Edward Whitgraues chamber ij^s^.[1]"

Fig. 10. Door-case and panelwork at Pembroke College.

"Item to y^e^ carpenters for theyre timber bestowed vpon y^e^ partition betwixt y^e^ studyes, y^e^ hearth peece, boards vnder y^e^ window towards ye backe lane: for remoouinge of ye study, layinge ye boards leauell where it stode before, and theyre wages................................00. 16. 04.[2]"

ornamenta Collegio clavis majoribus (ex judicio Magistri) affixa, si sine ejus consensu auferantur, furtum esto."]

[1] Junior Bursar's Accounts of Trinity College, 1598—99, *Dayes worke to Carpenters*. [Similar entries have been already quoted in the History of Christ's College, Vol. II. p. 200, *note*.]

[2] [Prizing Book of St John's College.]

[The walls of the studies were of reeds, covered with plaister, as shewn by the following entries from the Audit Book of Christ's College for 1564—65:

"Item for [the] chamber next ye chapell, seling for ij studies, selinge over ye same, for heare and reede to ye same xij^s. vj^d.
Item to Richard for clayenge ye studdies ij^s. vj^d."

In the King's College Inventory above referred to the studies are enumerated among the articles which passed from tenant to tenant, and in some cases had evidently been paid for so often that their full value had been refunded to the College. For instance, in "The lowe Fellowes Chamber next the gates" we find the following list:

"Inprimis a standing bedstead with a trundle beddstead.
Item the southe studdy free.
Item the other studdye x^s.
Item iij wyndowes glased with v double casements of wood and leaves for the windowes.
Item a portall and ij formes.
Item a table vpon a frame."

In "The first Scholers Chamber" there was "a studdye and a presse"; in the second "a studdye at vij^s. without furniture"; in the third "a study at xij^s.; another studdye at $xxiij^s$.; an old presse of boards converted into the raysing of 3 studdyes," and so forth. Again, in the *Gesta Book* of Caius College for 1657, leave is given to Mr Adamson "to take down one of the Studyes in the chamber under him, and that it bee set up againe when Mr Okey leaves the College"; and in 1659: "to convert the bed-place in Mr Hewe's chamber into a study."

The furniture, if we may take the above Inventory as a guide, was extremely simple. The beds must all have been placed in the great room, privacy being sought only in the studies. The articles which occur most frequently are: a standing bedstead; a trundle bedstead, which, when not wanted for use, would be placed under the former; a leaden water-cistern with a trough of the same material to wash in; wooden shutters for the windows; a plain wooden table, two forms, or a few stools, or a settle; a cupboard; a desk for writing on, and one or more shelves for books. The latter articles were usually placed in the studies, as appears from such entries as: "a study desked and shelved round"; "a studdye well desked on 2 sydes with 4 shelves"; "a wryting table or bord in the studdye." The following extracts illustrate this description, and afford additional evidence for the division of the studies as described by Professor Willis:

"The seconde midle Chamber.

Inprimis vij Iron casements.
Item vj woodden leaves for the wyndowes.
Item a presse for books in the vpper studdye with 4 shelves.
Item a locke, a handle, and 2 bolts, on the vtter Chamber dore.
Item a halfe head bedsteade of walnuttree varnished vpon layd in woorke.
Item a round table and vj playne Joyned stooles.
Item a foote pase before the Chimney.
Item a litle table in the lower studdye.
Item a laver with a spoute of leade.

The third middell Chamber.

Inprimis a playne ioyned oken portall.
Item iiij Iron casements and one of woodd.
Item a standing bedstead without pillers.
Item v woodden leaves for the windowes.
Item a locke and a bolt of the Chamber dore.
Item 2 casements of Iron in the lower studdye.
Item a locke on the same studdy Dore belowe.
Item a dore for the colehowse belowe.
Item a standing bedstead and ij casements in the lofte.
Item a table of waynscott and ij joyned formes in the Chamber.
Item a newe Cisterne or a troughe of leade in the Chamber.
Item waynscott before the said Cisterne and before the lesser northe wyndowe.
Item the great crests of oke for the hangings.

The third vpper Chamber.

Inprimis a trundle bedstead corded.
Item iij woodden Casements and ij Iron double Casements.
Item iiij woodden Leaves for the wyndowes.
Item a lead to wasshe with a cocke.
Item a studdye in the Chamber with lock and kay.
Item a woodden Casement in ye studdie.
Item iij shelves and ij desks.
Item a locke and kay and a handell on the Chamber dore.
Item a portall Dore to the vpper studdye.

The Chamber over the Treasurye.

Inprimis a bedstead.
Item a table, a benche, and a forme in the Chamber.
Item a parte of the nether gallary at xv^{s}.
Item a standing bed in the vpper gallary corded.
Item an vpper gallarye."

The chamber last mentioned was on the second floor over the great gate, the first floor being occupied by the treasury, or muniment-room. After the enlarged site had been obtained by King Henry the Sixth, this part of the older college was completed in a temporary fashion, and Loggan shews that the upper chambers, or, as we should call them, the second floor, from the south side of the gate to the north-west corner of the college, had windows in two rows, with a considerable interval between the rows. This arrangement would leave space sufficient for two narrow slips, one above the other, each called a gallery. The chamber over the pantry appears also to have been fitted with two similar small rooms, though the "gallery belowe," or "the lowe gallery," only is mentioned. The sixth and seventh upper chambers had each one gallery; and so had the fifth, sixth, seventh, and eighth middle chambers. In these rooms the word evidently signifies the narrow entresol over the vestibule and study. Subsequently it came to mean a garret, as in the contract for the Bishop's Hostel at Trinity College in 1669:

> "The said Building * * * to conteine above ground two storyes to the roofe * * * and a hansome gallary of a sufficient heighth to bee all under the roofe of the said building to conteine and be devided into five roomes or gallaryes, and every of those to have one chamber and one Studdy to them."

This is probably what is meant in the following extract from the Audit-Book of Jesus College for 1601—2:

> "Item to Mr Clarke towardes y^{e} building of his galery in y^{e} chamber wch was Mr Ducket's $xlvj^{s}$. $viij^{d}$."]

Before quitting this subject it should be pointed out that the system of providing these small cells for study was derived from monastic arrangements. In the statutes of the provincial chapter of Benedictines held at Northampton in 1343, the statute relating to the student-monks (*De studentibus*) makes provision for their occupation of chambers and studies (*camere et studia*)[1]. Again, the *carrells* of the monks of Durham, described in the following passage, were of the nature of studies:

"In the north syde of the Cloister, from the corner over against the Church dour to the corner over againste the Dorter dour, was all fynely glased, from the hight to the sole within a litle of the grownd into the Cloister garth. And in every wyndowe iij Pewes or Carrells, where every one of the old Monks had his carrell, severall by himselfe, that, when they had dyned, they did resorte to that place of Cloister, and there studyed upon there books, every one in his carrell, all the after noune, unto evensong tyme. This was there exercise every daie. All there pewes or carrells was all fynely wainscotted and verie close, all but the forepart, which had carved wourke that gave light in at ther carrell doures of wainscott. And in every carrell was a deske to lye there bookes on. And the carrells was no greater then from one stanchell of the wyndowe to another. And over against the carrells against the church wall did stand sertaine great almeries or cupbords of waynscott all full of Bookes, with great store of ancient manuscripts to help them in their study, wherein did lye as well the old auncyent written Doctors of the Church as other prophane authors, with dyverse other holie mens wourks, so that every one dyd studye what Doctor pleased them best, having the Librarie at all tymes to goe studie in besydes there carrells[2]."

1 "Apostolatus Benedictinorum in Anglia," Opera R. P. Clementis Reyneri. Fol. 1626. Appendix III. p. 162. The equivalent words in the margin are "camere et musæa." Ducange describes the word *studium* as "conclave ubi studetur," and as equivalent to the French "estude," a word still used for a lawyer's office.

2 "A Description or Breife Declaration of all the Ancient Monuments, Rites, and Customes belongeinge or beinge within the Monastical Church of Durham before the Suppression. Written in 1593." Ed. Surtees Society, 1842, p. 70. Compare also The Architectural History of the Cathedral and Monastery at Worcester. By Rev. R. Willis, p. 57. (Archæol. Journ. Vol. XX.)

IV.

THE MASTER'S LODGE[1].

THE Master of a college at the beginning dined and supped with the other members of the community and the servants in the common hall, and had a single chamber assigned to him. As it was shewn in the last essay that each chamber was usually occupied by two or more tenants, the exclusive use of one was a considerable privilege. It is also evident that in several colleges another chamber was assigned to the Head for the purpose of receiving guests, or of transacting business with the stewards and servants of the House. Two chambers, however, probably always on the first floor, because the "solars" (*solaria*) of the primitive buildings were preferable to the ground-floor rooms, or celars (*celaria*), appear to have been the utmost allowance. On this subject it will be desirable to investigate the provisions of the statutes of the colleges in both Universities.

Walter de Merton gives no directions for the lodging of his Warden (*custos*); but, as he directs that his scholars are to have a common table, presided over by the Warden and the other officers, it was clearly intended that he should dine in Hall[2]. The first statutes of Balliol College (1282) say nothing about the chamber of the Master (*magister*), but his

[1] [A small portion only of this Essay was written out by Professor Willis, but he had prepared such voluminous notes, and tabulated quotations from statutes and other documents, that it has been comparatively easy to complete it in accordance with his views; and the small number of passages included within square brackets shew that little, except the description of the furniture, has been added. For the history of individual Lodges the reader is referred to the separate collegiate Histories.]

[2] [Statutes of Merton College, Cap. 8. Commiss. Docts. (Oxford) Vol. I.]

daily presence in Hall is implied; the second statutes (1340) assign to him "a chamber for himself alone with a servant to wait upon him[1]." The statutes of Michael House (1324), the first given in Cambridge, assign to the Master the principal chamber (*cameram principalem*), and direct that he, with the scholars, the chaplains, and other members of the House are to have a common table[2]. At Oriel College, Oxford (1326), and at Queen's College in the same University (1340), the chamber of the Provost (*præpositus*) is not mentioned, but in both colleges he is to dine in the common hall. In the second statutes given to the former college (1329), he is permitted to dine apart when he chooses; and at the latter he is permitted to select a residence beyond the precincts, if his means permit, provided that the college be not neglected, and that no part of the additional expense be borne by it. At Pembroke College, Cambridge, founded 1347, the Master is to have the first choice of rooms, and to dine in Hall; the statutes of Trinity Hall (1352), and of Gonville Hall (1353), are silent on the point; in those of Corpus Christi College, founded 1352, and of Clare Hall, given 1359, the principal and best chamber is assigned to him for his exclusive use[3], and he is to dine in Hall; at King's Hall (1379—80) the Master's chamber is not mentioned, but, as it is part of his duty to assign the chambers to the other members of the college, the choice of the best is virtually given to himself; and we know from the list of the chambers in King's Hall, printed in the History of Trinity College[4], that the Master had a chamber on the first floor, with a study adjoining to it. He is further directed to dine in Hall with the rest of the community in terms nearly identical with those used for Michael House[5].

The first indication of the assignment of a second chamber

[1] [Statutes of Sir Philip Somerville, confirmed by Edward Balliol, King of Scotland, 1340. Ibid. p. xi.]

[2] [Statutes of Michael House; printed in The University of Cambridge from the earliest times to the Royal Injunctions of 1535, by J. B. Mullinger. 8vo. Camb. 1873, p. 640. "§ 6. Magister et scolares capellani et alii mensam communem habeant in domo prædicta. § 19. Habeat Magister cameram principalem."]

[3] [Statutes of Clare Hall, Commiss. Docts. I. 133, "Reservatâ semper Magistro soli camerâ dictæ nostræ domus principali et etiam meliori."]

[4] [History of Trinity College, Vol. II. p. 431.]

[5] ["Item habeant præfati Custos et scholares mensam communem, horis competentibus, simul epulantes decenter et honeste."]

to the Master is afforded by the ancient statutes of Peterhouse (1344). It is difficult to translate the passage literally, but the general sense is as follows:

"Whereas guests of the House, and stewards and bailiffs of the same, whether they reside in the House or at a distance from it, when they come to ask the Master's advice, and possibly to confer with him in private, are usually received in his chamber, because such business can be transacted more privately and conveniently in a chamber than in the hall; we appoint, and also enjoin, that, for these duties and for others which concern the House, the Master shall select one chamber, whichever he please, for his own use, and another with the advice of the Deans[1]."

It is further provided that the Master is to dine in Hall.

William of Wykeham proceeds upon a new principle at New College, Oxford (1400), by decreeing that his Warden (*custos*) shall have a separate residence:

"The Warden of our College shall dwell apart and separate within the precincts of our College in a residence of his own, which we have provided for him and his household over the west gate. This house we have caused to be built apart and separate in this manner in order that the Fellows and Scholars may not be disturbed and annoyed in their own pursuits by those varied occupations which the Warden, in distinction to the others, will find it his duty to undertake in transacting the business of the College."

The founder proceeds to prescribe for his Warden an annual stipend of £40, for the proper maintenance of his household, together with allowances of plate, kitchen utensils, horses, harness, and the like. When strangers come to see him, they and he are to be entertained in Hall at the college expense; and, for the promotion of good feeling between him and the Fellows, he is to dine in Hall on certain specified festivals, and to occupy the place of honour at the high table[2]. This statute is copied

[1] [Statutes of Peterhouse, § 7. Commiss. Docts. II. 11.]

[2] [Statutes of New College, Chap. xi. Commiss. Docts. (Oxford) I. 33. At Winchester College the Warden's residence was placed over the gateway which led from the first to the second quadrangle. By this arrangement he could see all that was passing in each. It is probable that a similar motive dictated the arrangement at New College, for it must be remembered that when first founded it consisted of a single quadrangle, and the Warden could therefore survey the whole of it from the windows of his chamber. Compare The Architectural Works of William of Wykeham, by C. R. Cockerell, in the Proceedings of the Annual Meeting of the Archæological Institute at Winchester, September, 1845. 8vo. London, 1846. At Gonville Hall (Vol. I. p. 166), and at Jesus College (Vol. II. p. 168), the Master's chamber was originally over the gate of entrance.]

almost word for word by King Henry VI. for King's College, Cambridge, but, with his usual anxiety to surpass previous efforts, he augments the stipend of his Provost to one hundred pounds, and prescribes that the household is to consist of at least one gentleman (*generosum*), three valets, and two grooms (*garciones*), with liberal allowance for commons, horses, &c. The King's design for his college includes a "Provostes loggyng" at the south-west corner of the quadrangle, with suitable offices connected with it, as previously explained [1].

King's College was succeeded after a short interval by Queens' College, and S. Catharine's Hall. In the statutes of the former the lodging of the President (*præsidens*) is not mentioned; in those of the latter two rooms are definitely assigned to the Master (*magister*), namely, the principal chamber above the hall, and another between the hall and the library. We find the same arrangement made for the Warden (*custos vulgariter* Gardeyn) at All Souls College, Oxford (1443); at Magdalen College in the same University (1479) the President is to have certain tower-rooms (*turris et cubicula*); but at Lincoln College (1479) the statutes follow the old rule, and prescribe that the Rector is to have no greater privilege than the first choice of rooms.

The statutes of Christ's College, Cambridge, given by the Foundress (1506), direct that the Master and Fellows are to dine together at the same table, because it is important that the college should be united, and be as it were one body under one head. The Master has a definite lodging appointed for him, "in those lower chambers which are under the primary chambers built for our own use [2]." These arrangements were followed at S. John's College (1530). The Master is to dine in Hall, and to occupy "those chambers which have been constructed for him [3]." At Jesus College in the same way definite chambers are assigned to the Master, and it was evidently intended that he should dine in Hall, for he is permitted, on special occasions, to take guests and certain of the Fellows, to dine with

1 [History of King's College, Vol. I. pp. 370, 374.]

2 [Statutes of Christ's College, Chap. vi. and Chap. xxxiv. Commiss. Docts. III. pp. 179, 199.]

3 [Statutes of S. John's College, Chap. xxx. and Chap. xxxii. Ibid. pp. 296, 299.]

him in his chamber[1]. In the statutes of the four following Oxford colleges, viz.: Corpus Christi (1517); Brasenose (1521); Cardinal College (in Wolsey's first statutes); and S. John's College (1555), a tower and chambers (*turris et cubicula*) are assigned to the Head; at Corpus Christi and St John's Colleges the President (*præsidens*) was to dine in Hall; in the statutes of Brasenose the table of the Principal (*principalis*) is not mentioned; and at Cardinal College the Dean (*decanus*) is expressly forbidden to dine with the Fellows except on certain specified festivals, on the principle that familiarity breeds contempt. At Emmanuel College, Cambridge, founded 1583—84, and at Sidney Sussex College, founded 1594, the Master is directed to occupy definite rooms which have been built for his special use.

This enumeration shews that the custom of allowing the Master to select his own room was gradually abandoned. When the plan best adapted for a college had been definitely settled, and the Master's Lodging had become a recognised element of collegiate architecture, a set of rooms proportioned to the magnitude and consequence of the establishment was erected for him from the beginning.

The favourite medieval arrangement of the Master's Lodging at Cambridge was to place it at the high-table end of the hall in continuation of the latter. It was thus placed at Corpus Christi College, Trinity Hall, and Pembroke College, in each case in buildings apparently erected in the fourteenth century; in King's Hall[2]; in the projected plans of Eton College and King's College (1448); at Queens' College (1448); at Peterhouse (1460); at Christ's College (1506); at S. John's College (1510); in the old court of Clare Hall (1521); at Emmanuel College (1584); and at Sidney Sussex College (1596). At Gonville hall (1441) the Master's chamber was separated from the hall by a considerable space, which included the library and the present combination room, but it was in contiguity with the chapel. At Michael House the Master's chamber was certainly on the first floor, because other chambers are described as beneath it, but of its relation to other offices we know nothing.

[1] [Statutes of Jesus College, Chaps. x., xix. Commiss. Docts. III. pp. 106, 113.]
[2] [History of Trinity College, Vol. II. pp. 442, 459.]

At Jesus College (1497) and at Magdalene College (1542), the existing monastic buildings give a peculiar character to the plan. This is especially true of the former college, where the Master's Lodge was placed in the first instance over the gate of entrance, and subsequently extended to the south-west corner of the cloister-quadrangle, in contact with neither hall nor chapel, but connected to both by means of the cloister. At Magdalene College it was situated, probably from the first, at the west end of the north side of the quadrangle, joining the chapel, but remote from the hall. At Trinity College it was placed by Nevile at the north end of the hall, but of necessity at some distance from the chapel. The present buildings of S. Catharine's Hall, King's College, and Downing College were erected subsequent to the Restoration, and their plans, formed in accordance with the change of manners in the University, have little in common with those of the older colleges.

[It should be further remarked that these medieval Lodges were generally so arranged that the Master could reach the principal offices of the college dryshod. At Peterhouse the Master's principal chamber was over the combination room or parlour, and by means of an external staircase he could ascend to his upper chamber, or descend to the parlour, hall, and garden. In after-times, when the new library and chapel had been built, his chambers communicated with both[1]. At Pembroke College, in the same manner, the Master's chamber was over the parlour, and by means of an external staircase he could ascend to his upper chambers and to the library, or descend to the hall and parlour[2]. At Gonville and Caius College one of the Master's chambers looked into the chapel; and Dr Caius rearranged them so that the Master could enter the chapel dryshod, and moreover built for him an external staircase on the west side, for more convenient access to his garden[3]. At Trinity Hall the Master could pass into the parlour, and from it to the hall or chapel. Moreover, by means of a passage on the top of the wall bounding the second court on the west, he could enter the library[4]. At Corpus Christi College the Master could

[1] [History of Peterhouse, Vol. I. pp. 20, 30.]
[2] [History of Pembroke College, Ibid. p. 130.]
[3] [History of Gonville and Caius College, Ibid. pp. 172, 200.]
[4] [History of Trinity Hall, Vol. I. pp. 223—226.]

enter the hall and library from his Lodge, and the gallery, built by Archbishop Parker, had a window looking into the chapel[1]. At King's College, though the Lodge was detached, the Provost had a private way into the chapel, which then contained the library[2]. At Queens' College the President had a private external staircase to his two chambers, the largest of which was over the combination room at the north end of the hall. From this room he could enter the library, and pass through it to the chapel. At the foot of his staircase was a vestibule with doors opening into the hall and parlour, and, in subsequent times, when the gallery had been built for his use, he had a second staircase at its north-west corner to give access to his garden[3]. At S. Catharine's Hall the Lodge seems to have communicated with hall and library[4]. At Jesus College the Master had a private staircase from the cloister to his Lodge (in what may be termed its second position), and a door opens out of it into the library[5]. At Christ's College the Master's chambers (when on the ground floor) opened into the hall, as at present; when he had moved to the chambers on the first floor reserved for the Foundress, he could command the hall and the chapel by windows looking into both; and by an external staircase could ascend into his upper chambers, or descend into the garden, hall, and parlour[6]. At S. John's College the arrangements were almost identical. An external staircase, at the junction of the hall with the combination room, led from the court to the Master's chamber, from which he had private access to the chapel, and, after the gallery was built, to the library also[7]. The following description of this Lodge, written in 1664, by Dr Michael Woodward, Warden of New College, Oxford, is well worth quotation. It must be remembered that the staircase mentioned is the one on the north side of the first court (F, fig. 15), not the external staircase in the second court.

[1] [History of Corpus Christi College, Ibid. pp. 266—270.]
[2] [History of King's College, Ibid. p. 534, *note*, pp. 540—548.]
[3] [History of Queens' College, Vol. II. pp. 21—36.]
[4] [History of S. Catharine's Hall, Ibid. p. 97.]
[5] [History of Jesus College, Ibid. p. 170.]
[6] [History of Christ's College, Ibid. pp. 217—219.]
[7] [History of S. John's College, Ibid. p. 312.]

"Being at Cambridge Apr. 29 1664, I visited Dr Gunning, Master of St John's College, the Scholars whereof are very numerous, about 300, as they say: more than in any House of Oxon by far. Dr Gunning did courteously entertain me—shewed me his Lodgings, which are very large—leading at the one end of them into the Library—which is very long, and fair, and full of books. The Cieling above is carved, and well wrought. Thence, after a cup of Sacke and some sweet bisket—(he desired me to dine with him)—I took my leave to return to my lodging—but before we went down the round stony staires, he shewed me his passage from out of his lodgings into the Gallery where their little Organ stands; and a seat there for himself, if he please, to hear Prayers, seeing all the Chapel, but the Scholars not seeing him, as in the King's Chapel. He went with me to the outer gate, and so we parted[1]".

These arrangements were carried out even in buildings erected during the sixteenth century; for at Trinity College the Lodge communicated with the library, as it still does with the hall, into which there is a door, and a window from one of the upper rooms; and at Emmanuel College and Sidney Sussex College, with hall, library, combination room, and chapel. The latest survival of this plan is to be found at Clare Hall, where the Lodge, commenced in 1705, communicates with the library, from which the Master can reach the hall by passing through the combination room. The small windows which overlooked the hall from the Master's chamber in some colleges were evidently borrowed from the domestic halls, where the domestic apartments were frequently provided with openings from which the lord could see what was going on in the hall below without being observed[2].

The external staircases at Pembroke College, and at Gonville and Caius College, and the garden-staircase at Queens' College, have been destroyed; but the others still remain. Descriptions of these will be found in the histories of the colleges to which they belong.]

After the Reformation the limited space allotted to the Head was found to be too small; partly from the necessity of exercising

[1] [This description was most kindly transcribed for me from one of Dr Woodward's diaries by the present Warden of New College. Dr Gunning had been chaplain at New College.]

[2] [Some account of Domestic Architecture in England from Richard II. to Henry VIII. By the editor of the Glossary of Architecture. 8vo. Oxford, 1859. Part I. p. 59.]

increased hospitality, but principally because the liberty of marriage, eagerly embraced by many of these functionaries, made it needful to provide for the accommodation of a family and a household. At Queens' College Dr Heynes (1529—37) was a married man, and his widow became the wife of his successor Dr Mey (1537—53). Dr William Chaderton (1568—97) was also married. At King's College Dr Cheke (1548—53), and Dr Goade (1569—1610), were both married. Dr Whitaker, Master of S. John's College (1586—95) was married twice; Dr Chaderton, Master of Emmanuel College (1584—1622), married his sister-in-law; Dr Matthew Parker married in 1547, while Master of Corpus Christi College; and probably other instances might be cited. Had not married Heads become numerous, Queen Elizabeth would hardly have issued her famous Order, 9 August, 1561:

"The Queen's Majesty, considering how the palaces and houses of cathedral churches and colleges of this realm have been, both of ancient and late time, builded and enclosed in severalty, to sustain and keep societies of learned men professing study and prayer, for the edification of the Church of God, and so constantly to serve the commonweal; and understanding of late, that within the houses thereof, as well the chief governors as the prebendaries, students, and members thereof, being married, do keep particular household with their wives, children, and nurses; whereof no small offence groweth to the intent of the founders, and to the quiet and orderly profession of study and learning within the same; hath thought meet to provide remedy herein, lest by sufferance thereof, the rest of the colleges, specially such as be so replenished with young students as the very rooms and buildings be not answerable for such families of women and young children, should follow the like example: and therefore expressly willeth and commandeth, that no manner of person, being either the head or member of any college or cathedral church within this realm, shall, from the time of the notification hereof in the same college, have, or be permitted to have; within the precinct of any such college, his wife, or other woman, to abide and dwell in the same, or to frequent and haunt any lodging within the same college, upon pain, that whosoever shall do to the contrary shall forfeit all ecclesiastical promotions in any cathedral or collegiate church within this realm. And for continuance of this order, her Majesty willeth, that the transcript hereof shall be written in the book of the statutes of every such college, and shall be reputed as parcel of the statutes of the same.

Given under our signet, at our town of Ipswich, the ninth of August, the third year of our reign[1]."

[1] [Correspondence of Archbishop Parker, ed. Parker Society, p. 146.]

This decree had the effect of removing the ladies from the college precincts. Baker observes, with reference to Dr Whitaker's wife, that she was "kept in town," in accordance with this "laudable injunction of Queen Elizabeth" as he terms it; which, he adds, was "generally observed until towards the times of usurpation, when all things run into confusion and wives with their dependances were brought in to the disturbance of scholars[1]." When Dr Goade was reproached with his marriage, he boldly replied: "My wyef is not kept within the quadrant of the Colledge, (wher as yet I think she neaver came twise) but in my lodging, being separate apart from the Colledge, more conveniently then eny other in the town[2]." The position of the Provost's Lodge of King's College, which had evidently been arranged in an exceptional manner from the beginning, has been already explained. No alteration would be required to adapt it to a new state of things; but elsewhere it became necessary to change a set of college rooms into a family residence. This could only be done by absorbing pre-existing college rooms in contiguity with the original Master's Lodgings, or by erecting additional buildings. The former course was adopted in almost every college, as has been already narrated in their separate histories, nor was annexation confined to chambers. At Corpus Christi College, Trinity Hall, and Christ's College, the Fellows yielded their combination room to the Master, and took another chamber instead of it for themselves. At Pembroke College, Gonville and Caius College, Queens' College, Jesus College, Christ's College, and Sidney Sussex College, the Master was allowed to use the audit-room as a dining room when it was not required for college business.

The Master's Lodge was frequently so situated that the addition of new buildings was impossible; but where such an enlargement could be carried out we find several instances of that remarkable feature of Cambridge Lodges, the Gallery, which appears to have been unknown at Oxford.

This feature seems to have proceeded naturally from the cloister of the earlier buildings. In all the regular societies of men in the Middle Ages, whether monastic, ecclesiastical, or

[1] [History of S. John's College, ed. Mayor, I. 186.]

[2] [Heywood and Wright, p. 232.]

scholastic, the confinement within walls made it necessary to provide some place for daily exercise. The cloister-walks were termed walking-places (*ambulacra*) or "deambulatories," in this sense; and the passages quoted below will shew that the words *alura* and *galeria* were used, in common with the above, with the same meaning[1]. Even in the present time the cloisters of Trinity College are commonly used for exercise in wet weather. [In France in the sixteenth century the alleys in a garden, arched over with a wooden trellis, and covered with ivy, were termed walking-places (*deambulationes*), or galleries (*galleries de charpenterie*[2]).]

It was explained in a former essay that the cloister was first introduced into collegiate architecture by William of Wykeham, but that his example was not followed at Cambridge. Galleries however, for the use of the Fellows, were built in at least five

[1] It appears from the passages collected by Ducange s. v. "galeria" that the word was used through the middle ages for a long corridor, "ambulacrum," or deambulatory; as for example: "In quodam superiori ambulacro sive quadam superiori Galeria ex parte australi ædium sive hospitii illustrissimi Principis et domini nostri domini Henrici VIII." Rymer, XIV. 390, col. 1, ed. 1704—35. "Galilæa" or "Galilee," according to the same authority s.v. "galilæa," was sometimes employed to signify the "ambulacrum" of a cloister. "Allorium," or "Alura," has the same general sense. In the following passage of Lydgate it seems to mean a vaulted passage under the houses of a street. He is describing the rebuilding of Troy by Priam, Book II. Chap. xi. (Ed. 1555):

"And thrugh the towne with crafty purueiaunce,
By great auise and discrete ordenaunce,
By compase cast and squared out by squyers,
Of pullished marble vpon stronge pyllers,
Deuysed were longe large and wyde
Of euery streate in the fronter syde
Freshe alures with lusty hye pynacles,
And mounstryng outward costly tabernacles.
Vauted aboue lyke tō reclinatoryes
That called were deambulatoryes.
Men to walke togithers twaine and twaine
To kepe them drye when it happed to rayne
Or them to saue fro tempest winde or thundre
If that them lyst shroude them safe there vnder."

Thus "galilæa"—"galeria"—alura"—"appear to be different forms of the same word, although each has some special application. [Compare also Architectural Nomenclature of the Middle Ages, p. 33.]

[2] [See the description of the Château de Montargis, in "Les plus excellents bastiments de la France," by Androuet du Cerceau; fol. Paris, 1576—79.]

colleges; Corpus Christi[1]; King's[2]; S. John's[3]; Trinity[4]; and Emmanuel[5]. These have all disappeared. Those for the use of the Master have on the contrary left sufficient traces of their existence to enable them to be described.

The known examples before the end of the reign of Queen Elizabeth are at the following Colleges: Trinity Hall[6], Corpus Christi[7], King's[8], Queens'[9], Catharine Hall[10], Christ's[11], S. John's[12], Magdalene[13], Trinity[14]. In all these Lodges galleries were erected in conformity with the domestic architecture of the period, when the gallery was a necessary feature of a gentleman's mansion. In a poem called "The Assembly of Ladies," printed in the old editions of Chaucer's Works, a mansion is thus described:

"The toures hie ful pleasaunt shal ye finde
With phanes fresh, turning with euery wynde;
The chambres and parlers of a sorte
With bay windowes, goodly as may be thought
As for daunsing and other wyse disport
The galeryes right well ywrought."

By comparing the plans of the colleges with the plan of Haddon Hall, it will be readily seen that the Master's gallery was arranged in connection with the College Hall and Parlour in the same relative position as the gallery of a mansion with respect to the Banqueting Hall and Withdrawing Room beyond. The addition of these galleries to a collegiate Master's Lodge, when taken in connection with the other arrangements now introduced, proves that at this time the Master's habitation was no longer treated as a superior set of chambers, but as a

[1] [History of Corpus Christi College, Vol. I. p. 260.]
[2] [History of King's College, Ibid. p. 569.]
[3] [History of S. John's College, Vol. II. p. 323.]
[4] [History of Trinity College, Ibid. p. 608.]
[5] [History of Emmanuel College, Ibid. p. 690.]
[6] [History of Trinity Hall, Vol. I. p. 223.]
[7] [History of Corpus Christi College, Ibid. p. 270.]
[8] [History of King's College, Ibid. p. 543.]
[9] [History of Queens' College, Vol. II. p. 30.]
[10] [History of Catharine Hall, Ibid. p. 97.]
[11] [History of Christ's College, Ibid. p. 217.]
[12] [History of S. John's College, Ibid. pp. 246, 314.]
[13] [History of Magdalene College, Ibid. p. 383.]
[14] [History of Trinity College, Ibid. pp. 607, 608, 622.]

dwelling-house. This principle had been laid down by Wykeham, but was never fully acted upon until after the Reformation.

[Of these galleries two only remain, at S. John's College, and at Queens' College. The former, built in 1599, though constructed as a gallery for the use of the Master in the first instance, is merely the first floor of a range of chambers undivided by partitions. The latter is undated, but it has been shewn in the History of Queens' College, Chapter IV., that it was probably built between 1537 and 1541. If that theory be correct, it is the first erected in Cambridge, if we except the still earlier one in the same college, and may be taken as a type of those which succeeded it. It is 80 feet long, 12 feet broad, and 9 feet high, built wholly of timber. The great beauty of its internal fittings, and its convenience as a means of communication between the two divisions of the Lodge, have combined to preserve it. It must be admitted, however, that it is extremely cold, and unsuited for any other purposes than those of a picture-gallery or a library. These considerations, with the perishable nature of the materials of which they were built, probably hastened the destruction of the galleries in other colleges.]

The plan of the first floor of the President's Lodge (fig. 1) shews that the gallery is lighted by a polygonal oriel and two bay windows on the south side, and by a semicircular oriel and two bay windows on the north side. None of these windows are opposite to each other. This disposition of the windows, which we find also in the gallery at Haddon Hall, appears to have been the usual arrangement employed in the galleries of the sixteenth century, and it was insisted upon by the great French architect Philibert De Lorme: "It will be better," he says, "and have a handsomer effect, if the windows of the two sides of a room be not set opposite to each other; for, if they be so, there will always be shadows and obscurities produced between the said windows, so as to make the rooms gloomy[1]."

[1] [NOVVELLES INVENTIONS POVR BIEN BASTIR ET A PETITS FRAIX, TROVVEES n'agueres par Philibert de L'orme Lyonnois, Architecte, Conseiller et Aulmonier ordinaire du feu Roy Henry, et Abbé de S. Eloy lez Noyon. fol. Paris. 1561. Book II. Chap. XI. fol. 52 b. The chapter is headed: "Comme on doit faire les fenestres croisees plus hautes que la naissance des poutres, à fin de donner meilleure clarté ou plus de iour dedans les lambriz." After describing the construction of the windows,

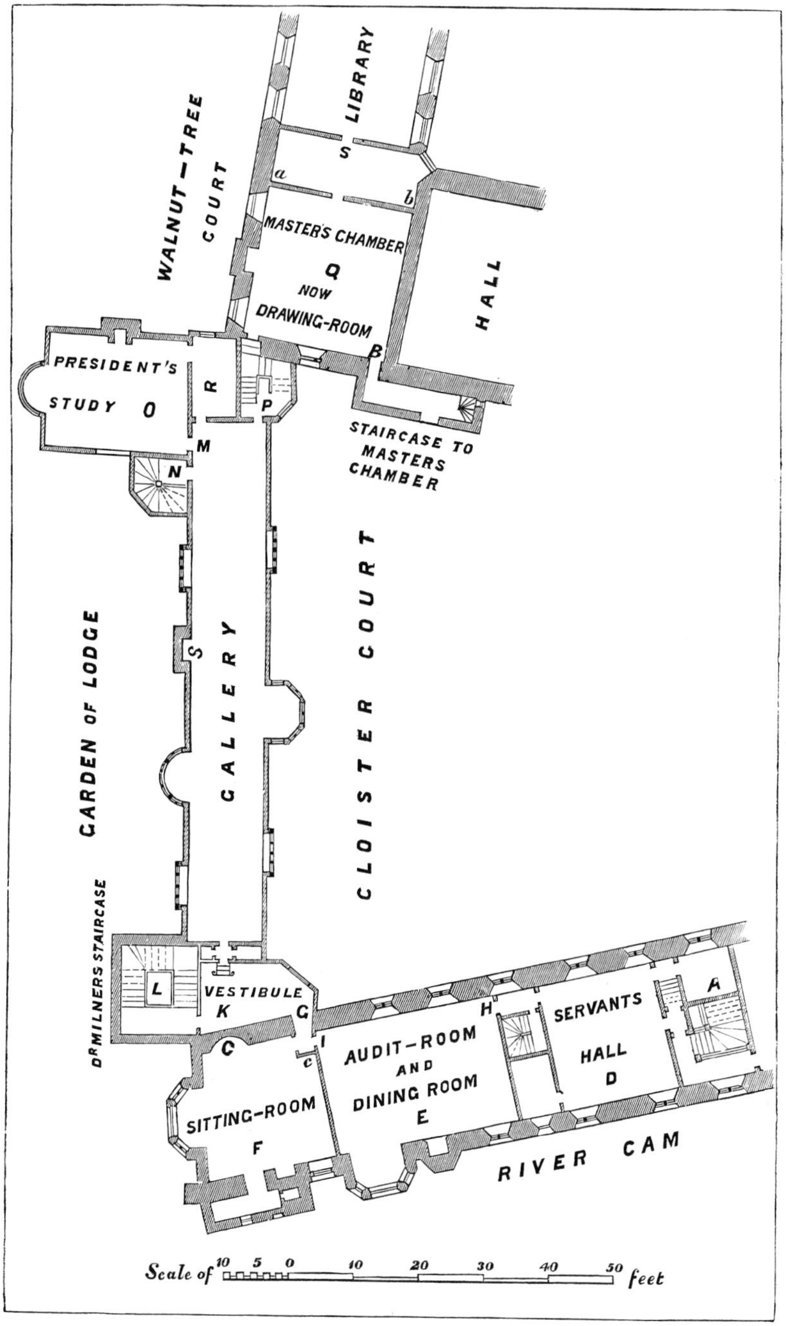

Fig. 1. Plan of the first floor of the President's Lodge at Queens' College. The letters refer to the description of the Lodge given in the History of Queens' College, Chapter IV.

As an illustration he refers to his building of the Château de Saint Maur des Fossés near Paris, "the first example in France which shewed how to observe the proportions and measures of Architecture"; the Salle and Gallery of the Château d'Anet; the "grande gallerie" which he made at Saint Ligier, and many others.

The inside of the court of Saint Maur is given by Du Cerceau. It has coupled Corinthian pilasters carrying an entablature with a high attic order like that of a triumphal arch, a portal in the centre with columns, and a pediment above the attic. The windows are placed in the alternate intercolumniations, so that each pair on one side of the apartment has a window opposite to it on the other. This principle is completely carried out in the gallery at Anet, which has five windows and a door on one side, and six windows and a door on the other, thus making six apertures and seven apertures which are placed each opposite to piers of the other sides respectively. The gallery forms one side of the second court of the château, and has the garden on a much lower level on its other side. A flight of steps from the door descends into it. The plan of the Tuileries also shews the piers of one side placed opposite to the windows of the other[1].

[We must next take brief notice of the arrangements of the Lodgings for the Head in the colleges at Oxford.]

At Merton College the Warden's Lodgings are said to have been built between 1455 and 1507. They form a separate mansion in the outer court, remote from the chapel and library, but connected with the east gable of the hall by a gateway leading into the quadrangle beyond. When first erected, they

he proceeds: "Il sera plus convenable et plus beau que les croisees ne soient point au droict l'une de l'autre: car si les fenetres sont à l'opposite l'une de l'autre, y a tousiours ombre et obscurité par les costez entre les dictes fenestres: laquelle rend ordinairement les lieux melancholiques. Qui ueut uoir cela par experience, le peut cognoistre au batiment que ie fis faire à sainct Maur des fossez pres Paris: lequel a esté le premier en France faict pour monstrer comme l'on doit obseruer les proportions et mesures de Architecture, en ce qu'il peut contenir. Aussi il se peut uoir à la salle et gallerie du Chasteau d'Annet: et à la grande gallerie que i'ay faict construire de neuf au chasteau de Sainct Ligier, en la forest de Montfort, qui est tres belle à uoir, estant accompaignee de deux pauillons et une chapelle au milieu. Il y a assez d'autres lieux esquelz i'ay ordonné tellement faire."]

[1] [This passage has been left exactly as Professor Willis wrote it, but it is extremely difficult to make out the arrangements which he describes from the plans and elevations given by Du Cerceau.]

must have been completely separate, for the gateway and the room above it are additions of the sixteenth century, and the quadrangle into which it leads, the east range of which abuts against the Lodgings, was completed in 1610.

At University College the Master's Lodgings were a separate house, or range of building, on the north side of the college, next to the street from which it was entered, completely external to, and projecting beyond, the old quadrangle, although in continuation of the line of the front towards the east. When first built they were contiguous to the hall, but remote from the chapel. These Lodgings remained until the building of the smaller quadrangle, which includes the Master's present residence, in 1719. They are therefore represented in Loggan's plate[1]. At present the Master is as remote from the hall as he formerly was from the chapel.

At Balliol College, which was wholly rebuilt in and after the reign of King Henry VI., the Master's Lodgings, as shewn by Loggan, are in the south-west corner of the quadrangle, occupying part of the west side of it. Their date is the latter end of the fifteenth century. They adjoin the south, or lower, end of the hall, but are remote from the chapel. They form, however, an integral part of the quadrangle, and of the principal front of the college. The part which looks eastward into the quadrangle is ornamented by a celebrated oriel-window of great beauty, proved, by the arms sculptured upon it, to have been built at the expense of William Gray, Bishop of Ely (1454—78)[2].

In the irregular group of buildings which constituted the college of Exeter when Loggan's view was published, the Rector is lodged in a low building in two floors on the north side of the quadrangle, opposite to the hall, between the chapel and the old north gateway-tower. Wood ascertained that this building, with the tower, had been erected about the year 1432, and was afterwards appropriated to the Rector[3].

[1] This view is copied, on a reduced scale, in Ingram's Memorials, University College, p. 10.

[2] It is delineated in Pugin's Examples of Gothic Architecture, Vol. I.; and in Skelton's Oxonia Antiqua, ed. 1843, Plate 22. [It must be remembered that the above description was written by Professor Willis before the modern rebuilding of Balliol College.]

[3] [Wood, ed. Gutch, p. 110.]

As no part of Oriel College is older than 1620, it is only necessary to say that the Provost occupies the western half of the north side of the quadrangle, remote from both hall and chapel.

At Queen's College, in the old buildings of which the aspect has been preserved for us by Loggan, the Provost's Lodgings were built in the first half of the fifteenth century. They were contained in a building with a separate roof, forming, together with the hall, the western side of the quadrangle. The north end of this Lodging was contiguous to the high-table end of the hall; the south-west corner touched the transeptal antechapel built 1518; and the south gable entered into the composition of the small subsidiary court containing the library. It was therefore conveniently situated with reference to those buildings; and, moreover, a covered way was provided from it to the chapel by means of a porch surmounted by an oriel, built at the same time as the antechapel, which stood at the junction of the two buildings. In the existing college the Provost is lodged on the west side of the principal quadrangle. He can approach the hall through the cloister, and the chapel through a passage on the north side of the hall.

At New College the Warden's Lodgings remain as Wykeham built them in 1380—the first of the kind, as already explained—occupying the space over the gate of entrance, and extending for a short distance to the south of it. These Lodgings have also, beyond the limits of the quadrangle, a private courtyard with the offices specified by the Founder. A comparatively modern arch, spanning New College Lane, connects these offices with the stables beyond. This range of outbuildings rather awkwardly narrows the approach to the college, which is compressed between them and the wall of the cloister (fig. 4, p. 256). These Lodgings are remote from the chapel, the hall, and the library.

At Lincoln College the Rector's Lodgings are at the south-east corner of the quadrangle, abutting upon the high-table end of the hall. In continuation of the hall they complete the east side, and also extend over a portion of the south side, and of the east side of the second quadrangle to the south of the former. They were built in 1465 by Thomas Beckyngton, Bishop of Bath and Wells:

"A token of this his generosity is yet remaining on the walls of the said fabrick, as well next to the quadrangle, as the common Walk or garden on the east side of the said Lodgings: which token is a Beacon over or on a tun, being a Rebus or name-device for the Benefactor, and commonly used before arms became frequent[1]."

At All Souls College the two chambers assigned to the Warden in 1445 are described as "one great chamber at the south-east corner of the buildings, and one chamber next to it on the other side of the stairs[2]." These chambers, of which the first was called "the great dining-room," and the second "the great bed-chamber," were situated over the second, or eastern, gateway, which gave admission from High Street into a subsidiary court on the east side of the principal court. These Lodgings were therefore external to the college, and remote from chapel, hall, and library. The Wardens gradually acquired possession of the room under the dining-room, and of the garrets over both rooms; and after the Reformation, Dr Robert Hoveden, the first married Warden, who held office from 1571 to 1614, erected an additional building on the east side. In 1703 Dr George Clarke, sometime Fellow, built for himself a house on ground adjoining to these old Lodgings, granted to him by the Warden and Fellows on condition that on his death it should revert to the college. Dr Clarke died in 1736, and from that time forward his house became the Warden's Lodgings, the old Lodgings being converted into rooms for a Fellow, and the buildings which join the old Lodgings to the new being erected at the expense of the college[3]. By this arrangement the Warden was placed at a still greater distance than heretofore from the principal college offices.

At Magdalen College the President's Lodgings are in a separate building or wing, external and at right angles to the cloister-quadrangle, presenting itself on the left hand of the entrance-court in the manner of an abbot's house. These Lodgings include rooms over the tower-gateway, one of which is still termed the Founder's chamber, together with two other rooms adjoining the muniment-tower. They are not contiguous to

[1] Wood, ed. Gutch, p. 244.

[2] Translated from an Injunction of John Stafford, Archbishop of Canterbury, dated 9 December, 1445. Commiss. Docts., Oxford, All Souls College, I. 72.

[3] [Wood, *ut supra*, p. 276. Ingram's Memorials, All Souls College, p. 19.]

hall or chapel, but the cloister supplies a covered way to both. These, or part of them, were probably the original Lodgings of the President. The wing above-described is the result of the usual expansion of this member of collegiate arrangement. Wood attributes it to Dr Laurence Humphrey, the first married President, who held office from 1561 to 1589[1].

At Brasenose College, which was for the most part erected in the time of the Founders, the Principal's Lodgings were over, and on each side of, the entrance-gateway; but, when Loggan's view was taken, they had extended along three quarters of the front, from the gate to the south-east corner of the quadrangle. These Lodgings were near the hall, but remote from the chapel in its original position. After the erection of the new chapel the Principal could easily reach it through the cloister by which it was connected with the old quadrangle. In 1770 the Principal was transferred to a private house at the southern extremity of the east front, extending to High Street, and the old Lodgings were converted into chambers.

At Corpus Christi College the President's Lodgings were at first in the same position as at Brasenose[2], but, when Loggan's view was taken, he was lodged in a detached *hospitium*, apparently a wooden building, placed diagonally, opposite to the south-west outer corner of the great quadrangle, against the wall of the garden of the Dean of Christ Church, with a separate entrance from the street. In 1773, Williams' delineations shew this *hospitium* enlarged by the addition of a south wing, and connected to the angle of the college, the corner chamber of which is also assigned to the President. The Lodgings have since been entirely rebuilt.

At Christ Church the Dean and each Canon had from the beginning a separate residence, with a private garden[3], though the Statutes, as quoted above, place the Dean in a tower, probably the entrance-gateway.

At Trinity College the President was placed on the

[1] Wood, *ut supra*, p. 322. Gutch notes, but without giving any documentary authority: "Dr Clerk tells me they were built 16 years after the College: finished about 1488."

[2] The Lives of William Smyth and Sir Richard Sutton, by Ralph Churton, 8vo. Oxf. 1800, p. 440. Ingram's Memorials, Corpus Christi College, p. 11.

[3] These are well shewn by Williams, Oxonia Depicta, fol. London. 1733.

eastern side of the quadrangle, as Loggan shews, opposite to the hall, and separated from the chapel by the intervention of the library. Dr Bathurst, President from 1664 to 1704, who largely contributed to the college buildings, as related above, erected at his own cost a building near the east end of the chapel, as an enlargement of the President's Lodgings.

At S. John's College the President's Lodgings are at the north end of the east side of the old quadrangle, which was erected in 1597, and formed no part of S. Bernard's College. In this position they abutted upon the chapel, but were remote from both hall and library. When Archbishop Laud's quadrangle was built in 1635, it was agreed, in accordance with his desire, that "thirty-nine feet in length of the north side should be added to the President's Lodgings," and moreover, "the west side (which hath a Cloister under it), half or more of it, containing six windows[1]."

At Jesus College, the Principal's Lodgings were not built until about 1625. They are contiguous to the chapel on the north side of the first quadrangle, and, besides, extend beyond the hall on the west side, so as to occupy a small portion of the east side of the second quadrangle.

At Wadham College the Warden's house occupies a moderate space at the western extremity of the north range of the quadrangle, terminating in a gable and oriel at the north end of the façade. It is remote from chapel, hall, and library.

At Pembroke College the Master was lodged, when Loggan's print was taken, in a considerable house outside the college, which it joined at the south-west corner of the quadrangle, with a separate entrance from the street. It was rebuilt in 1695, and gothicised, to match the new façade of the college, in 1829[2].

Loggan's picturesque view of Gloucester Hall shews that the Principal resided in a mansion of considerable extent, standing detached at the north-west corner of the quadrangle, in which the Prior of the student-monks had formerly resided.

[This survey gives the following results. In nine colleges at

[1] [Wood, *ut supra*, p. 548.]

[2] The original appearance of these Lodgings is shewn by Loggan, the second by Williams, and the third by Ingram, in an engraving which forms the frontispiece to his account of Pembroke College.

Oxford the Head lived from the beginning in a house which was either completely external to the quadrangle, or which extended beyond it, and was provided with a separate entrance, viz. at the colleges of Merton, University, New College, All Souls, Magdalen, Corpus, Pembroke, Gloucester Hall (afterwards Worcester). In the remaining colleges no uniform rule was maintained. At Queen's College and Jesus College it adjoined both hall and chapel; at Lincoln College the high-table end of the hall; at Balliol College the opposite end of the same building; at Exeter College and S. John's College the chapel; at Oriel College and Trinity College the library; at the colleges of Brasenose, Christ Church, and Wadham it was remote from all the college offices. It appears therefore that the Cambridge system of placing the Head in such a position that he could easily have access to the chapel, hall, or library, found no favour at Oxford, for at only one college, viz. Magdalen, was communication provided by means of the cloister. The curious fashion of placing the chambers of the Head over the principal gate of entrance, after it had been set by Wykeham, was followed at Magdalen, Brasenose, and Corpus. At All Souls' he was placed over the lateral gate.

The Master's rooms, in the first instance, like the ordinary chambers, had paved floors, strewed with rushes[1]. Even so late as 1606 the gallery attached to the Master's Lodge at Trinity College was paved with tiles; and it was not till 1689 that they were covered with matting[2]. The walls, on the other hand, appear to have been concealed from the earliest times with hangings of various descriptions, fastened at the top to a ledge of woodwork. In the first Inventory of the college property in the Provost's Lodge at King's College, dated 1451, four rooms have hangings of red worsted, and one of blue worsted[3]; say, frequently called "Norwich say," or green say, appears at King's College in 1562—3:

[1] ["Magnum Journale" of Queens' College, 1495—96, fo. 102 b. "Item pro scirpis pro camera magistri j d. q'." Ibid. 1512—13, fo. 256 b. "Pro .v. C et d. de scirpis pro camera magistri xj d."]

[2] [Jun. Burs. Audit Book, 1605—6. "To George Houlton for 600 paving tiles for our Master's gallery 3. 12. 0." Sen. Burs. do. 1688—89. *Extraordinaries.* "To Mr Shuter for matting the Lodge Gallery, for 461 yards of Matt 6. 9. 0."]

[3] [The notices of the furniture in the Provost's Lodge at King's College will all be found in a paper "On the Old Provost's Lodge at King's College" in the Camb. Antiq. Soc. Communications, Vol. IV. No. XXIII.]

"Item sol' magistro Nycholao Norgate de Norwyche for iiij peces of norwyche sayes to hange the new haull and the chamber next vnto yt in mansione magistri prepositi...vj li. xiij^{s} iiij^{d}.";

at Queens' College in 1563—64[1]; and at Trinity College in 1601, and in 1620:

"Item to an Vpholster for hanginge the greene sea in our master's chamber...iiij^{s}. vj^{d}[2]."

"For 22 yardes and halfe a quarter of say for the lodginge gallerie[3]."

At S. John's College the Master's chamber was hung with red say.

A kind of damask, called dornicks (or darnex), from its being made at Tournay in Flanders, was also frequently employed for the same purpose. At Trinity College, in 1590—91, eighty-two "yardes of dornix at ij^{s}." are provided for the Master's parlour; and at King's College in 1610—11[4], and at Queens' College in 1625—26, the bed-chamber of the Provost and President respectively is hung with the same[5]. Tapestry, usually called "arras," or "cloth of arras," was also employed for the same purpose. At Christ's College, in 1532, we meet with a charge "for lynyng for the arrace in the master's chamber xx^{d}."; at King's College, in 1570—71, "for mendyng M^{r} provestes arres clothes xiiij^{s}"[6]; and at Queens' College in 1690—91 "four pieces of Tappestry hangings for the great room in the Lodgings over the college Parlour[7]" are ordered, at a cost of £11. At S. John's College in 1681 the master's study is hung with gilt leather.

It was even more usual to conceal the walls with hangings of some kind of canvas, painted. They are described in the

[1] [Mag. Journ. 1563—64, fo. 43. "Item pro 10 vlnis et di' pro tapetiis de le saye in cubiculo presidentis xvj^{s}. viij^{d}. Item pro suendo idem tapetium vj^{d}."]

[2] [Jun. Burs. Audit Book, 1600—1601. *Extraordinaries.*]

[3] [Jun. Burs. Audit Book, 1619—20. *Extraordinaries.*]

[4] [Mundum Book, 1610—11. *Exp. necess.* "Solut' pro .60. virgis de peristromatibus communiter vocatis Dornicks pro adornatione novi cubiculi magistri Prepositi ad · 2j^{d} ob le virg' et pro portagio eiusdem de Londres 3^{s} 4^{d} in toto v^{li} v^{s} vj^{d}."]

[5] [Mag. Journ. 1625—26, fo. 22 b. "For dornicks for the master's bed-chamber ix^{s}. iiij^{d}."]

[6] [We meet with this tapestry again in 1603: Mundum Book, 1602—3, *Exp. necess.* "Solut' pro scowring and renewing the colors of the Arras hangings in ædibus magistri Præpositi, being 4 peeces iij^{li}. iij^{s}."]

[7] [Mag. Journ. 1690—91, fo. 253.]

Accounts and Inventories as "painted cloths." At Queens' College in 1532—33 a painter receives twenty shillings for painting the hangings in the President's parlour[1]; and at King's College in 1561—62 we meet with the following entries:

"Item sol' Roberto Tatam for xviij. yardes of canvas at ix. d. the yeard to make a border for the new haull in mansione m^ri^ prepositi .... xiijs.

Item sol' Rychard Crowe for payntynge the same border conteynynge xxxvj. yeardes at x^d^. the yeard .... xxx^s^.

Item sol' Roberto Tatam for xiiij. yeardes and a quarter of canvas at viij. d. ye yearde to make a border for the new chamber by the new haull............ ix. s. vj. d.

...Item sol' Rychardo Crowe for payntynge the same border conteynyng in lengthe xxviij. yeardes et dimid' at x^d^. the yeard...xxiij^s^. viij^d^."

At S. John's College in 1681 part of the Master's study is hung with "purple peinted stuff" in addition to the above-mentioned gilt leather; and in the next year more is ordered, to make curtains to hang before his books.

Towards the end of the sixteenth century and at the beginning of the seventeenth the use of wainscot became general[2], and entries frequently occur in the Accounts for wainscoting both the sitting-rooms and bed-rooms in the different Masters' Lodges. As these tell us nothing respecting the style of the woodwork, but simply record the fact that it was put up, they need not be quoted. At the same time greater luxury in the way of furniture was introduced. The simplicity of this in earlier times is shewn by various entries and inventories. Of the latter class of document we will quote the following, to which reference has been already made, from King's College. It is dated 3 July 1451:

"*The Parlour*

hanged with reed worsted, late bought, and j banker for the same (old): j cupbord cuvered with old tapstre work: j chere of turned werk: j table with a paire trestles: iij stoles: j firforke of yren broken.

In the Hall

ij tablez with ij paire trestles and ij fourmez.

[1] [Mag. Journ. 1532—33, fo. 179. "Item solui pictori Warde pro depictione ly hangingis pro conclaui presidentis, xx^s^."]

[2] [In some exceptional cases the Master's Lodge had been wainscotted earlier; as at Corpus Christi College, where the parlour and lower bedrooms were panelled with linen panelling, ornamented with gilt knobs, between 1443 and 1474. History of Corpus Christi College, Vol. I. p. 266.]

The chambre ouer the Parlour

hanged with blewe worsted; j bed hanged with blewe bokeram and a feble coueryng therto of blewe worsted, and j bed renning vpon whelez vnder the other grete bed, etc.

The litel Parlour at the Gate

hanged with reed worsted; j table; j paire trestles; j fourme; trussyng cofres olde.

The closet chambre

hanged with reed worsted.

The Provost chambre

hanged with reed worsted; an hanged bed of the same; j forme; j joyned stole; j litel folding trestel for a table standyng by the chymney to fore where the Provost sitteth."

This shews that in the wealthiest Lodge in the University there was then only one chair, that the tables were supported on trestles, and that those who used them sat on forms or stools.

Similar information is afforded by "An Inventorie of the Colledg stuff remaining in the Masters Chamber" at S. John's College, taken just a century later, 10 March, 1546. It will be remembered that in this college the Master had resided from the beginning in a set of chambers specially set apart for him.

"*In the great Chamber at the ende of the Hall.*

A Portal of wainscott.
Item Hangings of owld red sai.
Item an owld cupbord.
Item a great Chest with plaiars raiment.
Item a table, ij trestells, and ij formes.

In the Middle Chamber.

First a portall of wainscott.
Item a table and ij trestells, and one forme.
Item a great Cofer of wainscot with plaiars apparell.

In the inner Chamber.

First a portall.
Item a bedstok with cortins of dornix, and testerne of the same. now being in the treasuri chamber.
Item a table with a chaiar in the same.
Item a stilletorie of Lede.

In the Chamber over the Chapple.

A table with a couer ouer, sometime an Altare, of wood.

In the Studdie.

Little presses to lai in papers and books.

In the vpper Chamber over the Chappelle

ij standing bedstedds.
Item a long cofer without a lok.

Item in an oyer Chamber.

A standing bedsted, and a trundle bedd[1]."

More sumptuous furniture gradually became the fashion, of which a few articles may be noticed. At Queens' College in 1528 the President's bed was ornamented with hangings on which a boar-hunt was represented, and blankets and feather-pillows are mentioned as though they were unusual luxuries[2]; in 1585—86 the old cushions are covered with red leather, and six new "turkey cushions" are bought; in 1612—13 a sum of £10. 10*s.* 7*d.* is spent on "hanging and matting the master's bedchamber"; and in 1613—14 we find a charge for "a carpet of broade cloth in the master's lodgeinge." A "Needle-Worke Carpett for the Lodging" was bought at Trinity College in 1648[3], at a cost of £6. In 1609—10 the Provost's Lodge at King's College was refurnished, on occasion of the death of Dr Goade, and the following list of articles, bought for the use of his successor, gives a vivid idea of the richness of the furniture then in fashion:

"Solut' pro . 6. Turky work heades of stooles with white grounds and lylly potts in ædibus Magistri Præpositi	xxiiij^{s}.
Item pro . 6. Turky worke heads of a sad greene	xx^{s}.
Item pro . 12. frames, fringe, Nayles etc ad conficiendum les stooles	Liiij^{s}.
Item pro le great red-leather chaire printed with gould, et 2 low stooles eiusdem operis	xvj s.
Item pro . 6. high stooles covered with redd leather and printed with gould	xx^{s}.
Item pro a standing feile (*sic*) bedd, green say curtaines and vallance, a Testar with three Curtan rodds......	v^{li}. iij^{s}. iiij^{d}.
Item pro a great chayre..	xviij^{s}. viij^{d}.

[1] [S. John's College Inventories etc., 1516—95, fo. 61^{a}. The document was kindly copied by Henry Bradshaw, M.A., University Librarian.]

[2] [Mag. Journ. 1528—29, fo. 116 b. "Item pro nova veste stragulata lecti magistri cum diuersis imaginibus aprorum et hominum venaticorum xxxviij^{s}. iiij^{d}. Item eodem die pro pari lodicum de ly fusthian hoc est blankettes xv^{s}. Item pro duobus cervicalibus plumarum mollium vj viij^{d}."]

[3] [Sen. Burs. Audit-Book, 1647—48. *Extraordinaries.*]

Item pro a little backChaire embrodred	viij^{s}.
Item pro a large Arras Coverlett	viij^{li}.
Item pro a fether bedd and boulster	iiij^{li}. x^{s}.
Item pro a quiltedd wool mattres	xj^{s}.
Item pro . 12 . thrummed quishions...........................	xliiij^{s}. vj^{d}.
Item pro a redd lether chaire and two low stooles	x^{s}.
Solut' pro . 2 . tapetis communiter vocat' arrace carpetts in vsum magistri Prepositi in cubiculo Auditoris	vij li.
Solut' pro a hanging presse in vsum eiusdem	xl s.[1]"

Before concluding this part of our subject we will quote some extracts from the Inventory taken at Christ's College in 1688 when Dr John Covel was elected Master. It will be observed that chairs have taken the place of forms, that the tables are no longer supported on trestles, and that carpets have become articles of ordinary use.

"*In the Maister's Lodging and House.*

A peice of perpetuana (blew) in two peices now in the Lodgings[2].
A long Turkey Carpet in the Meeting Roome.
A long Table there.
A Court cupboard.
One two arm'd chair: ten lesser chairs, and two old ones.
A Square Table in the Study in the Lodgings.
A Long Table in the Study in the House[3].
Two old Court Cupboards, one now in Mr Finch's chamber, the other decaid.
One old Screen; the cloath now about the Sizar's Bed.
One Leather Carpet in the Star Chamber, another of green Bays.
The Foundress bed-settle.
Six Cushions Turkey worke."

The Lodge not unfrequently contained a private oratory or chapel for the Master's use, as has been already pointed out in the Histories of the several colleges. The Inventory of S. John's College quoted above mentions an altar which had once existed in the Master's study; and probably in most cases these private oratories were nothing more than a portion of one of the Master's rooms set apart for devotional use, with an altar at which he had license to say mass.]

1 [Mundum Book, 1609—10, 1610—11. *Expense necessarie.*]

2 [Audit Book, Mich. 1660—Lady Day, 1661. "For 11 yards of Perpetuana for ye Window in ye Lodgings £1. 18. 6."]

3 [A building beyond the quadrangle to the north, used by the Master as a private residence. History of Christ's College, Vol. II. pp. 212—13.]

V.

THE HALL, THE KITCHEN, ETC.[1]

[THE position of the Hall at Oxford and Cambridge with reference to the other parts of the collegiate quadrangle has already been fully considered in the essay on the Collegiate Plan (p. 267). We have now to investigate its original arrangement, so far as this can be discovered from the existing buildings, or from documentary evidence.]

As might be expected, the principal features of the domestic hall of the fourteenth and fifteenth centuries are reproduced in the collegiate hall[2]. The high-table for the Master and Fellows was always placed on a raised dais at the upper end, the tables in the body of the hall being at right angles to it. In the centre there was frequently a brazier, with a louvre above it to let out the smoke; the roof was of open timber-work; and at the lower end there was a screen with a music-gallery.

The side-windows, in some of the older halls, as for instance at Pembroke College, Trinity Hall, and Corpus Christi College, came to within a few feet of the ground; in the later examples they were placed much higher up, to allow of space for the

[1] [This essay, like the last, was not written out by Professor Willis, and the collections which he had made for it were less complete. He left, however, a large quantity of notes and headings, from which I have done my best to gather his intentions, and I have carefully investigated those points which he had evidently selected for illustration.]

[2] [The whole subject of medieval Halls is exhaustively treated in Some Account of Domestic Architecture in England, by T. Hudson Turner, 8vo. Oxford, 1851; and in the continuations of the work by the Editor of the Glossary of Architecture.]

wainscot which had by that time come into fashion. The lower half of these windows was often left unglazed, and closed with wooden shutters[1].

An oriel-window, placed near the upper end of one of the side-walls, is to be found in nine of the Cambridge halls, viz.: at the colleges of Clare Hall (as shewn on Hammond's plan), Trinity Hall, Queens', Jesus, Christ's, S. John's, Emmanuel, and Sidney. There is also an oriel-window in the hall of Eton College. At Trinity College there are two, opposite to each other, as ordered in the Will of King Henry the Sixth for the halls of Eton College and King's College, and there were formerly two in the old hall of Corpus Christi College. At Peterhouse, Pembroke College, Gonville Hall, S. Catharine's Hall, and Magdalene College, there was no oriel. At Peterhouse Loggan shews at the upper end of the hall, on the side next to the court, a long narrow window divided by a transom, coming down to a much lower level than the other windows; and at Magdalene College there is a similar arrangement. The hall of Pembroke College had a range of windows in the side-walls at a uniform height, no difference being made for the high-table. The arrangements of the old halls of Gonville Hall, King's College, and S. Catharine's Hall, have not been recorded.

[Open roofs of timber were originally employed in all the older Cambridge halls of which we have any information, except in that of Pembroke College, where the library was over the hall; but, as explained in the separate histories, they were frequently concealed in the course of the last century by a flat ceiling, probably for the sake of warmth. There was a louvre in the centre of the roof at Trinity Hall, Christ's College, S. John's College, Magdalene College, Trinity College, and Emmanuel College. At Trinity Hall and Christ's College the louvre was merely fitted with boards for ventilation; at Emmanuel College it seems, from Loggan's view, to have been latticed; but in the other colleges it was a lofty structure in stages, with glazed windows, and terminating in a cupola or spire, ornamented with a vane of ironwork. At Magdalene College each of the six sides appears to have carried a sun-dial when Loggan's view was taken.

[1] [History of Gonville and Caius College, Vol. I. p. 196.]

In place of the louvre, and occasionally in addition to it, we find a bell-turret, usually placed over the through-passage at the lower end of the hall, as at Peterhouse, Clare Hall, Corpus Christi College, Queens' College, S. John's College, Trinity Hall, and Christ's College. At Jesus College and Sidney Sussex College it was over the lower end of the hall, and may possibly have served the further purpose of ventilation. At Magdalene College it was over the buttery. In many cases this structure closely resembled the louvre in general appearance, and might easily be mistaken for it. At Peterhouse the base was utilised for a clock on the side next to the court.

An entrance-porch, a common feature in domestic halls, was very sparingly employed in either University. At Oxford it is found at Merton College, and at Queen's College, as Loggan shews; at Oriel College there is a beautiful example of singular and unique design, giving common access to both hall and chapel; and at New College access to the hall is provided through a tower-porch, the upper floors of which are used as muniment-rooms. The Will of King Henry the Sixth gives directions for the halls of Eton College and King's College, Cambridge, which would probably have resulted in structures similar to this, as previously explained[1]. None of the existing halls at Cambridge have a porch, except the hall of Trinity College; but it has been already shewn that one existed in the old hall of King's College[2], and at King's Hall[3].

There was a brazier in the centre of the floor at Gonville Hall, Trinity Hall, Corpus Christi College, S. John's College, Trinity College, and Emmanuel College. At Corpus Christi College the brazier was replaced by a fireplace between 1487 and 1515[4]; but at Gonville Hall it remained until 1792[5]; at Trinity Hall until 1742[6]; at S. John's College until 1865[7]; and at Trinity College until 1866[8]. On the other hand there is a large

[1] [History of King's College, Vol. I. Chap. iv.] [2] [Ibid. p. 324.]

[3] [History of Trinity College, Vol. II. p. 440.]

[4] [History of Corpus Christi College, Vol. I. p. 263.]

[5] [History of Gonville and Caius College, Ibid. p. 197.]

[6] [History of Trinity Hall, Ibid. p. 234.]

[7] [History of S. John's College, Vol. II. p. 308.]

[8] [The brazier which was then removed had been bought in 1702—3. Jun. Burs. Accounts: "For a firegrate for the Hall, £12. 00. 00."]

fireplace, apparently original, at the following colleges: Peterhouse, Pembroke, Queens', Jesus, Christ's; and in the comparatively modern halls of Clare Hall and S. Catharine's Hall. At Eton College three fireplaces were intended, but, as explained in the History, they were never completed.]

At the lower end of the medieval collegiate hall there were two doorways in the lateral walls opposite to each other. One of these opened into the quadrangle of the college, and was the principal entrance into the hall; the other opened into a secondary court or garden beyond, so that the lower end of the hall was constantly employed as a thoroughfare from one court to the other. In the halls of the nobility and gentry this passage was separated from the body of the room by a transverse screen of ornamental work with a door at each extremity; and over the passage thus formed there was often a music-gallery. The windows were glazed, and the walls below them were clothed with wainscot.

These luxurious arrangements, however, were not provided for students until a later period than the foundation of the colleges; and we must suppose that for the two first centuries of collegiate establishments the walls of the refectory were as bare as those of the chambers. The same simplicity prevailed in monasteries, for even in the luxuriant arrangements of Durham there is no mention of a screen in the refectory, or Frater House, but in 1518 Prior Castell wainscoted both sides of it, two yards and a half in height above the stone bench which ran along the wall, and upon which the monks sat at meat[1]. The hall of Eton College was not wainscoted till 1547, before which date the walls had been concealed by hangings, put up soon after the completion of the building[2]. The contract for the roof and fittings of the hall at Queens' College, Cambridge, in 1449 makes no mention either of wainscot or screen[3]; neither does the contract for various wooden fittings in the original buildings of S. John's College in 1516, although it includes five doors which "shall be in the Halle in the same College, that is to say two Halle doores, a Botery doore, a pantere

1 [Rites of Durham, *ut supra*, p. 68.]
2 [History of Eton College, Vol. I. pp. 414, 451.]
3 [History of Queens' College, Vol. II. p. 10.]

doore, and a doore leadynge towards the Maister's Loggyng[1]." This contract would naturally have mentioned the screen, had it been proposed to erect one, for it includes a variety of fittings about the college, in the chapel, library, chambers, etc.

The old plan of Trinity College, which has been explained to have been drawn about 1595[2], shews a screen with two openings in the hall which then existed, and in the Inventory relating to this hall given below, the mention of "the Stocks above the Screen" proves that there was a gallery. The wainscot under the windows is also mentioned. We are, however, unable to assign any date to these fittings. The hall now in use was begun in 1604, a contract to wainscot it was drawn 21 February 1604—5, and the screen was begun in the same year. This appears to have been the first hall which was erected in Cambridge complete with screen, and wainscot lining under the windows and behind the high-table, all of which still exist. The gallery was used for music on great occasions even during the present century[3].

These conveniences had been introduced much earlier into the older halls. The hall of King's Hall seems to have been wainscoted in 1511—12, and a screen above or behind the high-table to have been made in 1514—15[4]. In earlier times the walls had been concealed by hangings, which are first mentioned in the Accounts for 1338—39[5]. At Corpus Christi College the hall,

[1] [History of S. John's College, Vol. II. p. 244.]

[2] [History of Trinity College, Ibid. p. 466, fig. 10.]

[3] [Charges for musical instruments are frequent in the Accounts, for instance: Sen. Burs. 1595—96. *Extraordinarie Charges.* "Imprimis for a sett of newe vialls viij^{li}. Item for viall strings and mending the Colledge Instrumentes xij^{s}. Item for a sackbutt and the Carriage iiij^{li}. xj^{s}." The present Master of Jesus College, George Elwes Corrie, D.D., who proceeded M.A. 1820, remembers that the successful prizemen of the year used to be called up to receive their prizes between the courses at the Commemoration Dinner. A band was stationed in the music-gallery, which played *Rule Britannia* and *See the Conquering Hero Comes* alternately, as each undergraduate came forward for his prize. Those, apparently, were the only tunes which the musicians knew.]

[4] [Accounts of King's Hall, Vol. XXI. p. 197, 1511—12. *Expense circa Aulam.* "In primis solutum est Cristofero Bradbanke pro di C le wanscot iiij markes." Ibid. p. 18, 1514—15 (the volume is bound incorrectly). "Item solutum est sculptori in partem solucionis quatuor librarum pro quadam tectura super altam mensam xx^{s}."]

[5] [Ibid. Vol. I. p. 35. "Item pro j dosser empt' pro aula xvj^{s}. q^{a}. Ibid. Vol. III. p. 223, 1382—83. "Inprimis pro Canefas empt' pro Docer aule ix^{s}. j^{d}. Item in clauis et hokys pro Doc' aule viij^{d}. Item pro factura doc' v^{s}."]

now the kitchen, was "wainscotted and fitted with three screens" between 1523 and 1544[1]. In explanation of this statement it may be remarked that the screen in the hall of the Manor House at Great Chalfield in Wiltshire is in three separate parts, and evidently had no doors[2]; [and that the hall of the Chetham Hospital at Manchester, which is believed to have been completed about 1425, has at its lower end three original screens of oak, each about 8 feet high by 5 feet broad, one central, and one abutting against each side-wall. The central screen masks the two doors which lead to the butteries; the lateral screens those which lead to the cloisters and the outer court respectively. The cresting of the cornice of these screens, and the profile of their uprights, shew that there could never have been either music-gallery or doors in this hall.] The screen at Hampton Court, set up in the reign of King Henry the Eighth, had no doors to its two openings. The hall of S. John's College was wainscoted between 1528 and 1529, but, as mentioned in the History of the College (p. 309), there is evidence that a screen was then already in existence. The doors are modern. At Queens' College the walls of the hall were concealed by hangings until 1531, when it was elaborately wainscoted with linen panelling. The screen was probably of the same date. The doors were added in 1628[3]. At Trinity Hall the screen and music-gallery above it were not made until 1566, and the doors were not added until thirty years later, in 1596, the cost being defrayed out of a special bequest made for that purpose[4]. At Magdalene College the hall was not wainscoted until 1586, by the munificence of Mr Lucas; but nothing is said about the screen. The present panelwork, together with the screen and staircase leading to the Combination Room, was put up in 1719[5]. At Jesus College a screen is mentioned as in existence in 1567. It was replaced by a new one in 1610—11,

1 [History of Corpus Christi College, Vol. I. p. 263.]

2 [Examples of Gothic Architecture, by A. W. Pugin, and T. L. Walker, Architects, 4to. London, Vol. III. 1840, pp. 23—48, Plate XVII.]

3 [History of Queens' College, Vol. II. pp. 44—46. The hangings had been put up in 1504—5. A charge "pro nouis pendentibus siue anabatris aule" occurs in the Magnum Journale of that year, fo. 177 b.]

4 [History of Trinity Hall, Vol. I. pp. 233—235.]

5 [History of Magdalene College, Vol. II. pp. 364, 380—382.]

which in its turn was removed in 1703, when the present panelwork was erected. The hangings appear to have been first put up in 1569—70, and from the numerous charges for lining and repairs, must have consisted of tapestry, which extended beyond the dais, from an allusion to the "piece of Arresse over the chimneye[1]." At Gonville Hall the hangings (*peristromata*) were bought in 1481; but the panelwork appears not to have been put up until 1625, or shortly before[2]. At Pembroke College the walls of the hall were concealed by hangings as usual; but the screen was not put up until 1634[3]. At Peterhouse the hall was wainscoted in 1589—90; but the screen was not put up until 1638[4]. At Emmanuel College, where the hall had been wainscoted before 1589, the doors were not added until 1716[5]. At Trinity College the doors are evidently, by their style, much later than the screen. They were probably added either in 1698 or 1703, when the Accounts shew that extensive work was done to the screen by Austin.

At New College, Oxford, the hall was not wainscoted until 1532[6]; at Balliol College in 1539[7]; at Merton College in 1540[8]; and at Magdalen College in 1541[9].

In addition to the hangings which covered the side-walls, several colleges had pieces of tapestry over the dais. At Peterhouse "the Cloth of Arras" in the hall is mentioned[10]; at Clare Hall there were two pieces of tapestry, one of which represented the Story of the Turks[11]; at Trinity Hall there was a single piece representing a Roman Triumph[12]; at Eton College there were

1 [History of Jesus College, Vol. II. p. 161.]

2 [History of Gonville and Caius College, Vol. I. pp. 169, 197. Professor Willis infers the date of construction of the wainscot from the charge for painting it, which occurs in the Bursar's Accounts for 1625.]

3 [History of Pembroke College, Vol. I. p. 149.]

4 [History of Peterhouse, Ibid. pp. 19, 62.]

5 [Bursar's Accounts of Emmanuel College, *Exp. since* 29 *October*, 1716. "Paid Mr. Goodal Executor of Mr. Kettel for the Hall Doors 01 . 19 . 0."]

6 [Wood, *ut supra*, p. 194. Ingram's Memorials, New College, p. 20.]

7 [Wood, *ut supra*, p. 89.]

8 [Ingram's Memorials, Merton College, p. 13.]

9 [Wood, *ut supra*, p. 327.]

10 [History of Peterhouse, Vol. I. p. 19.]

11 [An early Inventory of the goods belonging to Clare Hall, preserved in the Master's Lodge, enumerates in the Hall: "Item j docer de tapstery precii xxvjs. viijd. Item j docer de rubeo say precii xxs. Item j docer depict' de historia ottomanorum precii xiijs. iiijd."]

12 [History of Trinity Hall, Vol. I. p. 233.]

two pieces, representing the Flight into Egypt, and Christ among the Doctors[1]; at Christ's College there was tapestry of some kind, but the nature of it has not been recorded[2]; and at S. John's College a piece of tapestry was given by the Countess of Shrewsbury in 1615, to replace an older one the presence of which may be inferred from a payment in 1610—11 for "a cord to hang the clothe in the hall[3]." The upper end of the old hall at Trinity College was also adorned in a similar manner, as shewn by the following Inventory, taken in 1560:

"*In the Hall.*

Imprimis Hanginges of Arrasse in the vpper end of the Hall, two grete clothes, tone aboue tother, and two lesse by the sides.

Item A mappe of thoole world sett in a Frame.

Item the Kinges Armes vppon the vpper Hanginges.

Item seven Tables.

Item three Joyned trustles vnder the highe table.

Item a joynid Chare for the maister.

Item three joynid fourmes for the highe table.

Item a joynid Cupbord in the grete wyndow and thre double casementes of Iron in it.

Item two single casementes in the wyndowe against the great wyndow.

Item a Latin bible and a standing lectron.

Item six playn fourmes for the syde tables.

Item a Payr of Stockes aboue the screne.

Item thre great dooble casementes of Iron beneth in the Hall one of tone side two of tother.

Item selyng of waynscott by the side of the Hall to the nether part of the wyndows.

Two Playt candlestyches Hanging of the wall[4]."

To this Inventory we will append another, taken at Emmanuel College, 22 October, 1589:

"*In the Hall.*

One table of deale for the Fellowes with 2 formes.

Four of deale for the Schollers, with 7 formes.

One of oak for the Steward, with two formes.

To every Table belongeth 3 Tressels.

Two syde Tables in the great wyndow with 2 formes.

[1] [History of King's College and Eton College, Ibid. p. 452.]

[2] [Audit-Book of Christ's College, 1577—78. *Exp. forinsece.* "Item to an Arris man for mendinge y[e] hanginges and cussinges in the dyninge chamber, xviij[d]."]

[3] [History of S. John's College, Vol. II. p. 311. Audit-Book, 1610—11.]

[4] [This Inventory and the following are preserved in the Treasuries of Trinity College and Emmanuel College respectively.]

A Chayre for the Mayster.
A deske to reade att.
Eight glass wyndowes with the Queen's Armes in both the baye wyndowes.
Four casements.
One hand dyall pertayning to the clock.
One movable hearth of Ironn.
Three benches.
Seeling of waynscott throwout the hall.
The Queenes Armes at the vpper end of the hall fayre gylt with our founders Armes vnderneath."

The three benches of the last Inventory no doubt refer to the seats which were fixed against the side-walls of the hall, and behind the high-table. In the hall of Trinity College those attached to the side-walls still exist, and that at the upper end was not removed until 1866. The practice of supporting the tables on trestles, and of seating everybody except the Master on forms, was so universal that it is needless to cite extracts from the Accounts in support of it[1].

[The forms, but probably only those at the high-table, were covered with cushions. As early as 1338—39 a "banker" is mentioned in connection with the hall at King's Hall[2]; but in later times cushions, stuffed with feathers, and covered with red leather or tapestry-work, are mentioned in other colleges. At Christ's College we find :

"Item for mending and newe lethering the Colledge Quisshens v^{s}.
Item for vij skyns of red lether for the same iiij^{s}. j^{d}.
Item for v pound of fethers for one of the colledge cusshins xxij^{d}."[3]

And again at Trinity College:

"For mending the six cushons in the Hall 00 . 01 . 06.[4]
For 14 Turkeywork Cushons for ye Hall 03 . 10 . 00."[5]

1 [The earliest instance I have met with is at King's Hall in 1523—24, when 2 tables and six "tripodes" were ordered; each table was to be 16 feet long, by 3 feet wide, and 2½ inches thick. In the Inventory from Clare Hall quoted above we find, in addition to the Master's chair: "Item j alia cathedra pro extraneo vel generoso precii xvj^{d}." Compare Some Account of Domestic Architecture in England, from Richard II. to Henry VIII. By the Editor of the Glossary of Architecture. 8vo. Oxford, 1859, Vol. I. p. 79.]

2 [Accounts of King's Hall, Vol. I. p. 35. After other charges for the Hall, "Item pro j Banker, iij^{s}."]

3 [Audit-Book, 1564—65, 1565—66.]

4 [Jun. Burs. Accounts, 1676—77.]

5 [Ibid. 1694—95.]

The wainscot above the high-table was in general more richly ornamented than the rest of the woodwork, with the exception of the screen. The finest example of this is to be found at S. John's College, as already described[1]. It was also usual to place the arms of the sovereign, with those of the founder of the college, in the centre of the gable-wall at this end of the hall, above the wainscot.

A lavatory, as in the domestic halls, was provided in those of some at least of the colleges, but, as no example has been preserved, we do not know in what part of the building it was usually placed. A lavatory of lead was made in the hall of King's Hall in 1399—1400[2], and indications of the existence of a similar convenience are to be found at Queens' College and at Christ's College, but in these latter instances the existence of the lavatory has to be inferred from the payments for towels. At Queens' College in 1579—80 "a towell of viij yeardes att xix*d.* the yarde for the Fellowes" is bought[3]; at Christ's College in 1554—55 "ix yeardes of Ossenbrydge for a towell to the hye tabyll"; and at Trinity College in 1612—13 "a hooke to hang a towell on in the hall" is paid for. The following curious document from the Register of Christ's College appears to indicate that at the end of the sixteenth century the custom of taking up food with fingers instead of forks still prevailed:

"It is agreed betwixte the m^r^ and the fellowes that they shall every one of them have ij table napkins bought by the Colledge of this condition that every fellowe at his departure shall deliver vnto the master ij whole table napkins for the use of his successoure, and this to be observed from time to time. Also it is agreed that if either fellowe or pensioner do wipe his hande or fingers of the table clothe he shall pay for every time j^d^. to the vse of the commins, whereunto the master and fellowes have set to theyre handes the . 24 . daye of October, 1575[4]."]

Stocks are included among the furniture of the hall at

1 [History of S. John's College, Vol. II. p. 309.]

2 [History of Trinity College, Vol. II. p. 439. In 1459—60 an entry occurs which shews that the lavatory was then external to the hall in the cloister: Accounts of King's Hall, Vol. XII. p. 271. *Expense circa Aulam.* "In reparacione lauacri in claustro ij^s^."]

3 [The Magnum Journale for 1530—31, fo. 137, records a repair "graduum ubi lavamus manus," but no hint of the situation of the lavatory is given.]

4 [Register of Christ's College, p. 1. Compare Some Account of Domestic Architecture in England from Edward I. to Richard II. By the Editor of the Glossary of Architecture. 8vo. Oxford, 1853, p. 64.]

Trinity College in 1560 (p. 361). They also occur in an Inventory of the hall of Emmanuel College, dated 5 May, 1642; and at Christ's College stocks are bought or repaired in 1624—25[1], but their position is not recorded. It may be presumed that they were intended for the punishment of undergraduates; but the only document affirming their employment for this purpose is a decree dated 8 May, 1571, in which John Whitgift, D.D., Master of Trinity College and Vice-Chancellor, and the other Heads, ordain, that no person *in statu pupillari* is to presume to bathe in a river, pond, or any other water within the County of Cambridge under pain of receiving a severe flogging in public in the common hall in the presence of the Fellows, Scholars, and all other members of his college; and, further, if the delinquent be a Bachelor of Arts, he is to have his feet tied, to be set in the stocks for a whole day in the common hall of his college, and to pay a fine of ten shillings towards the commons of all the members of the college before he is let out[2].

The duty of being regularly present in hall at dinner and supper, and of behaving, while there, with the utmost quiet and decorum, is insisted upon in nearly all the collegiate statutes of both Universities. In the course of the meal a portion of the Bible was to be read aloud by one of the scholars, during which reading silence was to be observed, or, if speech could not be avoided, remarks were to be expressed in Latin, Greek, Hebrew, or at least French. Penalties, more or less severe, were to be inflicted for disobedience. The injunctions enforcing these rules are expressed in such identical language in the successive codes of statutes, that it will be unnecessary to make more than one or two quotations from them at length. For instance, the statutes of Merton House (1270) and of Merton College (1274) prescribe a reader at meals, and silence while he is reading. If the scholars wish to converse in their chambers, they are to use Latin. These rules are enforced with greater minuteness by Archbishop Peckham, from whose injunctions (1284) the following curious passage may be translated:

[1] [Audit-Book of Christ's College, 1624—25. "To the carpenter for the stocks 0. 4. 8."]

[2] [Statuta Academiæ Cantabrigiensis, p. 453; copied by Dyer, Privileges of the University, I. 303.]

"In future ye are to have a reader at meals, whom we enjoin to read before you the *Moralia* of Gregory[1], or some other edifying work easy of comprehension; and we desire that ye keep silence while the reading is going on, lest the unbridled license of a garrulous tongue give evidence of an ill-ordered mind, as a depraved daughter follows the steps of an infamous mother. We give leave, however, to speak at all times both at meals and elsewhere, when there is necessity; but always briefly and modestly; as we read in the Gospel of S. John that Martha called Mary secretly[2]. All public conversation, however, must be carried on in a learned language[3]."

The next Oxford code, the statutes for Oriel College (1326), prescribes the reading of the Bible or of some holy book at meals; and directs that the students, even in their chambers, are to speak, as far as possible, in Latin, or at least in French. At Peterhouse, Cambridge (1344), the Deans are to decide "who is to read at table, what part of the Bible or other authentic Scripture he is to read, and at what period of the meal he is to begin his reading." Silence is to be observed, and any scholar who infringes this rule is to be punished at the discretion of the Master. The custom still prevailed at this college in 1629[4]. At Clare Hall it was provided that all the Fellows, Scholars, and Perendinants, should repair to the hall when the Bell rang, and there dine and sup together, because "not only is it decent and orderly, but tends to the common advantage, that members of the same family should not take their food in hiding-places and corners, like wild beasts, but in some common dining-room." As soon as the dishes were put on table, one of the scholars was to read a portion of Holy Scripture selected by the Master or his deputy; no language except Latin was to be used in hall, or anywhere else within the precincts of the college. At New College, Oxford (1400), the reading of the Bible in hall is directed, together with the use of the Latin language, both there and in all other parts of the college, cloister, and gardens. Moreover there is to be no lingering in hall after dinner or supper, except on Saints'

1 [S. Gregory the Great, *Moralia in Job.*] 2 [John xi. 28.]

3 [Commiss. Docts. (Oxford) Vol. I. Statutes etc. of Merton College, pp. 13, 26, 43. The original words of the last sentence are: "Ita tamen, quod literaliter omnia semper in publico invicem præferantur." In the statutes of 1270 the phrase is: "non aliter quam idiomate regulari."]

4 [Audit-Book, 1628—29: "Et de iiij^{d}. pro membranis in vsum Bibliotistæ legentis in aula."]

Days and holy days in winter, when a fire is lighted; on these occasions "a reasonable time may be spent in the hall in singing and in some other decorous recreation; or in the serious reading of poems, the chronicles of kings, the marvels of the world, and other subjects becoming the clerical profession[1]." Directions similar to these in principle, but less elaborate, are to be found in all the Oxford statutes down to those of Worcester College (1714). At Cambridge, reading during dinner was not always insisted on in the statutes, but it can be shewn that it was a matter of practice in every college except Magdalene. The statutes of Peterhouse and Clare Hall have been already quoted; those of Michael House do not mention the subject, but we learn from another document that two scholars were expected to read the Bible during dinner on alternate weeks, and that Latin was always to be spoken in hall[2]; those of King's Hall prescribed the use of Latin, or at least French, in hall, but are silent about the reader. We learn however from an entry in the Accounts for 1514—15 that a Life of Christ was read publicly, probably in the hall[3]. At Gonville Hall, Bishop Bateman directed that one of the Fellows, or some other person, should read the Holy Scriptures in hall[4], to which Dr Caius added that all the Fellows and pensioners were to speak Latin in hall and chapel, under pain of being deprived of their commons for the day during the greater part of which they had not used that language[5]. At Trinity Hall the statutes are silent, but we know from Cole's description of the hall that a "Desk for the Chapter in Latin while at Dinner and Supper" still existed, and was apparently still used, in 1742[6]. At Corpus Christi College the statutes prescribed the use of Latin in full term, and the reading

[1] [Commiss. Docts. (Oxford) Vol. I. Statutes of New College, p. 41.]

[2] [In the orders made by Michael House, 18 February, 1484, for the two scholars dependent on the bounty of Robert Turke and Bartholomew Seman, it is provided: "Item dicti duo scolares tenentur legere bibliam in aula tempore prandii alternando hebdomadas. Item continue in prandio et in cena loquentur Latinum et non Anglicum sine licentia magistri." Otryngham Book, fo. 33.]

[3] [Accounts of King's Hall, XXI. p. 18. "In primis solutum est pro quodam libro de vita Ihesu pro lectore biblie v[s]."]

[4] [A Latin Bible was bought for the Hall in 1624. History of Gonville and Caius College, Vol. I. p. 197.]

[5] [Commiss. Docts. II. pp. 229, 247.]

[6] [History of Trinity Hall, Vol. I. p. 233.]

of the Bible in hall by one of the poor Scholars[1]. At Eton College (1444) one of the collegers (*scholares*), deputed by the Head Master, is to read during dinner out of the Bible, the Lives of the Fathers, the Doctors of the Church, or some other devout work[2]. This custom was maintained until about twenty years ago, whenever the Provost and Fellows dined in hall. At King's College the provisions of Wykeham for New College were copied, as usual, almost literally, and the Mundum-Books contain numerous entries for binding and repairing the hall-bible. At Queens' College "a Bible to read in the Hall" was bought in 1590—91[3], and the statutes direct the Fellows to speak in Latin while there, unless the President or his deputy give them leave to speak in their mother tongue, under pain of a fine of one penny for each offence[4]. This injunction was affirmed towards the end of the seventeenth century by the following Orders[5]:

"Octob: 26: 1676. It was decreed by ye unanimous consent of ye President and Fellows that noething but Latine be spoken in ye Hall at dinner and supper (not onely in Term but out of Term) by all Gownmen constantly excepting All Scarlett-days, ye twelve days at Christmas, and commemoration of Benefactors. present and assenting Mr Vice-President [and 10 Fellows].

[*Signed*] H. James Præs.

Memor'. It was desir'd and consented to that English may be spoken on Sundays and Holidays, and ye Decree in force as to all other times.

Sep. 13. 1680. [Signed] H. J."

At S. Catharine's Hall a portion of the Bible is to be read daily in hall by a Bible-clerk, and no language but Latin is to be used, except on festivals, or when strangers are present[6]. At Jesus College no language but Latin is to be spoken within the college precincts, and as soon as the dishes have been put on the table, a portion of the Bible is to be read "after the manner of a lesson, in a loud clear voice[7]." This custom was still in force in 1664—65, from a charge in the Audit Book "for

[1] [Commiss. Docts. II. pp. 454, 458.]

[2] [Statutes of Eton College, etc., ed. Heywood and Wright, p. 532.]

[3] [Magn. Journ. 1590—91, fo. 25.]

[4] [Commiss. Docts. III. p. 31.]

[5] [Old Parchment Register of Queens' College, fo. 157 b.]

[6] [Commiss. Docts. III. pp. 83, 84.]

[7] [Ibid. p. 113.]

the Desk in the Hall which the schollars read upon." At Christ's College the statutes are silent, but the Accounts shew that the Bible was read in hall from the foundation to the end of the 17th century. "A lectryn to the byble in the hall" is bought in 1533—34; "a desk for the hall" in 1651—52; a "Latin Bible for the Hall" in 1661—62; and the Hall-Bible is bound in 1672. [The following amusing extract from one of the letters written by Joseph Mede, Fellow of Christ's College, to Sir Martin Stuteville, illustrates this part of our subject. The letter in which it occurs is dated "Christ's College, 9 Aprill, 1625," and in the earlier part of it the writer had mentioned the death of King James I.:

"I haue no more vnless I tell you a Colledge jest. Our boyes were so confounded with the feare of missing when they changed in the Grace *Carolum Regem* for *Jacobum Regem* that a Batchelor this week being *Lector Bibliorum* as he was reading in the Psalmes at dineing, lighting there vpon *Deus Jacobi* afore he was aware, corrected himselfe and read *Deus Caroli*, and presently apprehending his error said againe *Deus Jacobi*, but could scarce go on he was so amased[1]."

At S. John's College Bishop Fisher's statutes (1530) direct the habitual use of Latin, Greek, or Hebrew; and that one of eight students who are to serve in hall is to read the Bible during dinner[2]. The statutes given by Queen Elizabeth to Trinity College (1559—60) direct that

"Six or more Bible-clerks, who know how to sing, and have clear voices, shall be appointed by the Deans. These are to take weeks in turn, and on each day to chant a chapter of the Bible, so distinctly that all may hear, and pronounce the words so clearly and articulately that all may understand what they hear. The reader is to place his desk in the middle [of the hall], a little above the brazier; and while he is reading all the Fellows, Scholars, and Pensioners are to keep silence[3]."

These statutes, however, only confirmed an existing practice, for in the Accounts for 1554—55 a payment occurs "for a lectron in the Hall for the reading of the bible"; and "a latin bible and a standing lectron" are mentioned in the Inventory of the furniture

[1] [MSS. Harl. Mus. Brit. No. 389.]

[2] [Statutes of S. John's College, ed. Mayor, p. 38. These rules are repeated in Henry VIII.'s statutes, 1545.]

[3] [Statutes of Trinity College, in "Appendix to Reports from Select Committee on Education"; ordered by the House of Commons to be printed 5 June, 1818.]

of the hall taken in 1560 (p. 361). This lectern was afterwards replaced by another, of which it is recorded that:

"Robert Beaumont Master [1561–67] gave the Brass Stand or Rest for the Bible in the Hall, cum hac Inscriptione, nunc avulsâ:

Beaumontus Præses dedit atque volumina sacra
Dumtaxat voluit vetuitque Papistica ferre[1]."

At Emmanuel College (1585), the Bible is to be read in hall, and Latin is to be spoken, so far as the Master thinks it expedient; at Sidney Sussex College the statutes given by the executors of the Foundress prescribe the reading of the Bible at dinner and supper, but the use of Latin is not enforced[2].]

The custom of publicly reading the Bible in hall, which, as we have shewn, was nearly universal in the colleges of both Universities, was evidently borrowed from the monasteries. The following description, from the "Rites of Durham," may be cited as an example. The writer is describing the arrangements for the dinner and supper of the novices:

"At which tyme the master observed this holsome and godlie order for the contynewallie instructing of ther youth in vertew and lerning, that is, one of the Novicies, at the election and appoyntment of the master, dyd reade summe parte of the Old and New Testamment, in Latten, in dynner tyme, having a convenyent place at the southe end of the hie table with in a faire glasse wyndowe, invyroned with iron, and certaine steppes of stone with iron rayles of th' one syde to goe up to it, and to support an iron deske there placed, upon which laie the Holie Bible, where one of the Novicies elected by the master was appointed to read a chapter of the Old or New Testament in Latten as aforesaid in tyme of dynner, which being ended, the master dyd toule a gilden bell, hanging over his hed, therby givinge warnynge to one of the Novicies to cumme to the hie table and saie grace, and so, after grace said, they departed to their bookes[3]."

[No example of the desk which was used by the Hall-Reader has, so far as we are aware, been preserved in either University[4].

[1] [MSS. Baker XI. 321, MSS. Harl. Mus. Brit. 7038.]

[2] [Commiss. Docts. III. 505, 568.]

[3] [Rites of Durham, *ut supra*, p. 69. Among the "Catalogi veteres Librorum Ecclesiæ Cathedralis Dunelm." ed. Surtees Soc. 1838, p. 80, a catalogue occurs of the "Libri pro Refectorio"; explained in the sub-title to be intended "pro lectura in refectorio."]

[4] [The author of Some Account of Domestic Architecture in England from Richard II. to Henry VIII., published 1859, mentions (Part I. p. 71) that "a brass eagle remained till recently in Magdalen College hall, Oxford, from which Scripture was read during meals. When the custom ceased, the piece of furniture was discarded."]

From some of the notices which we have collected it would appear to have been a lectern such as is used in churches, and occasionally to have been raised on a half-pace, and to have had the book for the reader's use attached to it by a chain[1]. The desk which was used at Eton, at least in later times, still exists (fig. 1). It is a plain frame of hammered iron fastened to the western jamb of the oriel, so that the reader might have his face turned towards the high-table[2].

Fig. 1. Desk for the Bible-Reader in the Hall of Eton College.

The warming of the hall, whether effected by brazier or by fire-place, was evidently insufficient; for the stone floor was strewn with rushes in earlier times, as is frequently mentioned

[1] [King's College Mundum-Book, 1573-74 *Exp. necess.* "Item for a cheyne to the deske in the hall, x[d]."]

[2] [In the sixteenth century a lectern raised on steps seems to have been in use: Accounts, 1568—69. *Exp. necess.* "for makynge ij. halfe paces in the hawle for the bybeler to stand upon."]

in the Accounts of King's Hall, and towards the end of the last century, at least in Trinity College, with sawdust. It was laid on the floor at the beginning of winter, and turned over with a rake as often as the upper surface became dirty; finally, when warm weather set in, it was removed, the colour of charcoal[1].

The hall was used for other purposes besides dinner and supper. Disputations in some colleges were held there; and the presence of a map of the world, with which the halls of at least Trinity College (p. 361) and S. John's College[2], Cambridge, were furnished, may indicate that, in those colleges, the hall served for a lecture-room, as elsewhere for a theatre at Christmas. At Peterhouse in 1571—72 a stage was set up, and a comedy performed in the hall[3]; at King's College in 1548 a company of players belonging to the Duke of Somerset, Lord Protector, who was also Chancellor of the University, gave a performance in the hall, followed shortly by another given by the King's troupe[4]; at Queens' College in the same year a play was given, apparently in the hall, but the interpretation of the entries in the Account-Book is extremely difficult; and at Jesus College in 1577 the following decisive entry occurs:

> "Item delivered to Mr Wilshawe ye v^th^ of Januarie towardes the Stage and other charges of the Comedie played publiklie in the hawlle in Christmas. viz. Anno Domini, 1577."

At Trinity College the statutes given by Queen Elizabeth (in 1559—60) prescribe the annual performance of plays in the hall during the twelve days of Christmas under the direction of the nine lecturers (*lectores*). The head-lecturer (*primus lector*) is to

[1] [This description of the former condition of the Hall was communicated to a general meeting of the Fellows of Trinity College, 15 December, 1865, by Adam Sedgwick, M.A., Woodwardian Professor of Geology. He concluded his speech by saying "The dirt was sublime in former years."]

[2] [Audit-Book of S. John's College, 1519—20. *Custus Aule.* "j tabula de Cosmegraphia vj^s^. viij^d^. j pomponius mela super Cosmegraphia iiij^s^." It is worth noticing that Pomponius Mela was the only work on geography used at Eton College until within fifty years ago.]

[3] [Bursar's Accounts, 1571—72: "Et de vij^s^. vj^d^. Jacobo Silcocke edificanti theatrum in aula pro comedia. Et de ij^s^. vj^d^. pro duodecim libris candelarum pro comedia."]

[4] [King's College Mundum-Book, 1547—48. *Feoda et Regarda.* "Item 21mo. Junii famulo .D. protectoris exhibentis ludicra spectacula in aula collegii vj^s^. Item .2. Julii ludionibus regiis exhibentibus spectacula in Aulâ vj^s^."]

represent either a comedy or a tragedy; the remaining eight are to divide four plays among them, either comedies or tragedies, one of each being entrusted to two lecturers. The performances may be public or private. If these directions be not carried out, each lecturer who is to blame is to pay a fine of ten shillings. Plays were accordingly performed regularly in the hall of Trinity College for a considerable number of years, as shewn by the entries in the Audit-Book, but towards the end of the seventeenth century they were given up[1]. On the occasion of the visits of King James I. in 1615, plays, including the celebrated comedy *Ignoramus*, written by George Ruggle, Fellow of Clare Hall, were acted before him in this hall. Again, as Sir Symonds d'Ewes informs us, a play called *Stoicus vapulans*, "was very well acted in the hall of our house," namely, S. John's College, at Christmas, 1618[2]. It is much to be regretted that no record has been preserved of the way in which these plays were given. We may be sure that considerable splendour of decoration was successfully attempted, for otherwise Roger Ascham, writing from Antwerp to his friend Edward Raven, Fellow of S. John's College, 1 October, 1550, would hardly have tried to give him an idea of the magnificence of the city by saying that it surpassed all others which he had visited, as much as the hall of his college, when decorated for a play at Christmas, surpassed its appearance at ordinary times[3].

We must next briefly describe the position of the kitchen and other offices with reference to the hall.

The description and plan of Haddon Hall (p. 271) shews that the passage entered from the hall-porch contained, on the

[1] [The performances appear to have been the cause of considerable damage being done to the windows, probably by those who were not present. Charges such as the following are frequent: Jun. Burs. 1565—66. *Charges for the Hall.* "2° Feb. Item for settinge in of lvj quarrells of glasse wch wear broken at ye plaies iiij^s. viij^d. Item for repairinge of the hall after the plaies ended xij^d." In 1598—99 precautions were taken to prevent a repetition of this mischief. Ibid. *Extraordinaries.* "Item given to those that watched the glasse windowes one the Comodie night and for torches wch they vsed vi^s." For a disturbance of this kind at King's College in 1606—7, see Cooper's Annals, III. 24.]

[2] ["College Life in the time of James the First, as illustrated by an unpublished diary of Sir Symonds D'Ewes." 8vo. Lond. 1851, p. 61.]

[3] ["Rogeri Aschami Epistolarum Libri Quatuor." 8vo. Oxoniæ, 1703, p. 228.]

side opposite to the doors of the hall, three openings. That in the centre led, through a long passage, to the kitchen, and the two others, in this instance, opened into the buttery and wine-cellar respectively; the pantry being placed between the cellar and the kitchen, and entered from the passage leading to the latter. In most examples it is entered directly from the through-passage at the lower end of the hall.

This arrangement of three doors, leading to the buttery, kitchen, and pantry respectively, which Professor Willis calls "the triple arcade," was the normal arrangement of a medieval manor-house, and was copied in most of the older colleges at Cambridge. It may have existed at Peterhouse, where, as the plan shews, the buttery is entered from the through-passage, and the passage to the kitchen turns suddenly to the left, in a way which is probably the result of a modern alteration to enlarge the buttery. The plan of Trinity Hall, made in 1731, before the hall and offices were altered by Burrough, shews the triple arcade very distinctly. It also, in all probability, existed at Corpus Christi College, and at Magdalene College, and it is shewn on the old plan of Trinity College (History of the College, fig. 10). It may still be seen, unaltered, at Queens' College, at Christ's College, and at S. John's College.

A "double arcade," as Professor Willis calls it, existed at Pembroke College before the recent changes, as shewn on the plan of that college (fig. 2), and still exists at Emmanuel College, and at Sidney Sussex College[1]. In this arrangement there are only two doorways, one of which opens into the passage leading to the kitchen, the other into the buttery. It was adopted in the modern buildings of Clare Hall and S. Catharine's Hall.

The kitchen was in a line with the hall, and formed part of the same range of building, in all the colleges where the triple arcade is found, except Christ's College, where, though it is in a line with the hall, it is external to the quadrangle. It also formed part of one of the sides of the quadrangle at Trinity

[1] [Trinity College might be quoted as an instance of the double arcade, but it is probable that the third door existed there originally, and that it was removed (1771—74) when the present Combination Room was built, with the staircase leading to it. History of Trinity College, Vol. II. p. 606.]

College before the present hall was built; and it is similarly placed at Clare Hall and Sidney Sussex College. At Catharine Hall it is in the same line as the hall, but forms part of a separate building. At King's Hall it was placed on the north side of the hall, but in such a position that it formed one side of the quadrangle; at Gonville Hall it was external to the quadrangle on the west side; and in the buildings described for King's College in the Will of King Henry VI. it would have formed one side of a small court on the west side of the hall. The colleges of Jesus and Emmanuel present somewhat abnormal arrangements, both being founded on sites previously occupied by monastic buildings which were altered to collegiate use. At Jesus College the larder and kitchen form part of the range at right angles to the hall, while the buttery is beneath it; at Emmanuel College the buttery is in the range which contains the hall, but the kitchen is at right angles to it on the north. At Trinity College the kitchen is partly in the hall-range, partly external to it, an arrangement probably dictated for convenience of access.

The above enumeration has shewn that at Cambridge there were at least seven examples of "the triple arcade." At Oxford, on the contrary, no instance of it is to be found; and the kitchens are generally external to the original quadrangle, though in some instances they have subsequently been built into, and now form part of, a subsidiary quadrangle. External kitchens are to be found at the following fourteen colleges: Merton, University, Oriel, Queen's, New College, Lincoln, All Souls, Magdalen, Brasenose, Corpus, Christ Church, Trinity, S. John's, Wadham. At Exeter College, as shewn by Loggan, the hall, buttery, and kitchen formed the greater part of one side of the principal quadrangle, the kitchen being in the corner, between the hall-range and that at right angles to it; and a similar arrangement still exists at Jesus College. These, however, are exceptional instances, the external kitchen being evidently the arrangement which was preferred. Here again we have an instance of the imitative spirit which influenced collegiate architecture; for no sooner had this arrangement been once adopted than it was copied over and over again with slight modifications.

It was usual, as pointed out in the different collegiate historie to lay out a small garden contiguous to the kitchen for the use of the cook (*hortus coci*). A bakehouse, and, if practicable, a brewhouse, were also provided, especially in the early colleges. In connection with the former we find a barn at S. John's College, King's College, and Pembroke College. Storehouses for salt fish, and salt provisions generally, were also not uncommon. At King's College the early Account-books contain numerous entries referring to a slaughter-house, and a skin-house, in which the skins of the animals were dried before they were sold.]

VI.

THE COMBINATION ROOM[1].

A ROOM called the "Common House" or "Common Hall," and occasionally *Pisalis* or *Calefactorium*, formed part of every Benedictine Monastery[2]. It is even found noted on the plan of the Monastery of S. Gall in Switzerland which is believed to have been drawn in the ninth century[3]. It was always placed beneath the Dormitory, and looked out upon a garden or green. This room,

[1] [This Essay, like that on the Hall, had not been written out by Professor Willis, but the collections which he had made for it indicate very clearly what he intended to write. In consequence, though the greater part of the language is mine, I have not used square brackets until near the end, where the statements respecting the Common Room at Oxford, and the furniture of the Combination Room at Cambridge, depend for the most part on my own researches.]

[2] [Architectural History of the Cathedral and Monastery at Worcester. By Rev. R. Willis. 8vo. Lond. 1863, p. 68. Architectural History of the Conventual Buildings of the Monastery of Christ Church in Canterbury; by Rev. R. Willis. 8vo. Lond. 1869, p. 27.]

[3] [Description of the Antient Plan of the Monastery of S. Gall. By Rev. R. Willis. Archæol. Journ. Vol. v. 1848, p. 16. The word "Pisalis," spelt also "Piselis" and "Piselum," is explained by Ducange, among other definitions, as "conclave vaporario vel fornacula calefactum, unde Gall. *Poêle;*" and again, quoting the Acta Murensis Monasterii, "cœpit inde vir venerabilis Reginboldus cellam ordinare et construere, ædificavitque primum dormitorium, subtus autem Pisalem, congruaque habitacula alia fratribus constituit, et sic fundavit Monasterium." This was its situation at S. Gall, for one of the doors of the large room under the dormitory, lettered "calefactoria domus," which Professor Willis considers to have been the sitting-room, or common room, for the brethren, is lettered "egressus de pisale." This apartment is quite different from the Parlour, which was a long, narrow, room or passage, in which conversation was carried on with visitors, and orders given to the servants. (Ibid. p. 19.) A similar description of the Parlour at Christ Church, Canterbury, is given by Professor Willis (History, *ut supra*, p. 28); and occurs also in the Rites of Durham, pp. 44, 59.]

with traceried windows looking west to the water, and fitted up in the subvaults of the dormitory, still remains at Durham. Its original purpose is described as follows:

"On the right hand, as yow goe out of the Cloysters into the Infirmary, was the Commone House, and a Maister therof. The house being to this end, to have a fyre keapt in yt all wynter, for the Monnckes to cume and warme them at, being allowed no fyre but that onely, except the Masters and Officers of the House, who had there severall fyres. Ther was belonging to the Common House a garding and a bowling allie, on the back side of the said house, towardes the water, for the Novyces sume tymes to recreat themselves, when they had remedy of there master, he standing by to se ther good order.

Also within this howse dyd the Master therof keepe his *O Sapientia*, ones in the yeare, viz. betwixt Martinmes and Christinmes, a sollemne banquett that the Prior and Convent dyd use at that tyme of the yere onely, when ther banquett was of figs and reysinges, aile and caikes, and therof no superflwitie or excesse, but a scholasticall and moderat congratulacion amonges themselves[1]."

This "Common House" of the monks corresponds to the Oxford "Common Room" and Cambridge "Combination Room" in their earlier form, when there were no chimneys in the chambers, and a common fire was kept up in them for the scholars to warm themselves[2].

A large chamber on the ground-floor at the high-table end of the hall, with a door of access from the same, will be found in all the Cambridge colleges of which the medieval buildings remain (with the exception of Magdalene College), as at Peterhouse, Pembroke College, Trinity Hall, Corpus Christi College, Queens' College, Jesus College, Christ's College, S. John's College; and even at the later Colleges of Emmanuel and Sidney Sussex. At Gonville and Caius College it was at the high-table end of the old hall, but, like the hall, approached by a flight of stairs. At Corpus Christi College, Trinity Hall, and Christ's College, the chamber in question has been added to the Master's Lodge, and at S. John's College it has been pulled down, but in the other colleges enumerated it is still used as a Combination Room for the Fellows, and it may be inferred from analogy that it was erected for that purpose in all cases[3].

[1] [Rites of Durham, *ut supra*, p. 75.]

[2] [Architectural History of Worcester, *ut supra*, p. 68, *note*.]

[3] [The relation of the Master's Lodge to the Combination Room in the older colleges has been already discussed in the Essay on the Master's Lodge (p. 333).]

This chamber at the high-table end of the hall exists also at Hampton Court, and is shewn on the plan of Haddon Hall given above (p. 272). It is the origin of our modern "drawing-room," which is literally, the "withdrawing-room" for the occupants of the dais, into which they retired while those who occupied an inferior position were left to warm themselves in the hall.

It will, in the next place, be desirable to trace the different names by which this room was known at successive periods, and the different uses to which it was put either by custom or by statute.

The existence of such a room in connection with a college is first alluded to, so far as we have been able to discover, in the Accounts of King's Hall for 1423—24, when the Parlour (*parlura*) is wainscoted[1]. At Peterhouse in 1464 the fireplace of the Parlour (*parletum* or *parletorium*), then first constructed, is set up[2]; at Queens' College in 1493—94 the Parlour (*parloria*) is repaired[3]; in the statutes of Jesus College, given by Nicholas West, Bishop of Ely 1515—34, it is directed that the Master may occasionally invite strangers, and some of the Fellows, to dine or sup with him in the Parlour (*parlura*) or in his own chamber[4]; a room called "the parlour" is mentioned in the Accounts of Trinity College in 1564—65, and in several subsequent years; at Trinity Hall in 1584, Henry Harvey, LL.D. (Master 1560—84) bequeathed certain funds for the maintenance of a fire "for the use of the Company in the common Parlor[5];" at Emmanuel College the "common parlor" is mentioned in 1588, the year in which the buildings were completed[6]; at S. Catharine's Hall in 1632 "the parlor" is painted[7]; at Christ's College in 1669—70 and at Trinity College in 1683, furniture is bought for "the College Parlour[8]"; and at Trinity

[1] [History of Trinity College, Vol. II. pp. 444.]

[2] Bursar's Roll, 1463-64. Stone is purchased "pro le mantils caminorum in parleto et camera superiori."

[3] [History of Queens' College. Vol. II. p. 49.]

[4] [Commiss. Docts. III. 113.]

[5] [History of Trinity Hall, Vol. I. p. 225.]

[6] [History of Emmanuel College, Vol. II. p. 692.]

[7] [Audit-Book of S. Catharine's Hall, 31 March, 1631—32.]

[8] [These statements are supported by entries in the Bursar's Accounts.]

Hall Dr Warren, writing in 1730, describes the alterations made in that year to "the Parlour[1]." At Emmanuel College no other name appears to have been applied to the room, for "Emmanuel Parlour" is frequently alluded to in connection with Richard Farmer, D.D., Master 1775—97[2]. It is probable that the word "Parlour" was used in conversation to designate the common meeting-room of the Fellows even after it had come to be known by other appellations. At King's College the graces for Fellows obtaining the status of Bachelor of Arts and Master of Arts were always "propounded in the Parlour," until 1864. In the sixteenth century it is usually described in formal documents by the classical Latin word *conclave*[3]. In the later statutes of Peterhouse, given in the beginning of the sixteenth century, the chambers on the east side of the hall are assigned to the Master "except the common *conclave*," which is to be left open for the use of the scholars, or as we should now say, the Fellows, in winter. The room here specified may be identified with the ancient Combination Room of the college, formerly called "The Stone Parlour[4]." At Gonville and Caius College the same name was given to the old Combination Room, on the ground-floor under the south end of the hall. It is evident that this room had been used, like the Common House in a monastery, for the Fellows and Scholars to warm themselves in, for Dr Caius, describing the placing of a brazier in the hall in 1565, expressly says that before that date there had been no fire except in the Parlour (*conclave*), which had been found large enough to contain all the Fellows and Scholars. This room, being on the ground-floor, was probably found to be damp and gloomy, for in the statutes given by Dr Caius leave is especially given for the construction of a winter parlour (*conclave hybernum*) above it; and he further directs that

[1] [History of Trinity Hall, Vol. I. p. 225.]

[2] [Gunning's Reminiscences, ed. 1855, I. 158, 165.]

[3] [Ducange, after explaining this word by "Vestiarium, *Gardaroba*," proceeds to shew that it was the name given to the room in which the Cardinals met to elect the Pope. In support of this view he quotes Matthew Paris, ann. 1245: "Domini Papæ camera, quæ Conclave, id est Guardaroba dicitur." He further cites from the *Vocabularium* of Papias (XIth century): "Conclave, Locus inclusus vel munitus, sive domus quæ multis clauditur cellis, interior cella."]

[4] [Commis. Docts. II. 79. History of Peterhouse, Vol. I. pp. 20, 63.]

"twenty shillings annually should be spent on the purchase of coals or wood to maintain a fire during the winter season, but not all the year round, in either the Hall or the Parlour (*conclave*)." The old name recurs again in the Orders made in 1653 and 1656 respecting "the chamber over the Parlour[1]."

At S. John's College a new name is given to the room. Bishop Fisher's first code of statutes (1524), directs the Master to dine and sup with the Fellows in the Hall or Parlour (*cœnaculum*), a word which is repeated in both the later codes (1530 and 1545). This language appears to be exceptional, for we have not found the word elsewhere in documents of similar authority.

The term Combination Chamber, or Combination Room, now universally employed at Cambridge, first occurs, so far as we have been able to trace it, in the Senior Bursar's Accounts of Trinity College for 1650—51, when "a Table for the Fellowes Combination Chamber" is ordered. We next meet with it at Gonville and Caius College in 1658, when the new "Combination Chamber" is fitted up[2]. Again, when the north range of the new buildings at Clare Hall was built between 1683 and 1689, the "new Combination Chamber," there placed over the Buttery, is mentioned frequently in the Building Accounts. In 1693 the old room which it replaced is called "the Combination dineing room[3]." When S. Catharine's Hall was rebuilt in 1675 Cornelius Austin was paid for wainscoting "the Combination Room[4]." At Magdalene College in 1712 "a Combination Room was fitted up for the use of the Fellows[5]." At Christ's College in 1719 Dr John Covel, Master, speaks of the "common Combination Room[6]."

At Oxford in like manner every college has a "Common Room," as it is there termed, but in a totally different position from that which obtains at Cambridge for the Combination Room. At only one college, namely Exeter College, is it

[1] [Commiss. Docts. II. 260, 344. History of Gonville and Caius College, Vol. I. pp. 198—200.]

[2] [Ibid. Vol. I. p. 199.]

[3] [History of Clare Hall, Ibid. pp. 107, 108.]

[4] [History of S. Catharine's Hall, Vol. II. p. 102.]

[5] [History of Magdalene College, Ibid. p. 381.]

[6] [History of Christ's College, Ibid. p. 213.]

placed at the high-table end of the hall, with a door of communication from the same; and though Williams shews a similar position for it at Oriel College, no access to it from the hall is indicated on his plan. Elsewhere it is placed in any part of the college where a space sufficiently large for it could be found. This singular arrangement would naturally lead us to suppose that the Common Room did not enter into the original plan of the earlier colleges, but was adopted at a later period; and, in fact, according to Wood, Common Rooms did not come into fashion until the latter half of the seventeenth century. In his History of Trinity College the following passage occurs:

"Much about the same time, 1665, was a Common Chamber made up out of a lower room belonging to a Fellow, between the common gate and the south end of the public Refectory; to the end that the Fellows might meet together (chiefly in the evenings after refection) partly about business, but mostly for society sake, which before was at each chamber by turns. And this was done in imitation of other Colleges, that had began before, of which Merton College was the first, an. 1661[1]."

[The imitative spirit which distinguished collegiate architecture has been more than once insisted upon by Professor Willis, and he has pointed out the great influence exercised upon that architecture by William of Wykeham. It was shewn in the last essay that in his statutes for New College he permitted the Fellows and Scholars to assemble round the fire in the hall on festivals, and there devote a reasonable time to amusement. On ordinary days, as soon as Grace had been said, and the grace-cup had been passed round, the seniors were to retire to their studies, and on no account to suffer the juniors to linger in the hall. In consequence, no Common Room is found in Wykeham's buildings at New College, and the fashion having been thus set by an architect whose arrangements were so largely adopted in subsequent colleges, it was evidently considered unnecessary to provide a room for which he had set no precedent. The present Common Rooms at New College are in one of the buildings of the Garden

[1] [Wood, ed. Gutch, p. 528. In the History of Merton College, however (p. 11), his editor informs us that "the Combination Room," as he calls it, was built by the celebrated William Harvey, M.D., Warden 1645—57, in which latter year he died.]

Quadrangle, of which the ground-floor was anciently called "The Chequer[1]," and the first floor was used as the Law Library. This latter was converted into "a Common Chamber for the Society" in 1675, and a commodious passage made to it from the hall.

The furniture of the Combination Room at Cambridge in the sixteenth century appears to have been limited to tables and forms, which towards the end of the following century were replaced by chairs. At Trinity College in 1560 the Inventory quoted above (p. 361) dismisses the furniture of the Parlour in a single line:

"*In* [*the*] *Parlour*

Item a long table with two tristles and two long fourmes;"

and in 1576—77 "the newe parlour graunted by Mr Vicemaster and the Seniors" is provided with two tables and eight forms; at Queens' College in 1589—90 "a forme for the College parler" is bought; and at King's College in 1598 we meet with the following Inventory:

"The Newe Parlor.

Inprimis a fayre long table of waynscott with iij formes therunto belonging of waynscott.

Item a Courte Cubborde of waynscott.

Item the parlor all seeled with waynscott.

Item ij long Curten rodds with ij green say Curtens for the wyndowes.

Item a plate Candlestick.

Item [blank] Iron Casements[2]."

At S. Catharine's Hall in 1633—34 a payment occurs "for a round table for the parlour and for 8 stooles"; and another in 1639—40 "for 2 long formes for the Fellowes table in the parloure." The following Inventory taken at Emmanuel College in 1642 enumerates the usual table and forms, but adds a single

[1] [Wood, *ut supra*, p. 197. It appears from the contract with William Bird dated 12 April 1683, quoted above (p. 280), that this room was then called the "Masters Room," or the "Masters Common Room," for he covenants to "make a new Stone Window to the Chequer, under the great Window of the Masters Roome, corresponding to the Window on the other side; And shall erect a wall with Battlements on the Masters Common Roome answerable to the wall and Battlements of the other side."]

[2] [Camb. Antiq. Communications, Vol. III. p. 194.]

chair, which we may presume was intended for the use of the Master, as at Queens' College in 1605—6 a charge occurs "for mendinge the Presedent's chaire in the Parlor."

"In the Parlour.

Three Casements.
One Joyned Table with two leaves.
One new wainscot chaire.
Two joyned fourmes.
One framed bench.
Two wainscot portalls with 2 doores two latches and fower bolts.
A Chimney peece of wainscot.
Wainscot seeling round about with a Cupboord in the wall.
One rest to set the feet upon at the Table end.
A Cupboord for Plate.
A Table of Benefactors with a locke and chaine.
A paire of bellowes Tonges and fire shovell.
A Grat with two cheeks and an iron back."

When the new "Combination Chamber" was fitted up at Gonville and Caius College in 1656, the following entries occur in the Bursar's Accounts for the furniture:

"For 2 dozen of Russ. Leather chayres at 7^s. 6^d. each 9^{li}. For 3 great Russ. chayres 2^{li}. 8^s. For 6 tulip Velure cushions 1^{li}. 4^s. For 3 leather carpetts conteyning 42 skins 3^{li}. 3^s."

At Jesus College in 1665—66 "the Table and Forms in the Parlour" are mended; but in 1671—72 "six chairs in the Parlor" are paid for. At Christ's College in 1669—70 "the College Parlour chaires" are mended, an entry which implies that they had been in existence for some time. At Trinity College in 1674—75 "24 Chaires for the Common Chamber," together with "a Large Turkeyworke Carpett," and "a Lesser Turkeyworke Carpett" are bought, evidently part of a refurnishing according to new fashions; and at Emmanuel College in the following year a charge occurs "for 18 Russia leather Chayres for the Parlor." In 1685-86 a bequest for "wainscotting and adorning the Combination Room" at Queens' College was spent on the panelwork which still exists, and on the provision of chairs and cushions[1]; and in 1688 the following Inventory was taken at Christ's College:

[1] [History of Queens' College, Vol. II. p. 49, Magn. Jour n. 1685—86.]

"In the Parlor.

An Organ.
One Elbow Chair, Russia Leather. And a Cushion.
One dozen and a half of Plain Russia Leather Chairs.
Four Spanish Tables.
Three Cloath Carpets.
Two and twenty peauter Trencher plaits.
A paire of Scales, and weights.
A paire of Bellows, fire Shovel, tongues, forks, and grate.
Two brass candlesticks.
Adams large Map of England."

At Trinity Hall the forms were not replaced by chairs until 1730, as recorded by Dr Warren[1].

The walls of the Combination Room, like those of the chambers, were concealed by hangings, at least in some colleges. At S. John's College "paynted cloths for the low parlor" were bought in 1529; and at Queens' College in 1532—33 the hangings in the Parlour (*conclave*) were mended.

The Inventory taken at Christ's College in 1688 mentions a map of England in the Parlour; and in 1719 we find a "Great Map of the World" hanging there[2]. At Queens' College a map was bought for the Parlour in 1532—33, and another in 1547—48[3]. These are not described, but in 1694—95 a charge occurs for a "Chart of France for ye use of the Fellows in ye Parlour." The Parlour at this College contained also the Statutes of the realm, and the Adages of Erasmus, both chained for security of reference[4]. At Jesus College in 1752—53, "an Universal History Chart" was bought "for the Parlour[5]." A barometer was also a not uncommon article of furniture. The first instance of this is at Queens' College in 1687—88[6]. It is evident that the

[1] [History of Trinity Hall, Vol. I. p. 225.]

[2] [History of Christ's College, Vol. II. p. 214.]

[3] [Mag. Journ. 1522–33, fo. 186. b. "Item xvj^o. Januarii m^ro. Stapleton pro magna carta pendenti in conclaui iij^s. iiij^d." Ibid. 1547–48. fo. 160. "Item 2 novembris J. Skarlet bibliopole pro mappa vna cum junctura que pendet in conclavi xxij^s." Ibid. 1682–83. fo. 209. "For mending maps in the Parlour o. 2. 6."]

[4] [Ibid. 1537–38. fo. 36. "Item pro ornanda cathena et adfixione eiusdem cum libro statutorum regis in cœnaculo iiij^d." Ibid. 1563–64. fo. 37. b. "Item pro relegando et concatenando chiliad' Erasmi in conclavi xxij^d."

[5] [Jesus College Audit-Book, 1752–53. *Exp. Necess.*]

[6] [Magn. Journ. 1687–88. fo. 236 b. "Paid for ye Weather-Glasses in ye Parlour 2. 3. o." Christ's Coll. Audit-Book. December 1694. "Pay'd M^r. Carter for the Barometer in the Parlour 1. 10. o."]

Combination Room gradually came to be regarded as a common sitting-room for the Fellows, and was therefore fitted up in accordance with their tastes. We have seen that at Christ's College in 1688 it contained an organ; and at Trinity College in 1671—72 a charge occurs "for strings and mending ye violls in ye common chamber[1]." Writing-materials had been provided at the same college in 1657—58[2]; flowers were admitted at Queens' College in 1692—93[3]; and a card-table at Christ's College in 1716[4].

In conclusion we must briefly notice the benefactions made to certain colleges for a common fire, which indicate, more than any of the arrangements already noticed, that the hall and the parlour were considered to be places of meeting for social intercourse, in which it was desirable to promote comfort as far as possible. It will be observed that these benefactions were all made between 1535 and 1598, during which period the common fire was probably still the only one to which many of the inmates of the college had access.

In 1535, Thomas Thymbleby, Doctor in Decrees, gave 2 marks annually for a fire in the hall at Queens' College[5]. In 1556, Nicholas Shaxton, D.D., gave £20 to Gonville and Caius College, with which an annual rent-charge of twenty shillings was to be bought, for the perpetual maintenance of a fire on feast-days in winter in the hall or parlour. The same sum was given in 1565 by Humphrey Busby, LL.D., with minute directions as to the quantity of fuel to be consumed on each occasion[6]. In 1571 Matthew Parker, D.D., gave £100 to Corpus Christi

1 [Jun. Burs. Accounts 1671–72. *Extraordinaries.*]

2 [Ibid. 1657—58. "For paper bookes and a little pewter Standish for the use of the Comon Chamber 00. 13. 06."]

3 [Magn. Journ. 1692–93 fo. 8. b. "Paid for a Blew flower-pott for the Parlour 00. 03. 06."]

4 [Audit-Book of Christ's College, Feb. 9, 1715–16. "Paid Fore the Joyner for the playing Table in the Fell. parlour."]

5 [Le Keux's Memorials, ed. Cooper, I. p. 300. A special place was set apart in the college for the fuel thus obtained: Magn. Journ. 1534—35, fo. 209. "Item iiij Julii Dowsy et suo famulo pro vij diebus et di' in erigendis palis pro lignis D. Thymbleby vj^s. iij^d." fo. 209. b. "Item Johanni Banks pro resartione seræ et claui lignarii Doctoris Thymblebie iij^d."]

6 [History of Gonville and Caius College, Vol. I. p. 198.]

College for the maintenance of the hall fire[1]. At Trinity Hall the same Dr Busby, sometime Fellow,

"gave £20 for a common fire to be kept in College on every Sunday at dinner-time or supper-time from the feast of All Saints to Candlemas Day. For which he was enrolled among the Benefactors Sep. 1. 1572[2]."

This benefaction was augmented in 1584 by Henry Harvey, LL.D., who directed his heirs to deliver a certain amount of fuel yearly for a fire in the hall or parlour; and again by Benjamin Thorowgood, LL.B., in 1596[3]. In 1598, Richard Bunting bequeathed certain property to Christ's College, out of which the Society agreed to devote £5 yearly:

"to the end that in the time of Winter and cold seasons the common Fire and Fires in the Common Hall or parlour of the said College should be the better maintained and the charges thereof supported for the common use and benefit of the Master Fellows and Scholars of the said College[4]."

It should be further mentioned that at Sidney Sussex College in 1628 it was stipulated, in the deed by which Sir Francis Clerke founded certain Scholarships and Fellowships, that his Fellows should "partake in all College Offices, and in the Privilege of taking Pupils, and in the Use of the Garden, Library, and Parlour Fire"; and at Emmanuel College so late as 1639 we meet with a donation to the hall-fire:

"To Wilkin for charcoale for the Hall being the Lady Darell's guift .... 02 . 00 . 00[5]."

At Peterhouse in 1749 it was ordered:

"That a fire be made in the combination at noon to continue 'till two o'clock in the afternoon from the Audit 'till Lady Day, and that the money formerly allowed '*pro pyris solennibus* and for trenchers be applyed for that purpose.'"

Other arrangements for the comfort and recreation of the Fellows will be noticed in the Essay on the Tennis-court, Bowling-green, etc.]

1 [History, etc. by Robert Masters, p. 92.]
2 [Dr Warren's MS. p. 155.]
3 [Le Keux's 'Memorials,' ed. Cooper, i. p. 122. History of Trinity Hall, Vol. I. pp. 225, 233.]
4 [The deed, dated 1 May, 1598, is in the Treasury of Christ's College.]
5 [Audit-Book of Emmanuel College, *Expenses since 27 April*, 1639.]

VII.

THE LIBRARY.

CHAPTER I.

SURVEY OF THE COLLEGIATE STATUTES OF OXFORD AND CAMBRIDGE HAVING REFERENCE TO THE LIBRARY. SMALL NUMBER OF VOLUMES CONTAINED IN ANCIENT COLLECTIONS. EXAMPLES OF EARLY LIBRARIES. A LIBRARY FIRST INCLUDED IN THE PLAN OF A COLLEGE BY WILLIAM OF WYKEHAM; AND SUBSEQUENTLY ADDED GRADUALLY TO OTHER COLLEGES. POSITION OF LIBRARIES.

IT appears from some scattered notices that have been preserved, that books were bequeathed for the use of students even before the foundation of colleges. The earliest record of this kind of benevolent aid to learning is the gift of several copies of the Bible to the University of Oxford by Roger L'Isle or *De Insula*, Dean of York[1], in the early part of the thirteenth century. On this subject, however, we cannot do better than quote the sentences with which Wood prefaces his account of the Public Libraries of Oxford:

"Before I come to speak of those Libraries that have been made public, or built and appointed for public use, I shall make these observations, and then proceed.

I. That many books have been given to the University by Benefactors in old time, as appears from certain footsteps of antiquity, but what their names were I know not, only Roger, Dean of York, who 'bestowed several exemplars of the holy Bible to be used by the Scholars of Oxford under a pledge.'

II. That the said Books have according to their donors' minds been locked up in Chests, or chained upon desks in St Mary's Chancel and Church to be used by the Masters upon leave first obtained.

[1] [Le Neve (Fasti Eccl. Angl. III. 121) states that he was dean in 1221 and 1226, and that he died in 1235.]

III. That those Chests have had by the appointment of the Chancellor and Regent Masters, certain Masters to keep them and their keys, and also to receive pledges from such that borrowed any books from them.

IV. That the said Chests have stood in the old Congregation House, or in one of the Chapels joining to St Mary's Church.

V. That the way of keeping them in Chests continued till the Library over the Congregation House was built, and then being taken out, were set up in pews or studies (such as we have now among us) digested according to Faculties, chained, and had a Keeper appointed over them[1]."

When colleges arose similar donations were made to them by their founders or by subsequent benefactors, and thus in time considerable collections were amassed, and the Library became a recognised element of collegiate arrangement.

Rules for the management of the books occur in several of the earlier college statutes, and give such curious and authentic information on this subject that it will be worth while to review them somewhat at length.

In the statutes of Merton College, Oxford, 1274, the teacher of grammar (*grammaticus*) is to be supplied with a sufficient number of books out of the funds of the House, but no other mention of books occurs therein[2]. The explanatory ordinances, however, of Robert Kilwardby, Archbishop of Canterbury (1276), direct that the books of the community are to be kept under three locks, and to be assigned by the warden and sub-warden to the use of the Fellows under sufficient pledge[3]. In the second statutes of University College, 1292, it is provided, "that no Fellow shall alienate, sell, pawn, hire, lett, or grant, any House, Rent, Money, Book, or other Thing, without the Consent of all the Fellows"; and further, with special reference to the Library:

"Let every Book of the House, now given, or hereafter to be given, be lent by Indenture, that he that has it may be more fearful lest he loose it; and let one Part (of the Indenture) be kept in the common Chest, and the other with him that has the same: And let no Book,

[1] [Wood, History and Antiquities of the University of Oxford, ed. Gutch, 4to. Oxford, 1796. Vol. II. Part 2. p. 910. On the whole subject of medieval Libraries see Warton's History of English Poetry, ed. 1840, Dissertation II. "*On the Introduction of Learning into England.*" Vol. I. pp. lxxxii.—cxxxviii.]

[2] [Commiss. Docts. Oxford, I. 24. Statutes of Merton College, Cap. 2.]

[3] [Sketch of the Life of Walter de Merton. By Edmund [Hobhouse], Bishop of Nelson, New Zealand. 8vo. Oxford, 1859, p. 39.]

belonging to the House, be lent out of the College, without a Pawn better (than the Book), and this with the Consent of all the Fellows.

"Let there be put one Book of every Sort that the House has, in some common and secure Place; that the Fellows, and others with the Consent of a Fellow, may for the Future have the Benefit of it.

"That every Opponent in Theology, or Reader of the Sentences, or a Regent that commonly reads, when he wants it, shall have any necessary Book, that the House has, lent to him Gratis; and when he has done with it, [let him] restore it back to that Fellow, who had formerly made choice of it[1]."

The early statutes of Balliol College make no mention of books, and the Library, according to Wood, was not begun until 1431[2]. The statutes of Exeter College have not been printed, but the Library is mentioned as having fallen to ruin in the reign of Edward III., when, about 1374, "William Rede, Bishop of Chichester, gave towards its reparation twenty pounds, and twenty-five manuscripts to be put therein[3]." The statutes of Oriel College, dated 1329, lay down the following rules for the management of the books:

"The common books (*communes libri*) of the House are to be brought out and inspected once a year, on the feast of the Commemoration of Souls (2 November), in presence of the Provost or his deputy, and of the Scholars. Every one of them in turn, in order of seniority, may select a single book which either treats of the science to which he is devoting himself, or which he requires for his use. This he may keep until the same festival in the succeeding year, when a similar selection of books is to take place, and so on, from year to year. If there should happen to be more books than persons, those that remain are to be selected in the same manner[4]."

The last clause plainly shews how small the number of the books must have been when the statute was written. Their safety was subsequently secured by an ordinance of the Provost and Scholars, which, by decree of the Visitor, dated 13 May, 1441, received the authority of a statute. The high value set upon them is shewn by the extreme stringency of the penalties imposed for wilful loss or failure of restitution. After describing the annual assemblage of the Provost and Fellows, as provided in the former statute, the new enactment proceeds as follows:

[1] [Annals of University College. By William Smith. 8vo. 1728. pp. 37—39. The statutes of University College have not been printed.]

[2] [Wood, History and Antiquities of the Colleges and Halls in the University of Oxford, ed. Gutch, 4to. Oxford, 1786, p. 89.]

[3] [Ibid. p. 114.]

[4] [Commiss. Docts. Oxford. Vol. I. Statutes of Oriel College, p. 14.]

"Any person who absents himself on that day, so that the books selected by him are neither produced nor restored; or who, being present, refuses to produce or restore them; or who refuses to pay the full value, if, without any fraud or deception on his part, it should happen that any one of them be missing; is to be deprived of all right of selecting books for that year; and any person who wittingly defers the aforesaid production or restitution till Christmas next ensuing, shall, *ipso facto*, cease to be a Fellow.

Further, any scholar who has pawned or alienated, contrary to the common consent of the College, any book or any object of value (*jocale*) belonging to the college; or who has even suggested, helped, or favoured, such pawning or alienation, shall, *ipso facto*, cease to be a member of the Society[1]."

The statutes of Peterhouse, Cambridge, dated 1344, class the books of the Society with the charters and muniments, and prescribe the following rules for their safe custody:

"In order that the books which are the common property of the House, the charters, and the muniments may be kept in safe custody, we appoint and ordain that an indenture be drawn up of the whole of them in the presence of at least the major part of the scholars, expressing what the books are, and to what faculty they belong; of which indenture one part is to be deposited with the Master, the other with the Deans.

"The aforesaid books, charters, and muniments are to be placed in one or more common chests each having two locks, one key of which shall for greater security be deposited with the Master, the other with the Senior Dean, who shall cause the books to be distributed to those scholars who have need of them, in the manner which has been more fully set forth in the section which treats of the office of the Deans[2]."

That section (*De duobus Decanis, et eorum officio*), after providing that the Master and the Senior Dean (*primus Decanus*) are to take charge of the books, in terms identical with those just quoted, proceeds as follows:

"They are to distribute them to the Scholars in such manner as shall appear to them expedient; and further, they shall, if they think proper, make each scholar take an oath that he will not alienate any book so borrowed, but will take all possible care of it, and restore it to the Master and Dean, at the expiration of the appointed time[3]."

The statutes given by Bishop Bateman to Trinity Hall in 1350, which he copied for Gonville Hall in 1353, contain more

[1] [Commiss. Docts. Oxford. Vol. I. Statutes of Oriel College, p. 22.]

[2] [Commiss. Docts. II. 38. Statutes of Peterhouse, § 53. "*De omnibus Libris Domus, Munimentis, et Chartis custodiendis.*"]

[3] [Ibid. § 15, p. 17.]

stringent and explanatory rules than the above, many of them similar to those of University College, Oxford, but evidently written in contemplation of a more considerable collection of volumes. A list[1] of the books which he himself presented to Trinity Hall is appended to his statutes, and a special chapter (*De libris collegii*) is allotted to the Library. This curious and interesting document may be translated as follows:

"On the days appointed for the general audit of accounts [in the Michaelmas and Easter Terms] all the books which have been received, or shall be received in future, either from our own liberality, or from the pious largess of others, are to be laid out separately before the Master and all the resident Fellows in such manner that each volume may be clearly seen[2]; by which arrangement it will become evident twice in each year whether any book has been lost or taken away.

"No book belonging to the aforesaid College may ever at any time be sold, given away, exchanged, or alienated, under any excuse or pretext; nor may it be lent to anybody except a member of the College; nor may it be entrusted in quires, for the purpose of making a copy, to any member of the College, or to any stranger, either within the precincts of the Hall or beyond them; nor may it be carried by the Master, or any one else, out of the Town of Cambridge, or out of the aforesaid Hall or Hostel, either whole or in quires, except to the Schools; provided always that no book pass the night out of College, unless it be necessary to bind it or to repair it; and when this happens, it is to be brought back to College as soon as possible after the completion of the binding or the repair.

"Moreover, all the books of the College are to be kept in some safe room, to be assigned for the College Library, so that all the Scholars of the College may have common access to them. We give leave, however, that the poor scholars of the college may have the loan of books containing the texts of Canon and Civil Law[3] for their private use for a certain time, to be fixed at the discretion of the Master and the three Senior Fellows, provided they be not taken out of College; but the books of the Doctors of Civil and Canon Law are to remain continuously in the said Library Chamber, fastened with iron chains for the common use of the Fellows[4]."

William of Wykeham, in his elaborate statutes given in 1400 to New College, Oxford (§ 61 *De libris collegii*), adopted the above statute of Bishop Bateman, in fact copying literally,

[1] [This list is analysed below, p. 402.]

[2] [The words thus paraphrased are: "ostendantur realiter, visibiliter, et distincte."]

[3] [The corresponding statute for Gonville Hall allows the scholars to borrow the texts of Logic, Philosophy, and Theology, as well as those of Civil and Canon Law.]

[4] [Commiss. Docts. I. 432: copied for Gonville Hall, ibid. p. 236.]

or with very slight changes, the first two-thirds of it, but amplifying the clause which relates to lending the books. This clause, which largely extends the time during which text-books may be retained by students, shall be translated in full.

"The books in each faculty may be lent to poor Fellows and Scholars, for their own special use, by the method of a fresh selection in each year[1], provided they be not carried beyond the precincts of the college except for the purposes above rehearsed; but the Warden and the Senior Dean in civil law may distribute text-books in civil law to students of civil law, and text-books in canon law to students of canon law, for their own special use during the whole time they devote themselves to those faculties in our college, provided they do not possess such books of their own, but no person may keep more than two books of the same kind in this latter manner.

"The remaining text-books, should any be left over, and also the glosses or commentaries of the Doctors of civil and canon law, may be lent to the persons belonging to those faculties by the method of annual selection, as in the other faculties.

"The books which remain unassigned after the Fellows have made their selection (*ultra sortem sociorum*), are to be fastened with iron chains, and remain for ever in the common Library for the use of the Fellows.

"Moreover we appoint that in respect of all books or other property of whatsoever kind which shall be presented to the college during the life time of the donors or by testament, the will and appointment of the donors is to be precisely observed, provided that the rights and ownership of the college in the books and other property remain in force and be recognised for ever[2]."

This statute is repeated in the statutes of King's College, Cambridge, and in those of the Oxford colleges of All Souls, Magdalen, Brasenose, Corpus Christi, Cardinal College, and S. John's, with additions or omissions according to the taste of the respective founders. For instance, the permission to keep books during the whole of a student's term of residence does not recur in any of these statutes, except in those given to All Souls College in 1443, by Henry Chichele, Archbishop of Canterbury. His library-statute is in the main copied from that of Wykeham, but it contains some provisions which are either wholly original, or so much altered from Wykeham's as to have the importance of an original enactment. Wykeham had provided that after

[1] [The words thus translated are: "Permittimus quod libri...annuatim per modum novæ electionis poterint commodari."]

[2] [Commiss. Docts. Oxford, Vol. I. Statutes of New College, p. 98.]

the Fellows had made their selection the books left over, if any, were to be chained in the Library. Here however the books to be chained are made the subject of definite choice. The statute begins with the following clauses, the first of which is implied in Wykeham's reservation of the will of donors:

"The books in each faculty, which have either been given to the College, or acquired in some other way, may be granted to poor Fellows of the said College, for their special use, by the method of a fresh selection to be made by the said Fellows in each year;

"Except those books which, in obedience to the will of the donors, or the injunction of the Warden, the Vice-Warden, and the Deans, are to be chained for the common use of the Fellows and Scholars;

"Except the text-books in civil law, and the text-books in canon law, which we appoint to be distributed by the Warden and the Dean in law to students in those faculties respectively, for their own use during the whole time they apply themselves to those faculties in the aforesaid college, if they do not possess such books of their own; on the understanding that two books of the same description, or on the same subject, may in no case be lent to the same person. The remaining text-books, if any be left over, may be lent to the Fellows in those faculties, by the method of a fresh selection in each year, as in the other faculties[1]."

In these statutes the preparation of a catalogue is specially enjoined. Every book is to be entered in a register by the initial line of the second leaf, and every book given to the Library is to bear the name of the donor on the second leaf, or in some other convenient position. The books are to be inspected once in every year, after which the distribution, as above provided for, is to take place. Each Fellow who borrows a book is to have a small indenture drawn up containing the title according to the initial line of the second leaf, and an acknowledgment that he has received it. These small indentures are to be left in charge of the Warden, or, in his absence, of the Vice-Warden.

In the statutes of King's College, Cambridge, given by King Henry the Sixth, no addition is made to Wykeham's statute, but the clause enjoining the selection of particular books by those who were to use them is omitted, and does not reappear in any of the subsequent Cambridge statutes. In those of Magdalen College, Oxford (1473), no new principle is introduced. In those of S. Catharine's Hall, Cam-

[1] [Commiss. Docts. Oxford. Vol. I. Statutes of All Souls College, p. 54.]

bridge, given in or about 1475, the books are classed with the muniments of the college, and it is provided that on the audit-day in each year the whole collection, whether kept in the library or in the chapel, shall be inspected by the Fellows. None are to be removed out of college, except by consent of the Master and Fellows, and on production of sufficient security[1]. Again, at Brasenose College, Oxford (1521), no new principle is introduced; but at Corpus Christi College (1517), safe-guards against the indiscriminate chaining of books are insisted upon:

> "No book is to be brought into the Library or chained there, unless it be of suitable value and utility, or unless the will of the donor have so directed; and none is to be taken out of it, unless it so happen that there be there already a considerable number on the same subject, or that another copy in better condition and of greater value, to take its place, have been presented by some benefactor.
>
> "By this means those books which are of greater value, or which contain material of greater utility to students in each Faculty, will be stored up in the Library; while those which are not fit for the Library, or of which a sufficient number of copies already exist in it, may be distributed to the Fellows of the College, according to the system of indentures between the borrower and the President, or in his absence the Vice-President, or one of the Deans[2]."

The founder was evidently afraid of the Library becoming overcrowded, for he allows books to be sold, in the event of their becoming so numerous as to be no longer of any use to the Fellows for the purpose of being borrowed. A new principle of distribution makes its appearance in these statutes. Masters are to have works on Theology; Bachelors works on Philosophy and Greek Mathematics; Bachelors, Fellows, Scholars, and undergraduates, works on the Humanities and Greek Literature in general. This distribution is to be regulated by the President, one of the Deans, and an officer called Dispenser (*dispensator*) who apparently corresponded to what we should call a Librarian. In the rules for recognition of donors, and for keeping accurate catalogues, these statutes follow those of All Souls College. The statutes of Cardinal College (1527) and of S. John's College (1555) copy those of Corpus Christi College.

[1] [Commiss. Docts. III. 85.]

[2] [Commiss. Docts. Oxford, Vol. II. Statutes of Corpus Christi College, p. 90.]

Among the statutes of Lincoln College, dated 1479, we find the following relating to the books:

"The selection of books, which shall always be conducted in the following manner, shall take place at the first annual chapter.

"In the first place there shall be assembled together all those books of the College which the Rector and the majority of the Fellows shall have decided not to keep chained in the Library, but to circulate among the Fellows according to their selection. Next, the Rector or his deputy shall select the book which he may wish to study, and after him the Senior Fellow or his deputy shall select another, and so on. Should several books remain unselected, a second distribution shall take place, in the aforesaid order, the Rector first, and next his colleagues, or their deputies. Provided always that the selection of the Bachelors shall be strictly (*præcise*) limited to the books of Logic and Philosophy, and shall not extend to those of Theology.

"Each of these books is to be assigned under the security of an indenture, the counterpart of which is to be laid up on behalf of the College in a chest with three locks; and all these counterparts are without fail to be brought out and exhibited by the guardians of the chest once in each year at the great chapter.

"None of the aforesaid books are to be pledged, or pawned, or lent to anybody beyond the precincts of the College. Should this ordinance be contravened, the offender is not only to pay the value of any book which may be lost, but is to be deprived of commons for six weeks for each offence[1]."

In 1480 the following special additional statute was made for the Library at Peterhouse, Cambridge:

"In the name of God, Amen. As books are the most precious treasure of scholars, concerning which there ought to be the most diligent care and forethought, lest, as heretofore, they fall to decay or be lost, it is hereby appointed, settled, and ordained, by the Master and Fellows of the House or College of S. Peter in Cambridge, that no book which has been chained in the library there shall be taken away from, or removed out of, the library, except by special assent and consent of the Master and all the resident Fellows of the aforesaid College—it being understood that by resident Fellows a majority of the whole Society is meant.

"It is not intended that any book which has been given to the library on condition of being kept perpetually chained therein shall, by virtue of this statute, be on any pretence removed from it, except only when it needs repair.

"Every book in the library which is to be selected and distributed shall have a certain value set upon it by the Master and the two Deans, and indentures shall be drawn up recording the same.

[1] [Commiss. Docts. Oxford, Vol. I. Statutes of Lincoln College, p. 21.]

"Once in every two years, in the Michaelmas Term, a fresh selection and distribution shall be held of every book which is not chained in the Library—the precise day to be fixed by the Master and the Senior Dean.

"No book so selected and distributed shall pass the night out of College, except by permission of the Master and the President and the other Dean who is not President; provided always that the said book be not kept out of College for six months in succession.

"If it should happen that a given book be not brought in and produced on the aforesaid day of fresh selection and distribution, then the person who is responsible for it shall pay to the Master, or in his absence to the Senior Dean, the full value of the said absent book, under pain of being put out of commons until it be restored.

"Every Fellow who is not present on the aforesaid day shall appoint a deputy, who shall be prepared to bring in any books which may have been lent to him, on the day when a fresh distribution is to take place, under pain of being put out of commons[1]."

At Cambridge the statutes of Michael House, Clare Hall, King's Hall, and the colleges of Pembroke, Corpus Christi, Jesus, Christ's, S. John's, Magdalene, Trinity, Emmanuel, and Sidney, are all silent on the subject of books. Probably the rules of the Library were of the nature of bye-laws, and governed by special statutes like that imposed upon the Society of Peterhouse in 1480 which has been already quoted, or like the following for Pembroke College, where we find a Librarian appointed for the first time in a college at Cambridge:

"Let there be in the aforesaid House a Keeper of the Books, who shall take under his charge all the books belonging to the community, and once in each year, namely on the feast of the Translation of S. Thomas the Martyr [7 July], or at the latest within the eight days immediately following, let him render an account of the same, by exhibiting each book in order to the Master and Fellows.

"After they have been looked at, and their distribution considered by the Fellows, let him distribute them to each Fellow in proportion to his requirements. And let the said Keeper have ready large pieces of board (*tabulas magnas*), covered with wax and parchment, that the titles of the books may be written on the parchment, and the names of the Fellows who hold them on the wax beside it. When they have brought their books back, their names may be taken out, and they need no longer be held responsible for them, the Keeper alone remaining responsible for the whole collection. By these precautions he will never be in doubt about any book or its possessor.

"No book is to be taken away or lent out of the House on any pretext whatever, except upon some occasion which may appear justifiable to the major part of the community; and then, if any book be lent,

[1] [Commiss. Docts. II. 44.]

let a proper pledge be taken for it which shall be honorably exhibited to the Keeper[1]."

It is worthy of remark that the security of the Library is made the subject of statutory enactment. Wykeham orders:

"On the door of the said Library there are to be two great locks with two different keys, which are to be kept continually and carefully in the custody the one of the Senior Dean, the other of the Senior Bursar, as is proper. A third lock, commonly called a *clickett*, is to be placed on the aforesaid door, of which lock every Fellow of our College may have a single key. The door is to be locked every night with all the three keys aforesaid[2]."

In the statutes of King's College, Cambridge, the substance of these directions is repeated in the following form:

"On the door of the Library there is to be a lock, commonly called a *clikat*, and every Fellow of our College is to have a single key to it. The door is to be locked at night, but in the day-time the Provost, Fellows, and others resident in the house (*intranei*), are to have free access to the Library, provided only that they admit no strangers, except those for whom those who introduce them are prepared to answer at their peril[3]."

In this passage nothing is said about a great lock or locks, and any such custom, if it existed, seems to have fallen into disuse, for when, long after the foundation, in 1686, the rules quoted below were made, and a member of the college was appointed to take charge of the library, he was to be the sole keeper of "the Additional new Lock," which he was to lock at night, leaving to Fellows and others the same freedom as is here enjoined to use their ordinary key when the room was not so additionally secured.

At Oxford the statutes of All Souls College, Magdalen College, Corpus Christi College and S. John's College repeat the above clause, in nearly identical language, with the additional provision that, when strangers are introduced, the Fellow who introduces them is to remain with them during the whole time that they are in the Library. In the statutes of S. John's

1 [This Statute, or College order, unfortunately without date, is quoted in a short history of Pembroke College Library drawn up by Matthew Wren, D.D., while Fellow, as the preface to a volume preserved in Pembroke College Library, dated 1617, in which he recorded the names of those who had presented books to the Library.]

2 [Statutes of New College, *ut supra*, p. 98.]

3 [Commiss. Docts. II. 601.]

College it is further directed that a Fellow who wants to have a private key is to obtain leave from the President or Vice-President, with the exception of the seniors, who are to have their keys as a matter of right. If any Fellow should lose his key, his own key and those of all the others are to be renewed at his expense. When a Fellow leaves college, he is to deliver up his key to the President. At Exeter College in 1545 each Fellow might have a key, but if he lost it he was to pay a fine of five shillings[1].

[It is probable that similar arrangements for access to the Library were made in those colleges where the statutes are silent on the subject; but, as they would be of the nature of bye-laws, and subject to frequent alteration, they have seldom been preserved, and their existence has to be inferred from other sources of information. For instance, in the Accounts of King's Hall for 1394—95 there is a charge for a lock and thirty-three keys—evidently for the Master and thirty-two Fellows[2]; in those of Christ's College for 1549—50 for "a key to the librarie dore for Mr Percevall," one of the Fellows; in the *Magnum Journale* of Queens' College for 1587—88 "for a locke et 22 keys for ye librarie"; and lastly, at King's College, two sets of Rules, to be observed by the Librarian and by those who used the Library, drawn up, the one in 1686, and the other about 1709—10, may be quoted at length[3]:

"ARTICLES, CONDITIONS, and COVENANTS upon which the Provost and other Officers of King's Coll: in Cambridge have admitted Michael Mills Schollar of the said College to be the Keeper of the Publick Library of the said College.

"1. He is dayly to be personally present in the Library, once in the forenoon, and once in the afternoon, besides when at the usual times He opens the Library door. There is to be but one Key of the Additional new Lock, with which the said Mills is solely intrusted, and

1 [Register of Exeter College, ed. Rev. C. W. Boase, Oxford, 1879, p. xii.]

2 [History of Trinity College, Vol. II. p. 442.]

3 [An old copy of these Articles (1686), followed by the Orders (1709—10), the latter signed by the Provost and nine Senior Fellows, is framed in the college library. The Dean of Divinity had charge of the library by statute, and the office of Under Library-Keeper, created in 1686, was held by an undergraduate or by a bachelor of arts. Michael Mills was admitted scholar 1683—84: proceeded B.A., 1687—88; M.A., 1691. He died in college of small-pox 25 July, 1696, and was buried in the chapel behind the altar.]

if He hear of any other, he is to acquaint the Provost or Dean of Divinity therewith. And as often as any good and lawful Occasion shall call him from his attendance there, the Provost or Dean of Divinity is to be made acquainted with it, that some other may be deputed in his room.

"2. He shall take care of and oversee every thing that belongs to the said Library, that neither Globes, Maps, Tables, Pictures, or any other thing of that nature suffer by rude and ill usage; and He shall give notice to the Provost or Dean of Divinity of any, whom He shall perceive thus to abuse his priviledge, or tear, deface, or cut leaves out of any books.

"3. He shall place and keep every book in its respective Classis, and in the proper place of that Class. He shall permit and suffer Strangers to see the Library, if they please, but not as Students to make Use of any Book or Books without the Leave of the Provost or in his absence the Vice-Provost, or Dean of Divinity.

"4. He shall keep the Door of the Library loct with both Locks at all other times save the usual Library-hours.

"5. He shall take care that the Chappel-Clerk cause the Library to be swept weekly, and the Classes together with the Books be cleansed from Dust once a month, or make Complaint.

"6. He shall render a just Account of all the Books, and other things belonging to the Library, and committed to his Charge together with the keys, when the Provost shall call upon him so to do.

"7. For the rend'ring this his business about the Library more easy, each Person that makes use of any book or books in the said Library, is requir'd to sett 'em up again decently without entangling the Chains: by which is signified to all concern'd, that no person whatsoever upon any pretence is permitted to carry any Book out of the Library to their Chambers, or any otherwise to be us'd as a private Book, it being against the Statutes of our Coll: in y^t^ Case provided."

"ORDERS for regulating the publick Library in Kings Coll. [1709—10.]

"1. The Dean of Divinity shall have the supervising and general care of the Library with the Custody of the Key of the Inner Library, and the Keys of the several Classes and Press for small Books.

"2. That no Bible, or Commentator upon the Holy Scriptures, or Dictionary in whatsoever language, shall be lent out of the Library at any time, being books of Common and almost daily Use.

"3. That if any other Book shall here after be borrowed out of the Library for private Use, the Dean of Divinity shall take a Note for it under the borrowers hand, when he delivers it, And y^t^ ye s^d^ Book shall be return'd to the Dean to be put into the Library again in its place within 2 month, unless there appears a reason to the Provost and Dean of Divinity for his Keeping it longer.

"4. All the fellows and Scholars and all other persons allow'd the Use of the Library shall carefully set up the Books they use in their proper place without entangling the Chains.

"5. No Foreigner or Member of any other Coll: shall be allow'd to have a key or study in our Library, without the special Leave of the Provost.

"6. The Under Library Keeper shall once a day see whether any books are negligently left on the Benches, or desks, and put 'em up in their proper places, and shall give notice to the Provost or Dean of Divinity, if he discovers any one misusing his Privilege, by defacing, tearing, or cutting leaves or pictures out of any book.

"7. The Under Library Keeper shall take care that the Chappel Clerk do sweep the Library once a week, and clean the Classes together with the Books from dust once a month, or upon default the Under Library Keeper shall make complaint thereof to the Provost or Dean of Divinity."]

The foregoing survey of the clauses in the collegiate statutes affecting the Library—which, it may be remarked, are much more numerous and elaborate at Oxford than at Cambridge—will enable us to arrive at definite ideas respecting the methods of keeping and using the books which gradually came to be adopted.

The small collections of books, accumulated by the generosity of founders or benefactors from the beginning of the thirteenth century, were at first used by borrowing them for private study under proper pledges, indentures, or other necessary cautions, while those which had not been borrowed were kept in chests, or perhaps in bookcases, by persons deputed to the charge of them, whose duty it was to deliver and receive them back from the borrowers under the required formalities. The custom of meeting annually to choose books, or rather to divide them all amongst the Fellows in order of seniority, is first mentioned at Oriel College, Oxford, in 1329, but this custom was not universally accepted. It subsequently came into use at University College, and was adopted by Wykeham, and by those who copied his statutes. It is also ordered in the Library-statute for Peterhouse, Cambridge, which was quoted above (p. 395). But, on the other hand, it evidently was not contemplated in the first Library-statutes of Peterhouse, Trinity Hall, Gonville Hall, Catharine Hall, and Pembroke College, in which the books are to be borrowed at any time as required.

Besides this mode of using the books, the statutes of University College, dated 1292, order that one book of every sort that the House has shall be put in some common and secure place, in order that the Fellows, and others with the consent of a Fellow, may for the future have the benefit of it. These selected books, therefore, were not to be locked up in the chests, or allowed to be borrowed. Thus the common collection was virtually divided into what we should now term a Lending Library, and a Library of Reference, a division adopted by Bishop Bateman at Trinity Hall in 1350, and after him by every subsequent legislator in some form or other. [This principle of separation reappears in the subdivision of libraries into an outer and an inner room, containing respectively the books of less and greater rarity. The collection at Peterhouse was divided into select books (*bibliotheca secretior*) and books of ordinary use (*bibliotheca apertior*)[1]; at Queens' College, the books which might be lent (*libri distribuendi*) were kept in a separate room from those which were chained to the shelves (*libri concatenati*)[2]; at King's College there was a public library (*bibliotheca magna*) and a lesser library (*bibliotheca minor*)[3]; and the University Library was divided into a "common Library," placed in the south room, and a "private Library," placed in the east room, to which, until the latter part of the seventeenth century, only a few privileged persons were admitted[4]."]

Further, Bishop Bateman's statutes direct that the works of the Doctors in Civil and Canon Law are to be chained in the Library for the common use of the Fellows. This is the first mention of this method of preventing irregular borrowing[5]. It must be observed that he does not chain the whole of the Library of reference. Wykeham, on the other hand, simply directs that

[1] [Old Register of Peterhouse, p. 22]

[2] [Magn. Jour. 1498—99. "Item pro claui vbi ponuntur libri distribuendi viij^{d}." Ibid. 1561—62. "Item pro clave seræ bibliothece vbi libri concatenantur."]

[3] [Mundum Book, 1508—9. *Exp. necess.* "Item * * * pro reparacione fenestrarum vitrearum tam in Aula quam in Ecclesia et magna et parua librariis." Ibid. 1541—42. "Item * * * scopantibus vtramque bibliothecam." The Orders quoted above shew that this distinction was still maintained at the beginning of the 18th century.]

[4] [History of the Schools, Library, &c., Vol. III. p. 25.]

[5] [In 1284 Archbishop Peckham, as Visitor to Merton College, Oxford, had directed the purchase of three works on grammar: "which you are to keep chained somewhere (*alicubi*) over a decent table, in order that everybody may have free access to them for purpose of reference". Commiss. Docts. Oxford, Vol. I. Statutes of Merton College, p. 41.]

all the books left after the annual borrowing shall be chained, in which he is followed at King's College, Cambridge. This plan of selecting what books should be lent out, not what books should be kept in, was evidently disliked, for in the subsequent Oxford statutes, down to those of S. John's College inclusive, the Master and Dean are empowered to select the books which deserve to be chained, or retained in the Library, and which are thus excluded from the borrowing, as well as those which are retained and chained by the will of the donors. This practice appears to have been carried to an inconvenient extent, to judge from the limitations which have been already cited from the statutes of Corpus Christi College, Oxford.

[It happens unfortunately that very few catalogues have been preserved of the libraries referred to in the above statutes; but, if we may estimate the extent of the remainder from those of which we have some account, we shall see that the number of volumes contained in a collegiate library must have been extremely small. For instance, the catalogue[1] appended to Bishop Bateman's statutes, dated 1350, enumerates eighty-four volumes, classed under the following subjects, in two divisions[2], viz. those presented to the College for the immediate use of the Fellows (*A*); and those reserved for the Bishop's own use during his life (*B*):

	A	*B*
Books on Civil Law	7	3
Books on Canon Law	19	13
Books on Theology	3	25
Books for the Chapel	7	7
	36	48

At King's Hall, in 1394, eighty-seven volumes are enumerated[3]; but at Peterhouse in 1418 we find three hundred and two volumes, divided among seventeen subjects. The general heading of the catalogue[4] states that it contains "all the books belonging to

[1] [Printed in the Camb. Antiq. Soc. Communications, Vol. II. p. 73.]

[2] [The headings of the two lists are as follows: "Libri per nos de præsenti dicto nostro Collegio dati et in dicto Collegio ex nunc ad Sociorum communem usum perpetuo remansuri."

"Libri vero de præsenti per nos dicto collegio dati, quorum usum nobis pro vitæ nostræ tempore quamdiu nobis placuerit duximus reservandum immediate inferius describuntur."]

[3] [History of Trinity College, Vol. II. p. 442.]

[4] [This catalogue is written at the beginning of the old parchment Register of the College, preserved in the Master's Lodge.]

the house of S. Peter in Cambridge, both those which are chained in the Library, those which are divided among the Fellows, and those of which some are intended to be sold, while certain others are laid up in chests within the aforesaid house[1]." The subordinate headings may be translated as follows:

Books on Theology chained	61	
,, ,, assigned to the Fellows	36	
	—	97
Books on Natural Philosophy chained in the Library	32	
Books on Metaphysics[2]	3	
Books on Moral Philosophy	5	
Books on Natural Philosophy, Metaphysics, and Moral Philosophy, divided among the Fellows	19	
	—	59
Books on Astronomy		10
Books on Alchemy (*alkemomia*)		1
Books on Arithmetic (*arsmetrica*)		1
Books on Music		1
Books on Geometry		1
Books on Rhetoric		1
Books on Logic	5	
,, ,, divided among the Fellows	15	
	—	20
Books on Grammar		6
Books on Poetry chained	4	
Books on Poetry and Grammar assigned to the Fellows	13	
	—	17
Books on History (*Libri de cronicis*) chained		4
Books on Medicine chained	15	
,, ,, assigned to the Fellows	3	
	—	18
Books on Civil Law chained	9	
,, ,, ,, divided among the Fellows	20	
	—	29
Books on Canon Law chained	18	
,, ,, ,, to be divided among the Fellows[3]	19	
	—	37
Total		302

1 ["Registrum factum in vigilia natalis domini nostri Jesu Christi Anno ab incarnacione eiusdem M°cccc°xviij° de omnibus libris pertinentibus domui Sancti Petri Cantabr' tam cathenatis in librario (*sic*), diuisis inter socios, quam aliis quorum quidam exponentur vendicioni et aliqui reponuntur in cistis domus predicte."]

2 [It may be presumed that these books, and the others in the list about which nothing is said, were chained for reference.]

3 ["Libri juris canonici *diuidendi* inter socios." In the previous entries the books are described as "*diuisi* inter socios," or "*assignati* sociis."]

A catalogue of the University Library, which, as the present Librarian, Mr Bradshaw, has shewn[1], was made about 1435, enumerates only 122 volumes, distributed as follows:

[Books on General Theology][2]	53
Books on Scholastic Theology (*Theologia disputata*)	15
Books on Moral Philosophy	5
Books on Natural Philosophy	12
Books on Medicine (*medicinalis philosophia*) . .	5
Books on Logic	1
Books on Poetry	0
Libri sophisticales	1
Books on Grammar	6
Books on History (*Libri cronicales*)	0
Books on Canon Law	24
Total	122

The catalogue of the Library of Queens' College, dated 1472, enumerates one hundred and ninety-nine volumes[3]; the second catalogue of the University Library, dated 1473, three hundred and thirty volumes[4]; an early catalogue of the library of S. Catharine's Hall, one hundred and four volumes, of which eighty-five were given by the Founder[5]; and a catalogue of the old library of King's College, dated 1453, one hundred and seventy-four volumes. In these catalogues the books are not directly classed under heads, but arranged roughly, according to subject, in their respective cases.]

These examples, which we have no reason to regard as exceptional, are sufficient to shew that an ordinary chamber would be large enough to contain all the volumes possessed by a college, even after some of the more generally useful books of reference had been chained to desks for the resort of students. A century elapsed after the foundation of colleges before the real library was introduced, that is to say, a room expressly contrived for the purpose of containing books, of considerably greater

[1] [Camb. Antiq. Soc. Communications, Vol. II. p. 239.]

[2] [No heading to the first division of the list is given in the catalogue.]

[3] [Camb. Antiq. Soc. Communications, Vol. II. p. 165.]

[4] [Ibid. Vol. II. p. 258.]

[5] [Camb. Antiq. Soc. Quarto Publ., No. I. This catalogue represents the state of the library at the end of the fifteenth century, for it contains the books given by Richard Nelson, who founded a Fellowship in 1503, and probably gave his books at the same time, "sub ea condicione quod semper remanerent cum tribus sociis."]

length than the ordinary chambers, and provided with numerous windows on both sides corresponding to the desks or bookstalls, which, in college libraries, appear always to have been arranged at right angles to the walls, as at present.

The upper chamber (*solarium*) which Thomas Cobham, Bishop of Worcester, began to build over the old Congregation House on the north side of S. Mary's Church, Oxford, about 1320, for the reception of the books which he intended to present to the University, is the earliest of these libraries in existence. It still retains on the south side part of a range of equidistant single-light windows of the simplest character, which, as just stated, mark the distinction of the apartment. This room is about sixty feet long by nineteen feet broad, and, in its original state, had probably seven of these single-light windows on each side, and a window of two lights at the east end[1]. A long controversy between the University and Oriel College is said to have rendered the benefaction useless for more than forty years; and it was not until 1367 that the University, in full Congregation assembled, decided that a contemporary statute, regulating the use of Bishop Cobham's books, should be regarded as a statute of the University[2]. It is directed by this document that the books are to be chained, in proper order; and that the Scholars who wish to use them are to have free access to them at convenient hours (*temporibus opportunis*). Lastly, certain volumes, of greater value, are to be sold, to the value of forty pounds, or more, if a larger sum can be obtained for them, for the purpose of purchasing an annual rent-charge of sixty shillings, to be paid to a chaplain, who is to pray for the soul of the aforesaid Thomas Cobham, and other benefactors; and who is to take charge of the books given by him and them, and of all other books heretofore given, or hereafter to be given, to the University. The passing of this statute may probably be regarded as the first institution of the office of University Librarian.

The library of Durham College, now Trinity College,

[1] A view of this south side is given in The Archæological Journal, Vol. VIII. p. 132, to illustrate "Remarks on the Church of St Mary the Virgin, Oxford" by the Principal of Brasenose.

[2] [Wood, History and Antiquities of the University of Oxford, II. 911. Munimenta Academica, Rolls Series, I. 226.]

Oxford, is said to have been built in the reign of King Henry IV. (1399—1413) for the express purpose of containing the collection of books which Richard de Bury, otherwise Richard Angervyle, Bishop of Durham[1], had bequeathed in 1345, to the end that the students of Durham College and the whole University might, under certain conditions, make use of it. The books "more than all the Bishops of England had then in their custody[2]" were kept in chests, under the custody of scholars deputed for the purpose, until the library was built, and they were then deposited therein, in certain pews or studies to which they were attached by chains. The building remains, as the library of Trinity College, and occupies nearly the whole of the first floor of the east side of the quadrangle, but the books were destroyed or dispersed by the visitors of King Edward VI. soon after the dissolution of Durham College. [It is thirty-seven feet long by eighteen feet wide.] The present oak stalls or bookcases, four on each side, were erected from a bequest of Edward Hindmer, sometime Fellow, in 1618. [The rules which the Bishop drew up to regulate the use of his books are summarised in the nineteenth chapter of a treatise called *Philobiblon*, written either by himself, or under his direction, at Auckland, and completed 24 January, 1344. We will translate the following passages as most nearly concerning our present purpose:

"The books are to be entrusted to the care of five scholars of the Hall, appointed by the Master; of these five, three, and on no account a smaller number, may give out books for the use and inspection of students. If a book is wanted for the purpose of making extracts, or transcribing the whole, it is on no account to be taken beyond the precincts of the House.

When a scholar makes application for the loan of a book—and under these circumstances we make no difference between seculars and regulars—the curators are to investigate carefully whether they possess the book asked for in duplicate; if this be the case, they may lend it on receipt of a pledge of greater value, in their judgment, than the book itself. Moreover, a writing to record the loan of the book is to be at once drawn up, containing the names of the persons who lend it, and the name of the person who receives it, together with the day and year in which it is lent. Should the curators, on the contrary, find that the book asked for does not exist in duplicate, they are on no account to

[1] [For an interesting account of. this Bishop, see Warton, History of English Poetry, ed. 1840, Vol. I. p. cxv. *note*.]

[2] Wood, *ut supra*, p. 910.

lend it, except to one of the scholars of the Hall—unless it be wanted for reference within the precincts of the House—but it is not to be taken beyond the precincts.

Anyone of the scholars of the House may borrow a book of the aforesaid curators; a note being taken of his own name, and of the day on which he first receives it; but he may not lend the book entrusted to himself to anybody else, unless he obtain the consent of three of the aforesaid curators; in which case the name of the first borrower is to be erased, and the name of the second inserted in its place.

Each of the curators, on entering into office, is to promise that he will observe all these provisions; and whenever they receive a book, or books, they are then and there to swear that they will on no account apply it or them to any other use than reference or study; and that they will never carry, or suffer to be carried, it or them, beyond the City of Oxford and the suburbs thereof.

Once in each year, the curators are to give an account of the way in which they have performed their duties to the Master of the House and to those scholars of the same whom he may think proper to bring with him; or, if he be too much occupied, let him appoint three inspectors—other than the curators—who are to read through the catalogue of the books, and see that they have them all, either the actual volumes, or the pledges which represent them. * * *

Every borrower of a book is to exhibit it once a year to the curators, when, if he chooses, he may also inspect his pledge.

Should a book be accidentally lost, by death, theft, fraud, or carelessness, the person who loses it, or his surety, or his executor, is to refund the value of it, and take back the pledge.

Should any money, from any source whatever, fall into the hands of the curators, it is to be spent on the repair and improvement of the books, and on nothing else[1]."

The architect-founder of New College included in his design an extensive library, occupying about seventy feet of the first floor on the east side of the quadrangle, and characterised by a range of nine windows, of a different design to the others in the quadrangle, and of a much larger size, each being of two lights, divided by a transom. This library was considerably altered in 1675. As it then stood it was divided into two distinct apartments: the Arts Library, and the Law Library at right angles to the former[2], over the building called "The Chequer". In addition to these there was another chamber in the roof, over

[1] ["Philobiblon, sive de Amore Librorum et Institutione Bibliothecæ Tractatus pulcherrimus; cui accessit Appendix de MSS. Oxoniensibus;" opera et studio T. I. [Thomæ James]. 4to. Oxford, 1599, p. 58.]

[2] [See the ground plan of New College, given above, p. 256.] Loggan's views exhibit the Library in its old and new state.

the Arts Library, termed the Manuscript Library, a distinction plainly assigned after the invention of printing. In the above year, however, partly perhaps in consequence of a bequest of five hundred volumes from Michael Woodward, D.D., Warden 1658—75, the Manuscript Library was enlarged, and windows were inserted in it on the side next to the quadrangle, similar to those below. At the same time the Law Library was converted into a Common Chamber for the Society, the books therein being removed to the Manuscript Library, and the entrance changed from the north to the south end, the old entrance being converted into a passage to the newly made Common Room.

Here again we have an instance of the imitative spirit which exercised such a powerful influence on collegiate architecture. Before the foundation of New College, though the statutes which we have reviewed shew that the several founders contemplated the possession of an ample collection of books, no regular Library enters into the composition of the quadrangle of any college in either University, though most of them evidently had some room, or part of a room, in which their manuscripts were kept; but, after the example had been set by Wykeham, the plan of every subsequent college includes a Library of sufficient dimensions to subsist at least until the Reformation, if not until the present time; and, moreover, the older colleges added such a room to their existing buildings, or included it in the new quadrangle which they then began to erect in imitation of their more modern neighbours. It may therefore be stated, in general terms, that a Library, as we now understand the word, was not adopted as an element of collegiate architecture until after 1380, the date of the foundation of New College.

The first recorded work at Cambridge after this date is the building of the great quadrangle at Peterhouse. This included a library, begun 1431, which occupied the greater part of the west side of the quadrangle, and was probably about sixty feet long by twenty feet broad[1]. The will of King Henry the Sixth, dated 12 March, 1447—48, provides a noble library, one hundred and ten feet long by twenty-four feet broad, on the western side of the proposed quadrangle of King's College, [and on

[1] [History of Peterhouse, Vol. I. pp. 10, 16.]

the east side of the quadrangle of Eton College, a Library of the same breadth, and fifty-two feet long[1]]. At Queens' College, Catharine Hall, Jesus College, Christ's College, S. John's College, and Magdalene College, the Library formed part of the original quadrangle, either built or planned by the Founder, as has been already related in the separate collegiate histories. At Oxford, in the same way, the Library is included in the Founder's quadrangle at the colleges of Exeter, Lincoln, All Souls, Brasenose, Magdalen, and Corpus Christi.

We will next review the older colleges at the two Universities, and note the gradual addition of a Library to their buildings.

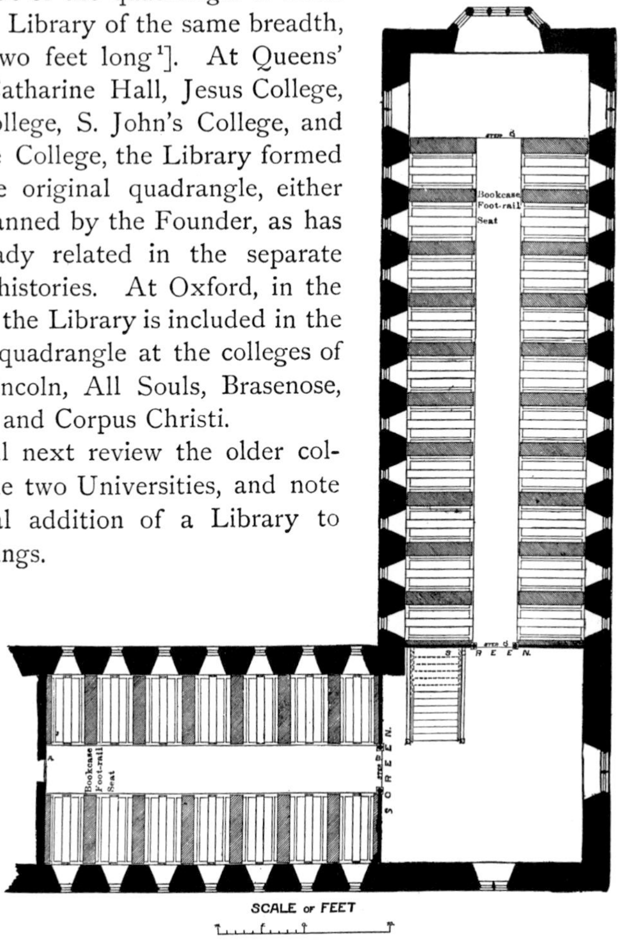

Fig. 1. Plan of the Library of Merton College, Oxford.

At Merton College, Oxford, founded about 1274, the Library is attributed by tradition to William Reade, Bishop of Chichester 1368—85, but, as explained above (p. 250), the history of the early buildings of Merton College is extremely uncertain, and the position of the Library which preceded that built by Bishop Reade in 1376, is unknown. Mr Gutch remarks with reference to it:

[1] [History of Eton College and King's College, Vol. I. pp. 356, 370.]

"The *Library*, before the present very ancient one, we know no more of, than that it was a room, at first with one Chest for books, and afterwards, as books increased, with more Chests in it[1]."

Bishop Reade's Library (fig. 1) occupies the greater part of the upper floor of the south and west sides of the small quadrangle to the south of the chapel, and is of considerable extent, having a total length of 133 feet. It retains unaltered its series of simple equidistant single-light windows, by which it is at once distinguished from the ordinary chambers.

At University College, Wood gives the following account of the Library:

"At first the Society kept those books they had (which were but few) in chests, and once, sometimes twice in a year, made choice for the borrowing of such as they liked, by giving a certificate under their hands for the restoring of them again to their proper place. At length when their first quadrangle was built [at the beginning of the reign of King Henry VI.], they appointed a place of stowage for them in an upper room at the west end of their Chapel, and what they procured afterwards, whether MSS or printed books, they added to the former[2]."

At Balliol College, Mr Thomas Chace (Master 1412—23) began the construction of the Library in 1431, after he had resigned his office. It was completed about 1477 by Mr Robert Abdy (Master 1477—94) assisted by a benefaction from William Grey, Bishop of Ely[3]. The total length of this Library is seventy feet, and the breadth twenty feet. It is lighted by a range of ten windows on each side, which still remain, each of two lights divided by a transom; but the interior was completely rearranged and altered by James Wyatt in 1792, when every vestige of antiquity was carefully obliterated. At Oriel College the first library, on the east side of the quadrangle, was not built until about the year 1444. Before that period the books "were reposed in chests, and by the Fellows of the House were borrowed thence upon certain pledges given in to the keepers of them[4]."

At Cambridge the Accounts of King's Hall shew that a new

[1] [Wood, History, etc., of the Colleges and Halls in the University of Oxford, p. 18, *note*.]

[2] [Ibid. p. 61.] [3] [Ibid. p. 89.] [4] [Ibid. p. 132.]

Library was begun in 1416—17, to replace an older and probably smaller building. The Library then built subsisted until the reign of Queen Elizabeth[1]. At Clare Hall a Library was being built between 1420 and 1430, and when the College was rebuilt after the fire of 1521, the Library occupied the whole upper floor of the north side of the quadrangle[2]. At Michael House the Library was extensively repaired, and possibly rebuilt, in 1425[3]. At Gonville Hall the first Library was built on the west side of the quadrangle in 1441, the books having previously been kept in a strong-room, as Dr Caius informs us[4]. A storey was added over the Hall at Pembroke College for a Library in 1452[5]. At Trinity Hall and Corpus Christi College the books were kept in an ordinary chamber, in the former at the east end of the chapel[6], and in the latter on the first floor next to the Master's Lodge[7], until after the Reformation.

When it became expedient or necessary, from the accumulation of books, to add a Library to a college of which the quadrangle was already completed, it was usually constructed as a wing jutting out from the exterior of the quadrangle, or as a completely detached building. These additions frequently became the nucleus of a new quadrangle, or served to complete one already commenced. For instance, the ancient Library of Queen's College, Oxford, founded about 1379, was a detached building, about forty feet long, in a small court at the west end of the chapel; and at Exeter College the "comely Library" which was built on the east side of the quadrangle about 1383, stood detached among its irregular buildings. With these exceptions, however, the examples of this mode of arrangement all date subsequently to the Reformation, as we will proceed to point out.

In 1588 Dr Andrew Perne planned the western portion of the present library of Peterhouse, Cambridge, which connected

1 [History of Trinity College, Vol. II. pp. 441, 459.]
2 [History of Clare Hall, Vol. I. pp. 78, 113.]
3 [History of Trinity College, Vol. II. p. 399.]
4 [History of Gonville and Caius College, Vol. I. p. 167.]
5 [History of Pembroke College, ibid. p. 138.]
6 [History of Trinity Hall, ibid. p. 226.]
7 [History of Corpus Christi College, ibid. pp. 253, 254, 262.]

the great quadrangle with the street[1]. In 1596 at S. John Baptist College, Oxford, a Library was projected into the garden from the south-eastern corner of the ancient quadrangle of Bernard College; and in 1631, William Laud, D.D., then Lord Bishop of London, who had been President 1611—21, commenced the addition of a second quadrangle to the first, under the direction of Inigo Jones, and,

"taking down the east window and the upper on the south side, did lengthen the Library towards the east twenty feet or thereabouts, and added another Library thereunto called the Inner Library (which taketh up the east side of the lesser Quadrangle) purposely to contain Manuscripts, all smaller books which might otherwise be in danger of being lost, any rarity that might be afterwards given, mathematical books and instruments, and other monuments of greater price[2]."

About 1600 the present Library of Trinity Hall, Cambridge, was built. This is a wing which projects in like manner into the garden from the north-western angle of the quadrangle, and as the Master's Lodge projects from the opposite, or south-western angle, a second court is formed, open on the west side to the garden[3]. In 1610 the foundress of Wadham College, Oxford, arranged her Library in a similar manner in her original buildings, with the exception, that the kitchen is below it, and the chapel forms the corresponding wing on the south[4]. In 1623 the Library at S. John's College, Cambridge, was erected in a similar position with reference to the second court; and between 1669 and 1671 the erection of ranges of chambers next the river, and on the south side, completed the third quadrangle of the college[5]. In 1663 the present Library of Brasenose College, Oxford, was built, which connects the south-east corner of the original quadrangle with the new chapel previously erected in 1656[6]. Thus a second quadrangle was formed, having the south range of the old quadrangle on the north side, the library on the east side, the chapel on the south side, and closed on the west side by an ornamental wall. In 1669, a new Library was built for Univer-

1 [History of Peterhouse, Vol. I. p. 28.]

2 [Wood, *ut supra*, p. 551. Ingram's Memorials, S. John's College, p. 13.]

3 [History of Trinity Hall, Vol. I. p. 226.]

4 [Wood, *ut supra*, p. 601.]

5 [History of S. John's College, Vol. II. pp. 264—271.]

6 [Wood, *ut supra*, p. 371.]

sity College, over the kitchen, which was external to the quadrangle on the south side[1]. This work, however, did not lead to any further increase of the college buildings. In 1676 the first stone was laid of the Library at Trinity College, Cambridge, designed by Sir Christopher Wren. Dr Nevile (Master 1593—1615) had previously formed a second court open to the west by erecting two parallel ranges of chambers projecting westwards from the exterior of the great quadrangle. This Library completed the court, and closed it on the west side, the north and south ranges being lengthened so as to connect them with it[2]. In 1677 the second quadrangle of Jesus College, Oxford, was added to and completed, part of the south side, and as much of the north side, having been erected about thirty-seven years before. Half of the first floor of the western side was appropriated to the Library, which, however, is not distinguished externally from the chambers[3]. In 1692 the present Library of Queen's College, Oxford, was built, as the west side of the new north quadrangle[4]. The present Library of Christ Church was begun in 1716, from the design of Dr George Clarke, Fellow of All Souls College, and completed in 1761. Before this Library was built the books belonging to the college had been placed in the ancient refectory of S. Frideswide. The new building forms the south side of the so-called "Peckwater" quadrangle, which had been brought to its present appearance a few years before, but it is completely detached at the angles. In the original design this Library stood upon an open cloister like that of Trinity College, Cambridge. This arrangement, however, was subsequently altered by walling up the arches to half their height, and placing windows in the rest of the space, so as to obtain more room for books and pictures[5]. In the same year, 1716, the Library of All Souls College was begun, from the design of Nicholas Hawksmoore. It was so planned as to match, in its external form, the ancient chapel, in order that the two

[1] [Wood, *ut supra*, p. 62.]

[2] [History of Trinity College, Vol. II. p. 480, pp. 531—550.]

[3] [Wood, *ut supra*, p. 583.]

[4] [Ibid. p. 157.]

[5] [Ibid. pp. 458, 460. In 1775 the old Library was converted into a lecture-room and chambers. A view of the exterior in the original state is given by Skelton, *Oxonia Antiqua Restaurata*, Plate 9; another, taken in 1833, will be found in Ingram's Memorials, Christ Church, p. 58.]

might constitute the north and south sides respectively of the new, or second, quadrangle which was subsequently completed[1]. In 1779 a new Library was built in the garden of Exeter College. It was a detached building, standing at right angles to the eastern side of the quadrangle, and between that and the Bodleian Library. It was designed by Mr John Townsend of Oxford[2]. [The present Library, begun in 1864, from the design of Sir George Gilbert Scott, occupies the same position as the old one.] In 1788 the third, or present, Library was built at Oriel College from a design by Mr James Wyatt. It is a detached building, which, like the Library of Christ Church, completes the second quadrangle begun seventy years before by the erection of the Robinson and Carter Buildings, which form the east and west sides respectively.

Another expedient to obtain more space for the Library was to transfer it to the old chapel of a college when a new one had been built upon a different site. This was done at Exeter College, Oxford, in 1625[3], and at Lincoln College in 1656[4]. The example was followed at Emmanuel College, Cambridge, in 1677[5], and at Pembroke College in 1690[6].

The positions of college libraries offer the very curious facts that the great majority of those which were built up to the beginning of the sixteenth century stand with their lateral walls facing east and west; those which were built after this to the end of the Commonwealth, including fourteen examples, face, without exception, north and south. Afterwards the contrary arrangement prevailed for a little while, but, on the whole, taking into account the remaining examples down to the present time, as many stand one way as the other.

The following sixteen libraries, erected before the beginning of the sixteenth century, face east and west: Merton College, Oxford (1376); New College, Oxford (1380); Queen's College, Oxford (1389)[7]; Exeter College, Oxford (1404); Peterhouse,

[1] [Wood, *ut supra*, p. 283.]

[2] [Ingram's Memorials, Exeter College, p. 14.]

[3] [Wood, *ut supra*, p. 115.]

[4] [Ibid. p. 248.]

[5] [History of Emmanuel College, Vol. II. p. 710.]

[6] [History of Pembroke College, Vol. I. pp. 136, 149.]

[7] [This library is shewn in Loggan's print of the college. The date is that given by Wood's edition, *ut supra*, p. 157, *note*, but it is very uncertain.]

Cambridge (1431); S. Bernard's College, Oxford (1436); All Souls College, Oxford (1437); the New Library, begun over the Canon-Law School, on the west side of the Schools Quadrangle, Cambridge (1438); Gonville Hall, Cambridge (1441); Oriel College, Oxford, First Library (1444); King's College, Cambridge, as designed (1448); Pembroke College, Cambridge (1452); Archbishop Rotherham's Library, Cambridge (1470); Jesus College, Cambridge (1505); Christ's College, Cambridge (1510); S. John's College, Cambridge (1516); Magdalen College, Oxford (1473).

The exceptions are: Bishop Cobham's Library over the Congregation House, Oxford (1320); the south wing of the Library at Merton College, Oxford (1376); Balliol College, Oxford (1431); Lincoln College, Oxford (1436); the upper story of the Divinity School, Oxford (1445); Queens' College, Cambridge (1448); the south wing of the Public Library, Cambridge (1457).

The following fourteen libraries, erected between the end of the sixteenth century and the Restoration, face north and south: Brasenose College, Oxford (1511); Clare Hall, Cambridge (1535); Christ Church, Oxford (1545); Trinity College, Cambridge, First Library (1560); Peterhouse, Cambridge (1589); S. John Baptist, Oxford (1596); Trinity Hall, Cambridge (1600); Sidney Sussex, Cambridge (1602); Wadham College, Oxford (1610); S. John's College, Cambridge (1623); Exeter College, Oxford, old chapel (1625); Jesus College, Oxford (1626); Oriel College, Oxford, Second Library (1637); Lincoln College, Oxford, old chapel (1656); the only exception being the additional wing at S. John's College, Oxford (1631), which faces east and west.

The following ten libraries, erected between the Restoration and the present time, face east and west: Brasenose College, Oxford (1663); University College, Oxford (1669); S. Catharine's Hall, Cambridge, as designed (1673); Trinity College, Cambridge (1676); Emmanuel College, Cambridge, old chapel (1678); Jesus College, Oxford (1677); Queen's College, Oxford (1692); Magdalene College, Cambridge, Pepysian Library (1703); Pembroke College, Oxford (1709); Worcester College, Oxford (1720). On the other hand, the following eleven examples face north and south: S. Catharine's Hall, Cambridge, as completed (1675); Clare Hall, Cambridge (1689); Pembroke College, Cambridge, old chapel (1690); Christ Church, Oxford (1716); All Souls College, Oxford (1716); Exeter College, Oxford (1778); Oriel College, Oxford (1788); Corpus Christi College, Cambridge (1823); King's College, Cambridge (1824); Gonville and Caius College, Cambridge (1853); Pembroke College, Cambridge (1875).

Vitruvius lays down the rule that libraries ought to face the east because their use requires the morning light, which will preserve their contents from decay; whereas, if the room should face the south or the west, they are liable to be damaged by damp and worms, which are nourished by moist winds[1]. [It appears probable that the first of these considerations influenced the builders of the early colleges, the inmates of which rose betimes, and would be glad to get as much light as possible for their studies. After the Reformation, however, when, as has been shewn in previous essays, the wealth of the country increased, and considerations of personal comfort began to be generally accepted, the library would be placed in the position which commanded the greatest amount of warmth.]

Ancient libraries were never placed on the ground, but usually on the first floor, or even higher, for the sake of preserving their contents from the damp to which ground-floors are necessarily subject. This excellent rule has been followed in modern examples, the only exceptions being the libraries of Pembroke College and Emmanuel College, at Cambridge, which, as already stated, were designed for chapels; and those of All Souls College and Exeter College at Oxford. There are also some other cases in which the necessity of obtaining space for increasing acquisitions has led to the occupation of chambers adjacent to and beneath the library, as at Queens' College, Jesus College, and the University Library, Cambridge; and at Christ Church and Queen's College, Oxford.

The additional precaution of admitting the air beneath the library by means of an open arcade or cloister was employed in several modern examples at the revival of classical architec-

[1] Vitruvius, "De Architectura," ed. Schneider, 8vo. Leipsic, 1807. Book vi. ch. 4.

ture. The additional library built by Inigo Jones at S. John's College, Oxford, in 1631, is the earliest example of this treatment. The open cloister, however, is only partially extended beneath the floor, as is also the case at Queen's College, Oxford, and in the Peckwater Library at Christ Church, as it was first built. But in the libraries of Brasenose College, Oxford (1663), and of Trinity College, Cambridge (1676), the cloister occupies the whole of the ground-floor. In the last example the air is admitted freely to traverse the space by grated windows in the river-front, as well as by the open arches next the court[1].

Dame Dorothy Wadham in 1610 prudently placed her library over the kitchen, by which dryness is no doubt effectually secured; and this example was followed at University College in the same University in 1669. The old library of Pembroke College, Cambridge, was placed over the hall; the present library of S. Catharine's Hall is in the same position; and the library of Pembroke College, Oxford, was removed in 1709, from a room over the south aisle of Aldate's Church to a room built to contain it above the hall[2]. At the colleges of Corpus Christi and Magdalene, Cambridge, the library was over the chapel, and it was similarly placed in the quadrangle of Clare Hall as rebuilt after the fire of 1521, and at Sidney Sussex College before the present chapel was built.

Libraries rarely face or join the street, the only examples at Cambridge being at Christ's College, S. John's College, the original design for S. Catharine's Hall, as shewn by Loggan, [and the University Library when Schools Street was a thoroughfare]; at Oxford at Brasenose College, and at All Souls College where the gable only stands in the street. The manifest reason for this is to prevent disturbance to students.

In the old examples the Library is not architecturally marked as a distinct building like the Hall or the Chapel; but it can generally be picked out from the ranges of chambers by the row of equidistant windows on either side already alluded to. Of these

[1] The room originally occupied by the Pepysian Library at Magdalene College, Cambridge, has also an open cloister beneath part of it, but the building was erected a considerable time before the adaptation of the room in question to the purposes of a Library. [History of Magdalene College, Vol. II. pp. 366—375.]

[2] [Wood, *ut supra*, p. 625.]

excellent examples still remain at Cambridge at Queens' College, Jesus College, and S. John's College.

Modern architects have often given a distinctive character to the Library. The Library built by Sir Christopher Wren at Trinity College, Cambridge, is the noblest and most successful example of this treatment.

CHAPTER II[1].

THE SYSTEM OF CHAINING BOOKS IN MEDIEVAL LIBRARIES. EXAMPLES FROM HEREFORD, LEYDEN, FLORENCE, ZUTPHEN, LINCOLN. THE CHAINING AND BINDING OF BOOKS ILLUSTRATED BY COLLEGIATE ACCOUNTS. CHAINING NOT ABANDONED UNTIL THE END OF THE LAST CENTURY. NAMES GIVEN TO BOOKCASES. SURVEY OF THE LIBRARY FITTINGS OF OXFORD AND CAMBRIDGE IN CHRONOLOGICAL ORDER.

[IT was shewn in the previous chapter that a medieval collegiate library was a long narrow room, lighted by equidistant windows on either side, and occasionally by a window at one end, in addition to those in the side-walls. The bookcases, and the seats for the readers, were placed at right angles to each side-wall; the former in the space between the windows, the latter in front of them. These primitive fittings still remain in the library of Merton College, Oxford; but, before attempting to describe them, or to trace the modifications which library-fittings have assumed at different periods, it will be well to explain the system of fixing the books to the shelves by means of chains—a system which was universally employed throughout Europe, both before and after the invention of printing, and which has been so frequently alluded to in the extracts cited from the collegiate statutes. This system has not survived in

[1] [Professor Willis had devoted much time and attention to the history of library fittings, but, unfortunately, he had not committed to paper anything except a number of notes and sketches. He had not even written out an account of the system of chaining books, which he intended to describe at length, as he states in more than one place. Under these circumstances I have endeavoured, by a careful study of all the examples of chained libraries which I have been able to discover, and of the ancient bookcases in the libraries of Oxford and Cambridge, to supply such a history as I conceive it was his intention to write.]

any library in either University, though, after it has been once understood, it is not difficult to detect more or less complete traces of it. It is therefore necessary, in order to explain it, to look elsewhere for an example. Single volumes are not unfrequently to be found chained in churches, but, so far as we have been able to discover, there are only three collections of books in England now attached to the shelves by chains, namely: the Chapter Library in Hereford Cathedral; a Library in the vestry of the parish Church of All Saints in the same city; and the Library attached to Wimborne Minster. These we have carefully examined, and will proceed to describe, by the help of the accompanying illustrations, reduced from drawings made on the spot[1]. In the next place we will examine the system adopted on the continent, which will be found, in some places at least, to differ materially from that which was adopted in England.

In the first of the above-mentioned libraries there are five complete bookcases (fig. 2) and the ruins of two others. Each

Fig. 2. Bookcase in the Chapter Library, Hereford Cathedral.

is 9 feet 8 inches long, 2 feet 2 inches wide, and about 8 feet high. The material is unplaned oak, very rough; the ends are

[1] [The drawings at Hereford were made by the permission, and with the kind assistance, of the Rev. John Jebb, D.D., Canon of Hereford.]

2 inches thick, made of three boards, fastened together with strong wooden pegs. The vertical supports which sustain the first shelf are also 2 inches thick; but the divisions between the upper shelves, made of rough boards which do not meet, and all the shelves are only one inch thick. The whole structure seems to be quite original, with the exception of the cornice, the brackets which support the desk, and the frames to contain the catalogue. The latter, which occur on three cases only, are known to have been added in the 17th century by Thomas Thornton, D.D., Canon Residentiary.

Fig. 3. Part of a single volume, shewing the clasp, the ring for the chain, and the mode of attaching it: Hereford.

The books, being all manuscripts, are still bound in their original boards, fastened together with clasps of leather. To attach the chain a narrow strip of flat brass is passed round the left-hand board, and riveted to it, in such a manner as to leave a loop in front of the edge of the board, wide enough to admit an iron ring, an inch and a quarter in diameter, to which one end of the chain is fastened (fig. 3). The book is placed on the shelf with the fore-edge turned outwards, and the other end of the chain is fastened to a second ring, rather larger than the former, which plays along an iron bar (fig. 4). For the two upper shelves these bars are

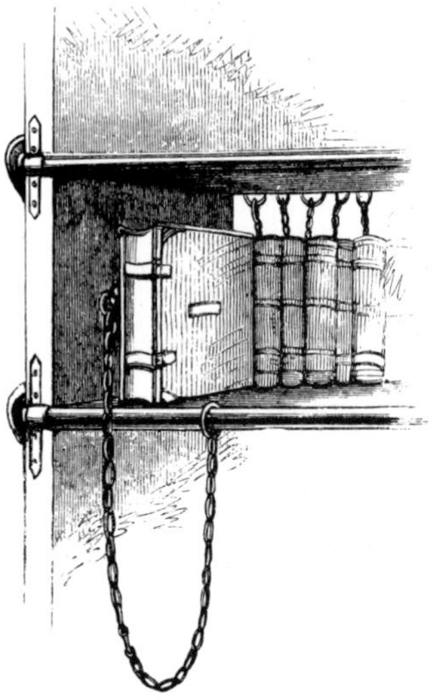

Fig. 4. A single volume, standing on the shelf, with the chain attached to the iron bar: Hereford.

supported in front of the shelf, at such a distance from it as to allow of easy play for the rings (fig. 2). Each bar extends only from partition to partition, so that three bars are needed for each shelf. For the lowest shelf there is a single bar only, set two inches behind the edge of the shelf, so as to keep the rings and chains out of the way of the desk. The bars for the upper shelves rest in iron sockets, screwed to the woodwork at the juncture of the horizontal shelves with the vertical divisions and ends respectively. The socket fixed to the end of the bookcase which stands against the wall is closed by an iron plate (fig. 5), so that the bar cannot pass beyond it. At the opposite end, that which would usually face the alley between the two rows of bookcases, the bars are secured by lock and key in the following manner. The whole system is shewn in the sketch of the complete bookcase (fig. 2); the sketches shewing the details of it will be referred to as we proceed. A piece of flat iron expanded into a triangle, is nailed to the end of the bookcase, just above the level of the uppermost shelf (fig. 2). Attached to this by a hinge is a hasp, or band of iron, two inches wide, and rather longer than the interval

Fig. 5. Iron bar and socket, closed to prevent removal of the bar: Hereford.

Fig. 6. Iron bar, with part of the iron plate or hasp which is secured by the lock and keeps the bar in place: Hereford.

between the two shelves. Opposite to each shelf this iron band expands into a semicircular plate to which a cap is riveted for the reception of the head of the socket in which the bar rests (fig. 6); and just below the middle shelf it drops into a lock and is secured by a key. A second hasp, similarly constructed, secures the lowest of the three bars; but, as that bar is behind, and not in front of, the shelf to which it belongs, the arrangements described above are reversed. One lock and key serves for the ironwork belonging to the three shelves.

Fig. 7. Piece of chain, shewing the swivel: Hereford. Actual size.

The removal of any of the volumes thus secured, or the addition of a new one, must have been a tedious and inconvenient operation. The bar would have to be withdrawn, and all the rings set free. Moreover, if this change had to be effected in one of the compartments remote from the end of the case which carried the lock, the bar belonging to each of the other compartments would have to be withdrawn before the required volume could be reached.

The chains are made of links of hammered iron, as shewn in the sketch (fig. 7) which represents a piece of one of them of the actual size. Most of them have a swivel in the centre, probably to prevent twisting. They vary somewhat in length, according to the shelf on which the books to which they belong are placed, it being obviously necessary to provide for the convenient placing of the books on the desk—the most usual dimensions being 3 feet 4 inches, 3 feet 6 inches, 4 feet 3 inches.

Each bookcase is provided with a desk just below the level of the lowest shelf; but, as in these examples the desks have evidently been altered, it will be better to reserve any description of this feature of a medieval bookcase until we come to other examples which have been better preserved. No books were placed below the desk.

At All Saints Church, Hereford, the books are arranged on three shelves carried along two sides of the room. The lowest shelf is three feet from the ground, and below it is a fixed desk, supported on legs. The ironwork, and the chains, so closely resemble those in the Chapter Library, from which they were not improbably copied, that they do not require a separate description. This example is a curious instance of the survival of the system of chaining down to comparatively modern times, for the collection was bequeathed to the parish by William Brewster, M.D., in 1715; and among the books chained are works published in 1706 and 1707.

At Wimborne Minster the books are placed in a small room, about fifteen feet square, over the vestry, a building in the Decorated style, situated between the south transept and the south aisle of the choir. Access to this room is obtained by a turret-stair at the south-west corner. It was formerly known as the Treasure House, but was fitted up as a Library in 1686, when the greater part of the books were given by the Rev. William Stone. Their arrangement therefore represents the fashions of a period long subsequent to that at which the bookcases in Hereford Cathedral were fitted up. There are two plain wooden shelves, carried round three sides of the room. The chains are attached to the right-hand board of each book, instead of to the left-hand board, as at Hereford, and they are made of iron wire, twisted as shewn in the sketch (fig. 8). The swivel, instead of being central, plays in a twist of the wire which forms the ring attached to the book. The iron bars are supported on eyes, and are secured by a tongue of iron passed over a staple fixed into the bracket

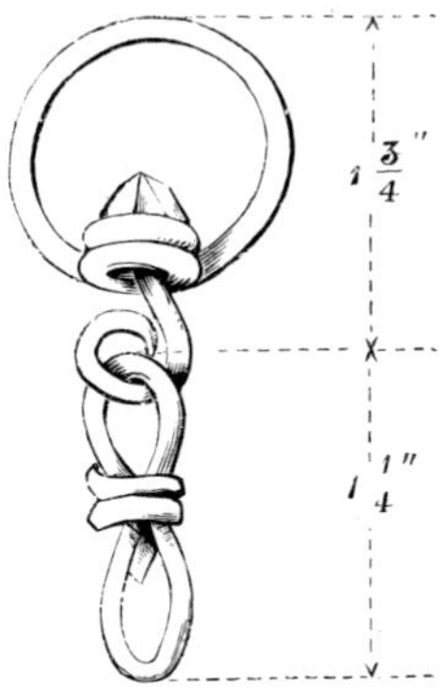

Fig. 8. Ring and links of chain: Wimborne Minster.

which supports the shelf (fig. 9). The tongue was originally kept in its place by a padlock, now replaced by a wooden peg.

Fig. 9. Iron bar, Wimborne; shewing the way in which it is secured to the bracket which supports the shelf.

No desk was attached to the shelves as at Hereford, but in lieu of it "there was a portable desk and stool, which the reader could bring near any shelf, and sitting sufficiently close for the chained book to rest upon the desk, he could peruse the volume there, and there only[1]."

A comparison of the evidence afforded by these three collections shews that in some English medieval libraries at least the books were ranged side by side as in a modern bookcase, with this exception, that the fore-edge and not the back was turned

[1] [Sketches of English Literature, by Clara Lucas Balfour, 12mo. Lond. 1852. Introduction. In the description of the Library there given the padlocks are specially mentioned. Compare also, A History of Wimborne Minster. 8vo. Lond. 1860; and Hutchins' Dorsetshire, Vol. II. p. 554.]

outwards. When the books were wanted for study they were taken down and laid on a desk, which, as we shall be able to shew from an examination of the older bookcases in the Oxford libraries, was usually bracketed to the framework of the case just below the lowest shelf. It followed therefore that out of each bookcase only so many books could be consulted at once as the length of the desk would accommodate; and it became necessary, for the convenience of students, to limit the number of shelves in each bookcase as much as possible, and to increase the number of cases and desks. In consequence it became usual to place only a single shelf, or at most two shelves, above each desk. This accounts for the large rooms required in early libraries for so few books. When the University of Oxford petitioned Humphrey Duke of Gloucester in 1444 to help them to build a new library, they specially dwelt upon the obstacles to study arising from the overcrowded condition of the old room. "Should any student," they said, "be poring over a single volume, as often happens, he keeps three or four others away on account of the books being chained so closely together[1]."

The books were ranged in the same manner in the library of the University of Leyden, as we learn from a print by Jan Cornelis Woudanus, dated 1610, a portion of which has been copied in the accompanying illustration (fig. 10)[2]. The print shews a long and lofty room, of moderate width. There are four large windows of three lights in each wall, extending from a few feet above the floor to the ceiling, and, from the way in which the light is made to fall on the bookcases, there was evidently a window in the end wall also. There were eleven bookcases on each side. Each bookcase appears to have contained only a single row of books, chained to a bar in front of the shelf, which was probably secured by a lock at one end of the bookcase. The desks were sloping, and, as the illustration

[1] [Macray, Annals of the Bodleian Library, p. 7.]

[2] [This illustration was made from a copy of the print in the British Museum, by kind permission of my friend Sidney Colvin, M.A., Keeper of the Prints. A view of the Leyden Library, closely resembling that from which the illustration has been taken, will be found in Illustrium Hollandiæ et Westfrisiæ Ordinum alma Academia Leidensis. 4to. Lugd. Bat. 1614. This view, reversed, is inserted in The Arts in the Middle Ages, by Paul Lacroix. Engl. transl. 8vo. London, 1870, p. 475.]

shews, at such a height above the ground that the readers were obliged to stand to consult the books.

The Biblioteca Laurenziana, or Medicean Library, at Florence, offers another type of the arrangement of chained books. The building, designed by Michael Angelo, was begun in 1525,

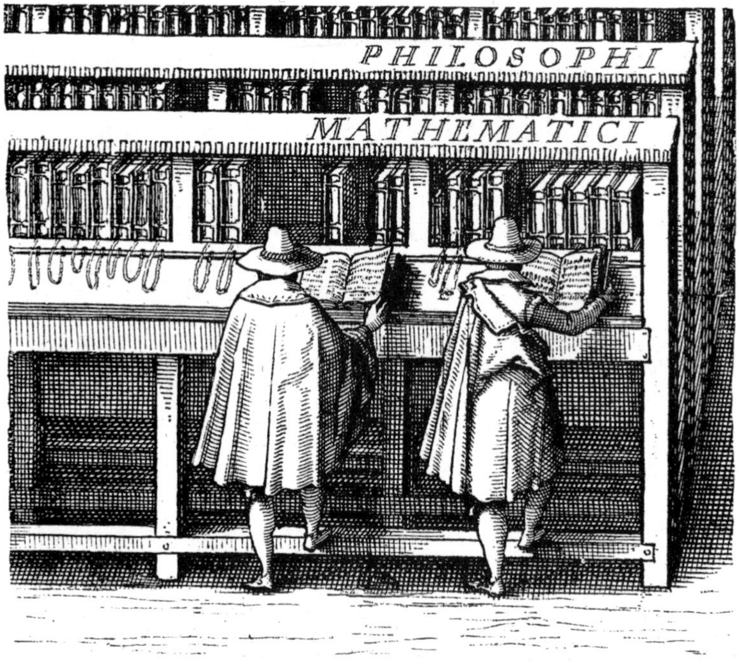

Fig. 10. Bookcases and desks in the Library of the University of Leyden; from a print dated 1610.

by desire of Pope Clement VII. (Giulio dei Medici), to contain the collection of books associated with the name of his ancestor Cosmo dei Medici. The bookcases, which are singularly beautiful specimens of woodwork, were executed, and probably designed without reference to Michael Angelo, by Antonio di Marco di Giano, called *il Carota*, and Gianbattista del Tasso. The material, walnut wood, was prescribed by the pope himself[1].

[1] [Life and Works of Michelangelo Buonarroti. By C. H. Wilson. 8vo. London, 1881. Chaps. XII. XIII. See also Vasari, ed. Milanesi, 1881, vii. 203.]

They are placed, as elsewhere, at right angles to the walls, on both sides of the room. Their general arrangement will be under-

Fig. 11. Bookcase and desk in the Medicean Library at Florence. From a photograph.

stood from the illustration (fig. 11). Each consists of a vertical central portion, to the end of which the catalogue is affixed. On one side of this there is a steep desk, on which the books are placed while they are being read, and beneath it a shelf, or cupboard, where they lie on their sides, one above the other, when not wanted for use. On the other side of the vertical portion is the reader's seat. The chain is attached to each book by a loop of iron inserted beneath the binding. The links are not of hammered iron as at Hereford (fig. 7), but of twisted wire, more like the later form in use at Wimborne (fig. 8). The bar of iron on which the rings at the opposite end of the chain are strung is placed in the space under the sloping desk. It is secured by a lock attached to the central bracket by which that space is divided[1].

This system of placing the books on a desk or lectern to which they were fastened by a chain appears to have been adopted in France, where elaborate bindings became the fashion at an early date. These were protected by elaborate bosses and corners of metal-work, which would of course effectually prevent the books from being ranged on shelves according to the usual English method.

There is a library at Zutphen in Holland, attached to the church of S. Wallburg, in which the books are chained to the desks in the following manner. Seats and desks are ranged round the room alternately, the desk being of a height convenient to be reached from the seat. The desks are double, like an ordinary church lectern, and the books lie upon the sloping portion, there being no shelf either above it or below it. Each book has a short chain attached to it by a ring fixed to the middle of the top of the right-hand board. The ring at the other end of the chain plays along an iron bar inserted into the upright ends of the desk one inch and a half above the top of the sloping

[1] [There is a single bookcase on this plan in the parish church of Waves Wootton, or, as it is commonly called, Wootton Wawen, in Warwickshire, with 9 volumes chained to it. It consists of a sloping desk, as at Florence, beneath which is a cupboard, closed by a long narrow door attached by hinges along its lower side. The books lie on their sides in this cupboard, at the back of which is the bar along which their rings are strung. All the volumes except one have the chain attached to the bottom of the right-hand board. The bookcase was evidently intended originally to be placed against a wall, for the legs at the back are quite plain, while those in front are more ornamental in style. The material is plain deal. I have not met with another example of this arrangement in England; and it appears not unlikely that the bookcase was copied—probably by description—from those at Florence. The books were given to the parish by George Dunscombe, fellow of King's College, Vicar, who died 1652. Harwood (Alumni Etonenses, pp. 229—30) mentions that they were kept in the vicarage-house, until, at the request of the people, they were chained to a desk in the south aisle of the church, 11 April, 1693.]

portion. At the end of the desk furthest from the wall the bar terminates in a hasp, secured in the ordinary manner by a lock. The chains resemble those at Hereford (fig. 7), but the swivel, instead of being central, is attached to the ring which plays along the bar. There are 18 desks, containing 316 volumes[1].

A desk similar to this in plan has been preserved in the Chapter Library at Lincoln, but it is provided with two shelves, a broad one below, and a narrow one above, the sloping portion, on either of which the books could be laid when not in use. The bar passes through the standards, at about six inches above the top of the desk.

The old Library at Pembroke College, Cambridge, was evidently fitted with sloping desks instead of shelves, but unfortunately we are wholly ignorant of their form and arrangement. Our knowledge of their existence is derived from a passage in Dr Matthew Wren's Account of the Library which has been already quoted (p. 396). It may be translated as follows:

> "I would have you know that in the year 1617 the Library was completely altered and made to assume an entirely new appearance. This alteration was rendered necessary by the serious damage, which, to our great sorrow, we found the books had suffered—a damage which was increasing daily—partly from the sloping form of the desks, partly from the inconvenient weight of the chains (*tum ex declivi pluteorum fabricâ, tum ex ineptâ mole catenarum*)."

The method of securing books to the shelves by chains, and of attaching the chains to the books, having been described, it will be interesting to quote a few illustrative passages from the collegiate accounts. These will be found to throw a good deal of light on the way in which books were bound, and upon the appliances required to carry out the operation.

When a book was given to a medieval library it was necessary in the first place to buy a chain, and, if the book were especially valuable, a pair of clasps; secondly, to employ a smith to put them on; and lastly, a painter, to write the name and classmark across the fore-edge. These processes were spoken of collectively as "chaining, howsing, and clasping," or simply, "chaining and desking." Strings were occasionally used

[1] [For this description I am indebted to my friends S. H. Vines, M.A., Fellow of Christ's College; and W. M. Fawcett, M.A. of Jesus College.]

instead of clasps; and the clasps themselves were made of strips of parchment or leather attached to metal plates. In some cases the external angles of the boards were protected by plates of brass or bronze, and bosses of the same material were fastened over the corners to prevent damage to the binding. Further, it was not uncommon to write the title, and the donor's name, on a piece of parchment overlaid with a thin plate of horn. The label, thus protected, was attached to the side of the book with narrow strips of leather laid along the edge, and fastened with small brass nails. A folio edition of Aristotle in the library of Peterhouse bears the following inscription, protected as above described: *Textus Aristotelis cum commentario Averrois ex dono magistri Willelmi Bacon quondam socii hujus Collegii.* The following entries, extracted from the Accounts of King's College, the University, S. John's College, and Queens' College, illustrate these various processes:

"Item pro cathenatione vij librorum, et howsing ac clasping, ut patet per billam M. Wodelark. .... ijs. xd[1]."

"Item pro cathenacione et cornu libri a magistro Doctore Fyrby uniuersitati legati .... iij^{d}[2]."

"Item pro vectura 3^{m}. librorum londonijs ex dono episcopi eboracensis .... xij^{d}.

"Item pro 3^{bus} cathenis pro eisdem libris............................ xvj^{d}.

"Item pro cathenacione eorundem et pro superscriptione......... viij^{d}[3]."

"Item for xiij yard and di' of sylke lace to stringe the new bookes for the lybrarye at iij^{d}. ye yarde .... iij^{s}. iiij^{d}. ob.[4]"

"Item to Philip Stacyoner for cornering, bossing, and chayninge Anatomiam Vessalii, [etc.] .... iij^{s}[5]."

"Item for twoe chaynes for the bookes [given by Mr Hollande] ...xij^{d}.
Item for .2. hookes for them ....iij^{d}.
Item horne and saddell nailes for the same bookes .... iij^{d}[6]."

"Item receaved of Mr Peter Shawe towards the cheyning and desking of his bookes given to the newe liberarie .... v^{li}[7]."

The next extract refers to the books given by Sir Nicholas Bacon to the University in 1574—75. The copper would be used for the slips passed round the board to secure the rings (fig. 3):

[1] [King's College Mundum Book, 1448–49.]

[2] [University Accounts, 1491-92, p. 47.]

[3] [Ibid. 1492–93, p. 63. The Archbishop of York alluded to is Thomas Rotherham.]

[4] [Audit-Book of S. John's College, 1560–61.]

[5] [Ibid. 1563–64, *Exp. Necess.*]

[6] [Magnum Journale of Queens' College, 1585–86, fo. 181.]

[7] [Sen. Burs. Accts. of Trinity College, 1600–1601. *Recepta.*]

"Item for 27 chaynes for the newe bookes in the librarye vij^{s}. vj^{d}. for 34 rynges xxij^{d}. for 4^{lb}. of copper ij^{s}. viij^{d}. for wyer iiij^{d}. for nayles ij^{d}. to John Sheres setting one 72 chaynes ij^{s}. and to Hillarye helping hym viij^{d}. and for setting on my Lorde Keeper's armes and wryting the names of the bookes and figures iij^{s}. vj^{d}. ....xviij^{s}. viij^{d}.[1]"

The most complete description of the whole process of chaining and binding a library which we have met with occurs in the Accounts of Eton College for 1519—20, and 1520—21[2], when the books, which, as explained in the History[3], were still in the vestry of the Church, were evidently rebound and re-arranged. In the first year 24 dozen chains of three sorts—explained in the next year's account to mean of three different lengths[4]—are bought; 48 iron bars for the rings to play upon; twelve locks, with a corresponding number of hasps (*claustra*) to secure the bars, and 4 keys—which would of course be kept in the custody of four officials of the college—; and lastly, a pair of pincers to cut the strips of brass or copper required for the attachment of the rings to the boards. The following is the text of this portion of the Account:

"Et pro xxiv duodenis cathenarum trium generum ad libros in bibliotheca cathenandos iiij^{li}. Et pro pari forpicum ad laminas eneas secandas ad fixuram dictorum librorum xvj^{d}. Et Roberto Oliuere fabro ferrario pro xlviij vectibus ferreis ad chatenas continend' pondere iij C et di C li, lvij^{s}. ij^{d}. Et eidem pro xij seris et totidem claustris et iiij clauibus precii capitis xx^{d}. xx^{s}."

In the next year a bookbinder named Andrew Lisley is employed for 199 days to bind and repair the books. He receives fourpence per day in wages, and one shilling per week in commons. The bursar buys for his use 20 calf skins, 36 white sheep skins, 3 large, and 3 small doe skins, 5 pig skins[5], and 28 red skins. After these different sorts of leather, the purchase is recorded of 100 plates of horn; 5000 copper nails—to be set round the edge of the boards, like bosses, to protect the binding—; 10 pounds and a quarter of strips of brass; 7 pounds of brass wire, the use

1 [University Accounts, 1574–75, fo. 129. b.]

2 [Audit-Book, 1519–20. *Custus templi.*]

3 [History of Eton College, Vol. I. p. 453.]

4 [In the Accounts for 1520–21 we find: "Et solvit pro .v. duodenis cathenarum maioris forme pro libris cathenandis in bibliotheca xx^{s}. Et pro sex duodenis cathenarum medie forme ix^{s}. Et pro j duodena cathenarum le bokill ij^{s}."]

5 [The words thus translated are: "pro quinque pellibus de le soure."]

of which it is difficult to explain; 27 pairs of clasps; and lastly, a quantity of green and red thread, glue of two kinds, and needles. The following is the text of the principal entries in this second portion of the Account:

"Et pro xx^{ti}. pellibus vitulinis vij^{s}. x^{d}. Et pro iij duodenis pellium ouillarum albarum ix^{s}. Et pro iij magnis pellibus damarum vj^{s}. Et iij aliis pellibus damarum iij^{s}. viij^{d}. et quinque pellibus de le soure v^{d}. in toto xv^{s}. viij^{d}. Et pro xxviij^{o}. rubris pellibus vij^{s}. iij^{d}. Et pro C laminis corneis iij^{s}. viij^{d}. Et pro v M^{l} clauiculorum cuperorum iuxta vij^{d} per mille ij^{s}. xj^{d}. Et pro decem libris lamine eree et quart' iiij^{s}. iiij^{d}. ob. Et pro vij^{li} eris tractilis le wire ij^{s}. iiij^{d}. Et pro ij duodenis le claspys et iij aliis paribus emptis a Lisleie pro libris edis iiij^{s}. Et pro filo ligatorio viridi et rubro xviij^{d}. Et pro glutino ad os et communi et acubus xvij^{d}[1]."

The dates of the extracts above cited shew that the medieval methods of chaining and binding were being still practised at the close of the sixteenth century. The following examples may be added to those which have been already collected. At Corpus Christi College Cambridge in 1554, it was ordered that the books bequeathed by Peter Nobys D.D. (Master 1516—23), should be taken better care of for the future, and, if the chains were broken, that they should be repaired at the expense of the college[2]. In 1555, Robert Chaloner, Esq., bequeathed his law books to Gray's Inn, with forty shillings in money, to be paid to his cousin, 'to th' entent that he maie by cheines therwith and fasten so manye of them in the Librarye at Grauisin [Gray's Inn] as he shall think convenyente'[3]. In 1573, Dr Caius directs by Will twelve copies of his own works to be given to his college 'there to be kepte as the other bokes are, and to be successivelye tyed with chaynes in the Librarye of the same College'[4]. In 1598 a chained library was presented to the parish-church of Grantham in Lincolnshire, and placed in a room over the south porch[5], approached by a circular stone staircase out of the church.

[1] [Audit-Book of Eton College, 1520–21. *Custus templi.*]

[2] [Masters, History, p. 62].

[3] ["The Guild of the Corpus Christi, York"; ed. Surtees Society, 1872, p. 206, *note.*]

[4] [Commiss. Docts. II. 309.]

[5] [These details have been most kindly communicated to me by my friend the Rev. George Maddison, M.A., formerly Vicar of Grantham. Compare also: Collections for the History of the Town and Soke of Grantham, by Edmund Turner, 4to. Lond. 1806, p. 29.]

As a general rule chaining was not discontinued until either a new library was built, or new fittings provided for an old one. Thus the books at Peterhouse were unchained as early as 1594, when they were moved into the new library; and it will appear below that at Cambridge there are no traces of chaining on any of the bookcases made in the course of the seventeenth century, except at Trinity Hall and King's College. Gonville and Caius College offers an exception to the rule, for, though the new bookcases were not made until 1675, the books were unchained in 1620 and 1621. In the Audit-Book for those years we find the following entries:

"Paid to Graves the smith for taking off ye chaines y^t^ were fastened to the bokes in ye Library.
Paid for carrying up to the treasury the chaines and the iron barres y^t^ were taken from the bokes and of the deskes in ye Library."

On the other hand benefactors to public libraries still directed their donations to be chained. The Will of Humphrey Chetham of Clayton in the County of Lancaster, dated 16 December, 1651, directs £200 to be spent on certain specified books, "to be, by the discretion of my Executors, chained upon Desks, or to be fixed to the Pillars, or in other convenient Places, in the Parish Churches of *Manchester* and *Boulton in the Moors*, and in the Chapels of *Turton*, *Walmesley*, and *Gorton*, in the said County of *Lancaster*[1]."

Of these bequests, the books and bookcases belonging to the parish-churches of Turton and Gorton still remain. At the former place both were thoroughly restored in 1855; at the latter the original arrangements have never been altered. The cornice and inscription of the Walmesley bookcase—the only part remaining of it—is now in the Chetham Hospital at Manchester. The bequest to the parish-church of Manchester itself has been wholly lost.

The bookcase at Turton[2], which now stands in the parish-church, on the floor in front of the pulpit, is a cupboard of dark oak 7 feet 5 inches long, by 3 feet 3 inches high, and 14 inches deep, with a pair of doors which close against a

[1] [Bibliographical Notices of the Church Libraries at Turton and Gorton; printed for the Chetham Society, 1855, p. 3.]

[2] [The front of this bookcase is figured on the title-page to the volume of the Chetham Society's publications already referred to.]

central division. On the cornice above these doors is the following inscription, carved in low relief:

THE GIFT OF HUMPHRY CHETHAM ESQVIRE. 1655.

When the doors are opened, the space within is found to be divided into two compartments by a vertical partition behind the interval which separates the doors. Each compartment is again subdivided by a horizontal shelf, in front of which are the iron bars to carry the chains of the fifty-two volumes which still remain. These bars, of which there is one for each division—are now immovably fixed to the ends of the case, and to the central partition, but their present position is of no authority, for, when the restoration of 1855 was undertaken, both shelf and bars had been removed, and the chains were wrapped round each volume to secure the loose leaves. The chains, of iron, tinned, are of the same type as those at Hereford, but the links are rather longer and narrower. They are attached to the volume in the same manner, either near the bottom of the right board, or near the top of the left board. The chains are just long enough to admit of the books being laid on the top of the case, which forms a desk at which they may be conveniently read.

The book-case at Gorton, now in the Committee Room of the National School, exactly resembles the one just described, except that it is 19 inches deep, and is raised upon four stout legs, 22 inches high[1]. On opening the doors, which shut against each other without any intervening partition, the interior is seen to be divided into two equal parts by a vertical partition, and again by a horizontal shelf. The shelf and the partition are both 9 inches deep, so as to leave a considerable interval in front of them. The bars—of which there is one for each division—rest in a socket pierced in a small bracket screwed to each end of the case, in such a position that the bar passes just in front of the shelf. A flat piece of iron, nailed to the central division, carries a short hasp, which passes over the junction of the bars, and is there secured by a lock. By this arrangement

[1] [The bookcase at Turton was originally raised on legs, of which the stumps still existed when the Illustration above referred to was taken, but in the course of the restoration they were concealed by a modern plinth.]

no person could have withdrawn either bar, unless possessed of the key. There are scars on the lower edge of the case, and on the legs, which seem to indicate that there might once have been a shelf. Otherwise the books, when read, must have rested on the reader's knees.

Besides these parochial libraries, Mr Chetham directed the foundation of a Hospital for poor boys, and a Library, in Manchester. For these purposes he directed his executors to purchase an ancient building called *The College*, or, *The College House*, which is known to have been completed before 1426, by Thomas, Lord de la Warre, as a college in connection with the adjoining collegiate church, now the Cathedral[1]. After minute directions respecting the foundation and management of the Hospital, the Will proceeds:

"Also I give unto my said Executors one Thousand Pounds, to be by them bestow'd in such Books, as [they] shall think fit for, or towards a Library within the Town of *Manchester*, for the Use of Scholars, and others well affected, to resort unto;

And if the said College or College House in *Manchester* may be obtained and purchased as aforesaid; then I would have some convenient Part or Place thereof, or therein, such as my Executors * * * shall think fit to be the Place for the same Library * * *; and if the same cannot be obtained, then I leave the Election of the same Place for the said Library to the Discretion of my said Executors * * *; so as the same be in some of the Chapels in the said Church of *Manchester*, if the same can be obtained; or elsewhere in the Town of *Manchester;* the same Books there to remain as a public Library for ever; and my Mind and Will is, that Care be taken, that none of the said Books be taken out of the said Library at any Time.

And my Will and Mind is, that the same Books be fixed, or chained, as well as may be, within the said Library, for the better Preservation thereof[2]."

Possession having been obtained of the college, as directed by the Will, the Library was placed in two long narrow rooms on the first floor, the original destination of which is uncertain. They are at right angles to each other, and have a united length of 137 feet 6 inches, with a breadth of 17 feet. The Hospital was formally opened 5 August, 1656; and, 21 May, 1657, the establishment of the Library was commenced:

[1] [The architectural history of these buildings has been admirably worked out, with numerous illustrations, in Old Halls in Lancashire and Cheshire, by Henry Taylor, Architect. 4°. Manchester, 1884, pp. 31—46.]

[2] [The Last Will of Humphry Chetham, [etc.]. 4°. Manchester, n. d. p. 42.]

"Ordered * * * that the somme of one Thousand pounds More bee with all possible and convenient speed bestowed and wared in such Books as may be judged vsefull for the library[1]."

Unfortunately no accounts have been preserved of the fitting-up of the library; but it appears probable that the existing fittings, though they have been extensively altered from time to time, are in the main those which were originally put up. The bookcases, of oak, are placed in medieval fashion at right angles to the windows. They are 10 feet long, 2 feet wide, and were originally 7 feet high, but have been pieced apparently twice, so that they now reach as high as the wall-plate. Each pair of cases is 6 feet apart, so as to make a small compartment, closed by wooden gates, which now open in the middle; but a lock attached to one side of the end of each case indicates that originally the gates were in one piece. The cases are quite plain, with the exception of a few panels at the end. On the uppermost of these, which is oblong, and extends from side to side of the case, the subjects of the works are written: as, PHILOSOPHIA; and beneath, in smaller characters, *Mathematica, Physica, Metaphysica.* The alterations made in the cases since their original construction have been so thorough[2], that all indications of chaining have been obliterated, but a reference to the earliest account-book which has been preserved, that namely beginning 20 April, 1685, shews that the founder's directions were obeyed:

"20 Apr. 1685.	To James Wilson for Cheining ten books	0	2	6
" 1686.	———— for making 26 large Claspes and Cheining 26 bookes	0	4	4
9 Mar. 1686—87.	———— for Cheining and Clasping 12 doz. bookes	00	18	00."

Chains were evidently kept as a part of the stock-in-trade of the library, to be used as required, for, at the end of an Inventory taken 18 November, 1684, we find:

[1] [Minute-Book of the Overseers of the Chetham Library.]

[2] [It is probable that these alterations took place in consequence of the following Order: "Tuesday, 24 July, 1787. That a Committee be appointed to inspect the Library along with the Librarian, consisting of the Treasurer [etc.]; And that such Committee snall have power to repair and make such Alterations in the Library as they may think proper." No Order for taking off the chains has been discovered.]

"Alsoe in the Library two globes; three Mapps; two queres of larg paper to make tables; a paper fol-booke; A Ruleing penn; 24 dossen Chains; A geniological roul; and a larg serpent or snaks skin."

In 1659 the executors of John Selden gave his books to the University of Oxford, on the condition, among others, "That the said Bookes may bee within the space of twelve moneths next ensuing placed and chayned." This condition was faithfully observed, as appears from Loggan's print of the interior of the Bodleian Library, and from the University Accounts for 1659—60, which record an outlay of £25. 10*s.* on chains[1]. In the Will of Matthew Scrivener, Rector of Haslingfield in Cambridgeshire, dated 4 March, 1687, the following passage occurs:

"I give fifty pounds in trust for the use of the public Library [at Cambridge], either by buying chains for the securing the books at present therein contained, or for the increase of the number of them[2]."

The library over the porch of the parish church at Denchworth, Berks, was built in 1693, and "stocked with one hundred books, well secured with chains[3]." It has been already mentioned (p. 423) that the library in the parish church of All Saints, Hereford, was chained so late as 1715.

In the course of the eighteenth century however the practice was finally abandoned. At Eton College in 1719 it was "Order'd to take ye Chains off ye Books in ye Library, except ye Founder's Manuscripts[4]"; at the Bodleian Library, Oxford, the removal of them began in 1757[5]; at King's College, Cambridge, the books were unchained in 1777[6]; and at Brasenose College, Oxford, in 1780[7].

We must next briefly investigate the terms applied to book-

[1] [Wood, History and Antiquities of the University of Oxford, ed. Gutch. II. 943. Annals of the Bodleian Library, Oxford. By Rev. W. D. Macray. 8vo. 1868, p. 86.]

[2] [Documents relating to St Catharine's College, ed. H. Philpott, D.D. p. 125.]

[3] [Notes and Queries, 6th Series, Vol. IV. p. 304. The library was destroyed in 1852, when the church was restored by Mr George Street, Architect, and the books were removed to the Vicar's house.]

[4] [Eton College Minute Book, 19 December, 1719.]

[5] [Macray, *ut supra*, p. 86.]

[6] [King's College Mundum Book, 1777: "*Smith's work.* 'To a man's time 9 Dayes to take the Chains of the books £1. 7*s.* o*d.*'"]

[7] [This date rests on a college tradition communicated to me by my friend Falconer Madan, M.A., late Fellow.]

cases at different periods. In the Middle Ages the word most commonly in use was "stall" (*staulum, stalla, stallus or stallum*). The catalogue of the University Library made 1473 begins: *In primo staulo communis librarie in parti boriali continentur xix^cim libri,* the names of which are set down in order. Each stall contained a single shelf only, or at most two shelves, as will be explained below, and the books placed upon it or them were usually on the same subject, and considered to form but one group, in whichever direction the volumes might be turned. In the early catalogue of the Library of S. Catharine's Hall the books are placed in "*Prima Stalla*", "*Secunda Stalla*", and so forth. At Queens' College, in 1545—46[1], the same word is used; and at S. John's College in 1556 a charge occurs "for mending one of the locks in the stalles of the librarye v^d[2]." At the same college the woodwork of the new library, begun 1623, is described collectively as "the seats[3]"; with which may be compared a payment at Peterhouse in 1633—34, "*pro novis sedilibus in Bibliothecâ*[4]". In the catalogue made at Queens' College in 1472, by Andrew Doket, the first President, the stalls are marked with the letters of the alphabet, A, B, C etc., and each is called a "step" (*gradus*). For example, at the end of the list of books in the first stall, is the note, *Gradus A continet* 5 *libros ad presens.* In 1667 the University Librarian is directed by Grace of the Senate (16 December) to arrange the books on seats (*in subselliis collocare*).

In the catalogue of the University Library, dated 1584, the word "class" (*classis*) is used interchangeably with the ancient "stall," and afterwards superseded it entirely. For instance, when a Syndicate was appointed in 1713 to provide accommodation for Bishop Moore's Library, the bookcases are described as *Thecæ sive quas vocant classes*[5]. Gradually, as we learn from the tract on the arrangement of the library published by Conyers Middleton in 1723, the term was extended from its medieval signification to include not only the books on both sides of

[1] [Magn. Jour. 1545—46, fol. 132. 'Item resartienti seras stallorum in bibliotheca.']

[2] [S. John's College Audit Book 1555—56. *Exp. necess.*]

[3] [History of S. John's College, Vol. II. p. 270.]

[4] [History of Peterhouse, Vol. I. p. 33, *note.*]

[5] [History of the Schools, etc. Vol. III. p. 30.]

a book-case, but also those in the shelves under one of the windows next to it; and one of the author's chief reasons for publishing his tract was to suggest the arrangement which has since been adopted, namely, that the term should be applied to the compartment formed by the shelves under a given window, together with those on the sides of the bookcases to the right and left of a spectator facing it[1].

Besides these terms, the word "desk" is occasionally applied to a bookcase. In the above-mentioned catalogue of the University Library, after enumerating the stalls and their contents on the north side of the room, the compilers of the catalogue pass to the south side. The entry referring to the first bookcase is in the usual form: *In primo staulo ex parte australi continentur* 15 *libri;* but the second is changed to: *In secundo desco continentur* 17 *libri*, and so on; the word "desk" being used for the remaining eight bookcases. In the accounts of Exeter College, Oxford, for 1392, a charge occurs for placing certain books on desks (*pro imposicione in descis*)[2]; and in the building contracts for S. John's College, Cambridge, in 1516, the "desks in the Library" are enumerated with the rest of the woodwork[3]. At the same college in 1633, we meet with a charge "for desks for litle bookes in the Librarie j^li^ iiij^s^"; and in 1635, "for turning and making two narrow dores for one of the deskes v^s^"; "for turning and making sixe narrow dores for one side of the deske, and both sides of the other deske in the library." At the end of the century Sir Christopher Wren describes his proposed bookcases for the new library at Trinity College, which were to be placed against the side-walls, as well as at right angles to them, as "the deskes[4]".

We will next examine the furniture of collegiate libraries. In this particular Oxford is richer than Cambridge; for though Cambridge possesses several splendid sets of bookcases made in the seventeenth and eighteenth centuries, it cannot boast of a continuous series of examples so interesting historically as those

1 ["Vellem sane, ut *tota illa area*, quæ (ad formam literæ H dimidiatæ) *forulis* sub fenestra positis, *duabusque hinc inde alis* constet, *unicam* tantum *Classem conficiat, unica Alphabeti litera distinguendam*." Bibliothecæ Cantabrigiensis Ordinandæ Methodus, Works, iii. 484.]

2 [Register, etc., of Exeter College, Oxford, ed. Rev. C. W. Boase, Oxf., 1879, p. 3.]

3 [History of S. John's College, Vol. II. p. 244.]

4 [History of Trinity College, Vol. II. p. 535.]

of Oxford, or which shew so many traces of the ancient method of chaining. In the first place we will describe the library of Merton College, which has been so little altered that it may be taken as the type of a medieval college library.

The ground-plan (fig. 1) shews that the library now occupies the whole of the first-floor of the south side of "Mob Quadrangle," and the greater part of the same floor of the west side. It consists, however, practically of two rooms, having a uniform width of 20 feet 6 inches, to which the space in the angle between them forms a common vestibule. The western room, called by tradition "New Library," is 38 feet 6 inches long measured from A to B: the southern room, or "Old Library," is 56 feet 6 inches long, measured from C to D. Each of these rooms is separated from the vestibule by a wooden screen of Jacobean work, and the walls at the north and east ends respectively are ornamented with oak panelling and enrichments in plaster-work above belonging to the same period, as does the staircase through which the vestibule is now entered. It may be concluded, therefore, that considerable changes in the interior of the library were effected during the seventeenth century. The staircase, as at present arranged, is evidently the result of an alteration, for the stone arch at the bottom of it has heavy iron staples on its inner side, which shew that it was once closed by a door, before the present stairs were extended into the jamb, in such a manner that no door could possibly be hung there. The external doorcase, however, in the south-west angle of the court, through which the staircase is approached, shews, by the superior ornamentation of its spandrils, by which it differs from all the other arch-ways, that it must always have been the entrance to some apartment of importance, and it may be safely concluded that the stairs leading to the library were always in the same place, though differently arranged. The door at the north end of the western library (A, fig. 1) is evidently part of the alterations made in the seventeenth century; to which period we ought perhaps also to refer the addition of the open space at the east end of the south room, which is reported by tradition to have been once a chamber appropriated to a Fellow, though it is difficult to understand how it could then have been approached. In all other respects the library maintains its ancient arrangements. The windows, with the exception of those in the vestibule, and at the end of the south library, are all of one light, trefoiled. These are evidently original. The ancient bookcases and seats remain in both rooms, and, though the two sets differ slightly in height and other details, there can be little doubt that they are those set up when the library was either built, or rearranged, by Bishop Reade at the end of the fourteenth century. The cornices and terminal pediments are part of the additions made in the seventeenth century.

Both rooms are floored with rough oak planking: on this are laid two sleepers parallel with the side-walls (fig. 1), the one next the central alley being roughly chamfered. Into these the book-cases and the seats are morticed. The central alley, five feet wide, is paved with encaustic tiles; by which arrangement it is at a slightly higher level than the flooring on each side of it. In the western room there are six complete bookcases, and two half-cases, on each side; in the southern room there are ten complete cases on each side, and one half-case against the screen. These cases are all set at right angles to the main walls, their ends occupying the greater part of the space between the windows, while the bench for the reader is similarly placed,

Fig. 12. Bookcase, desk, and seat in the Library of Merton College, Oxford.

opposite to each window. The illustration (fig. 12)[1] shews one of these cases, with the corresponding seats, from the west side of the western room. Each case is 7 feet 6 inches long, and 2 feet 6 inches wide. The material is oak, very coarse and rough, as at Hereford. The ends are occasionally as much as three inches thick, and at the end next to the wall are shaped roughly with an adze. The cases in the western library are 6 feet 2 inches high and 18 inches wide. In the southern library they are of the same width, but three inches higher. Most of the desks remain. They are immovable, nailed to rough brackets, and have a slit two inches wide, on the side next to the book-case, in order to let the chains pass through. Each bookcase is separated, by a vertical partition, into two divisions. At present there are three shelves; one on the same level as the desk, and two above it. Originally, however, there was only one in this interval. This appears from examination of those cases to which the iron sockets which originally supported the bar are still affixed, and from one of the half-cases in the south room (E, fig. 1) which still retains a portion of the ironwork. For the shelf which intervened between the desk and the cornice there was an iron hasp to hold the bar in place exactly resembling that at Hereford (fig. 2); and the lock which secured it was a few inches above the desk. The scar left by its removal has been indicated on the sketch (fig. 12). The books which stood on the shelf at the level of the desk, without reference to the direction in which they were turned, were all chained to a single bar in the centre of the standard, secured by a separate hasp and lock. The traces of the nails which secured the former, and the scar left by the removal of the latter, may be distinctly seen on every one of the cases in the western library. It is evident that there was no shelf below the desk. Two books are still attached by chains to the bar in the bookcase in the southern library above referred to. The chains and rings resemble those described above (figs. 3—7), and are attached to the books in the same manner. The book-cases are about 4 feet apart, and in the centre of the interval is the reader's seat, a plain wooden bench, 9 inches wide.

The arrangements for the safe-keeping of the books, and the

[1] [The "sleeper" next the wall has, through inadvertence, been omitted from this sketch.]

accommodation of the readers, which we have just described at Merton College, seem to have set the fashion, at least in principle, for other Oxford libraries, but, as books increased in number, it became necessary to make the cases which contained them proportionately larger. We shall not, therefore, find an exact copy of the Merton College bookcases in any other library, but only adaptations of their method. The earliest library, after that at

Fig. 13. Bookcase, desk, and seat in the Library of Corpus Christi College, Oxford.

Merton College, in which the original fittings have been preserved is that of Corpus Christi College, built between 1516 and 1528. In the former year the charter was given, and in the latter the founder, Bishop Fox, died[1].

[1] [Wood, *ut supra*, p. 399, says that "the fabric of the College was totally built in the Founder's time."]

The library occupies the first floor of the south side of the quadrangle opposite to the entrance. It is 79 feet 6 inches long by 21 feet broad, with ten equidistant windows, about 3 feet 6 inches apart, on each side. At the west end there is an inner library, occupying the angle between the south and west sides of the quadrangle. On each side there are nine bookcases (fig. 13), closely resembling in their general arrangements those at Merton College. They are, however, much larger, each being 8 feet 6 inches high, 2 feet wide, and divided by partitions into three compartments, as at Hereford, instead of into two. A joint across each end just above the pediment of the frame for the catalogue—which by its style is evidently Jacobean—seems to indicate that these cases were heightened before chaining fell into disuse, so as to provide two shelves above that on the level of the desk. If this conjecture be correct the number of shelves was originally identical with that at Merton, the shelf now inserted below the desk being evidently modern. It should also be mentioned that in order to provide more room for books a modern shelf, omitted in the sketch, has been inserted in the upper division; so that there are now five shelves between the floor and the cornice. The desks appear to have been slightly altered, the bracket which supports them being now over the hole for the lowest bar, and the original hinges have been replaced by modern ones. Moreover there is now no slit to admit the chains. No books preserve their original chains, but the ironwork by which the bars were secured still remains on all the bookcases. A comparison of the sketch (fig. 13) with that of one of the Hereford bookcases (fig. 2) shews that the two systems are identical. In front of each window there is a reader's seat. It will be seen that comfort had begun to be considered when it was put up, and that it was made double, with a partition to lean against.

At S. John Baptist's College the library was built in 1596, and we may presume was fitted up soon afterwards, as Wood records numerous donations of books in the years immediately succeeding, and the appointment of a keeper to take charge of them in 1603[1]. This library, on the first floor of the south side of the second quadrangle, is 112 feet long by 26 feet wide, with

[1] [Wood, *ut supra*, p. 551.]

eight windows of two lights in each wall. The bookcases, of which there are eight on each side between the windows, with a half-case against the west wall, exactly resemble those at Corpus Christi College, except that they are rather larger, being 10 feet high, and 2 feet 6 inches wide. They have a classical cornice and terminal pediment. Modern shelves set against their ends conceal the traces which doubtless exist of the iron-work. The desks have not been altered. Each is in two divisions, as at Corpus, separated by a central bracket, and it has the slit to admit the chains. The long iron hinges are evidently original. The seats resemble those at Corpus.

Between 1598 and 1600 Sir Thomas Bodley refitted the library over the Divinity School. It is 86 feet long by 32 feet wide, with 10 two-light windows on each side. At right angles to these walls, which face north and south, there are nine book-cases on a side with a half-case at each end. Here again we find so close a resemblance to the cases at Corpus Christi College, that a particular description is unnecessary. It should be noted, however, that, as at S. John's College, they had been made of a greater height (8 feet 4 inches) in the first instance, so as to accommodate two shelves above that on the level of the desk. These shelves are proved to be original by the existence of the plates of iron which originally carried the sockets for the bar, at the juncture of the shelves with the upright divisions. The rest of the ironwork has been removed, and it is difficult to detect traces of its former existence, because modern shelves have been set against the ends of the cases. The hole for the lowest bar, however, remains in the same relative position as at Corpus Christi College; and, as the ironwork for supporting the bars is identical with what still remains there, it seems safe to conclude that no new principle was introduced. The desks are modern, but the large and ornamental brackets which support them are original, and the iron hooks still remain by which they were prevented from falling when turned up. The position of these hooks shews that each desk was 19 inches broad. There were originally seats between each pair of cases, as may be seen in Loggan's view of the interior of the library, where their ends are distinctly shewn.

The bookcases in the library of Trinity College, which, as

mentioned above, were set up in 1618, have been greatly altered, and carried up to the ceiling, so as to accommodate the largest possible quantity of books. It is, however, still possible to detect the original portion of them, which, like those we have been examining elsewhere, was 8 feet high by 2 feet wide. Traces of ironwork still exist, and the hole for the lowest bar may be found under the first shelf.

The present library of Jesus College was built between 1677 and 1679, in which year the books were moved in[1]. It occupies the south half of the first floor on the west side of the second quadrangle, and projects slightly beyond the south range, so as to give opportunity for a picturesque gable, in which there is a large window of four lights. The library is 68 feet long by 21 feet 6 inches wide. In the west wall there are nine windows of two lights; but in the east wall there are only six, the range being interrupted by the abutment of the south side of the quadrangle against the wall of the library. The bookcases, of which there are nine on each side, arranged as usual at right angles to the walls, reproduce the type with which we are already familiar. There are two original shelves above that on the level of the desk; the desk itself has evidently once been pierced with the usual slit to admit the chains; and the traces of the ironwork shew that it was arranged on the usual method. It is probable that these bookcases were made in 1679, expressly for use in the new library; for Wood records that for forty years previous to this date the books belonging to the college "were laid in an upper room or loft over those chambers that are above the Buttery and Kitchen." The cases therefore could not have been removed from the earlier library, which was built in 1626 and pulled down in 1639; and their severe archaic appearance must be due to the fidelity with which the earlier specimens were copied by the carpenter who made them. Their cornices, and the frames to contain the catalogues, are in the florid style of the period. Seats are still to be found between those bookcases which retain their desks.

The six sets of bookcases which we have described establish the correctness of the view advanced at the outset, namely, that a certain fashion of bookcases and seats was adopted

[1] [Wood, *ut supra*, p. 583.]

in Oxford at Merton College in the fourteenth century; that the pattern there set was enlarged and developed at Corpus Christi College at the beginning of the sixteenth century; and, further, that the bookcases there set up served as a model which was followed at S. John's College (1596), the Bodleian Library (1600), Trinity College (1618), and Jesus College (1677). The most curious instance, however, of the way in which a type once adopted was regularly copied by successive artists remains to be described.

It was mentioned above (p. 415) that the library at Queen's College was begun in 1692. The architect is said to have been Nicholas Hawkesmoore, to whom the fittings, put up in the first fourteen years of the eighteenth century[1], are also ascribed. This library is 123 feet long by 30 feet wide. There are ten bookcases on each side at right angles to the walls between the windows. Each case is about 11 feet high, and 2 feet 6 inches wide; but, though their ornamentation is in the style of the period, of which they are splendid examples, their general design exactly reproduces the old type. In their original state they were provided with desks, though there is no evidence that the books were chained; they had only two shelves above that which was on the level of the top of the desk; and there was a double seat between each pair of cases. The space above the second shelf, between it and the cornice, was occupied by a cupboard, handsomely ornamented with carved panels, for small books or manuscripts[2]. In fact, the only innovation which the designer of these remarkable cases permitted himself to employ was to make the moldings of their cornices continuous with that of the panelwork which he carried along the sides of the room and into the jambs of the windows. The space below the desk

[1] [This date is given on the authority of the present Provost, John Richard Magrath, D.D.]

[2] [A view of the Library in its original state is given in Ingram's Memorials, Queen's College, p. 12. An article in Notes and Queries, 6th Ser. iv. 442, by the Rev. Robert Lowes Clarke, M.A., Fellow and Librarian, contains the following passage: "The bookcases were fitted with reading desks, as at the Bodleian, and there were fixed oak seats in each recess. These were convenient in some ways, and helped to make the room seem a place for study rather than a store for materials, but they made the lower shelves hard of access, and were removed in 1871 to give room for new cases."]

was utilised for books, but, as these were found to be inconvenient of access, the desks and seats were taken away in 1871, and dwarf bookcases provided in front of the windows.

If we next examine the library-fittings at Cambridge, we shall find that no library was fitted up at an early date in such a manner as to command the imitation of posterity. Each library, so far as we can judge from the examples which have come down to us, was fitted up according to individual taste, without reference to a common original. Moreover, in several colleges the

Fig. 14. Bookcases and seats in the Library of Trinity Hall, Cambridge, made 1626—45.

position of the library has been altered since the original foundation, in some cases more than once, and advantage was taken of each change to furnish it afresh with new fittings in the style of the period. This has been the case at Peterhouse, Clare Hall, Pembroke College, Gonville and Caius College, Corpus Christi College, Magdalene College, S. Catharine's Hall, Christ's College, and S. John's College. The same remark applies also to the University Library.

The library of Trinity Hall is that which has been least altered. A general description and history of it has been given already in the History of the College[1]. It is on the first floor, 65 feet long by 29 feet wide, with eight equidistant windows in each side-wall, and a window of four lights in the western gable. There are at present five ancient book-cases and six seats on each side, placed as usual at right angles to the side-

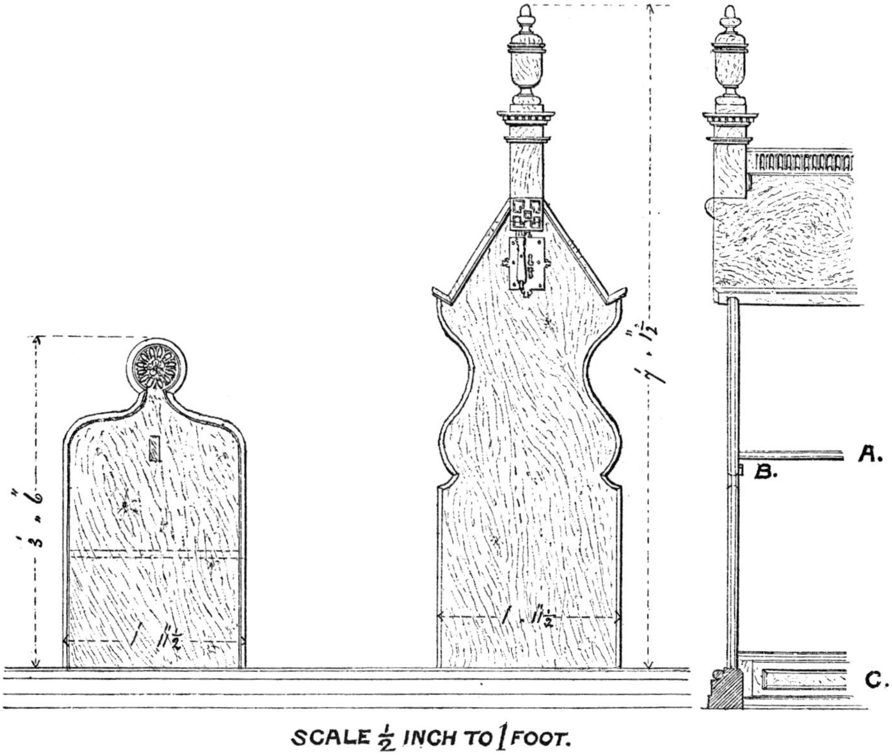

Fig. 15. Elevation of bookcases and seats in the Library of Trinity Hall, Cambridge.

walls, in the interspaces of the windows, and in front of the windows, respectively. The library was built about 1600, but the fittings are later, having evidently been put up during the mastership of Thomas Eden, LL.D. (Master 1626—45), as his

[1] [History of Trinity Hall, Vol. I. p. 226.]

arms appear on the end of the bookcases. They are therefore a remarkable instance of a deliberate return to ancient forms at a time when a different type had begun to be adopted elsewhere. The cases and seats (figs. 14, 15) are set on two sleepers, as at Merton College, Oxford (fig. 12). They are of oak, 6 feet 7 inches long, and 7 feet high, measured to the top of the ornamental finial at the ends, and 2 feet wide. In their general outline and plan they offer a remarkable resemblance to those at Merton, but there are some equally remarkable features which are quite original. There is a sloping desk at the top, beneath which there was a single shelf for books (A, fig. 15). The books were chained to an iron bar which passed under the desk, and through the two vertical ends of the case. At the end farthest from the

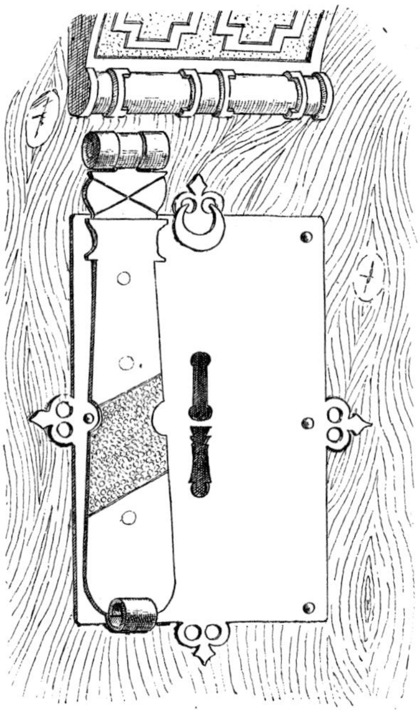

Fig. 16. Lock at the end of the bookcases in the Library of Trinity Hall, Cambridge.

wall, the hasp of the lock is hinged to the bar, and secured by two keys (fig. 16). The bars and locks remain, but the chains have been long since removed. The position of the bar renders it probable that each chain was attached to the top, and not to the side, of the book which it secured. Beneath the shelf there was a sliding desk, as is proved by the existence, on most of the cases, of the slip of wood (ibid. B) on which it rested. At the bottom of the case there was a plinth (ibid. C), replacing the bar in this position elsewhere. The reader could therefore consult his convenience, and work either sitting or standing.

A somewhat similar arrangement had been adopted in the library of Queens' College[1], which forms part of the original buildings completed in 1448. The cases have been altered at least twice, and, moreover, their ends are now concealed by modern shelves placed at right angles to them; but the general plan of the earliest arrangements can be recovered without much difficulty. The original library was about 43 feet long by 20 feet wide, lighted by six equidistant windows, each of two lights in the north and south walls. Against each of these walls there were six original bookcases of oak, very coarse and rough. The ends were of the same shape as those at Trinity Hall, to which they may have served as a model, and at the top there was a double sloping desk, with a single shelf for books beneath it. The seats have disappeared, but it is easy to see that they existed, for the books could only have been consulted by readers who sat in front of them. The total height of the cases from the floor to the top of the sloping desk is unusually low, being only 4 feet 2 inches; and the interval between the floor and the shelf is only 15 inches. No traces of chaining now remain, but numerous entries in the Accounts for chains, locks, and iron-work, prove the former existence of the system.

In the library of S. John's College we meet with the first indication of a more modern form of bookcase. This library was built between 1623 and 1628[2]; and the beautiful fittings which are actually in use at the present day were provided during the same period. This "curious specimen of Jacobean Gothic," as Professor Willis terms it, is 110 feet long, by 30 feet broad. It has an original boarded roof, ten lofty pointed windows on each side, each of two lights, and an oriel at the west end. The

1 [History of Queens' College, Vol. II. p. 50.]

2 [History of S. John's College, Vol. II. pp. 263—271.]

principal bookcases (fig. 17) stand at right angles to the walls, in the spaces between the windows. Their general arrangement will be understood from the illustration. They are 8 feet 2 inches high, and 2 feet 3 inches broad. It will be observed that they are no longer detached from the side walls, as in the

Fig. 17. Bookcases in S. John's College Library, Cambridge, made 1623—28.

older examples, but their cornice is continuous with that of the panelwork which lines the walls and the window-jambs. Professor Willis has left the following notes upon them: "they have been considerably altered by changing the levels of the shelves. The plinths originally ran round the sides of the case. There was a rich pilaster in the middle of each [below the central bracket], and a broad member along its side in continuation of that which remains at the end above the arches." In making this criticism Professor Willis was probably guided by the arrangement of the bookcases at King's College (fig. 20) which were put up in 1659, or of those at Clare Hall, to be described below. No traces of chaining[1] remain, but the catalogue of the books contained in each case was still written on the inside of two panels at the end farthest from the wall. In addition to the tall bookcases between the windows low detached cases were placed in front of each window. These are evidently, by their style, of the same date as the others, and may be identified with "the lesser seats" referred to in the building-accounts (p. 270). They were originally 5 feet 6 inches high, and 2 feet broad, with a sloping desk on the top, on which books could be laid for study. These "subsellia," as Professor Willis calls them, were all raised to a height of nearly 7 feet in 1741 and 1742[2], in order to accommodate more books, with the exception of two at the entrance, one of which is shewn in our illustration. No fixed seats were provided in this library, but a number of moveable stools. It should be mentioned, in conclusion, that these bookcases are placed, like the older examples, on two "sleepers." The floor in the central alley between the cases is now raised, but it was originally, as at Trinity Hall, at the same level as the floor on which they stand[3].

These fittings were copied at Clare Hall in 1627, when the library, then above the old chapel, had new cases provided for it. The present library was completed about 1693, and fitted up as Cole says, writing in 1742, "à la moderne, with the Books ranged all round it, and not in Classes as in most of the rest of the Libraries in other Colleges." The older library, according

[1] [An entry in the Audit-Book for 1630–31: "Paid for 2 cheynes for the Librarye j^{li}. vj^{s}. $viij^{d}$." probably refers to the chaining of some particular volumes, as the price far exceeds that commonly paid for ordinary chains.]

[2] [College Order 1 June, 1741: "Agreed to raise all the middle classes in the library": Ibid. 12 July, 1742: "Agreed to raise all the classes in the library, except the two classes next the door." Baker's History, Ed. Mayor, p. 1036. Mr Mayor suggests that the additional room was required for the books bequeathed by Thomas Baker, who had died in 1740.]

[3] [The floor is shewn at the original level in the view of the Library by Westall in Ackermann's Cambridge, Vol. II. p. 91.]

to the same authority, was "fitted up with wainscote Classes on both sides." When it was pulled down in 1763, these classes were removed to the new library and ranged round the room[1]. It is easy to detect their original arrangement, for in six of them one end is left rough, and in the remaining four it appears to have been finished at a later period in imitation of the older work. In design and ornamentation they are almost identical with those at S. John's College; but are rather smaller, being 6 feet 10 inches long, 7 feet 6 inches high, and 2 feet 2 inches broad. They have been slightly altered to provide additional accommodation for books, but the plinth, 14 inches high, is still carried along the sides in the manner which, according to Professor Willis, was originally employed at S. John's College. No trace of chaining can be detected.

The old library of Peterhouse, begun 1431, was another example of the normal arrangement of such a room in the middle ages. It was about 60 feet long by 20 feet wide, with a range of equidistant two-light windows in either wall, and a window of three lights at the north end. It was fitted up with desks, i.e. bookcases, between 1447 and 1450, and the provision of locks for these desks in the latter year indicates the presence of the usual ironwork[2]. The catalogue of books made 1418, which has been analysed above (p. 403), shews that even then the college possessed an extensive collection, to which Dr Perne's printed books were added in 1589. His Will, dated 25 February, 1588, gives some interesting glimpses of the conditions of the library at that period. After providing for the building of a new "Colledge Librairie," he directs that "all my bookes bequeathed in this my testament be layed and chayned in the old Librarie of the Colledge"; and that the Keeper of the Library "suffer none of the sayed bookes to be lent to anie person out of the sayed Librairie, but he to see all my bookes that I shall give to the Librairie to be bound with chaines at my coaste. And the names of the bookes that be set in euerie stall to be written in the end thereof, with my name in euerie of the said Bookes." As Dr Perne's Library was "supposed to be the worthiest in all England[3]," immediate facilities would of course be provided

[1] [History of Clare Hall, Vol. I. pp. 107, 113.]

[2] [History of Peterhouse, Vol. I. pp. 12, 16.]

[3] [MSS. Baker XXIV. 250.]

for consulting it; and we may therefore safely conclude that the room in which it was deposited would be fitted up with bookcases and seats, in the usual manner. His books were unquestionably chained in it as he directed, for when they were moved into the new library in 1593—4, one of the entries under the heading "Dr Perne's Foundation" (*Fundatio Doctoris Perne*), is a charge for taking the chains off the books[1]. The new library was probably fitted up, in part at least, with the cases already in use. The present fittings were put up between 1641 and 1648, after the room had been lengthened eastwards[2]. There are seven compartments on each side, made by six bookcases and two half-bookcases against the east and west walls. The walls are panelled, but the bookcases stand at right angles to them independent of the panelwork. Their general plan will be understood from the sketch (fig. 18). When first put up they were 8 feet 6 inches high, as may still be seen at

[1] [History of Peterhouse, *ut supra*, pp. 28—30.]

[2] [Some of the entries having reference to these fittings under the heading *Bibliotheca* in the Bursars' Rolls have been quoted already (Hist. of Peterhouse, Vol. I. p. 33), but the cases are so interesting that it is worth while to transcribe the whole series in this place:

		£	*s.*	*d.*
1641—42.	"Pro fabris scriniariis pro extruendis tribus novis Thecis	30	0	0
1642—43.	Inprimis numeravit scriniario Ashley pro tribus novis Thecis ...	30	0	0
	Item Anthonio Faulkner	14	0	0
	Item pro scriniariorum operâ extraordinariâ	1	6	0
1643—44.	*Inprimis* numeravit scriniario Ashley pro Thecis novis	19	0	0
	Item Anthonio Faulkner pro opere scriniario	1	2	6
1644—45.	Item numeravit scriniario Ashley pro Thecâ novâ et Tabulâ ...	11	5	0
1645—46.	Item numeravit scriniario Ashley pro Thecâ novâ et Tabulâ ...	12	0	0
	Item numeravit scriniario Ashley pro fenestra orientali	10	0	0
1647—48.	Item numeravit scriniario Ashley pro Thecis novis et Tabulis...	11	17	0
1655—56.	Scriniario pro fabrica novi vestibuli et scriniorum............	17	6	8
	Carpentario pro opera circa fabricam novi vestibuli		9	6
	Fabro ferrario pro ferramentis circa novum vestibulum et scrinia	3	5	10
	Total	161	12	6"

If we deduct from this total the payments for the east window (£10. 0*s*. 0*d*.) and those for the Vestibule, by which the two compartments at the west end are probably meant (£21. 2*s*. 0*d*.), there remains £130. 10*s*. 6*d*. This sum, allowing £10. 0*s*. 0*d*. for each bookcase, at which rate Ashley was paid in 1642—43, and 1643—44, is sufficient to provide the 12 bookcases and the 2 half bookcases at the east end. The sums which Ashley received after 1643—44 were probably payments on account.]

the west end of the room, on each side of the entrance; but at some subsequent period the others have been raised to a height of 11 feet, so as to touch the ceiling. The inserted portion has been cleverly made to correspond in style with the older work, but it may be readily detected by the deal lining. Each book-case is 7 feet 2 inches wide, and 2 feet 2 inches broad, divided into two compartments by a broad central pilaster. Professor

Fig. 18. Bookcases in the Library of Peterhouse, Cambridge, made 1641—48.

Willis notes that the names of the books were written in the panels of each of these pilasters, but these lists no longer exist. The three cases on each side nearest to the door have a semi-circular pediment. This has been removed from the others, to admit them beneath the ceiling. No indications of chaining are to be found on any of these cases, and therefore no benches were provided in front of them for readers. Instead of these a seat, 12 inches broad, and 23 inches high, appears on the side of each bookcase, forming the top of a complete "podium," the uppermost member of which is returned across the face of the end, or standard. The ends of the "podium" are concealed by richly carved wings, like those in the Medicean Library (p. 427). Most of these seats have been removed to provide additional room for books; but they still remain on the cases on each side of the two fireplaces in the south wall, and on those which form the first compartment on each side of the room at the

Fig. 19. One of the bookcases in the south room of the University Library, Cambridge, made 1649.

west end. In these compartments the seat is carried along the north and south walls as well as along the bookcases.

With these bookcases at Peterhouse should be compared those in the south room of the University Library, which were put up shortly after 1649[1]. The close general resemblance between the two sets, in design and arrangement, will be recognised from the illustration (fig. 19). The plinth, however, or "podium" as Professor Willis terms it, has been dropped to the height of a step, and the carved wing which was used in the former example to conceal the end of the seat, is here reversed, and used merely as an ornament. No traces of chaining appear on these bookcases.

Fig. 20. Bookcase in the old Library of King's College, Cambridge, made with the bequest of Nicholas Hobart, 1659.

We come next in order of time to the bookcases made for King's College in 1659 and 1677 with the bequests of Nicholas Hobart and Thomas Crouch[2]. One of the former (fig. 20), and

[1] [History of the Schools, etc., Vol. III. pp. 27, 28.]
[2] [History of King's College, Vol. I. pp. 538, 539.]

two of the latter, still remain in their original positions. They have suffered but slight alterations. These bookcases, which are precisely similar in style and plan, have several details in common with those in S. John's College library, as originally constructed. Like them, they have a lofty plinth, a broad member interposed between the first and second shelf, and a central vertical pilaster. As at Peterhouse and the University Library they are set on a step or "podium." With these resemblances

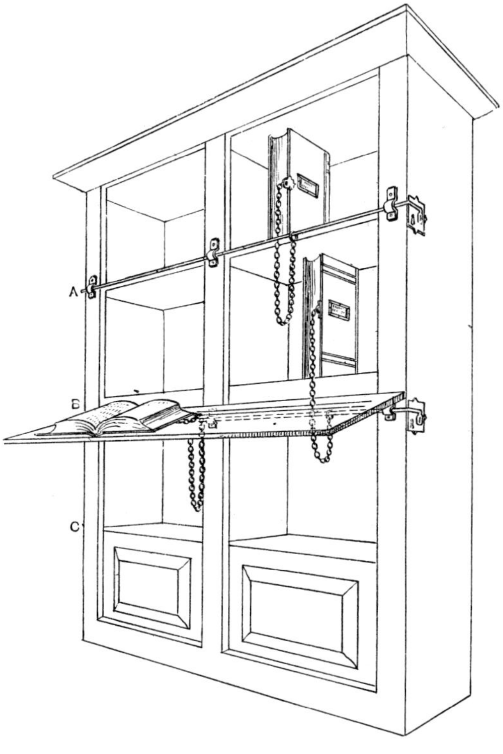

Fig. 21. Diagrammatic sketch of the bookcase shewn in the last figure, with a restoration of the ancient system of chaining; from a sketch by Professor Willis.

to cases in which books were arranged as at present, it is curious to find the usual indications of chaining, which we know from other sources was not given up in this library until 1777 (p. 437). These indications have been interpreted by Professor Willis with his usual ingenuity, and from a rough pen-and-ink sketch drawn by him the accompanying diagrammatic view (fig. 21) has been drawn, with some slight alterations. The two locks, from their position in relation to the scars which it is easy to detect on the same level as the upper shelf (*A*), and at a short distance below the shelf next to it (*B*), evidently secured the iron bar for the books which stood on those shelves. This bar must have turned round the end of the case, and have been fastened there with a hasp in the usual manner. Immediately below the second shelf (*B*) a piece of wood has been let in of a different quality from that of which the bookcases are made, evidently to fill up a vacancy caused by the removal of some portion of the original structure. This insertion has been made on all three bookcases. If we suppose that it indicates the former presence of a desk for reading at, we shall find that the bookcase, when complete, bore a close resemblance to some of those still in existence at Oxford. It is probable that no books stood on the lowest shelf (*C*), for it was not usual either to place books under a desk, or to make a single bar do duty for two shelves on different levels. Without the hypothesis of a desk it is difficult to understand how the books could have been consulted, for the floor of the chapel was fully occupied by bookcases, of which we know that there were three, in addition to the two against the east and west walls[1].

The bookcases in the library of Jesus College were put up between 1663 and 1679[2]. They are plain structures of oak, 8 feet long, 7 feet 9 inches high, and 2 feet wide. Each is placed at right angles to the side-walls, in the spaces between the windows, and immediately below a principal of the roof, to which it is connected by a turned shaft of wood. The walls are not panelled. A broad central pilaster separates each case into two divisions, and it is set on a "podium" 7 inches high and 8 inches broad, which extends unbroken from end to end. No traces of chaining are to be found on any of these cases.

This library has been very little altered, and the present bookcases no doubt stand in the same places as those which we may

[1] [This is specially mentioned in the description of the Library written by Cole in 1744 and quoted in the History, Vol. I. p. 539.]

[2] [History of Jesus College, Vol. II. p. 165.]

suppose were put up by Bishop Alcock. The subject of the books contained in each class was notified in the stained glass of the adjoining window. On the west side the original quarries have been replaced by square panes, probably for the sake of uniformity with the rest of the windows in the court; but on the east side, most of the original glass, with its inscriptions, has been preserved. Each light of each window contains Bishop Alcock's emblem, a cock standing on a globe. Every window, therefore, contains a pair of birds, which look towards each other; that is, the beak of the bird in the left-hand light is turned towards the right; that of the bird in the right-hand light is turned towards the left. Beneath each bird, in a single diamond-shaped pane, is a small inscription containing half the designation required; while above, attached to the bird's beak, is a label bearing a suitable text. The following enumeration begins at the door, which is at the north end, and the lights of the windows (marked *a*, *b*) are taken in the same order.

WINDOW I.

a. Phi
Honora . medicum . [propter] . necessitatem . ecci . 28°. [Ecclus. xxxviii. 1]

b. sica
Langor . prolixior . grauat . medicum . ecci . 5°. [Ecclus. x. 11]

WINDOW II.

a. Lex
Parauit . in . iudicio . tronum . suum . Ps°. 9°. [Psalm ix. 7]

b. Ciuilis
Honor . regis . iudicium . diligit . Ps°. 98°. [Psalm xcix. 4]

WINDOW III.

a. Lex
[Cock and text wanting]

b. [wanting]
Lex . tua . meditacio . mea . est . Ps°. 118°. [Psalm cxix. 174]

WINDOW IV.

a. Lex
Legem . statuit . ei . in . via . quam . elegit . Ps°. 24°. [Psalm xxiv. 12]

b. Canonica
Legem . pone . mihi . domine . viam . iustificacionum . tua[rum] . Ps°. 118°. [Psalm cxix. 33]

WINDOW V.

a. Ysaias
Audite . celi . et . auribus . percipe . terra . quoniam . deus . locutus . est . Isaie . j. [Is. i. 2]

b. [Designation, cock, and text wanting]

WINDOW VI.

a. Marcus
[Cock and text wanting].

b. Matheus
[Cock and text wanting]

WINDOW VII.

a. Lucas
[Cock and text wanting]

b. Johannes
[Cock and text wanting]

The above list shews that in this library the three principal faculties, Divinity, Law, and Physic, were represented, and that, as elsewhere, Divinity occupied the end of the room farthest from the door.

Four cocks, with labels and texts, which evidently, from their style, formerly belonged to this series, are now incorporated with the modern glass in the windows of the hall. The labels bear the following texts :

WINDOW I.

a. Loquebar . de . testimoniis . tuis . P°. 118°. [Psalm cxix. 46]

b. Euangelizo . vobis . gaudium . magnum . luc. 2°. [Luke ii. 10]

WINDOW II.

a. Sed . secundum . dei . eloquia . viuere . Crī super. ioh[1].

b. Liber . generacionis . ihū . xpi . Math. j°. [Matth. i. 1]

Of these four texts that in Window I, *a,* may safely be assigned to Window III, *a,* in the library, where the designation *Lex* still remains without a text. This leaves the texts denoted I, *b,* II, *a,* II, *b,* in the hall to be placed in the library. The text in Window II, *b,* must belong to S. Matthew (Window VI, *b*), and that in Window I, *b,* with equal certainty to S. Luke (Window VII, *a*). We find nothing belonging to S. Mark, but the text in Window II, *a,* seems almost certainly to refer to S. John (Window VII, *b*). From the position of the cocks (which in the windows of the hall face each other in the same way as in the library) it follows of necessity that S. Matthew and S. Luke must have occupied the right-hand lights, *b,* of their respective windows. S. Mark and S. John would then occupy the left-hand lights, *a,* of their windows, as the text which we have just assigned to S. John actually does in the hall (Window II, *a*). If we allow ourselves to suppose that the glass at present in

[1] [The commentary by S. John Chrysostom on the Gospel of S. John.]

Window VI of the library stood originally in Window VII, and that the glass at present in Window VII stood in the lights marked *b* and *a* in Window VI (and it is almost needless to say that there has been much dislocation of the glass), we find that the last two windows in the room would have contained the four Evangelists, beginning from the further end, namely, S. Matthew, S. Mark, S. Luke, and S. John.

It appears from this arrangement that, with the exception of two designations and two texts and emblems, the glass of all the fourteen lights of the seven windows on the east side of the library is still preserved, while nothing whatever is preserved for the west side. This leads to the conclusion that the west side was re-glazed at a time when no interest was felt in the preservation of such remains of antiquity.

The bookcases with which the south room of the University Library was fitted in 1649, were copied almost exactly at Gonville and Caius College when that library was refitted in 1675[1]. When these bookcases were removed into the new library in 1853, they were raised to the ceiling, so that they have now a height of 11 feet 9 inches. They have the step or "podium," carried without interruption along their sides, and "wings" at the ends. There is a heavy projecting cornice, but no pediments. It is, however, probable that these existed originally, but that they were removed when the cases were heightened.

The same type reappears at Emmanuel College, where, as related in the History, the old chapel was fitted up as a library in 1679[2]. The arrangement of the bookcases which, with some unimportant modifications, was afterwards carried out, was suggested to Archbishop Sancroft by William Dillingham, D.D. (Master 1653—62) in the following passage of a letter dated 15 July, 1678[3]:

"And I may give your Lordship an account also of Emman. library; I have observed the windows etc. in the old chappel, and do not doubt but it may make a very convenient library, the walls are good and dry;

[1] [History of Gonville and Caius College, Vol. I. p. 200.]

[2] [History of Emmanuel College, Vol. II. p. 710.]

[3] [MSS. Tanner XXXIX. 65. Dr Dillingham was ejected from the Mastership in 1662, and succeeded by Dr Sandcroft.]

the dampnes that appeares being only from the floore wch may be remedyed by raising the floore to the levell of the foot-pace of the Bachelors seates; and the widenes being 27 foot, nine on each side may be sett off for the length of the Classis, and the middle walk wilbe 9. f. broad. The windows being but 4 on a side will admitt but 3 Classes between y^m and at each end an halfclassis; but the distance between the windows and wideness of the window is such that there may be very well an interclassis against the midst of every window as high as the soyle of it about 6 foot high to come as farr out as the higher classes wch may be 8 foot high. So there will be in effect 8 Classes on each side, of 9 foot length, wch will containe thrice so many bookes as yet they have. This is the summe of what Mr Vice Chancellor[1] and I had discourse upon, at my being lately there."

The library is 60 feet long by 27 feet wide, having three windows in each of the east and west walls, and a window of four lights at the north end. The sills of these windows are 5 feet 6 inches above the floor, and the windows in the side-walls are 6 feet wide, and reach as high as the roof. The room is therefore admirably lighted. When first fitted up for books, cases were placed at right angles to the walls between each pair of windows, and also in the space beyond the windows at each end, so that there were five bookcases on each side, besides two half-cases at each end, set against the north and south walls. These cases were evidently copied from those in the south room of the University Library, which they resemble in all important details, but they are somewhat larger. Each is 9 feet 6 inches high, by 2 feet 3 inches broad, and 9 feet 8 inches long. The ends are ornamented in the same way as the pattern cases; and they have wings, and a continuous step along the sides like those at Gonville and Caius College[2].

There are similar cases in the library at Christ's College, but their date is unknown, and they have evidently been a good deal altered. The lower member, that to which the wing is attached, is of the same height as in the two last examples, but the step, which is continuous along the sides, is only four inches

1 [Thomas Holbech, D.D. Master of Emmanuel 1676—80.]

2 [Professor Willis notes of these cases: "The principal stalls like Caius and Bancroft's [the cases in the south room of the University Library made originally for Archbishop Bancroft's books] with some variations. The large ones have a full entablature running round the side; no pediment, but in lieu a handsome blank escutcheon."]

high. The cornice has a very wide projection, and a richly ornamented entablature, treated like that at Peterhouse (fig. 18).

The bookcases with which the old chapel of Pembroke College was fitted in 1690[1] were evidently suggested by the same original as the last three examples. They are 8 feet 7 inches high, 2 feet wide, and 6 feet 9 inches long. The ends are ornamented with a semicircular pediment, beneath which is a band of fruit and flowers in high relief. Wings of peculiar design, rather lower than usual, flank the lower member of the composition; but there is no step, and, instead of it, a plinth extends along the whole side of the case. These cases were placed at right angles to the walls, between the windows, of which there are six on the north side and four on the south side; and, as at S. John's College (fig. 17), the flat surface of the wall, beside and below the windows, together with the window-jambs, were clothed with panelwork, the cornice of which was continuous with that of the cases.

In all these examples the central pilaster has disappeared, probably for the sake of providing additional space for books, and is replaced by a division about half an inch wide.

In the libraries which we have hitherto examined, the bookcases have been placed at right angles to the main walls, which have usually been left bare; or, at any rate, have not been utilised for the accommodation of books. To account for this it must be remembered that these libraries were either the original medieval rooms, or else were built on medieval models, with the windows close together, and coming down to within a short distance of the floor; and again, that those who made the bookcases were in the habit of copying the designs of their predecessors, without venturing to introduce any important innovation.

In 1695, however, Sir Christopher Wren completed the new Library for Trinity College[2], in which he had designed the wood-

[1] [History of Pembroke College, Vol. I. pp. 136, 149. Since the building of the new Library this room has been converted to the purposes of a lecture-room, and only four complete cases and two half-cases remain at the east end. The ends of the others have been preserved as part of the panelwork of the walls.]

[2] [History of Trinity College, Vol. II. pp. 531—551. Sir Christopher Wren's Memoir, quoted below, has been printed entire, pp. 534—537.]

work as well as the building. The memoir which accompanied his drawings shews that he deliberately placed the windows so that they might "rise high and giue place for the deskes against the walls", and that he gave special attention to the best method

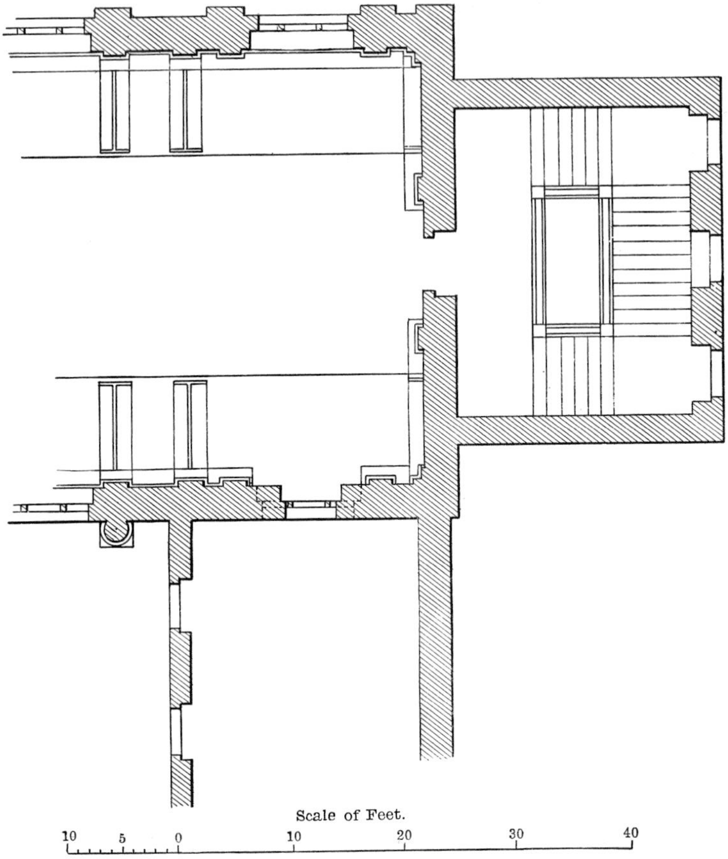

Fig. 22. Part of Sir Christopher Wren's ground-plan for Trinity College Library to shew the arrangement of the bookcases.

of arranging the books, and providing students with opportunities for consulting them. This part of his work he describes as follows :

"Fig. II.

Shewes halfe the ground plot of the upper floor, the entrances from the staireccases, and the disposition of the shelues both along the walls and breaking out from the walls, wch must needes proue very convenient and gracefull, and the best way for the students will be to haue a little square table in each Celle with 2 chaires. The necessity of bringing windowes and dores to answer to the old building leaues two squarer places at the endes and 4 lesser Celles not to study in, but to be shut up with some neat Lattice dores for archives."

A portion of the ground-plan here referred to, shewing the north end of the library, is here reproduced (fig. 22), together with a view of part of the east side, shewing one of the compart-

Fig. 23. Interior of the north-east corner of Trinity College Library, shewing the bookcases, table, desk, and chairs, designed by Sir Christopher Wren.

ments or "Celles," with its table, revolving desk, and stools (fig. 23), beyond which is one of the "lesser Celles" closed with doors. The floor upon which the bookcases stand is raised higher than that of the central portion of the library; and the cases themselves have a height of 11 feet 10 inches. The great depth of the plinth recalls the plan of some of the older book-cases, but here it is utilised for cupboards. The decorative part of the work has been fully described in the History of Trinity College already referred to. The workman who made the bookcases under Wren's direction was Cornelius Austin.

The influence of Wren can easily be traced in all the library fittings put up in the course of the next century, with the single exception of the cases in the west room of the University Library, put up by John Austin in 1715[1]. That room, as the ground-plan given in the History of the Schools shews, is long and narrow, and of no great height. It was therefore impossible to adapt it to the purpose of a library in any other way than by increasing the number of windows, and placing the cases at right angles to the walls between them according to medieval precedent. It was therefore wisely determined to make the cases resemble generally those in the south room. They are 9 feet high, 2 feet 2 inches wide, and 9 feet 4 inches long, with a plinth 9 inches high, and a deep projecting cornice. The ends are plain, ornamented with two panels in relief, and a semicircular pediment.

The first work done after Wren had carried out his innovations at Trinity College was the provision of additional fittings to the library of Emmanuel College, between 1702 and 1707[2], to accommodate Archbishop Sancroft's books. An intermediate case, as suggested in 1678 by the writer of the letter already quoted, was set up in front of each window, and in addition, the tall cases provided in 1679 were moved forward for a short distance, and shelves in continuation of them were placed against the side-walls. These additions may easily be detected by the absence of carving in the frieze of the cornice. The intermediate cases are of the same length and breadth as the others, but only 7 feet 3 inches high.

The influence of Wren is more distinctly seen in the library of S. Catharine's Hall, which was fitted up, according to tradition, at the expense of Thomas Sherlock, D.D., probably while Master,

[1] [History of the Schools, etc. Vol. III. p. 32.]
[2] [History of Emmanuel College, Vol. II. p. 710.]

an office which he held from 1714 to 1719[1]. The room is 63 feet 6 inches long by 22 feet 10 inches wide; and it is divided by partitions into a central-portion, about 49 feet long, and a narrow

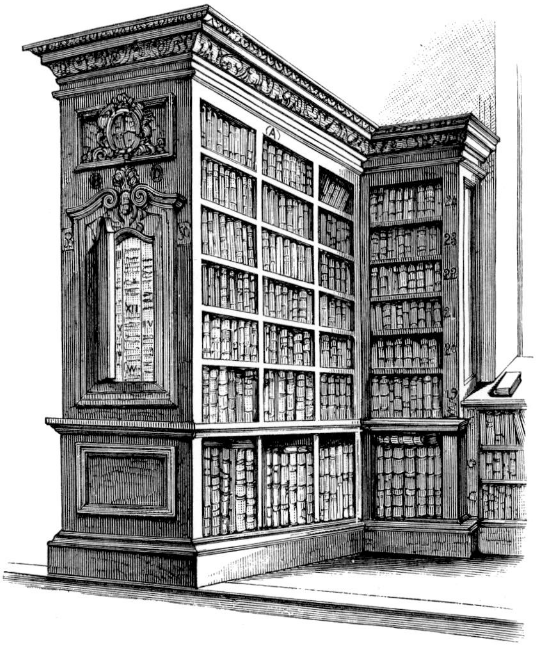

Fig. 24. Bookcase in the north room of the University Library, Cambridge, designed by James Essex, 1731—1734.

room at each end, 12 feet long. Each of these latter is lighted by windows in the north and south walls; the former has

[1] [It was shown in the History of S. Catharine's Hall, Vol. II. p. 102, that the "Hall, Combination Room, and room over that," were wainscoted by Cornelius Austin between 1674 and 1677. At that time it was proposed to complete the quadrangle by the addition of an east side which should contain the library. When that scheme was abandoned, the whole space over the Combination Room and Hall, being probably unappropriated, was assigned as a library. The exact date of Sherlock's benefaction has not been recorded, but the author of Cantabrigia Depicta, pub. 1763 (p. 59), mentions "the Library, a very handsome Room, lately fitted up and enlarged at the sole expence of the Rev. Dr *Sherlock*, late Bishop of *London;*" and Carter, whose History was published in 1753, speaks of it as "a large Room, and well Classed," as though it had been fitted up for some time.]

windows in the south wall only. The central portion is divided into three compartments by bookcases which line the walls and project from them at right angles; in the two smaller rooms the cases only line the walls, the space being too narrow for any other treatment.

The north room of the University library was fitted up as a library by James Essex, father of the architect, between 1731 and 1734[1]. A glance at the ground-plan of the first floor (History of the Schools, etc. fig. 9), shews that Wren's example was followed as far as the nature of the room would permit. Wherever a blank wall could be found, it was lined with shelves, and the cases placed at right angles to the side-walls were continued over the narrow spaces left between their ends and the windows. One of these cases, from the south side of the room, is here shewn (fig. 24). The shelves under the windows were added subsequently. A similar arrangement was adopted for the east room in 1787—90[2], as the same plan shews.

The library of Sidney Sussex College was fitted up by James Essex, the architect, in 1778[3]. In designing the fittings he followed the same system as at the University Library, placing his cases at right angles to the walls, but returning them over the space left between their ends and the windows, so as to utilise the whole surface of the walls for books. Half-cases are set against the north and south walls. There are three cases on each side of the room between the windows, each 9 feet high, 7 feet 4 inches long, and 2 feet 2 inches wide. In addition to these, dwarf cases are placed in front of each window, each 5 feet 2 inches long, 3 feet 3 inches high, and 2 feet 2 inches wide.

The library in each college was considered to be the proper place of deposit for portraits and busts of founders and benefactors, together with curiosities of various kinds. In addition to the necessary furniture it is usual to find a pair of globes, with other scientific instruments and appliances, as for instance a human skeleton, enclosed in a case of oak, commonly fitted with a glazed door. These, or at any rate the cases which once contained them, are still to be met with in the libraries

[1] [History of the Schools, etc. Vol. III. p. 74.] [2] [Ibid. p. 77.]
[3] [History of Sidney Sussex College, Vol. II. p. 749.]

of Clare Hall, and of the Colleges of King's, Queens', Jesus, Trinity, Emmanuel, and Sidney Sussex[1].

It should be remarked, in conclusion, that a close analogy can be traced between the monastic and the collegiate library. At Durham[2], for instance, the books were at first kept in various places. The earliest catalogue, undated, records the books kept in a single press (*armariolum*[3]), without mentioning its position. The second, made in 1391, records those kept in the common press (*commune armariolum*) within the treasury (*spendimentum*); the third, of the same date, records those in "the inner library called the treasury" (*libraria interior quæ vocatur spendment*); and a fourth, those in the chancery (*cancellaria*). This language indicates the division into an outer and inner library which subsequently became so usual, and shews further, that here, as in the earliest colleges, books were classed with money and valuable documents. The books were not collected into a single room until Prior Wessington built a library, between 1416 and 1446, over the treasury, between the Chapter House and the south wall of the south transept of the cathedral. At Hexham the library was in a similar position, and the stone staircase leading to it from the south transept of the church still remains. At Christ Church, Canterbury[4], the library was not built until about the same time as that at Durham, namely, between 1414 and 1443, by Archbishop Chichele.]

1 [These skeletons evidently belong to the time when human anatomy was studied in the Colleges instead of in the University Lecture-rooms. Various romantic legends which have been invented concerning them have been collected in the Cambridge Portfolio, p. 339; that relating to the skeleton in King's College Library, preserved by Cole, has been already quoted, Vol. I. p. 539.]

2 [Catalogi veteres librorum Ecclesiæ Cathedralis Dunelm. Ed. Surtees Society, 1838.]

3 [In classical Latin *armarium* signified a money-chest, or cupboard, and in medieval Latin, according to Ducange, a place in which books were stored. The diminutive form (*armariolum*), according to the same authority, usually signified either an aumbry for the altar-vessels, or the small cupboard in which the Host was reserved. In England however it clearly had the same meaning as *armarium*.]

4 [An Architectural History of the Conventual Buildings of the Monastery of Christ Church in Canterbury. By Rev. R. Willis. 8vo. Lond. 1869, p. 67.]

VIII.

THE

TREASURY OR MUNIMENT ROOM[1].

FOR nearly four centuries after the foundation of colleges, money could only be invested in real property, tithe rent charges, advowsons, or plate. The last, as has been shewn in more than one collegiate history, was regarded as a temporary investment which could be realised when any extraordinary repair of the building was required, or any other unexpected contingency rendered a large expenditure necessary[2].

When a legacy was bequeathed to a college, with special directions respecting the use to which the money was to be applied, it was kept in a chest, out of which a certain sum was taken in each year, until the whole was expended. This is illustrated by the following extract from a document drawn up by the Master and Fellows of Peterhouse respecting a sum of £40 bequeathed to them by Henry Horneby, D.D., Master, who died 12 February, 1517–18. The receipt of the money is acknowledged, and it is covenanted:

"that the said summe of xl *li* shalbe put by the sayd Maister * * * and Felowes into a certeyn chiste of the same collegge, wheryn was wonte to be keped the money of Mr John Warkeworthe [Master

[1] [For this essay Professor Willis left only a few notes. I have tried to work it out after the pattern of those for which he had prepared more copious materials.]

[2] [Sales of this kind took place at S. John's College in 1635–56 (Vol. II. p. 294); at Corpus Christi College in 1648 (Vol. I. p. 256); and at Christ's College in 1702 (Vol. II. p. 210.)]

1473—1500], and by the right and consent of the said maister of the collegge or his deputie, and the keper of the same chiste for the tyme beyng, ther shall be taken oute of the same summe of xl *li* euery yer by the space of x yers next ensuyng after the date herof iiij *li*, whiche iiij *li* shalbe delyeurd yerly to the stuward of the said Collegge for the tyme beyng or to some other Felowe[1]."

In the same way the yearly revenues of every college were kept in chests in some secure place, and the sums required for the weekly expenditure were withdrawn by the proper officials. At the end of the year the balance in hand was placed to the account of different funds, as at present, each of which, in some cases, had a separate chest, and the actual sum was deposited therein in gold, silver, and copper coins. When a loan was effected, to facilitate which there were special loan-chests, the borrower deposited some object of value as a pledge in the chest out of which his loan had been taken, and it remained there until the loan was repaid[2].

The chests in which these precious articles were deposited were made of stout oak planks, from two to three inches thick, bound with iron bands, and secured by locks and padlocks with different wards, so as to require the presence of several officials at the same time to open them. In addition to the security gained by such expedients, the statutes of nearly every college in both Universities enjoin the safe keeping of the chests, the common seal, the valuables (*jocalia*) of the House, the charters, royal letters patent, and other important documents, to which books are not unfrequently added. It will be interesting to review these injunctions somewhat at length.

Beginning with Cambridge, the statutes of Michael House, given soon after 1324 by Hervey de Stanton, direct that the

[1] [Treasury of Peterhouse, "Collegium" Box, A. 15.]

[2] [The most striking instances of this kind of security for money are to be found in the Accounts of the Proctors of the University, preserved in the Registry. In the earliest Inventory of the contents of the University Chest delivered by the out-going to the in-coming Proctors, dated 17 October, 1431, we find the following: "It' Magister Johannes Bernarde debet xx marcas quod non incepit in iure caucio pro quibus habebatur in cista communi liber sextus decretalium qui vendebatur pro xl^s." Subsequently, in nearly every year a list occurs headed: *Cautiones deliberate novis procuratoribus et iam in cista posite.* If we take the year 1516–17 as an example we find deposited in the University chest 12 spoons, a salt-cellar, a gold signet-ring, a crystal cup (*mirra*) etc.]

Master and Scholars are to have a common chest, with three keys, for the safe keeping of their charters, writings, and other similar documents; that of these keys one is to be retained by the Master, the others by two of the chaplains, specially selected for that office by the Master and scholars[1]. At Peterhouse (1344) the books, charters, and muniments, are classed together, and they are all to be kept in one or more chests, locked with two locks, one key of which, for greater security, is to be retained by the Master, the other by the Senior Dean. Nothing is said about the place in which these chests are to be kept; but, wherever it was, it was not considered to be sufficiently safe, for in 1489 John Alcock, Bishop of Ely, Visitor of the College, directed the selection of some more secure spot for the custody of the valuables, and of the balances remaining in the hands of the Bursars after the yearly accounts had been made up; and further, that there should be three keys instead of two, the third to be retained by one of the Fellows[2]. At King's Hall the provisions were similar to those for Michael House[3]. At Clare Hall (1359) the common seal, together with the original statutes and ordinances, and the balance left in the hands of the bursar after the annual audit, are to be kept in a common chest with three locks. One key of a particular make (*unius fabricæ*) is to be retained by the Master; the other two, of a different make (*diversæ fabricæ*), are to be retained by two of the Fellows, annually elected for this duty[4]. At Pembroke College, Gonville Hall, Trinity Hall, and Corpus Christi College, we find similar provisions, expressed in language so nearly identical with that of the statute for Clare Hall, that they need not be quoted. At Pembroke College a special room called a Treasury (*thesauraria*) is mentioned for the first time, but the only object of value directed to be kept in it is

[1] [Printed in The University of Cambridge from the Earliest Times to the Royal Injunctions of 1535: by J. B. Mullinger. 8vo. Camb. 1873, p. 640.]

[2] [Commiss. Docts. II., p. 38, *De omnibus libris Domus, Munimentis, et Chartis custodiendis.* For Bishop Alcock's ordinance see p. 91.]

[3] [The statutes of King's Hall are in the Treasury of Trinity College. They are printed in Rymer's Fœdera, VII. 239.]

[4] [Commiss. Docts. II. pp. 126, 127. *De Munimentis et Sigillo Communi; De computo reddendo.*]

the Register, into which all letters patent are to be faithfully transcribed[1].

At Oxford Walter de Merton does not give directions on this subject in any of his codes of statutes; but as early as 1276, Robert Kilwardby, Archbishop of Canterbury, among other ordinances promulgated in explanation of Merton's statutes, prescribes that the bursars are to keep the muniments in a chest under three locks[2]. The statutes of Balliol College and Oriel College are silent, but those of Queen's College direct that the custody of the Common Seal and other valuables is to be entrusted to the Provost, the Bursar, and the Chamberlain, who are to keep them in a chest with three locks[3]. The same provisions recur in the statutes of Lincoln College.

In the statutes which we have hitherto analysed, though the security of the chests in which the valuables of each college are to be deposited is insisted upon, no special room is set apart to contain them. Nor did the earlier colleges adopt any uniform rule in this respect, or assign a position of special security to their Treasury. The one exception to this general statement is afforded by Merton College, Oxford, where the treasury, said to have been built about 1310, is an independent structure in two floors, "built entirely of stone, with vaults to the lower rooms and passages, and a stone roof to the upper chamber. No wood is employed in any part of the structure, and it is consequently fireproof[4]."

It was reserved for William of Wykeham, in his elaborate statutes for New College (1400), to introduce a Treasury into the collegiate plan, and to give such minute directions concerning it, that it will be worth while to translate from his fiftieth statute, "*Of the Seal and the Common Chests*," those passages which concern our present purpose:

"Moreover we direct the aforesaid Warden and College to have a common seal, and common depositories or chests, which for greater

[1] [Commiss. Doc^ts. II. p. 201. *De Electione Officiariorum et de Bonorum Domus cura atque administratione.*]

[2] [Sketch of the Life of Walter de Merton. By Edmund [Hobhouse] Bishop of Nelson, New Zealand. 8vo. Oxford, 1859, p. 39.]

[3] [Commiss. Doc^ts. (Oxford), Vol. I. Statutes of Queen's College, p. 11.]

[4] [Some Account of Domestic Architecture in England, from Edward I. to Richard II. By the Editor of the Glossary of Architecture. 8vo. Oxford, 1853, p. 193.]

security are to be stored up in a certain building, after the manner and form of a tower, situated in front of the hall door, adjoining to the said hall, and divided into four rooms, counting from the ground upwards.

"The common seal, together with all valuables, sums of money, and muniments concerning our college, are to be preserved with the greatest care in this building in the following manner.

"The lower or ground floor room is to contain vessels of brass or tin (*stannea*), and other articles which are not required for the daily use of the Fellows. Of this property two bursars are to keep the keys.

"The room over this—the second counting from the ground—is to contain, in chests made for the purpose, all the registers, with all copies or transcripts of Papal Bulls, charters of kings and other lords, our own statutes and ordinances, and the muniments and evidences of all kinds belonging to the college; all rolls of accounts; and all sums of money required to meet the daily and weekly expenditure. The room and the chests are to have three different keys, of which one is to be retained by each of the three bursars.

"The room over this—the third counting from the ground—is to contain, in a certain chest made for the purpose, all the valuables, and vessels of gold and silver, which are rarely required for the daily use of the college, and all sums of money remaining in the hands of the bursars after payment of the daily, weekly, and annual expenditure; Papal Bulls and suits arising out of them; appropriations of churches; charters of kings and other lords; the original book of our statutes and ordinances for our college at Oxford; the book of the statutes for our college near Winchester, both sealed with our episcopal seal; all other letters, writings, and muniments with seals attached to them, and all original documents whatsoever concerning our college. On the door of this room there are to be four different locks, with four keys belonging to them; one of these the Warden is to keep in his own custody, the other three are to be divided between the three bursars. In the same way the aforesaid chest is to have as many locks with as many keys; the first of these is to be kept by the Warden; the second and third by two other persons, men of approved discretion. but not officials, specially elected for this purpose; the fourth by the bursar who shall happen to be of the most advanced age.

"The room over this—the fourth and last counting from the ground—is to contain, in chests made for the purpose, vestments, cups, and other ornaments of the church of greater value and importance; hangings of cloth of gold and of silk, and other articles appointed to be used as well in the chapel as in the hall of our college. The door of this room is to have three keys; to be kept by the Vice-Warden, the Senior Bursar, and the senior Dean respectively. The chest aforesaid is to have three different locks, the keys of which are to be kept respectively by the Warden, the junior Dean, and one of the more discreet graduates of our college, to be elected by a majority of the Fellows who are graduates[1]."

[1] [Commiss. Docts. (Oxford), Vol. I. Statutes of New College, pp. 83—86, Cap. 50, *De sigillo et arcis communibus*.]

This tower was built, as the statute directs, in a commanding position at the south-east corner of the hall, above the roof of which it rises several feet. The rooms on the ground floor and first floor are narrowed by the width of the stairs leading to the hall, as the plan shews (p. 257), but the two uppermost floors occupy the full area of the tower, and are each about 20 feet square. These, the muniment-rooms proper, have never been altered in any way, and still preserve their floors of encaustic tiles, and their presses to contain papers, of a date which is probably but little posterior to that of Wykeham. A similar muniment-tower was built at the north-east corner of the chapel at Winchester College, and the arrangements of it were provided for by a statute identical with that for New College[1].

The example set by Wykeham naturally called forth several imitators. At All Souls College (1443) Archbishop Chichele employs Wykeham's own words, and directs the common seal, and the common chests, to be placed over the gate of entrance, in a building "after the manner and form of a tower," having two floors. The room on the lower floor is to contain the registers, all copies of documents, and the money set apart for weekly expenditure. The room on the upper floor is to contain the plate, the originals of the aforesaid documents, and all the money left in hand after payment of yearly expenses. Minute directions are added for the safe custody of the keys of the chests, the rooms, and the door at the foot of the stairs leading up to them[2].

At Magdalen College (1479) the founder, William Waynflete, copies Wykeham still more closely. After directing the common seal and common chests to be kept in a room next the hall, he prescribes the construction of a separate tower next the chapel, in two floors. The room on the lower floor is to contain the valuables, the plate which is not often required for use, and the money saved out of daily expenditure, which is to be retained for the defence of lawsuits, and for the purchase of estates. The

[1] [The statutes of Winchester College have not been published, and I owe to the kindness of my friend T. F. Kirby, M.A., Bursar, a transcript of Section XXXIII., *De sigillo et arcis communibus.*]

[2] [Commiss. Docts. (Oxford), Vol. I. Statutes of All Souls College, p. 52. *De custodia communis sigilli et munimentorum ad Collegium pertinentium.*]

room on the upper floor is to contain other sums to be devoted to the above purposes, and also to the repair of sudden disasters which may befall the college estates by fire or other accidents, and all the muniments, distributed in various chests, originals and copies being kept separate. The keys of the chests and of the doors are to be all different, and entrusted to different officials of the college[1]. This tower, with the "vice", or turret-stair, leading up to it, exists unaltered, and the two rooms in it are still devoted to their original purpose of muniment-rooms.

At Brasenose College the money received by the bursars is to be kept in the treasury (*thesauraria*), in a common chest with three keys, one of which is to be retained by each bursar, and the third by the Principal. The other valuables are to be kept "in a safe and strong building within the precincts of the college, to be arranged and reserved for that purpose," but no special directions are given respecting its position[2].

At Corpus Christi College the founder, Richard Fox, Bishop of Winchester, whose statutes were given in 1517, returns to the principle of a tower—presumably the gate of entrance—in the upper chamber of which the surplus funds, the valuables, and the muniments, are to be preserved. Minute directions are given for keeping the documents relating to different properties distinct; and for placing originals in a different chest from copies. The same statute prescribes the establishment of two loan chests (*cistæ mutui*), the one to contain two hundred marks, the other one hundred[3]. These statutes are copied at the colleges of Christ Church and S. John's. The statutes of Balliol College (1507)[4], and those of Jesus College (1622)[5], mention a treasury (*domus thesauraria*), but without defining its position; those of Pembroke College (1629)[6] direct the

[1] [Commiss. Docts. (Oxford), Vol. II. Statutes of Magdalen College, pp. 73—76. *De sigillo communi et ejus custodia, et cistis communibus. De evidentiis, munimentis, et aliis scriptis, secretè et securè conservandis.*]

[2] [Ibid. Statutes of Brasenose College, p. 14. *De electione bursariorum et eorum officio*, and p. 35, *De custodia jocalium, ornamentorum, librorum, et aliorum bonorum.*]

[3] [Ibid. Statutes of Corpus Christi College, pp. 91—94. *De cistis et sigillo. De evidentiis, munimentis, et scriptis.*]

[4] [Ibid. Vol. I. Statutes of Balliol College, p. 13.]

[5] [Ibid. Vol. III. Statutes of Jesus College, pp. 49, 66.]

[6] [Ibid. Statutes of Pembroke College, p. 21.]

selection of "a convenient place within the college precincts," to contain the chests for the muniments, the money, and the plate. This statute is copied at Worcester College (1698)[1].

Returning to Cambridge, we find that King Henry VI.'s designs for Eton College and King's College, which, as has been already pointed out, were evidently suggested by those of Wykeham for Winchester College and New College, both include towers, which the statutes shew to have been intended for treasuries. At Eton College the quadrangle was to be entered through "a faire tour and a gate hous," the destination of which is explained by the thirty-fifth statute, which directs that the common seal and the common chests are to be kept "in a building constructed by Ourselves for this purpose over the gate of Our Royal College." It was to be divided into two floors, of which the lower was to contain the seal, the registers, all copies of documents, account-rolls, and the money required for the daily and weekly expenditure; the upper was to contain relics, valuables, gold and silver plate, the originals of all documents, and the balances of money left in the hands of the bursars after the annual audit[2]. At King's College a gatehouse is ordered, "with iij chambres ouer the gate euery aboue other," but nothing is said about the use to which they are to be put. As in the case of Eton College, however, this is explained by the forty-eighth statute (*Of the seal and common chests*), which is closely copied from Wykeham's corresponding statute for New College translated above, with this exception, that it enumerates three rooms instead of four, the list of articles to be placed in the lower room (*inferior sive bassior camera*) being omitted altogether, and those for the second room being transferred to it.

At Queens' College no Fellow, nor even the President himself, is to enter the tower, or public treasury (*ærarium*) alone, but is always to take with him the two bursars or their deputies. Money, valuables, and evidences, are all to be kept there, and no document is to be sealed in any other place, for the seal may never be removed thence, except on special occasions by leave of the President and a majority of the Fellows. It was evidently

[1] [Commiss. Docts. (Oxford), Vol. III. Statutes of Worcester College, p. 45.]

[2] [History of King's College and Eton College, Vol. I. pp. 356, 369. Statutes of King's College and Eton College, ed. Heywood and Wright, pp. 126, 572.]

to be locked with three keys, for it is directed in a subsequent statute that the keys are to be kept by the President and the two bursars[1].

At S. Catharine's Hall the directions are of similar import, but expressed more briefly. The common seal, the muniments, etc., are to be kept in a tower or treasury (*thesauraria*), in which the sealings are to be held. The box containing the seal is to have three locks of different make, and the three keys belonging to them are to be kept by the master and two of the Fellows[2]. At Jesus College[3] (1515—34) and at Christ's College[4] (1506) the position of the treasury, in both called (*thesaurarium*), is not defined, and the safekeeping of its contents is enforced in terms so closely resembling those already quoted for other colleges that they need not be further discussed. The statutes which Dr Caius gave to his college (1558–72), mention a treasury (*ærarium*), in which documents are to be read aloud before they are sealed, but he does not define its position[5]. At S. John's College the statutes of Bishop Fisher (1530), and those of King Henry VIII. (1545), copy the statutes of Corpus Christi College, Oxford. At Trinity College the statutes of King Edward the Sixth and those of Queen Elizabeth place the Treasury in the lesser tower (*in minore turre*)[6]. The statutes of Emmanuel College and Sidney Sussex College copy those of Christ's College.

It will be interesting, in the next place, to note how far the elaborate provisions which we have been reviewing were obeyed, at least at Cambridge. Before the end of the fourteenth century the treasury could hardly be said to enter into the collegiate

1 [Commiss. Docts. III. 34. Stat. 18. *De custodia publici ærarii*, and p. 48. Stat. 35. *De electione Officiariorum.*]

2 [Ibid. p. 85. Stat. 5. *De custodia sigilli communis et munimentorum ac librorum collegii.*]

3 [Ibid. p. 118. Stat. 26. *De cista communi, et sigillo communi.*]

4 [Ibid. p. 180. Stat. 8. *De tuta rerum custodia;* and p. 191. Stat. 25. *De præfecto cistæ communis.*]

5 [Ibid. II. 288. § 81. *De obsignandis scriptis.*]

6 [History of Trinity College, Vol. II. p. 632. The passage from the statutes of King Edward the VI. is quoted in the same volume, p. 460, *note*. The statutes of Queen Elizabeth (printed in Appendix (B) to Reports from Select Committee on Education, &c., 1818) direct the Bursar to keep money in the Treasury (*ærarium*). This is afterwards spoken of as the tower, and lastly (Cap. XXXIV.) as "the lesser tower".]

plan. At only four colleges have we distinct evidence of its existence as a separate room, namely at Peterhouse, Pembroke College, Gonville Hall, and Trinity Hall. At the two first-mentioned colleges it was over the buttery, at Gonville Hall over the ante-chapel, and at Trinity Hall on the ground floor at the east end of the chapel. Wykeham in 1380 placed his treasury in a separate tower, erected for the purpose, and King Henry VI., in imitation of him, placed it over the gate of entrance to his intended college, and, so far as we can ascertain, in the same position in his first buildings, commonly called the Old Court of King's College, where the room on the first floor over the gate was unquestionably used as a treasury from the earliest times. The position of the treasury at King's Hall is somewhat uncertain, but as we find it occupying the second floor of King Edward's gate before the removal of that gate to its present position, it is probable that it was placed there from the first erection of that gate. If this be so, the first assignment of that position to the treasury at Cambridge may be claimed for King's Hall. At Queens' College and at Christ's College the treasury has always occupied the first floor over the gate of entrance; and at S. John's College the second floor over the same gate. At the colleges of Emmanuel and Sidney Sussex no definite position has been assigned to it.

It has never been the custom, at Cambridge, so far as we are aware, for the Master and Fellows to meet in the treasury to transact business, or to affix the college seal to leases and other documents. At Trinity College and King's College sealings take place in the chapel. At many colleges, however, there was a room set apart for this purpose, which in several cases has now become part of the Master's Lodge. At Peterhouse this room was called the chapter-house (*domus capitularis*), but all record of its position is lost; at Pembroke it was on the first floor over the Combination Room, and used by the Master as a dining-room; at Gonville and Caius College it was over the ante-chapel, and was used in the same way by the Master; at Corpus Christi College it was a room in what afterwards became the Master's Lodge; at Queens' College a room on the first floor of the west building, used by the President as a dining-room, is still called the audit-room; at Jesus College it was a room on the first floor, called the "Conference Chamber," between the Library and Master's Lodge (by which it has been absorbed), and probably, in its original state, approached by an external staircase; at Christ's College it was called the "Meeting Room," and is now the Drawing Room of the Master's Lodge; at S. John's College it was on the ground floor next the large Combination Room; at Trinity College it was a room in the Master's Lodge, the position of which has been forgotten; and at Sidney Sussex College the dining-room of the Master's Lodge is termed the audit-room.

A room which should serve the double purpose of a treasury and an audit-room was a feature introduced into the collegiate statutes, if not into the collegiate plan, from the monasteries. At Durham the following interesting description of the treasury has been preserved:

> "In the weast alley of the Cloysters, towards the north ende, undernethe the Dorter, and adjoyning unto the staires that go up to the Dorter, is * * * a strong howse called the TREASURE HOWSE, where all ther treasure was kept, having a strong door and two locks. * * * Within the said treasury was a strong iron grate, set fast in the groundwork, in the roof, and in either wall, the breadth of the house, so fast as not to be broken, and in the midst of the grate a door of iron, according to the workmanship of the grate, with a strong lock upon it and two great shuts of iron for the said door. And within the said grate was a four-square table, covered with a green cloth, for the telling of their money. Within this treasury were likewise the Evidences of the house and the Chapter seale, as also the Evidences of several gentlemen's lands in the country, who thought them safer there than in their own custody[1]."

This description shews that the treasury was divided by an iron grating into two rooms. The whole apartment was called Spendment or Splendment (*Spendimentum*), and we learn from existing records that through the bars of the grating money was received and paid, and, especially, that the servants of the convent received their wages. The room further served the purpose of an outer and inner library, as shewn above (p. 471)[2].

At Christ Church, Canterbury, the treasury occupied the first floor of a building adjoining S. Andrew's Chapel, now the

[1] [Rites of Durham, p. 71.]
[2] [Catalogi Veteres, *ut supra*, p. vi.]

vestry, on the north side of the Cathedral, out of which a staircase gave access to it[1]. In the middle ages vestry (*vestiarium*) and treasury (*thesaurarium*) were synonymous terms, for the first is defined by Ducange to be a place used not only for the keeping of vestments, but also of the valuable ornaments, vessels, and even money, of the church. The treasury at Canterbury probably served this double purpose, which, as shewn above, was also contemplated in many of the colleges in both Universities.

Besides the treasury, another building appears in monasteries, called the "Cheker" or "Chekker," which, as Professor Willis has pointed out, was a counting-house (*scaccarium*) in which the bursar and other officers transacted business. At Christ Church, Canterbury, the bursar's "Cheker" adjoined the Infirmary[2], as at Durham, where each officer of the monastery had his separate "Cheker[3]." The term was still used at New College, Oxford, during the last century, to designate a building situated at no great distance from the treasury, and probably used, as some of the rooms adjoining it are at present, as a bursar's office[4].]

1 [This "noble and unique room," as Professor Willis terms it, is fully described by him in The Architectural History of the Conventual Buildings of the Monastery of Christ Church in Canterbury, pp. 74—79.]

2 [Architectural History, etc. *ut supra*, p. 100.]

3 [Rites of Durham, pp. 82—85.]

4 [Essay on the Collegiate Plan, p. 280.]

IX.

THE CHAPEL.

CHAPTER I.

THE FIRST COLLEGES HAD NO PRIVATE CHAPELS. USE AND APPROPRIATION OF PARISH CHURCHES AT OXFORD AND CAMBRIDGE. INCONVENIENCE OF THIS. PRACTICE OF THE MEDIEVAL CHURCH WITH REGARD TO PRIVATE CHAPELS.

ALL scholars residing at the Universities, or at any other place of study, were legally parishioners, for the time being, of the church of the parish in which they happened to be lodged[1]; and, as colleges could not aspire to the privilege of a private chapel until they had risen to some importance, no other place than the parish

[1] According to Lyndwood, Provinciale, fol. Oxon. 1679, p. 233, they were classed under the head of travellers (*peregrinantes*), who "cujuslibet ecclesiæ parochiani existunt. Unde et scholaris, divertens se ad studium, dum ibi moratur, efficitur pro tempore parochianus ejus, in cujus parochia degit." It must be remembered that all persons were bound to attend Divine Service, that is, Vespers, Matins, Hours, and more especially Mass, on Sundays and the greater Festivals, in their own parish church. On other days the laity were not required to attend service, unless they wished to do so. Every priest had authority on those days to eject parishioners of other parishes before the Mass began. Laymen were strictly enjoined to receive the Sacrament on Easter Day, Pentecost, and Christmas Day, if not oftener; and this in their own parish church, unless during a journey, or by special licence (Ibid. p. 231). It was not expected that scholars should attend all the week-day services. For instance, in Walter de Merton's statutes dated 1274, it is directed: "Horis canonicis et celebrationi missarum [scholares] intersint diebus festivis et aliis *quantum eis vacaverit*."

church seems to have been contemplated by the first founders for the devotions of their beneficiaries. As every collegiate community was essentially a religious community, studying Theology and Canon Law, and for the most part preparing for Holy Orders, the attendance of students on divine service was regular and constant; and to enable this to be carried on with the least loss of time and inconvenience it was desirable to select a site as near to a parish church as possible. This is remarkably shewn at Cambridge, where Peterhouse, Clare Hall, Gonville Hall in its first position, and Corpus Christi College, were placed in actual contiguity with the churchyards of their respective parishes of S. Mary the Less, S. John Baptist, S. Botolph, and S. Benedict. Pembroke Hall was nearly opposite to S. Mary the Less, and not far from S. Botolph, while Trinity Hall was separated only by Clare Hall from the parish church of S. John Baptist. [At Oxford on the contrary no college except Merton College is at the present day in actual contiguity with a parish church; but, as at Cambridge, the early colleges were compelled, in default of chapels of their own, to use parish churches.] Balliol College used an aisle of the neighbouring church of S. Mary Magdalene; Exeter College S. Peter's in the East, and subsequently, on removing to a new site, S. Mildred's; University College and Oriel College both used S. Mary's; and Lincoln College, as will be explained below, was actually founded in the church of All Saints which it adjoined.

Amongst other provisions for increasing the revenues of colleges, founders and benefactors naturally had recourse to the appropriation of livings, a practice which originated as a convenient contrivance for improving the endowments of religious houses, which in many respects resembled the new colleges, and in consequence served as models for parts of their organisation.

The founders of the early colleges, in evident imitation of the collegiate churches previously established, were especially desirous of obtaining the advowson, and, where possible, the appropriation, of the parish churches near which their buildings were placed; but, as the increase in the number of colleges brought two or more into the same parish, it was of course impossible for every college to obtain the appropriation of its parish church. In such cases the members of the nascent college attended their parish church as ordinary parishioners until they were able to provide better accommodation for themselves.

Every episcopal act of appropriation contains the condition that the persons who are thereby permitted to appropriate the proceeds of the living to their own use shall make a competent provision for the spiritual cure of the parish. This is generally directed to be effected by a perpetual vicar, chosen upon each vacancy by the impropriators, and by them presented to the Bishop for admission, with a competent salary, residence, etc., subject to his approval, and generally minutely detailed either in the act of impropriation or in a subsequent document. [Let us take as an example the church of Litlington in Cambridgeshire, which now belongs to Clare Hall. The advowson had been given to University House by Elizabeth de Burgh. Shortly after, the Master and Scholars addressed a petition to Simon de Montacute, Bishop of Ely, setting forth the poverty into which, without any fault of theirs, they had fallen, and praying him to allow them to appropriate the rectory. The Bishop consented, on certain conditions, which are minutely set forth in the deed of appropriation, dated 7 September, 1338. The vicar is to have a suitable stipend (*congruens portio*), which stipend is to be perpetual. It is to consist of all customary oblations, all burial fees (*mortuaria*), all bequests, the smaller tithes (the nature of which are carefully enumerated), and, lastly, an annual stipend of five marks, paid quarterly. Moreover a site is to be assigned to him in the garden of the rectory on the west side of the church, on which a dwelling-house is to be built for him and his successors, together with a convenient piece of ground adjoining thereto. On the aforesaid site the Master and Scholars are to build him a vicarage, consisting of a hall, a chamber, and a kitchen, unless some house belonging to a chantry in the church can be obtained, by consent of all those who have any interest in it. In consideration of these privileges the vicar is to supply the church with service-books, and to pay the archdeacon's dues; but all other payments, ordinary and extraordinary, are to be made by the Master and Scholars and their successors. If these conditions be accepted, they may take possession of the church on the death of the present rector, without any authority from the

Bishop or his successors, saving always the rights of the Archdeacon[1].]

In all acts of appropriation of town livings in the neighbourhood of the respective colleges, the colleges were permitted to retain the cure of souls in their own hands, and to serve the parish by stipendiary chaplains, or, as they were called, parochial chaplains, appointed by themselves from time to time, generally from the Fellows of their own college, and without reference to the Bishop, so that all chance of interference and of dispute concerning the parochial services would be avoided.

This example was set in the foundation of the first college. Even in his first establishments at Maldon and Farleigh[2], Walter de Merton was careful to obtain from the Bishop of Winchester the appropriation to his scholars of their respective parish churches, the advowsons (or right of patronage) of which he had previously given to them. These churches were to be served by perpetual vicars. For his Oxford college he began by acquiring in 1265 vacant ground in contiguity with the parish church of S. John Baptist, to which ground the advowson of it belonged, and he also purchased the advowson of the more distant parish church of S. Peter in the East. These two churches were canonically appropriated to the college by the Bishop of Lincoln in 1266 by one and the same deed[3]. The former was intended for the ritual use of the scholars, the latter merely for their better support, and accordingly the services of the latter are in the deed consigned to a vicar, while the services of the former are to be performed by the four ministers of the altar who formed part of the community of the college, and who are designated chaplains in the statutes[4], and also in the Papal Bull

[1] [The deed is copied from Bishop Montacute's Register by Baker, MSS. Vol. XIX. fol. 1. MSS. Harl. Mus. Brit. 7046.]

[2] Maldon is near Kingston, and Farleigh is a small parish on the chalk hills south of Croydon, between Sanderstead and Chelsham. Both are in Surrey. The first is about 50 miles from Oxford in a direct line, the second 10 or 12 miles farther.

[3] [Printed in The Account of Pythagoras's School in Cambridge. By Joseph Kilner: Appendix, p. 66.]

[4] [These officials are most usually designated ministers of the altar (*ministri altaris*), words which occur even in the statutes of 1274 (Commiss. Docts. (Oxford) Vol. I. Statutes of Merton College, p. 26, cap. 9. *De ministerio altaris*). In a later

of 1280, which allows "four chaplains to celebrate mass for ever in the church of the aforesaid House, canonically granted to the same[1]." These chaplains thus became the parochial ministers of the church, but being, as part of the foundation, otherwise provided for than as vicars in other churches, the tithes or oblations have belonged to the college from the time of the appropriation of this church, as may be seen in the rentals and accounts. The chaplains, however, besides the benefits they have from the college as chaplains, have their dues for marrying and burying, etc. as personally and accustomably belonging to them.

The founder, as in the common case, which evidently served him as a model, of the transformation of a parish church into a collegiate church, set about rebuilding it in order to provide a spacious quire for the reception of his scholars and chaplains, and for the due performance of their religious rites, apart from those of the parish. This magnificent quire was so far completed in 1277, twelve years only after the appropriation, that the high altar was dedicated; but the building-accounts shew that the work went on for ten years or more afterwards, probably in the tower-arches. It was then suspended, and resumed in the fifteenth century, when the church was re-dedicated (in 1424), probably on account of the completion of the transepts, to which period their architecture belongs. The tower was finished about 1451[2]. The nave was never carried on, but the arches intended to communicate with its central and side aisles are still to be seen, and, although walled up, give sufficient evidence that a nave formed part of the plan.

In the foundation of Peterhouse at Cambridge in 1284, Hugh de Balsham, then Bishop of Ely, followed the example of Merton in placing his students in the immediate neighbourhood of the church of S. Peter, re-dedicated afterwards as S. Mary the Less, which he himself, as uniting in his own person the founder of the college and the Bishop of the diocese, appropriated to the

chapter of the same code, however, they are called chaplains (*capellani*), ibid. p. 33. Their number was to be four if the funds of the House permitted it, if not, three at least.]

[1] [Kilner, *ut supra*, pp. 62, 79.]

[2] [The Building-Accounts of this tower from 20 May, 1448, to 9 May, 1450, have been printed by J. E. Thorold Rogers, History of Prices, III. 720—737. Professor Willis has sketched the history of Merton College chapel in the essay on The Collegiate Plan, pp. 251, 258.]

House in 1285, empowering the scholars to serve the church by a parochial chaplain[1]. [This church was used as a chapel by the members of Peterhouse until their present chapel was consecrated in 1632. It was rebuilt in 1352, when the construction of a spacious quire for the use of the college, which would have occupied five severies of the existing church, seems to have been intended, probably in imitation of Merton's work. There is no evidence to shew how the western portion, for the use of the parish, was to have been completed; but, as explained in the History of the Church[2], the building-work was evidently interrupted, and the western portion finished in a later style.]

The parish church of S. Mary at Oxford was given and appropriated to Oriel College by the founder, King Edward the Second, 26 April, 1326, but in this appropriation a vicar was appointed for the parish[3]. The statutes enjoin attendance on divine service in this church, and the maintenance of two chaplains to say daily masses therein for the souls of the founder and others[4].

The foundation of Michael House at Cambridge is contemporary with that of Oriel College. The founder, Hervey de Stanton, in the words of his chronicler,

"having resolved to found a college of chaplains and scholars, first bought the advowson of the church of S. Michael in Cambridge from Dera de Madingley for one hundred marks of silver, together with a certain messuage to which the advowson was said to belong. * * * Next he bought, also for one hundred marks, another messuage for the aforesaid scholars to dwell in[5]."

The Bishop of Ely's licence for the appropriation of the church contains, among other grounds for giving his consent, the following express statement:

"because, as your permanent habitation is situated in the parish of the aforesaid church, you will be able to celebrate mass in that church,

[1] [Baker's History of S. John's College, ed. Mayor, I. 25. Commiss. Docts. I. 3. The church had been previously appropriated to S. John's Hospital.]

[2] [History of Peterhouse, Vol. I. p. 52.]

[3] The Antient and Present state of the City of Oxford, [etc.] By Mr Anthony à Wood and the Rev. Sir T. Peshall, Bart. 4to. Lond. 1773, p. 56.

[4] [Commiss. Docts. (Oxford), Vol. I. Statutes of Oriel College, p. 12.]

[5] [Otryngham Book, fo. I.]

and to perform your other religious duties therein at proper hours, as it is fit you should do, in greater tranquillity, from having, to all future time, the cure of souls entrusted to you[1]."

Hervey de Stanton rebuilt the church from the ground, arranging the plan (fig. 1) so as to suit the purpose he had in view of employing it as a collegiate parish church; and, dying at York in 1327, his remains were, in accordance with his own instructions, conveyed to Cambridge, and buried in the church, in the middle of the chancel, amongst his scholars[2]. He had charged his executors with the care of finishing the church and House which he had begun, and of completing the establishment of a perpetual chantry for his soul, the building of which it appears that he had also commenced in his lifetime.

Of University House, Cambridge, the next foundation in order of time, we can only suppose that the scholars attended their parish church of S. John Baptist, commonly called S. John Zachary, to which their dwelling was contiguous, and as they continued to do after the name was changed to Clare Hall; for the statutes of that House, dated 1359, appoint six of the Fellows to be chaplains, and direct that one of them is to celebrate daily, in the parish church, a mass in honour of the Blessed Virgin at early morning (*summo mane*), so that all the Fellows may attend before they go to the Schools. Daily mass is also to be celebrated in the same church, at which all the chaplains and scholars (*pueri*) are to be present, unless prevented by study or other reasonable excuse[3]. It is clear, however, that this church was not appropriated to either college.

[1] [The conveyance from Dera de Madingley to Hervey de Stanton is dated 9 September, 1323; the Bishop of Ely's licence 3 March, 1324—25. The latter has been printed in the appendix from the original in the Treasury of Trinity College, where both deeds are preserved.]

[2] [Hervey de Stanton's will is dated 26 August, 1327. By a codicil dated 31 October following he desired to be buried in St Michael's Church. In the course of the action brought against his executors respecting their administration of his effects, they justify the great expense of the funeral by stating that: "in vita sua dixit, voluit, et mandauit, quod corpus suum traderetur sepulture in ecclesia Sancti Michaelis predicti in medio cancelli inter scholares suos, et ideo funus suum de Ebor' ad eundem locum ducebatur." The will and the other documents belonging to it are preserved in the Treasury of Trinity College.]

[3] [Commiss. Docts. II. pp. 129, 141.]

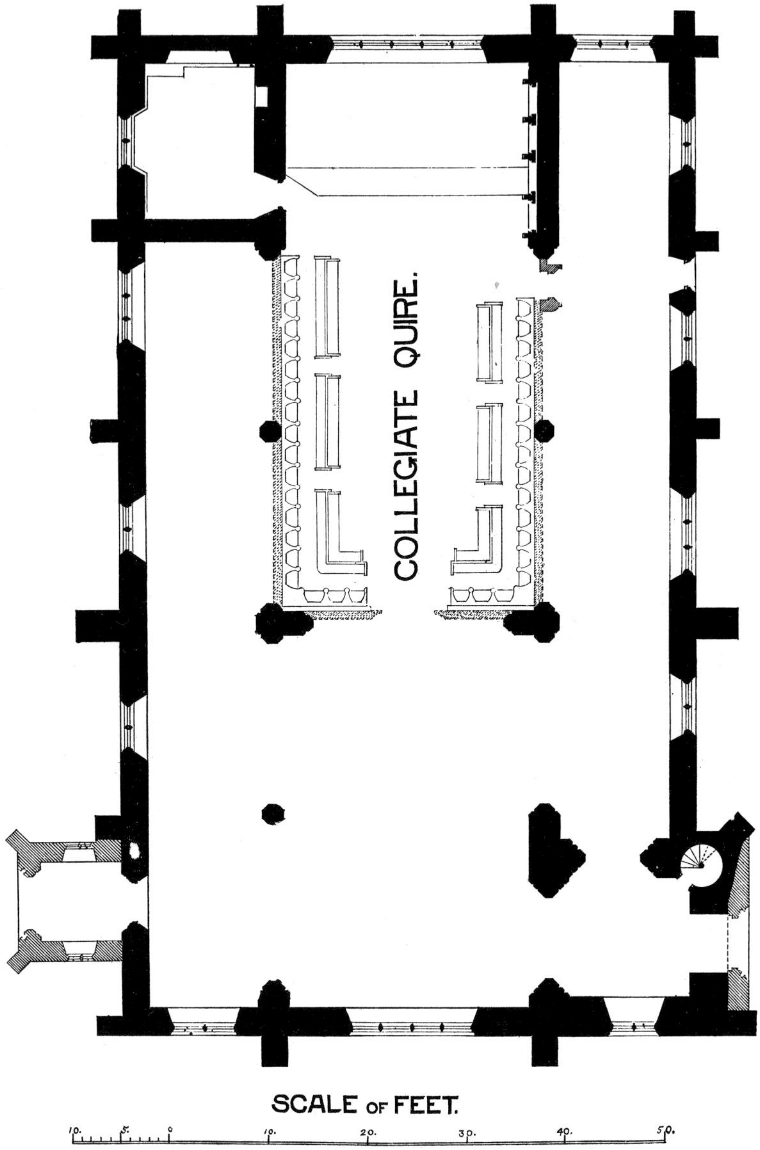

Fig. 1. Ground-plan of S. Michael's church, Cambridge, reduced from a ground-plan made by Sir G. G. Scott in 1849. The walls distinguished by hatching were put up under his direction at that time.

King Edward the Third, by letters patent, dated 25 July, 1342, gave to his college of King's Hall, Cambridge, the church of S. Mary the Great, evidently to serve the purpose of a college chapel, although it was not in the same parish, the college being at that time wholly contained within the adjoining parish of All Saints. The episcopal licence of appropriation[1], dated 19 October, 1343, contains a clause identical in substance with that which I have just quoted from the appropriation-deed of S. Michael's, though expressed in rather different language, with this exception, that the scholars in the case of S. Mary's are described as residing in the same *university*, instead of in the same *parish*. In the case of S. Michael's the parish services are not mentioned; in that of S. Mary's the college is to be responsible for their proper conduct by a chaplain, who is to be in priest's orders, and to whom a suitable salary is to be paid by the college out of the revenues of the church[2]. Both these churches, however, as well as the church of S. Peter (afterwards S. Mary the Less), are shewn to have been customarily served by parochial chaplains, and not by vicars, by a list of the patrons, vicars, etc. in the diocese of Ely, inserted in the Register of William Gray, Bishop of Ely 1454—79[3].

The colleges of Pembroke, Gonville Hall, and Corpus Christi were founded within five years of each other (1347—52), and very nearly in contiguity, though in the distinct parishes of S. Peter, S. Botolph, and S. Benedict. It is probable that the members of Pembroke College would use their parish church of S. Peter for their devotions, until they obtained a chapel for themselves. The foundress spared no pains to obtain this privilege, but, before it was granted to her, she contemplated the appropriation of the neighbouring church of S. Botolph. We learn this from the history of that church, to be narrated below; and further, in the original undated draft of her statutes, she directs her two priests to celebrate in the chapel of the house, *or in their church should they have one annexed to the*

1 [The deed is printed in the Appendix, No. II.]

2 The Register of Bishop Montacute (MSS. Baker XIX. 6, MSS. Harl. Mus. Brit. 7046) contains the following entry respecting this appropriation: "Collegium tenetur ad sustentationem capellani et ad solutionem 4 solidorum annuatim Archidiacono pro recompensatione damni."

3 MSS. Baker XXX. 101.

house[1]. But in her remodelled copy of the same statutes, as finally adopted and confirmed by the Bishop of Ely in 1347, the clause in italics is omitted.

The advowson of S. Benedict was purchased by the founders of Corpus Christi College in 1350[2], and the royal licence for the appropriation of the same was obtained in 1352[3], but, for some reason not recorded, it was not canonically confirmed, or at least was not acted upon, for the college continued merely to exercise their right of presentation for successive rectors until 1578, when Richard Cox, Bishop of Ely, formally appropriated the church to the college[4].

In 1353 the college of Corpus Christi obtained the original site of Gonville Hall, in contiguity, as before mentioned, with the churchyard of S. Botolph, by exchanging for it the ground in S. Michael's parish to which Gonville Hall was removed. The deed by which this exchange was ratified contains the curious provision that the college of the Annunciation, as Gonville Hall was then designated, should procure for the college of the Gild of Corpus Christi all the rights which the Countess of Pembroke and her college possessed with respect to the church of S. Botolph, and should bear all the expenses of the transfer. It appears from this deed, the only record remaining concerning this matter, except the allusion to an appropriated church already quoted from her statutes, that the Countess of Pembroke had purchased, or at least had made progress in a design for purchasing, the advowson of S. Botolph, which belonged at that time to the convent of Barnwell, for the use of her own college, part of which was situated in that parish. In consequence of the above transaction the advowson of the church became, in 1353, after some disputing, the property of Corpus Christi College, but the rectory was never appropriated to it. By these transfers the college was placed in two parishes, and

[1] [This draft is preserved in the Treasury of Pembroke College, A. 12, l. 94. With the view of securing the right of appropriating a church she sent a proctor to Rome in 1359. Ibid. A. 4.]

[2] [Josselin, § 3. (Camb. Antiq. Soc. 8vo. Publ. 1880.)]

[3] [Commiss. Docts. II. 445.]

[4] Masters, History, p. 115. The deed of appropriation has been copied by Baker, MSS. XXX. 162. Lysons mentions (Cambridgeshire, p. 198) that it was one of the last rectories ever appropriated. [The History of the Church has been narrated at length, Vol. I. pp. 271—285.]

in contiguity with their respective churches at the extremities of the site, both being the property of the college, so far as the right of presentation went. By the statutes of 1356 the members of the college were bound to attend divine service daily, either in the church of S. Benedict or in that of S. Botolph. The advowson of the latter was sold to Queens' College, which is wholly situated in that parish, 12 January, 1459—60, with the sole reservation that the members of Corpus Christi College might still use the church for the services to which they were statutably obliged, but it has never been appropriated to Queens' College[1].

The next example of appropriation of a parish church to a college occurred at Oxford, in connexion with the foundation of Lincoln College. The description of this college in the preamble to the letters patent granted by King Henry the Sixth, 13 October, 1427, unlike that of other colleges, runs in the terms of the foundation-deed of a collegiate chantry. Richard Flemmyng, Bishop of Lincoln, was empowered

"to found a certain College or Society of one Warden or Rector, and seven Scholars, in the Church of All Saints in Oxford, which was then of the patronage of the said Bishop; and to unite, annex, and incorporate the said Church of All Saints, and the Churches of St. Mildred and St. Michael at the north gate, which were in his patronage also in right of his Bishopric; and the said Churches so united annexed and incorporated, to name them the Church of All Saints; and the same Church to erect and change into a Collegiate Church or College; and to the said Church so erected or changed, to unite, annex, and incorporate a certain Chantry in the Chapel of St. Anne within the said Church, of the patronage of the Mayor of the Town of Oxford for the time being; provided that daily Mass and other Suffrages be duly performed in the Chapel, according as the foundation thereof requireth, for the souls of the Founder and others. That there should be also two moveable Chaplains (*capellani removibiles*), to be put in and out at the pleasure of the Rector, that should serve in the said Church, and undergo the cure of souls there. That the said College be called THE COLLEGE OF THE BLESSED VIRGIN MARY AND ALL SAINTS, LYNCOLN, IN THE UNIVERSITY OF OXFORD. That the said Rector and Scholars be perpetual Parsons of the said Church [etc.][2]."

[1] [History of Corpus Christi College, Vol. I. p. 243. The deed of exchange is printed in the notes to the edition of Josselin above referred to. Compare also Masters' History, pp. 16, 20; and Searle's History of Queens' College, p. 67.]

[2] Wood, *ut supra*, p. 236. Commiss. Docts. (Oxford) Vol. I.; Statutes of Lincoln College, p. 4.

At Cambridge the last[1] instance of similar appropriation is that of the parish church of S. Edward to Trinity Hall in 1446[2]. This complicated transaction shall be narrated as briefly as possible. Clare Hall and Trinity Hall continued to use their parish church of S. John, the patronage of which, as well as that of S. Edward, belonged to the convent of Barnwell, until the plans of King Henry the Sixth for extending the site of King's College made it necessary for him to obtain possession of S. John's Church, and eventually to pull it down. The necessity for doing this must have been evident for some years before it was carried into effect, for so early as 1444 Trinity Hall negotiated for the acquisition of S. Edward's Church with John Langton, Chancellor of the University, and one of the Royal Commissioners for the acquisition of the new site. By a deed dated 8 June, 1444, Langton agreed "in all godely hast" to "labour and do his ful part and diligence to gete the Patronage of the Vicarage of the Church of S. Edward's of the Towne of Cambrigge,...and to appropriate the said Churche at the next vacacion thereof to the propre vse of the said College," and Simon Dallyng, Master of Trinity Hall, engaged to pay him 100 marks for his trouble. Clare Hall, though likely to be as much inconvenienced as Trinity Hall by the loss of S. John's Church, does not appear to have moved in the matter in any way. Two years afterwards, 20 February, 1446, the king obtained the advowsons of the two churches from Barnwell Abbey, and conveyed the advowson of S. Edward's, with the rights of appropriation, to Trinity Hall, 21 March following, on the condition of the appointment of a proper chaplain (*capellanum idoneum*) to conduct the parish services, who should be appointed by the college, and be capable of being removed by the same authority. It is probable that the new site had been by this time cleared for building, for on the last day of July in the same year the Bishop of Ely, at the instance of the

[1] Excepting of course the above-cited appropriation of S. Benedict to Corpus Christi College in 1578, which had been legally authorised in 1352.

[2] [The history of this transaction has been fully related in a paper printed in the Cambridge Antiquarian Society's Communications, Vol. IV. No. XX., in the appendix to which all the documents relating to it have been printed. For the position, etc. of the Church of S. John see History of King's College, Vol. I. pp. 340, 548.]

parishioners of S. John, appointed a commission to inquire whether a union of the parishes of S. John and S. Edward might not be desirable; and, after some unavoidable delay, he declared the two parishes to be united, and appropriated to Trinity Hall.

The church of S. Edward, a ground-plan of which is here given (fig. 2), is of the Decorated period, consisting of a nave and chancel with side-aisles. But the side-aisles of the chancel are broader than those of the nave, and extend one arch farther westward than the chancel. They are in fact chapels, the result of an alteration in the original church in the fifteenth century, to which their details belong; and the parish records furnish evidence that the north chapel, together with the chancel, belongs to Trinity Hall, and the south chapel to Clare Hall[1]. It may be conjectured that these two Societies had attached chapels of this kind to their original parish church of S. John; and that after the destruction of that church and the union of the parishes, similar chapels were added to the newly-acquired church of S. Edward. The style of the architecture of the two chapels corresponds very well with this supposition[2]. The parish registers shew that members of Trinity Hall and Clare Hall have been buried in these chapels, and that S. Catharine's Hall also has used the south chapel for the same purpose.

The examples given above include all the cases of appropriation of parish churches in Cambridge and Oxford for the purpose of collegiate worship. It will be seen that I am not here alluding to the appropriated benefices, of which every college has acquired a certain number as a source of revenue and patronage.

The inconvenience and loss of time consequent upon attendance at a parish church, unless in immediate contact with a college, soon led to attempts to obtain permission for the erection

[1] [Cambridge Borough Rate Report, pp. 17, 29.]

[2] [Professor Willis gave a lecture at Cambridge in 1858 or 1859 on the architectural history of S. Edward's Church, but unfortunately it was not reported, and he did not himself preserve any notes for it. The parts of the church erected at different periods are distinguished on the plan by different hatchings. The tower is Early English, the nave Decorated. A restoration of the church, including a new vestry, was commenced in 1858, and continued in 1859, when a new east window was inserted to commemorate the ten years incumbency of the Rev. Harvey Goodwin, who was made Dean of Ely in the former year.]

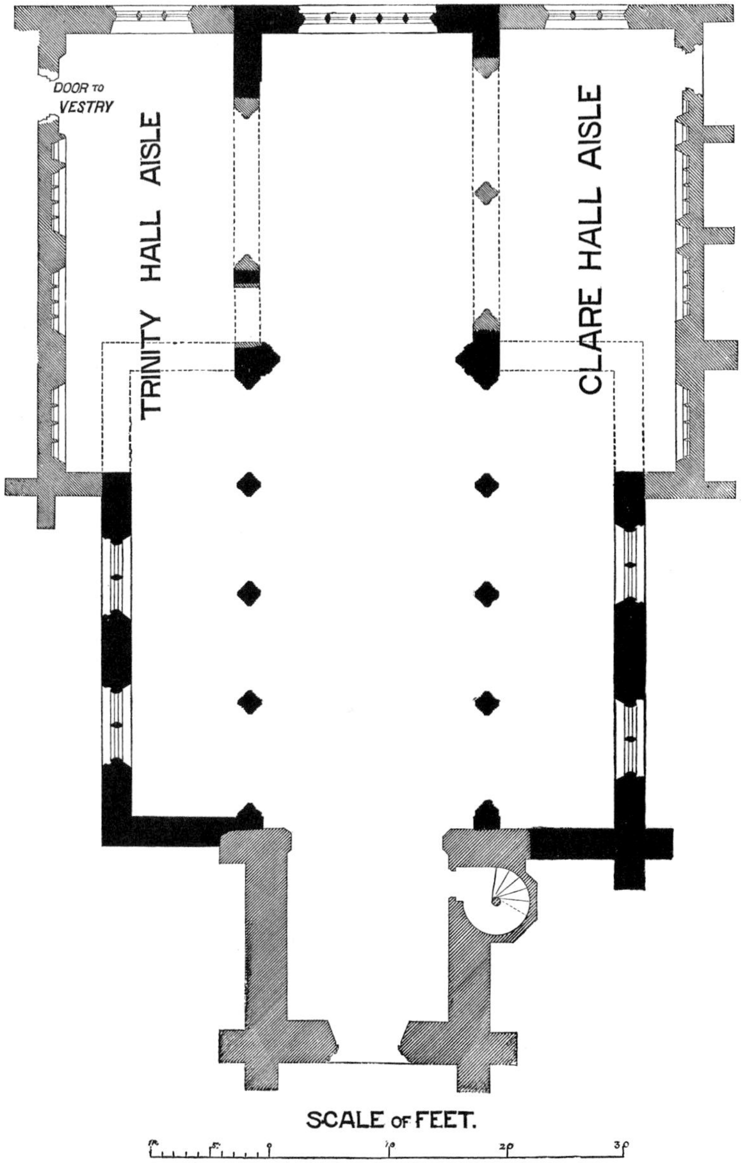

Fig. 2. Ground-plan of S. Edward's Church, Cambridge, reduced from a ground-plan made by Professor Willis in 1858. The probable original extent of the chancel, and of the aisles of the nave, is indicated by dotted lines.

of private chapels within the walls. But it appears that at first this privilege was granted with great reserve and unwillingness by Popes and Bishops. The early licences do not extend to the administration of the sacraments, and there is in all cases a strict caution to preserve the rights and dues of the parish church. In fact, the first chapels were mere oratories, and the parish church was still resorted to for the greater ceremonies and sacraments. Gradually, however, as the collegiate system became established, and the colleges increased in riches and influence, more extended privileges were granted to them, and many of the college chapels of the later foundations were from the first completely emancipated from parochial interference, and were even allowed the privilege of sepulture.

On the other hand Papal Bulls and episcopal licences for the erection of intramural chapels were sometimes obtained by the early colleges, and allowed to lie idle for many years, either because they hoped to obtain more extensive privileges, or because want of funds prevented them from erecting and furnishing the chapel after permission had been obtained. The records of most of the early colleges contain privileges of this kind dated long before the building of their chapels. As the parish church could be resorted to for the performance of their sacred duties, the chapel was not so absolutely necessary as the chambers and the refectory, without which the establishment could not be carried on.

To understand the successive steps by which the college chapel became an integral part of the system it may be well to state in a few words the practice of the medieval church with respect to chapels.

Everyone was freely allowed to have an oratory in his house for simple prayer, for matins, and for other hours, but the licence or permission of the Bishop was required to allow a priest to celebrate mass in such an oratory, consecration not being necessary, or even thought desirable. The canons and constitutions of the Church enjoin the Bishops to use great reserve in giving licences for private chapels, except in special cases, such as the residence of families at a great distance from a consecrated church, or for other pressing reasons, and even then the permission must not be extended to the greater festivals, upon which attendance in the parish church was indispensable. No bells were allowed to be used in such oratories without episcopal authority[1].

But the use of private chapels was also circumscribed and limited by the necessity of protecting the privileges of the parish churches, and the incomes of the parish ministers; for the oblations which formed a considerable part of their maintenance were offered by the people to the priest in the mass on certain festivals, and also at weddings, funerals, and other ceremonies. Such oblations were held to belong to the priest who held the cure of the church, and whose office it was to pray for the sins of the people, and not to other priests celebrating therein, into whose hands the oblations were delivered[2]. The establishment of a private chapel in a parish for the use of persons who would otherwise have frequented the church was an injury to the parish priest, whose oblations would have suffered proportionally had he not been protected by a compromise. Hence it is that the licences for private chapels, although some, or all, as the case might be, of the above regulations for the compulsory attendance at the parish church are usually dispensed with, all contain a clause in reservation of the rights of the parish church which cannot be better explained than by extracting a part of the sixteenth constitution of Othobonus (1268):

> "When a Bishop, upon sufficient reasons shewn by a private person who is desirous of obtaining a chapel of his own, concedes the privilege, he invariably inserts in the licence that this must be done without prejudice to the rights of others. Wherefore we ordain that every chaplain ministering in a chapel which has been licensed with a clause securing the rights of the mother-church, shall, under pain of suspension, deliver freely to the Rector all oblations, and all other things which, if he had not received them, would have been directly given to that church[3]."

[1] [*Oratorium* verò dicitur quod non est ædificatum ad missam dicendam, nec dotatum, sed ordinatum ad orandum. Et tale Oratorium potest quis ædificare sine consensu Episcopi, tamen sine licentia Episcopi non potest ibi celebrari; sed hanc licentiam non concedet is majoribus Festivitatibus. Fiunt enim hujusmodi Oratoria ad orandum, non ad celebrandum, nisi auctoritas Episcopi interveniat, vel aliud privilegium a Sede Apostolica impetretur. Lyndwood, *ut supra*, p. 233.]

[2] [Lyndwood, *ut supra*, p. 111.]

[3] [Constitutiones Legatinæ sive Legitimæ Regionis Anglicanæ D. Othonis et D. Othoboni, Cardinalium, et Sedis Romanæ in Anglia Legatorum. Fol. Oxon. 1679,

The concluding words are modified by the commentator, so as to shew that these dues might either be overridden by some special indulgence, or ancient privilege to the contrary, or commuted for a fixed annual payment to the Rector. In the licence pecuniary compensations are usually claimed for the Bishop, Archdeacon, and others whose dues suffer from the diminution in the value of the livings occasioned by these chapels.

A good example of a permission to have a private chapel is afforded by a Bull of Pope Alexander the Sixth, dated 25 June, 1501. Robert Drury, proprietor of the manor of Hawstead in Suffolk, had represented that his house was more than a mile distant from the parish church, and that he and his family were frequently prevented from attending service by bad weather, and the dangerous condition of the roads. Under these circumstances the Pope allows him to have mass celebrated on a portable altar in his unconsecrated private chapel, without leave of the diocesan, on all festivals except Easter-Day, the rights of the parish being reserved, but all other rules and constitutions, including those of Otho and Othobonus, being dispensed with[1].

It would be easy to give numerous instances of the manner in which dependence on the mother church was recognised, if we had space to do so. The following passage, however, so nearly concerns our present subject that it deserves quotation:

"When Chappels were first allow'd to our colleges in *Oxford*, it was generally provided that such liberty should be no prejudice to the Parish Church, and that the Scholars of every such house should frequent the said Parochial Church in the greater solemnities of the year. Which custome does still prevail at *Lincoln* college, where the Rector and Fellows on *Michaelmass* day go in their respective habits to the Church of S^t^. *Michael*, and on the day of *All Saints* to the Church of *All-hallows*[2]."

In an essay on college chapels it is plainly superfluous to inquire concerning the parochial rights of Baptism or Matri-

p. 111. Cardinal Ottoboni, afterwards Pope Adrian V., was sent to England as Legate by Pope Clement IV., in which capacity he attended the Anglican Council held in S. Paul's Cathedral, London, May, 1268.]

[1] [Bibl. Top. Brit. V. 120. An interesting figure of a portable altar is given on Plate IV.]

[2] Kennett: Parochial Antiquities, 4to. Oxford, 1695, p. 595.

mony, but a few words may be said on Sepulture. The characteristic privilege of a parish church is to have a font and a cemetery, but the parish had no power to compel the burial of a parishioner therein. For the canons, from a very early period, decree that every one ought to be buried in the sepulchre of his ancestors, but that if any person desire to be deposited elsewhere, as, for example, in some favourite religious house, he shall not be hindered, provided only that a share, called "the canonical portion[1]," of the special oblation or bequest which, by will, according to the custom of the middle ages, was assigned to the church selected by the testator for his burial-place, should be reserved to the parish church of his residence.

CHAPTER II.

ORATORIES. PORTABLE ALTARS USED IN THEM. CONSECRATION OF CHAPELS. USE OF CHAPELS FOR OTHER PURPOSES THAN DIVINE SERVICE. SKETCH OF THE GRADUAL INTRODUCTION OF A SEPARATE CHAPEL INTO THE COLLEGIATE PLAN AT OXFORD AND CAMBRIDGE, WITH SPECIAL REFERENCE TO THE PRIVILEGES OBTAINED IN EACH CASE.

[WE will next examine the conditions under which the Chapel, as we understand the term, became part of the collegiate plan. It will be found that this investigation gives the following results: at first a licensed room either replaced the parish church, or was used in addition to it, for the less solemn services; and, in the second place, a private chapel was not desired until the necessity for it had been demonstrated by long experience, when the privilege was reluctantly conceded by the ecclesiastical authorities, with immunities from parochial and other rights which became more and more substantial as time advanced.

[1] [The canonical portion was usually a third of the bequest, but was allowed to vary according to local custom. Particulars relating to mortuaries and other matters foreign to our immediate purpose which I have not pretended to give, may be found in Lyndwood, and in the ordinary works on Ecclesiastical Law.]

Oratories, or small private chapels, licensed under the conditions just described, were not uncommon in Cambridge. They were either private to the Master or one of the Fellows[1], or appointed for the use of the whole collegiate body. The latter was the destination of the oratory in two floors at Corpus Christi College, built between 1487 and 1515[2]. The rooms, and the gallery through which they were approached, have been but little altered, and are the only specimen remaining in the University of these curious medieval substitutes for chapels.]

When mass was said in them it was necessary to use a portable altar, or, as it is frequently called, a "super-altar" (*superaltare*), because it was laid upon the unconsecrated altar which had been erected in the chapel at the time of its construction. This portable altar usually consisted of a small thin stone, consecrated, and set in a wooden frame. It was the practice of medieval Bishops

> "to consecrate a good number of these altar-stones at the same time, so that they might have them at hand ready for distribution through the diocese, or to bestow upon such of their flock among the laity whose wealth allowed them to keep a private chaplain, or whose old age, ill health, the length and badness of the road to the parish church, warranted them to ask, and the prelate to grant, the leave of having Mass said at home within their private chapel. A like indulgence was sometimes too accorded in favour of gilds, the brethren of which, though individually poor, might thus have, through the services of the brotherhood's priest, the same religious comforts in sickness, as the knight or earl. Such a grace was sometimes furthermore enhanced by the additional privilege of being able to carry about, and having Mass celebrated upon, the altar-stone, in any decent and becoming place[3]."

That such altars were used at Cambridge is shewn by the Inventory of Queens' College, made 12 October, 1496, which enumerates nine portable altars ready consecrated (*altaria portabilia sanctificata*), and by the licence granted to Bishop Fisher to consecrate portable altars at S. John's College. In the accounts of Exeter College, Oxford, for 1556, a charge of

[1] [History of Queens' College, Vol. II. p. 43; and the word *Oratory* in the Index.]

[2] [History of Corpus Christi College, Vol. I. pp. 285—288.]

[3] Rock, Church of our Fathers, I. 247. [The author carefully distinguishes between these and the super-altars properly so called, to which he devotes a long description (pp. 249—263).]

sixpence occurs "for a consecrated super-altar[1]." Similar altars are also in all probability meant by the "xij superaltariez" enumerated in the earliest list of chapel-furniture at King's College, drawn up in 1453[2]. Their use is illustrated by the following curious passage translated from the statutes of Queen's College, Oxford:

"Neither the Provost, nor any one of the scholars, is to be allowed an Oratory or a private chapel in his chamber or adjoining to it, except in case of sickness; and for the duration of such sickness only may they be permitted to arrange for the hearing of Mass in their chambers on a super-altar placed upon a moveable table[3]."

The consecration of every Cathedral, Conventual, or Parochial, church within two years after its completion, was ordered by the first constitution of Otho, dated 1237[4]. From the language used it would appear that the custom had been much neglected at that period; but it may be doubted whether a more regular observance of it was effected by that enactment. [It has been shewn in the separate Histories that several of the Cambridge Chapels erected before the Reformation were probably only licensed. Indeed it is only for the chapels of King's Hall, Gonville Hall, and Trinity Hall, that we have certain evidence of consecration; though, as will be explained below, the chapels of King's College and Queens' College ought perhaps to be added to this list. The following curious narrative of what happened at Clare Hall, when visited by Queen Mary's Commissioners in 1557, is worth quotation in this place, though its authority is doubtful, and it is not endorsed by anything stated in the official account of the proceedings drawn up by John Mere, Registrary[5]. In their perambulation of the University, when the Commissioners

"came into Clare-hall and entered into the chapel, which was their ordinary custom to do first of all, wheresoever they came, they perceived there was no sacrament, as they call it, hanging over the altar.

The which thing being taken in great displeasure, Ormanet [one

[1] [Register, etc. *ut supra*, p. 38.]

[2] [The Ecclesiologist, XX. 313. History of King's College, Vol. I. p. 535.]

[3] [Commiss. Doc^{ts}. (Oxford), Vol. I. Statutes of Queen's College, p. 33.]

[4] [Constitutiones Legatinæ, etc. *ut supra*, p. 6. Cardinal Otho, legate of Pope Gregory IX., presided at the Anglican Council held in S. Paul's Cathedral, November, 1237.]

[5] [Lamb's Documents, p. 211.]

of the commissioners and the pope's datary] calling to him the master of the house, told him what a great wickedness he had, by so doing, brought upon himself and all his house: for, although he were so unwise to think it no shame at all, yet unto them it seemed an inexpiable offence. The old man being amazed and looking about him how he might answer the matter, while he went about to purge himself thereof, made the fault double: he said it was a profane place never as yet hallowed nor consecrated with any ceremonies. At that word, the commissioners were yet more astonied, demanding whether he himself, or any other, had used to sing mass there or no. When he had confessed that both he himself and others also had oftentimes said mass there: 'O thou wretched old man,' quoth Ormanet, 'thou hast cast both thyself and them in danger of the grievous sentence of excommunication' [1]."

It is evident that both the oratories and the regular chapels were used for other purposes than divine service without any objection being raised to such a practice. The students of Corpus Christi College used their oratory for lectures and acts, as well as for prayers; and when they petitioned Sir Nicholas Bacon to build a separate chapel they stated "that there is in the saide Colledge never a convenient place for the company of the saide howse to repaire to devine service, nor to vse the exercises of learninge that by thorder of the same howse ought to be kept and observed[2]." The performance of plays in the antechapel of King's College in 1564, on the occasion of Queen Elizabeth's visit, is well known, and the quire was used for declamations, and even for degree-examinations, down to 1851. At Trinity College declamations, no matter on what subject, are still delivered in the chapel. Plays were also performed in the chapel at Jesus College in 1567—68, and 1568—69;

"Item a bunche of glasse for the chappell after y^e playe......ij^s. vj^d [3].
Item spent at the playes in the chappell laid out by Mr Day and Wod [2 Fellows] vt patet per eorum billas .... $iiij^{li}$. vj^s"] [4].

The first attempt to obtain a private chapel was made at Oxford by Balliol College in 1293, about twenty years after the establishment of the Society in old Balliol Hall. The following history, condensed from the narrative of the foundation and progress of the college, drawn up by Henry Savage, Master

[1] Fox, Acts and Monuments, ed. 1563, p. 1545. Ed. 1843—49, viii. 275.
[2] [History of Corpus Christi College, Vol. I. pp. 286, 289.]
[3] [Audit-Book of Jesus College, 1567—1568. *Exp. necess.*] [4] [Ibid. 1568—69.]

1650—72, under the title *Balliofergus*[1], will shew how charily the Bishops proceeded in licensing collegiate chapels, until colleges had risen to importance, and a sufficient number of chapels had been sanctioned to afford a precedent.

"*Anno Dom.* 1293. *Oliver* [Sutton] Bishop of Lincoln did grant to the *Master* and *Scholars* License, That, in as much as by reason of the frequency of Disputations and Lectures, they could not attend Divine Offices of the Parish Church, then in the Patronage of the Abbot of St *Mary Oseney*, they might celebrate them in their own Oratory within the House, not prejudicing the Parish-Church in regard of Oblations and Obventions: Provided also, That they visited the Parish Church in the greater Solemnities of the Year, as other Scholars were bound to do to the Parishes wherein they lived, as in the said Grant is signified, wherein no leave was given them of celebrating the Sacraments, which was that which the House aymed at, not onely as a convenience, but an advantage to themselves; but was never granted them till it was done by the Authority of the Pope, though they afterwards prepared a better Fabrick, which they called by the name of St *Katerine's Chappel.*

Anno Dom. 1310. Hugo de Warkeneby, and William de Socham, gave us four Messuages with the Area adjoyning, and the Appurtenances, in the Parish of St *Mary* the Virgin, in the street of the School of Arts, to find some Chaplain in the *Chappel of St Katerine* within our House, *for the daily Celebration of Divine Offices.*

Anno 13 Edward II. (1319—20), twelve Acres of Medow, commonly called *Bayly-mead*, were given by Mr *Hunsingoure* to the Master and Scholars, to find a chaplain for the celebration of Divine Offices in the Chappel of St *Katerine*, within the Mansion of the said Master and Scholars. * * *

And now we having, by the charity of our Benefactors aforesaid, gained two Chaplains, others began to entertain thoughts of a more elegant Chappel for us, *Anno Domini*, 1327. * * * And now as we had License from Oliver [Sutton] Bishop of *Lincoln*, to celebrate Divine Offices in our own Oratory, within our House, as hath been said: The same was obtained from his Successors *John* [Dalderby], *Henry* [Burwash], *Thomas* [Beck], which appears under the Seal of the said *Thomas* Bishop of *Lincoln*, *Anno Dom.* 1346. The same License also, and upon the same Conditions as all former were, was given by *John* [Bokyngham] Bishop of *Lincoln*, *Anno* 1368. In which last, our Oratory is called St *Katerines Chappel*, and in none of the former. But as in those there was a tacite, so here was an express exception of administring the Sacraments therein: A thing very strange, when upon the Petition of the House Pope Urban [the Fifth] had given a License for it in the second Year of

[1] Balliofergus, or a Commentary upon the Foundation, Founders, and Affaires of Balliol Colledge. By Henry Savage, Master of the said Colledge. 4°. Oxford, 1668, pp. 30, 33, 34, 35.

his Pontificate [dated 16 April, 1362], as appears by the Record thereof (the hindrance whereof had been Oblations and Obventions, the great Sore of those times, which was not endured to be touched)[1]."

It is evident from this narrative that a room in the college had sufficed as an oratory until 1327, when the contributions of certain benefactors enabled a chapel to be built.

The episcopal founder of Exeter College built an intramural chapel for his scholars soon after their removal to Stapledon Hall, part of the present site,

"for, finding it troublesome to his Scholars to attend divine offices in the parish Church, which they could not well do without neglecting philosophical exercises, he procured license of Henry, Bishop of Lincoln, an. 1321, to build one: which being confirmed the year following by the Dean and Chapter of the said place (saving the rights and oblations due to the Rector or Vicar of the parish Church wherein the said Chapel was to be built), a fair Chapel, with convenient rooms under it, was finished before the year 1326; for then, as I find, upon the desire of the Founder, license was granted to him by the said Bishop of Lincoln, that he might consecrate the greater altar of the Chapel of Stapledon Hall, then lately built, to the honour of the Blessed Virgin Mary, S^t. Peter the Apostle, and S^t. Thomas the Martyr[2]."

This account appears to imply a consecration of the building, for a fixed altar was never consecrated in an unconsecrated room. This is therefore the first known instance of a consecrated college chapel; for that of Balliol was not finished for some years afterwards, nor is it certain that it ever rose from the condition of a licensed chapel to that of a consecrated one.

It is in the statutes of Queen's College, Oxford[3], given in

[1] The terms of the Bull, quoted by Savage, p. 36, are as follows: "Nos * * * ut in capella predicta singuli vestrum qui fuerint in presbyteratus ordine constituti * * * Missam et alia divina officia, etiam in festis maioribus summissa et alta voce iure Parochialis Ecclesie et cuiuslibet alterius in omnibus semper salvo celebrare valeatis * * * indulgemus." This language does not authorise the administration of the Sacraments, as the author of *Balliofergus* imagines, neither does it free the college from duties to be done, or dues to be paid, to the Parish Church (as he proceeds to say it does in the passage which follows the end of our quotation), but the reverse. It would seem that the author refers to some other Deed not transcribed, for it can hardly be supposed that he would fall into the not uncommon mistake of confounding a permission to perform Mass with one to administer the Sacraments.

[2] Wood, *ut supra*, p. 115.

[3] Commiss. Doc^ts. (Oxford), Vol. I. Statutes of Queen's College, p. 26.

1340 by the founder, Robert de Eglesfield, that we find for the first time a chapel within the walls expressly mentioned in the original scheme of a college, and contemplated as part of the system of the establishment. "I will," says the founder, "that a chapel, situated within the mansion, be erected and maintained there for ever, to the honour of God, his Blessed Mother, and All Saints; which chapel shall bear the name of the chapel of All Saints for ever." In other parts of the same statutes, however, in directing the services to be performed, he mentions "the chapel within the House, or the parish church, if it should happen that one be annexed and appropriated to the college." Like Hervey de Stanton, he gives directions for his burial amongst his scholars:

"In order that my scholars may preserve a special recollection of myself, I will that my body be buried in sight of them, in the chancel of their chapel or parish church, even though it should chance to have been buried after my death in some other place; in which event I will that they cause it to be removed and buried in the place indicated above for it[1]."

These statutes contain also the first example of a complete choral establishment for a college on a large scale. There were to be thirteen chaplains, from among whom were to be chosen: a Dean, two precentors, a sacrist, a Bible-reader, an almoner, and a bursar's clerk; and besides, a certain number of poor boys to officiate as choristers, with two teachers in music. Minute directions are also given for the services, vestments, tapers, and ritual arrangements generally. In accordance with his intentions here recorded the founder obtained the consent of the King and the Pope to build a chapel, but it was not completed until 1382, when licence was obtained from the Bishop of Lincoln to celebrate in it, but it was not consecrated until 17 December, 1420[2].

About thirty years after the foundation of Queen's College, University College (in 1369) "obtained licence of the Diocesan to perform service" in an oratory within their own House, "and had afterward, 1390, an altar consecrated therein[3]."

The attendance of the scholars of Oriel College upon their

[1] Commiss. Doc[ts]. (Oxford), Vol. I. Statutes of Queen's College, p. 36.
[2] Wood, *ut supra*, p. 159 and *note*. [3] Ibid. p. 62.

parish church of S. Mary had been rendered especially troublesome and inconvenient, as Wood remarks, "because of the daily and sometimes hourly meetings there of the University," but nevertheless they endured the inconvenience for nearly fifty years, for it was not until 2 March, 1372, that they

"obtained license from John Bokygnham, Bishop of Lincoln, 2 March 1372, to celebrate divine offices in a Chapel in the said College '*constructa vel construenda,*' for then, as it plainly appears, Richard Earl of Arundell had at his own charges begun and pretty well carried on a Chapel on the south side of the College[1]."

In every collegiate foundation at Oxford subsequent to Queen's College the chapel appears as an essential and recognised part of the collegiate system and its buildings, with the sole exception of Lincoln College, which, as above described, resembles a chantry-college more than a college of students. At New College, Bernard College (afterwards S. John's)[2], All Souls College, and Corpus Christi College, the chapels were carried on simultaneously with the rest of the buildings. The first stone of Magdalen College was the first stone of the chapel, laid in the middle of the high altar, 5 May, 1473. Wolsey's original plan for Christ Church included a chapel on a grand scale on the north side of the present quadrangle, the foundation of which was begun, and the walls carried up in some places more than three yards above the ground. At the second foundation, however, this chapel was abandoned, and in 1638 a range of chambers was erected on the site[3]. The cathedral church of S. Frideswide, which the magnificence of the Cardinal had destined merely for a place for private prayers and theological exercise, became the college chapel.

At New College, the next in order of foundation after Queen's College, a new principle was introduced. In all pre-

[1] Wood, *ut supra*, p. 133. Wood mentions "another license from the Bishop of Lincoln, dated 3 December, 1437, whereby it was granted to the scholars of S. Mary of Oriel that they might perform service in a chapel within the precincts, in honour of the Virgin Mary." It is evident from existing examples that it was required that the licenses for these chapels should be renewed from time to time by successive Bishops, except in the case of the larger foundations, whose chapels had special privileges.

[2] [Wood states (Ibid. p. 554) that this chapel was not consecrated until 1530, after it had become the chapel of S. John's College.]

[3] Wood, *ut supra*, p. 447.

vious cases of chapel-licences the rights of the parish had been carefully guarded. Here, however, William of Wykeham obtained papal authority to set apart the central area of the cloister for a burial-ground, and erected a belfry on the north side of it. [Further, the statutes of New College contain minute directions for the services to be held in the chapel, not merely on week-days, but on Sundays and the greater festivals, of which a list is given. On those specified days the Warden, or one of the principal and more dignified personages in the college (*alius de principalibus et dignioribus personis ipsius collegii*), was to officiate at high mass, and at the other prescribed services[1]. Here, in fact, an example was set (which subsequent establishments were not slow to follow) of making a college extra-parochial in regard of those rites which had hitherto been performed in the parish church. Unfortunately the documentary evidence is imperfect, and we do not know the full extent of the immunity from parochial rights which Wykeham was able to obtain, nor by what authority the prescribed services were inserted in the statutes. His cloister-cemetery, together with three of the bells, was consecrated 19 October 1400[2], but no record appears to have been preserved of the consecration of the chapel, a ceremony which could hardly have been omitted.

This partial exemption from parochial rights received a further development in the next foundation, that of All Souls College.] Archbishop Chichele began the acquisition of a site for his college in 1437, and while the buildings were in progress Richard Andrews, whom he had selected as the first Warden, was despatched to Florence, to solicit from Pope Eugenius IV. a confirmation of the charter granted to him by King Henry VI. The Bull which the Pope issued, 21 June, 1439, gives leave not only to erect a chapel, but to lay out a cloister within the precincts of the college for the burial of the dead. The chapel might be consecrated by any Bishop whom the founder thought proper to select; service might be performed in it even while the town lay under an interdict; the Warden, Fellows, and clergy might dispense with the authority of the Ordinary, of the Provost

[1] [Commiss. Docts. (Oxford), Vol. I. Statutes of New College, p. 68. *De modo dicendi missas matutinas et alias horas canonicas in capella collegii.*]

[2] Wood, *ut supra*, p. 182.

of Oriel College, and of the Vicar of the parish church of S. Mary, in the celebration of mass, of the rite of extreme unction, and other religious ordinances; nor were they to attend service in that church or pay any customary dues to it, previous papal edicts, and the constitutions of Otho and Othobonus, notwithstanding. The chapel was consecrated by the Archbishop himself in 1442, and in the following year a composition was made with Oriel College, in virtue of which it was agreed that on payment of 200 marks the Warden and Fellows of All Souls should be acquitted for ever of all dues payable to the aforesaid church. The cloister was not completed until 1491, and was afterwards consecrated for the burial of the dead, processions, etc.[1]

Magdalen College obtained exemption from all tithes and parochial dues by agreeing (10 April, 1480) to pay a yearly pension of twenty-six shillings and eightpence to Merton College as patrons of the parish church of S. Peter in the East[2], in lieu of all demands; and a similar arrangement was made in 1517 by Corpus Christi College, with reference to the parish church of S. John Baptist[3]. Both these colleges acquired the right of sepulture; the former in a cemetery at the west end of the chapel[4], the latter in the cloister, the position of which has been already described (p. 263).

[Brasenose College was content with a small unconsecrated oratory on the south side of the quadrangle over the buttery until the completion of the existing chapel, which, with the adjoining cloister, was consecrated 17 November, 1666[5].]

Turning now to Cambridge, we find four Colleges founded before Queen's College at Oxford, namely Peterhouse, Michael House, University House (afterwards Clare Hall), and King's Hall; and four between Queen's College and New College, namely, Pembroke Hall, Gonville Hall, Trinity Hall, and Corpus Christi College. No chapel licences, however, exist for these colleges before 1340, the date of Queen's College, Oxford.

[1] [Wood, *ut supra*, p. 305. Life of Henry Chichele, Archbishop of Canterbury, By O. L. Spencer. 8vo. Lond. 1783, pp. 158—160. Appendix, No. V., where the Papal Bull is printed.]

[2] Chandler's Life of Waynflete, p. 143.

[3] Wood, *ut supra*, p. 400.

[4] Ibid. p. 347.

[5] Ibid. p. 373.

Peterhouse was so conveniently placed in contact with the churchyard of S. Peter's, afterwards S. Mary the Less, that a separate chapel could be dispensed with, and it is clear that none existed until the present building was consecrated in 1632[1]. In the same way Michael House used the church of S. Michael, though at a somewhat inconvenient distance from its gates, until it was absorbed in Trinity College[2]. [Clare Hall stood in the same relation to S. John's, as Peterhouse to S. Peter's, and no private chapel was therefore necessary until after the destruction of that church. Even then, however, as shewn above, no separate building was erected, for we need not suppose that the chapel, respecting which several notices have been collected in the History of the College[3], was anything more than a specially licensed room. The only episcopal licence referring to this college, which we have been able to discover earlier than 1535, when a chapel was undoubtedly built, occurs in the register of Thomas de l'Isle, Bishop of Ely 1345—62. It is dated 27 April, 1352, and authorises the Master or any one of the Scholars, provided he be in priests' orders, to say Mass in any place suitable and proper for that purpose, without prejudice to the rights of the parish church, so long as

1 [History of Peterhouse, Vol. I. pp. 40, 51.] The licences from the Bishops of Ely there quoted refer to special occasions when it was necessary to leave the parish church for a brief period, and do not imply the existence of a separate chapel.

2 The Registers of the Bishops of Ely give four licences: (1) Simon de Montacute licenses John de Illegh (16 May, 1341) "quod posset celebrare in quodam Oratorio constructo infra Hospitium magistri et Scholarium Domus S. Michaelis Cantab. per triennium." MSS. Cole XXIII. 17. Add. MSS. Mus. Brit. 5824. (2) Thomas de l'Isle licenses (16 Feb. 1346) "Magistro Roberto de Mildenhale magistro Domus S. Michaelis Cantab' quod posset celebrare Divina et etiam facere celebrari in loco ad hoc ydoneo et honesto infra Domum predict' durante infirmitate suâ, et quod posset eligere confessorem." Ibid. p. 64. (3) The same Bishop licenses (11 June, 1351) "Magistro Johanni de Runham magistro Domus [etc.] quod posset celebrare Divina in Oratorio infra Hospitium suum absque prejudicio [etc.] et singuli Socii sui dicte domus Presbyteri possent celebrare quotiens et quando eis viderint expedire." Ibid. p. 87. (4) John de Fordham grants (7 March, 1392) "Magistro et Sociis Domus [etc.] licentiam celebrandi in Capella sive Oratorio vel in aliquo loco honesto infra dictam Domum ac ad audiend' Divina in eadem Capella sive Oratorio * * * per alios Capellanos idoneos in sua presentia ad beneplacitum Domini duraturam." MSS. Baker XXXI. 231. It is evident from these documents that a regular chapel was never erected.

3 [History of Clare Hall, Vol. I. p. 80.]

the parish church of S. John lies under an interdict[1]. The absence of other documents may perhaps be explained by the destruction of the college muniment-room in the fire of 1521[2]. At King's Hall an oratory was built and furnished between 1420 and 1424[3], but a separate chapel was not begun until 1464, and was not consecrated until 1498—99[4]. The licences for these have not been preserved.]

The efforts which the Countess of Pembroke made to obtain for her college the privilege of a separate chapel, or, to quote the endorsement of the first of the Papal Bulls authorising it, *pour avoir une franche capelle*, were mentioned in the previous chapter; and her wealth and position no doubt enabled her to bring considerable influence to bear upon the Papal Court. The small extent of the privileges which, notwithstanding her exceptional position, she succeeded in obtaining, affords a striking illustration of the reluctance of the Popes to interfere with existing custom. We will quote the second of the two Papal Bulls which she obtained, that of Urban the Fifth, dated 6 August, 1366. It allows the building of a chapel with a belfry, the celebration of masses and other Divine Offices, and dispenses with episcopal jurisdiction; but it reserves all the rights of the parish, and does not confer the right of burial.

"Urbanus episcopus, seruus servorum dei, Dilectis filiis Custodi et Collegio clericorum Scolarium Aule de Valense marie Cantabrigie Eliensis dioceseos salutem et apostolicam benedictionem.

Piis fidelium votis, illis presertim que diuini cultus augmentum et animarum salutem respiciunt, libenter annuimus, et fauorem apostolicum liberaliter impertimur.

Sane pro parte vestra, et dilecte in Christo filie Nobilis mulieris Marie de Sanctopaulo Comitisse Pembrochie, nobis nuper exhibita petitio continebat quod ipsa Comitissa, que vestrum collegium aule de Valense marie fundasse dicitur pariter et dotasse, ad huiusmodi cultus augmentum et vestrarum consolacionem eciam animarum, infra

[1] [MSS. Baker, Vol. XL. p. 181. The words of the entry are: "1352. 5 Kal Maii. Dominus concessit licentiam magistro et Scolaribus Domus de Clare Cantebrig' pro singulis eorum in ordine sacerdotali constitutis, ut possent celebrare Divina in aliquo loco ad hoc ydoneo et honesto, et per alios facere celebrari presbyteros absque preiudicio parochialis ecclesie. Et hoc quousque relaxatum fuerit interdictum Ecclesie Sancti Johannis in cuius parochia conversantur."]

[2] [History of Clare Hall, Vol. I. p. 79.]

[3] [History of Trinity College, Vol. II. p. 443.]

[4] [Ibid. pp. 449—451.]

Septa dicte Aule unam Capellam cum Campana et Campanili in qua Scolares dicti vestri Collegii, qui sacerdotes fuerint, per se, uel alios sacerdotes ydoneos, missas et alia diuina officia celebrare possint, fundare et construere desiderat et proponit. Quare pro parte vestra et ipsius Comitisse fuit nobis humiliter supplicatum vt eidem Comitisse fundandi et construendi Capellam predictam ac vobis faciendi alia premissa licenciam concedere de benignitate apostolica dignaremur.

Nos igitur qui augmentum et salutem huiusmodi intensis desideriis affectamus, eiusdem Comitisse ac vestris in hac parte supplicacionibus inclinati, eidem Comitisse fundandi et construendi Capellam huiusmodi, ac vobis quod in ipsa Capella missas et officia celebrare ut prefertur licite ualeatis, cuiuscunque licencia minime requisita, plenam et liberam auctoritate apostolica licenciam elargimur, iure parochialis ecclesie et cuiuslibet alterius in omnibus semper saluo; ac prouiso quod saltem unus ex dictis scolaribus qui sunt uel erunt pro tempore presbyter existat qui missas in dicta capella postquam constructa fuerit teneatur et debeat celebrare.

Nulli ergo omnino hominum liceat hanc paginam nostre concessionis infringere uel ei ausu temerario contraire. Si quis autem hoc attemptare presumpserit indignationem omnipotentis dei et beatorum Petri et Pauli Apostolorum ejus se nouerit incursurum.

Datum Avinioni viij Id. Augusti Pontificatus nostri Anno Quarto[1]."

In 1352 Thomas de l'Isle, Bishop of Ely, on the petition of the Master and Fellows of Trinity Hall, then recently founded, gave licence that they might erect within their habitation a proper and decent chapel or oratory, in which, always without prejudice to the parish church, they might freely celebrate divine service, or cause the same to be celebrated in their presence by a proper chaplain; and in the next year he issued a licence in the same words to the College of the Annunciation (as Gonville Hall was then termed) which in that year had been transferred to its new site by Bishop Bateman, the effectual founder of the college. Neither of these licences was acted upon for a considerable period. It has been already explained that in the 15th century Trinity Hall added an aisle to S. Edward's Church in lieu of a private chapel within the college precincts, which was not consecrated until 1513[2]; and that the chapel at Gonville Hall was not completed till 1393, when a Bull of Pope Boniface the Ninth authorised the celebration of masses and other divine offices in the chapel of the college, without requiring the Bishop of Ely's licence, provided that the

[1] [Treasury of Pembroke College, A. 10.]
[2] [History of Trinity Hall, Vol. I. p. 220.]

rights of the parish and all others were respected. A century later it was consecrated by John Alcock, Bishop of Ely, and in 1500 a Bull of Pope Alexander the Sixth authorised the college not only to celebrate, but to reserve, the Eucharist, and to bury the dead[1].

Corpus Christi College continued to use their appropriated church of S. Benedict until 1578, when a separate chapel was built.

[King Henry VI. was more successful than his predecessors had been in obtaining special privileges for his intended college. The existing chapel of King's College was begun in 1446, and in the previous year, 29 November, 1445, a Bull was issued by Pope Eugenius the Fourth, very similar in character to that which he had issued for All Souls College, Oxford, six years before. This remarkable document, after giving authority for the chapel, and for a cemetery adjoining it, in which not only members of the college, but others who wished to have their graves there, might be buried, proceeds to specify a series of unusual privileges. The consecration of the chapel might be performed by any Catholic Bishop whom the Provost and Scholars chose to select; mass and all other divine offices might be celebrated in it, and all the Sacraments of the Church administered to the entire collegiate community without distinction; these services might be performed even before the break of day, and when the town lay under an interdict; the Provost and Scholars might prove wills; they were to be excused payment of the canonical portion of any bequest; they were to be entirely independent of all parish rights of every description, whether pecuniary payments, or the obligation to attend services; they were to apply all oblations to their own use; all provincial constitutions were to be set aside in their favour; and lastly, by a separate Bull bearing the same date as the preceding, they were to be exempted from the authority of the Metropolitan, the Bishop and Archdeacon of Ely, and the Chancellor of the University[2].

[1] [History of Gonville and Caius College, Vol. I. pp. 166—168, 190. Blomefield (Collectanea, p. 43), mentions a tradition that the North Aisle of S. Michael's Church was used as a chapel by Gonville Hall.]

[2] [From the Register of Papal Bulls in the Muniment Room of King's College transcribed about 1453.]

The right of sepulture here granted enabled the founder to include in the plan of his projected college a cloister-cemetery —a feature manifestly borrowed from New College, Oxford—which was consecrated by William Waynflete, Bishop of Winchester, 2 November, 1446, and actually used for the burial of many members and servants of the college[1]. The persons to whom this privilege might be granted were limited by the fifty-first statute, in which, after directing in general terms the continual supervision and repair of the buildings, the founder proceeds:

"In the same way they are to supervise and repair, as in duty bound, the cloister of the King's College, within which cloister or cemetery no buildings are to be constructed except those constructed by ourselves. We give leave however that the Fellows, the Scholars, the Chaplains, the Clergy, and all other persons who may chance to be buried in the open air within the aforesaid cloister, may have tombs or monuments or buildings to mark their places of sepulture constructed, provided always that the permission of the Provost be first obtained. Within the precincts of the church, on the other hand, no person may be buried, except the Provost, the Vice-Provost, a Master in Theology, or a Doctor in some other faculty, provided he be a Fellow of the College, or some person of noble rank or a special friend[2]."

No subsequent college was equally fortunate. The licence granted to Queens' College by William Gray, Bishop of Ely 1454—78, dated 12 December, 1454, follows the old models. It is addressed "to the students of the college who are in priests' orders," and allows them to celebrate divine service in the usual terms, and with the usual reservation of the rights of the parish. The burial of the dead is not mentioned, but this privilege must have been implied, for thirty years afterwards Andrew Doket, the first President, desired to be buried in the chapel[3]. At S. Catharine's Hall the licence, dated 26 September, 1478, is in similar terms[4]; and even at Christ's College the influence of the Lady Margaret could not obtain from her stepson James Stanley,

[1] [History of King's College, Vol. I. pp. 369—372, 466, 489.]

[2] [" Statutes of King's College," etc. ed. Heywood and Wright, p. 134.]

[3] [History of Queens' College, Vol. II. p. 36. The Bishop's licence is printed at length in Mr Searle's History, p. 44.]

[4] [History of S. Catharine's Hall, Vol. II. p. 87. MSS. Baker, VII. 18. MSS. Harl. Mus. Brit. 7034.]

Bishop of Ely 1506—15, any wider privilege than that of celebration in the usual form, and reservation of the Eucharist; but he specially reserves the parish rights. His licence is dated 12 December, 1506[1]. In S. John's College no licence of the kind we are discussing has been preserved; but only one authorising Bishop Fisher to consecrate altars, portable altars, vestments, etc.[2] It may be suggested in explanation that the ancient Hospital had doubtless been consecrated, and that the building which replaced it would not require a second performance of the same ceremony[3].]

After the Reformation a chapel was included in the plan of every newly founded college; and, moreover, some of the older colleges, which had hitherto been content with a parish-church, added a private chapel to their buildings, while others replaced their old chapel by a new one. At Cambridge there are in all eight post-Reformation chapels, commenced in the following order: Trinity College (1555), Corpus Christi College (1579), Emmanuel College (1584), Sidney Sussex College (1602), Peterhouse (1628), Pembroke College (1663), S. Catharine's Hall (1699), Clare Hall (1763). At Oxford the list includes the colleges of Jesus, Wadham, Pembroke, Worcester.

The rite of consecration, as is well known, was laid aside at the Reformation, and no form was provided for it in the English Liturgy, those times, as Heylyn remarks, being more inclinable to the pulling down of old churches than the building up of new ones. This probably explains the fact that the first chapels erected at Cambridge after the Reformation were not consecrated, those namely of Trinity College (so far as we know), Corpus Christi College, Emmanuel College, and Sidney Sussex College. The chapel of Peterhouse is an exception, having been consecrated as soon as completed (17 March, 1632), by

[1] [History of Christ's College, Vol. II. p. 194. MSS. Baker, IX. 225. MSS. Harl. Mus. Brit. 7036.]

[2] [History of S. John's College, Vol. II. p. 242.]

[3] [It is shewn in Le Keux's Memorials, ed. 1847, Vol. II. p. 250, that "at first the brethren of this house were obliged to attend divine service and bury their dead in the parish church; but in the time of Bishop Eustace [1198—1220] they were allowed to have a chapel of their own, and an annual payment of 3*s.* was made to the church in recompense of all damages it might sustain thereby." The ordinance of the Bishop here referred to is given at length from MSS. Cole III. 67.]

Francis White, D.D., Bishop of Ely, through the influence, no doubt, of the Master, Dr Matthew Wren.

This state of things, taken in connexion with the general neglect of ecclesiastical ceremonial which is alleged to have prevailed at Cambridge at the close of the sixteenth and the beginning of the seventeenth century, engaged the attention of Archbishop Laud, who persuaded King Charles I. to submit the University to his visitation as Metropolitan. Laud's reasons for this step, which was notified by him to the University, 12 May, 1635, are stated by his biographer and panegyrist as follows:

"Many things had been done at *Cambridge* in some years last past, in order to the Work in hand; as beautifying their Chappels, furnishing them with Organs, advancing the Communion Table to the place of the Altar, adorning it with Plate and other Utensils for the Holy Sacrament, defending it with a decent Rail from all prophanations, and using lowly Reverence and Adorations, both in their coming to those Chappels, and their going out. But in most Colledges, all things stood as they had done formerly; in some there were no Chappels at all, or at the best, some places used for Chappels, but never Consecrated.

In *Sidney* Colledge the old *Dormitory* of the *Franciscans* (on the *Site* of which *Friery* the said Colledge was built) was after some years trimmed and fitted, and without any formal Consecration converted to a *House of Prayer*; though formerly, in the opinion of those who allowed thereof, it had been no better nor worse than a *Den of Thieves.* The Chappel of *Emanuel* Colledge, though built at the same time with the rest of the House, was both irregular in the situation, and never Consecrated for Divine and Religious uses.

And what less could this beget in the minds of the Students of those Houses, than an Opinion touching the indifferency of such Consecrations, whether used, or not, and at the last a positive Determination, *That the continued Series of Divine Duties in a place set apart to that purpose, doth sufficiently Consecrate the same?*"

The intended visitation never took place, for

"The Troubles in *Scotland*, and the Disturbances at home, kept it off so long, that a greater Visitation fell upon the Visitor, than could have hapned unto them. Howsoever, the bare reputation of it did prevail so far, that many who were slack or fearful in embelishing their Chappels and publick Places of Divine Worship, went on more confidently than before; insomuch that not only in the Chappels of some private Colleges, but in S^{t}. *Maries* Church it self, being the Publick Church of that University, the Table was railed in like an Altar, towards which many of the Doctors, Scholars, and others usually bowed[1]."

[1] Cyprianus Anglicus: by P. Heylyn, D.D., fol. Lond. 1668, pp. 314, 315. Cooper's Annals, III. 267.

In anticipation of it, however, Laud obtained a detailed report from Matthew Wren, D.D., then Bishop of Ely, dated December, 1639, which confirms what was said above:

"It was presented unto me, That in the Colledges of Emanuel, Sidney, and Corpus Christi, there have been Roomes built within the memory of man, which are used for common Chappels, wherein they have dayly prayers, and do Preach there, without any faculty or license granted unto them so to do; And wherein also they ordinarily celebrate the holy Communion, The said places never having been consecrated thereunto [1]."

The ceremony of consecration was resumed at the Restoration. It was performed for the chapels of Pembroke College, Emmanuel College, S. Catharine's Hall, and Clare Hall as soon as they were completed; and also for that of Corpus Christi College, after it had been used without consecration or licence for eighty-four years. The episcopal act of consecration—which took the place of the old episcopal licence—invariably begins with setting the chapel apart for ever from all secular and profane uses. Leave is then given for the performance of divine service in any language or dialect commonly understood of the congregation; for catechising the young; for the administration of the sacraments; and for the burial of the dead. Lastly, all privileges which have ever been conferred upon any chapel, or which belong of right to any, are to be conferred upon the one then consecrated[2]. The rights of the parish are not alluded to[3].

[1] [Canterburies Doome, by William Prynne. Lond. 1646, p. 127. Compare History of Peterhouse, Vol. I. p. 46, and that of Emmanuel College, Vol. II. p. 700.]

[2] [The following passages from the Act of Consecration of Corpus Christi College Chapel, dated 21 September, 1662 (MSS. Baker VI. 21. MSS. Harl. Mus. Brit. 7033), contain the essential portions of the document:

"Nos Matthæus [Matthew Wren, Bishop of Ely 1638—67] * * * capellam hanc ab omni communi et prophano usu in perpetuum seperamus, seperandamque semper esse decernimus, et soli divino cultui, ac divinorum celebrationi addicimus. * * * Licentiam * * * concedimus ad rem divinam inibi faciendam, nempe ad preces publicas et sacram Liturgiam cætui suo quacumque in lingua aut idiomate ab ipsis communiter intellecto recitandum; ad verbum Dei sincerè et fideliter proponendum atque prædicandum; ad Neophytos suos catechyzandum in fide Christi; * * * ad Sanctissima Sacramenta quoties par erit in eadem ministranda; ad mortuos suos si ita voluerint sepeliendos; atque ad cætera quæcunque heic peragenda quæ in aliis Capellis Collegiorum communiter possunt et solent fieri. * * * Privilegiis insuper omnibus et singulis in aliqua capella usitatis, aut alicui capellæ in hac universitate competentibus, etiam et hanc Ædem, ad omnem Juris effectum, munitam et stabilitam esse volumus."]

[3] [It is worth remarking that when Downing College petitioned the Bishop of Ely

[The history of each chapel has been already so fully considered in connexion with that of the college to which it belongs, that it is needless to print any inventories of plate, relics, vestments, etc., of which many have been preserved, and some printed elsewhere. One curious custom, however, deserves notice. Long after the Reformation, and evidently without attaching any ritual significance to the practice, it was usual to use incense in college chapels. The extracts already cited from the accounts of King's College shew that it was there used on important festivals and public occasions[1]; but at Christ's College in 1583—84 "fracensence in the chappell" is charged for without any special reason being assigned for its use; and at S. John's College the following entries occur:

1564—65. "Item for franckinsense to ayre the Chapell j^{d}ob."
1565—66. "Item for frankinsense to perfume the Chapell ij^{d}."
1567—68. "Item for frankinsense when Mr Woodward was buried iiij^{d}."
1579—80. "For perfume to the Chappell iij^{d}." "For frankensense to the chappell j^{d}."

At Jesus College in 1590 we find a charge "for junipers to ayre the chapel," and in 1597 and 1612 for "perfume and frankincense" in the same building, on all three occasions to be used on S. Mark's Day (25 April); and at Trinity College in 1615: "Item for perfume for the chappell against Trinity Sunday vj^{d}."

At Jesus College in 1579—80 there is an entry for "cheyninge xij bookes with staples to them in the chappell ij^{s}"; but the subjects of the books thus carefully guarded have unfortunately not been recorded.

The statutes of certain colleges were chained in the chapel. In the original statutes of Christ's College, drawn up by Bishop Fisher in or about 1506, this is specially directed to be done:

"In order that no scholar may be ignorant of the statutes of the college, we desire that true copies of them may be fastened by a small iron chain to a stall in the chapel, so that every scholar may be enabled to have access to them[2]."

in 1814 to consecrate a cemetery within their precincts, he, being unable to attend in person to consecrate, licensed their cemetery "for the interment of the Bodies of the Members and Inhabitants of the said College, * * * saving and reserving all fees, dues, and perquisites to the perpetual curate or minister of the parish of S. Benedict."]

[1] [History of King's College, Vol. I. p. 524.]

[2] [Commiss. Docts. III. 204.]

In the statutes which he gave to S. John's College in 1524 the clause is slightly altered, the statutes being directed to be chained in the vestry, and the permission of the master or the deans is to be obtained whenever any scholar wishes to have access to them[1]. At Jesus College, Oxford, the statutes, given in 1622, are to be chained in the chapel; and at Queens' College, Cambridge, they were actually so chained[2].

The public reading of the statutes in the chapel is directed in several colleges. At Jesus College, Cambridge, they are to be read twice a year by one of the Fellows; at Brasenose College, Oxford, at least twice; at S. John's College, Oxford, three times; at Cardinal College, Oxford, Wolsey orders that the whole college is to meet in the hall three times in the year, and proceed thence to the chapel, where the Dean, or the Senior Canon present, is to read the statutes slowly and distinctly[3]; at Trinity College, Cambridge, the Elizabethan Statutes (1560) assemble the whole college at the end of each term in the chapel, at one o'clock in the afternoon, where "a fourth part at least of the statutes shall be read by the Deans, by which means the whole of them will be read through within the year, to the end that everyone may fully understand his duty, and having been made acquainted with it, may execute it to the best of his ability." At Pembroke College, and at Worcester College, Oxford, the statutes are to be publicly read in the chapel or the hall, once at least in each year.

Lastly, it should be mentioned that at two colleges, namely, Christ's College and Trinity College, a special servant was kept to exclude dogs from the chapel[4].]

1 [Statutes of S. John's College, ed. Mayor, p. 332.]

2 [Magn. Jour. 1561—62, fol. 11 b. "Item pro ligatione statutorum et catenatione eorundem in sacello ij^s. viij^d."]

3 [Commiss. Docts. (Oxford) Vol. II. Statutes of Cardinal College, p. 137.]

4 [Audit-Book of Christ's College, 14 Dec. 1721. *In the Chappel.* "Paid Salmon the Dogwhipper a year ending at Mich. last 1. 0. 0." 20 Oct. 1722. "To Salmon, Whipper of the Dogs out of the chappel to Mich. ½ year 0. 10. 0." Sen. Burs. Accts. of Trinity College 1636—37. "To him that should keepe dogges out of ye chappell xxvj^s. viij^d."; a charge which recurs in each year for some time.]

APPENDIX.

I. *John Hotham, Bishop of Ely, gives licence to Michael House to appropriate the parish church of S. Michael, Cambridge*, 3 *March*, 1324.

Johannes permissione diuina Eliensis episcopus, dilectis in Christo filiis magistro et scolaribus domus scolarium sancti Michaelis Vniuersitatis Cantebr' Eliensis dioc', salutem.

Pastoris officium summe decet, vt circa pietatis opera, et presertim que ad salutaris discipline diuinique cultus augmentum tendere dinoscuntur, continuo se exhibeat liberalem, sollicitum, pariter et attentum.

Sane licet dilectus filius noster dominus Heruicus de Stanton, vestri ac dicte domus vestre et collegii vestri fundator, ipsam domum et collegium eo proposito laudabili vt vos et successores vestri in eadem domo temporibus perpetuis indeficienter studio Literarum, Philosophie videlicet et Theologie, ac diuino obsequio sub certis modo et forma per ipsum statutis insisteretis, et ad honorem dei proficeretis in scienciis antedictis, fundauerit pia mente; Nosque ac nostrum Capitulum Eliense vestrum collegium approbauerimus, tanquam rite canoniceque fundatum; vobis tamen pro vestra et vestrorum successorum sustentacione imposterum competenti iuxta ipsius desiderium nondum ita sufficienter in redditibus possessionibus seu proventibus annuis prouiderat quin, ob defectum congrue sustentacionis huiusmodi, nisi vobis et vestris domui seu collegio supradictis aliunde subueniretur vberius, vos aut successores vestros ab insistencia studendi vt predicitur et profectu in scienciis huiusmodi et diuini cultus obsequio faciend' cogi posse miserabiliter imposterum (quod perquam dolendum foret) desistere, sicque collegium vestrum et dicti fundatoris vestri laudabile propositum predictum (quod absit) posse deficere verisimiliter formidatur;

Ad quorum releuamen et aliqualem suplecionem idem fundator vester zelo comendabili feruenter anelans nobis instanter et sepius supplicauit quatinus ecclesiam Sancti Michaelis Cantebr', cuius fructus et obuenciones ad sustentacionem proprii sacerdotis vix sufficere dinoscuntur, et cuius Jus patronatus ad vos ex collacione dicti fundatoris vestri pertinet, ex causis premissis, necnon pro eo quod in eiusdem ecclesie parochia perpetuo residentes eo quietius ad missas in eadem ecclesia celebrandas et alia diuina obsequia perficienda intendere possitis horis congruis prout decet quo curam animarum perpetuam habueritis in eadem, vobis vestreque domui et collegio prefatis appropriare paterna clemencia curaremus, in vestros proprios vsus perpetuo possidendam;

Nos igitur attendentes ex vestri et successorum vestrorum in domo et vniuersitate predictis litterarum studio huiusmodi ac diuino obsequio cui estis astricti insistencia, profectuque per vos in dictis scienciis faciendo fructum oportunum in vniuersali Dei ecclesia que ad sui regimen viris litteratis noscitur indigere posse multipliciter obueniri; pensantes eciam fore pium ne dum domos seu collegia huiusmodi studencium construere et fundare quin immo iam constructa et fundata ad honorem Dei et ea fundancium animarum salutem confouere ac in suis necessitatibus et indigenciis, ne in eisdem studentes et in sciencia proficere cupientes egeant in futurum, misericorditer releuare, quia inuenimus causas predictas fore euidenter vtiles, iustas, et veras, tractatu vnanimi et sollempni cum summa diligencia cum Capitulo nostro Eliensi prehabito, premissisque et ceteris omnibus et singulis interuenientibus que de iure requirebantur in hac parte, prefatam ecclesiam sancti Michaelis Cantebr' nostre dioc' Eliensis vacantem per resignacionem Edmundi de Twamhille nuper Rectoris eiusdem ecclesie coram nobis in manus nostras simpliciter factam et per nos admissam; cum manso eidem ecclesie deputato, aliisque suis Juribus et pertinenciis vniuersis vobis domui ac collegio vestris prefatis pro vestra et vestrorum successorum scolarium in vniuersitate Cantebr' predicta litterarum studio in eadem domo actualiter intendencium et ministrorum vestrorum et suorum sustentacionis subsidio secundum formam et modum per prefatum dominum Heruicum seriosius ordinatos:

Ex causis predictis quas euidenter vtiles, iustas, veras, et sufficientes, fore reputamus et pronunciamus, quantum in nobis est appropriamus, annectimus, conferimus et concedimus in proprios vestros vsus possidendam,

Saluis semper in omnibus nobis et nostre ecclesie Eliensi que debent de consuetudine vel de iure in huiusmodi appropriatis ecclesiis reseruari; iuribus eciam Archidiaconalibus in omnibus semper saluis.

In cuius rei testimonium sigillum nostrum presentibus est appensum.

Dat' London in hospicio nostro in Holbourne v^to^ Non. Marcij. Anno domini millesimo trescentesimo vicesimo quarto.

II. *Simon de Montacute, Bishop of Ely, gives licence to King's Hall to appropriate the parish church of S. Mary the Great, Cambridge*, 19 *October*, 1343.

Simon permissione diuina Eliensis Episcopus, dilectis in Christo filiis.. Custodi et Scolaribus Aule Scolarium Regis Cantebr' nostre dioc' salutem, cum benedictione et gracia redemptoris.

Pastoris officium ... (as above) attentum.

Sane peticio vestra nobis exhibita continebat, quod licet Serenissimus Princeps et Dominus dominus Edwardus Dei gratia tertius post Conquestum Rex Anglie illustris, vestri ac aule vestre predicte et Collegij vestri fundator, ipsam aulam et Collegium eo proposito laudabili, vt vos et Successores vestri, videlicet vnus Custos et triginta duo Scolares in vniuersitate Cantebr' in aula predicta perpetuis temporibus indeficienter studio literarum in Scienciis liberalibus ac diuino obsequio sub certis modo et forma per ipsum statuendis insisteretis; et ad Dei honorem ac fidei Catholice et regni sui Anglie fulcimentum proficeretis in eis dudum fundauerit pia mente; nosque ac nostrum Capitulum Eliense vestrum Collegium approbauerimus tanquam rite canoniceque fundatum: Vobis tamen et Collegio vestro, pro vestra et successorum ac seruitorum vestrorum sustentatione perpetua, ac oneribus tanto Collegio incumbentibus supportandis, juxta ipsius desiderium, propter varias guerrarum turbaciones et alias causas arduas multipliciter prepeditus, nondum sufficienter in redditibus possessionibus seu proventibus annuis prouiderat; ymmo verius vestri adhuc redditus et proventus ita sunt notorie tenues et exiles, quod nisi vobis et vestris aule seu Collegio supradictis aliunde subueniatur et prospiciatur vberius, vos aut successores vestros ab insistentia studendi, vt predicitur, et profectu in Scienciis huiusmodi et diuini cultus obsequio faciend' cogi posse miserabiliter imposterum, quod perquam dolendum foret, desistere; ac Collegium predictum et dicti fundatoris vestri laudabile propositum, quod absit, posse deficere verisimiliter formidatur;

Propter que nobis per vos humiliter extitit supplicatum, a nobisque sepius et instanter petitum, quod ob hoc et alias causas iustas veras et legitimas nobis pro parte vestra seriatim expositas, Ecclesiam parochialem beate Marie Cantebr' dicte nostre dioc', cui cura iminet animarum, iam vacantem, cuius fructus redditus et prouentus annui sex marcarum et dimid' summam prout de illis secundum taxacionem vel alias pro decima est amplius persolutum, nequaquam excedunt, et cuius ecclesie ius patronatus ad vos ex collatione dicti fundatoris vestri pertinet, ex hujusmodi causis, necnon pro eo quod, in eadem vniuersitate perpetuo residentes eo quiecius in ecclesia predicta in missis celebrandis et aliis diuinis obsequiis horis congruis poteritis interesse ; vobis et successoribus vestris ac aule et Collegio prefatis vnire et annectere, ac in proprios vsus vestros perpetuis temporibus possidendam concedere dignaremur ;

Nos igitur attendentes ex vestri et successorum vestrorum, in aula et vniuersitate predictis, studio literarum insistentia profectuque per vos in dictis Scienciis faciend' fructum oportunum in vniuersali Dei Ecclesia posse multipliciter obuenire ; pensantes etiam fore pium, nedum domos seu Collegia huiusmodi studencium construere et fundare quin immo iam constructa, et ad honorem Dei et ea fundancium animarum salutem fundata, confouere, ac in suis indigenciis ne studentes et in sciencia proficere cupientes egeant, in futurum misericorditer releuare, super omnibus et singulis causis supradictis, inquisicionem tam per clericos quam per laicos in forma iuris iuratos et examinatos, concurrentibus omnibus que de iure in ea parte requirebantur, vocatisque omnibus qui de iure in ea parte fuerant euocandi, fieri fecimus diligentem.

Et quia per eandem inquisitionem et alia legitima documenta, habitis etiam super premissis omnibus cum Capitulo nostro Eliensi deliberatione et tractatu simul in communi semel et pluries prout decuit diligenti, inuenimus luculenter totam prefatam suggestionem vestram ac omnes et singulas causas supradictas veras fuisse et esse, et prefatam peticionem vestram piam fore et consonam racioni, vobisque per vestrum procuratorem habentem a vobis plenam et legitimam potestatem, in hac parte coram nobis sufficienter comparentibus, et pronunciationem super premissis per nos fieri humiliter supplicantibus, auctoritate Dei et nostra Diocesana, pronunciamus et declaramus in hiis scriptis omnes et singulas causas memoratas, ad faciend' appropriacionem hujusmodi, legitimas veras et sufficientes et canonicas fuisse et esse, ac adeo racionabiles et iustas, quod ad vnionem annexionem et concessionem atque appropriacionem dicte ecclesie beate Marie Cantebr' vt supra petitur faciend', est merito procedend'.

Vnde nos, interuenientibus omnibus supradictis, iuris ordine et solempnitate debita in hac parte in omnibus obseruatis, Christi nomine inuocato, predictam Ecclesiam beate Marie Cantebr' dicte nostre Diocesis nunc vacantem, cum omnibus et singulis ipsius Ecclesie fructibus et prouentibus ac iuribus et pertinenciis vniuersis, de consensu Capituli nostri Elien' antedicti, ac nostri Archidiaconi Elien' in cuius Archidiaconatu dicta Ecclesia beate Marie situatur, prehabito cum eodem Capitulo nostro super hiis solempni debito et diligenti tractatu, atque consensu omnium et singulorum aliorum, quorum interest, concurrentibusque omnibus et singulis que in hac parte de iure requirebantur, vobis et Successoribus vestris ac aule vestre predicte annectimus unimus appropriamus, et in proprios vsus vestros concedimus in hiis scriptis perpetuo possidendam.

Volumus insuper, concedimus, statuimus, et ordinamus, quod liceat vobis et quod liberam habeatis facultatem per vestrum procuratorem ad hoc specialiter constitutum, prefatam Ecclesiam beate Marie cum omnibus suis iuribus et pertinenciis vniuersis auctoritate presencium, nulla alia auctoritate nostra seu licencia vel successorum nostrorum exspectata, ingredi, et in vsus vestros proprios imperpetuum possidere pariter et habere, omnesque fructus redditus et prouentus eiusdem Ecclesie integre percipere, ac de eisdem et quibuscumque iuribus et pertinenciis eiusdem Ecclesie libere disponere, prout Vobis et Successoribus vestris videbitur expedire.

Statuimus insuper et ordinamus, ac de consensu Capituli nostri prelibati et Archidiaconi supradicti decernimus in hiis scriptis, quod vos * * * prefate Ecclesie parochiali populo et parochianis eiusdem, per sacerdotem ydoneum deseruiatis et faciatis laudabiliter in diuinis et animarum cura prout ius exigit congrue deseruiri, et eidem Capellano de ipsius Ecclesie fructibus et prouentibus per vos et successores vestros congruam sustentacionem prouideri.

Volumus etiam * * * quod vos, Custos et scolares predicti, * * * soluatis * * * dicto .. Archidiacono Eliensi et cuicunque Archidiacono qui pro tempore erit, seu procuratori eiusdem sufficientem in hac parte potestatem habenti, de Ecclesia beate Marie predicta ac de fructibus et prouentibus eiusdem, annis singulis, ad festa Sancti Michaelis et Pasche, in eadem Ecclesia, imperpetuum, unam annuam pencionem quatuor solidorum sterlingorum, pro equali porcione in recompensacionem dampnorum quorumcunque que iidem Archidiaconi incurrere poterunt in futurum, racione appropriacionis ecclesie prelibate.

Ad quam quidem dicte pensionis annue solucionem singulis annis imperpetuum, prefatis terminis et loco, Archidiacono Eliensi cuicunque qui pro tempore erit, fideliter faciendam, vos .. Custodem et scolares et successores vestros de consensu vestro expresso sententialiter et diffinitiue condempnamus canonice in hiis scriptis, ac vos et successores vestros oneramus ad eandem pensionem, .. Archidiacono Eliensi cuicunque qui pro tempore erit, terminis et loco suprascriptis, annis singulis persoluendam.

Decernimus insuper et ordinamus, vos .. Custodem et scolares predictos vestrosque successores, qui pro tempore eritis seu erunt, fore quotiens opus fuerit eciam per quascunque censuras Ecclesiasticas compellendos, ad dictam pensionem terminis et loco predictis .. Archidiacono Eliensi cuicunque qui pro tempore erit annuatim imperpetuum ut premittitur persoluend'.

Que omnia et singula statuimus, diffinimus, decernimus, volumus, et ordinamus futuris temporibus imperpetuum obseruari; Saluis in omnibus episcopalibus iuribus et consuetudinibus ac nostre Cathedralis Eliensis Ecclesie dignitate.

In quorum omnium et singulorum robur et testimonium sigillum nostrum presentibus duximus apponend'.

Dat' apud Elm quartodecimo Kalend' Novembr' anno Domini millesimo trecentesimo quadragesimo tertio et translationis nostre septimo.

X.

THE STYLE OF COLLEGIATE BUILDINGS:

AS MODIFIED BY THE REVIVAL OF CLASSICAL ARCHITECTURE, AND BY THE INFLUENCE OF INDIVIDUAL ARCHITECTS.

[POINTED architecture was succeeded by a style, which, for want of a better name, is usually termed the Renaissance. It was the intention of Professor Willis to prepare an essay on the introduction and gradual development of this style at Oxford and Cambridge, during the sixteenth, seventeenth, and eighteenth centuries; and, from the small portions which he was able to complete, it is easy to see that it would have been a most masterly performance. Unfortunately the essay was left, not only unfinished, but in such a fragmentary condition that it may be doubted whether the author had quite made up his own mind as to the best method of treating the subject. Under these circumstances it would be useless to try to finish it; and, after very careful consideration, it has been thought better to print the paragraphs which he had written, with just so much connecting matter as either arose directly out of them, or appeared indispensable for their comprehension. Lastly, an attempt has been made to complete his catalogue of architects[1].]

The history of the Renaissance can be followed in the

[1] [With this fragment by Professor Willis should be compared an essay by Orlando Jewitt: "On the late, or debased, Gothic Buildings of Oxford, from the reign of Elizabeth to the end of the seventeenth century." Arch. Journ. VIII. pp. 382—396.]

Universities with greater precision than elsewhere, because of the number of dated examples, and my purpose in the present chapter is to sketch that history.

To call the Renaissance a revival of classical architecture is perhaps too strong an expression; for, during the centuries which elapsed between the extinction of that architecture, and the decadence of medieval architecture, a total change had taken place in domestic and social habits, and great improvements had been made in the mechanism of structure, in the art of preparing materials, and in decoration, especially by the introduction of glass. As the temples of the Pagans were unfitted by their structure for the Christian ritual, so their palaces and houses were equally unsuited to the public and private life of the fifteenth century; and the Renaissance is nothing more than a compromise between the desire to reproduce the forms of classical architecture which the revival of classical literature had brought into favour, and the necessity of retaining the structural arrangements which were too intimately connected with the building arts, and the habits and customs of society, to be abandoned.

The problem was first attacked and solved in Italy, and many modifications in the classical forms necessarily arose, borrowed from the arrangements of Italian domestic and ecclesiastical architecture. In France and in Holland the new fashion received other changes which were mingled with those contrived in Italy. [We received it partly from Italy, partly from the two last-named countries, for Henry VIII., in imitation of Francis I. of France, superseded the workmen of his own country by foreigners, introduced from Italy and elsewhere.]

The mode in which the new decorative forms were introduced, by the gradual and increasing application of them, in successive buildings, to the accustomed mechanical arrangements of the structures, is exhibited in the two English Universities with peculiar distinctness. They each present a group of numerous buildings exhibiting every phase of the transition, for the most part of known date, and, further, executed by architects mentioned by name, whose influence can be traced in successive works. My purpose is to sketch the history of the transition from these buildings alone.

[We will begin by enumerating those builders whose names are associated, during the above-mentioned period, with the designs of the buildings on which they were employed, and indicate briefly their most important works[1]. It will be seen that they arrange themselves naturally in two categories: those who respected medieval architecture and used its forms, with certain modifications; and those who adopted a classical style, either because they despised medieval architecture, or because their employers would not allow them to use it.

At the commencement of the period we are considering, a building-contract, like the corresponding documents during the middle ages, is careful to specify the number of floors, doors, windows, chimneys, etc. which the proposed building is to contain; but, unless some well-known building is directed to be copied, the style is very rarely alluded to. This leads to the conclusion that it was left to the builder, either because, from the prevalence of a given style at the date of the contract, all reference to the subject would have been superfluous, or because he could be trusted to invent a suitable treatment for himself. A builder therefore—or, as he is usually designated, a freemason—combined in his own person the functions of architect and builder, as we understand the terms; and it will appear in the course of the following enumeration, that the same person was often as willing to undertake small repairs as to design important buildings.

The first architect mentioned in connexion with a collegiate building is Theodore Haveus of Cleves, who was employed by Dr Caius to erect a sundial of peculiar construction in the court of which the foundation was laid in 1565. He is described by his employer as "a skilful artificer and eminent architect[2]"; but there is no ground for assuming that he designed any part of Caius College except the dial thus specially commemorated. This view is confirmed by his portrait, preserved in the college library, in which a mathematical figure is placed by his side, intended probably as a reference to the dial, for designing which

[1] [In order to avoid encumbering the notes with numerous references, the reader is referred to the Index for the passages in the different Histories in which the works of each Cambridge builder are mentioned.]

[2] [History of Gonville and Caius College, Vol. I. p. 182.]

it was thought proper to do him honour. Tradition has given to Dr Caius himself the credit of having been his own architect; but it is specially recorded that the Gate of Honour was built after his death "according to the very form and figure which Dr Caius in his lifetime had himself traced out for the architect[1]"; a sentence which shews that though he might have suggested designs, another person had been employed to execute them. A second tradition makes Dr Caius bring the design with him from Padua, where he resided in 1541. He returned to England, however, in 1544, twenty years before he began to build at Cambridge, and it is not likely that he could have conceived the exact plan of the buildings he proposed to erect so long before. Moreover the style employed at Padua is wholly different from his. Pointed architecture was never really adopted in Italy, and the buildings of the University there, with which he was of course familiar, for they were completed about 1493, are in a heavy classical style with none of that admixture of earlier forms which is so characteristic of his work. It is, however, just possible that the inscription on his foundation-stone: *Io. Caius posuit sapientiæ*, and the words which he uttered when he laid it[2], *Dico istud ædificium sapientiæ: pono hunc lapidem in fundamentum ædificii, in incrementum virtutis et literarum, in nomine patris et filii et spiritus sancti*, may have been suggested by the inscription on the entrance to the University at Padua, in which the same thoughts are expressed: *Sic ingredere ut te ipso quotidie doctior, sic egredere ut indies patriæ Christianæque reipublicæ utilior evadas;* words which may be rendered: *So enter that thou mayest become daily more learned; so leave that day by day thou mayest become more useful to thy country and to Christendom.* The theory put forward by Mr Wilkins[3], that John of Padua was the architect of whom we are in search, appears to rest on no better foundation than the fortuitous coincidence of the dates of Dr Caius' return to England in 1544, and King Henry the Eighth's grant of a pension to the architect[4]. It was probably

[1] [History of Gonville and Caius College, Vol. I. p. 178.]
[2] [Ibid. pp. 171, 172.]
[3] [Vetusta Monumenta, London, 1747—1842, Vol. 4.]
[4] [Rymer, Fœdera, ed. 1704—35, Vol. XV. p. 34.]

suggested to Mr Wilkins by the Paduan tradition which we have just mentioned.

Twenty years after Dr Caius had commenced his buildings, we meet with the name of Ralph Symons, a native of Berkhampstead, in Hertfordshire. His reasons for leaving his native place and settling in Cambridge have not been recorded, but after the completion of his first work, the building of Emmanuel College (begun about 1584), to the satisfaction of his employers, he obtained from them the lease of a house in Preachers' Street, now S. Andrew's Street, and he appears to have resided in Cambridge until 1605, when he is described as "late of Cambridge[1]." At Emmanuel College, his work consisted principally in adapting to collegiate use the remains of the Dominican convent, which seem to have been extensive, and his only original work there was a range of chambers on the south side of the first court, called "The Founder's Range," the aspect of which, before it was altered, has been preserved to us by Loggan. It is in three floors, the uppermost of which is a garret-floor lighted by wall-dormers, and it is distinguished by a total absence of ornament.

Symons was next employed at Trinity College, and, if the evidence stated in the History[2] be trustworthy, it was under his direction that the great court was set out, the ranges of chambers which interfered with its symmetry pulled down, and a design given for the new hall. In these new works he evidently felt obliged to make the new buildings harmonise with the old, and to copy medieval forms in preference to producing those of his own time. The great court was commenced in 1593 and practically completed about 1600; and, if Symons was really the architect of the hall, he resumed work at Trinity College in 1604. This however must remain doubtful.

Meanwhile (1596—98) he had built the new college of Sidney Sussex, so far as it was carried forward in the first instance, namely, the three-sided quadrangle consisting of parallel ranges of chambers, connected by a range on the east side containing the hall, kitchen, and Master's Lodge. In this building he returned to the simple forms which he had already employed at

1 [History of S. John's College, Vol. II. p. 257.]

2 [History of Trinity College, Vol. II. Chapter III.]

Emmanuel College. Loggan's view[1] shews similar windows, and a similar arrangement of wall-dormers, in both colleges. At Sidney Sussex College two specimens of genuine Renaissance work were introduced, namely, the porch to the hall and Master's lodge, and the fanciful gatehouse in the west wall, through which the college was entered.

Between 1598 and 1602 Symons executed his principal original work, the second court of S. John's College, for which, as shewn in the History, he undoubtedly made the design, in conjunction with Gilbert Wigge, a freemason like himself. These buildings, the general style of which will be understood from Loggan's view, reproduced in the History (fig. 3), shew a remarkable recurrence to medieval forms in the windows and door-cases, and the gate-house leading to the third court is a close copy of a medieval design. The influence of a more modern style can only be detected in the cresting of the oriels. The gables are of the old form, but the eaves have been replaced by battlements.

It has been suggested by Professor Willis that Symons may have designed Nevile's Court at Trinity College, begun about 1612. This, however, could hardly have been the case, unless indeed he returned to Cambridge for the express purpose of doing so. Moreover, as he lost the use of one of his hands in the course of his work at S. John's College, and also became involved in a law-suit with his employers there which was not settled before 1610, it appears more probable that his departure from Cambridge implies a retirement from business.

Gilbert Wigge, the mason associated with Symons at S. John's College, appears as the sole builder of the range next to the street in the Walnut-tree Court of Queens' College (1616—19). This range, when first completed, must have closely resembled the second court of S. John's College in general design; but it was worked in a less pretentious and elaborate style.

While Symons and Wigge were at work at Cambridge, a remarkable series of buildings was being executed at Oxford; namely, the addition of a third storey to the quadrangle of New College, begun towards the close of the sixteenth century;

[1] [These views have been reproduced in the History of Emmanuel College, fig. 3; and in that of Sidney Sussex College, fig. 4.]

Sir Thomas Bodley's refitting of the Library over the Divinity School, 1597—1602; the new quadrangle at Merton College, built by Sir Henry Savile between 1608 and 1610; the "pro-scholium" to the Divinity School with the Library above it, begun 1610; Wadham College, 1610—13; and the Schools' quadrangle, 1613—19. In connexion with these several names of builders occur. John Acroyde, of Halifax, contracted to execute all the stonework of Merton College new buildings, 28 January, 1609[1]. Before this he had done work for Sir Thomas Bodley at the Library; and, as he is mentioned in one of his letters as "the New-College Workman[2]," it is probable that he had something to do with the work which was then proceeding, or had been only lately finished, at that college. He died 11 September, 1613, and was buried in Great S. Mary's Church, in the Register of which he is commemorated as "chief Builder of the Schools[3]." It is therefore probable that he took part in the work done to the Schools after the first restoration of the Library. Two workmen named Bentley are also mentioned in connexion with the same buildings, one of whom, J. Bentley, is stated to have been "one of the chief Masons that built the Schools, and *Merton College* New Buildings[4]." Thomas Holt, of York, executed the carpenters' work at Merton College in 1609; and subsequently, if we may believe his epitaph, became the "architect of the Public Schools." He died in Oxford, 11 September, 1624, and was buried in the church-yard of Holywell[5].

The next Cambridge builder who executed a series of works of importance is John Westley. He first appears as the contractor for the so-called Brick Building at Emmanuel College, begun 1632—33, if indeed he did not build the range at S. Catharine's Hall on the west side of Dr Gostlin's court, which is referred to in the contract for the building at Emmanuel College as

[1] [Memorials of Merton College. By Hon. G. C. Brodrick, Warden. 8vo. Oxford, 1885, p. 71.]

[2] [Hearne, Reliquiæ Bodleianæ, p. 311.]

[3] [Peshall, p. 69, where the date is given 1631, but this is clearly a mistake, as pointed out by Dr Ingram, Public Buildings of Oxford, *The Schools*, p. 12.]

[4] [Peshall, p. 84, quoting the Register of S. Peter's in the East.]

[5] [Peshall, Appendix, p. 25, gives his epitaph, from Wood's MSS.]

a pattern to be followed. In 1637 he lengthened the chapel of Gonville and Caius College, and in 1638 began the rebuilding of Clare Hall. He is not mentioned as having given the design for that beautiful work, which exhibits such a remarkable combination of medieval and Renaissance treatment; but, as we find the Bursar, Mr Barnabas Oley, speaking of him as "that good workman that built the colledge," it is more than probable that, like Symons at S. John's College, he designed the building which he afterwards executed. The east range and the south range were completed, and the foundations of the west range laid, under Westley's superintendence, after which the work was suspended. He died in 1656.

Among the workmen engaged in the rebuilding of Clare Hall we meet with Thomas Grumbold. Like Symons and Westley he is described as a freemason, and in subsequent years other members of the family are occasionally found working under known architects; but their names are associated with a sufficient number of original designs to be included in this enumeration. The family came to Cambridge from Raundes in Northamptonshire, a place famous for its quarries, and therefore likely to produce good stonemasons[1].

The east gate of Clare Hall was built by Thomas Grumball (as the name is there spelt) in 1639, and in the following year he designed the bridge leading to the then newly acquired walks. It is probable that he may be identified with "Grimball

[1] [Much interesting information about Raundes will be found in "The History and Antiquities of Northamptonshire, compiled from the manuscript collections of the late learned Antiquary John Bridges, Esq." By the Rev. Peter Whalley, 2 vols, fol. Oxf. 1791: "This lordship is famous for its quarries of rag-stone. The stone raised here, from the beauty of its grain, and firmness of texture, is usually called *Raundes* marble. It is generally thick set with a great variety of shells; and seemeth to be that kind of marble, which the *Italians* have named *Nephiri*. In many of the best seats in the county, are chimney pieces and window slabs of this stone." Vol. II. p. 185. "At *Raundes* was born *John Grimbold*, who built *Trinity* college library, and part of *Clare* hall in *Cambridge*, who died lately, advanced in years." Ibid. p. 188. This statement is slightly inaccurate. The mason employed at Trinity College library was Robert Grumbold. For Raundes and its quarries compare also "The Natural History of Northampton-shire; with some Account of the Antiquities." By John Morton, M.A. Fol. Lond., 1712, p. 107.

The parish registers of Raundes, for searching which I have to thank the Rev. Hugh Bryan, the present Vicar, contain numerous entries of marriages, births, and deaths of members of the Grumbold family.]

the free mason" who was employed on the stone-work of S. John's College library in 1625. Thomas Grumbold died at Cambridge in 1657[1]. His business devolved upon Robert Grumbold, son to Edward and Mary Grumbold, who was born at Raundes in 1639[2]. He passed the greater part of his long life at Cambridge, where he died, aged 82, 7 December, 1720[3].

It will be impossible to do more than indicate some of Robert Grumbold's more important works. At first he was employed as a workman on the west range of Clare Hall, and next at Christ's College and S. Catharine's Hall. In 1676 he was master-mason at the building of the new library of Trinity College; in 1677 he altered the central arch of the cloister at Emmanuel College, then in process of erection; in 1678 he superintended a general repair at the Regent House; in 1679 he made the north window of Emmanuel College library; in 1680—81 he did work to "Nevile's Gate" at Trinity College; in 1681—82 he built Dr Babington's chambers, and the "Tribunal," in Nevile's court at the same college; in 1684 he designed and executed the new hall at Clare Hall; in 1687 he gave a design for a new chapel at S. John's College; in 1695 he submitted a scheme for laying out the Physic Garden; in 1696 he drew a plan for a new printing-house; in 1701 he put sash-windows into the Master's Lodge at Trinity College; in 1703 he built the piers at the entrance-gate of Jesus College; it is probable that he designed the chapel of S. Catharine's Hall, consecrated 1704; in 1705—6 he finished the west front of Clare Hall; in 1709 the cloister at Peterhouse was altered "according to a paper delivered by Mr Grumbold"; in 1714 he ashlared the gate-house and part of the west front of Christ's College; in 1715 he altered the Civil Law School, now the west room of the University Library, for the reception of Bishop Moore's books; and in 1716 he rebuilt the fountain at Trinity College.

[1] [His gravestone may still be seen against the west wall of the churchyard of S. Benedict, with the inscription: "Here lyeth the Body of Thomas Grumbold Free-Masson, Who Was Buried ye 15th of August Anno dom. 1657"; and in the Register for the same year we find "Goodman Grumbold buried August 15."]

[2] [The register of Raundes has the following entry: "1639, Robert Grimbole, son of Edward and Mary, Bap. June."]

[3] [His gravestone, on the south external wall of the chancel of S. Botolph's Church, bears the following inscription: "Here lieth in hope of a Joyfull Resurrection, the Body of Robt. Grumbold who died Decem^{er}. 7. 1720. Aged 82 Years."]

The only work of importance by Inigo Jones (1572—1653) in either University is the east side of the second quadrangle of S. John's College, Oxford, begun 1631. His claims to have designed the detached building at Christ's College, Cambridge, have been discussed in the History of the college, and dismissed. He is also recorded as the architect of the walls and gate of entrance to the Botanic Garden, Oxford (1632).

Sir Christopher Wren (1632—1723) is the reputed architect of the cloister and chapel at Brasenose College, Oxford (1656), the design of which "strongly marks the period of transition from our ancient architecture to the modern, and is singularly interesting as a connecting link[1]"; in 1663 he designed the chapel of Pembroke College, Cambridge; in 1664 the Sheldonian Theatre, Oxford; in 1665 the second court of Trinity College, Oxford; in 1666 the chapel of Emmanuel College, Cambridge; in 1676 the library of Trinity College, Cambridge; in 1682 the Ashmolean Museum, and the completion of the entrance-gateway of Christ Church, Oxford; in 1691 he was consulted respecting the design for the chapel of Trinity College, Oxford; and in 1710 is said to have designed that of Queen's College in the same University, the further buildings of which were completed by his pupil Nicholas Hawkesmoore.

Wren was generous in giving advice, and it is probable that Hawkesmoore, who became his pupil at the age of eighteen, consulted him respecting most of his works. It is certain that when he was requested to give a design for the new buildings of King's College, Cambridge, in 1713, he sought Wren's advice, and that the Provost met Wren at his house[2]; and there is good reason for believing that he had acted in a similar manner at S. John's College, Cambridge, in 1669. In this way we may explain the tradition that Wren designed the chapel at Queen's College, Oxford, of which Hawkesmoore was unquestionably the architect, for he built the library in 1692, and the quadrangle next to the High Street in 1710. Hawkesmoore was also the architect of the new buildings at All Souls College (1720—34); and, as shewn above (p. 281) exerted his influence successfully to persuade

[1] [Ingram's Memorials, Vol. II., Brasenose College, p. 15.]

[2] [History of King's College, Vol. I. p. 557; of S. John's College, Vol. II. p. 274, and *note*.]

the authorities to preserve their ancient quadrangle, as superior to any modern buildings which they were likely to get built for them. A similar respect for antiquity is evident in his attempt to preserve the plan of King Henry the Sixth, with its cloister and belfry, at King's College[1]. Hawkesmoore executed no works at Cambridge. He died in 1736.

The garden-court at New College, Oxford, built 1682—85, was designed by William Bird, Mason, of the same place.

Sir John Vanbrugh (1666—1726) was the architect of the Clarendon Press at Oxford, completed 1713.

James Gibbs was employed at Cambridge in 1722 to design the Senate-House and adjoining buildings, of which, as already narrated, the Senate-House was the only part executed; and at the same time he built the Fellows' Building at King's College, part of a larger design which, like the former, was never completed. At Oxford he built the Radcliffe Library (1737—49), for which Hawkesmoore had submitted an unsuccessful design when it was proposed to build it as an addition to the Bodleian. He died in 1754[2].

Two amateur architects, Henry Aldrich, D.D., and George Clarke, LL.D., appear at Oxford as the contemporaries of Wren, Hawkesmoore, and Gibbs. The former was Dean of Christ Church from 1689 to 1710, in which year he died. During that period he is said to have designed the chapel of Trinity College in 1691, but he probably only made suggestions to Dr Bathurst, before Wren was consulted[3]; in 1705 he built three sides of the Peckwater Quadrangle at Christ Church[4]; and in 1706 the building at Corpus Christi College, erected at the sole expense of the President, Thomas Turner, D.D.[5] Dr Clarke, Fellow of All Souls College from 1680 to his death in 1736, was the intimate friend of Dr Aldrich, and assisted him in his architectural works, designing the library of Christ Church, begun 1716, on the south side of the Dean's new quadrangle. Tradi-

[1] [History of King's College, Vol. I. p. 558.]

[2] [Walpole, ed. Dallaway, IV. 73; Memorials of the Public Buildings of Oxford, by Rev. J. Ingram, D.D., Radcliffe Library, p. 13.]

[3] [Wood, History and Antiquities of the Colleges and Halls, etc., ed. Gutch, p. 530, *note*.]

[4] [Ibid. p. 453.]

[5] [Ingram, Memorials, Vol. II., Corpus Christi College, p. 15, *note*.]

tion assigns to him some share in the design for the new buildings at his own college, to which he was a generous benefactor, but, like other amateurs, he probably only made suggestions to Hawkesmoore. There are better grounds for believing that he was the architect of the new buildings at Worcester College, begun 1720, but not completed until after his death, partly with funds bequeathed by himself[1].]

We have next to notice the works of a gentleman at Cambridge, an amateur like Aldrich and Clarke, who exercised a great and permanent influence on collegiate architecture. This was Mr James Burrough, son of James Burrough a Physician of Bury St Edmund's in Suffolk, where he was born 1 September, 1691. He was educated at the Grammar School there for eight years, entered at Gonville and Caius College at Michaelmas 1708, proceeded to the degree of B.A. in 1711, and of M.A. in 1716. In 1727 he was made one of the Esquire Bedells of the University, and, 27 February, 1754, was elected to the Mastership of his college, an office which he held until his death at the age of 73, 7 August, 1764. During his University career he practised architecture to a considerable extent, but in what manner his previous education had prepared him for it does not appear. His works are certainly not characterised by great artistic power, and are all in the tamest Italian style.

The design for the Senate-House, commenced in 1722, and completed in eight years, has been attributed to him, and it is in truth an extremely elegant and beautiful piece of architecture. But in the University accounts the name of Gibbs, the celebrated architect, appears alone as architect, or, in the language of the day, surveyor, and he is paid accordingly for the plan, as well as for the superintendence of the work, no mention being made of Burrough, and the whole design is engraved in his published works. We can only conclude that Burrough had no other share in the work than that of suggesting the general arrangement, and of taking an active part in the promotion and management of the building. [This view is confirmed by the order which the Syndics made, 8 March, 1721—22: "that Mr James Gibbs do take

[1] [Ingram, Memorials, Vol. II., Worcester College, pp. 9—13. On both these architects see Walpole, ed. Dallaway, IV. 75, *note.*]

with him to London Mr Burrough's Plan of the Intended publick Buildings and make what improvements he shall think necessary upon it, and that the said Mr Gibbs be imploy'd and retain'd to supervise and conduct the said work[1]." On the other hand, it is clear that his contemporaries in the University believed that he had really designed the Senate-House. Cole, writing shortly after his death, says, "his skill in Architecture is evident from the Theatre or Senate House designed by him"; and he begins his account of the acceptance of Wright's design for the façade of the Library in 1754 with the words: "Sir James Burrough had built the Senate House on a most elegant Plan[2]"].

In 1728 he probably designed the Italian cupola over the Combination Room at Gonville and Caius College, of which he was then Fellow and Bursar; and in 1729 he appears in the accounts of his college as directing repairs and improvements in the Master's Lodge.

In 1732 he was employed at Queens' College to convert the hall into an Italian chamber, receiving 25 guineas as a fee for his trouble; in 1735 he "beautified" the chapel of Emmanuel College; and in 1736 gave a design for a new building at Peterhouse of which the north wing only was erected. For the design of this work he received a piece of plate worth £10, and at the conclusion of it in 1744, "in consideration of his designing and overseeing the execution of the new building," a further gratuity of £50. He was therefore acting at this time as a professional architect. In 1742 he designed the new altar-piece and wainscoting in the chapel of Corpus Christi College, and between that year and 1745 had the charge of the works by which the court of Trinity Hall was Italianized and converted into the aspect which it bore until the fire of 1852[3]. He was also responsible for the internal fittings of the hall, and further, gave a design for rebuilding the library and Master's Lodge in the Italian style. The engraving of this design, pub-

1 [The whole question has been fully discussed in the history of the Senate-House, Vol. III. pp. 43—55. The sums paid to Gibbs are given in a note, p. 54.]

2 [Ibid. p. 64.]

3 Part of this work had been carried on under James Essex the builder, father of the architect of the same name, but Burrough had probably given the design. [History of Trinity Hall, Vol. I. pp. 226—229.]

lished in 1745, is signed "James Burrough, Architect." The hall of Sidney Sussex College, which was similarly transformed between 1747 and 1749, may be attributed to him, or at least to his example.

In 1751 he designed the Doctors' gallery in the University church of S. Mary the Great[1], and in the same year the ashlaring of Gonville court and the rebuilding of its northern side, in exact imitation of the court of Trinity Hall, was carried out. In 1754 he undertook the direction of an Italian transformation of the medieval quadrangle of Peterhouse, in precisely the same manner as that of the two previously cited colleges. Besides these works Burrough [had some share in the alteration of Nevile's Court at Trinity College in 1756; and was suggested as the architect for the Ramsden building at S. Catharine's Hall in the following year. He also gave a design for an altar-piece for King's College Chapel, which was probably too incongruous in style to be accepted. Lastly, he] is recorded as the architect of the chapel at Clare Hall and of the west front of Emmanuel College. But he did not live to carry either of these designs into effect. The first stone of the former was laid 3 May, 1763, the year before his death, and the work was carried out under the management of James Essex, who received, "for his drawing of plans, measuring of work, and for all his other care and trouble," the sum of £200. It is remarkable that in the same building-account a sum of twenty guineas is set down as a "gratification to the heirs of Sir J. Burrough." This chapel, like all his work, is in the Italian style, and of the Corinthian order. It is placed in a favourable position, projecting from the north-east external angle of the quadrangle,

[1] [Syndics, of whom Mr Burrough was one, were appointed to build what was afterwards called the Doctors' Gallery, 28 October, 1751. Burrough's share in the work rests on the authority of Cole, who, writing in 1757, says: "By the advice and contrivance of my worthy friend James Burrough * * * the Chancel is quite altered, and the Church appears to much less advantage than it used to look: for the Stalls and fine Screen are taken down in the Chancell, and a Gallery built with an arched top of Wainscot, highly ornamented indeed with Mosaic carving, but very absurd in the Design." The builder employed was Essex, and the University Audit-book shews that the first payment to him was made in 1754, and the last in 1760. The side-galleries had been erected in 1735. See Annals of the Church of S. Mary the Great, by the Rev. E. Venables: Camb. Antiq. Soc. Octavo Publ. No. x. pp. 92—97.]

so as to exhibit its southern side, and eastern gable, to great advantage. The interior is elegant and cheerful, but necessarily deficient in solemnity. It is approached through an octagonal vestibule, lighted by a lofty dome crowned by a lantern.

The records of Emmanuel College shew that our architect had submitted a plan in 1752 for rebuilding the hall-range, or north side, of that college, and also the west, or street side. Some of the details, however, being objected to, the plan was not executed; and in 1760 the rearrangement of the hall-range was entrusted to James Essex. In 1769 it was decided to revert to Burrough's plan for rebuilding the west front, [but the original design, as a contemporary writer records, was "departed from in almost every instance, and in some considerably improved[1]." The façade, as we see it, is practically the work of James Essex.]

Before leaving Sir James Burrough and his works, it will be interesting to quote some of the particulars which Cole[2] has preserved of his last illness, and his estimate of his character. After mentioning his death, he proceeds:

"In a Letter from a Friend dated King's College, July 25, 1764, I had before expected this News of my worthy Friend's Death:

'Sir James Burrough about 3 Weeks since was struck with a fit, something of the Apoplectick Kind, and has continued since dangerously ill. He has a sore Leg that threatens a Mortification—a Habit of Body that shews a great Tendency to a Dropsy. These, with an Asthma, and 74 years of Age, are such Circumstances, that his Friends cannot flatter themselves with Hopes of his long Continuance among them. Last Friday he was seized with a chilley Fit, which alarmed them much: but since he is somewhat better.'"

Upon this letter he makes the following remarks:

"Sir James * * * was a Suffolk man, and died a Bachelor; was a great Virtuoso in Painting, Prints, and Medals, of which he had a very choice and valuable Collection; his Skill in Architecture is evident from the Theatre or Senate House, designed by him. He was always my particular Friend and Acquaintance, and was as honest and worthy a Man as ever lived: but being a very large and corpulent Man, who lived freely and used no Exercise, it is no wonder he fell into so ill an Habit of Body; or rather that he lived so long."

[1] [History of Emmanuel College, Vol. II. p. 714, *note*.]

[2] [MSS. Cole, Vol. XXXI. Add MSS. Mus. Brit. 5832, fol. 83 *b*.]

Cole's friend and correspondent, the Rev. Edward Betham, of King's College, sent him the following account of Sir James Burrough's last moments, in a letter dated 14 August, 1764:

"Sir James departed this Life on Tuesday, August the 7th, about 5 o'Clock in the Afternoon. From the first of his Illness, there were little or no Hopes of Recovery: yet he himself seem'd insensible of the least Danger: during the whole Time he was in tolerable good Spirits, saw every Day, and seemed pleased with, Company. He would talk, as usual, about Affairs of the College, and particularly of Repairs which were then in Hand. The very Tuesday on which he died Mr Essex (the Builder) was with him after Dinner for half an Hour, talking upon that Business. He was buried about six o'Clock in the Evening on Fryday, August the 10, according to his own Desire, in the Antichapple of the College Chapel."

While Burrough's influence was paramount in the University, we meet with a curious evidence of the prevailing fashion in the design proposed by Robert Masters, the author of the History of Corpus Christi College, for the enlargement of the same[1]. The publication of this piece of amateur architecture [in 1747, was the occasion for an amusing controversy in the following year between Mr Masters and Mr Essex, then a young man of twenty-six, who claimed to be its real author[2].] The design exhibited a quadrangle open to the street on the west, in two storeys with garrets, in evident imitation of the courts of the medieval colleges, one of which, Trinity Hall, had been then recently clothed in Italian masquerade by Burrough. But the plan is most judiciously arranged, so as to spare the ancient quadrangle, and to preserve the chapel, guided by the feeling of respect and attachment which every member of a college must, or ought to, retain for the buildings in which he has received his education. This feeling was totally absent from the mind of Burrough.

The architect mentioned in the last paragraph, Mr James Essex, was [the son of a Cambridge builder, or, as he is usually designated, a joyner[3]. The father was evidently a man of distinction in his trade, and we find him employed to make

[1] The plan will be found in Masters' History of Corpus Christi College, 4to. Cambridge, 1753.

[2] [The controversy with Essex has been related in the History, Vol. I. p. 298.]

[3] [As for instance in the repairs done to Christ's College Hall, in 1723, Vol. II. p. 220, *note*.]

the sash-windows and put up the wainscot in the Senate-House, 1724—25; to fit up the old Regent House for the reception of Bishop Moore's library (1731) in the course of which work he apparently designed the bookcases; to remove the staircase and lengthen the west room, 1732; to alter the hall of Queens' College, 1732—34; and to ashlar the court and façade of Trinity Hall, 1742. He died in 1749[1].

James Essex, his son, was born in 1722[2], and passed his whole life at Cambridge, where he died of a paralytic stroke[3], 14 September, 1784, in his sixty-third year[4].]

Cole, writing in 1776, informs us that he "was put to Schole for grammatical Learning under Mr Heath, Fellow of King's College, the Master of the College Schole kept in the New Brick Building at the S. E. end of the Chapel, and now totally neglected[5]." Be this as it may, his writings as well as his works shew him to have received a more than usually good education. We find him first employed in 1750 to alter [the "Square Room" at the University Library; but the work done at that time consisted of little more than the addition of wire doors to the bookcases to fit them to contain MSS., and the construction of a new roof with a glazed cupola. Moreover it is possible that he may have had his father's designs to guide him. His first original work, begun 1755, is the] rebuilding of Nevile's Court at Trinity College, which, from the perishable stone and clunch of which it was built, had fallen into a ruinous condition. [As explained in the History of the College, (p. 529)] only the general appearance of the original was preserved, the florid Jacobean decoration being swept away, and the picturesque gablets replaced by a straight balustrade.

[In the following year Essex gave a design, much admired at the time, for rebuilding the river-front of Queens' College. The only portion executed is a] stack of chambers at the south-west angle of the college. It was begun in 1756 and finished in

1 [Register of S. Botolph's Church: "17 February, 1749. James Essex buried."]

2 [Ibid.: "James, the son of James Essex was baptized 25 Aug. 1722."]

3 [Bentham's Ely, Appendix, p. 138.]

4 [The inscription on his monument in S. Botolph's Church is: "James Essex, A.S.S. Eminent for his Skill in Architecture and Antiquities, who died Sept. 14, 1784. Aged 63."]

5 [Athenæ Cantabrigienses. Add. MSS. Mus. Brit. 5868, p. 72.]

1760. In the words of Dr Plumptre (President 1760—88): "It was planned and executed by Mr Essex, an eminent architect and man of good understanding and character in Cambridge[1]." It is a handsome Italian building in three floors.

At S. Catharine's Hall James Essex is recorded as the architect under whose direction the Ramsden Building on the south side of the quadrangle opposite to the chapel was erected in 1757, the houses next to the street pulled down, and the present arrangement of the grove, railings, and approach, laid out and completed[2].

[In 1758 he was employed to ashlar the south side of the interior of the quadrangle of Christ's College, a work which he continued in subsequent years, until the whole quadrangle had been similarly treated. In 1760 he began the transformation of the hall of Emmanuel College; in 1762 he altered the combination room of Jesus College, and designed and built the bridge at Trinity College, for which he received £50; in 1764 he was employed, after the death of Sir James Burrough, to complete the chapel of Clare Hall.

In 1766 he undertook a more important work, namely, the completion of] the west gable of the Senate-House, which had remained for forty years in a state of rough brickwork, awaiting the termination of the battle between the Attachment and Detachment parties. [For this he submitted two designs, the first of which was considered to be too plain, and he was requested to prepare a second, more in conformity with the style of the already completed east end. This was accepted and executed.

In 1769 he was employed to build the street front of Emmanuel College, for which a design had been given by Sir James Burrough in 1752.] It is a low range of chambers in two floors, connecting the extremities of the north and south sides of the quadrangle. It has an Ionic tetrastyle in the centre, with a pediment above, and engaged columns. Three archways in the inter-columniations seem to have been intended as

1 [History of Queens' College, Vol. II. p. 18.]

2 [Professor Willis criticises the Ramsden Building in the History of S. Catharine's Hall, Vol. II. p. 106; and the alterations to the intended design for the college in the essay on the Collegiate Plan, Vol. III. p. 277.]

entrances. The pediment with its entablature is unskilfully connected with the parapet which crowns the chambers, and it stands as a detached wall above, unprovided with the transverse roof which its introduction naturally supposes.

In 1770 he designed the Italian building at the south end of the hall at Trinity College, which was begun in the following year, and completed in 1774[1]. This building, though incongruous in style, is skilfully arranged, and comprises a large and small combination room with a handsome staircase, commodious butteries, pantries, additional space to the kitchen, and several sets of chambers. Two years afterwards, in 1772, the south side of the first court of S. John's College was altered into the same style as the Trinity College building, under the same architect, a proceeding of which even his contemporaries disapproved[2]. An additional storey was added, and the front wall next the court was entirely rebuilt of stone in the prevalent fashion. The wall next the lane, however, was merely raised higher in white brick, and the windows inserted in this additional part were constructed so as to conform with the old ones below which remained undisturbed. This is the last of the series of melancholy attempts made during the last century to convert the medieval style of our colleges into Italian by a mere mask of ashlar.

In the following year, 1773, Essex altered the chapel of Queens' College, "though it seemed to want it very little," as Cole remarks[3]; and published a design for rebuilding Corpus Christi College in the Italian style, and in the form of a single quadrangle open to the street on the west[4]. This plan, which fortunately was never carried out, would have swept away the whole of the ancient buildings of the college. Yet, as we shall shew presently, he was a devoted admirer of medieval archi-

[1] [15 December, 1770. "Ordered by the Master and Seniors that £2000 in the old SS. Annuities left by D[r] Smith be sold and applied towards the new Building in the great Court, and the painted Window in the Library." The work had however been practically decided upon a few months earlier, for in the Accounts of the Junior Bursar for the year ending at Michaelmas, 1770, £200 is advanced "for the purchase of Bricks, etc. on Account of a new Combination Room to be built."]

[2] [See Cole's remarks, Vol. II. p. 318.]

[3] [History of Queens' College, Vol. II. p. 41.]

[4] [History of Corpus Christi College, Vol. I. p. 300.]

tecture. In 1775 he was commissioned by Sidney Sussex College to rebuild the east side of the second quadrangle which contains the library and the chapel. The former chapel, being in a ruinous condition, was pulled down, and the first stone of the present laid, in 1776, as already related[1]. These buildings were plain, with sash-windows.

Notwithstanding the fashion for employing an Italian style on all occasions, medieval architecture was gradually rising into favour during the period we have been reviewing, and Essex was one of its most ardent admirers. His drawings and manuscripts, preserved in the British Museum, shew how carefully and systematically he had attempted to study its principles, and his works at Ely, and at King's College, Cambridge, prove that these studies were carried on with the view of restoring that architecture to practice. [His remarks on Lincoln Cathedral, read to the Society of Antiquaries in 1775, begin as follows:

> "If the principles of Gothic architecture are now but little known, the various styles of building which come under the denomination of Gothic, are pretty well ascertained; and as the former, if well understood, and properly applied, would be useful to modern professors of architecture, so the latter may be usefully applied by the lovers of antiquities to illustrate and correct the different historical accounts which antient writers have left us of many elegant structures which once adorned this kingdom."

As early as 1756, at the very time that he was employed to destroy the Jacobean ornamentation of Nevile's Court at Trinity College, and to pull down the medieval buildings of Queens' College in order to make way for his own work, he issued proposals (dated 1 October, 1756) for engraving views, plans, and sections of King's College Chapel, "being so remarkable a structure, as to be admired and held in the highest esteem by all that have seen it, as well foreigners as English." He proceeds to inform the public that

> "on account of the late repairs, there have been more opportunities of taking proper dimensions than are likely to happen again, (and of which such use has been made, that very few more will be wanting for the purpose) whereby the proportions of its parts, and the design of the architect, are better understood than they have hitherto been."

[1] [History of Sidney Sussex College, Vol. II. p. 742.]

In conclusion he states the design of the work which, if he can obtain adequate encouragement, he proposes to publish. It would evidently have been a regular architectural history of the chapel. He intends, he says,

"to give about 15 plates of the building, explaining the various designs and proportions of its parts; with a plan of the college, as designed by the founder, and a printed explication of the whole; with some historical account of the building, extracted from the original contracts for the materials and particular parts of the work; the contracts themselves, or extracts from them, to be printed in an appendix, together with some remarks on that kind of building, and comparisons made with other buildings in the Gothick stile[1]."

We may presume that supporters were not forthcoming, for the work made no farther progress. His interest, however, in medieval architecture and antiquities continued unabated until the close of his life, as shewn by the valuable series of papers which he contributed to the *Archæologia*, the last of which was read to the Society of Antiquaries after his death. Moreover, he had collected materials for a history of Gothic Architecture, on which his friends set a high value, and tried in vain to persuade him to publish. Tyson, writing to Gough in 1779, exclaims:

"I cry when I think that Essex's materials must be lost to the world in a few years, and with them all real knowledge of that singular art; for no one alive understands the technical part but himself. Can't you buy, borrow, or steal them?[2]"

His name is associated with several works of merit in the style which he so much admired.] In 1757 we find him at Ely Cathedral repairing and fortifying the wood-work of the Dome and Lantern. He also restored the upper part of the eastern gable to the perpendicular, and designed the new roof for the Presbytery. About 1770 he directed the removal of the choir stalls from their ancient position to the Presbytery, and designed the choir screen, a most creditable performance for that time, when the difficulty of getting works executed in a forgotten style was so great[3]. In 1771 he designed and set up the panel-work

[1] [The "Proposals" are printed at length in Gough's British Topography, I. 237.]

[2] [Nichols, Literary Anecdotes, VIII. 656.]

[3] [Extracts from Mr Essex's Report on the dangerous condition to which the

and stone canopies at the east end of King's College Chapel, which, with due allowance for these difficulties, must be considered a remarkable work. He also made an altar-piece, and laid down a new pavement, at Lincoln Cathedral[1], repaired the tower of Winchester College Chapel, and made a survey of Canterbury Cathedral[2].

This statement of the real predilections of this able and ingenious architect shews that, if left to himself, he would have preserved medieval architecture instead of destroying it. It must be concluded, therefore, that in those cases in which he has obtruded the Italian style into medieval courts, he was acting in obedience to the instructions of his employers.

[With Mr Essex our enumeration of architects must end; and we will proceed in the next place to investigate the principal characteristics of architecture during the period of their influence.]

There are some elements of classical decoration which are so different in character from those of medieval architecture as to be at once recognised even by an untutored observer, however much they may be disguised by irregularities of capitals, moldings, crestings, or fanciful surface-ornament. Amongst such elements may be reckoned in the first place the predominance of flat surfaces, and rectangular edges of openings, which lingered in the Romanesque styles, but vanished when pointed architecture was established. They were superseded by obtuse angles,

Lantern at Ely had been brought by neglecting proper repairs, are given in Stewart's Architectural History of Ely Cathedral, p. 126; and his plan for removing the stalls into the Presbytery, in Bentham's Ely, p. 285. It should be mentioned that he took care to preserve, in the west face of the organ-screen, some fragments of an arcade, of delicate workmanship and good design, of earlier date than the stallwork, evidently the remains of some important structure in the church which had been destroyed.]

[1] [For this work he received a silver salver bearing the following inscription: "Voted, in the year 1784, by the Dean and Chapter of Lincoln, to Mr James Essex, Architect, In token of their respect for his abilities, and in acknowledgement of his assistance, which he so readily lent, in settling the mode of the new Pavement and other repairs of the Cathedral Church of Lincoln." For this information I have to thank his descendant, Miss Marian Hammond.]

[2] [For further particulars of Mr Essex see Cooper's Annals, IV. 412; Bentham's Ely, Supplement, p. 138.]

Fig. 1. One bay of the west side of the Roodloft, or Organ-screen, in King's College Chapel, probably erected between 1531 and 1535.

or by rectangular edges set in a diagonal position. Other characteristics are the column or pilaster bearing an entablature composed of an architrave, frieze, and cornice; an arch with flat architrave-molds on imposts or pilasters, and set in a frame composed of two columns bearing an entablature. An obtuse pediment replaces the old gable.

When the revival of classical architecture commenced in the University we find these elements, and similar ones, applied to individual members of a building only, and the remainder retaining its medieval character. Gradually, however, as the newer fashion took root, it absorbed the different parts one after another, until at last the medieval character wholly disappeared.

Wood-work and entrances were the first to receive the change, and the wooden screen of King's College Chapel, dated 1531—35 (fig. 1), is the earliest piece of classical architecture in Cambridge; a rich and pure specimen of Italian Renaissance traversing an interior equally admirable as the culminating work of the Perpendicular style in stone, the more valuable because, as a royal work, it is certain that the best architects and artists were employed upon the whole composition whether of one material or the other. Similar characteristics are to be observed in the wooden gallery of the President's Lodge at Queens' College, and once existed in that of Trinity Hall also, to judge by the windows as shewn in Loggan. [The former example was probably built about the middle of the sixteenth century, and the panel-work, which is full of classical details, was put up by Dr Humphry Tyndall (President 1579—1614) before 1600. With respect to the exact date of this beautiful work, the following statement may be added to the information already collected:

"Queenes Colledge, where the Masters lodging hath beene lately very much enlarged and beautified, partly at the charge of Doctor *Tyndall* Master there, Deane of Ely, and of the house, to the summe [of] foure or fiue hundred pounds[1]."

In both these examples some of the windows have external pediments. Renaissance details are also abundant in the woodwork of the hall of Trinity College (1605), and in the niches

[1] [Synopsis Papismi; by Andrew Willet, fol. Lond. 1600, p. 961.]

which Nevile added to the gates of entrance between 1597 and 1615.]

The gateways of Caius College are the first specimens of the revival in stone-work. The Gate of Virtue (1567) is, on the east or entrance-side (fig. 2), a remarkably pure and elegant specimen of the period, and its windows, though divided into three lights by mullions, have yet an Italian air given to them

Fig. 2. East front of the Gate of Virtue at Gonville and Caius College, built 1567.

by the flatness of the mullion and the square sinking on its face. On the west side, next to the court (fig. 3), the great arch is four-centered, and the composition has in other ways a mixed character, possibly given to it for the express purpose of making it harmonise with the chapel. The Porta Honoris (1575), erected from the especial device and instruction of Dr Caius, has also a four-centered arch, but in all other respects is purely of the Renaissance on both faces. Yet the ranges of chambers erected at the same time are medieval, but of the simplest character, in doors, windows, and general appearance, as shewn in the two illustrations.

The tower-gateway of Clare Hall (1638) is a very striking example of a composition of pure Renaissance in itself, but forming part of a façade containing medieval windows with arch-headed

Fig. 3. West front of the Gate of Virtue at Gonville and Caius College, built 1567.

lights, and crowned with a battlement. The archway presents an interesting example of the late use of fan-vaulting.

In the same way the western portal of Great S. Mary's Church (1576), the arches of entrance to the chapel of Corpus Christi College (1584), to Magdalene College (1585), and to the hall of Pembroke College (1635)[1]—each of them small but

[1] [The portal of S. Mary's Church was destroyed in 1850; of Corpus Christi College Chapel in 1823; and of Pembroke College Hall in 1862.]

complete specimens of pure classical renaissance work of a single storey in height, were applied to buildings of a medieval character, two of which were erected before the Reformation. The portal of Emmanuel College (1584), the entrance gate-house of Sidney Sussex College (1595) with a four-centered arch and a classical entablature (both now destroyed); the hall-porch at the same college (destroyed); and the porches to the Master's Lodge at Trinity College (1602), and to the Hall (1604), are all good examples of the same style. The gate called "Nevile's Gate" at the same college (fig. 4), which probably originally formed part of the decoration of Nevile's court, and was removed to the end of the avenue in 1680—81, when it was extensively repaired and altered, should not be forgotten in this enumeration.

The Fountain in the centre of the Great Court of Trinity College (fig. 5) is a charming example of an isolated and complete composition of the English Renaissance, though, as explained in the History (p. 630) some of the original features were removed in the repairs of 1661—62, 1672—73, and 1716.

The parapets, or upper termination of the walls, underwent a transformation which has assuredly no derivation from any classical form, but was purely structural. The humble chambers of the early colleges, as explained in a former essay[1], had tiled roofs, terminating in eaves, and the superior buildings only had battlemented parapets. Garrets in the roof formed no part of the original ranges of chambers in either University, although occasional specimens even of wall-dormers occur from the middle of the fourteenth century in other examples of domestic architecture; and in France they were commonly employed in the fifteenth century. When garrets began to be formed, their window-frames were of wood connected with the frame-work of the roof by trimmers let in between the rafters, and set considerably within the line of the wall. [The rafters were often the limbs of trees used as they were felled, but admirably ceiled with rough plaster, two to three inches thick, laid on a deep bed of the long rushes found in the fens. This ceiling was carried over the stud-work by which the whole area was partitioned out into rooms. But these half-storeys

[1] ["The Chambers and Studies"; pp. 297—327.]

Fig. 4. East front of Nevile's Gate, Trinity College.

Fig. 5. Fountain in the Great Court of Trinity College, begun 1601—2.

were badly lighted, and hence no doubt it came to pass that the roof-dormers very soon became wall-dormers, rising in a line with the main walls of the buildings which carried them. This change naturally led to a corresponding transformation of the walls themselves.]

During the reign of Queen Elizabeth, in the buildings of Caius College (1565), and in Dr Harvey's works at Trinity Hall, we find for the first time the front of several dormer-windows

Fig. 6. Buildings of the Third Court of S. John's College, 1669—71.

carried up in masonry in continuation of the wall. They are not however arranged with regard to symmetry. At Emmanuel College, Sidney Sussex College, the second court of S. John's College (all the work of Ralph Symons), and in Nevile's Court at Trinity College, as well as in the walnut-tree court at Queens' College, the Perse Building at Caius College (destroyed 1868), and the second court of Pembroke College, these wall-dormers are arranged at equal distances along the length of the whole

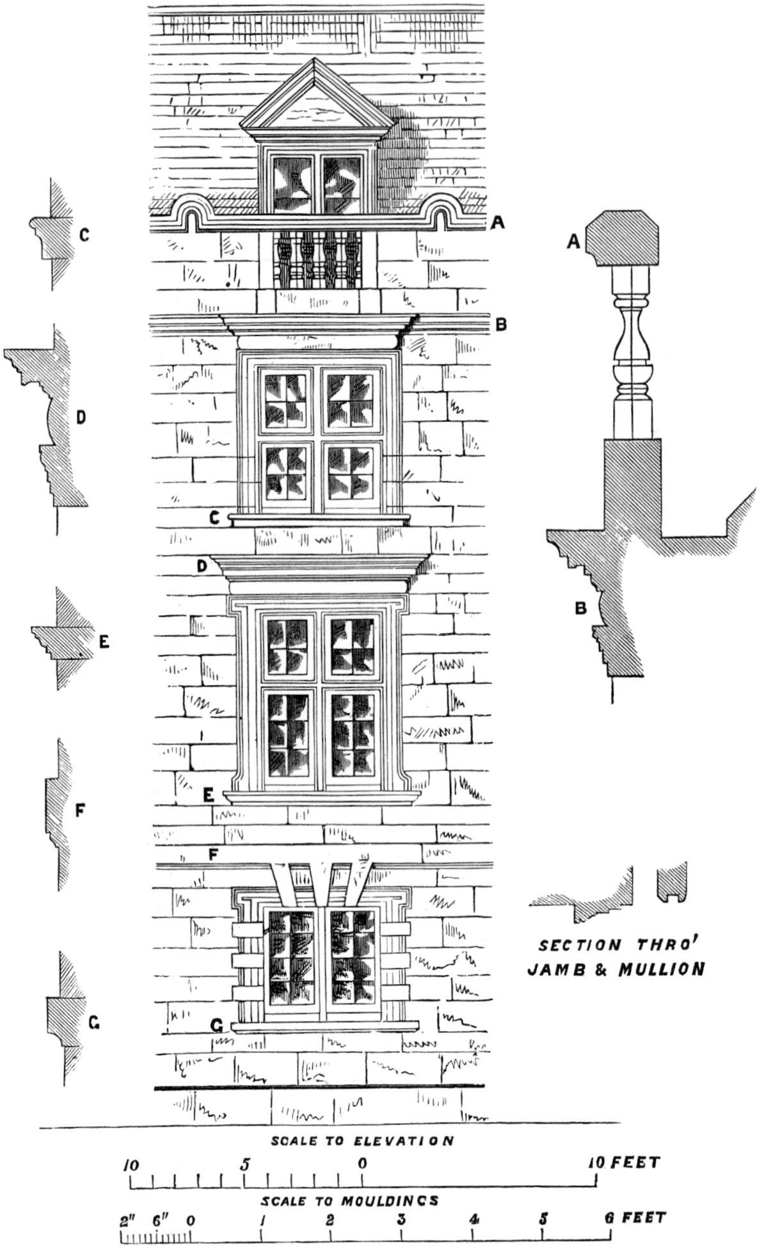

Fig. 7. One bay of the Fellows' Building at Christ's College, 1640—42.

building, cresting it as it were with a battlement of gigantic "merlons," separated by short intervals of eaves, or, as at S. John's College and in Nevile's Court at Trinity College, by a short parapet[1]. In all these examples, which extend to the year 1617, the gables are of the old triangular form; but in the Brick Building at Emmanuel College (1633), and (fig. 6) the buildings in the third court of S. John's College (1669), their outline is made up of ogees and semicircles, and the "merlons" are no longer the fronts of dormers, but are small and unpierced. The purer building of Christ's College (1640) still retains these semicircularly capped "merlons" on a still smaller scale, but they are connected by short ranges of genuine balustrades (fig. 7); and henceforth the dormer-windows, when employed at all, are set back as a part of the roof, and subordinated as much as possible, in order to preserve the long horizontal upper line of the walls, which is one of the characteristics of Italian architecture.

[Similar wall-dormers were introduced at Oxford during the same period, but amongst them there is a favourite and picturesque oriel window given to the dormer gables of which there are no examples at Cambridge. The only specimens now to be seen are above the library at Merton College (1589), and at S. Alban's Hall; but they are shewn by Loggan in the front chambers of Merton College, in the roof of the Warden's Lodgings at New College, in the kitchen of Brasenose College, the street front of Corpus Christi College, the so-called "cocklofts" added to Trinity College by Dr Kettell, and to S. Mary Magdalen Hall by Dr John Williamson, at the beginning of the reign of King James I., and at Pembroke College.

Fig. 8. Window in the north wall of the Library-range at Queens' College.

Picturesque examples of the elaborate gable-cresting of the time of James I. are to be found in the kitchen-building of S. John's College

[1] [It must be remembered that in citing these examples Professor Willis refers to their original condition, as shewn by Loggan.]

(1615), at Oriel College (1620), at University College (1634), and in the second court of Jesus College.]

As a general rule, windows are the last members of a building which assume the classical dress, [but gradual changes in their treatment may be noticed long before the employment of classical forms became general.]

In the older colleges the windows of the upper chambers are pointed, and divided into two lights by a monial which branches over the light-heads. Those of the lower chambers are square, and are also divided by a monial. Windows of this character may still be seen at Corpus Christi College, in the north garden of Trinity Hall, and at Queens' College (fig. 8). They are shewn by Loggan in the street-front of the latter college, in the court of Gonville Hall, and in the library of Pembroke College.

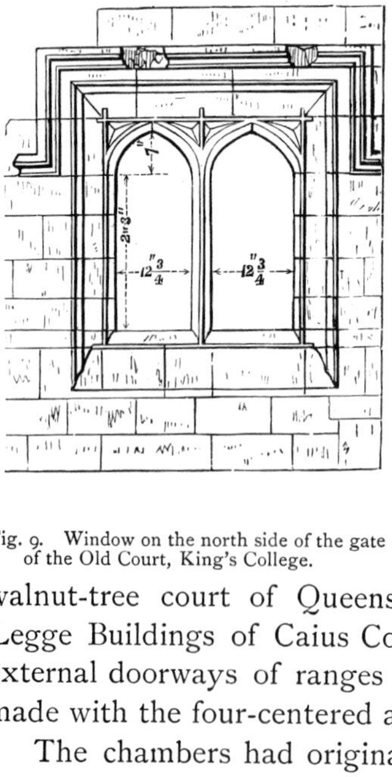

Fig. 9. Window on the north side of the gate of the Old Court, King's College.

Hoodmolds are never employed for the windows of the early collegiate buildings, except for those of halls and chapels. In the later buildings of Cambridge we find hoodmolds given to the windows of King's College (fig. 9), of the old court of Jesus College, of the Master's Lodge and some other parts of Christ's College, of both courts at S. John's College, of the street front of Magdalene College, of the ground floor rooms in the great court of Trinity College, of the walnut-tree court of Queens' College, and of the Perse and Legge Buildings of Caius College. They are also given to the external doorways of ranges of chambers, which continue to be made with the four-centered arch.

The chambers had originally bare walls, and naked joists or roof-timbers overhead. Wainscot and plaster began to take their place even during the reign of King Henry the Eighth[1].

[1] [Compare Josselin's account of the gradual alteration in the chambers at Corpus Christi College (Vol. I. pp. 251—254), and the essay on "Chambers and Studies," p. 320.]

These changes, following the changes in habits, were not confined to the interior. Chimney-stacks were added to many chambers which had had no fireplace provided in their original construction. The narrow windows of the old time began to be enlarged, and thus the exterior walls changed their aspect. In the hall of Trinity College, completed 1605, the lights of the windows are four-centered; in the Brick Building of Emmanuel College, completed 1634, and in the range of chambers on the east side of the entrance-court of Jesus College, completed 1643, they are round-headed; but in other respects collegiate buildings retained their medieval character. As a general rule ranges of new chambers continued to be provided with rectangular windows divided by monials into two or three lights, each light being "hansed" or arch-headed, as shewn in the accompanying example (fig. 10) from the library of Trinity Hall, built in the reign of Queen Elizabeth. This fashion lasted down to the building of Clare Hall, begun 1638, where, as we learn from Loggan, the window-heads were originally arched. In the range which contained the old library of Trinity College, built 1599—1600, the window-heads are polygonal (fig. 11). In a few examples erected in the second half of the sixteenth century the arch-heads are omitted, and the openings are rectangular, apparently in imitation of wooden window-frames, as in the pensionary of Corpus Christi College (1569), at Emmanuel College (1584) and Sidney Sussex College (1596), both the work of Ralph Symons, in the pensionary of Christ's College (1613)[1], and in the range of cham-

Fig. 10. Window on the north side of the Library at Trinity Hall.

[1] [These windows are shewn in Loggan's Views, which have been reproduced in the Histories of the different colleges referred to. At Emmanuel College they are to be seen in the range on the west side next the street, interspersed with others of the more ancient type, which probably mark the portions of the Dominican buildings which were preserved.]

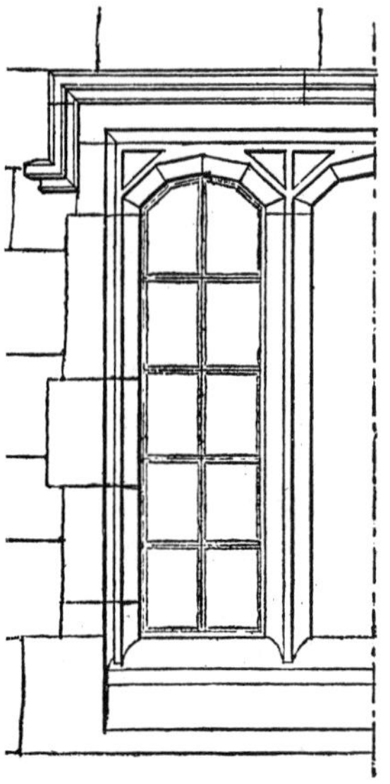

Fig. 11. Window on the south side of the old Library-range at Trinity College.

Fig. 12. Window in the Fellows' Building at Christ's College.

bers on the west side of Dr Gostlin's court at S. Catharine's Hall (1634—36). Windows on a similar plan, divided into nine lights of unequal size by two vertical mullions and two transoms, appear in the Dominican refectory which Symons converted into a chapel.

In the new building of Christ's College (1642), the windows (fig. 12) assume the totally different form of a single monial with a transom, which is characteristic of French domestic architecture [from the days of Francis the First to the beginning of the seventeenth century. Sir Robert Hitcham's building at Pembroke College, built 1659—71, contains both this window, and also the plain rectangular window divided into three lights by vertical mullions (fig. 13), which had been introduced at a somewhat earlier date. A still more characteristic example of what we will term the French window may be cited from the kitchen-range of Clare Hall, built 1689 (fig. 14).] This pattern immediately superseded the old one, and was employed in every building of the University until it was itself supplanted by the sash-windows of William and Mary's time. Dr Bentley appears to have been the first who introduced sash-windows into Cambridge. He fitted the Master's Lodge at Trinity College with them in 1700. The example set by him was followed at Clare Hall, where the north half of the river-front was built by Grumbold between 1709 and 1715 after the same design as the southern half. But sash-windows were now employed, and the mullion and transom of the older design were at the same time cut away from the southern portion in order to make it harmonise with the new work. Sash-windows were also used at

Fig. 13. North front of the west end of Sir Robert Hitcham's Building at Pembroke College, built 1659—71.

Trinity Hall, and at Corpus Christi College. [Similar windows had been introduced into the Provost's Lodge at Eton College in 1689—90.] The introduction of these sash-windows in place of the ancient mullioned window was much more destructive of the architectural character of the colleges than any other change, from the glaring discrepancy between them and the other arrangements of the original buildings.

[The complete renaissance window so common in the works of Inigo Jones and Sir Christopher Wren was no doubt suggested by the tabernacles of the Pantheon; but examples of this purely classical style are not so frequent in Cambridge as in Oxford, though they are used in the Senate-House and in one or two other buildings.]

In the majority of the works that we have hitherto surveyed, the style of architecture, although gradually wandering from medieval models, and introducing details borrowed from the classical styles, has yet not presented a sudden and violent contrast between the old buildings and the new. The mullioned windows of the collegiate buildings of the reigns of Queen Elizabeth and King James I. form a connecting link between the old and new styles that could not be broken by the sparing use of the classical orders in the gates of Caius College, or by the introduction of moldings of classical form arranged in the manner of medieval string-courses, or applied to monials. There appears to have been an attempt throughout these additions to harmonise them with older work by retaining forms such as the four-centered arches which we find in the gateways of Caius College, or by actually imitating a previously existing structure, as was done at Jesus College, where the range on the east side of the entrance-court is copied, with only slight and obvious modifications, from the original work of Bishop Alcock. Caius College in fact presents a more striking contrast to older works than any succeeding building, with the exception of Clare Hall, which presents a Renaissance gateway, flanked by win-

Fig. 14. Window in the kitchen of Clare Hall, built 1689.

dows still subdivided by monials into two or three narrow lights. Finally, the new building at Christ's College gives the first distinctly separated specimen, as isolated in design as in position, of a new architecture which retained no decorative features in common with medieval buildings.

In following henceforward the history of collegiate architecture to the beginning of this century we have but to record the erection of a succession of structures, which although for the most part attached to existing colleges, are designed in the style of their day without the least attempt on the part of the architect to harmonise them with their then despised neighbours. They form a most valuable series of examples of the variation of taste; many of them are excellent pieces of art, the work of eminent architects; and all are worth preserving and studying as historical monuments.

[In many of the repairs and alterations undertaken at the beginning of the last century, we find an indisposition to change the older style. For instance, when] Grumbold rebuilt the north and south cloister of Peterhouse in 1709, he substituted an Italianised design for the picturesque Jacobean Gothic of the original[1], yet in the windows he employed the cruciform mullions [which, as explained above, were first employed at Christ's College in the middle of the previous century]. In 1712 the street front of Pembroke College was cased with stone, and five years afterwards the inside of the old court was similarly treated. Up to this time the walls had been simply plastered. The ashlaring towards the street was a continuation of Sir Christopher Wren's new range of chambers erected in 1664. In this work, both within and without, the window-frames and monials, as also the pointed door-cases of the original building, were retained, and the architectural character of the whole was therefore very little disturbed[2]. In 1715, upon occasion of the presentation of Bishop Moore's Library to the University by King George the First, the upper floor of the west side of the

1 [The old and new designs are given in the History of Peterhouse, figs. 14, 15. At present, as the woodcut shews, the windows exhibit only one central vertical mullion, and there is no evidence that a horizontal mullion ever existed.]

2 [History of Pembroke College, Vol. I. pp. 147—149. The name of the builder who superintended these changes has unfortunately not been preserved.]

Schools Quadrangle underwent a transformation which greatly deteriorated it, as may be seen by comparing its present appearance with Loggan's view. Nevertheless it is evident that Grumbold, to whom the work was entrusted, intended to respect the original style[1].

[Unfortunately, however, this respect for ancient buildings was not of long duration.] At Oxford the old quadrangles were pulled down and rebuilt on a larger scale in the new and consistent style of the period. But at Cambridge (except at S. Catharine's Hall) we were content with the attempt to clothe our ancient colleges with a modern dress, which did not suit their proportions, and was at once detected by the gateways and other parts of the older structures which admitted of no disguise. Had the architectural work of the University been limited to the erection of new chambers, and additional courts, or even to the substitution of complete buildings for older ones pulled down, we should have welcomed these works as historical monuments, shewing, in conjunction with their predecessors, the gradual increase and progress of these institutions. But, unfortunately, here as elsewhere, the requirements of altered habits, and the introduction of new fashions of decoration, led to the alteration of the older buildings, and transformed them from architectural monuments into anomalous and mutilated structures.

[These changes, which affected the general structure of the colleges, as well as particular buildings such as the hall or the chapel, have been already described, as far as Cambridge is concerned, in the different Histories. The following table, in which the most important works done at Oxford during the corresponding period have been included, will be useful in pointing out the gradual progress of the desire for change, and the influence of particular architects at a given time. It will be understood that, as a general rule, the dates represent the time when the work was begun.

KING HENRY VIII.

1531—35. Organ-screen of King's College Chapel.

QUEEN MARY.

1555. Chapel of Trinity College.

[1] [History of the Schools, etc. Vol. III. pp. 29—33.]

Queen Elizabeth.

1565—75.	Caius College court, Porta Honoris, etc.
1569.	Pensionary at Corpus Christi College.
1576.	West doorway of Great S. Mary's church.
1579.	Sir Nicholas Bacon's chapel for Corpus Christi College.
1580.	Storey added to buildings of New College, Oxford.
1583—84.	Lady Bacon's doorway to chapel of Corpus Christi College.
1584.	Foundation of Emmanuel College; Symons, architect.
1585.	Sir C. Wray's doorway to Magdalene College.
1593.	Nevile alters the great court of Trinity College.
1596.	Foundation of Sidney Sussex College; Symons, architect.
	Ceiling to "catalogue-room" at University Library.
	Library of S. John's College, Oxford.
1597.	Sir T. Bodley repairs Duke Humphry's Library at Oxford, and adds a new roof.
1598.	Second court at S. John's College; Symons, architect.
1600.	Library at Trinity Hall.
1602.	Fountain in the great court of Trinity College; Library at Oxford reopened.

King James I.

1604.	Hall at Trinity College.
1608.	New quadrangle at Merton College, Oxford.
1610.	North side of second court of Pembroke College.
	Foundation of Wadham College; eastern wing of Bodley's Library and Proscholium of Divinity School, Oxford.
1612.	West side of second quadrangle of Lincoln College, Oxford.
1613.	Schools quadrangle, Oxford; Thomas Holt, architect: Wadham College opened.
1614.	Nevile's court at Trinity College completed.
1615.	Chapel of Jesus College, Oxford.
1616.	Range of chambers in the walnut-tree court at Queens' College; Wigge, architect.
1617.	Perse Building at Caius College; Hall of Jesus College, Oxford.
1619.	Legge Building at Caius College.
1620.	Quadrangle of Oriel College, Oxford.
1623.	Library of S. John's College (Jacobean Gothic).

King Charles I.

1626.	Library of Jesus College, Oxford.
1628.	Sir F. Clerke's building at Sidney Sussex College; Chapel of Peterhouse (Jacobean Gothic).
1630.	Staircase of Christ Church Hall, Oxford.
1631.	Second quadrangle of S. John Baptist College, Oxford; Inigo Jones, architect: chapel of Lincoln College.
1632.	Gate of entrance to Botanic Garden, Oxford; Inigo Jones, architect.

1633. Brick building at Emmanuel College; Westley, architect: Library at Peterhouse lengthened.

1634. Wainscot and screen in Pembroke College hall; chambers on west side of Dr Gostlin's court at S. Catharine's Hall.

West side of the quadrangle of University College, Oxford, rebuilt; Congregation House and west wing of Bodley's Library.

1635. Front of University College, Oxford.

1637. Porch of Great S. Mary's church, Oxford; Quadrangle of Oriel College, Oxford, rebuilt.

1638. New building at Jesus College.

1638—42. New buildings and bridge at Clare Hall; Westley, architect (?).

1639. Chapel of University College, Oxford.

1640. Second quadrangle of Jesus College, Oxford.

1640—44. Fellows' building at Christ's College.

COMMONWEALTH.

1656. Chapel and cloister at Brasenose College, Oxford.

1659. South side of second court of Pembroke College (eastern portion) begun with Sir R. Hitcham's bequest.

KING CHARLES II.

1663. New chapel at Pembroke College; Wren, architect.

1664. Sir Robert Hitcham's cloister at Pembroke College.

Sheldonian Theatre, Oxford; Wren, architect.

1665. Second quadrangle of Trinity College, Oxford; Wren, architect.

1668. New chapel at Emmanuel College; Wren, architect.

1669. The Bishop's Hostel at Trinity College; south half of the west front of Clare Hall; third court of S. John's College.

1673. Rebuilding of S. Catharine's Hall.

1676. Library of Trinity College; Wren, architect.

1679. New building (Pepysian Library) at Magdalene College in progress.

1682. Garden-court at New College, Oxford; William Bird, architect.

Tower-gateway at Christ Church, Oxford, completed; Wren, architect.

1683. Hall, Combination Room, and butteries at Clare Hall.

Ashmolean Museum, Oxford; Wren, architect.

WILLIAM AND MARY.

1689. Kitchen at Clare Hall.

1691. Chapel at Trinity College, Oxford; Wren and Aldrich, architects.

1692. Library at Queens' College, Oxford; Hawkesmoore, architect.

1695. Chapel at S. Catharine's Hall.

1700. Master's Lodge at Trinity College altered and sashed by Dr Bentley.

QUEEN ANNE.

1705. Northern half of west front of Clare Hall; Peckwater quadrangle, Christ Church, Oxford, rebuilt; Aldrich, architect.

1706. Chapel at Trinity College altered; Turner building at Corpus Christi College, Oxford.
1710. Quadrangle of Queen's College, Oxford; Wren and Hawkesmoore, architects.
1711. Clarendon Press, Oxford; Vanbrugh, architect.
1712. West front of Pembroke College ashlared, without change of style.

KING GEORGE I.

1714. Foundation of Worcester College, Oxford. Hall of Magdalene College, Cambridge, altered, flat ceiling.
1714—16. West front of Christ's College ashlared.
1716. West room at University Library altered.
Fountain at Trinity College rebuilt; Library at Christ Church, Oxford; Clarke, architect. New Quadrangle of All Souls College, Oxford; Hawkesmoore, architect.
1718. Additional storey to south side of entrance-court at Jesus College; sash-windows inserted.
1719. Second quadrangle of University College, and Robinson building at Oriel College, Oxford.
Founder's Range at Emmanuel College rebuilt.
1720—59. New Buildings of Worcester College, Oxford.
1722. New Senate House; Gibbs, architect.
1723. Hall at Christ's College altered; flat ceiling.
1724. New building at King's College; Gibbs, architect.
1725. Library at Eton College.

KING GEORGE II.

1732. Hall at Queens' College altered by Burrough and Essex, flat ceiling.
1733. Chapel at Magdalene College altered, flat ceiling; new quadrangle begun at Magdalen College, Oxford.
1736. New Building at Peterhouse; Burrough, architect.
1737. Radcliffe Library, Oxford; Gibbs, architect.
1738. Part of west front of Christ's College ashlared.
1742—45. Principal court of Trinity Hall ashlared by Burrough; hall and east front altered; scheme for rebuilding second court.
1747. Hall of Sidney Sussex College altered, flat ceiling.
1751—54. Gonville court ashlared and partly rebuilt.
1754. Quadrangle of Peterhouse ashlared; Burrough, architect. East room and façade of University Library; Wright, architect.
1755. Nevile's court at Trinity College rebuilt; Essex, architect.
1756. New building at Queens' College; Essex, architect; east front and gateway of Jesus College, Oxford.
1757. Ramsden building at S. Catharine's Hall; Essex, architect.
1758—69. Interior of court of Christ's College ashlared; Essex, architect.

KING GEORGE III.

1760. Hall of Emmanuel College altered by Essex, flat ceiling.

1762.	Battlements at Clare Hall replaced by balustrades.
1763.	Chapel of Clare Hall; Burrough and Essex, architects.
1769.	West front of Emmanuel College ; Essex, architect.
1770.	Combination Rooms at Trinity College ; Essex, architect.
1771.	East end of King's College Chapel decorated by Essex.
1772.	First court of S. John's College altered by Essex ; Radcliffe Observatory, Oxford, Keene and James Wyatt, architects.
1773.	Chapel at Queens' College altered by Essex, flat ceiling: south side of first court of S. John's College altered by the same.
1776.	New Chapel at Sidney Sussex College.
1788.	Library of Oriel College, Oxford; James Wyatt, architect.
1789—92.	Chapel at Jesus College altered, flat ceiling.
1815.	Alteration of windows in west front of Clare Hall.

Before leaving the subject of these later changes, it will be interesting to note the impression they made on a contemporary, Sir John Cullum, a man of taste and refinement, who, revisiting the University in July, 1775, makes the following remarks in his diary:

"While I was rambling about the University this afternoon and revisiting those Scenes, where I spent so delightfully a considerable Part of ten Years in the Prime of Life, it was with Pleasure I observed the great Improvements that have been here since I have known the Place. Within so short a Time as 25 Years, ten out of the sixteen Colleges have received, not only Occasional Repairs, but very great Embellishments or Additions, and I must particularly congratulate the noble Chapel of King's College upon its new Gothic Altar Piece, which it owes to the superior Taste of Mr Essex. How few of our venerable Cathedrals have escaped without some inconsistent Mass of Grecian Architecture! what a Pity it is that the Town, to aggravate the narrowness and windings of its streets, should still continue one of the worst paved in the Kingdom[1]."

In conclusion, we will enumerate, as briefly as possible, those architects who successively gained the confidence of the University of Cambridge during the present century.

William Wilkins was the architect of the new college of Downing, 1801; of the bridge at King's College, 1819; of the King's court at Trinity College, and the new buildings at

[1] [MS. Diary, 1 July, 1775. Mr Cullum matriculated as a pensioner at S. Catharine's Hall, Lent Term, 1752. It may be conjectured that the ten Colleges referred to are Peterhouse, Clare Hall, Caius, Trinity Hall, King's, Queens', S. Catharine's Hall, Christ's, Trinity, Emmanuel.]

Corpus Christi College, 1823; and of the new buildings at King's College, 1824.

Anthony Salvin built the new front of the Master's Lodge of Trinity College, 1841; commenced the restoration of Jesus College chapel, 1846; enlarged the Master's Lodge at Trinity Hall, and rebuilt the east front, 1852; built the new hall, library, etc. at Gonville and Caius College, 1853; built a new façade to the building between the great gate and chapel of Trinity College, 1856; designed and built the two Master's courts at Trinity College, 1860—68; and, lastly, the New Museums for Natural Science, 1863.

Sir George Gilbert Scott restored the parish church of S. Michael, 1849; the parish church of S. Mary the Less, 1857; repaired the roof of King's College chapel, 1860—63; built the new chapel and Master's Lodge, and lengthened the hall, at S. John's College, 1862; built the new wing of the University Library, 1864; restored the hall and combination room at Peterhouse, 1868; and built a new range of chambers at the south-east corner of King's College, 1870.

Alfred Waterhouse was the architect of the new court at Gonville and Caius College, 1868; of the new range of chambers at Jesus College, 1869; of the Master's Lodge and range of chambers next Trumpington-street at Pembroke College, 1871; of the new range of chambers at Trinity Hall, 1872; of the new hall at Pembroke College, and of the alterations to the hall at Jesus College, 1875.

William Milner Fawcett, M.A., of Jesus College, altered the Hall and Library at S. Catharine's Hall, 1868; built the Cavendish Laboratory, 1872; restored the east front of Queens' College, and built the new Master's Lodge at S. Catharine's Hall, 1875; built the new work-rooms and class-rooms for Zoology and Physiology, 1876; and the new lecture-room and chambers at King's College (facing Scott's building), 1883.

Arthur William Blomfield, M.A., Trinity College, lengthened the chapel of Corpus Christi College, and decorated the chapel of Trinity College, 1870; built the new Master's Lodge at Emmanuel College, 1871; a new oriel for the combination-room at the same college, and two new ranges of chambers at Trinity College, 1876.

George Gilbert Scott, junior, sometime Fellow of Jesus College, rebuilt the hall of Christ's College, 1875; completed the restoration of the east end of the parish church of S. Mary the Less, 1876; and built two new ranges of chambers at Pembroke College, 1880, besides lengthening the chapel, and repairing the west range of the old buildings next Trumpington Street.

Basil William Champneys built the Selwyn Divinity School, 1877; and the new Museum of Classical and General Archæology, 1882.

In addition to these series of works, the Gisborne court at Peterhouse, 1825, was built by William M'Intosh Brookes; the new court at S. John's College, 1826, by Messrs Rickman and Hutchinson; the University Press, 1831, by Edward Blore; the new Master's Lodge at Magdalene College, 1835, by John Buckler; the University Library, 1837, by Charles Robert Cockerell, who was subsequently called in, in 1845, to complete the Fitzwilliam Museum after the death of Basevi, the original architect, in the same year; the chapel and hall of Queens' College were restored by G. F. Bodley, 1858 and 1861; the hall of Clare Hall was altered, 1870, by Sir M. Digby Wyatt; the entrance-hall of the Fitzwilliam Museum was decorated, 1871, by Edward M. Barry, who also added to the buildings of Downing College, 1873; and the south and west fronts of Magdalene College were restored in 1873 and 1875 respectively by F. C. Penrose, who is also the architect of the new buildings at S. John's College, begun 1885.]

XI.

THE TENNIS-COURT, THE BOWLING GREEN, THE GARDEN, ETC.

WHEN the collegiate system was fully developed, it was intended, at least at Cambridge—to which this essay must be in the main restricted—that the inmates of each house should find within the precincts all that could be required for their daily life; not merely for their devotions, their food, and their instruction, but also for their exercise and amusement. The younger members of the society were not allowed to go into the town or country unless attended by an older person; and they were specially forbidden to indulge in the habitual amusements of young men of the day. Tennis, bowls, and archery being among the permitted exercises, we shall find that provision was made for them, especially for the two former.

Of the sixteen Cambridge colleges, nine had tennis-courts, thirteen had bowling-greens, and eight had both. Peterhouse had a tennis-court; Clare Hall a bowling-green; Pembroke College a bowling-green[1]; Gonville and Caius College[2] and

[1] [The tennis-court at Pembroke College has been omitted from this enumeration, because, so far as we are aware, it was always let on lease; and the ground on which it stood was not hired by the college until 1609, by which time the court had probably been already built.]

[2] [No bowling-green is marked on Loggan's map or print for this college; but the lawn in the Fellows' Garden in front of the Perse Building, as shewn in his print, looks as though it were intended to be used as a bowling-green.]

Trinity Hall neither; Corpus Christi College, King's College, and Queens' College, both; S. Catharine's Hall, a bowling-green; Jesus College, Christ's College, and S. John's College, both; Magdalene College, a bowling-green; Trinity College and Emmanuel College, both; Sidney Sussex College, a bowling-green. The tennis-courts have all been pulled down; but a bowling-green still exists at the following colleges: Pembroke, Queens', Jesus, Christ's, S. John's, Trinity, Emmanuel, Sidney Sussex.

Besides the provision made for games, it will be desirable to notice more fully than was possible in the separate histories some other adjuncts to colleges; such as the gardens, the summer-houses, or galleries, the baths, and the pigeon-houses.

TENNIS-COURT.—The position and history of each tennis-court (*sphæristerium*) has been noticed in the separate collegiate histories, to which the reader is referred for detailed information. Unfortunately the date of foundation of most of the courts belonging to the earlier colleges is unknown, and therefore nothing definite can be ascertained respecting the period at which the game first became popular in the University. The earliest reference to it which we have met with is at Corpus Christi College, where, as Josselin[1] tells us, the walls of a building which had been intended for a bakehouse and granary were carried up to their full height between 1487 and 1515, and used as a court to play hand-tennis in (*locus quo pila palmaria luditur*), until 1569, when it was turned into rooms for students. The second tennis-court was probably built soon afterwards. It is shewn in Hammond's map of Cambridge, dated 1592, and in Loggan's view of the college, taken in, or about, 1688. At Queens' College the tennis-court was in use before 1531, when a small repair to it appears in the accounts[2]. It was built of brick or stone, for in July, 1583, a workman is employed for four days and a half, "in tylinge and coping the Tennys corte wall[3]." It is mentioned last in January, 1585, when a small payment occurs for "blacking

[1] [Josselin, Historiola, §§ 21, 74. Camb. Antiq. Soc. Octavo Publications, 1880.]

[2] [Magn. Jour. 1530—31, fo. 139. "Item in die sancte Etheldrede pro reparatione spheristerii vj^{d}."]

[3] [Ibid. 1582—83, fo. 165.]

y[e] wales of y[e] tennis cort[1]." At Christ's College the tennis-court was completed in 1564—65. The material employed was brick[2]. At Trinity College the tennis-court in its first position, near the south-eastern corner of the college, was probably built soon after the foundation. It was necessary to pull it down in 1598—99, to make way for the completion of the great court, but it was rebuilt in 1611 at a cost of about £120. At S. John's College in the same way there were two courts. The first was built in 1573—74, on the outside of the court to the west, near the Master's garden. The following entries, which are all that relate to it, indicate a wooden building, of no great size; but they may refer to a repair, and not to a first construction:

"Item for xxxviij^{li}. of Ironworke for the tennis courte at ij^{d}. the pownde, vj^{s}. iiij^{d}.

Item to iij carpentars for settinge vp the tennis court iiij dayes apece, xij^{s}.

Item to Robert Nicolson for his scruse, vj^{d}.

Item to ij laborers iiij dayes a pece ramminge the spurres (*sic*) and digginge places to sett them in at the tennis courte v^{s}. iiij^{d}.[3]"

This court was granted to the contractors for the second court, and pulled down in 1598, or at the beginning of 1599. It was rebuilt on the opposite side of the river in 1602—3, at a cost of £79. 14*s*. 0*d*.[4] This sum, however, does not represent the whole cost, for in 1597—98 a subscription was got up for it, the amount of which was handed to the bursar, and entered by him among the receipts. This is the court shewn by Loggan (fig. 1). In construction it evidently exactly resembled that at Christ's College, of which a portion is shewn in Loggan's view, projecting from behind the Fellows' building.

In the same way at Jesus College a tennis-court, which is frequently referred to in the accounts from 1566—67, when it is first mentioned, was rebuilt in 1603—4. As at S. John's College, a subscription defrayed some part of the cost—in this case

1 [Ibid. 1584—85, fo. 175 b.]

2 [Audit-Book, 1597—98. *Exp. forinsece.* "Item for Brick and workmanship about the Tennis Court as appeareth by bill x^{li}. i^{s}. x^{d}.]

3 [Audit-Book of S. John's College, 1573—74, *Reparationes domi.*]

4 [Ibid. 1602—3. *Reparationes domus*, with which should be compared a separate account at the end of the volume, headed: "Expenses aboute the Teniscourte the former yeare."]

evidently by far the larger part—for the rebuilding is disposed of in the following entry :

"Item towards the building of the teniscourt, besides a pretor collected amongst y^e^ schollers viij^li^. vij^s^. vj^d^[1]."

Fig. 1. The Tennis-Court at S. John's College ; reduced from Loggan's print, taken about 1688.

[1] [Audit-Book of Jesus College, 1603—4, *Reparationes.*]

At Emmanuel College the tennis-court was probably built soon after 1584. Loggan's view (fig. 2) shews it after it had been unroofed in 1633. The buttresses indicate solidity in the walls, which were no doubt built of brick or clunch.

Fig. 2. The Tennis Court at Emmanuel College; from Loggan's print, taken about 1688.

Most of the tennis-courts appear to have been open. This was probably the earlier arrangement, for the two which we know to have been roofed, namely that at Corpus Christi College, and that at Emmanuel College, were built respectively about 1569 and 1584. The roof of the former appears in Loggan's view of the college; and the roof of the latter is mentioned in the contract for the Brick Building dated 1633. The tennis-court at King's College was also roofed, for in 1569—70 a payment occurs "for tylyng the tennys courte"; and so was that at Pembroke College, but, as it was extensively altered, if not rebuilt, in the last century, its arrangements throw no light on those of the older courts.

It will not, however, be difficult to discover the general plan of the Cambridge tennis-courts, on the assumption that they were all similarly arranged, by comparing Loggan's views of the two courts mentioned above with the description of those in use in France in 1767, as set forth in a treatise called *Art du Paumier-Raquetier, et de la Paume*, by M. de Garsault, and published at Paris in that year[1]. He describes two courts, the one called *le jeu à dedans*, the other *le jeu quarré*. The essential difference between them is that the former has a passage, with a penthouse roof, carried along one side and both ends (the passage at one end being termed *le dedans*, and used for the accommodation of

[1] [The translation of M. de Garsault's treatise given below is quoted from The Annals of Tennis, by Julian Marshall, 4to. London, 1878.]

spectators, as in modern courts[1]), while in the latter the passage is carried along one side and one end only.

It will appear, as we proceed, that the Cambridge courts belong to the latter category, and we will therefore quote so much of M. de Garsault's description of *le jeu quarré* as is necessary for its adequate comprehension.

"Every Tennis-Court is a long rectangular building, contained by four walls. The ground, which this carcase should include, will be 90 feet long and 36 feet broad, so that, when all the internal constructions are made, the area of the court shall be 90 feet long by 30 feet broad. * * * On each side-wall seven timber-posts shall be placed, at equal distances from each other. These posts shall be 14 feet high, and shall support the main roof; it is through the spaces intervening between these posts that light is admitted throughout the court; and, for this reason, the building must be placed somewhat apart from other houses or great trees, so as not to be darkened. This then, is what may be called the carcase of the building; let us now pass to the interior constructions.

At 5 feet distance from the inner side of one of the side-walls, and parallel with it from one end to the other, a low wall is built, of various heights, that is to say, 7 feet high at each end, for the distance of 18 feet on the left side, and 13 feet on the right side; all the rest of the wall shall be 3 feet 4 inches in height. Now, as the two ends of this wall, raised to the height of 7 feet, must receive a wall-plate to run at that height from one end to the other, seven light, round, wooden, posts, turned like little pillars, are fixed upon the low wall to support it. * * * Upon the wall-plate is placed the lower edge of a wooden roof or pent-house, the top of which rests on the side-wall; and the whole of this forms a long corridor, called the *gallery*. At right angles to this gallery, and 5 feet inside from the gable on the left, another low wall is built. This wall supports another pent-house, similar to the first, and they are joined together in their angle of intersection.

In the gable at the other end of the court, there is on the level of the floor a square opening [called *le petit trou*] 16 inches each way, contrived in the thickness of the wall of the gable itself. At the point where the gallery ends, a board (*l'ais*) is attached, 1 foot in breadth and 6 feet in height, behind which a hollow is made, the effect of which is that the board, not touching the wall, except at its edges, gives a different sound, when struck by a ball, to that given by the wall.

The whole area of the court is paved with flags of Caen stone, each 1 foot square, making 90 rows of flags; and the ceiling, level with the tops of the great posts first mentioned, shall be of fir boards.

[1] [It must not be supposed that a court with a *dedans* is a modern invention, for Mr Marshall gives a ground-plan (p. 15) of a court so arranged which was built by Francis I. in the Louvre.]

The post [which stands at the centre of the internal wall described above] shall be pierced at five feet from the floor with a hole, through which must pass a central cord, from which a net shall hang down to the floor. This cord crosses the whole width of the court, separates it into two equal parts, and is attached, at the same height of five feet, to a hook fixed in the main wall opposite; and, in order to stretch it more or less, a winch is placed in the low wall, below the [above-mentioned] post, and holds one end of the cord; the latter, for appearance sake, is covered with a tissue of strong thread; and this cord, with its net, hangs gradually lower and lower by its weight as it crosses the court, so that it is hardly more than two feet and a half high in the centre. The winch serves to raise it more or less, according to the wishes of the players [1]."

The view of the tennis-court at Emmanuel College (fig. 2) distinctly shews the gallery with its penthouse roof resting against one of the side-walls, the board (*l'ais*) in the gable wall close to the point at which the gallery abuts against it, and the hole called *le petit trou* at the opposite corner, close to the ground The second gallery, which, as the description has told us, is always opposite to *le petit trou* and *l'ais*, is concealed by the gable-wall against which it rests. The court of S. John's College is evidently on the same plan as that of Emmanuel College, but it is drawn from such a point of view that the only distinctive point shewn in it is *le petit trou*. Both courts are subdivided by a cord, from which a fringe [2], instead of a net, seems to be suspended; and both are entered by a door opening into the gallery. This door is distinctly shewn in the S. John's College court (fig. 1); and its presence in that at Emmanuel College may be inferred from the path leading up to it.

In some colleges the money derived from letting the court to players was paid into the hands of the bursar, and brought to account as an extraordinary receipt. For instance at Trinity College in 1586—87 we find: "Receyved of Gentlemen for the tennis court 8^{li};" in 1588—89, £13. 10*s*. 0*d*. from the same source; and in 1590—91, £9. At S. John's College this money was applied to the increase of the servants' wages. In 1595—96 we find: "The increase of ye Laundresse wages of ye tenis court gaines, xvj^{s}. viij^{d}."; and in the following year: "To ye porter for his wages out of ye gain of ye tenis court vj^{s}. viij^{d}."

The popularity of tennis at Cambridge at the beginning of the seventeenth century is attested by the way in which the

[1] [Marshall, *ut supra*, p. 35.]

[2] [Ibid. p. 61.]

courts which it had been found necessary to pull down to make way for other buildings were at once rebuilt in new positions. Similar evidence is supplied by Bishop Earle's Microcosmography, first published in 1628, where, among the characteristics of "A meere young Gentleman of the Vniuersitie," is set down "his proficiencie at Tennis, where when hee can once play a Set, he is a Fresh-man no more[1]." The following rules for the management of the tennis-court were made at Emmanuel College in 1651[2]. They are signed by nine fellows:

"Octob. 29. 1651. For the better regulating of the Teniscourt it is ordered by the Master and Fellowes unanimi consensu, that the key of it shalbe in the keeping of the Deane, who is to take care that the doore be kept lockt, and none suffered to play dureing the howers herafter mentioned, vizt. from one of the clock till three in the afternoone, and from eight of the clock at night untill tenn the next morning; unlesse any of the Fellowes shall desire to play there in any of those howers, who may take any fellow commoner wth them; yet soe as that they cleare the court, shutt the doore, and returne the key to the Deane at theire comeing away."

The same hours for play are indicated at Peterhouse in the conditions imposed on the lessee of the tennis-court in 1667 and 1677: "that the scholars shall freely play with their owne Balls and Rackets from eleven of the clock until one, paying nothing for the same; and at other times when the Master or Deans shall allow them[3]."

In the following century tennis gradually went out of fashion, but it was evidently still played to a certain extent, for in 1719 four Bachelors of Arts were suspended from their degrees by the Vice-Chancellor "for being caught at a tumultuous and disorderly meeting at the Tennis Court"; and the celebrated Regulations promulgated by the Duke of Newcastle, Chancellor of the University, in 1750, enumerate the tennis-court among places of amusement to which undergraduates were likely to resort:

"Every person *in statu pupillari* who shall be found at any coffee-house, tennis-court, cricket-ground, or other place of publick diversion and entertainment, betwixt the hours of nine and twelve in the morning, shall forfeit the sum of ten shillings for each offence[4]."

[1] [Wordsworth's University Society, etc., p. 377.]

[2] [Order-Book of Emmanuel College, p. 57.]

[3] [History of Peterhouse, Vol. I. p. 27.]

[4] [Wordsworth, *ut supra*, pp. 178, 666. Cooper's Annals, IV. 278.]

Before this time, however, some tennis-courts had been pulled down—probably because play in them had ceased to be popular. The court at Trinity College was pulled down in 1676, to make way for the library, and was not rebuilt; those at Christ's College and Corpus Christi College were pulled down in 1711 and 1756 respectively; and that at Emmanuel College before 1746, when the ground-plan by Essex, reproduced to illustrate the History, was taken.

BOWLING-GREEN.—As was the case with tennis, it is impossible to discover when bowls were first introduced into the University, but, as "a bowlinge allie for the Novyces sume tymes to recreat themeselves[1]" existed at Durham, and probably at other monasteries also, we may safely conclude that it would be included among the other arrangements introduced at an early period from monasteries into colleges. The earliest allusion to a place to play bowls in which we have been able to discover, is at Queens' College in 1609—10, when "a bord to set at the end of the bouling alley" is charged for[2]. This expression probably refers to what was subsequently called a bowling-green[3], for in 1629—30 the gardener is paid for extraordinary work "about the bowling *alley*," and for "sodding the bowling *alley*"; but in 1634—35 the seat in the bowling *green* is painted[4]. As no further charges of importance having reference to the bowling-green occur in the accounts for subsequent years, it may be taken for granted that the bowling-green mentioned in 1634—35 is that shewn by Loggan in 1688. It was then in the same situation as at present. At S. John's College the bowling-green is first mentioned in 1625, but as already in existence, and it was probably laid out soon after 1610—11, when the ground of which it forms part was purchased; at Jesus College it had been laid out before 1630—31, when work is done to it; at S. Catharine's Hall it was

1 [The passage from "The Rites of Durham" in which this sentence occurs will be found at length in the Essay on "The Combination Room," p. 377.]

2 [Magn. Jour. 1609—10, fo. 130 b.]

3 [Strutt, Sports and Pastimes, ed. 1831, p. 268, shews that a bowling-alley was covered in, in contrast to the bowling-greens, which were open.]

4 [In the same way at Jesus College the bowling-green is called the bowling-alley. In 1630—31 we find in the accounts: "to the gardner for worke about the bowling ally (*sic*) ix^{s}."; in 1631—32, "the bowlinge alley and Fellowes garden"; and in 1641—42: "To John Hibble for a seat in ye bowling alley iiij^{s}."]

laid out in 1637, as soon as a convenient site had been obtained; at Emmanuel it was already in existence in 1638; at Trinity College it was laid out in 1648; at King's College it is first alluded to in 1658, and at Christ's College in 1686. These dates shew that bowls were most popular at the same period as tennis, namely in the first half of the seventeenth century; for, had it been necessary or desirable to lay out a bowling-green at an earlier period, colleges with a large site, as S. John's, Trinity, and King's, could easily have done so.

By examining Loggan's views of the different colleges a good idea may be formed of the appearance of the bowling-greens in his time. Privacy, and warm shelter for the spectators, were evidently much sought after, for the bowling-greens are usually encompassed by lofty clipped hedges, or even walls, and provided with seats, or arbours, usually raised on a low terrace, and placed in such a position as to get the greatest amount of sun.

ARCHERY.—The practice of archery in Cambridge by the townspeople is commemorated by the name Butt Green, given to the common south of Jesus College[1]; and the name Butt Close, given to the common on the west bank of the River Cam, opposite to King's College, would seem to indicate that that ground was put to a similar use by the members of King's College. It must, however, be admitted that the accounts of that college do not contain any entries having reference to the practice, and that in the controversy with Clare Hall in 1636—37 respecting the alienation of a piece of this ground, archery is not once alluded to, though King's College was obviously anxious to make the case for refusing to comply with the request of their neighbours as strong as possible.

Again, at S. John's College, Bishop Fisher's statutes, dated 1530, expressly except bows and arrows, if used for recreation, from the list of arms which scholars are forbidden to carry; an exception which is repeated in the second set of statutes, dated 1545[2]. It is therefore remarkable that we find no reference to

[1] [It may be conjectured that members of the University used the Town butts, from an entry in the Accounts of Christ's College for 1594—95: "Item given towards the towne buttes iij^{d}."]

[2] [Statutes of S. John's College, ed. Mayor, p. 134.]

archery in the accounts, and that Roger Ascham's treatise, Toxophilus, first published in 1545, when he was still resident at S. John's, should contain no allusion to his own practice of an accomplishment to which he evidently attached so high a value. It may, however, be inferred that archery was practised at Cambridge during the time that he resided there (1530—48), not only from his own enumeration of the evils which befell the University (S. John's College being taken as a type) at the accession of Queen Mary in 1554, among which we find "honest pastimes joyned with labour left of in the fieldes," with "shoting" appended in the margin[1]; but also from a letter written by Dr William Turner, Physician to the Lord Protector Somerset, and afterwards Dean of Wells, who, describing his intercourse with Nicholas Ridley at Pembroke College between 1526 and 1540, says: "his behaviour was very obliging and very pious, without hypocrisy or monkish austerity; for very often he would shoot in the Bow, or play at Tennis with me[2]."

At other colleges, however, we meet with distinct evidence of the practice of archery. Butts are mentioned at Peterhouse in 1588—89, and again in 1613[3]. They were probably set up in the grove to the west of the college. At Queens' College the garden opposite to the college gates, called "the tennis-court yard," was used for archery until 1587, when a payment occurs "for castinge down the buttes in the Tennis court yarde[4]." We must not infer from this entry that archery was discontinued by members of the college, for in 1629 the Corporation of Cambridge objected to their habit of digging turf "in the Green by Newnham for the repairing of their butts, without any leave or license[5]"; and in 1662 and following years a number of small payments are made "for scouring the ditch by the Butts," "for makeing the hedge behinde the Butts," "for hedging and mowing the Butclose," and the like, from which we may infer that the butts were then placed in the field on the west side of the river. They

1 [The Scholemaster, ed. Mayor, p. 165.]

2 [Strype, Ecclesiastical Memorials, ed. Oxf. 1822, iii. 386.]

3 [Audit Roll of Peterhouse, 1588—89, "pro ostio arbusti prope les buttes"; Ibid. 1613—14, "ostium circa les Butts."]

4 [Magn. Journ. 1586—87 (March), fo. 187. History of Queens' College, Vol. II. p. 54.]

5 [Cooper's Annals, iii. 214.]

are last mentioned in 1682—83. At Christ's College the orchard to the east of the college was used for archery. In the audit-book for 1591—92 we find:

"Item for making y^e buttes in y^e Orcharde vj^s. $viij^d$.
Item to Cutchie for turfe to y^e sayd buttes $viij^s$."

This last entry is repeated in the accounts for 1610—11. At Trinity College we find similar evidence, though the ground where the butts were placed is not defined:

"Jun. Burs. Accounts, 1643—44. For setting up a Butt in y^e Garden	o.	18.	o
Ibid. 1647—48. To y^e workemen for y^e Butts	1.	5.	o
— 1650—51. Paid ye hired gardiner for a p^r. of Butts	o1.	o4.	oo."

Garden.—The records of several colleges shew that a garden was laid out and planted as soon as possible after the foundation of the House, but rather for the purpose of securing a supply of fruit and vegetables, than as a place for recreation. For instance, at King's Hall, in 1338—39, only three years after Robert de Croyland had sold his property to King Edward III., the wages of the gardener (*serviens in gardino*) occur in the accounts, with charges for nailing up and pruning the vine, which was probably trained over the house. In subsequent years similar charges are frequent. In 1362—63 the ground between the college and the river was laid out as a garden, and a workman is paid at the rate of threepence a day for four days to make the beds (*herbaria*); but, with the exception of a charge for "persily sed" in 1341—42, and for saffron in 1383—84, the accounts throw but little light on what was planted in them. At Pembroke College the garden dates from 1363, when the Foundress bought a piece of garden-ground already in cultivation[1]; but the loss of the early account-books prevents our having any detailed information respecting the use made of it by the college. At Peterhouse the account-roll of 1374—75 contains a set of charges which shew that the extensive ground belonging to the college was being cultivated. There was a kitchen-garden, for which seeds of parsley, cress, garlic, leeks, saffron, and vegetables in general, are bought; and, besides this, a considerable space was laid down

[1] [History of Pembroke College, Vol. I. p. 122.]

in clover or vetches, as four bushels of seed are paid for[1]. In 1815 this garden was still "well stocked with culinary vegetables[2]."

At King's College a garden—probably a kitchen-garden—was laid out in 1451—52, and seeds of various sorts were bought for it in 1467—68. At this college there was a large orchard, in which crab-apples were extensively cultivated, and used for the manufacture of verjuice, evidently a kind of cider. In 1468—69 we meet with a charge for crushing the apples, and extracting fifty-two gallons of verjuice, at the cost of a halfpenny for each gallon[3]. A similar charge occurs in 1478—79; and so late as 1579—80 a fresh planting of crabtree stocks is recorded. Crab-stocks were also planted at Queens' College in 1519—20[4], probably for the same purpose. At this college the garden on the west bank of the river was laid out in 1499—1500[5], and has been used as a vegetable and fruit garden ever since.

We will next notice, very briefly, some of the plants of which the names occur most frequently in the account-books of the different colleges.

Allusions to saffron are numerous. When saffron was extensively used in cookery and medicine, both for home consumption and for exportation, it was in Cambridgeshire and the adjacent counties of Norfolk, Suffolk, and Essex, that the crocus which produces it (*Crocus sativus*) was chiefly cultivated[6].

[1] [" In cultura orti cum aratro et seminatione xvj d. It^m in quatuor bussellis viciarum pro semine xxj d. In purgacione riviarii in orto xj sol. In potu dato eis iiij^or d. In alleo iiij^or d. It^m semine de cresse j d. It^m in semine petrosilli j d. It^m in semine de saffrey j d. It^m in fossura curtilagii xij d. It^m in oleribus v d. It^m in porris x d. It^m in falcacione viciarum iiij^or d. It^m in paryng de croco xx d. It^m pro paryng alterius loci iiij d."]

[2] [Ackermann's History, p. 9.]

[3] [Mundum-Book, 1468—69. "Item sol'. xxj. et xxiij^cio. die Augusti pro expensis factis circa collecclonem le . Crabbez . pro . le . Veriuse. Et pro le hoggishede pro eodem xiiij^d. Item sol' pro le Stampyng de le Crabbez. viz. pro iiij duss' et iiij^or. lagenis de le veriuse, pro qualibet lagena ob. ij^s. ij^d." The measure called a *lagena* ought, according to Ducange, to contain twelve pounds weight of water. A gallon, which has been used as the nearest English equivalent, actually contains nine pounds, twelve ounces.]

[4] [Magn. Jour. 1519—20. "Item cuidam homini de Brynkley pro xxxvj crabbestckkis plantatis in orto ex opposito magne porte collegii xxij^d."]

[5] [History of Queens' College, Vol. II. p. 56.]

[6] [In the History and Antiquities of Hawsted and Hardwick, in the County of

It is not surprising, therefore, that it should have found its way into college gardens. We meet with it first at King's Hall in 1383—84. In 1454—55 the planting of the garden of Pembroke College with saffron, "to the public advantage of the college," is mentioned among the good deeds of Lawrence Booth (Master 1450—80)[1]. At King's College we find it in full cultivation in "the little garden," which, as we have shewn elsewhere[2], was situated between the bridge and Clare Hall, in 1466—67[3]. A similar entry occurs at Queens' College in 1523—24[4]. At Peterhouse a portion of the ground to the west of the college, called the grove (*virgultum*), was set apart for the cultivation of the crocus, and the following curious entries occur respecting the way in which the saffron was prepared:

> "1518—19. Et de v^{s} pro vj ly howys ad purgand' terram Croci in virgulto...et de viij^{d} ob. pro faccione quadrati ad caminum croci...
>
> 1520—21. Et de xiij^{d} pro colleccione ac preparacione croci, viz. quadraginta unc'. Et de xj^{s} vij^{d} pro purgacione terre croci. Et de iiij^{d} pro duobus modiis ly chercole ad eundem crocum. Et de vij^{d} pro reparacione fornacis in coquina pro fabricatura ly kyll ad crocum[5]."

In explanation of the above extracts we will quote the careful description of the mode of preparation, communicated to the Royal Society in 1728 by James Douglass, M.D., based upon observations collected "up and down all that large Tract of Ground that lies between *Saffron-Walden* and *Cambridge*, in a Circle of about ten Miles Diameter."

Suffolk, by the Rev. Sir John Cullum, Bart., 4to. Lond. 1813, p. 221, *note*, the following references to the former cultivation of the Saffron Crocus occur: "Chiefly cultivated in Norfolk, Suffolk, Essex, and Cambridgeshire; now, I believe, only in the last. Several pieces of land in this county (Suffolk) still retain its name; at Fornham St Genevieve is a piece called the *Saffron Yard*; another at Great Thurlow, the *Saffron Ground*; and a piece of glebe land near Finningham Churchyard, the *Saffron Pans*, or Panes, so named, I suppose, from the slips, or beds, in which the plants were set."]

[1] [History of Pembroke College, Vol. I. p. 138. In the Accounts for 1444 we find: "recept' pro 15 modiis croci (pro singulis 5 d.) 6^{s}. 5^{d}."]

[2] [History of King's College, Vol. I. p. 569.]

[3] [Mundum-Book, 1466—67. *Exp. necess.* "Item sol' pro eradicacione croci in paruo orto collegii vj^{d}. Item sol' Rogero Hunt iij^{cio} die Septembris pro le paryng croci in paruo orto collegii ij^{d}."]

[4] [Magn. Jour. 1523—24, fo. 58. "Item pro ly parynge de horto ubi crescit crocus, cum mundatione ejusdem xvj^{d}."]

[5] [Similar entries occur in the two following years.]

"The Chives [or filiform *stigmata*] being all picked out of the Flowers, the next Labour about them is to dry them on the Kiln [*caminus*]. The Kiln is built upon a thick Plank (that it may be moveable from Place to Place) supported by four short Legs. The Outside consists of eight Pieces of Wood, about three Inches thick, joined in Form of a quadrangular Frame [*quadratum*], about twelve Inches square at Bottom on the Inside, and twenty-two Inches at Top, which is likewise equal to the perpendicular Height of it. On the Foreside is left a Hole about eight Inches square, and four Inches above the Plank, through which the Fire is put in. Over all the rest, Laths are laid pretty close to one another, and nailed to the Frame already mentioned, and then are plaistered over on both Sides, as is also the Plank at Bottom very thick, to serve for a Hearth. Over the Mouth, or widest Part, goes a Hair-Cloth fixed to two Sides of the Kiln, and likewise to two Rollers, or moveable Pieces of Wood, which are turned by Wedges or Screws, in order to stretch the Cloth. Instead of the Hair-Cloth many People now use a Net-work of Iron-wire, with which it is observed, that the Saffron dries sooner, and with a less Quantity of Fewel; but the Difficulty of preserving the Saffron from burning, makes the Hair-Cloth be preferred by the nicest Judges in drying.

The Kiln is placed in a light part of the House, and they begin by laying five or six Sheets of white Paper on the Hair-Cloth, upon which they spread the wet Saffron, between two and three Inches thick. This they cover with other Sheets of Paper, and over these lay a coarse Blanket five or six times doubled, or instead thereof, a Canvas Pillow fill'd with Straw, and after the Fire has been lighted for some Time, the whole is cover'd with a Board, having a large Weight upon it.

At first they give it a pretty strong Heat, to make the Chives sweat, as their Expression is; and in this, if they do not use a great deal of Care, they are in Danger of scorching, and so of spoiling all that is on the Kiln.

When it has been thus dry'd for about an Hour, they take off the Board, Blanket, and upper Papers, and take the Saffron off from that that lies next it, raising at the same time the Edges of the Cake with a Knife. Then laying on the Papers again, they slide in another Board between the Hair-Cloth and under-Papers, and turn both Papers and Saffron upside down, afterwards covering them as above.

This same Heat is continued for an Hour longer; then they look to the Cake again, free it from the Papers and turn it; then they cover it, and lay on the Weight as before. If nothing happens amiss, during these first two Hours, they reckon the Danger to be over; for they have nothing more to do, but to keep a gentle Fire, and turn their Cake every half Hour, 'till it be thoroughly dry; for doing which as it ought, there are required full twenty-four Hours.

* * * * * * *

Their Fire may be made of any kind of Fewel; but that which smoaks the least is best, and Charcoal for that Reason is preferred to any other[1]."

[1] [Phil. Trans. 1727—28, Vol. XXXV. p. 570. Compare also: Pharmaco-

Vines were cultivated not only for the sake of the grapes they produced, but also for the shade they afforded; but it is probable that the former reason dictated the planting of them in the first instance. The accounts of the Gild of Corpus Christi for 1348 contain a charge "for splentes for the vineyard[1]"; and one of the pieces of ground composing the site of Physwick Hostel included a plot of vines (*parcella de vynes*) in 1369[2]. We meet with a vineyard (*vinearium* or *vinetum*) at several colleges. At King's Hall in 1418—19 a charge occurs for pruning the vineyard (*pro putacione vinearii*), and a similar charge in 1452—53 (*pro truncacione vinetorum*). In this instance the vines were attached to poles which rested on forked sticks, as shewn by charges for "crutches" and "rails[3]." This vineyard appears to have been maintained at Trinity College, for in 1550—51 the gardener is paid "for cutting ye vynes for ye space of iij dayes." At King's College also there was evidently a vineyard of considerable extent, for in 1483 seven gallons of "verjuice" were made from the grapes[4]. At Queens' College there was evidently a regular vineyard, for in 1510—11 a labourer is employed in the garden for four days "circa ly vynes"; and in 1524—25 the vineyard (*ortus vinearum*) is specially mentioned. In 1538—39 a frame for the vine is made, which is shewn by the cost to have been an extensive structure[5]; and in 1575—76 we meet with a set of entries which indicate a trellis, with the uprights resting on stone posts. The structure thus formed was probably arched over one of the alleys, so as to form a walking-place or gallery :

graphia, by Flückiger and Hanbury, 8vo. Lond. 1879; and Woodville's Medical Botany, Vol. III.]

1 [First Report of the Hist. MSS. Commission, 1870, p. 65.]

2 [History of Trinity College, Vol. II. p. 415.]

3 [Accounts of King's Hall, Vol. vi. p. 254 (the Account should probably be referred to 3 Hen. V. 1415—16): "Item pro xj kroochys pro vineis et quinque raylys ij^{s}. vj^{d}. It' pro liij peciis pro vineis vij^{s}. viij^{d}." Ibid. Vol. vii. p. 122 (1425—26): "In meremio pro reparacione vinearum. In Crochis et rayles et Sparres v^{s}. viij^{d}."]

4 ["Item solut' Thome Figge septimo die Septembris pro pressyng vij lagenarum de verjus de Grapys collegii iij^{d}."]

5 [Magn. Journ. fo. 47. "Item G. Persono fabro materiario pro materie ad abricam erigendam viti, xxv^{s}. x^{d}." With this may be compared an entry in 1548—49 (ibid. fo. 173): "Item 23 Martii pro perticis salicum ad vineam et pro opera illius qui eas supposuit vinee, xj^{d}."]

"Item for xvij foote of squared stoon for the post of the vines frame to stand on...v^{s}. viij^{d}.

Item to Robert Geordenor Carpenter and vij of his men for xj dayes woorke setting vppe the frame of the vine in the fellowes garden...xxviij^{s}. vj^{d}.

Item to Thomas Thatcher and his men for iij dayes woorke in framing the stones to sett the vyne's frame on, and making holes in the wall for the same...v^{s}. iiij^{d}.

Item to the frenche man for iij dayes work and a haulf in setting uppe and planting the fellowes vine...iij^{s}. vj^{d}."

A similar entry occurs in the accounts of Jesus College for 1572—73:

"Item to John Munde and John Richardson eche of them iij daies and dimid' sawynge tymber for A frayme for the vines in o^{r}. m^{rs}. gardeyn and the fellowes gardeyn y^{e}. 22th. of februarij after xij^{d}. a pece y^{e}. daye...vij^{s}."

These galleries are shewn in more than one of the views of French country-houses given by Du Cerceau in Les plus excellents bastiments de France, published in 1576—79[1]; and the employment of a Frenchman at Queens' College furnishes additional evidence in favour of a similar structure having been then erected there. Again, at Christ's College, in 1596—97, a carpenter is paid "for mending the frame of the vine in the fellowes garden."

Hops were grown at King's College. Part of the ground on the west side of the River Cam, called the "Laundress Yard[2]," was laid out as a hopyard. The first notice of this use occurs in the accounts for 1573—74, where we find the following entries:

"It' for setting up the hop poles...vj^{d}.

It' pro 2^{bs}. bigatis le pooles for the hoppe yarde...x^{s}. x^{d}."

Mulberry trees were extensively planted in the gardens of at least three colleges at the beginning of the seventeenth century. The sudden increase in the cultivation of this tree in England at that time was due to the action of King James I., which we find described as follows in Stow's Annals, under the year 1609:

"It is not very many yeeres since the Kingdomes of Spaine and Portugall haue obtayned the perfection of breeding silke-wormes, and

[1] [Compare the Essay on "The Master's Lodge," p. 338.]

[2] [History of King's College, Vol. I. p. 570.]

making of silke, neyther is it but twentie yeeres since the first generall making of silke came into France, which knowledge France had from Spaine and Italy, euery of which Nations by time and time haue brought therby not onely good imployment of their poore and idle people, but also great profite to each common-wealth: the which his Maiestie well knowing, and being desirous by all laudable meanes to imploy his poorest Subiectes, and preferre the general profite of this kingdome, and hauing made sundry trials and experiments that silke wormes would liue and breed in England: And that of their silke here was made sundry things, as peeces of Taffeta, Stockings, and Sowing silke, equall to the best that is made in Granado: And as apt to take all fine coullours; whereupon the last yeere, and this spring, according to the Kinges expresse order, vpon apparant reason and likelihood of great vtilitie to this kingdome: there were many hundreth thousands of yoong Mulberrie trees brought out of France, and planted in many Shires of this Land: And manie began to breed wormes and make silke, and albeit this is the first publique notice of keeping wormes and making silke in England, yet true it is that many yeeres past there were diuers industrious gentlemen y^{t} kept wormes and made good silke, amongst which of late yeeres, William Staledge Comptroller of the Custome house, hath taken ingenious paynes in breeding wormes, and making of fine silke for all vses: he had a patent for seauen yeeres to bring in Mulberry seed, and this yeere he and monsieur Verton by order from the king planted Mulberry trees in most shires of England[1]."

The "kinges expresse order" mentioned in the above passage, took the form of a "Letter to the Lords *Lieutenants* of the several *Shires* of *England*," dated 16 November, 1608, in which they were enjoined

"to take occasion either at the *Quarter-Sessions*, or at some other publique place of meeting, to perswade and require such as are of ability (without descending to trouble the poore, for whom we seeke to provide) to buy and distribute in that County, the number of ten thousand *Mulberry-plants*, which shall be delivered unto them at our City of etc. at the rate of 3. farthings the plant; or at 6*s*. the hundred, containing five score plants[2]."

M. François de Verton, Sieur de la Forest, the French gentleman who was appointed by the Earl of Salisbury, then Lord Treasurer, to carry out the distribution of the plants, having made a progress through the counties of Hertford, Suffolk, Norfolk, Cambridge, Huntingdon, Bedford, Buckingham, Northampton, Warwick, Leicester, Nottingham, Derby,

[1] [Annals, ed. Howe, 1615, p. 895.]

[2] [King James's Letter is printed in Samuel Hartlib his Legacie, 4to London, 1651, p. 74.]

Stafford, Chester, and Lancaster, addressed a report to his master at the conclusion of his first journey. His success in inducing those whom he met to become purchasers appears to have been only moderate, but, interesting as the document is, we can quote only one passage, that namely which concerns Cambridge:

"Dudit lieu [Bury S. Edmunds] j'allay a Cambridge, ou je trouuvé les escolliers assez morfondus. Toutefois My lord de Bathe prist 600 des Meuriers, et quelques aussi furent prins[1]."

The word *morfondus* may be translated, "they took the matter coolly"; and in fact three colleges only, Jesus, Christ's, and Emmanuel, obeyed the royal injunctions. Their purchases were all made in 1608—9. In the accounts of the two first we find: "Item for 300 mulberrye plants xviij^{s}."; an entry which occurs also at Emmanuel College, with a slight variation: "For mulbyrie plants at ye king's appoyntm^{t}. 300. xviij^{s}." It was suggested in the History of Christ's College (p. 227) that the old mulberry tree, traditionally associated with the name of Milton, may be the last survivor of the three hundred then bought.

It may be worth recording that at Queens' College apricots were planted in 1634—35[2], and asparagus in 1688—89[3]; and that at Jesus College in 1647—48 there is a charge, among other plants, "for Quince trees in the Fellows' Orchard."

By the end of the seventeenth century, when Loggan's prints were taken, gardens had become exceedingly elaborate. It will be interesting to go through the colleges in order, and notice some of the features which he has perpetuated. For further particulars the separate histories should be consulted.

At Pembroke College the Fellows' Garden is divided into two plantations of trees, with the bowling-green between them. These three divisions are separated by thick hedges, one of which is clipped into an imitation of battlements. A broad gravel-walk is carried round the whole, sheltered by a high boundary-wall. Carter, writing in 1753, describes this garden

1 [This document is preserved in the Public Record Office. See Calendar of State Papers (Domestic), for the year 1609.]

2 [Magn. Jour. 1534—35 (June). "To Mr Farloe for Apricock trees and carriage 0. 13. 0."]

3 [Ibid. 1688—89 (April). "100 Asparagus Plants."]

as "a large spot of ground, wherein is a good Bowling-Green, but what it is chiefly noted for, is a long and fine Gravel-Walk, at the foot of a South Wall, which is counted one of the warmest Winter walks in the University." The Master's garden is much more elaborately laid out, with rectangular flower-beds on gravel. One of these is arranged to represent a sundial, with a large wooden gnomon in the centre, and the figures worked (apparently) in box. The whole is surrounded by a carefully clipped box-edging.

At Gonville and Caius College the Master's Garden is laid out even more formally than at Pembroke College, with low clipped hedges separated by gravel-walks; and at Trinity Hall part of it is in the French style, with geometrical flower-beds on gravel. The wall which faces the south is covered, as usual, with fruit-trees.

At Corpus Christi College the most was made of the small ground at the disposal of the Fellows. Though only about 185 feet long by 130 feet broad, it contains a tennis-court, a summer-house or gallery, and a bowling-green, besides a certain amount of what looks like kitchen-garden. Notwithstanding its small area, it was evidently much admired, for Carter says: "The *Fellows Gardens* are very Pleasant, having a grand *Bowling-green*, a beautiful *Summer-house*, with variety of Wall and other Fruit, all which are kept in excellent order."

At Queens' College the Fellows' Garden is surrounded by a high wall, with fruit-trees trained against it, as at present. Rather more than half the garden is occupied by the bowling-green. A broad gravel-walk is carried round the whole ground; and smaller walks subdivide the portion laid out as a garden. One of the beds contains a sun-dial, closely resembling that at Pembroke College. The Master's Garden is divided by walks into four squares, all differently arranged. Three have oblong flower-beds; the fourth contains a small French garden, of geometrical design. On the west side there is a large pigeon-house, and also a curious battlemented structure, the flat top of which is approached by a flight of external stairs. It seems to have been intended to command a view of the river[1].

[1] [The probable use of this building is discussed in the History of Peterhouse, Vol. I. p. 27.]

At Jesus College a formal French garden is shewn in the space eastward of the first quadrangle; and the Master's Garden has geometrical flower-beds, with yews clipped into concentric circles separated by wide intervals. The extensive ground beyond the immediate precincts of the college buildings was left in its natural state.

At Christ's College the Fellows' Garden is laid out with much less formality than elsewhere. It is divided into two nearly equal parts by an avenue of lofty trees extending from one end of it to the other. At the further end of this avenue there is a summer-house, an elaborate classical structure with a pediment on each of its four sides; a second summer-house stands near the south boundary of the garden. There is a small bowling-green; but, with this exception, most of the ground is planted with trees, so thickly as to form a grove rather than a garden. The Master's Garden is planted regularly, with rows of young trees; and it presents the unusual feature of a large pond. Loggan's carefully drawn view shews beehives in a sunny situation under one of the boundary-walls; posts with lines for drying clothes; and a watch-dog. The garden between the south range of the first court and the lane now called Christ's Lane[1], is laid out with the usual formal beds and gravel-walks. Near the street we see four geometrical beds arranged symmetrically round a large vase which contains a shrub.

At Emmanuel College the garden has the curious feature of an arbour arched over the central walk. The map shews that this strange device must have been at least 190 feet long. Unfortunately the accounts do not give any clue to the date of its construction, or to the nature of the plants with which it was covered; but, from the notices which we have collected above, it may be conjectured that vines would be employed. The arrangements of the rest of the garden do not call for special remark.

At Sidney Sussex College half the Fellows' Garden is laid out as a bowling-green, separated from the remaining portion by a clipped hedge. The rest is partly a grove, partly a flower-garden, with elaborate geometrical beds, arranged round

[1] [In the next century this garden was considered the private property of one of the Fellows. History of Christ's College, Vol. II. p. 224, *note*.]

a central circular elevation, covered with smaller beds, and crowned by a sundial. The Master's Garden is laid out in a similar style, but with less elaboration.

At S. John's College the walks are unfortunately not shewn by Loggan, but numerous entries in the accounts shew that they were laid out elaborately. Among the decorative features there was a covered walk, or arbour, first made in 1685, as recorded in the accounts for 1685—86: "To Solomon Bones for 600 Poles to make y[e] Long Arbour in y[e] Inward Walks last year, 4. 1. 0." It was made still more substantial in 1691—92: "To James Nottingham for worke done in y[e] Walks in raising y[e] high Arbor with bricks. * * * To John Adams Carpenter for Materialls and worke in raising y[e] high Arbor in y[e] Fellows Walks." This arbour probably resembled the structure noticed above at Emmanuel College.

SUMMER-HOUSE.—In several gardens we find solid structures of stone or brick, usually called "galleries," or, as we should say, summer-houses. As most of these have been already noticed in the separate histories, we need not do more in this place than briefly notice their existence. The most important and substantial, so far as we can judge, was "the gallery in the fellowes orchard" at Corpus Christi College, built 1648, a view of which appears in Loggan's print. It was in two floors, the lower of which was occupied by a colonnade. Loggan shews four arches of stone, divided by stone pilasters, on the north side, over which are four windows of two lights, and an oriel-window at the east end. Loggan also shews a large square summer-house, built 1680, in the Fellows' Garden at Emmanuel College, and a smaller one in the Master's Garden. The former resembles a Swiss *châlet*, the upper floor being wider than the ground-floor, and the roof having projecting eaves. As the cost of the two buildings did not exceed £22, the material used was probably wood. At Sidney Sussex College Loggan shews a curious polygonal building in the Fellows' garden. Like the two former, it was in two floors, with windows of five lights on each floor on each side, so as to admit the greatest possible amount of light and air. The summer-house in the garden of Christ's College has been already noticed.

Besides these, of the appearance of which we are able to form a tolerably accurate idea, a "fellowes gallerie" at St John's College is alluded to in 1604—5; at Trinity College in 1570—71; and at King's College in 1468—69. An "old Summer House, built over the river," once existed also at Trinity Hall. The summer-houses at King's College and St John's College were in a similar position.

BATH.—Of the baths which formerly existed in the University, two only remain, namely, at Christ's College and at Emmanuel College, but the existence of others can be traced. On this subject we find the following statement, written in 1748:

"And here it may be proper to take notice, that Cold-baths are much resorted to by the students of *Cambridge* at present, of which there are several in the College Gardens; but the best is two Miles West of the Town, near the Village of *Madingly*[1]."

The description of Peterhouse, in the same work, contains the following statement:

"There is a Grove South of the College, and a large Garden beyond, abounding with all manner of Wall-fruits, and a Cold-bath, much frequented by the Students[2]."

This Bath was still in existence in 1815, when Ackermann's History states that "a cold bath is one of the valuable appendages of the place[3]." At Clare College there was a bath, lately removed, in the basement of the west range, between the gate leading to the walks and the south-west corner of the quadrangle; and Carter, writing in 1753, makes the following statement respecting one at Pembroke College, at the end of his description of the gardens:

"There are besides several other Gardens, belonging to the Apartments of particular Fellows, in one of which, is another small and simple, yet well contrived Water-Work, which is continually supplying a large Cold-Bath with fresh Water; the over-plus of which runs through the Second Court, and so into the King's Ditch[4]."

Lastly, it should be mentioned, that when the New Master's Lodge at S. Catharine's Hall was built in 1875, advantage was

1 [The Foreigner's Companion, etc., p. 52.] 2 [Ibid. p. 18.]

3 [Ackermann, History of the University of Cambridge, i. 9.]

4 [History of the University of Cambridge, p. 78.]

taken of the cellars of one of the houses adjoining, to construct a bath for the use of the undergraduates.

MODE OF LAYING OUT THE QUADRANGLE.—When quadrangles were first built, the central space was evidently laid out as a garden, with shrubs and flowering plants, bordered with privet, rosemary, or sweetbriar; and in some cases furnished with seats[1] and arbours[2]. In the sixteenth century this fence was exchanged for wooden railings. By the end of the following century a greater formality had been introduced. The varied garden had been replaced by grass-plots, on which single trees were planted; and the use of wooden railings had ceased to be general. When Loggan's views were taken, there were none in the courts of the following colleges: Peterhouse, Clare Hall, Pembroke, Gonville and Caius (Caius Court), Trinity Hall, Queens', S. Catharine's Hall, Jesus, Christ's, St John's; but they still existed at Corpus Christi, Magdalene, Trinity, Emmanuel, Sidney Sussex. We will go through the colleges in order, and point out the appearance which their courts then presented.

At Peterhouse the court had been planted with privet in 1601[3]; but by 1688 this had been replaced by four rows of cypresses; one along the north side of the grass-plots, one along the south side, and two forming an avenue leading to the west door of the chapel. Between this avenue and the other rows, there was on each side a row of fir-trees. At no other college was the court planted so formally as at this.

At Clare Hall four large trees are shewn, one in the centre of each of the grass-plots into which the area of the court is divided.

The small extent of the principal court of Pembroke College did not admit of trees; but the second court has a row of seven trees along its eastern side, and a smaller tree appears in the centre of one of the two grass-plots.

[1] [Account-roll of Peterhouse, 1589—90. "Et de viij^d^. Swayne reparanti sedilia in Area."]

[2] [Accounts of Jesus College, 1596—97. "Item for 8 spaces for the arbor in the quadrangell ij^s^. viij^d^. Item to Richarde Bridges for 300 setts of whytethorne for the arbor in the quadrangell xviij^d^."]

[3] [Account-roll of Peterhouse, 1600—1601. "Et de xviij^d^ Williams operanti circae ligustrum in area et de iij^d^ pro radicibus ligustri."]

At Gonville and Caius College two trees at least are shewn in Gonville Court, one at the north-east and one at the north-west corner of the grass-plot, which is bounded by low railings, with posts at intervals. None appear in Caius Court; but an avenue of trees (as at present) leads from the Gate of Humility to the Gate of Virtue, and the Perse Court has a grass-plot with a tree in the centre, and a row of trees along its western side, close to the wall of the Fellows' garden. Posts and rails are carried round two sides of this grass-plot; and another row of rails, in the centre of which is an entrance flanked by two lofty posts, divides the whole court from the above-mentioned avenue[1].

At Trinity Hall there is a large fir-tree[2] in the centre of the eastern half of the principal court; and a small clipped yew at the south-west angle of the western grass-plot.

At Corpus Christi College there is a single large tree near the north-east corner of what was then the principal court. The grass-plots are defended by railings, subdivided, at intervals of a few feet, by tall and low posts, set alternately.

At Queens' College a fir-tree is shewn towards one side of the principal court, and there was probably a second opposite to it on the other side, the view of which is intercepted by the upper storey of the gate of entrance. There is also a single tree in the second court, as high as the eaves of the President's Lodge.

At Jesus College a large and spreading tree, known to have been a walnut-tree[3], stands in the centre of the first court.

At Christ's College there are no trees in the court, but one large tree—nearly twice as high as the chapel—stands in the yard between the chapel and the Master's "private Lodge," and a smaller tree a little to the eastward of it.

At S. John's College the grass-plots in the first court are edged with what the accounts shew to have been rosemary and sweetbriar.

At Emmanuel College there is a single tree in the centre of

[1] [Loggan's view of Gonville Court has been reproduced in the History of Gonville and Caius College, fig. 2: and that of the Perse Court in the Essay on "Chambers and Studies," p. 298.]

[2] [For the history of this tree see Vol. I. p. 216, *note.*]

[3] [History of Jesus College, Vol. II. p. 180.]

the principal court. Railings are shewn both in this court and in the first court. They were set up in 1613, and probably replaced the quick which had been planted in 1589[1].

At Sidney Sussex College the second court has a row of trees along the south and west sides, behind high posts and rails, and two trees on the grass-plot—one in the centre, the other close to the chapel.

PIGEON-HOUSE.—It may be gathered from the collegiate histories, that a pigeon-house once existed at every college except Clare Hall, Magdalene, and Sidney Sussex; and it is possible that there may have been one at these colleges also, for the early accounts of the two first-mentioned have not been preserved, and those of the last have not been examined in detail.

In the fifteenth and sixteenth centuries a pigeon-house was evidently regarded as a necessity, to be built as soon after the foundation of the college as possible. At King's Hall the pigeon-house was built in 1414—15; at King's College in 1449; and at Queens' College in 1505—6. At Peterhouse the date of erection has not been discovered, but the building is frequently mentioned in the early account-rolls; at Pembroke College it is shewn standing in the orchard on Lyne's map, dated 1574; it was built at Gonville Hall in 1536, as recorded by Dr Caius; at Corpus Christi College in 1547, by Matthew Parker, a work thought worthy of special commemoration by his panegyrist Josselin; at Jesus College in 1574; and at S. John's College in 1622, but the work then done was evidently only a rebuilding of an older structure.

Some of these pigeon-houses must have been of considerable size; that at S. John's College cost £109. 17*s.* 2½*d.*, and those at Queens' College and Jesus College had windows, for at the former in 1537—38, "Thirteen feet of glass for the windows of the pigeon-house" are paid for; and at the latter in 1575—76 we find, "for glasing ye doue-howsse conteyninge xliiij^{o} fott of glasse xxij^{s}."

The young birds were sold, probably in most cases for the use of the Hall, and occasionally a profit was realised, as at

1 [Audit-Book, 1588—89. "To Midleton for quicksett to sett the court wth iij^{s}." Ibid. *Exp. since* 20 *Apr.* 1613. "For rayling ye court, over and besyde ye bachalors monyes, xij^{li}. v^{s}. viij^{d}."]

King's Hall in 1416—17[1]. On this subject the following order, made at S. Catharine's Hall in 1560, is worth quotation:

"M^{d}. y^{t} y^{t} was Decreed ye xxviij day of September An^{o} Dni 1560 by ye whole consent off ye m^{r} and ye fellows off thys college y^{t} ye pygeonse off ye sayd college should be solde into ye commons for iiijd a dosyne and not above; and also yff ye m^{r} or any off ye fellowse wold bye off ye same for y^{er} owne vse in ye college they shall pay vjd a dosynne and not above; and ye rest to be sold for ye most advantage; all ye profyt off ye wch duffhousse to be devyded quarterly amongst ye m^{r} and fellowse off thys college[2]."

In the course of the seventeenth century the practice of keeping pigeons fell gradually into disuse. At Jesus College the pigeon-house was let on lease in 1633, and at Peterhouse in 1675. By the end of the century nearly all had been pulled down, for Loggan's accurate views shew a pigeon-house at three colleges only, viz. at Trinity Hall, at Queens' College, and at Christ's College; and in the two latter the building is in the Master's garden, and therefore was not the public property of the college. At Trinity Hall, however, the pigeon-house was still in use in 1730, as recorded by Warren.

Some curious notices of the articles required for keeping and feeding the birds occur in the accounts. At Peterhouse in 1546—47 four gallons of wort were bought to wash the nests; but the entries which recur most frequently have reference to the purchase of cummin-seed, a favourite lure[3], or salt, usually under the form "salt-cat" or "salt-stone." For instance, at Queens' College in 1578—79 we find:

"Item ij salte stones for ye fellowes pigeon howse iij^{s}. iiij^{d}.
Item a salte stone for ye m^{r} hys pigeon howse xvij^{d}.";

and at Jesus College in 1593—94 "for barly, comyn, and sault for ye doves iij^{s}. ii^{d}.," and, strangest entry of all, in 1651—52, "for a roasted dogg and comin seeds 00. 02. 00." Birds of prey, more numerous three centuries ago than at present, had to be guarded against, and birdlime for that purpose was purchased at Queens' College in 1513—14[4].

[1] [History of Trinity College, Vol. II. p. 441.]

[2] [Register of S. Catharine's Hall, I. A.]

[3] [Magn. Journ. of Queens' College, 1559—60, fol. 268 b. "Item pro cumino ad alliciendas columbas, v.d."]

[4] [Ibid. 1513—14, fol. 268 b. "Item x^{o} die novembris dedi ad jussum Mr Wahan

In explanation of the above-mentioned articles of food we will quote a few passages from John Moore's "Columbarium: or the Pigeon-House," first published in 1735[1].

"*The Salt Cat*

"Being thus enter'd on the Head of Diet, it necessarily leads us to consider a certain useful Composition call'd by the Fanciers a Salt Cat, so nam'd, I suppose, from a certain fabulous oral Tradition of baking a Cat * * *, with Cummin-Seed, and some other Ingredients as a Decoy for your Neighbour's Pigeons; this, tho' handed down by some Authors as the only Method for this Purpose, is generally laught at by the Gentlemen of the Fancy, and never practis'd.

The right Salt Cat therefore is, or ought to be, thus made: Take Gravel or Drift-Sand, Loom, such as the Brick-Makers use, and the Rubbish of an old Wall, or for want of this a less Quantity of Lime, let there be a Gallon of each; add to this a Pound of Cummin Seed, a Handful of Bay-salt, or Salt-Petre, and beat them all up together into a kind of Mortar * * *, and your Pigeons will take great Delight in it. * * * *

The Cummin-Seed, which has a strong Smell in which Pigeons delight, will keep your own Pigeons at home, and allure others that are straying about, and at a Loss where to fix upon a Habitation."

SWAN-HOUSE.—Allusions to a building called the swan-house in the accounts of King's College and Trinity College, suggest the collection of a few notes on the practice of keeping swans at those colleges and elsewhere.

At King's College swans are first mentioned in the accounts for 1554—55. After this we hear no more of them until 1570—71, when several entries occur:

"Item pro 4 modiis et di' le malte pro sagmacione Cignorum iij^{s}. x^{d}.
Item Jacobo Beckwith for vppyng ye Swannes and wynteryng them vt patet per billam .... xxiij^{s}.
Item for an action entred agaynst Cole of Horningsay for kyllyng a colledge Swanne .... xviij^{d}."

In 1571—72 the swan-house is mentioned for the first time, and in 1575—76 and following years "malte to fatt the swannes" is charged for. In 1600—1601 the following entries occur:

"Item solut' Fox le Clayer pro mending the Swanhouse walles iiij^{d}.
Item solut' Peere pro fabricanda fenestra in le Swanhowse ... xij^{d}."

tunc vices vice presidentis gerentis Johanni Fenys ad emendum viscum quo caperet aves deuorantes collumbas collegii ijd."]

[1] [Reprint by W. B. Tegetmeier, 8vo. London, 1879, p. 14.]

A longer entry than usual in 1641—42 shews that the college had then nine swans:

"Solut' Richardo Roby le Swanhopper pro le 9 Swans 1^{l}. 9^{s}.; et pro 9 dayes charges boat and man 1^{l}. 10^{s}.; et pro stipend' 1^{l}.; in toto vt patet per billam .... 3. 19. 0."

We have not been able to discover when the keeping of swans was given up.

At Trinity College, in 1550—51, the Junior Bursar pays "to goodman Gamsler for his fee for kepyng our Swans, vj^{s}. viij^{d}."; and, in the following year, "vnto Ball for his costes in ye marking tymes of Swannes ij^{s}. vj^{d}." The existence of a swan-house in the seventeenth century is shewn by sundry small payments for its repair, but its position is not known. A payment in 1662—63, "For the Alienacion of the Swanne marke, 00. 07. 08," though not easy to understand, proves at any rate that the college had a distinctive swan-mark of its own. In the eighteenth century five swans were kept. A yearly payment "to ye swan herd for feeding 5 Swannes" is entered regularly in the accounts down to 1782, after which year it does not again occur.

At Jesus College the following entry occurs in the accounts for 1601—2:

"Item to Cutbert Browne Swanherde for wintering 83 Swans xxvii^{s}. vj^{d}."

In succeeding years we meet with the following particulars:

1602—3. "Item giuen Bond for going to St Iues about our swan-marke .... xij^{d}.
Item ye swanherd for vpping swans .... ij^{s}. ix^{d}.
Item wages to ye swanherd .... vj^{s}. viij^{d}.

1603—4. Item to the swanherd when he brought a note of the swans .... v^{s}.

1607—8. Item to the swanheard (*sic*) for wintering 48 swans at 8^{d}. ye swan .... xxxij^{s}.

1608—9. Item to Arthur Jourdan of Willinghame for vpping of 7 brood of Swans, whereof ye Colledg hath 13 birds .... ij^{s}.

1609—10. Item to Arthur Jourdane for his charges about ye swans, and for taking vp halfe a dosen agaynst Christmas .... vj^{s}. viij^{d}.

1617—18. Item to a man of Bassingborne at our m^{r}. his appointment for looking to our swannes for ye space of two yeares .... x^{s}.

1619—20. For fatting and bringing of two swans at ye auditt iij^{s}. vj^{d}."

Similar entries occur down to 1628—29, after which year nothing having reference to swans has been detected in the accounts. It is evident that the birds were kept at a distance from Cambridge, probably at Willingham, for the purpose of supplying the fellows' table with a delicacy on special occasions.

The accounts of Christ's College shew that their swans were kept in the same way, on one of their estates, probably at Bourne in Cambridgeshire. They are first mentioned in 1594—95, when five shillings are given "to a Swaner for bringing a swane mark, and for markinge of 6 signetes giuen by Mr Collet of Burne"; but, as they are alluded to only twice afterwards, in small payments made "to the swanner" in 1596—97, and 1597—98, we ought perhaps to conclude that the keeping of them was discontinued after the latter date.

It should also be mentioned that swans were kept at Eton College, and that, probably, as explained in the History, one of the chambers on the first floor of the quadrangle was assigned to the swanherd[1].

At the present time swans are kept at S. John's College and at Emmanuel College; but we believe that at both these colleges the introduction of them is of comparatively recent date.

Swans were not the only birds kept in colleges. A raven was bought at Peterhouse in 1635—36[2]; and a pair at Queens' College in 1673—74, and again in 1737—38. An eagle appears in Loggan's view of the Great Court of Trinity College, for which a perch was bought in 1683—84, and a tub in the following year. A second eagle was kept at the same college in 1744—45. Lapwings were kept in Queens' College garden in 1708—9, and 1736—37.

BARBER'S SHOP.—The statutes of several colleges include a barber (*tonsor* or *barbitonsor*) among the servants who are to receive yearly wages. At Peterhouse he is to be paid twelve shillings yearly, "for shaving the beards and cutting the hair of

[1] [History of King's College and Eton College, Vol. I. p. 438, *note*. The Eton College swan-mark has been engraved by Yarrell, British Birds, ed. 1856, III. 226, 229. We cannot discover that any Cambridge swan-mark has been preserved.]

[2] [Account-roll, 1635—36: "Pro corvo in usum collegij, js. vjd."]

the Master, Fellows, scholars, and all other officers, as often as they require it[1]." Similar provisions will be found in the statutes of King's College, Jesus College, Christ's College, S. John's College, Trinity College, and Sidney Sussex College.

As early as 1454 we find a special locality in college assigned to the barber, and called the barber's shop (*barbitonsorium*)[2], at King's College. At Christ's College in 1657 "the Barber's chamber," and "the Barber's Roome" are mentioned. At Trinity College one of the old buildings near Bishop's Hostel was assigned to the barber. This fact rests on a college tradition[3]; but an entry in the Junior Bursar's accounts for 1695—96, for repairing "the vault in the grass-plot next ye Barber's shop"; and another in those for 1731—32 for leadwork to "the Bow window over the Barber's Shop," shew that that name was given to the place where he performed his duties.

STANGATE HOLE.—A place called Stangate Hole, Stangate Hall, Staincoat Hole, and Staincoat Passage, is mentioned in the accounts of Queens' College, Christ's College, S. John's College, and Trinity College; but unfortunately in such a manner as to give but little information about it. A note in explanation of the name, and of the use to which the place was put, is to be found among the collections of Dr Thomas Parne, who resided at Trinity College from 1714 to 1749, and who therefore must have been well acquainted with the customs of his own time. He is describing part of the Master's Lodge:

"Y^{e} Comedy room included both ye long Room where ye bow windows are, and some of ye present Master's Parlour, when they used to have leave to keep Christmas; ye Senior Soph and Bachelor were masters of ye Revels and ordered all things in College. One came with drums, the other with trumpets before him; ye fellows dined and supped promiscuously with ye scholars. They had a Pole or Colestaff, which they called ye Stang, on which servants and Scholars were carried by

1 [Commiss. Docts. ii. 84. For several amusing anecdotes respecting College Barbers, which it would be beside our purpose to quote in this place, see Wordsworth, University Society, etc. pp. 130—138.]

2 [King's College Mundum-book, 1453—54. "Johanni Cryspe carpentario pro labore suo et filii sui per tres dies circa facturam Muri inter cameram Janitoris et barbitonsorium per diem x^{d}. ij^{s}. vj^{d}."]

3 [Wordsworth, *ut supra*, p. 132.]

way of Punishment, the latter chiefly for missing Chapel. Stangate Hole was ye Place where this instrument of discipline used to be deposited[1]."

In the Scholars' Book of King's College—a traditional record of what each scholar was expected to do when he first became a member of the college—the new scholar is directed "to stand in the Stangate hole before grace, [and] under the Organ loft at Chappel." This passage leads us to conclude that just as a person standing under the organ-screen in chapel might take part in the service without being actually one of the congregation, so a person standing in Stangate Hole might be considered as virtually present at grace in hall, though not yet allowed to be there as of right, and that therefore Stangate Hole must at least have communicated with the hall. At Trinity College in 1703 the Junior Bursar mentions it in connection with the Buttery: "for 40 Quarries of glass in ye Butt' and Standgate hole"; and it was evidently, from other entries, a room of considerable size, lighted by a large window, and having a hatch of its own. The following extracts from the accounts give the most interesting particulars concerning it, and further, shew the curious changes of the name at different periods. In 1582—83, we meet with a payment for mending "standgate hole walles"; and for "makinge a paire of newe hookes for the hatche in stangat hole"; in 1599—1600, for "a new nosle of the lanthorne in stangate hole"; in 1612—13, "for 8 foote of newe glasse for the windowe in the Stangate Hole"; in 1614—15, for "setting in hookes and staples in the entrance into stangate hole," for "a new dore at the entrance into the stangate hole," and "a double dore in stangate hole"; in 1694—95, "for 4 foot of paving in Stangate hole"; in 1696—97, for "a deal for ye bench in Stangate Hall"; in 1703—4, "for a Lintell in Standgate hole window 11 foot long, and worke about shoreing up ye floore, and fixing ye Lintell"; in 1760—61, "for mending the windows in Stangate Hole"; in 1766—67, for

[1] [History of Trinity College, Vol. II. p. 624. In "A Collection of *English* Words not generally used," etc. by John Ray, ed. 1768, p. 57, we find, s. v. *Stang*: "This Word is still used in some Colleges in the University of *Cambridge*; to *stang* Scholars in *Christmas* time, being to cause them to ride on a Colt-staff, or Pole, for missing of Chapel." The punishment called "riding the stang" is described in A Glossary of North Country Words, by J. T. Brockett, Newcastle, 1846, ii. 155; and in Chambers' Book of Days, ii. 510.]

"mending staincoat Hole"; and, in 1768—69, "for work done in the Stangate Hole."

At S. John's College in 1782, it was "agreed that at the end of Stain coat passage doors be put up[1]"; and at the present day the passage from the hall screens to the kitchen is still called "Stankard Hole," a manifest corruption of the older name. It is therefore probable, that at this college, as at Trinity College, Stangate Hole was near the Buttery, for the passage leading from the hall-screens to the kitchen has the buttery on one side of it, and the pantry on the other. In confirmation of this view we find in the accounts for 1758—59 a payment for "ceiling Kitchen, and cleaning that and Staincoat Hole." On the other hand, in 1593—94 we have: "for mending S^{r} [blank] chamber in ye stangate hole ij^{s}. ix^{d}.," as though some special part of the college was then so termed.

At Queens' College Stangate Hole is mentioned four times in the accounts between 1617—18 and 1638—39, but only in connection with small repairs, which throw no light upon its position.

At Christ's College it is mentioned only once, in 1590—91: "for mending Stangate Hole."

On the whole, it may be concluded from these extracts, that the name, Stangate Hole, was applied in several colleges to a sort of lumber-place, where, among other things, the "stang" was kept; and that at S. John's College, and at Trinity College, it either formed part of the Buttery, or was close to it.]

[1] [Baker's History, ed. Mayor, ii. 1087.]

ADDITIONS TO THE THIRD VOLUME.

Schools, Library, Senate-House.

p. 118, l. 20. Since writing the History of the Library, an opportunity of studying Mr Cockerell's design has been afforded, through the kindness of Mrs Frederick Pepys Cockerell, who has most generously placed in my hands, for presentation to the University, a complete set of ground-plans, elevations, and detailed working-drawings, not only for the north wing, but also for the remaining portions, which the architect then believed would shortly be begun. The proposed dimensions and arrangements shall be briefly described.

The ground-plan is endorsed: "This was the last plan, made while the north wing was being erected, 1837 and 1838." It therefore shews that wing, as at present. This being masked, to a certain extent, by the Senate-House, the portico is placed symmetrically with respect to the rest of the façade, which projects fifteen feet in front of the north wing. The portico, set on a plinth extending the whole width of the façade, is twenty-two feet in depth, with nine columns in front, and one at each end, as shewn in Mackenzie's engraving, the authority for which was probably supplied by Mr Cockerell.

The central quadrangle, round which the buildings are grouped, measures 100 feet from north to south, by 92 feet from east to west. The ranges of building which form the sides of this are of different width, an arrangement rendered necessary by the irregular nature of the ground, and the varied purposes for which they were intended. The north side is 38 feet wide between walls, the east side 52 feet, the south side 33 feet, and the west side 48 feet at the south end, diminished to 37 feet at the north end. These buildings are divided in the following manner.

A door from the portico gives access to a vestibule, from which a visitor can either ascend the staircase to the library, placed, as at present, in the south-east corner, or proceed forwards to a corridor, which extends along the whole west side of the east range, so as to provide access dryshod either to the schools in the south range, or to the museums in the north range. A second entrance from the portico gives access to the Vice-Chancellor's room and the Registry; and a third to a lecture-room at the north end, communicating with the Geological Museum.

The south range contains four schools in the following order, beginning at the east end: Divinity, Arts, Physic, Law. At the west end of this range is a lecture-room, entered from a vestibule exactly opposite to, and corresponding with, the vestibule already described in the east range. This vestibule provides access to the quadrangle from Trinity Hall Lane.

The west range contains two buildings only: a large lecture-room, on the north side of the above-mentioned vestibule, communicating with the Mineralogical Museum, which adjoins it on the north.

The north range contains, at the west end, a Botanical Museum (to be entered either from the Mineralogical Museum, or by the existing staircase at the west end); a Zoological Museum (entered by a separate door from the quadrangle, and communicating with the Museums east and west of it); and, at the east end, a Geological Museum. In other words, the architect intended to accommodate three sciences in the space which is now barely sufficient for Geology. The party-walls being in the same positions as at present, Geology, in this primitive scheme, would have been restricted to the room now used as a lecture-room; Zoology would have occupied the central room, or principal Museum of Geology; and Botany the western division of it.

The Library occupies the first floor. It is entered at the east end of the south range, through a vestibule, containing the ticket-office, and a passage to the east room. By this means no one could enter or leave the library without being seen by the person in charge of the office. The irregular shape of the west side gives space for two librarians' rooms, lighted from the west, without encroaching on the space for the library.

p. 124. At the end of 1883 the want of space for books in the Library induced the Syndicate "to consider whether it might not be possible to make some use of the Arts and Law Schools, by refitting them in such a manner that the walls could be furnished with closed book-cases, while the body of the room could be made even more convenient than it is at present for general University purposes, such as Acts, Examinations, Discussions, Lectures, and Board and Syndicate meetings[1]." They proposed to deal with the Arts School in the first instance, for the alteration of which they subjoined a detailed scheme, prepared by W. M. Fawcett, M.A., architect. Their report having been confirmed by the Senate, 13 December, 1883, the work was carried out early in the following year. It was in the course of this that the discoveries already mentioned (p. 92), were made.

At the beginning of 1885 (6 May) a report of the Librarian to the Syndicate, recommending that the Law School should be given up to the Library, was published to the Senate. The following passage explains the changes suggested, which will be readily understood by reference to the plan (fig. 9).

"If the Law School were given up to the Library, as well as the small room adjoining at the west end, which communicates with the Arts School on the north, and with the lobby between it and the Syndicate room on the west, a considerable portion of the School might be assigned as a workroom, for which the situation would be admirably fitted, and the rest of the School might be furnished so as to hold a number of books which it is desirable to have within easy reach of the entrance to the Library. A doorway from the west side of the space at the foot of the great staircase would lead at once into the Law School and thus create a through communication between the various parts of the Library[2]."

The Senate having accepted this suggestion (18 June, 1885), the Syndicate obtained from Mr Fawcett a detailed plan for carrying out the necessary changes, which was embodied in a second report dated 25 November. It was confirmed by Grace, 17 December, 1885, and the work is now (April, 1886) in progress.

Before the commencement of these alterations to the Law

[1] Report of Library Syndicate, 14 November, 1883. Camb. Univ. Reporter, p. 177.

[2] Camb. Univ. Reporter, p. 680.

School, the statue of *Glory*, which had been placed at the east end of the School on its removal from the Senate-House in 1807, as above related (p. 61), was transferred by Grace of the Senate to the Fitzwilliam Museum[1].

Museums and Lecture Rooms for Natural Science.

p. 151, l. 24. Cole has preserved[2] an interesting description of the gateway of the Augustinian Friary, which stood on the north side of their ground, next Pease Hill, as that part of the Market Place is still called. The volume contains a transcript of Warren's work on Trinity Hall, which was completed, as recorded above (Vol. I. p. 237), in 1730, and the description is given as a note to the following passage:

"The Place where these St Austin's Fryers dwelt, was, I think, where Mr Buck now lives, in Free School Lane; and also where Mrs Wigmore now lives, where the Gate belonging to the House lets out towards the Pease Market Hill."

Upon this Cole proceeds as follows:

"Mrs Wigmore kept a Boarding Schole there for young Ladies, and was a very flourishing Schole before the late Wm Finch pulled [down] the old venerable Gateway, like a College, and much like that of Trinity Hall, having a large Portal and a smaller Wicket close to it, fronting the Pease Hill, in the very Place and on the very Spot where Finch built a good square Brick House. I am afraid the Lovers of Antiquities must be at a Loss for this old Gate Way, which I perfectly well remember; but was not so early initiated into these Studies at that Time. I have a copy of their Refectory, still standing [see above, p. 130], and which Mr Buck inhabited, in my Vol. 42, p. 261, tho' it is drawn rather too squat and short. Finch, an ironmonger, and very rich, out of Misery and Covetousness, only bought Part of the Scite: he might, and anyone but a Tradesman would, have purchased the Whole, it is lucky his Want of Taste prevented it: what he refused now makes the Botanic Garden. Wm Cole. Wedn: Mar: 29. 1780."

Mr Finch bought the property, described as a "Messuage or Tenement and premises in Saint Edward's parish," 1 June, 1720, and "pulled down most of the Old Buildings and built a very Capital Mansion house, Coach House, Stables, and Offices upon the Ground where the same stood, which house he resided in

[1] Camb. Univ. Reporter, 1885, p. 416.

[2] MSS. Cole, lviii. p. 47. Add. MSS. Mus. Brit. 5859.

many Years before his Death," which took place in or shortly after 1761. In 1783 (9 April) the house was bought by John Mortlock, Esq., and is now (1886) the residence and bank of Edmund John Mortlock, Esq. The position of the gateway of the Friary, which probably stood in the centre of the north side of their house, can therefore be identified with certainty[1].

Having become the owner of this house, Mr Mortlock bought the adjoining ground, as above related; and, in all probability, pulled down the Refectory shortly afterwards, for it is covenanted in the conveyance that he shall "at his costs and charges take down the said Capital Messuage or Tenement, and remove and carry away all the Materials and Rubbish thereof, and erect and support a Brick Wall to separate the Ground so agreed to be sold to him from the rest of the said Botanic Garden Ground."

The Hall.

p. 360, l. 15. The statement that the existing doors were added to the hall-screen at Trinity College in 1698 or 1703, is incorrect. The view of the interior of the hall, by Pugin, in Ackermann's Cambridge, published 1815, shews doors solid for only about four feet from the floor; above this solid portion are vertical bars set in a frame.

In addition to the pieces of tapestry in college halls here recorded it should be mentioned that at King's College in 1458—59, we meet with charges for the repair of hangings embroidered with lions, in addition to green hangings[2]. It may be conjectured that the former would ornament the dais, the latter the side-walls.

p. 364, l. 4. There were also stocks in hall at King's College, as we learn from an entry in the Mundum-Book for 1599—1600:

"Solut' Peer for a new payr of Stocks et a newe desk in aulâ, ij^{s}."

[1] These particulars have been ascertained from an examination of the title-deeds, which have been most kindly lent to me by my friend Mr Mortlock. The words between inverted commas in the last paragraph are quoted from the abstract of title.

[2] Mundum Book, 1458—59. "Item sol' ix^{no}. die maii Johanni Warner scissori pro labore suo circa reparaciones vestium aule viridum per iiij^{or}. dies et per totidem noctes xx^{d}. Item Johanni Reder xxviij^{o}. die maii in partem solucionis maioris summe sibi debite per collegium pro filo laneo per ipsum empto pro reparacione vestium aule cum leonibus ij^{s}."

The Library.

p. 425, l. 20. The inconvenience of having to consult chained books is insisted upon in the following description of the Bodleian Library, written in 1748:

"Nor is the Disposal and Ordering of their Books much approv'd; for the Books of the Principal Benefactors having a particular Place assign'd to each of them, a Student must run from one End of the Room to the other to consult Authors which treat of the same subject; for the Books being chain'd down, there is no bringing them together, even in the Library, much less can the Student consult them in his Study[1]."

p. 471. It should also be mentioned that the custom of borrowing a volume for a year, and at the end of it solemnly returning it, and then selecting another, had been practised in monasteries long before it was introduced into colleges. In illustration of this the following passage may be translated from the rules drawn up for the Order of S. Benedict by Archbishop Lanfranc:

"On the Monday after the first Sunday in Lent, before the brethren enter the chapter-house, the librarian (*custos librorum*) is to display the books on a carpet stretched on the floor, with the exception of those which have been lent out to read during the preceding year; these the brethren are to bring with them, each carrying his own in his hand. Of this duty they should be reminded by the librarian, on the preceding day. When they are assembled, the passage out of the Rule of S. Benedict on the observance of Lent is to be read aloud. A Sermon having been preached on that duty, the aforesaid librarian shall read a statement of the distribution of the books among the brethren during the preceding year. As each of them hears his name read out, he is to return the book which had been entrusted to him for reading the year before; and, if any one of them is conscious of not having read through the book which he has received, let him fall on his knees and ask forgiveness for his fault. When this is over, the aforesaid librarian shall assign another book to each of the brethren; and, when the distribution is over, he shall make a list of the books and their recipients[2]."

1 "The Foreigner's Companion through the Universities of *Cambridge* and *Oxford*," etc. p. 27.

2 Lanfranci Opera, ed. Giles, Oxford, 1844, i. 98. This passage was kindly sent to me by my friend the Rev. G. F. Browne, B.D., S. Catharine's Coll.

GLOSSARY.

THE following abbreviations have been used: *Arch. Nom.* for: "Architectural Nomenclature of the Middle Ages." By Robert Willis, M.A. 4to. Camb. 1844. Camb. Antiq. Soc. Quarto Publ. No. IX. *Gloss. of Arch.* for: "A Glossary of Terms used in Grecian, Roman, Italian, and Gothic Architecture." 8vo. Oxford, 1850. *Finchale Priory*, for "The Charters of Endowment, etc., of the Priory of Finchale, in the County of Durham," ed. Surtees Soc. 1837.

ANTIQUE or ANTYK: a term used in woodwork, usually to denote a special kind of border or crest. In the account for wainscoting Queens' College hall (ii. 62), it is also applied to the heads used in decoration. It probably signifies there what we should call classical. In the "Rites of Durham," p. 9, we find "curious *antick* worke, as beasts and men upon horsebacks, etc."

ARRIS: the edge of a stone or piece of wood; Old French *areste*, now *arête*. Arch. Nom. p. 24.

ASHLAR, ASSHELER, or ASCHLER: hewn or squared stone used in building. The word usually occurs in combination, as: "assheler rough scapled, or assheler chapman ware"; "perpendaschler" or "parpin aschler," *q. v.* etc.

ASHLAR PIECES: in carpentry, short upright pieces about 3 feet high, fixed between the rafters and the floor in garrets, in order to make more convenient rooms by cutting off the acute angles at the bottom. Gloss. of Arch. *s. v.* The word occurs in the contract for timber-work to be supplied to Trinity Hall, 1374, i. 238; and in the similar documents for Queens' Coll. ii. 8, 10.

AT: preposition used between a Christian name and a substantive to describe the person mentioned by means of his residence. The following combinations have come under our notice: Christopher att Wode (Eton Building Acts.): Gerardus at y[e] pond (Roll of S. Mary's Gild, Treasury of Corp. Chr. Coll.): Johannes atte Cherche de Teuersham: Johannes in the Lane de noua Wyndesor, John at Gate, (Eton Building Acts.): Johannes at Wode (Acts. of King's Coll.): Richard atte hatch: Roger atte Strete (Eton Building Acts.): Simon ad aquam: Symon at y[e] Watyr (Roll of S. Mary's Gild, *ut supra*): Thomas atte le, spelt Ateleye in the conveyance (Eton Building Acts.): William atte Conduit: William atte Ree. In the last example *atte* is for "at the."

BANKER: a cushion. "Item ij *bankeres* de rubeo say precii vj[s]. viij[d]." Inventory of Clare Hall (iii. 360, *note*).

BASTARD: Audit-book of S. John's Coll. 1524–25: "Item payd to John Turner in full payment for wrytting a stattut boke in a *basterd* hand vj[s]. viij[d]. Item...in p[t] of payment for wrytting a stattut boke in a smaller hand vj[s]. viij[d]." In French *lettre bâtarde* is: "une sorte de lettre qui est entre la lettre ronde et la lettre italique." Dict. de l'Academie, ed. 1814.

BEAM FILLING: "pro le *beamefillinge* le gallery," i. 73. It probably means the filling up of the spaces between the beams to keep out the weather. Comp. Fabric Rolls of York Minster, ed. Surtees Soc. p. 250: "Chorus ecclesie est defectivus in coopertura et muris lapideis, et *bemefillyng*, et quod pluit multociens super altare, etc."

BEAVER: a term of carpentry; "5 foote of oake *Beavers* for Mr Smith Stairs"; Acts. of Jun. Burs., Trin. Coll. 1701–2.

BECKETT or BEKETTE: a word applied to stone cut in a particular form. Acts. of King's Hall, ii. 442, note 4. In the contract for the Second Court of S. John's Coll. (1598) it is provided that "the chimneys with their *becketts* shalbe of good whit ston" (ii. 252). In the contract for Bishop's Hostel (1669) the word is similarly used (ii. 557). Loops of rope round the gunwale of a life-boat are called *beckets.* Penny Mag. 19 May, 1832, p. 66. In Wright's Glossary the word is said to mean a mantelpiece in Northamptonshire. As applied to a chimney it may signify the projecting molding which in late work is frequently carried round the chimney-stack near the top.

BEDMOLDING: in Grecian and Roman architecture, the moldings of a cornice immediately below the corona. Gloss. of Arch. *s. v.* ENTABLATURE.

BEGINNER: the first pieces of stone or wood. In a window the commencement of the monials. The word often occurs in the Acts. of King's Hall and elsewhere: "Et de ixs. in vj. *begynners* pro fenestris." Peterhouse Bursar's Roll, 1462–63.

BENCH-TABLE: explained by Prof. Willis (Arch. Nom. p. 28) to mean the stone seat which runs all round the inside of the wall of a church.

BENT: "a *bent* for the Parlour 00.01.08." Magn. Journ. of Queens' Coll. 1672–73, p. 160. The word may signify rushes.

BERNE: "werkemen dryving the *berne* into the quadrant of the College." Building Acts. of Eton Coll. 1447–48, i. 389, *note* 1.

BICE or BISSE: a grayish blue colour (i. 519, ii. 199, *note* 1), from the French *couleur bise.* Comp. Italian *bigio.* The word is still used. In the Acts. for wainscoting S. John's Coll. hall (1528–39) "*byse* paper" occurs (ii. 309, *note* 2).

BILEXION: a molding carried round the panels of doors when they project beyond the plane of the framing; "large faire pannells and *balection* molding." Contract for Pembroke Coll. Chapel, 1664; i. 156; i. 104, *note* 2.

BLEW ORCH, and BLEW YONDE: shades of blue used in fresco painting; i. 412, *note* 3. It has been suggested by Prof. Skeat that *blew yonde* is an English form of *ultramarine*, and short for "blue of beyond sea."

BOKILL: a chain for books, the smallest of three specified kinds; iii. 431, *note* 4.

BOLLE: a ball; ii. 448, *note* 5.

BOROW: surety; i. 310.

BOUGHT: bend, curve; ii. 564.

BOWKE: "of the which Rodeloft the utter parte toward the *Bowke* of the same Chirche," contract for Eton Roodloft, 1475, i. 596. *Bowke* is the old spelling of *bulk*, German *bauch*, the belly. Halliwell (*s.v.* Bouke) shews that it is used for the interior of a building.

BRACE or BRASE: any oblique piece of wood that is used to *brace* and bind together the principal timbers of a frame, as of a roof (iii. 95, fig. 21).

BRISSEL CLOTH: "Item payd for xxxvij elles of *brissel clothe* at vd. ob. ye ell for the scolers table xvijs vd." Christ's Coll. Audit-Book 1532–33. "Item for a *brissels tycke* into the master's lodgin xxxijs." Magn. Journ. of Queens' Coll. 1585–86, fo. 181 *b*.

BURGUNDY GLASS: frequently contrasted in contracts with Normandy glass; and also used alone; i. 205, 543 *note* 3; ii. 572.

BYRTUR: In the account of the entertainment of King Henry VII. at King's Hall in 1505–6 we find: "It' solutum est in aduentu regis pro duobus *byrturs* et duodecim rabbettes iiij^{s}. vj^{d}." Halliwell *s.v.* says that *birt* is a turbot. Prof. Skeat suggests that *byrturs* may be an error for *byttturs*, i.e. bitterns.

CALABS or CHALYBS, steel: occurs only in the phrase "pro empcione Liiij garb' *calabis*," i. 389, note 3. Comp. Finchale Glossary, *s.v.* calibs.

CANDLE-BEAM: "Roodelofte and Candell beame," ii. 243.

CANTWISE: in the contract for the Legge Bg. it is provided (i. 207) that the chimneys are to be brought up *cantwise* i.e. cornerwise. It is explained (Gloss. of Arch. p. 107) that *cant* or *canted* is a term in common use to express the cutting off the angle of a square. The view of the Legge Bg. (iii. 298) shews that the chimneys were set in such a way that an angle, instead of a flat side, was turned towards the spectator. An oriel window is sometimes called a *cant* window (Gloss. of Arch. *ut supra*). *Cant* is simply corner; see Skeat's Dict. *s. v.*

CARRELL: a small study, iii. 327. At Finchale Priory the word is spelt "caroll."

CARSY: Acts. of King's Coll. 1615–16: "Sol' pro a yard et quarter of green *carsy* at 5^{s}. the yard, vj^{s}. iij^{d}." Carsy is the old form of *kersey*, a coarse woollen cloth.

CASEMENT: a deep, hollow molding: Gloss. of Arch. *s.v.*

CASSHEPEED: see TABLE.

CAST OF BREAD: Eton Acts. 1443. "Watkyn Wynwick for ij *cast* of brede and vij galons of Ale" i. 389, *note* 1.

CELAR: a room on the ground-floor, as contrasted with a solar, a room on the first floor. This is well illustrated by the enumeration of the rooms at King's Hall, ii. 431, and by the following passage quoted in Anstey's Munimenta Academica, i. 227: "statutum est quod libri legati dictæ Universitati ponantur in solario ad hoc specialiter deputato, super *cellario* in quo Regentes communiter congregantur."

CELATURA: plastering or wainscoting of walls. See SEELING, and Gloss. of Arch. *s.v.* CEILING.

CERUSE: whitelead, ii. 199, *note* 1.

CHAIRE-ORGAN: The word chaire-organ occurs at King's Coll. 1606, i. 519; at Trin. Coll. 1609–10, ii. 575; and at S. John's Coll. 1697–98: "To Robert Dalton for painting and guilding y^{e} *chaire organ* in the Master's Lodging per billam 0.10.0." May not *chare*, service, explain both *chaire*-organ, and *chare*-roof? A chaire-organ is a small organ which does the service of the larger one; and the chapel of King's Coll. is to be roofed with a supplementary stone roof which is to do the service of the usual wooden roof.

CHAMERANT or CHAMERAUT: a word of frequent occurrence in lists of worked stones. It is probably the same as "chaumeres," which Prof. Willis explains (Arch. Nom. p. 57) by "*jawmers*, i.e. stones for the jambs" of windows or doors. In the Acts. of King's Hall (ii. 445 *note*) we have "chamerantz pro magna porta," i.e. stones for the jambs of the great gate.

CHAMFER: an arris or angle which is slightly pared off is said to be *chamfered;* a *chamfer* resembles a splay, but is much smaller: the words apply to woodwork as well as to stones.

CHAPMANWARE: occurs in the combinations "ashlar chapmanware," and "paces chapmanware."

CHARE-ROOFED: In the Will of King Henry VI. the chapel of King's Coll. is directed to be "embatelled, vauted, and *chare rofed*" (i. 369). This is usually explained to mean "roofed with hewn stone"; chare being a supposed corruption of *quare* "to cut into pieces" (Halliwell). Comp. *quar*, "a quarry." See CHAIRE-ORGAN.

CINDULA: explained by Ducange, *s. v.* scindula, to mean split wood used for roofing. Comp. modern English "shingle."

CIROTHECA: a glove.

CIRPA: a rush (ii. 448, *note* 1), a corruption of the classical *scirpus*.

CLABBORD: wood for building-purposes: "all maner of wood, waynscote, clabbourd, tymbre"; ii. 469. "Clapboard, a board cut ready to make casks, etc." Bailey's Dict.

CLADÆ: laths. Eton Coll. Building Acts. i. 387, *note* 3.

CLAUSTRUM: court, or cloister, according to the context.

CLERIESTORY or CLERESTORY: any window, row of windows, or openings, in the upper part of a building. Gloss. of Arch. *s. v.* In the contract for a range of chambers at S. Cath. Hall, 1611, it is provided that there shall be bay-windows next the court,—"and convenient lights on thotherside by Cleriestories" (ii. 111).

CLICKETT or CLIKAT: a small lock, for which a number of keys were provided, as we should say, latch-keys (iii. 397). The word is still used in Shropshire near Craven Arms. See Miss Jackson's Glossary.

COBIRONS: irons to support fire-logs, andirons. "Item for mendynge both ye greate cobyerons belonginge to ye parloure xiiij^d^." Magn. Journ. of Queens' Coll., 1565—66, fo. 52 *b*.

COPEROSE: occurs in a list of painter's colours, ii. 199, *note*. Comp. modern *copperas*.

COPOROWNE or COPPORON: Prof. Willis explains (Arch. Nom. p. 32) that the rising part of a battlement is called a "cop," in distinction to the "crenels" or "spaces." In the Acts. for building King Edward's gate at Trin. Coll. (ii. 446, *note* 3) "*copporons* peces" are probably part of the battlements. In other passages the word seems to mean pinnacles, or even chimneys (ii. 438, *note* 5); as also in the Acts. of King's Hall for 1431–32, "Item xxxij crawfett, et xvj clampes pro caminis iungent' *copporons*."

CORBEL-TABLE: explained by Prof. Willis (Arch. Nom. p. 29) to mean "the upper table below the battlements, which derives its name from the sculptured flowers or knots [corbels] at equal distances, with which it is commonly decorated."

CORPORASSE: the cloth on which the consecrated elements were laid in the Mass; i. 551, *note* 1.

CORRODIUM, CORRODY: a right to board, lodging, and other necessaries, claimed by founders of religious houses, and sometimes created by grant of the house itself. Oliver, Monast. Exon. *s.v.*

COUNTERPAINE: the counterpart of a legal document, ii. 735.

COUNTERPOINT: a counterpane. Acts. of Christ's Coll. 1531–32: "for mendyng of y^e^ *cownter poynt* in ye M^rs^ chamber."

COUPLES: see SPAR.

COURT-CUPBOARD: iii. 353.

COWESEE: "item for iij elles of *cowesee* holland at xxij^d^. the ell v^s^. vj^d^." Jun. Burs. Acts. Trin. Coll. 1564–65. *Cowesee* may mean stitched; Fr. *cousu*.

COWTRE: "all the stallez of the Quere from the *cowtre* upward": Contract for Eton Roodloft, 1475, i. 597. May *cowtre* be a contracted form of cowntre = counter?

CRAGG: occurs only in the phrase "a *cragg* of sturgeon," ii. 692, *note* 4. "*Crag*, the neck." Bailey's Dict.

CRESSES: crests, i. 207.

CRICKET: a small stool; "For a *cricket* for the Vice-Master to kneel upon ix^s^." Sen. Burs. Acts. Trin. Coll. 1641–42; see also ii. 709, *note* 2.

CRIPPLE-ROOF: ii. 112. In some parts of England *cripples* are bent timbers: and a *cripple-roof* is probably one made of them, in distinction to a hipped roof, which is made of straight timbers.

CROCEILE: a building adjoining Eton Coll. church, perhaps a transept, i. 395.

CROSS SOMMER: a main beam of a floor or roof. Gloss. of Arch. *s. v.* SOMMER.

CROSSE DORMAUNTES: beams forming part of a floor or roof, explained and figured, iii. 94—96. Comp. also i. 311.

CROSSE-GARNET: a hinge. Audit-Book of S. John's Coll. 1601–2: "for a paire of crosse-garnetts for the dore of the leades of Mr Presidents Chamber xd.": Jun. Burs. Trin. Coll. 1614–15: "Item a paire of crosgarnetts for a dore coming out of the Mrs lodging." Comp. also i. 108, *note*. Gloss. of Arch. *s. v.* GARNETT.

CROSSE QUATERS: quatrefoiled openings (*quaters*) so arranged that the lines between them intersect each other at a right angle. Described and figured, ii. 497.

CROWNE-TREE: the highest beam of a roof, the ridge-piece.

CURTILAGE: a word of frequent use in medieval conveyances. Cowell (Interpreter, ed. 1727) derives it from the French *cour*, and explains it to mean "a yard, backside, or piece of ground lying near a dwelling-house, where they sow hemp, beans, and such like". Compare Italian *cortile*, and old French *courtil.*

CUSTODIA: a guard, a term of book-binding. Acts. of King's Hall, 1421–22, *Exp. circa novam librariam:* "Item pro viij pellibus percamini pro custodiis, xijd."

CYNCTOURS: "the temporary support placed under vaults and arches to sustain them while they are in building" (Gloss. of Arch. *s. v.* CENTERING), ii. 445.

DEAMBULATIO: a gallery, iii. 338.

DICHEADED: an epithet for nails, i. 74; perhaps *thick*headed.

DIKKAR: ten of anything. Sen. Burs. Acts. Trin. Coll. 1553—54. "It' to John Barbour for a dikkar of knives."

DIUISA: a stream of water, ii. 190, *note*.

DO: in the sense of "cause." "The same shall do make and be brought to London," Eton Contract, 1442, i. 386; "Walter Nicholl shall make, or do to be made," 1475, i. 597; comp. also i. 309, 311, 336.

DOBLETTES or DOWBLETTES: a term for worked stone, ii. 442, *note* 4.

DOCELETTES: do., ii. 445, *note* 1.

DOCER or DOSSER: a hanging at the back of the high-table in hall; iii. 358, *note* 5; 360, *note* 11. Spelt also *dorser.*

DOLE: defined by Cowell as "a part or portion, most commonly of a meadow, in which several persons have shares"; ii. 409. A *dole* is described, with figures, in Hone's Everyday Book.

DORMANTES or DORMANS: i. 311, ii. 698; see CROSSE DORMAUNTES.

DORNICK or DORNAR: a kind of coarse cloth originally made at Tournay, called in Flemish, Dornick: i. 419; ii. 608; iii. 349.

DREWILL: "Item ij *drewills* ponderant' iiijli, vijd." Acts. of King's Hall, 1431–32.

ENDSTONES: a term for worked stones, i. 391, 392.

ESTRICHBORD: a particular kind of planking, of uncertain derivation, i. 389, *note* 3. Acts. of King's Hall, 1431–32: "Item pro xv. *hestrysbord* viz. waynscot vjs. viijd." The Finchale Glossary gives "bordis de Estland or Estland bordis. Boards, or timber, from Norway." *Estrich* may be a corruption of Östreich or Eastland, whence "Eastland boords" (Arch. Nom. p. 23). See RIGALBOARD.

EVESBORD: ii. 446, *note* 2; the board which underlies the tiles at the lower edge, or *eaves*, of a sloping roof.

EXCELSES: garrets, i. 206; explained and figured, iii. 305, 306.

EXENNIUM: a complimentary present, or Xenion. Comp. Ducange, *s. v.*

FASTINGHAM: the beginning of Lent, ii. 572.

FAUCE BOTERACE: i. 309. Explained by Prof. Willis (Arch. Nom. p. 76) as "a buttress with a false bearing," one which does not "stand fairly and directly upon a foundation."

FELEWELL: a term for worked stone. Acts. of King's Hall, 1428–29. "Item pro viij peciis de *felewell.*"

FERMENT: ironwork, *ferramenta*, i. 401.

FEY: to clean. Sen. Burs. Acts. of Trin. Coll. 1550–51. "It' to a laborer for *feynge* of y[e] kinges diche in y[e] frears vj[d]."

FLASH: Jesus Coll. Acts. 1574–75: "Item to the Plummer one day for settinge in lead over the chappell on the north side of the steple where the *flasshes* were taken awaye, and for souldringe xij[d]."

FLORISHED GLASS: a kind of glass, defined in the foll. passage from the Eton Coll. Building Acts. i. 394, *note* 3: "Vitri operati picti vocati *florisshed glasse* cum diuersis ymaginibus." It is there contrasted with "powdred glasse" ibid. note 1: "vitri operati vocati powdred glasse cum xij ymaginibus prophetarum." Comp. also i. 393, *note* 3; 403, *note* 4.

FLOWER-GENTLE: amaranth, i. 180, *note.*

FOOTCLOTH: "Doctors in their formalityes and vpon their footscloths," iii. 35; a term usually applied to housings of cloth hung on horses.

FORMPIECES: pieces of stone shaped for tracery; "form" being the medieval word for a stone frame, or seat, for glass. Arch. Nom. pp. 48, 49.

FOTHER: a measure, usually of lead, varying in diff. parts of the country. London and Hull, 19½ cwt.: Derby, 22½ cwt.: Newcastle, 21½ cwt.: Whitaker's Almanack, 1876, p. 810. It was also used for rope and lime. Acts. of King's Coll. 1483: "It' pro x. fother cordarum"; Ibid. 1573: "pro vno foder le lyme."

FOURE: a term applied to the divisions of glass in a window; ii. 571. *Foure* may perhaps be a translation of "*quarrell.*"

FRANCHESE: in the phrase "franchesies and liberties," ii. 469. Ducange explains *franchisia* as: "Districtus seu territorium certis privilegiis et juribus donatum, quo sensu *Franchisia* idem quod aliis *Septena*, *Banleuca.*"

FRENCH EAVES, FRENCH PANEL: ii. 564, 699.

——— ROOF: in the contract for Bishop's Hostel at Trin. Coll. ii. 557, a *French roof* is probably a high-pitched roof.

FRET: "a *frette* to hang vppon the rooffe with croked battones and strayte battones," ii. 564; "three rowes of large square pannells...which will proue the best *fret*," ii. 535. In these passages the two ideas of ornamentation by crossed or interlacing lines, or by roughening the surface, both appear (Gloss. of Arch. *s. v.* FRET).

FRETTISH: to ornament, ii. 260; evidently from the medieval verb *frectare.*

GALLERY: for the various uses of this word see the INDEX.

GARBA: a sheaf, orig. of corn; but applied to denote a certain quantity of other substances, e.g. steel, i. 389, *note* 3.

GARYTE or GARRET: orig. a watch-tower; ii. 403, 404, *note* 1.

GEMEWES, GEMMERS, GYMMOWS, GEMOYS: hinges. The word, which is very common, is variously spelt: King's Coll. Mundum Book (1502–3) *Custus ecclesie:*

"Item Otte fabro pro duobus Seris et duobus clauibus cum ij paribus de *gemewes* in quadam Cista pro libris Cantuum reponendis xiiij^d^."; Ibid., 1555–56: "Item sol' pro le *gymmows* pro hostio in le conductes court, iiij^d^."; "Item for a new wooden casement to one of my chamber wyndowes wth two *gemmers* to it xviij^d^." Magn. Journ. of Queens' Coll. 1565–66, fo. 52 *b*. The word is derived from the Latin *gemellus*, double.

GENERALL: a yellow colour used in fresco painting, i. 412, *note* 3.

GIRT, GIRT-HOUSE: *Girt* is a beam of particular dimensions (i. 311); and also a standard of measure, i. 156. *Girt-house* (ii. 111) is probably a range of building composed principally of such timber.

GLOGGES: timber, probably, like *girt*, of a particular size. "Item iisdem Joanni et Philippo pro dissecatione magnorum lignorum siue *le glogges* ad eundem murum." Mag. Journ. of Queens' Coll. 1552–53, fo. 214 *b*.

GLOMERIA: the derivation and meaning of this word are uncertain. The Master of *Glomery* had the direction of the school of grammar, but the office evidently involved more than this (iii. 2, and *note* 3). Prof. Skeat considers that *glomery* is another form of gramarye, i.e. grammar.

GOGION or GOODYON: an iron spindle for a wheel. Jun. Burs. Acts. Trin. Coll. 1550: "payde for two *goodyons* to repare a whelebarow ij^d^." Ibid. 1556–57: [to the smith] "for mending a *gogion* for one of ye whelebarowes, j^d^." It is also used for iron applied to stonework (Fabric Rolls of York Minster, ed. Surtees Soc. *s.v.*). The English word gudgeon is still used in the same sense.

GOOTWICH: a kind of cloth, or canvas. Acts. of King's Coll. 1544–45: "Item pro xiiij vlnis *Gootwich* pro borders in aula ij^s^. iiij^d^. ob. Item pictori pingenti le *Gootwich*, x^s^. ij^d^."

GOSFOTE: possibly a kind of hinge. It occurs in the Building Acts. of Eton Coll. quoted i. 417, *note* 1.

GRAIL: a service-book, in Latin *gradale*. Acts. of Christ's Coll. 1554–55. "Item for a *gralle* to ye chappell, xiij^s^. iiij^d^." Ibid. S. John's Coll. 1554–55. "Item for a newe *graill* prycked in parchemente, xl^s^."

GRASTABLE: a term for worked stones in the Building Acts. of Eton Coll., i. 391; see TABLE.

GRECE or GRESE: a step; i. 355, ii. 10. This is the plural form of the old English *gre*, a step.

GRESYNGE: used apparently for a staircase; "tymber for *gresynges* and midel walles," ii. 10.

GROGERAN: a coarse stuff, in French *gros-grain*. Acts. of King's Coll. 1615–16. "Sol' pro 2 yards of wrought *grogeran* at 10^s^. 6^d^. the yard xxj^s^"; bought for use in the chapel.

GROUNDS: foundations, i. 387, and *note* 4; see also TABLE.

GROUNDCILLS: a foundation. In carpentry, the beam laid along the ground for the rest of the work to stand upon, i. 205, 238, 388, *note* 5; ii. 198, *note* 2. A verb to *groundsill* was also used, i. 392, *note* 1.

GROUND-TABLE: see TABLE.

GYNNE: a piece of machinery; in French *engin*, i. 608. Comp. Skeat's Dict. *s.v.*

GYSTE: a joist, *q.v.*

HAIR-CLOTH: a coarse cloth principally used in building operations, ii. 488, *note* 3, and sometimes for other purposes, as for altar cloths, i. 221, *note*.

HALF-STOREY: the third floor in ranges of chambers, extending into the roof for a short distance, ii. 249. For a complete explanation see the Essay on *Chambers and Studies*, iii. 297–311.

HAMBOROW: Acts. of Christ's Coll. 1605–6: "Item for .24. yards of *hamborowe* 23^{s}." The word usually means a horse collar.

HANGEDAX: a latch, ii. 442, *note* 1. In the Acts. of King's Hall the word is variously spelt: *hagodatrys, hagoday, hagodday, hafgooddays.*

HANSE: the curve or spandrel of an arch; Gloss. of Arch. *s.v.*

HANSE HEAD: the stonework composing the arch of a window, door, etc., i. 207.

HARLYNG-RODS: Acts. of King's Coll. 1570–71: "Item for a lode of *harlyng roddes* pro ede columbaria, viij^{s}."

HEART-LATH: a kind of lath, usually contrasted with *sap-lath.* Contract for Bishop's Hostel, 1669, ii. 558. "All the said particions to be lathed with good sound lath, *heart* and *sapp* to be mingled." Comp. also ii. 697.

HETHSTON: a kind of stone frequently mentioned in the Building Accounts of Eton College; e.g. i. 392.

HEWSTON of KENT: a stone (hewn stone?) frequently mentioned in the same Acts. e.g. i. 399; probably the stone called Kentish rag, which is extensively used in the Church (p. 424).

HOBBLEDINS: Acts. of King's Coll. 1589–90, among a number of entries recording the purchase of timber; "Item solut' Atkinson pro dimid' bigat' de *hobbledins* v^{s}."

INKLE: a kind of tape. Jun. Burs. Acts. Trin. Coll. 1619–20: "For silke and *inckle* for the [curtains in the Master's Lodge] ij^{s}. iiij^{d}."

INTAYLER: a carver; comp. Skeat, Dict. *s. v.* ENTAIL.

INTEGA: a mat or cushion, i. 76. The word does not occur elsewhere, but the meaning is decided by the next entry: "pro aliâ *mattâ* in sedem ministri." The Latin word *teca* signifies a case, mod. English *tick*, for a bed.

JENTACULUM: an entrance-feast. It was apparently obligatory on a freshman to give one of these on coming to college, ii. 440, *note* 3.

JOINT-TABLE: see TABLE.

JOIST: the horizontal timbers in a floor, on which the flooring is laid (Gloss. of Arch. *s.v.*). The word is variously spelt: GYSTE; IOYCE; JESTYS.

JOPPY: a term of carpentry, used to define a certain part of a roof, but the explanation is exceedingly difficult, as Prof. Willis admits (Gloss. of Arch. *s.v.* JOPY, JAWEPIECE). In the contract for the roof of the Library it has been interpreted to mean a cornice (iii. 95, fig. 21; comp. also ii. 10); but in the contract for the roof of S. Benedict's ch. (i. 283, 284, fig. 15), a triangular piece of wood interposed between the principals and the spars forming the roof, in fact, a jaw-piece.

JUSS: Acts. of S. John's Coll. 1639–40: "To Miton his allowance for his *Jusses* this quarter xiij^{s}." Ibid. 1640–41: "To Miton for his allowance in *iusses* this quarter xiij^{s}." Possibly *juss* is a corruption of *ioutes*, pottage (Prompt. Parv. p. 265).

KEY: the great stone placed at the intersection of the ribs of a vault, and usually decorated with sculpture, ii. 446, *note* 3 (Arch. Nom. p. 43).

KING'S-TABLE: a term for worked stone supplied to King's Hall, ii. 440, *note* 4. Prof. Willis (Arch. Nom. p. 36), basing his explanation on the use of the word at Ely, considers that it means a special ornament used there, and called King's table because imitated from the King's seal. This ingenious explanation does not suit the passage quoted above, where the stone is used for the steps of the oven. It is probably a workman's term, the signification of which is now lost.

KNEELER: "cornises and kneelers over everie window of free stonne," i. 205. A knee, or *kneeler*, was the return of the dripstone at the spring of the arch (Gloss. of Arch. *s. v.* KNEE). In the contract for the Legge Bg. (i. 207) *kneelers* are joined with whelmers. In the Gloss. of Arch. *s. v.* WHEELERS and KNEELERS, the former are described to be the level stones of a battlement, the latter the upright.

LAGENA: a measure of liquids. Its capacity is discussed, iii. 579, *note*. Comp. Finchale Priory, Glossary, *s. v.*

LATCH: to cover with lath, ii. 252; probably an error for *latth*.

LATEYS: a lattice, ii. 449, *note* 4. It is also spelt *lettesse*. Acts. of S. John's Coll. 1574–75, "For *lettesse* for the Master's gallery, xvij^s. ij^d."

LAYSTOWE: a dunghill, i. 222.

LEEDLATHS: a kind of oak-laths, iii. 93.

LEGEMENT, LEGEMENT-TABLE: a term for worked stones in the Building Acts. of Eton Coll. and elsewhere; i. 386; ii. 445, *note* 1. See TABLE.

LETTOUR: a reading-desk, ii. 243. Comp. Skeat's Dict. *s. v.* Lectern.

LIERNE STOOD: the king-post of a wooden roof, described and figured, iii. 95, fig. 21. Here *stood* is stud; see STODYS.

LIMNER: Acts. of S. John's Coll. 1634–35: "P^d. Parrett for washing the *limner* in the chappell last quarter and this quarter, iiij^s."

LINTHIAMEN: a sheet, ii. 444, *note* 2.

LIRE: Acts. of King's Coll. 1503–4: "Item sol' Thome Hoggekyng pro *liryng* de hangyng pro aula communi xij^d."

LOCKETT: in ironwork, the cross-bar of a window, ii. 252.

LOCKRAM: a cheap kind of linen. Skeat, Dict. *s. v.* (Comp. i. 442, *note*.)

LOPP ET CROPP: faggot wood, i. 391, *note* 3, and Eton Building Acts., *passim*.

LUTHERAN WINDOWS: Contract for Bishop's Hostel at Trin. Coll. 1669: "with hansome Lutheran windowes in the roofe," ii. 557; contrasted (p. 558) with the "transome windowes" used in other parts of the building. The windows in the roof, which have not been altered since Loggan's print was taken about 1688, are dormer-windows of two lights, surmounted by a pediment.

MARCH-PANE: a kind of cake, the recipe for which is given by Halliwell, *s. v.*

MEDLEY: a kind of cloth, i. 382, *note*.

MENSULA: a board, ii. 446, *note* 5.

MEREMIUM: timber.

MERLON: "the solid part of an embattled parapet, standing up between the embrasures, sometimes termed a *cop*." Gloss. of Arch. *s. v.*

METEYERD: a measuring rod, a yard in length, i. 309. Comp. Levit. xix. 35.

MINIONS: see MONYELL.

MISA: money spent, French *mise*. It usually occurs in the phrase "pro misis et exspensis," ii. 437, *note*.

MODRESTONE: a name for stone brought to Eton Coll. i. 386, *note* 2. It is occasionally spelt MOLDRESTONE, i. 388.

MOLD or MOOLD: the pattern drawn by masons as a guide for shaping their stones, i. 385, 610. Medieval masons usually used boards to draw their patterns on: "pro tabula ad *moolde* petre vocat' nowell," ii. 442, *note* 4; and in the Acts. of King's Hall for 1414–15, "Item pro j planch de fir for *moldyngbord* ij^s." Comp. Arch. Nom. p. 22.

MOLNIE: Acts. of King's Coll. 1677–78: "Solut' Grumbold lapicide pro reparand' le *molnie* in novo templo, ut per billam patet, 1. 8. 0." Prof. Skeat suggests that for *molnie* we should read *moline*, which means (1) an iron such as is fixed in the centre of a millstone: (2) a cross *moline*, as in heraldry.

MONYELL: the vertical bars of stone which divide the lights of a window. Prof. Willis (Arch. Nom. p. 47) derives the word from the French "*moyen*, qui est au milieu," and decides that the original form of the word is *monial*. It occurs, variously spelt, in nearly all the Acts. of stone delivered for building operations. Comp. Skeat, Dict. *s.v.* Mullion.

MOTEY: a kind of yellow, i. 395, *note*; ii. 199, *note* 1.

MUSTARDYBILES: a colour applied to woollen cloth. "Et in xij Virgis panni lanei coloris *mustarddybiles*," i. 382, *note*. In a will, dated 1499, printed by Oliver (Monast. Exon. p. 278), we find: "tres curtas togas, quarum una viridis coloris, altera murey, tercia *mustardevillys*." He notes that the word "has been plausibly derived from Montivilliers in Normandy (called Moustier Villiers in the 15th cent.), the seat of a supposed manufactory."

NESSETE or NESSITT: a word which occurs in the account for altering the great gate of Trin. Coll. in 1614–15, ii. 488. It seems to mean a stone niche.

NORMANDY CANVAS: Acts. of Christ's Coll. 1555–56: "Item for xxiij yeardes of *Normandy canvas* to make tabyll clothes and panifer pokes xxiij^{s}."

———— GLASS: frequently contrasted in contracts with Burgundy glass, and also used alone; i. 615, 616, 617, 618.

NOWELL or NEWELL: the central column round which the steps of a circular staircase wind (Gloss. of Arch. *s. v.*), ii. 442, *note* 4.

OGGES: a word which occurs in a list of worked stones brought to King's Hall in 1428–29: "Item pro iiij ped' de *Ogges*." Can "ogee" be meant?

ORB: a blank window or panel (Gloss. of Arch. *s. v.*). The meaning of the terms "orbys, or crosse quaters," i. 610, is explained in the text, p. 497.

ORDINAUNCE: in the contracts for King's Coll. i. 608, 610, 613, the word seems to mean things ordered, builder's "plant."

ORNELL: a kind of stone brought from London to Eton Coll. i. 386, 388. Prof. Willis (Arch. Nom. p. 25) includes "urnell" among names of stones "which are plainly local, and apply to the quarries whence they are brought, or to the rough shapes of them, rather than to their office in the structures."

ORPMENT: a colour (ii. 199, *note* 1), lit. gold paint. Skeat, Dict. (*s. v.*), defines it as "yellow sulphuret of arsenic."

OSMONDES: occurs in a list of ironwork supplied to Eton Coll. 1443–44, i. 389, *note* 3.

OSSENBRIDGE, OSTENBRIDGE, OZENBRIDGE: a kind of linen used for towels. Acts. of Christ's Coll. 1554–55, "It' for ix yeardes of *ossenbrydge* for a towell to the hye tabyll, iiij^{s}. vj^{d}." Magn. Journ. of Queens' Coll. 1571–72, fo. 92. "Item of *Ostenbriges* .6. yardes and a half xxxv^{s}. ix^{d}." Acts. of S. John's Coll. 1594–95. *Exp. aule.* "For 120 elnes of whyt *ozenbridg* for 4 towels, xvij^{s}. vj^{d}."

OVER END: opposed to nether end, ii. 8.

PACES, and PACES CHAPMANWARE: names of stone supplied to Eton Coll. 1445–46, i. 393. A *pace* is "a broad step, or slightly raised space round a tomb, etc." (Gloss. of Arch. *s. v.*).

PALISER: a workman employed to drive in *pales*, or stakes for fencing, i. 387.

PANDOXATRIA: a brewery. See Ducange, *s. v.* pandox, and pandoxare.

PARE: to weed, applied to beds of saffron, iii. 579, *note* 1; 580, *note* 3.

PENISTONE: a kind of coarse woollen cloth. Halliwell. Univ. Accounts, 1589–90: "Item...for five yardes three quarters of greene *penistone* to lay before the doctors in the Chauncell of St Maries in the sermons times, xx^{s}. ij^{d}." Acts. of S. John's Coll. 1611–12: "For 6. yards of greene *pennistone* att 4^{s}. 4^{d}. the yard for the lodging xxvj^{s}."

PERIMENT; a pediment. Act. for wainscoting the hall of King's Coll. i. 452, *note*. (Comp. Arch. Nom. p. 37, *note*.) The word is spelt *perriment* at Trin. Coll. in 1603–4: ii. 575, *note* 1.

PERPENDASCHLER: hewn or squared stone faced on both sides (Arch. Nom. p. 24); spelt also *parpinaschler*. To this we should prob. refer the "xxxiij ped' de *perpoynt*'" bought for King's Hall in 1428; ii. 445, *note* 1.

PERPETUANA: a kind of stuff, used for curtains. Blue *perpetuana* is used in King's Coll. chapel, 1633–34 (i. 523). Comp. Acts. of Chr. Coll. 1660–61: "For 11 yards of *perpetuana* for ye Window in ye Lodgings, 1. 18. 6."

PES PAULI: a measure of length, occasionally used in conveyances of pieces of ground, i. 338, *note* 2; ii. 406, *note* 1. Mr J. G. Nicholls (Gent. Mag. Sept. 1852, p. 276) quotes a conveyance of land in Marylebone, which shews that the foot there referred to was actually inscribed on one of the columns in the Cathedral Church of S. Paul as a standard; "Terra quidem messuagii habet in latitudine xxxij pedes et dimidium; in longitudine lvij pedes, per pedem Algari qui insculpitur super basim columpnæ in ecclesia Sancti Pauli."

PESS: a hassock. Acts. of Jesus Coll. 1596–97: "Item for *pesses* for the chapel, ix^{d}." Ibid. King's Coll. 1609–10: "Item solut' pro .20. virgis de rushmatts et .3. *pesses* in vsum ecclesie, ix^{s}. iiij^{d}." Ibid. S. Cath. Hall, 1623–24: "Six *pesses* for the chapell." Ibid. Chr. Coll. 1702–3: "*pesses* in the chapel."

PESSULUS: a bolt, ii. 34, *note* 3. Vid. Ducange, *s. v.*

PIPIO: a young pigeon, ii. 441, *note* 2.

PLAVNCHERS: boards. Trin. Hall contract, 1374, i. 238. Comp. Fabric Rolls of York Minster, ed. Surtees Soc. *s. v.* "*Planchæ* de quercu et fraxino" occur at Finchale Priory, p. ii.; French *planche*.

PLANCHER: to fit wood to a particular position, i. 11.

PLASTRA: "*plastra* de paressh," plaster of Paris, occurs in the Eton Coll. Building Acts., i. 391, *note* 4.

POLEYN: "cera de *poleyn*" and "cera *poleyn*" occur in the Eton Coll. Building Acts., i. 391, *note* 4. *Poleyn* may mean Bologna, whence E. "*polony* sausage."

POLUBRUM: an alms-dish, i. 76. The word properly signifies a laver.

POPILL-BORD: wood used for the roofs of studies, ii. 446, *note* 5; probably made from the wood of the poplar, still called *popil*, or *popple*, in Essex.

POWDRED-GLASS: see FLORISHED GLASS.

POWNT: to point, or renew the mortar in walls, i. 9, *note* 4.

PRASSA: a word which occurs in a list of moveable furniture (*necessaria mobilia*), specified as not included in a contract, i. 390, *note* 1. It may perhaps be identified with the lectum pressur' at Finchale Priory, explained in the Glossary as "a bed capable of being *compressed* into a small space during the day-time."

PRESS-MONEY: money paid for expenses of journey etc. to workmen pressed by virtue of a royal commission, ii. 568, *note* 3.

PREST: ready-money advanced. The word often occurs in wage-books and contracts. "One hundreth poundes sterling unto Barnard Flower the Kinges Glasier *in way of prest* towardes the glaising of the Great Churche," i. 499. Comp. also p. 612, where the word occurs several times; "threescore poundes *as in a prest*," p. 617. It occurs again at the building of Christ's Coll., ii. 198. Skeat (*s.v.* press) quotes from Froissart: "And he sent thyders .iii. somers [sumpter mules] laden with nobles of Castel and floreyns, to gyve *in prest* to knyghtes and squyers, *for he knewe well otherwyse he sholde not haue them come out of theyr houses.*"

PRETOR: a subscription. "A *pretor* collected amongst yᵉ schollers," iii. 570.

PUNCHION: in carpentry, a short upright piece of wood used in framing a wooden roof (Gloss. of Arch. *s.v.*). It is described and figured, iii. 95, fig. 21.

PUNCTUATIO: the pointing of walls, i. 14, *note* 2. The word was used in the same sense at Finchale Priory.

PURCHOLIS: a portcullis, ii. 571.

PURLINS: in carpentry, the horizontal pieces of timber which rest on the principals, or main rafters, of a roof, and support the common rafters. Gloss. of Arch. *s.v.* Described and figured, iii. 95, fig. 21.

PYKE-WALL: a wall terminating in a gable; French *mur à pic*. Comp. Gloss. of Arch. *s.v.* GABLE.

QUARTER-BOARD: board to make partitions. In medieval carpentry, *quarters* are the posts in partitions, called also uprights, and studs (Gloss. of Arch. *s.v.*).

QUATERS: see CROSSE-QUATERS.

RANGE: a word used in an act. for stained glass, ii. 571.

RATELY: in proportion to; "as moche money as shall suffise to pay the Masons and other *rately* after the numbre of workemen," i. 608.

RAY CLOTH: a superior kind of cloth, bought for the livery of the master-mason at Eton Coll., i. 382, *note*. Striped cloth, from the Latin *radius*.

REDE or REEDER: a thatcher. Hugo le *Rede* is mentioned at Peterhouse (i. 4, *note*); and the Act. Roll of the same coll. for 1411 contains a payment "Thome *Reder* pro coopertura coquine." Reeds were commonly used for roofs and partitions. In the contract for the Perse Bg. 1617, it is provided "that all the said chambers ...shall be...seeled with lime and haire layd on *reed*," i. 205; and in that for S. John's Coll. 1598, "all the roomes shalbe well plaistered ouerhead with good *reed*, lime, and hare," ii. 252. In the contract for Bishop's Hostel, 1669 (ii. 558), it is specially provided: "no *reed* to be vsed in anie part of the said building."

REGARDUM: a gift, made usually to a servant, for extra work, or to a messenger who brought a present.

REVE: an officer, a churchwarden, i. 282.

RIGALBOARD: a word frequently occurring in lists of building-materials. Timber from Riga in Russia was largely imported, through Holland, into England, and is probably the "Eastland timber" which is elsewhere spoken of as "estrich borde," *q.v.* Comp. an article in The Builder, iv. 365, on "Riga and Dutch Wainscot for Building Purposes."

RINGOLD: a term of carpentry applied to boards, perhaps local. In the Acts. of King's Hall between 1366 and 1370 we find "It' in v. tabul' vocatis *ringoldes* empt' pro ostio pincerne (bake-house)." Again, in 1421–22: "It' pro j tabula de *Rynggold*, xiiijᵈ."

ROBYNETTE: occurs in a list of machinery, or "plant," of which the contractors for the vault of King's Coll. Chapel are to have the use, i. 608. Probably a spout; French *robinet*.

ROCH: a colour, ii. 199, *note* 1.

ROUME: a term for the divisions of panelwork: "To Arnold Pinckney joyner for seling the upper end of ye chapple being xxiiij *Rovmes* at v^s. a *Rovme*," ii. 570, *note* 1.

RYFANT GABLETTES: a small gable, the outline of which is an ogee arch; i. 497.

SALT-CAT: a food for pigeons, described, iii. 593, 594.

SAP-LATH: contrasted (ii. 558, and elsewhere) with heart-lath, *q. v.*

SCABELLUM: a hassock, i. 76.

SCANNUM or SCAMNUM: a low table, a bench. Ducange, *s. v.*

SCANSILE: a pair of steps, a scaffold for painters to stand on, i. 412, *note* 3.

SCANTLING: a pattern, French *échantillon*. "Timber well tried, hewed, and sawen to a scantlin herin expressed," i. 310. Comp. Gloss. of Arch. *s. v.*

SCRUSE: a carpenter's tool, a screw-driver, or auger. Acts. of S. John's Coll. 1573–74: "Item to Robert Nicolson for his *scruse*, vj^d."; Ibid. King's Coll. 1636–37; "Solut' Henrico Mann [a carpenter] pro opere in reparand' le Chapell roof. Item eidem pro conducione le *skrewes*."

SCUES: a word of common occurrence in lists of worked stones, e.g. i. 392. Prof. Willis (Arch. Nom. p. 30) decides that a *skew* is the sloping face of a coping.

SEELING: commonly used for panelwork as well as plasterwork; e.g. "the wainscot-seeling of our master's parlour," ii. 608, *note* 3: 309, *note* 2.

SEERGHYS or SERCHES: a word of occasional occurrence in lists of worked stones, ii. 442, *note* 4. The meaning has not been ascertained.

SELIO: a division of an acre (from the French *sillon*, a furrow), the precise size of which was regulated by custom. A piece of the site of Pembroke Coll., containing about half an acre, is described in 1389–90 as *una selio*, i. 123, *note* 1. Mr Seebohm (The English Village Community, pp. 2, 3) shews that the *selio* was a piece of ground separated from the ground next to it by a turf-balk, and that it sometimes contained an acre, sometimes a half-acre.

SENGRENE: house-leek, i. 180, *note;* lit. evergreen, A. S. *singréne*.

SENGULAR PRINCIPALLS: shorter beams in a roof, placed between the principal rafters. Described and figured, i. 283.

SESTROLL: "The comen lane equall with the *sestroll* pertaynyng vnto the Kynges halls Cundytte," ii. 398. As this lane (King's Hall Lane) is known to have had the aqueduct in question carried along it (ii. 428), it is manifest that the word *sestroll* must mean the channel, or pipe, in which the water ran. It is probably an equivalent of *sestron*, a cistern, Halliwell.

SEVERANT-TABLE: see TABLE.

SEWLYS: a term for worked stone, probably denoting sills.

SHEND: to damage, to upset, i. 383.

SHERE: to cut out, of cloth; i. 382, *note*.

SHOTT: a term of carpentry: "all the boards to be well *shott* and plained," ii. 558. Comp. Skeat Dict. *s. v.* Wainscot, pp. 692, 833.

SHOULDER: Acts. of Peterhouse, 1438–39, "*schulderyng* de le gystes"; which Prof. Willis explains to mean, "to cut the shoulders of joists," i. 11. A "shouldering-piece," in carpentry, is what in stonework is termed a corbel (Gloss. of Arch. *s. v.* BRAGGER).

SKOUCHON ANGLERS: see SQWYNCHYN CREST.

SOLAR: a room on the first floor, ii. 431. Comp. i. 252, and *note*. See CELAR.

SOLYS: a term for worked stone, evidently identical with SEWLYS, i.e. sills. It occurs in the Bursar's Roll at Peterhouse for 1462–63, in conjunction with "monyell" and "begynners."

SOMER PIECES: a term for worked stone, occurring in the Acts. of King's Hall, ii. 445, *note* 1.

SOMERE: In carpentry a *sommer* is a main beam, or girder, in a floor (Gloss. of Arch. *s. v.*). It is also written *sumer*, and *summer*, i. 238; and in the contract for the roof of S. Benet's, ch. i. 282, we meet with *somere trees*.

SOWTHELASES, SOWTLASES, SUCHLATES: a term used in medieval carpentry-work, the meaning of which is lost. In the first contract for timber-work at Queens' Coll. (1448) we find: "all the *sowthelases* and the asshelers," ii. 8: in the second do. (1449), "all the *sowtlases*, asshalers, walplatz and jopees," ii. 10; and in the similar contract for Trinity Hall (1374), i. 238, "wyndbems, *suchlates*, asthelers." The same kind of timber is evidently intended in all three cases.

SPANISH BROWN: Acts. of King's Hall, 1501–2: "It' pro vna libra de vermilon, viij^{d}. It' pro *Spanysshe brenne* iiij^{d}."

SPAR: a name applied to pieces of timber of various kinds, such as quarters, rafters, etc. (Gloss. of Arch. *s. v.*). In the Trin. Hall Contract (i. 238), *spars* are joined with couples (*copulas*), or rafters framed together in pairs with a tie (Gloss. of Arch. *s. v.* COUPLES).

SPEER: a screen, ii. 433. The screen across the lower end of the hall in domestic buildings of the middle ages. Gloss. of Arch. *s. v.*

SPICE HOUSE: In the Jun. Burs. Acts. Trin. Coll. for 1598 repairs are paid for in: "the *spice house*"; "Mr Dickenson's *spicehouse*"; and "Sir Walton's *spice house*." A small room or cupboard is probably meant, in which eatables, in the most general sense, were kept: Ital. *Spezieria*.

SPINDLE: In the contract for the woodwork of Corp. Chr. Coll. chapel (1579, i. 311) we find: "for the *spindle* a pece xviij foot longe iiij vnch square."

SQUARE PECES: a term for worked stone supplied to King's Hall, ii. 445, *note* 1. It occurs frequently in these Acts.

SQWYNCHYN CREST: the ornament of the interior arch of a window. In old French, the interior edge of the window side or jamb was called *escoinsson* or *écoinson*, in English, *scoinson*. In medieval windows this interior edge is often ornamented with a shaft carrying an arched rib (Gloss. of Arch. *s. v.* ESCOINSON; Arch. Nom. pp. 56, 57). This arrangement will be understood from the drawing of a lancet-window at S. John's Coll. ii. 300, fig. 20. The ornamented rib or arch might easily be called by workmen the crest; and the word *scoinson* be corrupted by oral repetition into *sqwynchyn*. The "*skouchon* anglers" which are contrasted in lists of worked stones (i. 386) with "square anglers", are evidently the stones required for the edge, or *scoinson*.

STANDER: Jun. Burs. Acts. Trin. Coll. 1614–15: "Item for mending our Master's *stander*, and adding one pound of iron to yt, iij^{s}. iiij^{d}."

STANDISH: an inkstand. Jun. Burs. Acts. Trin. Coll. 1655–56: "For a *standish*, paper, and quills for the Librarie." Ibid. 1657–58. "A little pewter *standish* for the use of the Common Chamber." Acts. of S. John's Coll. 1697–98: "For a new *standish* for Audit Chamber, o. 3. 6."

STANK: a dam. Acts. of S. John's Coll. 1710–11: "To...carpenter for worke done in making a *stanke* at ye end of ye Library 5. 17. 1.," in connection with repairs to the west end of the Library.

STATERA: a steelyard, a balance, used for weighing stone; ii. 440, *note* 4. The word occurs also at Finchale.

STODYS: The word occurs in an account for timber supplied to King's Hall, ii. 443, *note* 3 and elsewhere. It is evidently the modern *studs*, the intermediate posts in partitions or woodwork, termed also uprights, or quarters.

STOREA: a straw-mat, in this account (i. 75), a hassock.

STORVYN: "alle this tymbir shalbe white oke, not doted, nor *storvyn*, nor sappy," iii. 93. *Storvyn* is evidently the past participle of *sterven*, to die; mod. E. *starve*.

STORY: in windows, the divisions into which a window is divided by the transom. In the act. for glass supplied to Trin. Coll. chapel (ii. 571), where the windows are separated by a transom into two divisions, "the loweste *storie*" and "the seconde *storie*" are mentioned. The word became in Latin *historia* (i. 405, *note* 2), which in turn was translated into the English *history*.

STOW-BRICK: "the walls of the said building shalbe all of well burned Stow-brick," ii. 557, from Stow, a village in Norfolk, ii. 251.

STRING: a term for timber, the precise meaning of which has been lost. Magn. Journ. of Queens' Coll. 1559–60, fo. 271: "Item pro .6. pedibus le tymber vocat' le *stringes* ad gradus novos conficiendos in cubiculo magistri ij^{s}. vj^{d}."

STUD: see STODYS.

STULP: a post, i. 139, *note* 1. Magn. Journ. of Queens' Coll. 1604–5, fo. 101: "Item to ye carpenter for setting up a *stulp* viij^{s}. iiij^{d}."

STURES: a particular kind of timber mentioned in the contract for timber-work at Trin. Hall (1374, i. 238), in connection with dormants and joists. At Finchale Priory the word is spelt *Stowris*, and is explained to mean "hedge or other stakes, here used in building a house in which the partitions appear to have been of wattle or wicker work, plastered with lime." "*Stowr*, a hedge-stake; also, the round of a ladder"; Bailey's Dict.

SUMER or SUMMER: see SOMERE.

SYNAXIS: the assemblage of Christians for the Eucharist, Σύναξις, i. 75.

SYNDON: muslin, i. 76.

SYNOPER: a red ochre, found near Sinope. It is mentioned by Pliny. In the list of colours (ii. 199, *note* 1) we should read "Synoper red okyr."

TABLE: This word is explained as follows by Prof. Willis (Arch. Nom. p. 25, foll.): "The face of a medieval wall is ornamented with horizontal moldings at different levels, which form basements, separate the stories of the building, and crown its upper portions. The general terms for these moldings were *table*, *tablement*, or *tabling;* sometimes with the addition of various distinctive epithets. These terms are either derived from the Latin *tabulatum*, a floor or storey of a building, whence we easily pass to those moldings which indicate on the outside of the building the position of the floors and roof; or else from the nature of these moldings, which are wrought on the edge of thin and *tabular* stones."

The usual distribution of the *table-moldings* of a gothic base will be understood from the accompanying sketch of the basement-profile of Eton College chapel (fig. 1)[1]. The lowest part of the wall (A) is succeeded by a plain slope (B), then a second flat surface (C) corresponding to the *truncus* or *dado* of the classical stereobate, then a second slope (F), which is more commonly a projecting molding, as at D. The first slope (B) is the GROUND-TABLE, GRASS-TABLE, or earth-table; and the remaining base-tables, whatever may be their number, were termed LEDGEMENT-TABLES.

[1] This diagram is copied from the Arch. Nom. Plate III. fig. 11. In the actual church the lower portion (*AB*), or ground-table, is repeated, as shewn in the text, Vol. i. p. 429, fig. 22.

The word *leggement* simply implies lying or horizontality (Arch. Nom. p. 27); but, as all *tables* are horizontal, the epithet cannot be in this case applied in its general sense, but may fairly be taken in the more limited one of a basement, the whole mass of which lies on the ground below the wall.

Prof. Willis next shews that the *ground-table* was, in all probability, immediately succeeded by the *ledgement-table* (F, fig. 1).

In the contract with the quarry-men of Kent for stone for Eton Coll. (i. 385), it is provided that they shall supply 416 "fote of *legement table* bering ful joyntes at ye lest iij ynches or more clene apparailled in the forme that ys callid casshepeed"; and, in the next year, 324 "fote of tweyne *legement tables*," with 416 "fote of Seuerant table."

It was shewn in the text (i. 423) that the church to which this contract refers was pulled down by Henry VI. in order to enlarge the dimensions—a fact of which Prof. Willis was not aware when he wrote his Architectural Nomenclature; but, as his explanation of the terms used fits the existing base-moldings extremely well, we proceed to give it. It is possible that when the church was rebuilt, the design of the lower part of the walls was not altered.

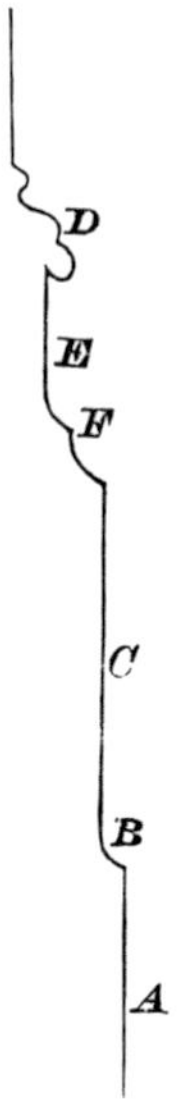

Fig. 1.

The ground-table (B) is succeeded by an unusually high plain portion of wall (C), above which is the first *ledgement-table* (F). The "legement table in the forme that ys callid casshepeed" is part of this table, worked with a CASEMENT (*q. v.*), which, by a misreading or misunderstanding, has been turned into *casshepeed.* The "tweyne *legement tables*" of the next year include the remainder of F, and the whole of D; and the basement is said to have a tweyne or double ledgement-table, because there are two, F and D. JOINT-TABLE, which occurs occasionally, is probably a general term for any table, of which the pieces were jointed, ready for use.

Prof. Willis (ibid. p. 29) agrees with the derivation of SEUERANT-TABLE from the French *severonde*, the eaves of a house, and considers that it refers to the gable-coping, for which *Crest-table* would be another name.

The lowest member of the base-tables (B, fig. 1) was also sometimes called WATER-TABLE, as in the contract for the Legge Bg. i. 206; but Prof. Willis decides (Arch. Nom. p. 35), that this word "may be defined to be a plain projection or set-off, one that allows the water to trickle down the wall, in opposition to the *larmier* or throated table, which throws the water off."

TABLE-WALL: a term for worked stone, supplied to King's Hall, ii. 440, *note* 4; "pro centum pedibus et di' de *tabyll* et gabyll wall." According to Prof. Willis' definition of *table* (*q. v.*) the word signifies stone with a molding attached to it, or else a general term for one of the *tables* described above.

TAILOR'S YARD: the length of the diff. pieces of ground through which the conduit-pipe of the Franciscans (afterwards of Trin. Coll.) ran, is given (1434), in *virgæ cissoris*, ii. 427, 678: and the dimensions of part of the site of the Grey Friars, leased 1547, in *taylors yerdes*, ii. 727.

TALSHIDE: wood cut into billets, i. 388, *note* 2; 391, *note* 3. The charge is always "for felling, drying, splitting, and making" so many *talshides*, as though the word meant a bundle of wood ready for burning. From the French *tailler* and M. English *shide*, a thin board.

TALWODE: wood cut (*taillé*) to make billets of. The word is of frequent occurrence in the Building Acts. of Eton Coll. under the head of *focalia;* e.g. i. 389.

THROWEN: turned. "*Throwen* pillars of wainscot" are mentioned in the contract for the woodwork in Trin. Coll. chapel, 1556, ii. 564. The orig. sense of the verb "to throw" was to turn or twist; hence a turner's lathe is still called *a throw*.

THRUMMED: in the conjunction "thrummed quishions," iii. 353. Here *thrummed* means furnished with *thrums*, or fringed ends.

TILESHERD: broken pottery, i. 393.

TOOM: "for clensing and tooming down the work on both sides of the building," i. 110, *note*. Can *toom* be a corruption of *coom*, to remove dirt?

TOWARD: in the possession of, i. 597; "that oon parte of this indenture *toward* the forsaid Walter."

TRANSERMUM: a word used in the fittings of Peterhouse chapel, i. 76; where it evidently means the iron crossbar of a window.

TRANSOME: a horizontal mullion, or crossbar, in a window; used in the sense of a reredos, ii. 576

TRIMMER: "a piece of timber inserted in a roof, floor, wooden partition, etc. to support the ends of any of the joists, rafters, etc. which cannot, from particular circumstances, be made to bear upon the walls or upon any of the main timbers." (Gloss. of Arch. *s. v.*)

TUNTIGHT or TONNETIGHT: In the Building Accounts of Eton Coll. stone is frequently paid for by the number of *tonne tights*, i. 399. Occasionally the word occurs in the Latin form *doliatum*, i. 389, *note* 2. *Tun tyght* occurs also in the Acts. of King's Hall, ii. 439, *note* 2. Evidently the quantity which a large barrel contained, and the amount which it weighed, were originally expressed by the same word, *ton* or *tun*.

TURKESS: to alter; explained at length by Prof. Skeat, N. and Q. 4 Mar. 1882. Acts. of Christ's Coll. 1548–9: "Item for *turkessing* a locke and making six keys to yᵉ doore of yᵉ librarie ijˢ. viijᵈ." Ibid. 1554–55. "It' to yᵉ tayler for *turkesyne* of yᵉ hangynges in our master's Chamber xxᵈ." Ibid. Magdalene Coll. 1586–87: "It' .4. spoanes (*sic*) and *turkisshinge* .2. oulde." Ibid. Trin. Coll. 1554–55: "Moyn the Smith. Item for altering and new *turkesing* the gemmars of the lesse windoys in the bed chamber xvj."

TURKEY WORK: a term occurring frequently in lists of furniture, e.g. "six cushions of turkey worke," iii. 353.

TOUCH-STONE: a kind of very hard black granite, i. 294.

TYPE: a small cupola (Gloss. of Arch. *s.v.*).

USE BOARD: Jun. Burs. Acts. Trin. Coll. 1661–62: "23 foote of *useboard* ouer Mʳ. Thorndick's and Mʳ. Stedman's chambers." Probably a corruption of evesboard, *q.v.*

VAWCER, VOUSER, VOWSER, WAWCER: a word of common occurrence in all lists of worked stones. In modern nomenclature it is spelt *voussoir*, "the wedge-shaped stones with which an arch is constructed" (Gloss. of Arch. *s.v.*).

VENTES: in the Acts. of King's Hall we find so many feet of "*venttes* crest" and "*ventes* pro enbatylment" paid for (ii. 445, *notes* 1, 3). A *vent* is the opening in a battlement, commonly called the crenel, embrasure, or loop, in distinction to the raised part, called merlon, or cop (Gloss. of Arch. *s. v.* BATTLEMENT).

VICE or VISE: a spiral staircase, the steps of which wind round a perpendicular shaft or pillar, called the *newel* (Gloss. of Arch. *s.v.*).

VIDIMUS: a pattern to be followed in executing stained glass, i. 616.

VOIDER: a basket or tray for carrying away broken meat, Halliwell. Magn. Journ. of Queens' Coll. 1702–3, fo. 50: "Item for a *voiders* for y[e] Fellows Table 0 . 3 . 6.'

VOLE: Magn. Journ. of Queens' Coll. 1625–26, fo. 22: "to the plummer for mending the *vole* in the fellows' garden."

WAINE: "...well seasoned deales without *waine* or sapp," ii. 558. Halliwell gives *waime* as a Suff. word meaning a flaw or tear.

WALL-PLATE: the horizontal beam laid at the top of a wall immediately beneath the roof (Gloss. of Arch. *s.v.* PLATE).

WALYSSH BLANKET: a Welsh blanket; bought for the beds of the workmen at King's Hall, 1427–28, ii. 444, *note* 2.

WARD: "a dore into the said cloistre *ward*, and outward noon," i. 369.

WARE: "one thousand pounds be bestowed and *wared* in books," iii. 436. To lay out labour, money, etc.: a north-country word. Halliwell. It is still used in Yorkshire. "To *ware* one's Money, to bestow it well, to lay it out in Ware," Ray.

WATER LEAVES: Acts. of S. John's Coll. 1576–77: "For xxxvj. pounds of Leade to make *Water Leaves* for the walls over the tower and chappell...iij[s]. vj[d]."

WATER-TABLE: see TABLE.

WHELMERS: see KNEELERS.

WHITE-STONE: a term for clunch, a stone extracted from hard beds low down in the chalk, and much used for building purposes. Bonney, Camb. Geol. p. 75.

WIND-BEAM: a crossbeam used in the principals of many ancient roofs, occupying the situation of the *collar* in modern king-post roofs (Gloss. of Arch. *s.v.*). In other words the *wind beam* is the horizontal beam above, and parallel to, the tie beam, connecting together the two vertical posts, or king-posts, at the point where they touch the sloping portion of the roof. Comp. i. 310; ii. 9, 698.

WYDDROUGHT: "a house for the common *wyddrought* of the said college," ii. 245. Acc. to Halliwell *Wydraught* is a sink, or drain. "*Wydraught*, a water-course, or water-passage; a sink, or common shore" [sewer]; Phillips (1706). The spelling here used gives the etymology: *wyddrought* is 'wide draught,' i.e. *chief* drain, *main* sewer.

XYLINUM: cotton, i. 76; a word used by Pliny.

INDEX.

Yonge, Ri. (Bp. of Rochester, 1404–19): gives £20 to build King's Hall library, ii. 441, *note*
Yonne, Margaret, i. 162, *note*
York, See of: arms on Trin. Coll. fountain, ii. 631
——, Joh.: makes new chaire-organ for Trin. Coll. chapel, ii. 575

ZOOLOGY: Museum suggested in connexion with new Library, 1829, iii. 102; omitted from second scheme, 1830, 110; where placed in Cockerell's final design, 601, see New Museums
Zouch, Eudo de la (Chancellor, 1396–1400): decrees a service for the repose of the souls of Sir William Thorpe and Grace his wife, 1398, iii. 10
Zutphen, in Holland: library at described, iii. 428